THE JOHNS HOPKINS

MEDICAL GUIDE TO

HEALTH
AFTER 50

THE JOHNS HOPKINS

MEDICAL GUIDE TO

HEALTH
AFTER 50

- More Than 100 Illustrations
- A 20-Page Body Atlas
- An Easy-to-Use A-Z Format

Medical Editor
Simeon Margolis, M.D., Ph.D.

Prepared by the Editors of *The Johns Hopkins Medical Letter: Health After 50*

Tess
Press

For updated health and medical information, visit the Johns Hopkins Health After 50
web site:http://www.johnshopkinshealthalerts.com/health_after_50

Published by Tess Press
Black Dog & Leventhal Publishers, Inc.
151 West 19th Street
New York, NY 10011

ISBN: 978-1-60376-233-6

Library of Congress Cataloging-in-Publication Data is on file at Black Dog & Leventhal
Publishers, Inc.

Cover design by Christina Gaugler

Manufactured in China

The Johns Hopkins
Medical Guide to Health After 50

Thomas Dickey
Executive Editor

Samantha B. Cassetty
Senior Editor

James W. Brown, Jr.
Assistant Editor

Timothy Jeffs
Art Director

Bree Rock
Production Associate

Carney W. Mimms III
Production Database Designer

John Vasiliadis
Production Database Programmer

Tom Damrauer, M.L.S.
Chief of Information Resources

**Robert Duckwall, Caitlin Duckwall,
Craig Durant**
Medical Illustrators

Johns Hopkins
Health After 50 Publications

Rodney Friedman
Editor and Publisher

Joan Mullally
Business Development and Licensing

Barbara Maxwell O'Neill
Associate Publisher

Contributors to this Guide include the following faculty at The Johns Hopkins University School of Medicine:

LAWRENCE J. CHESKIN, M.D.
Associate Professor, International Health
Director, Johns Hopkins Weight Management Center

GARY GERSTENBLITH, M.D.
Professor, Medicine, Cardiology Division

SERGEY V. KANTSEVOY, M.D., PH.D.
Assistant Professor, Medicine
Director, Endoscopy Training and Certification

JOHN P. KOSTUIK, M.D.
Professor, Orthopedic Surgery and Neurosurgery
Chief, Spine Division

RAFAEL H. LLINAS, M.D.
Assistant Professor, Neurology
Director, Stroke Neurology, Johns Hopkins Bayview Medical Center

HARRY A. QUIGLEY, M.D.
Professor, Ophthalmology
Director, Glaucoma Service and Dana Center for Preventive Ophthalmology

CHRISTOPHER D. SAUDEK, M.D.
Professor, Medicine
Director, Johns Hopkins Diabetes Center
Director, General Clinical Research Center

KAREN L. SWARTZ, M.D.
Assistant Professor, Psychiatry

LORA BROWN WILDER, SC.D., M.S., R.D.
Assistant Professor, Medicine

The following organizations have cooperated with Johns Hopkins in providing material for this Guide:

American Academy of Dermatology
American Academy of Otolaryngology— Head and Neck Surgery
American College of Obstetricians and Gynecologists
American Foundation for Urologic Disease
American Lung Association
American Sleep Disorders Association
National Cancer Institute
National Institute of Dental and Craniofacial Research
National Institute of Diabetes and Digestive and Kidney Diseases
National Institute of Neurological Disorders and Stroke
Weight-Control Information Network

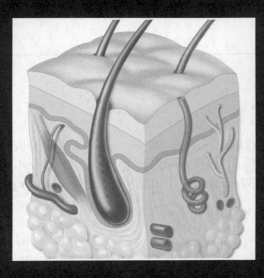

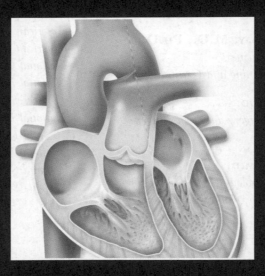

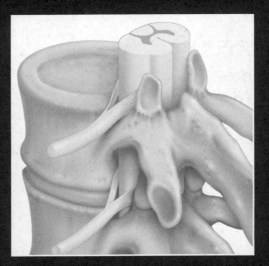

Contents

Introduction

Many medical encyclopedias have been written for the general public; this guide, too, is intended for consumers, but it differs from others by specifically focusing on the major health concerns of people over 50. *The Johns Hopkins Medical Guide to Health Over 50* provides entries on more than 100 major medical disorders that primarily affect people at midlife and beyond.

The entries, which are organized in an A to Z format (indexed on pages 76-80), cover ailments that affect virtually every part of the body. Each entry includes information on symptoms, causes, complications, diagnostic procedures, prevention strategies, and the most current treatment options for a specific problem or a set of related problems.

In particular, you will find in-depth explanations of chronic health problems associated with aging—including high blood pressure, coronary heart disease, stroke, diabetes, osteoarthritis, dementia, and various types of cancer. These disorders have become the leading causes of mortality and disability in the United States and other Western societies. The Guide describes advances in treating these disorders as well as how changes in diet and other lifestyle habits can often reduce the risk of disease or contribute to managing a chronic condition more effectively.

The benefits of living a healthy lifestyle are described in greater detail in the section on disease prevention that begins on page 12, where you will find advice and guidelines on topics such as exercise, diet, quitting smoking, alcohol consumption, and weight control—all of which not only can help prevent serious illness, but also help you feel younger and more energetic than people who ignore healthy habits. This section also explains which screening tests can benefit healthy people and how often the tests should be done.

How to Use This Book

The purpose of this Guide is to provide a ready reference source of available knowledge rather than to report the most recent developments in the field. The Guide can help you to become well-informed about a health problem that may affect you or a member of your family—and it can point you toward topics and issues you may want to bring up with your own physician.

Certainly the information presented here is not meant to substitute for the advice of your physician. But each of the entries in the Guide will help you gain a familiarity with the vocabulary of the disorder that concerns you, provide you with helpful explanations of the disorder, and serve as a good starting point for further conversations with your physicians or with health-care organizations that can provide additional information and assistance. We expect that, in this way, the Guide will be a valuable asset in helping you take control of your own health and medical care.

Most of the information in the Guide has been written directly by physicians at Johns Hopkins Medicine, which brings together the faculty physicians and scientists of The Johns Hopkins University School of Medicine with the organizations, community physicians, and professionals of The Johns Hopkins Hospital and Health System. The authors include members of the editorial advisory board of *The Johns Hopkins Medical Letter Health After 50* as well as other specialists who are practicing clinicians and on the teaching staff at Johns Hopkins.

Other information comes from some of the leading health information organizations in the United States, which are identified on page 7 and at the end of any entries to which an organization has contributed material. Each organization had already subjected its material to an extensive review process by doctors who are recognized authorities in their fields. Specialists at Johns Hopkins have given this material an additional review.

Throughout the entries on disorders, certain key points and topics are given emphasis in text highlighted in a blue tint. A **"Hopkins dome" icon** indicates that this text is from Johns Hopkins physicians; text that doesn't carry a Hopkins dome contains material from one of the contributing organizations.

At the back of the Guide you will find advice about how to locate information on health-care providers, hospitals, and health insurers—along with an extensive listing of health information organizations and support groups organized by disorders.

Hopkins dome icon

Disease Prevention

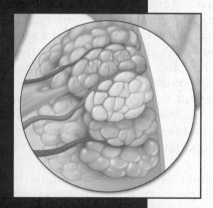

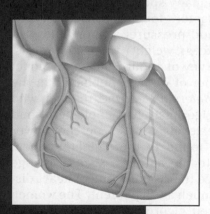

As millions of baby boomers slide into middle age, there has never been a better time to enter the second half of life. During the last century, life expectancy in the United States increased dramatically, from age 47 in 1900 to age 76 today. In the first decade of the 20th century, only about one in five Americans lived to celebrate their 65th birthday. At the beginning of the 21st century, at least 70 percent will achieve this milestone. Rare a hundred years ago, centenarians today number an estimated 100,000 worldwide. By the year 2050, many experts believe that the average adult will live about 83 years.

Older Americans are also remarkably healthy. According to surveys conducted by the MacArthur Foundation, no significant physical or mental disabilities are reported by 89 percent of those between 65 and 74, 73 percent of those between 75 and 84, and 40 percent of those over age 85. Even when faced with disability, only a small fraction of the elderly require nursing home care.

A healthy middle and old age cannot be taken for granted, however. Nearly half of older Americans suffer from arthritis, about one third have high blood pressure or heart disease, and more than one tenth have diabetes. Cancer, osteoporosis, and chronic obstructive pulmonary disease (chronic bronchitis or emphysema) are also prevalent.

These illnesses, and the disabilities that frequently accompany them, can often be delayed until very late in life. Extensive research has shown that genes account for only about one third of the problems associated with aging. Lifestyle factors, which have a greater impact on health during middle and late life than in early adulthood, account for the rest. Also, experts now recognize many measures that are likely to increase longevity and delay the onset of disabling illnesses.

What follows is an overview of the disease prevention recommendations from the board members of *The Johns Hopkins Medical Letter Health After 50* newsletter. More detailed information on key recommendations is presented on pages 18-54—along with advice on the preventive screening tests offered by the health-care system.

Exercise: A Potent Antidote for Aging

The board members of *The Johns Hopkins Medical Letter* unanimously recommend exercise as the single most important anti-aging measure anyone can follow, regardless of age, disability, or general level of fitness. A sedentary lifestyle accelerates nearly every unwanted aspect of aging. Conversely, physical activity slows the erosion of muscle strength, maintains better cardiovascular and respiratory function, limits the risk of developing diabetes and helps to prevent osteoporosis by increasing bone mass. Exercise also facilitates digestion, promotes efficient bowel function, reduces insomnia, and lessens the risk of depression.

Older adults who exercise regularly typically outperform nonexercisers half their age in many sports and usually have fewer risk factors for heart disease (such as high blood pressure, a poor lipid profile, and excess weight) than nonexercisers. In a survey of about 5,000 men and an equal number of women, published in the *Archives of Internal Medicine*, the men who exercised vigorously had cholesterol and triglyceride levels 9 to 27 percent lower than those found in the sedentary men. According to the authors, such a change could reduce the risk of dying of heart disease by as much as 25 percent. The women who reported vigorous exercise also had better lipid profiles than their sedentary counterparts.

In a recent report, the American College of Sports Medicine recommended that, to be effective, an exercise program should include the following components: aerobic exercise such as running or cycling, which increases the demand placed on the cardiovascular and respiratory systems; *strength training* using light weights or one's own body weight to work major muscle groups; and stretching to achieve and maintain flexibility in joints and muscles.

As for the amount of exercise you should get, some experts recommend expending 2,000 to 3,000 calories per week above your normal sedentary baseline—the equivalent of jogging about four miles a day, five days a week. But research has shown that less rigorous activity is highly beneficial. For example, one study found that taking a brisk 30-minute walk three times a week can reduce blood pressure by an average of 10 mm Hg/ 8.6 mm Hg.

How much exercise you can and should do depends on your general health and present level of fitness. Because older, unconditioned muscles and bones are more vulnerable to injury, commitment and constancy are important: Exercising regularly is the best means of protection.

To ensure success, begin any exercise routine gradually, and check with your doctor before starting, especially if you are over 50. If you have never exercised before, your doctor may refer you to a physical therapist or other specialist who can offer instruction. (For more information on starting an exercise program, see page 21).

Other Preventive Lifestyle Choices

Experts on aging generally agree that a prescription for mid- and late-life health should also include the following:

- **Eat a healthy diet.** A diet that is rich in fruits and vegetables cuts the risk of colorectal cancer in half, substantially reduces the risk of coronary heart disease and diabetes, and decreases common gastrointestinal problems such as diverticulosis (protrusions in the inner lining of the intestine) and constipation. Switching from a high-fat to a low-fat diet often reduces total cholesterol by about 10 mg/dl. It also produces small but significant declines in blood pressure. For the steps you can take to help ensure a healthy diet, see pages 30-33.

  A sound diet can theoretically provide all the vitamins and minerals you need, but it occasionally falls short. Despite their best efforts, some adults in their 60s and older are deficient in vitamins B6 and B12, folic acid, vitamin D, and calcium. A standard multivitamin can fill in most of these gaps. But older adults, especially women, should generally also take a calcium supplement. When coupled with a proper diet, a 500-mg supplement may be sufficient to meet the daily need (1,500 mg). See pages 33-36 for more information on the judicious use of dietary supplements.

- **Achieve and maintain a healthy weight.** The complications of excessive weight—including type 2 diabetes, high blood pressure, coronary heart disease, gallbladder disease, and sleep apnea (intermittent cessation of breathing during sleep)—are second only to smoking as a preventable cause of deaths.

  Using body mass index (BMI) as the criterion (see page 37), about 61 percent of American adults are either overweight or obese. One survey found that, at any given moment, almost 28 percent of men and more than 43 percent of women are trying to lose weight. Yet despite all the

Preventive Medication

Certain drugs can now be used to prevent several common medical problems, chief among them coronary heart disease (CHD). When lifestyle measures fail to lower blood pressure and blood cholesterol, both of which are risk factors for CHD, drug therapy should be considered. Many drugs can effectively lower high blood pressure (see page 391); statins are generally chosen for high cholesterol (see page 241).

Most older adults should take aspirin (one 325-mg adult tablet every other day or one 81-mg baby aspirin daily) to decrease the risk of CHD and possibly colorectal cancer. Aspirin is not appropriate for everyone—for example, people with a bleeding ulcer or a history of hemorrhagic stroke, or those taking anticoagulants such as warfarin (Coumadin), should refrain. Be sure to discuss aspirin therapy with your doctor, rather than starting it on your own (see page 379).

In postmenopausal women, early research suggested that hormone replacement therapy (HRT), usually a combination of estrogen and progesterone, might help reduce the incidence of CHD and also preserve bone mass. But more recent evidence strongly suggests that HRT may actually increase the risk of heart attack, stroke, and breast cancer. Consequently, experts no longer recommend that it be used for disease prevention. Instead, women should use medications targeted at specific risk factors.

Although many other hormones, including dehydroepiandrosterone (DHEA), growth hormone, melatonin, and testosterone, are periodically touted in the media, there is too little evidence to recommend any of them for general anti-aging purposes—and they may, in fact, be harmful. However, doctor-supervised use of melatonin may be helpful for certain types of insomnia, and testosterone may restore sex drive in men with abnormally low testosterone levels.

time and money invested in trying to slim down, excessive weight gain remains a persistent problem for millions.

If you are one of them, don't despair. Shedding even a few pounds can significantly improve general health. Properly implemented lifestyle measures can be highly effective—and, if they fail, certain medications or even surgery may be an option for those who are severely overweight. (See pages 37-43 for more information on weight control.)

- **Don't smoke.** A pack-a-day smoker is four times more likely to develop congestive heart failure than a nonsmoker. Those who smoke half a pack a day are twice as likely to develop the condition. Smokers also have a greatly increased risk of lung cancer.

But it's never too late to quit. Five years after they stop, ex-smokers have about the same risk of developing coronary heart disease as someone who has never smoked, regardless of age, number of cigarettes smoked daily, and years spent smoking. In most instances, lung cancer risk returns to normal after 15 years. Quitting also decreases the risk of stroke, some other cancers, chronic bronchitis, and emphysema. It may also improve circulation and the cosmetic appearance of the skin. (See pages 44-45 for advice on the best methods for quitting.)

- **Avoid excessive alcohol consumption.** One glass of wine or spirits daily is acceptable and may even provide some cardiovascular benefit. But if you don't drink, don't start. The drawbacks of excessive consumption—possible addiction, liver disease, and even cancer—are too significant and unpredictable to warrant adopting the practice (see page 47). Furthermore, because age slows alcohol metabolism, the effects of alcohol are more pronounced in older adults.

- **Avoid excessive sun exposure.** Aging skin and eyes are vulnerable to sun damage because protective pigment diminishes over time, permitting greater penetration of harmful rays. Although a small amount of sunlight is needed to produce vitamin D, too much sun exposure increases the risk of skin cancer. In addition, the sun can cause significant cosmetic damage. Most wrinkles, discoloration, and texture changes are directly related to sunlight (see page 636).
- **Reduce stress.** Studies show that stress and anxiety impair the immune system and increase susceptibility to illness. Some of the ways to cope with stress are meditation, yoga, and exercise. Find the technique or combination of techniques you prefer, and make a point of setting aside time to practice them. Studies also show that positive social interactions, including sexual activity for those who desire it, lower the level of stress hormones in the blood, help preserve cognitive function, and prevent depression.
- **Challenge the mind.** Over time, short-term memory and reaction time decline, and it takes longer to acquire new information. But it's still possible to learn new skills and maintain old ones. Three key factors predict strong mental function: regular physical activity, strong social support, and belief in your ability.

Just as for younger people, regular exercise provides numerous physiological benefits for individuals over 50 that cannot be gained in any other way. Only a regular program of exercise allows older people to maintain, or increase, their stamina, strength, and flexibility. Yet while most people are aware of the health benefits of keeping fit after 50, many aren't certain what a well-rounded exercise program entails. This section can help you get started on a safe, lifelong commitment to exercise.

Aerobic Exercise

Virtually everyone knows that regular aerobic exercise (activities that prompt the heart to pump at an elevated rate for an extended period) is one of the best prescriptions for a long and healthy life. The cardiovascular benefits of walking, jogging, cycling, and swimming are well-established, and it is becoming increasingly clear that the benefits of these aerobic activities extend far beyond the heart.

Yet, according to the Centers for Disease Control and Prevention (CDC), fewer than one quarter of American adults exercise enough to achieve these benefits. The problem is that many people—especially older adults, whose ability to exercise is frequently impaired by chronic health problems—remain sedentary because they mistakenly believe that aerobic exercise requires vigorous activity.

In reality, nearly everyone can benefit from a modest amount of aerobic activity. Furthermore, even ordinary daily activities—vacuuming, mowing the lawn, or taking the stairs instead of an escalator—can help preserve the function of the heart and lungs, keep bones strong, enhance psychological well-being, and possibly even help protect against Alzheimer's disease and some cancers.

Fewer Heart Attacks
and Strokes

A sedentary lifestyle contributes to 250,000 deaths per year in the United States—about 12 percent of the total—usually due to coronary heart disease (CHD) or medical problems that raise the risk of CHD (especially diabetes and obesity). When combined with a poor diet, physical inactivity is the second most common (and preventable) underlying cause of death in the United States. People who do not exercise have a 30 percent to 50 percent greater risk of high blood pressure and are almost two times more likely to develop CHD than those who are active.

Aerobic exercise can turn around these rather grim statistics. A study in the *Archives of Internal Medicine*, for example, followed more than 30,000 people age 20 to 93. Those who consistently exercised, played sports, or biked to work were significantly less likely than their sedentary peers to die of any cause over that time period. Compared to the inactive subjects, the highly active people were about half as likely to die and the moderately active people were about one third less likely, during the 14 years of the study. This benefit increased with age, especially in women. Other studies have confirmed a similar effect in men.

Research has documented that aerobic exercise reduces the risk of CHD-related death by about 25 percent in people with established CHD. And for the first time, aerobic exercise was recently linked to a reduction in strokes, the third leading cause of death in the United States. A report in the *Journal of the American Medical Association* in 2001, based on data from over 72,000 women age 40 to 65, found that performing 30 minutes of moderate to vigorous exercise, including brisk walking or jogging, almost every day, cut the risk of ischemic stroke by 30 percent. The risk of hemorrhagic stroke was cut by 20 percent. Similar data are not yet available for men.

Aerobic exercise delivers these benefits by affecting four major CHD risk factors: diabetes, high blood pressure, obesity, and lipid (cholesterol and triglyceride) levels.

Reductions in Diabetes and Blood Pressure

Exercise reduces the risk of developing diabetes and may increase the lifespan of people with diabetes by helping insulin to work more efficiently and thus lowering blood glucose levels. A study in the *New England Journal of Medicine* examined more than 500 men and women at risk for diabetes because they were middle-aged, overweight, and had borderline-high blood glucose. Men who received counseling on techniques for effective weight loss, making dietary changes, and boosting exercise were 58 percent less likely to develop diabetes. Other studies have shown that exercise reduces complications and extends life after diabetes is diagnosed.

A variety of mechanisms account for the blood pressure-lowering effects of aerobic exercise. In general, regular aerobic workouts increase the amount of blood ejected from the heart with each contraction. Exercise also promotes more efficient use of oxygen. Both of these effects lower blood pressure during exertion and while at rest. Recently, researchers have also discovered that aerobic exercise helps to prevent age-related deterioration of the endothelium (cells lining the blood vessels), which can lead to atherosclerosis

(thickening and hardening of the arteries), the formation of blood clots, and reduction of blood flow in the coronary arteries. Exercise promotes blood flow to the heart by increasing the formation of nitric oxide, which is produced by the endothelium and signals the coronary arteries to relax when the heart needs more blood.

Less Obesity, Improved Lipid Profile

Aerobic exercise can decrease the ill effects of obesity, a risk factor for both diabetes and CHD. Benefits may accrue in older adults by reducing body fat by as little as 1 percent to 4 percent—even though weight may not decline. Additionally, exercise lowers triglyceride levels and raises levels of high density lipoprotein (HDL, or "good") cholesterol. These improvements may be related to both a reduction and a redistribution of body fat. Aerobic exercise diminishes body fat, which is particularly associated with an increased risk of CHD and diabetes.

Stronger Bones, Joints, and Lungs

Weight-bearing aerobic activities—walking, stairclimbing, and running—can help prevent osteoporosis (weak bones that break easily) and fractures resulting from falls, the leading cause of injury-related deaths among people age 65 and older.

In one study of postmenopausal women, participation in a one-year walking program modestly improved bone mineral density of the spine. Aerobic exercise also strengthens leg muscles, which helps to stabilize joints and further reduces the likelihood of falls. Another report found that leg strength increased up to 13 percent in 26 women age 63 to 86 after they bicycled twice a week for 10 weeks.

Exercise can also ease the pain and physical impairment characteristic of arthritis.

Disease Prevention

In a study of 439 men and women over age 60 with osteoarthritis of the knee, the exercisers had less discomfort and better physical functioning than the nonexercisers. Such benefits can be attributed to increased strength and joint stability, weight control (because excess pounds increase pressure on joints), and wider range of motion in the joints. Swimming, a gentle form of aerobic activity that is not weight-bearing, is particularly beneficial for people with arthritis and osteoporosis. Adding strength training to any aerobic regimen provides even greater bone, joint, and muscle benefits, regardless of general health (see page 22).

The more efficient oxygen usage promoted by aerobic exercise also improves respiratory function, which is especially helpful for those with respiratory ailments such as asthma, emphysema, or chronic bronchitis. In addition, exercise has been shown to improve mood and self-esteem. Accumulating data suggest that regular vigorous aerobic exercise also lessens depression in patients with moderate to severe symptoms.

Fewer Cancers, Improved Memory

While not as well documented, mounting evidence suggests that regular aerobic exercise may reduce the risk of developing certain types of cancer, particularly colon, lung, prostate, and breast cancer. It is believed that the lower risk is due to immune system improvements or more efficient elimination of free radicals—highly reactive molecules that can damage or kill important cellular components such as DNA or cell membranes. In patients already diagnosed with cancer, preliminary studies show that exercise has a positive physical, mental and emotional effect; it improves strength, the performance of daily activities, and the ability to battle the nausea and fatigue caused by chemotherapy.

Regular exercise may also help prevent mental decline. Tests of the cognitive abilities of nearly 6,000 women age 65 and older over a 6- to 8-year period showed a slight benefit from exercise: The most active women (who walked an average of nearly 18 miles per week) experienced a 17 percent decline in memory, compared with 24 percent among the women who walked the least (an average of about a half mile per week). A 5-year study of people age 65 and older found that participants who were most active were half as likely to develop Alzheimer's disease and about 40 percent less likely to experience dementia or mental impairment than those who were inactive. Researchers speculate that the lower blood pressure and blood cholesterol levels associated with exercise may protect the brain just as they do the heart.

Exercise Risks

Exercise should not hurt or leave you feeling exhausted—although some temporary soreness, slight discomfort, or mild weariness is common and acceptable after working out. The most frequent problem—injury to muscles or joints—is usually caused by exercising too hard for too long. Such injuries can be avoided by gradually building up to a comfortable, yet challenging, level of exertion. If pain lasts more than a day or two, contact your doctor.

Because the likelihood that chronic medical conditions might be worsened by exercising improperly, it's important for people over 50 to see a doctor before embarking on a new exercise program. This caution is especially important for those who have previously led a sedentary lifestyle. Anyone

Keeping an Exercise Program Simple

To walk or run or bicycle…to work out intensely or moderately…to exercise every day or every other day… Although different and sometimes contradictory advice abounds, the basic elements of an exercise program designed to enhance health are clear: Include about 30 minutes of moderate aerobic exercise on most days, along with regular strength training and stretching. This recommendation is backed by the Centers for Disease Control and Prevention and the American College of Sports Medicine. In reviewing all of the available evidence on physical activity and health, an expert panel convened by these two organizations concluded that adults should accumulate 30 minutes or more of physical activity on most, preferably all, days of the week.

Here are some additional guidelines:

- An aerobic activity does not have to be formal exercise, such as jogging, cycling, or aerobic dance, but should be performed at moderate intensity—the equivalent of walking at a pace of three to four miles per hour. Work hard enough to raise your heart rate, but not so hard that you cannot carry on a conversation.

- The 30 minutes of activity need not take place at one time. Short bursts of activity for 8 to 10 minutes, three times a day, are enough, as long as they are performed at moderate intensity. Such activities include walking up stairs, walking short distances, and doing calisthenics or pedaling a stationary bicycle while watching television. Gardening, housework, raking leaves, dancing, and playing actively with children can also count—as long as the level of intensity corresponds to brisk walking.

- According to the panel, people who perform lower-intensity activities should do them more often, for longer periods of time, or both. And, of course, those who prefer more structured exercise can continue to benefit from it. The key is to pick activities that you enjoy and to tailor them to your own particular ability, guided by the advice of your doctor.

- Though rare, an unusual amount of exertion may trigger a heart attack in individuals with an otherwise sedentary lifestyle. Thus, physical activity should be incorporated into one's lifestyle gradually, with a slow and steady increase in intensity.

who has coronary heart disease or is at high risk for developing it should also see a doctor before beginning any new physical activities, even moderate ones.

For people who already exercise, new symptoms or any changes in the body's response to exercise should also prompt a consultation.

Strength Training for Better Health

While the key role that aerobic activities play in preventing illness or relieving symptoms remains undisputed, most experts now consider that strength training (exercise that forces the muscles to contract against an external weight or other resistance) is equally important.

Evidence for the benefits is so overwhelming that the American College of Sports Medicine now recommends strength training, also known as weight or resistance training, for virtually everyone over 50. Strength training reduces the risk of falls—a leading cause of death among Americans age 65 to 84—by 10 percent to 20 percent. By providing greater support for the spine, weight training can improve posture, ease chronic back pain, and delay or eliminate the bone loss and brittleness that characterize osteoporosis. Like aerobic exercise, resistance training also improves cardiovascular health and helps prevent or retard obesity and diabetes.

Fortunately, it is never too late to begin—or to reap substantial rewards. Resistance training can increase strength and mobility even among those who are well into their 90s. But after mid-life, certain precautions should be observed.

Proven Health Benefits to Strength Training

Muscle mass declines dramatically after middle age—by approximately 15 percent per decade beginning at age 60, and even more after age 80. This loss of strength, combined with age-related deficits in balance and coordination, are largely responsible for the falls suffered each year by one of every three American adults over 65. Strength training is the only type of exercise that can substantially slow and even reverse these declines, dramatically lowering the risk of falls and fractures, building atrophied muscles, and making joints stronger and more flexible. Investigators at Tufts University found that when nine frail 90-year-old nursing home residents used leg weights for two months, their muscle mass increased by an average of 10 percent. Five of the residents walked faster after completing the training. Two were able to walk without their canes, and one who initially could not rise from a chair without support was able to do so unassisted.

In another Tufts study of 40 healthy but sedentary women age 50 to 70, high-intensity strength training two days a week for a year increased bone mass in the hips and spine by about 1 percent, exchanged about 3 lb of fat for muscle, and improved balance by about 15 percent. In contrast, the women who remained sedentary lost about 2 percent of bone mass and 1 lb of muscle, while their balance declined by approximately 8 percent.

An article in *Circulation* reported that strength training was as effective as aerobic exercise in increasing HDL cholesterol and lowering both LDL cholesterol and diastolic blood pressure (the lower number in a blood pressure reading) in healthy adults and low-risk men with heart disease. No data are available on women with coronary heart disease (CHD), but there is every reason to believe that these women would also benefit.

While strength training was slightly less effective in reducing systolic blood pressure (the higher number), a study published in Hypertension, which involved over 300 people, showed that this form of exercise can reduce resting systolic blood pressure by 2 percent and diastolic blood pressure by 4 percent, amounts substantial enough to decrease the risk of stroke and CHD. Although both studies focused on middle-aged people, results were so encouraging that the authors recommended strength training for all older adults.

By increasing metabolism, thereby burning fat and helping to keep weight and blood sugar in check, strength training offers important advantages for people with diabetes. It is also frequently recommended for people with arthritis. Although working out with weights cannot reverse arthritic changes, regular weight training can alleviate symptoms by improving range of motion and strengthening the muscles, tendons, and ligaments that surround arthritic joints.

How to Begin Strength Training

While most people over 50 can begin weight training if they observe certain precautions, there are some exceptions. Most people with chronic diseases can undertake a moderate strength training program if their condition is stable. Those with muscular or skeletal injuries, osteoporosis, hypertension, or other cardiovascular problems, or who smoke or haven't recently been physically active, should first consult a doctor. Men—and probably women—with stable, well-controlled mild to moderate heart disease can usually proceed after receiving their doctor's approval.

Numerous studies have reported few orthopedic problems and no increased risk of heart attack or other CHD problems attributable to weight training. But people with any type of unstable disease should not perform either strength training or aerobic exercise until their doctor is confident that the condition has been properly treated and brought under control.

It's also helpful to see a trainer (preferably someone certified by the American College of Sports Medicine or American Council on Exercise) for at least a few sessions. He or she can train you, identify any muscle imbalances—generally the lower back, abdomen, and (particularly in women) the upper arms and shoulders are weakest—and develop an appropriate series of exercises. It should involve all the major muscle groups in the arms, legs, shoulders, and trunk.

The exercises on pages 24-25, which are aimed at different muscle groups, are examples of basic exercises for beginners.

At a gym, you can begin a strength-building program on machines that allow you to focus on specific muscle groups with less worry about doing anything wrong (for example, extending beyond a muscle's proper range of motion). Also, your body is stabilized, so it doesn't require as much balance.

Ultimately, though, free weights provide a better overall muscular workout—precisely because they require you to use your whole body for both balance and stabilization. (They also have the advantage of being smaller and mobile, and so are easier to use at home.) Most people progress to working out with free weights as exercise becomes more comfortable.

Try to find a trainer who understands the special needs of older adults. For instance, while all people should avoid holding their breath when lifting weights, correct breathing is especially important to avoid spikes in blood pressure in people with cardiovascular disease. Similarly, people with osteoporosis risk spinal fractures if they cross their legs or bend at the hip at more than a 90-degree angle.

Also, trainers routinely recommend that people who have never exercised should perform aerobic activity regularly before they consider weight training. But experts also say that frail, elderly people can reduce their risk of falls and injury by strengthening their legs, arms, and trunk muscles through resistance training before engaging in aerobic exercise.

Basic Strength Training

The exercises at right are a good way to get started on basic strength training at home. If you are over 50, check with your doctor before embarking on a strength training program. Once you receive the go-ahead, it is always worthwhile to seek expert instruction at a local gym or university-based wellness facility, or from a qualified personal trainer. A trainer will probably design a program containing at least eight to ten exercises that should be performed two to three times a week.

If the exercise causes pain—aside from the slight discomfort that is a normal part of working out—stop at once. It's okay to be a little sore afterward; that's the only way you improve. But if pain persists for several days, you should be evaluated by a doctor. And don't try to accomplish too much too soon. Most strength training injuries are related to overuse: You should try to get fit in three to six months, not three to six weeks.

People usually begin by working out twice a week before increasing to three to four times a week, alternating muscles to allow them the 48 hours they need to rest.

The following guidelines can help make workouts rewarding and safe:

- **Warm up before each workout**—by jogging in place for a few minutes or using a treadmill or exercise bike. Then do some basic stretches (see page 28).

- **For exercises with weights, start with light weights.** You should be able to lift each weight 10 to 15 times without straining.

- **Start with one set of each exercise.** While younger people are usually instructed to strength train to near fatigue, the American College of Sports Medicine advises only one set of 10 to 15 repetitions for most people over 50 to prevent injury.

- **As your muscles adapt, gradually increase the weight**—but just by 5 to 10 percent. The goal is to continue taxing your muscles somewhat without overdoing it. If you can't repeat an exercise 10 times, the new weight is too heavy.

- **If you do more than one set,** rest for a minute or two between sets.

- **Move slowly and smoothly through the full range of motion.** Lifting and lowering the part of the body you are exercising in a slow, controlled manner reduces the chance of injury and soreness. Don't lock your knees or elbows when they are involved in an exercise, since doing so puts excess stress on the joint itself.

- **Breathe evenly** with every repetition. Exhale while you lift, inhale when you bring the weight down. Holding your breath can raise blood pressure suddenly.

- **Cool down after your workout.** Repeat a warm-up activity for a few minutes, then do some stretches to help muscles recover.

Upright row (for upper back, shoulders, and arms). Standing with your feet shoulder-width apart and knees slightly bent, hold dumbbells side by side at thigh level (palms toward thighs). Slowly pull them up to your collarbone, until elbows are just above shoulder height. Slowly lower, and repeat.

Curl down, or negative sit-up (for abdominals). Start by sitting with your knees bent, feet flat, and arms reaching forward. Slowly lower yourself to the floor to a count of 10. Sit back up (using your arms if necessary), and repeat.

Curls (for biceps). Sit leaning forward with your legs slightly spread and one hand on your thigh. Keeping the other elbow on the other thigh, hold a weight so that your forearm is horizontal. Slowly curl the weight up and in toward your chest; repeat. Switch arms.

Triceps extensions (for triceps). Supporting one knee and hand on a bench or chair, hold a weight at the side of your chest, keeping your arm bent so that your elbow is far behind you. Without moving the elbow, extend your arm behind you. Return to starting position; repeat. Switch arms.

Dumbbell squats (for buttocks, quadriceps, and hamstrings). Holding dumbbells (with palms inward), stand with your feet hip-width apart; don't lock your knees. Keeping your weight on your heels, contract your abdominal muscles and bend your knees, lowering your upper torso. Don't go lower than the illustration shows. Slowly straighten up; repeat.

Push-up #1 (for upper body). Place your hands slightly wider than shoulder width; keep your feet together, with knees locked. Start with your elbows straight, but never locked. Bend your elbows to lower your body, and try to bring your chest to within an inch of the floor. Keep your body in a straight line, from head to ankles, throughout the movement. Move up and down slowly, with abdominal muscles tightened. Repeat 10 to 15 times.

Push-up #2 (easier version). Same as at left, but keep your knees on the ground and feet raised. Don't put your weight on your knee caps, but rather just above them; you can use a cushion. Don't arch your lower back. Lower, lift, and repeat.

The Benefits of Staying Flexible

Although most people are aware of the health benefits of keeping fit after 50, many aren't certain what a well-rounded training program entails. In a recent report, the American College of Sports Medicine recommended flexibility exercises (stretching), along with aerobic (cardiovascular) exercise and strength training.

As we age, flexibility decreases owing to loss of water content in the intervertebral disks and other age-related tissue changes. Research has shown that inactivity also plays a role: muscles need to be used regularly to keep them from weakening and stretched regularly to keep them from tightening. If you're inflexible, it's more difficult to perform everyday activities, such as putting on shoes and socks and getting in and out of the car, and falls are more likely.

Types of Stretching

There are two major types of stretching: static (or passive) and dynamic (or active). Static stretching involves slow, gradual, controlled elongation of the muscle through its full range of motion. Dynamic stretching employs a bouncing technique. Static stretching is recommended more frequently since it is less stressful and easier to perform without injury. Dynamic stretching is generally reserved for sports training. It is not recommended for older adults or nonathletes.

When properly performed, static stretching increases flexibility by encouraging joints and muscles to utilize their full range of motion. The result is improved balance and greater agility, better posture, and less susceptibility to fatigue and pain. A study in the Journal of Gerontology evaluated 103 men and women age 65 years and older who were free from

cardiovascular disease and musculoskeletal problems. Over a 12-month period, those who performed static stretching exercises reported greater improvements in levels of generalized body aches than those who underwent strength training.

Static stretching also enhances physical performance, since flexible muscles react faster and with more force than inflexible ones. Stretching can also help to reduce anxiety, muscle tension, blood pressure, and breathing rate in people who are physically and emotionally tense. The resulting mental and physical relaxation may enhance mental alertness and minimize the risk of joint injuries, muscle strains, and sprains.

Most experts believe that less flexible muscles and connective tissue restrict joint mobility and boost the likelihood of injury. But there are no definitive data to support this assumption.

Getting Started with Stretching

Static stretching is considered beneficial for almost everyone, regardless of their general health. But if you have strained muscles; any back, neck, bone, or joint problems such as rheumatoid arthritis, osteoarthritis, osteoporosis, or compression fractures (breaks caused by ordinary forces on weakened bone); or have had a hip or knee replacement, consult your doctor before beginning a stretching program.

People with conditions such as CHD, chronic obstructive pulmonary disease (an umbrella term used for both chronic bronchitis and emphysema, which primarily affect longtime smokers), or diabetes also require medical guidance.

The exercises on page 29 provide a basic routine of static stretches. Most experts agree that static stretches should be performed to the point of mild discomfort, but never stretch so far that you feel acute pain. While stretching can help alleviate muscle tension, it can also cause soreness when overdone.

If you are just starting a stretching program, therefore, you should be especially careful that you don't overstretch a muscle. As long as your stretch is slow and deliberate, you can safely lengthen a muscle beyond its normal reach as you develop flexibility.

If you feel unsure about stretching technique, you can ask for expert help in designing a stretching program from a certified personal trainer. If you're looking for a more structured stretching program, also consider yoga. A 5,000-year-old physical and mental discipline involving moving and stretching from one posture into another, yoga provides strength and flexibility to the whole body while it relaxes and calms.

Basic Stretching

Proper technique is important when you are performing stretches because stretching incorrectly—or when you shouldn't—can do more harm than good. Moving the wrong way can cause tiny tears in muscles and connective tissue, which may leave scar tissue after healing. The scar tissue may then tighten the muscle, decrease flexibility, and possibly increase susceptibility to pain and injury.

The most important caveat is to warm up muscles before starting to stretch, because stretching without any preparation—while the muscles are cold—may cause injury. If stretching will be your only physical activity of the day, warm up first by walking, pumping your arms, doing light calisthenics, or performing another low-intensity cardiovascular activity for 10 to 15 minutes. Then do 10 to 15 minutes of stretching.

For people who work out regularly, 5 to 10 minutes of light aerobic exercise can suffice as a warm-up. This warmup is generally a slower or gentler version of the usual workout or a series of slow, rhythmic exercises that target larger muscle groups. Riding a bicycle or walking work well. The warm-up should be followed by gentle stretching, a full cardiovascular or strength training workout, and a final stretch. This is the best time for the final stretch because the high muscle temperature after the warm-up and full workout reduces the potential for soreness and stiffness.

The following safety principles apply to all types of static stretching:

- **Stretch your entire body,** from head to foot, in any order that feels right to you; the best strategy varies from person to person. Focus on the body's major muscle groups, including calf, thigh, and hip muscles, lower and upper back muscles, neck, and shoulders. Don't neglect the knees, feet, and ankles. Keep your body properly aligned, as uncontrolled twisting or turning can lead to injury. Incorporate a full range of motion—both side to side and front to back—where appropriate.

- **Hold each pose at least 30 seconds.** One 30-second stretch is more beneficial than two 15-second stretches.

- **Don't bounce or kick.** Repeated brief stretches of a muscle can increase stiffness and susceptibility to pain and offer no benefit. They simply result in a reflex contraction of the muscle, similar to how the leg bounces when a doctor taps your knee.

- **Move slowly and gently.** Vigorous stretching or jerking into a stretch can put undue stress on the ligaments and tendons, tearing them or decreasing joint stability.

- **Breathe.** Holding your breath while you stretch can cause muscles to contract and blood pressure to rise. Regular breathing will deepen the stretch. Begin by exhaling and extending the muscle, breathe slowly and deeply while holding the stretch, and inhale when returning to a relaxed position.

- **Don't lock your joints into place when you straighten them.** They should remain very slightly bent.

- **When lying on your back, move one leg at a time.** Sudden movements with both legs can strain the muscles and ligaments of the lower back.

- **Make sure it feels good.** If not, your technique is incorrect or you may have a medical problem. Stop and check with your doctor before continuing a stretching program.

Neck stretch. Tilt your head to the right, keeping your shoulders down. Place your right hand on the left side of your head. Gently pull your head toward your right shoulder and hold for 10 to 30 seconds. Switch sides and repeat.

Hip stretch (for hip flexor). From a kneeling position, bring right foot forward until knee is directly over ankle; keep right foot straight. Rest left knee on floor behind you. Leaning into front knee, lower pelvis and front of left hip toward floor to create an easy stretch. Hold for 10 to 30 seconds, then switch legs and repeat.

Calf stretch (for gastrocnemius and soleus muscles). Stand 2 to 3 feet from a wall, with your feet perpendicular to wall in the position shown, and lean against wall for 10 to 30 seconds. Keep your feet parallel to each other; make sure your rear heel stays on floor. Switch legs and repeat. Variation: keep your rear knee slightly bent during stretch.

Thigh stretch (for hamstrings, in back of thigh). Lie on back. Place a rope loosely around the sole of one foot, grasping both ends with both hands. Contracting the front of your thigh, lift that leg as high as possible, aiming your foot toward ceiling. "Climb" hand over hand up the looped rope to lift your leg gently, keeping upper body on floor. Keeping tension on the rope and using it for gentle assistance, hold stretch for 2 seconds. Don't pull your leg into position—that can cause knee problems. Repeat 8 to 10 times, then switch legs.

Outer thigh Stretch (for iliotibial band). Placing your left hand against a wall for balance, place your left foot behind and beyond your right foot. Bend your left ankle and lean into the wall. Hold for 10 to 30 seconds, then switch and repeat.

Lumbar stretch (for lower back). Lying on your back, clasp one hand under each knee. Gently pull both knees toward your chest, keeping your lower back on the floor. Hold for 10 to 30 seconds, relax, then repeat.

Disease Prevention

The right diet is a powerful weapon against several chronic diseases. The amount and types of food you eat may determine whether and when you develop a life-threatening disorder, such as coronary heart disease (CHD), cancer, obesity, diabetes, or a disorder that reduces the quality of life, such as macular degeneration or osteoporosis. For example: about 35 percent of all cancers are related to dietary factors, but a high intake of fruits and vegetables can cut cancer risk in half.

Surveys show that most people recognize the importance of a healthy diet, but they don't always follow one. For example, in an American Dietetic Association survey, 72 percent of people over age 55 said that diet and nutrition were important to them, yet only about half reported that they were consuming a healthy diet. Moreover, two-thirds of Americans eat more than the recommended amount of total and saturated fat, according to a U.S. Department of Agriculture (USDA) survey; the National Cancer Institute found that the average intake of fruits and vegetables is 3.4 servings per day—the minimum recommendation, met by just 23 percent of the population, is 5 servings a day. The USDA also found that people who do eat vegetables tend not to eat the most nutritious ones: Only 9 percent of fruit and vegetable eaters chose dark green leafy vegetables, and only 8 percent ate deep yellow or orange vegetables.

Among the factors that contribute to these discrepancies between knowledge and action are restraints on time, the ready availability of packaged and processed foods, people's perception that they will have to give up favorite foods, confusion over conflicting information about nutrition, and the belief that dietary changes made later in life are of little consequence.

Fortunately, changing dietary habits in middle or even old age is not difficult and can significantly influence health. In fact, age-related body changes make it even more important to pay attention to the foods in the diet and the nutrients they contain: Older adults face a diminishing ability to absorb and utilize certain nutrients and often experience a change in appetite due to age or life circumstances. Nevertheless, most people can achieve a healthy diet merely by adding certain flavorful foods to their diet, while cutting back on—but not eliminating—other less healthful foods.

The Keys: Variety and Moderation

Food supplies not only the energy we need to function but also the nutrients that are required to build all tissues (bone, muscle, fat, and blood) and to produce substances required for the chemical processes that take place within our bodies millions of times a day. There are two broad categories of nutrients: macronutrients—carbohydrates, protein, and fats—which supply energy and are needed in large amounts to maintain and repair body structures; and micronutrients, the vitamins and minerals required in small amounts to help regulate chemical processes and maintain bones. Fiber, technically not a nutrient, is also part of a healthy diet.

Below are 12 guidelines for a healthy diet. Every meal doesn't have to meet all these guidelines. What's important is that you apply them to your eating pattern over the course of several days or a week

1. Emphasize fruits, vegetables, and grains. Most experts recommend a high-carbohydrate/low-fat diet with a semi-vegetarian focus. According to this school of thought, 50 to 60 percent of calories should come from carbohydrates, 10 to 20 percent from protein, and 30 percent or less from fat. (Some experts have set 35 percent as the outer recommended limit for fat intake.) To achieve these targets,

grains, vegetables, and fruits should make up the bulk of your diet. Many of these foods are also a good source of vitamins, minerals, and dietary fiber (see below). Try to get nine or more servings of fruits and vegetables daily and six or more servings of grains or grain products (preferably whole grains).

2. Cut back on foods high in fat. A certain amount of fat is essential for your body to function properly. But because fat is a concentrated source of calories—it contains 9 calories per gram, compared with 4 calories per gram in carbohydrates or protein—a high-fat diet can contribute excess calories that lead to weight gain. Also, many foods that are derived from animal sources, including meats and dairy products, contain saturated fat and cholesterol; both (but especially saturated fat) raise blood levels of total cholesterol and LDL ("bad") cholesterol, a major risk factor for coronary heart disease (CHD). In some studies, a high intake of animal fat has also been associated with an increased risk of certain cancers, especially colon and prostate cancer.

3. Reduce your intake of trans and saturated fats. Along with trying to keep fat intake to 30 percent or less of total calories, you should aim to limit your intake of saturated fat to 10 percent or less of total calories. Rather than calculating percentages, it's easier to reduce your intake of foods high in saturated fat. These include red meats, dark meat poultry, poultry skin, whole-milk dairy products, butter, and products made with coconut, palm, or palm kernel oils. Also included are packaged foods made with hydrogenated oils; these contain trans fats, which may be more dangerous than saturated fats (see page 32).

4. Substitute unsaturated fats for saturated ones. Another way to reduce the intake of saturated fat in the diet is to replace it with oils containing monounsaturated fats and, to a lesser extent, polyunsaturated fats. Monounsaturated fats—which are plentiful in olive oil, canola oil, avocados, and some nuts—lower total blood cholesterol levels without reducing levels of HDL ("good") cholesterol. Polyunsaturated fats, found in vegetable oils (such as safflower, sunflower, and corn oils), nuts, and fish, also lower total cholesterol levels, though large amounts may reduce HDL cholesterol levels as well.

    Some studies have suggested that certain polyunsaturated fats called omega-3 fatty acids, which are found in oily fish such as salmon, tuna, and sardines, have a heart-protective benefit by making blood platelets less likely to clot, which in turn may reduce the chance of a heart attack. Eating fish twice a week (8 ounces total) is associated with a reduced risk of CHD.

5. Consume foods high in dietary fiber. Experts recommend that everyone over 50 consume at least 21 to 30 grams of dietary fiber (from food, not supplements) each day. Fiber is found only in plant foods, which contain varying proportions of insoluble and soluble fiber. Whole grains are an especially good source of insoluble fiber, which can help prevent constipation and diverticular disease. Some studies have shown that consuming soluble fiber—found in oats, oat bran, legumes, barley, citrus fruits, prunes, and apples—can help lower blood glucose and cholesterol levels. High-fiber foods are generally good sources of vitamins and minerals as well.

6. Watch the amounts of foods you eat. Nutrient and calorie needs for good health

The Insidious Fat

Dietary fats are composed of various combinations of saturated, monounsaturated, and polyunsaturated fatty acids, and come in solid or liquid form. Fatty acids are differentiated by how many hydrogen atoms they contain: Saturated fats hold all the hydrogen atoms they can carry; monounsaturated fats are missing a single pair of hydrogen atoms; and polyunsaturated fats are missing two or more pairs.

Saturated fats, which are solid at room temperature and are found primarily in animal foods, have long had the reputation of being the most harmful type of fat. But recent studies suggest that trans fatty acids—a type of fat that is widely used in commercially processed foods—pose an even greater risk.

Trans fatty acids are present in small amounts in natural foods, but the major dietary sources are margarines and commercial baked products such as chips, cookies, and cakes. In making these products, food manufacturers typically use modified polyunsaturated oils. Because polyunsaturated oils are liquid, manufacturers add hydrogen atoms (a process known as hydrogenation) to make vegetable oils firmer and less likely to spoil. This hydrogenation process transforms many of the unsaturated fatty acids in oils, making them more saturated and changing their structure in other ways that makes them into "trans" fatty acids.

Studies have shown that these trans fats are even more harmful to health than saturated fats because trans fats raise the ratio of LDL to HDL cholesterol more than saturated fats. A recent study also showed that a high intake of trans fatty acids was associated with a significant increase in the risk of diabetes.

For some years, nutrition labels on packaged foods have indicated how much total and saturated fat a product contains, but not the amount of trans fats. The Food and Drug Administration (FDA) requires trans fat information as of 2006. In the meantime, read labels to check for hydrogenated or partially hydrogenated fats on packages of baked goods and snack foods. Also cut down on stick margarine and fried fast foods—both major sources of trans fats.

vary from person to person. How many servings of foods you should eat daily depends on your gender, body frame type, and level of physical activity. In general, sedentary women and some older individuals need about 1,600 calories per day. Active men and very active women need about 2,800 calories daily. (For information on calorie intake and its effect on body weight, see page 39.)

7. Limit your sodium intake. Consuming less than 1,500 mg of sodium per day can help control hypertension and, in turn, lower one's risk of CHD. You can accomplish this by using less salt at the table and in cooking, and by avoiding foods that are high in sodium (for example, processed meats such as sausages, cured ham, and hot dogs; canned or dried soups; ketchup; and most cheeses).

8. Eat foods rich in antioxidants. Antioxidants are substances that help the body neutralize free radicals—chemical compounds that oxidize LDL and make it more likely to deposit in arteries. It is possible that LDL oxidation can be diminished by a substantial intake of foods containing the naturally occurring antioxidants beta-carotene, vitamin C, and vitamin E.

Carotenoids are found in dark green vegetables and yellow and orange vegetables and fruits. Good sources of vitamin C include citrus fruits, berries, red and green peppers, broccoli, brussels sprouts, and dark leafy greens. (Vitamin E is hard to obtain from foods alone, as explained on page 34.)

9. Consume plenty of calcium. This mineral is crucial for building strong bones, and helps maintain bone strength for a lifetime. Calcium intake is especially important for women, whose bone density declines dramatically after menopause. Men and women over 50 should consume 1,200 to 1,500 mg of calcium daily to help slow the bone loss that occurs with aging. The best food sources for calcium are milk and other dairy products, and you should chose only low-fat varieties (which contain just as much or more calcium than high-fat products). Fortified cereals and calcium-fortified orange juice are also good sources. Other nondairy calcium sources include white beans, broccoli, canned salmon and sardines eaten with the bones, and dark leafy greens such as kale and arugula.

   Many people may have trouble obtaining the recommended level through foods alone, and can use supplements to make up for calcium shortfalls (see page 35).

10. Consume sugary foods in moderation. Sugar is a simple carbohydrate that can provide energy. It is not linked to serious health disorders, but it can cause tooth decay. From a dietary point of view, the chief problem with sugar is that it doesn't provide the nutrients present in foods high in complex carbohydrates (grains, vegetables, legumes, and fruits). And in many commercially prepared foods, a high sugar content is usually matched by a high fat content. If you eat a balanced, nutritious diet, following the guidelines given here, moderate use of sugar is perfectly acceptable as a way of enhancing the taste of certain foods and beverages. (People with diabetes needn't avoid sugar, but do need to be careful about sugar consumption, as explained on page 278.)

11. Drink enough water or other fluids. Using thirst as your guide, drinking sufficient amounts of fluid (which may include juices, milk, and other nonalcoholic beverages as well as water) each day can help prevent constipation and dehydration. Keeping well hydrated is especially important for people living in warmer climates.

12. If you drink alcohol, drink moderately. Experts recommend that men not have more than two alcoholic drinks per day; women should limit themselves to one drink per day. (A drink is defined as 12 ounces of beer, 5 ounces of wine, or 1.5 ounces of 80-proof spirits.) Alcohol consumption at this level may reduce the risk of CHD, but heavy alcohol consumption can lead to a variety of health problems, especially several types of cancer. Also, people with certain disorders should avoid alcohol altogether (see page 47).

Dietary Supplements: Are They Necessary?

While no supplement can replace a healthy, well-balanced diet, it can sometimes be difficult to get sufficient amounts of certain vitamins and minerals from foods, especially for older individuals. As you age, food intake can be limited by a variety of factors, such as living alone (which makes it harder to shop and cook) or difficulty chewing and swallowing due to tooth loss or dental disease. Even when you eat right, some age-related changes decrease the body's ability to absorb certain nutrients. For these reasons, some older adults often don't get enough vitamins and minerals and should consider supplements. Other individuals who may also need supplements include vegetarians, pregnant women,

Questions About Vitamin E

A number of observational studies over the past two decades suggested that taking vitamin E supplements could help coronary heart disease (CHD)—specifically, acting as an antioxidant to slow the development of coronary atherosclerosis by preventing harmful oxidation of LDL cholesterol. However, several prospective trials carried out in recent years found that vitamin E supplementation did not lower the number of cardiovascular events in patients with known CHD. Though many people with CHD are taking vitamin E supplements, the available evidence makes it unlikely they will obtain any benefit.

It has also been suggested that the antioxidant effects of vitamin E may protect against cancer and eye diseases such as cataracts, as well as boost the immune system. Since vitamin E is found mainly in nuts, seeds, and vegetable oils—and even these foods contain only small quantities—it is difficult to obtain enough vitamin E through food. At the same time, the amount of vitamin E needed to obtain any benefit has not been established.

People taking anticoagulant medications, such as warfarin (Coumadin), should be aware that they may not be able to take vitamin E because it may enhance the anticlotting effects of anticoagulants. If you take one of these drugs, check with your doctor before you start taking vitamin E.

and people who are on strict diets or are lactose intolerant.

Supplement Guidelines

Although the need for supplements is a matter of some controversy, most experts agree that four nutrients may be useful to take in supplement form—calcium, vitamin D, vitamin B12, and folic acid. Not only have studies shown that these essential nutrients (which are discussed below) protect against disease, but they can be difficult to obtain from food sources). While it's also considered healthful to increase your intake of vitamins C and B6, for example, supplements are generally unnecessary because these nutrients are relatively easy to obtain from food. Vitamin E is another nutrient that isn't easily available from food, but there is controversy about the value of taking supplements (see text box above).

Before taking any supplement, you should remember a few caveats. First, supplement pills cannot substitute for food, since they do not provide other important nutrients found in food—such as fiber and protein—that contribute to your health and well-being. In addition, supplements are not cure-alls and should be considered as only part of a healthy lifestyle that includes a well-rounded diet and exercise.

Finally, always remember to follow dosage recommendations. Taking higher doses than advised is not necessarily better and, in fact, may be harmful. (Vitamin D, for example, is toxic when taken in large doses.) The figure most often placed on supplement labels is the daily value (DV). It corresponds to the recommended dietary allowance (RDA), the amount of a specific nutrient necessary to meet the nutritional requirements of nearly all healthy people in a specific age and gender group. Three units of measure are used: International Units (IU), micrograms (mcg), and milligrams (mg).

You may want to consider a multivitamin for some your nutrients (see the text box on page 35). A good multivitamin should supply the amounts you need of folic acid and vitamin B12. But calcium, and possibly vitamin

D, may need to be taken in separate pills in order to obtain adequate amounts.

Calcium

Essential for building and maintaining healthy bones, calcium both helps create strong bones when you are young and protects against bone loss and osteoporosis as you age. For example, a recent review found that bone loss was slowed or halted in 16 of 19 studies of postmenopausal women taking calcium supplements. Unfortunately, many people do not get enough of this mineral, often because they have reduced their intake of dairy products in order to follow a low-fat diet. Women and men over age 50 need 1,200 mg per day, and should try to consume 1,500 mg. People unable to reach these amounts from food sources should take supplements.

Calcium is always found in combination with another chemical component, such as carbonate or citrate. Calcium carbonate pills should be taken with meals since the presence of gastric acid improves calcium absorption. To improve absorption, you should take no more than 500 mg of calcium at one time, and never exceed 2,500 mg a day, because higher intakes have been linked to kidney stone formation. (However, diets low in calcium also increase the risk of kidney stones.)

Vitamin D

This vitamin is also essential to protect against osteoporosis, since it enhances calcium absorption. Normally, vitamin D is manufactured in the skin during exposure to ultraviolet light from the sun, but the ability to form vitamin D decreases with age. By age 70, vitamin D production is only 30 percent of what it was at age 25. In addition, fewer older people drink milk, the other main source of vitamin D, and they are less able to absorb the amounts that they do consume. The National Academy of Sciences (NAS) recently

Getting the Most from a Multivitamin

Today, health-conscious shoppers face hundreds of supplement products, many of them with labels that make questionable advertising claims. Here are some tips to keep in mind when making a selection.

Take a basic multivitamin. Most products contain 100 percent of the recommended dietary allowance (RDAs) of all the essential vitamins, except biotin and vitamin K, which are easy to obtain from foods. They also contain a percentage of the RDAs of key minerals. Products formulated for seniors typically contain less iron and vitamin A and more calcium, vitamin B12, and vitamin B6.

Choose tablets. Tablets are cheaper than gels, capsules, and liquids—and you can feel confident choosing inexpensive drugstore brands. Laboratory tests have shown that the various brands of multivitamin tablets contain what their labels indicate—and that the most expensive brands are no better than the cheapest ones.

Don't double up on your multivitamin. You may get too much of some nutrients.

Avoid supplements that supply more than 100 percent of the recommended daily values for vitamin A and iron. Your body's need for these nutrients declines with age.

Don't pay for worthless features, such as "all-natural," timed-release, or chelated (a chemical formulation said to promote absorption).

Avoid taking vitamin or mineral supplements that also contain herbs. Although a few herbs may hold some therapeutic promise, most have unproven benefits and some could be harmful. If you choose to take an herb, research it carefully, purchase it separately, and tell your doctor that you take it.

increased their recommended vitamin D intake to 400 IU for adults age 51 to 70 and 600 IU for adults over 70. Avoid intakes over 2,000 IU since too much vitamin D can be toxic, and cause lethargy, vomiting, constipation, and excessive thirst and urination.

Vitamin B$_{12}$

This vitamin is necessary for many essential processes in the body, but it becomes increasingly difficult to obtain from food as you age. Between 10 percent and 30 percent of older people lack the acid in their stomach necessary for the separation of vitamin B12 from food, and many of the foods that contain it—such as meat and eggs—have been eliminated or cut back due to their fat and cholesterol content. In fact, the NAS advises that all people over 50 meet their vitamin B12 needs with a supplement or through fortified foods. The current RDA is 2.4 micrograms per day.

Folic Acid

This B vitamin assists in protein metabolism and has been shown to decrease birth defects, such as spina bifida, by 50 percent. As a result, the federal government now requires that enriched grains, including cereal and pasta, be fortified with additional amounts of folic acid. The NAS recommends that all women of child-bearing age get 400 mcg of folic acid from supplements and/or fortified foods in addition to the folate that is naturally present in food. In addition, the RDA for folic acid was recently raised to 400 mcg per day for all adults. Folic acid from supplements and fortified foods is actually better absorbed than naturally occurring folic acid.

Folic acid can also lower blood levels of the amino acid homocysteine. High homocysteine levels are a risk factor for cardiovascular disease, and together with vitamin B6 and B12, folic acid helps reduce homocysteine levels in the blood. While no study has proven that taking folic acid supplements decreases the risk of cardiovascular disease, research has shown that people with the highest levels of homocysteine have more than twice the risk of cardiovascular disease than those with the lowest levels; and people with the lowest blood levels of folic acid have a 69 percent greater risk of death from CHD than those with the highest levels.

The one danger of a high folic acid intake is that it can mask the symptoms of pernicious anemia, a condition caused by a lack of vitamin B12, which is more common in older individuals. For this reason, people taking folic acid supplements should take vitamin B12 as well.

The complications related to excessive body weight—which include type 2 diabetes, high blood pressure, coronary heart disease, osteoarthritis, and gallbladder disease—are second only to tobacco-related complications as a cause of preventable deaths. Moreover, studies have shown that people who are significantly overweight can often decrease their risk for these medical problems by losing a modest amount of weight—even as little as 5 percent to 15 percent of body weight. In many cases, weight loss can improve symptoms of obesity-related disorders, or slow or even reverse disease progression.

Yet in the face of increasing publicity about the health risks of being overweight, and despite spending billions of dollars annually on products and programs aimed at people eager to be thinner, millions of Americans are chronically overweight.

Over the past three decades, Americans have heeded public health warnings and significantly cut their intake of dietary fat. For example, according to a study published in 1997, Americans reduced their average consumption of total fat by 6 percent between 1987 and 1992, achieving an average intake of 36 percent of total calories. (The intake currently recommended by most experts is 30 percent or less of total calories.)

Despite this progress, however, the percentage of overweight and obese adults in the United States has risen dramatically since the 1980s. Results of the most recent National Health and Nutrition Examination (NHANES), an ongoing study conducted by the Centers for Disease Control and Prevention (CDC), indicate that an estimated 61 percent of U.S. adults are either overweight or obese, defined as having a body mass index (BMI) of 25 or more. The surge is especially significant for obesity, defined as having a BMI greater than or equal to 30. From 1980 to 1999, the percentage of obese individuals nearly doubled, from approximately 15 percent of the population to an estimated 27 percent. (To determine your BMI, the medical standard used to define overweight and obesity, see page 458.)

What's more, obesity appears to be on the rise among all segments of the American population, especially children and adolescents, as well as in people from all ethnic backgrounds. Perhaps most unsettling, the obesity epidemic is not limited to Americans, but—with the increased urbanization of the world's population—is now occurring globally.

Are You at a Healthy Weight?

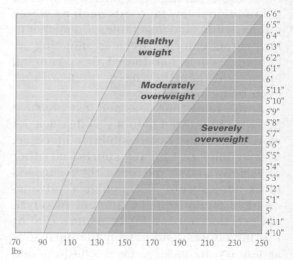

The chart above, from the U.S. government, is an approximate guide to healthy and unhealthy body weights. It uses body mass index (BMI)—which measures weight in relation to height—to show that health risk increases at higher levels of overweight and obesity (severe overweight).

Why Obesity Has Risen

How can people decrease their intake of fat and still gain weight? Dietary fat does not appear to be a major contributor to the growing prevalence of obesity in our society. And, despite the attention devoted to the genetics of obesity, genetic factors do not seem to be a key culprit. Instead, most experts point to our environment, which encourages both an excessive intake of calories and decreased physical activity.

Our society now has an unprecedented abundance of convenient, inexpensive foods, which are available almost everywhere. In addition, portion sizes have grown larger, especially at restaurants, where patrons have become accustomed to expecting large quantities of food in order to feel they're getting their money's worth. Although an increasing number of reduced-fat products are available, even these are often high in calories compared to traditional low-fat foods such as whole grains, fruits, and vegetables. Consequently, overall calorie intake is climbing as people become habituated to consuming more food than they need, often without even being aware of it.

At the same time, less and less physical activity is required in today's lifestyles. As work and family responsibilities increase, many adults give up any sports and other physically active pastimes they engaged in as adolescents. Technological advances have minimized the amount of physical exertion needed for transportation or routine chores, and have made most jobs sedentary in nature. Even children and adolescents are getting less exercise, as they spend more time indoors (increasingly because of concerns about their safety), where they watch television and play computer games.

Thus, while genetic susceptibility and dietary fat intake certainly play a role, the current obesity epidemic is believed to arise primarily from a combination of decreased physical activity and increased caloric intake. Unless lifestyle conditions change, obesity rates will continue to rise and, consequently, so will the rates of obesity-related health problems. But if weight gain can be curbed and eventually reduced, the frequency of these health problems will drop correspondingly.

Complex Mix of Factors

In theory, weight control is a simple matter of balancing energy intake (the calories supplied by food) with energy output (the calories expended by physical activity and metabolism). To lose weight, all you need to do is expend more energy than you take in.

In practice, however, the equation is clearly not that simple. While the basic principle of energy balance remains true, several mechanisms—genetic, metabolic, and environmental—govern how your body uses and stores energy. At the same time, controllable factors—such as how much you eat, inappropriate psychological responses to food, and a lack of exercise—play a critical role in the development of obesity.

Heredity. Heredity clearly plays some role in the risk of becoming obese. For example, studies show that 80 percent of children born to two obese parents will themselves become obese, compared to 14 percent of children born to normal-weight parents. Research on identical twins shows similarly high rates of heritability.

However, studies comparing the weights of adoptees to the weights of their biological and adoptive parents indicate that genetic factors are responsible for only about 33 percent of the variance in weight, a figure experts believe is more accurate. Heredity seems to influence the number of fat cells (adipocytes) in the body, how much fat is stored, where it is stored, and some aspects of metabolism. About 80 percent of children who are obese become obese adults; yet only 20 percent of obese adults were obese as children.

Studies have also shown that a genetic predisposition to becoming overweight can be overcome. In one study of 485 pairs of female twins, the amount of physical activity appeared to be a significant factor in determining body weight. Physically active women had 9 pounds less body fat than their sedentary twin sisters.

Caloric intake. Regardless of genetic predisposition or any other factors, you cannot gain weight without consuming more calories than you burn. Thus, one study found that "diet resistance"—the inability to lose weight even on a reduced-calorie diet—may be explained by under-reporting food intake and over-reporting exercise. The study participants reported eating less than 1,200 calories a day, yet they were unable to lose weight. In comparing figures the subjects reported in their food/activity diaries to their actual calorie intake and level of physical activity, the researchers found that they had underestimated their calorie intake by 47 percent and overestimated their energy output by 51 percent.

Even small excesses in calorie intake—too small to measure accurately in the most rigorous study—can contribute to obesity over the long term. For example, if a person overeats by just 25 calories a day, he or she will consume 9,125 excess calories over the course of a year, and so gain 2 1/2 lbs (a pound of body fat is equivalent to 3,500 calories). A woman weighing 125 lbs who starts this pattern at age 20 would weigh 175 lbs by the time she is 40.

To point to overeating as the cause of obesity is overly simplistic, however. It doesn't explain why one 125-lb woman needs 1,800 calories a day to meet her body's energy needs and avoid losing weight, while another 125-lb woman struggles to avoid gaining weight on 1,200 calories a day. Many other factors are at work, including metabolism and physical activity. Nevertheless, obese persons must be consuming more calories than required by their individual make-ups and activity levels; otherwise they would not store excess body fat. Thus, it is essential to reduce caloric intake in order to lose weight.

Physical activity. Variations in physical activity can have a tremendous impact on total daily energy expenditure. A sedentary person may burn just a few hundred calories above his resting metabolism rate (RMR) while going about daily activities (such as working and performing household chores), whereas an athlete can burn an additional 3,000 calories each day through vigorous exercise. Regular exercise not only burns calories, but also builds lean muscle mass and raises RMR because muscle requires more energy to maintain. According to a report by the Surgeon General on physical activity and health, 60 percent of Americans are not regularly active, and 25 percent are not active at all. This low level of activity may be the most important factor responsible for the high and rising rate of obesity in the United States.

Behavioral and psychological issues. Several psychological factors affect weight control. The message to eat often comes from external cues rather than hunger—noon means it's time for lunch, for example. Food and emotions are closely linked; many people use food for comfort or to release tension. Eating too quickly can lead to taking in more calories than are needed to satisfy hunger. The amount of exercise a person engages in is also shaped by habit and attitudes toward physical activity.

How to Lose Weight

Even if some of the components involved in weight regulation are beyond your control, environmental factors have a significant impact. By manipulating these factors to your advantage, you can successfully lose weight and keep it off.

Successful weight loss requires a three-pronged approach: changing behavior patterns, making dietary adjustments, and increasing physical activity. Culled from medical research, the guidelines given here incorporate strategies employed by people who have lost weight and kept it off. (Some people who are chronically obese and/or have other medical problems may also, in consultation with their doctors, consider medication or surgery—see pages 459 and 461. But these options are only for some patients and only after diet and exercise have failed.)

Be motivated. An ability to alter lifelong attitudes toward diet and exercise may ultimately be the key to successful weight management: You must be motivated enough to change habits not for a few weeks or months, but for a lifetime. The importance of this resolve cannot be underestimated. The desire to lose weight must come from within, rather than from external pressures. A person who wants to shed 20 lbs to please a spouse is not likely to be as motivated, or as successful, as someone whose goal is to improve health or increase self-esteem.

Choosing the right time to start a weight-loss program is also important. People under stress or pressure may not be able to devote the considerable attention and effort required to make lifestyle changes.

Set realistic goals. Remember that weight tables give estimates of ideal weights; you can probably be healthy at weights above "ideal" if you have a nutritious diet and get some exercise. Instead of attempting to lose a specific number of pounds, make it your goal to adopt healthier eating and exercise habits. If you are obese and feel compelled to set a weight goal, losing 10 to 15 percent of your current body weight is a realistic objective. The safest rate of weight loss is 1/2 to 2 lbs a week.

If your weight is stable, cutting out about 500 calories a day usually achieves this weekly goal. As a rule of thumb, the average woman who is dieting should consume at least 1,200 calories a day and the average man at least 1,500.

Take advantage of exercise. Cutting caloric intake is one way to lose weight, but such asceticism is hard and can be frustrating. Combining exercise with reduced calories is more successful than dieting alone as the way to lose weight and keep it off.

Step 1: Eating Right

Diets work when you make permanent, balanced changes in what and how much you eat. Think of healthy eating as being on a calorie-nutrition budget. You have just so many calories available to "purchase" the nutrition you need.

Spend your calorie budget on basics first. Start with foods providing carbohydrates—vegetables, fruits, bread, cereal, rice, pasta, and other starchy, low-fat foods. Then add good sources of protein—lean meat, poultry, fish, low-fat dairy products, eggs, nuts, dry beans, peas, and legumes. Finally, limit the amount of fats and oils you consume. (See pages 30-32 for more advice on adopting a low-fat, high-complex-carbohydrate diet.)

Packaged foods that are "fat-free" can help you limit fat intake, but only if you use them as substitutes for higher-calorie foods and don't replace the calories you have saved with something else. Ordering a cheeseburger with a bag of fat-free chips isn't a

High-Protein Diets

Most fad diets point to some miracle food that you should either eat plenty of or avoid altogether to help you shed pounds for good. Among the most popular of these are high-protein, low-carbohydrate diets, such as the Atkins diet, Protein Power, and The Carbohydrate Addict's Diet, which all but eliminate carbohydrates and replace them with additional protein. This approach boils down to a diet rich in animal products such as meat, eggs, and cheese, but with few grains, fruits, and vegetables. Such diets produce a state known as ketosis, in which increased breakdown of fat forms appetite-suppressing substances called ketone bodies.

Ketosis may cause dehydration, dizziness, weakness, or headaches. Despite these effects, such diets are probably not harmful for short periods in healthy people. They can, however, be dangerous for people with known or hidden heart or kidney problems. And metabolic changes caused by these diets can also alter the effects of medications, particularly antihypertensive drugs. Therefore, high-protein diets should be adopted only under a doctor's supervision.

The long-term risks are of greater concern. Prolonged ketosis can cause kidney damage. Also, a diet high in animal protein is high in fat and lacks adequate vitamins, minerals, and fiber, which may increase the risk of cancer, osteoporosis, and, especially, heart disease.

High-protein diets are appealing because they often result in rapid weight loss, at least initially, due to the loss of body water. However, people tend to regain the weight eventually—a problem with all fad diets—because most people can stick with this type of food restriction for only a limited period of time. The safest and most effective way to lose weight is a balanced, low-calorie diet combined with regular exercise.

reasonable weight-loss strategy. However, if you're in the habit of eating an ounce of regular potato chips every afternoon, switching to a few low-fat whole-grain crackers will save you a considerable number of calories (and also provide important nutrients).

Step 2: Becoming Active
Burning more calories by boosting your activity level is an effective way to achieve and maintain weight loss. Your long-term goal should be to get at least 30 minutes of physical activity most days of the week—in truth, not a demanding task, yet one accomplished by fewer than 25 percent of adult Americans. Achieving significant weight loss, though, may require 60 to 90 minutes of exercise per day.

Walking is usually the easiest exercise for most people. Even people with severe heart disease or arthritis can benefit from a walking program tailored to their abilities. Strength training is also important because building muscle boosts the overall rate at which the body burns calories.

If you are over 50, be sure to talk to your doctor before starting any type of exercise program. If you don't like to exercise, keep in mind that being physically active throughout the day—by consistently taking the stairs instead of the elevator, for example, or parking at the back of the lot instead of near the front—can be helpful. (See page 21 for more detailed exercise guidelines.)

Step 3: Reinforcements
In addition to eating right and making time for exercise, the following measures have proven to be effective for anyone motivated and ready to lose weight.

Seek support from family and friends. People who receive social support are more successful in changing their behaviors. Ask family and friends for help, whether this means keeping high-fat foods out of the house or relieving you of some chore so that you have time to exercise. You may also be more motivated to exercise if you work out with a friend or family member.

Make changes gradually. Trying to make too many changes too quickly can leave you feeling overwhelmed and frustrated. Instead, ease into exercise; don't overdo it. Incorporate low-fat eating in stages. For example, if you typically drink whole milk, switch to 2 percent milk, then to 1 percent, and then to fat-free milk.

Eat slowly. Many people consume more calories than needed to satisfy their hunger because they eat too quickly. Since it takes about 20 minutes for the brain to recognize that the stomach is full, slowing down helps you feel satisfied on less food.

Eat three meals a day, plus snacks. Skipping meals is counterproductive, as is severely reducing food intake, since such strict changes are impossible to maintain and are ultimately unhealthy. People who restrict their eating habits too rigorously often have an "all or nothing" approach: Once they "go off" their diet, they tend to abandon all efforts and find it difficult to return to healthy eating.

Evaluate your relationship to food. Behavioral and emotional cues frequently trigger an inappropriate desire to eat. The most common cues are: habit, stress, boredom, emotions, and the use of food as a reward. Many people also relate food to love or care and derive comfort from it. Although eating may seem to soothe uncomfortable feelings, its effect is temporary at best and ultimately does not solve any problems. In fact, it may distract you from focusing on the real issues.

Record your progress. Start a food diary and exercise log to keep track of your accomplishments. Such detailed diaries may seem cumbersome, but they can help you stay motivated, and reviewing the entries can reveal any problem areas. In addition, the information can help your nutritionist or doctor facilitate treatment.

Recall your other accomplishments. Over your lifetime you have probably been successful in tackling many difficult tasks—quitting smoking, learning a new skill, or advancing in the workplace, for example. Reminding yourself of past achievements can help you feel more confident about making the changes that will lead to weight loss.

Don't try to be perfect. While losing weight requires significant changes in eating and exercise habits, not every high-fat food must be banished forever, and you needn't exercise vigorously every day. High-fat foods can be eaten once in a while without hindering weight loss, and it's also acceptable to miss an exercise session.

Step 4: Maintaining Weight Loss
Keeping weight off is often a bigger challenge than losing weight; the majority of people who embark on diets quickly regain the weight they have lost. However, about 20 percent of dieters do succeed in achieving permanent weight loss. What distinguishes people who maintain their weight loss from those who lose and then regain weight? The few studies that have examined this question suggest that the answer lies in the use of coping strategies.

The National Weight Control Registry (NWCR) is a database of about 3,000 people who have lost an average of 66 pounds and maintained that weight loss for 5 1/2 years. By studying this group of people, researchers have gained insight into what behaviors these weight loss maintainers have in common. For example, maintainers eat a low-fat, high-carbohydrate diet; engage in exercise for about an hour each day; self-monitor their weight (three quarters of registry members weigh themselves weekly); and eat breakfast. While maintaining weight loss seems like a formidable task, participants in the NWCR report that weight maintenance becomes easier over time. Based on NWCR participants, researchers predict

that people who maintain their weight loss for more than three years will likely have long-term success.

The good news is that if you've lost weight sensibly by following the guidelines outlined here, you have already learned much of what you need to know about successful weight maintenance. For the most part, all you need to do is to continue the behaviors and activities that helped you lose weight initially.

Disease Prevention

Cigarette smoking kills more than 400,000 Americans each year. It plays a role in the leading causes of death—cancer, heart disease, and lung disease—and accounts for $50 billion of annual health-care expenditures. Quitting lowers the risk of getting and dying of these illnesses. So why do people keep smoking?

Why It's Hard to Quit

Giving up cigarettes is harder than giving up heroin, according to people recovering from these addictions. With every puff from a cigarette, a smoker inhales 4,000 chemicals, many toxic and one—nicotine—highly addictive. Within seconds, nicotine unleashes a flood of brain chemicals (including dopamine, norepinephrine, and serotonin) that causes the smoker to feel alert and to enjoy a sense of pleasure. Because the body adjusts to and craves heightened levels of these chemicals, some people experience intense withdrawal symptoms—including irritability, difficulty concentrating, anxiety, and depression—when trying to quit smoking.

On top of the physical addiction, psychological, behavioral, and environmental factors make quitting smoking especially hard. A smoker may come to associate cigarettes with enjoyable experiences such as socializing with friends or the cup of coffee that starts the day every morning. Or people may smoke to calm their nerves during stressful situations. While giving up cigarettes requires a tremendous amount of determination, sheer willpower is often not enough. Only about 5 percent of those who quit "cold turkey" are successful. The good news is that many cessation aids are available that can dramatically increase a smoker's chance of putting out that last cigarette.

Nicotine Replacement Therapy

Pharmaceutical nicotine administered via chewing gum, skin patch, nasal spray, or inhaler can substitute for the nicotine in cigarettes. It lessens both the craving for and the withdrawal symptoms from the drug. A smoker trying to quit may use nicotine replacements anywhere from a few weeks to a few months, depending on the level of addiction. During that time (each product has a suggested duration of use), the dose is gradually tapered. Studies evaluating different nicotine replacement therapies show that they all work about equally well and yield roughly twice the success rate of a placebo.

People who smoke more than 20 cigarettes a day often require higher doses of nicotine for a longer time than those who smoke less. They may also benefit from using more than one nicotine replacement therapy at a time or adding a different cessation aid—some form of social support or an antidepressant.

Nicotine gum tends to work best for lighter smokers. It can be purchased over the counter (OTC) in 2-mg and 4-mg doses (a piece of the 2-mg gum delivers about the same amount of nicotine as a cigarette). Nicotine gum should not be chewed like normal gum. Chew it slowly, until you feel a mild tingling. Then place it between your gum and cheek for a few minutes. Continue this process for half an hour, then discard the gum. Many people find they need 10 to 15 pieces a day during the first week after quitting.

Transdermal nicotine patches, which deliver nicotine through the skin, can also be bought OTC. Use a dose that corresponds to the number of cigarettes you smoke. For example, if you are a pack-a-day smoker, you may want a patch that delivers 21 or 22 mg of nicotine over 24 hours. Likewise, if you smoke two packs or more daily, you might require a patch that delivers 42 to 44 mg of nicotine a day. Minor skin irritation can occur, so don't apply them to the same spot every time.

Nicotine nasal spray, available by prescription only, delivers a strong dose of nicotine into the nostril, where it is absorbed very quickly. This rapid delivery method may help heavy smokers. Headaches, watering eyes, and nasal/throat irritation are not uncommon in the first few days of use, but these effects generally wear off within the first week.

Nicotine inhaler, a recent product also available by prescription, resembles a cigarette holder and delivers about 4 mg of nicotine. As the device can be held and inhaled like a cigarette, this product might be the best choice for those who enjoy the ritual of smoking.

Beyond Nicotine

Despite their usefulness, nicotine replacement therapies don't work for everyone. Interestingly, nicotine seems to matter more to men than to women. In most of the studies evaluating nicotine replacements, men do better than women. Similarly, smokers with a history of depression tend not to do as well using nicotine replacement therapies alone. These findings suggest that some smokers who are trying to break the habit may need some form of behavioral intervention, such as individual counseling or participation in a smoking cessation group.

Behavioral therapy. Research shows that nicotine replacement therapy increases the chance of success, but the best results are achieved in conjunction with behavioral therapy, which helps patients learn to avoid being around cigarettes, smokers, and things that trigger their desire for a cigarette. Therapy can also address emotional triggers that cause a smoker to light up. The hardest time, say experts, is the first two weeks after quitting. If someone can go for two weeks without smoking a cigarette, he or she has a much better chance at long-term abstinence than someone who cannot.

Antidepressants. Bupropion (Zyban), by affecting some of the same neurotransmitters as nicotine, reduces both nicotine cravings and withdrawal symptoms during cessation attempts. A recent study revealed that 23 percent of those taking bupropion, compared with 12 percent of those taking a placebo, were smoke-free after one year. That's about the same long-term success rate as is seen with nicotine replacement therapies. In addition, people taking bupropion gained much less weight than those taking a placebo. So bupropion might be a good cessation aid for smokers concerned about gaining weight after quitting. Another antidepressant—nortriptyline (Aventyl, Pamelor)—has proven to be an effective stop-smoking tool, although it is not approved for this purpose.

Combination Therapy

Research indicates that combining therapies may be the most effective way to quit smoking. While the patch and bupropion used individually are more effective than a placebo in helping people to quit smoking after a month, the two used together achieve the greatest cessation rate. Likewise, adding some form of counseling or behavioral therapy to drug treatment can increase a smoker's chance of quitting for good.

In recent years, numerous studies have shown that moderate alcohol consumption offers some appealing health benefits. For example, moderate drinkers are less likely to have heart attacks and strokes—and are even less likely to die from these conditions—than teetotalers. This evidence is so strong that dietary guidelines issued by the United States Department of Agriculture (USDA) in 2000 acknowledge the cardioprotective benefits of alcohol for men over age 45 and women over age 55. Not only is it acceptable for older adults to have a glass of wine with dinner, the guidelines say that doing so may help the heart.

Research suggests that alcohol consumption may be associated with noncardiac benefits as well. Surprisingly, when more than 8,500 men between ages 30 and 79 were evaluated at a clinic in Texas, those who had 5 to 10 alcoholic drinks a week had a much lower risk of developing type 2 diabetes than those who drank less. And a German study found an inverse relationship between alcohol intake and infection with *Helicobacter pylori*, the organism that causes 90 percent of stomach ulcers. In this evaluation of nearly 1,800 people, the percentage of subjects infected with *H. pylori* declined as alcohol consumption rose.

But before uncorking the beer, wine, or champagne, consider the risks. While moderate alcohol consumption may be healthy for some people, many should abstain—and drinking too much can have serious health consequences. Furthermore, age-related changes in how the body processes alcohol make older adults particularly vulnerable to the negative effects of excess consumption.

The Key: Moderation

Any possible health benefit alcohol may deliver is negated once consumption goes beyond a certain point. Based on the current evidence, USDA guidelines recommend limiting daily alcohol intake to one drink for women and two drinks for men. One drink is the equivalent of 12 oz. of beer, 5 oz. of wine, or 1.5 oz. of 80-proof distilled spirits. The guidelines also suggest consuming alcohol with food to slow its absorption.

While one to two drinks a day are considered safe and even healthy for many people, a greater intake is potentially hazardous. Heavy drinking not only increases a person's chances of having an automobile accident, committing suicide, and acting violently, it can also cause the very health problems tempered by moderate drinking. In the diabetes study mentioned previously, an alcohol intake of more than 10 drinks a week was associated with a twofold increase in the risk of developing type 2 diabetes. In fact, the researchers found evidence suggesting that high alcohol consumption was a major contributing factor in 24 percent of their diabetes cases.

The much-touted cardioprotective effect of alcohol is limited to one to two drinks per day as well. While studies have consistently shown a 20 percent to 40 percent reduction in heart attacks among moderate drinkers compared with nondrinkers, the benefit is offset when consumption exceeds this amount. Heavy drinkers are at greater risk for other types of heart disease and other serious medical problems. Stroke protection, too, is lost with heavier consumption. In a study that appeared in the *Journal of the American Medical Association*, people who had only one or two drinks daily had a 45 percent lower risk of ischemic stroke (a stroke caused by a blocked blood vessel) than those who drank no alcohol. But heavy drinkers had three times the risk of ischemic stroke. Long-term, excessive consumption can also lead to high blood pressure, cirrhosis of the liver, cardiomyopathy (an enlargement of the heart), malnutrition, and certain types of cancer.

Women and older adults should be particularly cautious about how much alcohol they consume. Aging reduces the amount of water in body tissues, and women typically have less water in their tissues than men of comparable height and build. Because alcohol is soluble in water, it tends to dissolve more slowly in older adults and women than in young men. Thus, women and older adults become intoxicated after fewer drinks, and the effects of alcohol last longer. In addition, women appear to have smaller amounts of the enzyme that metabolizes alcohol than men do. As a result, alcohol stays in their bodies longer.

When to Say No

Regardless of age, anyone who has uncontrolled hypertension, liver disease, kidney disease, pancreatitis, or congestive heart failure should abstain from alcoholic beverages. And clearly, anyone who is prone to alcohol abuse or addiction, or who exhibits violent behavior after drinking, should abstain.

People with high blood levels of triglycerides (a type of fat, or lipid) should also consider abstinence, because alcohol increases the blood level of these potentially harmful lipids. You can find out your triglyceride values as part of a complete lipid profile, which also includes values for total cholesterol, high density lipoprotein (HDL) cholesterol, and low density lipoprotein (LDL) cholesterol (see page 50).

Abstinence is also necessary for people who take medications that interact with alcohol. These include a long list of prescription and over-the-counter (OTC) drugs, including popular OTC pain relievers such as aspirin, ibuprofen (Advil), and acetaminophen (Tylenol). Drug interactions are listed on the package information that comes with both prescription and OTC medications. You should also discuss the possibility of alcohol/drug interactions with your physician and pharmacist.

Alcohol and Cancer

Heavy drinking increases the risk of several cancers—notably, cancer of the mouth, esophagus, pharynx, larynx, liver, and pancreas. In the last decade, considerable attention has been focused on a possible association between alcohol and breast cancer. An analysis of multiple studies published in the mid-1990s found that having two alcoholic drinks per day raised a woman's chances of developing breast cancer by nearly 25 percent. The reasons for this link are unclear, but researchers speculate that alcohol slowed the metabolism of estrogen. Prolonged exposure to high levels of estrogen over a lifetime has been linked to a higher breast cancer risk. One report found that heavy drinking led to a threefold increase in circulating estradiol (a type of estrogen) in women on hormone replacement therapy (HRT), but not in women who weren't on HRT. Although more research is needed to make any recommendations, abstaining from alcohol might offset the slight increase in breast cancer risk associated with HRT.

The effect of light drinking (one drink per day) on breast cancer risk has been controversial. But an evaluation of two generations of women may have settled the dispute. The subjects were part of the famous Framingham Study, a massive epidemiologic research effort that has been culling health information about residents of Framingham, Massachusetts, since 1948. Among 2,764 women who were followed for more than 40 years and 2,284 of their daughters who were followed for more than 20 years, light drinking did not

Alcohol Is Alcohol

Red wine has a reputation for being the most cardioprotective type of alcohol, possibly because it contains more antioxidants. But evidence strongly suggests that there is little difference in the health effects—good or bad—among red wine, white wine, or any other type of alcoholic beverage.

In modest amounts, alcohol in any form increases HDL ("good") cholesterol and lowers LDL ("bad") cholesterol. Much of alcohol's benefit on CHD can be credited to this action. Alcohol also appears to prevent strokes and heart attacks by enhancing the blood's ability to break up clots that have formed.

increase breast cancer risk. Nor was breast cancer risk affected by the type of alcohol consumed.

Summing Up: Recommendations for Alcohol Consumption

1. If you don't currently drink alcohol, don't start. Experts do not recommend that teetotalers begin drinking alcohol; instead, they should take other steps to reduce their risk of CHD, including the diet and exercise measures covered earlier in this section.

2. Men should limit their intake to one to two alcoholic drinks per day. This amount is enough to reduce CHD risk, but has little negative impact on health.

3. Women who have no CHD risk factors should limit alcohol intake to fewer than seven drinks per week. Having a few drinks per week probably does not increase the odds of getting breast cancer, but it is not known whether this amount of alcohol helps to prevent CHD.

4. Women who have CHD (or who are at increased risk) should have no more than one drink per day. For such women, the benefits of moderate alcohol consumption may outweigh the risks. (However, there are many ways to reduce CHD risk, but few known ways to reduce the risk of breast cancer.)

5. Remember that heavy alcohol consumption is a health risk. Heavy drinking (more than one to two alcoholic drinks per day) can cause a variety of life-threatening diseases.

6. People with hypertriglyceridemia, pancreatitis, liver disease, porphyria, uncontrolled hypertension, and congestive heart failure should avoid alcohol—as should anyone with a past or current problem with alcohol. And of course, everyone should abstain from alcohol when driving.

A screening test can be defined as any type of health evaluation—including labwork, physical exams, and imaging procedures such as x-rays—that is intended to identify health problems in people who have no signs or symptoms of the disease. Like the lifestyle measures discussed in this section, screening tests are intended to help people live longer, healthier lives—specifically, in the case of screening tests, by detecting a disease at its earliest and most treatable stage. An increasing number of tests have been developed in the past several decades. However, the benefits and limitations of screening tests are matters of continuing debate, as are the issues of who should receive particular tests and how often they should be administered.

Potential Drawbacks of Screening

To be useful, a screening test must accurately detect a disease; effective treatments must be available; and early intervention must be able to reduce suffering or save lives. One widely successful screening test is the Pap smear—a simple test for identifying cervical cancer at an early stage that is almost always curable. The test has certainly saved many lives. Yet, experts disagree on how often a Pap smear should be done.

Indeed, even the most valuable tests have limits. Though some tests are highly reliable in detecting disease, no test is 100 percent accurate. Screening tests typically produce a certain number of false-negatives, meaning that the disease is present, but test results are normal. Tests can also produce false-positives, meaning results are abnormal even though disease is not present. Some tests carry slight but definite health risks—for example, colonoscopy, unquestionably a valuable tool for early detection of colon cancer, carries a small

risk of bowel perforation. Even if a test is risk-free, a positive result can often lead to additional, and often more invasive, diagnostic tests that may pose some risks. Finally, even the most accurate screening test offers little benefit if early diagnosis and treatment do not influence the outcome of a disease.

When Is a Screening Test Appropriate?

At present, based on the results of large-scale scientific studies, only a limited number of screening tests are recommended for use in the general population. These include blood pressure and blood lipid and glucose measurements, vision and hearing exams, and certain screening tests for colon, breast, and prostate cancer. Many other tests are considered beneficial for selected individuals, primarily people at high risk for a particular disease. In certain cases, widespread screening may be recommended for a rare disease if has severe consequences and can be treated effectively.

If you have questions about whether you need or might benefit from a particular screening test, consult your physician, who can help make informed decisions that are tailored to your particular circumstances.

Screening Guidelines

Many different health organizations and groups—government agencies, professional associations, and nonprofit groups—have issued guidelines that outline which screening tests are appropriate and how often they should be performed. Among the recommendations that have received the most attention are those made by the U.S. Preventive Services Task Force (PSTF), a government-sponsored group of experts who have reviewed evidence on the usefulness of different measures, including screening tests for preventing various illnesses. Also widely acknowledged are guidelines from the American Cancer Society, The American

Heart Association, The American Diabetes Association, the American College of Physicians, and the National Cholesterol Education Program.

Guidelines from various organizations can differ, especially with respect to the age when screening should begin and the frequency of testing. The following pages cover the screening tests most often performed on healthy adults age 50 and older. The recommendations are based on a review of existing guidelines by specialists in various medical fields at Johns Hopkins. In many cases, screening tests are recommended on an annual basis; however, in some instances, more frequent monitoring and additional tests may be called for.

Remember, too, that these are guidelines. In deciding whether a test is appropriate for you, your doctor will consider such factors as your age, risk factors, any coexisting disorders, and your attitude about various outcomes and potential side effects of different screening tests.

Recommendations for All Adults

Tests considered useful for all adults include those for coronary heart disease (CHD), diabetes, glaucoma, hearing loss, thyroid disease, colorectal cancer, and skin cancer,. The medical advisors for this book unequivocally recommend these tests for all adults. In addition, all women should be screened for breast cancer, cervical cancer, and osteoporosis, while men should seriously consider getting screened for prostate cancer, as explained on page 53.

Blood pressure measurement. Most experts suggest that all healthy adults (those who do not have high blood pressure) should get their blood pressure checked every two years. Generally, a diagnosis of hypertension should be based on the average of two or more readings taken at each of two or more visits after an initial screening. People with high blood pressure require more frequent evaluations (see the chart on page 387).

Lipid profile. To identify people at risk for CHD, the National Cholesterol Education Program, sponsored by the National Heart, Lung, and Blood Institute, recommends a fasting lipid profile (a blood test obtained after a 12-hour fast) for adults over 20 at least every five years. The test measures total cholesterol, low density lipoprotein (LDL) cholesterol, high density lipoprotein (HDL) cholesterol, and triglycerides. More frequent monitoring may be necessary for older adults who have abnormal results or have other CHD risk factors. (See page 236 for more information.)

Blood glucose measurement. To promote the early detection of diabetes, and thus help reduce the risk of its complications, the American Diabetes Association recommends that all individuals age 45 and older have a blood glucose test every three years. The presence of certain factors that heighten the risk for developing diabetes should prompt earlier and more frequent testing. Risk factors include: obesity; having a first-degree relative with diabetes; being a member of a high-risk ethnic group (including African American, Hispanic, and Native American); delivering a baby weighing more than nine pounds; or being diagnosed with gestational diabetes. The blood glucose test can detect diabetes in its early stages and identify people who are at increased risk for the disorder. (See page 270 for more information.)

Screening for thyroid disease. The American Thyroid Association recommends a test for thyroid disease for all adults every five years beginning at age 35 with an inexpensive blood test for thyroid-stimulating hormone (TSH). People with known thyroid problems, a family history of thyroid disorders, or other

Vaccines

Vaccination is another important aspect of disease prevention. Vaccines work by "tricking" the immune system: When a vaccine is introduced into the body, it activates specialized white blood cells (B cells and T cells) that recognize and eliminate potentially harmful microbes, usually bacteria or viruses. Whenever B and T cells become active, they give rise to memory cells—B cells that retain the ability to recognize the invading microbe and trigger an immune response if the microbe enters the body again. Following vaccination, the memory cells can recognize and respond to specific disease-causing organisms, and the resulting immunity protects you from the disease.

Which vaccinations you need depends on your age, general health, and lifestyle. The shelf life, side effects, and effectiveness of a particular vaccine vary, as do the duration of immunity and the number of doses required to produce immunity. The following is a general guide for those over 50.

Flu. An annual flu shot is recommended for everyone over age 50; it is especially important for people who are frail or have chronic medical problems.

Pneumonia. The pneumococcal pneumonia vaccine is recommended for everyone over age 65, all nursing home residents, and anyone with a serious illness. If first given after age 65, only one pneumonia vaccination is usually necessary. A pneumonia booster is needed after five years if the original vaccination was given before age 65.

Tetanus. Adults of all ages should be vaccinated against tetanus. Vaccination requires three doses spread out over two years, followed by booster shots every 10 years.

Hepatitis B. The following people should be vaccinated against hepatitis: dialysis patients, people with sexually transmitted diseases or who have multiple sex partners, homosexual men, people who use intravenous drugs, health-care workers, police officers, firefighters, people who work or live in homes for the mentally and physically disabled, and anyone who lives with a hepatitis B carrier. A series of three shots confers lifelong protection.

Childhood diseases. Older adults should consider vaccination against certain childhood diseases (such as chicken pox, mumps, measles, and rubella) if they never had them.

risk factors—which include pernicious anemia and adrenal insufficiency—should be monitored more frequently.

Screening for glaucoma. While glaucoma cannot be prevented, early detection—by measuring intraocular pressure, examining the optic disc, and testing visual fields—allows treatment that may prevent damage to the optic nerve. A common recommendation is an examination every two years after age 50 in whites and after age 40 in African Americans. Cardiovascular disease, diabetes, and high degrees of myopia (nearsightedness) appear to increase the risk of nerve damage from glaucoma. People with such risk factors may need more frequent screening. An annual exam is advisable by age 65.

Although glaucoma screening is offered in many settings, ophthalmologists produce the most reliable results. They are well acquainted with the appearance of the optic disc and can make the most educated assessment of its condition. A thorough eye examination to evaluate other aspects of vision and eye structures should also be done at this time.

Hearing exam. The PSTF recommends that primary care physicians screen for hearing impairment by interviewing patients during regular check-ups, counseling them about the availability of hearing aid devices, and referring them to hearing specialists when abnormalities are detected.

Screening for colon cancer. According to guidelines endorsed by the PSTF, the American Cancer Society, the American Gastroenterological Association, and several other organizations, screening should begin at age 50 with an annual *fecal occult blood test* (FOBT); it involves placing a small amount of stool on a card that, under laboratory analysis, can reveal traces of blood that may be a sign of cancer.

A second recommended test is *flexible sigmoidoscopy*, which should be performed at age 50 and at least every five years thereafter if no abnormalities are uncovered. The test involves insertion of a flexible, lubricated viewing instrument (a sigmoidoscope) into the rectum and sigmoid colon. Sigmoidoscopy is best performed by gastroenterologists, who are more experienced than primary care doctors in recognizing abnormalities and knowing when to biopsy them. A *digital rectal exam* (DRE) should accompany each sigmoidoscopy. During a DRE, the doctor inserts a gloved, lubricated finger into the rectum and feels for abnormalities.

Other screening options include *colonoscopy*, which inspects the entire colon through a scope, or a *barium enema*, which provides an x-ray view of the colon. Which option you choose depends on your preferences and your doctor's recommendations.

Anyone at increased risk for colorectal cancer, especially those with a history of suspicious lesions or a family history of colorectal cancer, requires more frequent monitoring and a colonoscopy.

Screening for skin cancer. The American Cancer Society recommends that everyone over age 40 have an annual total skin examination performed by a dermatologist or other physician trained to recognize skin cancer. People who have had any type of skin cancer or precancerous lesions should discuss with their doctor whether they need a more aggressive monitoring program.

In addition, experts recommend regular self-exams: ideally once a month, or at least every three months. Suspicious lesions should be examined by a dermatologist and biopsied if necessary. Skin inspections are particularly important for people with a fair complexion, a history of frequent sunburns, a great deal of lifetime sun exposure, or a family history of skin cancer.

Recommendations for Men

Prostate cancer is the second most common cancer among North American men (after skin cancer). The screening test for prostate cancer, known as PSA—for prostate specific antigen, a protein produced by cells in the prostate—has been available for some years, but recommendations concerning its use remain controversial.

The American Cancer Society and the American Urological Association are strong advocates of a PSA test, along with a digital rectal examination (DRE). Their recommendations call for annual testing to start at age 50, or at an earlier age in men who are at elevated risk (African-American men, men with a family history of prostate cancer, and, possibly, veterans exposed to Agent Orange). Currently, however, the PTSF does not recommend the PSA as a general screening test.

Critics of PSA testing argue against universal screening largely because there is no proven relationship between prostate cancer death rates and PSA testing. In addition, they note that PSA testing often prompts a biopsy that may be unnecessary, since the PSA test cannot distinguish between early cancers that will become life-threatening and those that will remain harmless. Also, treatments for prostate cancer may be ineffective or cause side effects that may reduce the quality of life.

Although PSA testing is far from perfect, men should seriously consider having the test because the potential benefits of early diagnosis are so great and PSA screening is so simple. The test can be performed using the same blood sample drawn to measure cholesterol. A prostate biopsy is warranted when a doctor suspects the possibility of prostate cancer after feeling a prostate abnormality during a DRE or when PSA is elevated. The biopsy takes no more than 30 minutes and can be performed in a urologist's office.

Whether you decide to have a PSA test depends on a number of factors, including your willingness to undergo treatment should prostate cancer be found, and whether your life expectancy is greater than 10 years. (Overall, about 70 percent of men choose testing.) While many professional organizations recommend that men have an annual PSA test beginning at age 50, researchers at Johns Hopkins— drawing on data from the Baltimore Longitudinal Study on Aging—suggest it may be prudent to have a PSA test and DRE at age 40, again at age 45, and then, beginning at age 50, every other year. Ultimately, decisions regarding prostate cancer screening should be made in consultation with your physician.

Recommendations for Women

Experts recommend routine screening for the following diseases in women over 50.

Breast cancer. As with the PSA test for men, the value of routine mammography is currently under debate because some recent research has cast doubt on whether mammography saves lives.

Most breast cancer experts acknowledge that mammography is not perfect.

The test misses 10 percent to 15 percent of breast cancers, particularly in younger women whose denser breasts make mammograms more difficult to interpret. Mammograms may also uncover an early but very aggressive cancer that proves incurable. In addition, mammograms produce many false-positives that result in additional—and frequently invasive—testing. Over 10 years, about a quarter of women undergoing annual screening have an abnormal mammogram; 80 percent to 90 percent of these turn out to be harmless.

The widespread adoption of screening mammography has greatly increased the detection of small tumors called ductal carcinoma in situ (DCIS). Many DCIS tumors remain noninvasive (harmless), but it's not yet possible to distinguish between those that will stay harmless and ones that will become invasive and life-threatening. Thus, the management of these tumors presents a dilemma.

The debate concerning the precise impact of mammography on breast cancer mortality will not be settled conclusively for some time. Meanwhile, recently updated recommendations from the National Cancer Institute, the American Cancer Society, and the PSTF suggest regular screening mammography—every one or two years—for all women over 40. Mammography is the best tool currently available for detecting early tumors, and early detection affords women more treatment options.

In addition to mammography, most experts recommend an annual clinical breast examination and a monthly breast self-exam (see page 155).

Cervical cancer. Women over 50 should routinely have the Papanicolaou (Pap) test for cervical cancer. An internal pelvic examination should also be done at this time. Some primary care doctors and all gynecologists do the procedure, which generally

Improving Mammogram Accuracy

You can improve the interpretation of your mammogram by going to the same radiologist for each exam and making sure that new films are compared to old ones. If you move or change doctors, request that your records (including the films) be transferred. In addition, choose a practice that frequently interprets mammograms, as studies suggest that accuracy is directly related to volume. Lastly, avoid deodorant, talcum powder, lotion, or perfume on your breast or underarm area on the day of the exam. Aluminum flecks in these substances may appear on the mammogram and reduce its accuracy.

causes little discomfort and takes only a few minutes.

Some experts advise that Pap screening need only be performed at three-year intervals in some women, or can be discontinued in women over 65 who have had normal findings on three consecutive tests and in women who have had the cervix removed at the time of a hysterectomy. However, the medical advisory board for this book supports annual testing for most women regardless of age. Three-year intervals are acceptable only for women who have had the cervix removed, and then only in women who have no personal or family history of cervical abnormalities, uterine cancer, or endometrial cancer.

Osteoporosis. The National Osteoporosis Foundation, in collaboration with a number of major medical organizations, recommends that the following women should be screened for osteoporosis: all women 65 or older; postmenopausal women who have one or more risk factors; and all postmenopausal women who have had a recent fracture, particularly of the vertebrae or hip—the two most common osteoporosis fracture sites.

In addition to menopause—which significantly increases the risk of osteoporosis—risk factors for the disorder include white or Asian ethnic background, a family history of osteoporosis, cigarette smoking, a thin or frail physique, a lack of exercise, a diet low in calcium, the use of certain medications, and a number of other factors related to lifestyle and health (see page 484).

Women who fall into any of these categories should undergo a bone mineral density (BMD) scan—a noninvasive, 15-minute procedure that involves exposure to minimal amounts of radiation (far less than a conventional chest x-ray). Several different types of BMD tests are available (see pages 484-485).

Body Atlas

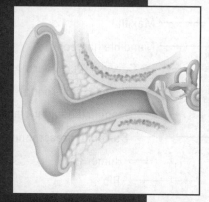

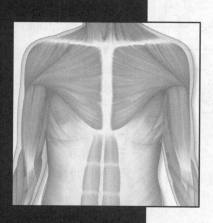

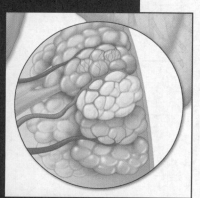

The human skeleton is made up of 206 bones, providing a rigid framework that gives shape and form to the body, protects and supports the internal organs, and works with the muscles to allow body movements. The bones are largely composed of living tissue that is constantly being remodeled. They also store important minerals, such as calcium and phosphorus, and house the bone marrow, which manufactures new blood cells. Bones are attached to each other by fibrous bands of connective tissue called ligaments. The joints—junctions where two or more bones meet—are lined with cartilage, a tough, elastic connective tissue that is also found in various other parts of the body, such as the outer ear.

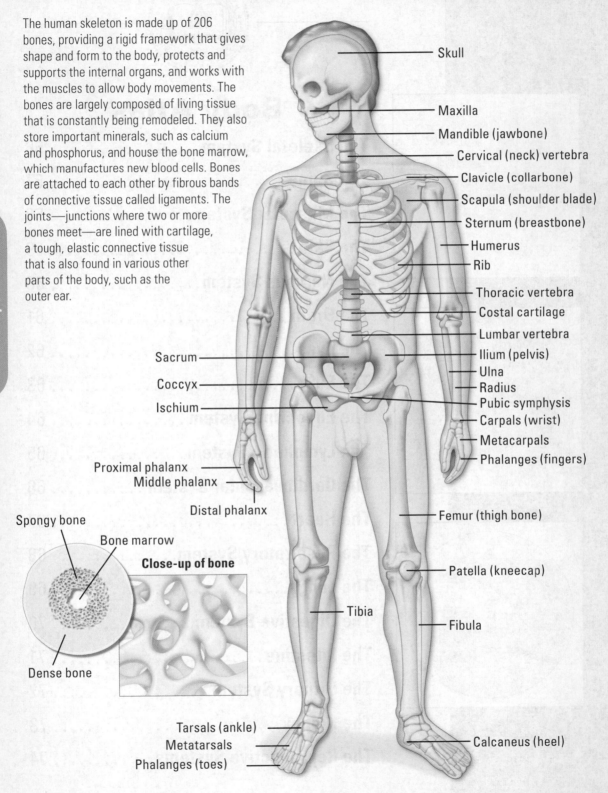

Skull
Maxilla
Mandible (jawbone)
Cervical (neck) vertebra
Clavicle (collarbone)
Scapula (shoulder blade)
Sternum (breastbone)
Humerus
Rib
Thoracic vertebra
Costal cartilage
Lumbar vertebra
Ilium (pelvis)
Ulna
Radius
Pubic symphysis
Carpals (wrist)
Metacarpals
Phalanges (fingers)

Sacrum
Coccyx
Ischium

Proximal phalanx
Middle phalanx
Distal phalanx

Femur (thigh bone)

Patella (kneecap)

Tibia
Fibula

Spongy bone
Bone marrow
Close-up of bone
Dense bone

Tarsals (ankle)
Metatarsals
Phalanges (toes)
Calcaneus (heel)

Designed to hold the body upright and also to protect the spinal cord, the spine forms an S-shaped curve that extends from the base of the head to the pelvis. It contains 33 bones called vertebrae: the smallest vertebrae are the delicate cervical bones of the neck that support the head; beneath these are the larger thoracic vertebrae that bear the weight of the arms and legs; the largest vertebrae, the lumbar vertebrae in the lower back, carry the weight of most of the body. Separating the vertebrae are fibrous discs that prevent vertebrae from grinding against one another and give the spine its flexibility. At the base of the spine, nine fused vertebrae make up the sacrum (the back wall of the pelvis) and the coccyx (tailbone).

Body Atlas

Cervical

Thoracic

Lumbar

Sacrum

Coccyx

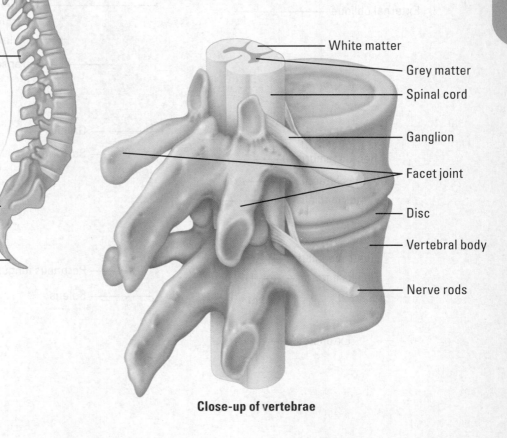

White matter

Grey matter

Spinal cord

Ganglion

Facet joint

Disc

Vertebral body

Nerve rods

Close-up of vertebrae

The more than 600 muscles that cover the skeleton give the human body its characteristic shape. The muscular system consists of the large skeletal muscles that provide support and enable us to move; the cardiac muscles of the heart; and the smooth muscles found in our internal organs. Only skeletal muscles are under our voluntary control. Responding to signals from the nervous system, they contract and relax to allow movement, locomotion, and facial expression. The involuntary contractions of the cardiac and smooth muscles are stimulated by signals from the nervous system and hormones from the endocrine system.

Frontalis
Temporalis
Orbicularis oculi
Orbicularis oris
Sternocleidomastoid
Trapezius
Omohyoid
Deltoid
Pectoralis major
Biceps
Triceps
Serratus anterior
Pronator teres
Rectus abdominis
Extensors
Flexors
Tensor fasciae latae

Brachioradialis
External oblique

Gracilis
Sartorius
Adductor
Rectus femoris
Vastus lateralis
Vastus medialis

Gastrocnemius
Tibialis anterior
Peroneus longus
Soleus

Extensors

The largest organ in the body, the skin serves as a barrier to injury and infection. It consists of two layers: the epidermis, the thin outer layer, and the dermis, a thicker layer that contains hair follicles, blood vessels, nerves, and sweat and oil (sebaceous) glands. Beneath the dermis lies a supportive, fatty layer of subcutaneous fat. The cells at the base of the epidermis continuously divide to produce new cells, which gradually die. Dead cells move up to the surface of the epidermis, where they are shed or rubbed off.

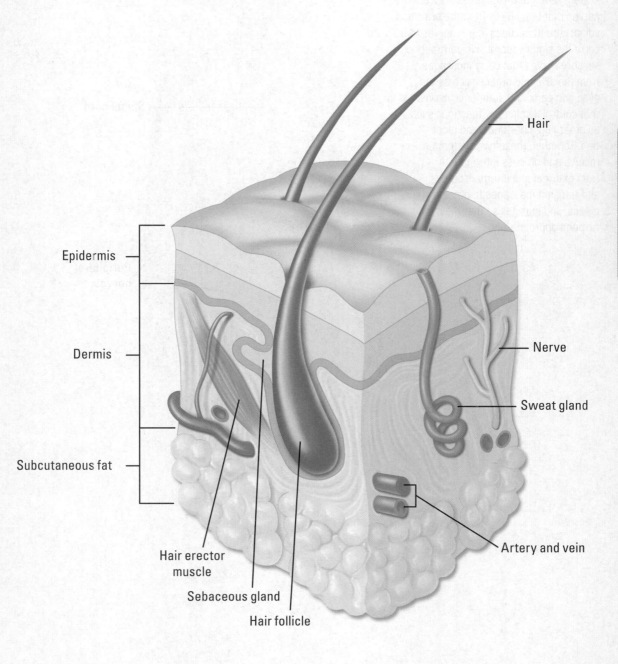

Hair

Epidermis

Dermis

Nerve

Sweat gland

Subcutaneous fat

Artery and vein

Hair erector
muscle

Sebaceous gland

Hair follicle

The central nervous system consists of the brain, the body's primary control center, and the spinal cord, the main conduction pathway for nerve signals to and from the brain. The peripheral nervous system refers to the complex network of nerves that branch out from the brain and spinal cord. It includes motor nerves that carry the signals for muscle contraction; sensory nerves that carry messages from the skin and organs such as the eyes and ears; and autonomic nerves that control involuntary functions such as breathing, heartbeat, and digestion. Together, these two systems receive and process information from external and internal sources, and transmit messages to organs, glands, and muscles so that they respond appropriately.

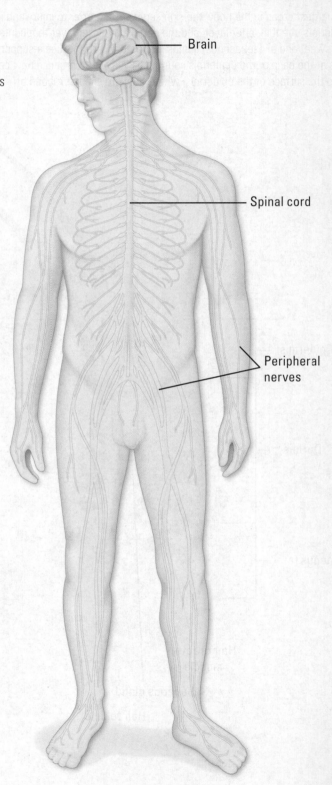

Brain

Spinal cord

Peripheral nerves

The brain is a complex organ that regulates most body functions. Each region of the brain has unique responsibilities such as interpreting sensations like pain and arousal (thalamus); coordinating movement (cerebellum), temperature regulation (hypothalamus), and breathing (brain stem); and enabling language, memory, and emotions (cerebrum).

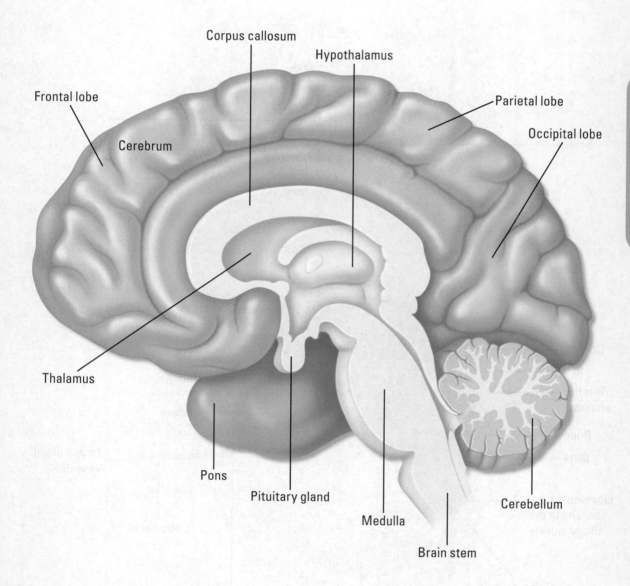

Corpus callosum

Hypothalamus

Frontal lobe

Parietal lobe

Cerebrum

Occipital lobe

Thalamus

Pons

Pituitary gland

Medulla

Brain stem

Cerebellum

Body Atlas

The eye is a complex structure that sends nerve impulses to the brain when stimulated by light rays. It is composed of several layers that surround the the vitreous humor, the gel-like center. In the front of the eye are three visible structures: the iris, the colored circle in the middle of the eye; the pupil, the dark opening at the center of the iris; and the sclera, the white outer layer. Inside the sclera lie two more layers. The middle layer, the choroid, contains a dark pigment that minimizes scattering of light inside the eye. It is rich in blood vessels that supply nutrients to the retina, the eye's innermost layer, which consists of light-sensitive nerve tissue. The retina receives an imprint of an image, which is sent via the optic nerve to the brain.

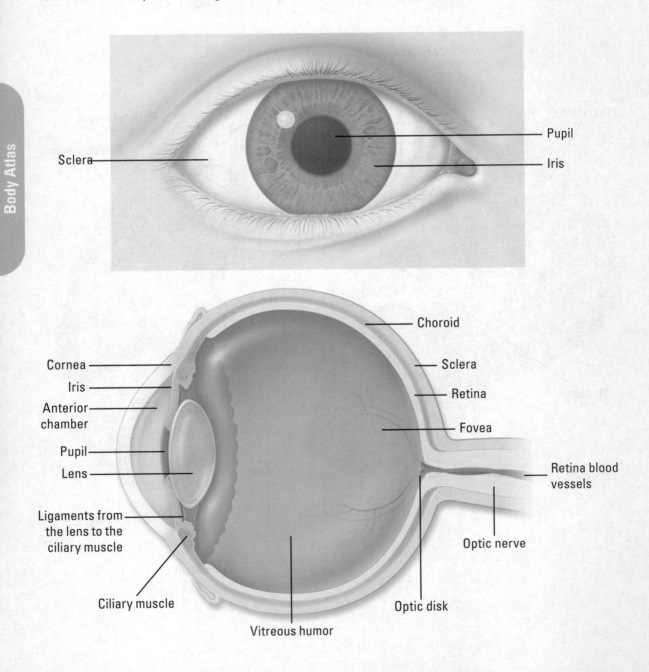

Sclera

Pupil

Iris

Choroid

Cornea

Sclera

Iris

Retina

Anterior chamber

Fovea

Pupil

Lens

Retina blood vessels

Ligaments from the lens to the ciliary muscle

Optic nerve

Ciliary muscle

Optic disk

Vitreous humor

Each ear is divided into three distinct segments: outer, middle, and inner ear. The outer ear consists of the visible, external folds of cartilage and a canal that leads into the middle ear, which includes the eardrum and three bones: the malleus, stapes, and incus. These bones amplify and conduct sound signals to the inner ear—a structure composed of the cochlea and the semicircular canals. The cochlea converts sounds into electrical nerve impulses that are then sent, via the auditory nerve, to the brain, where sound is interpreted. The semicircular canals are responsible for maintaining a person's sense of balance.

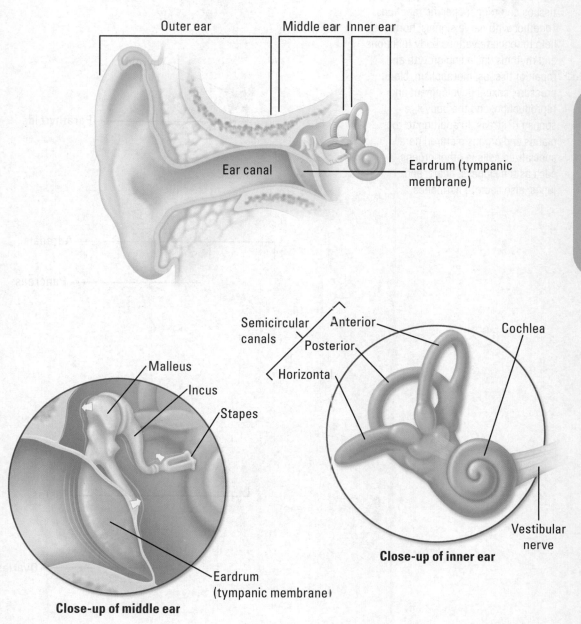

Outer ear   Middle ear Inner ear

Ear canal

Eardrum (tympanic membrane)

Semicircular canals

Anterior

Posterior

Horizonta

Cochlea

Malleus

Incus

Stapes

Vestibular nerve

Close-up of inner ear

Eardrum (tympanic membrane)

Close-up of middle ear

Body Atlas

The endocrine system—which, along with the nervous system, oversees the body's internal communications—consists of glands that produce hormones and secrete them into the bloodstream. Hormones act as chemical messengers that travel to their target organs or tissues and trigger specific reactions. Together with nerve signals, hormones help to regulate various body functions and rhythms, including growth and repair of tissues, metabolism, blood pressure, sexual development and reproduction, and the body's response to stress. In addition to the glands and organs pictured here, specialized cells in other organs, such as the kidneys, heart, and lungs, also secrete hormones.

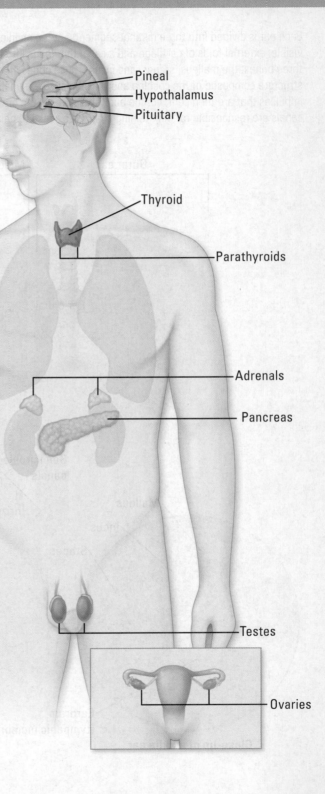

Pineal

Hypothalamus

Pituitary

Thyroid

Parathyroids

Adrenals

Pancreas

Testes

Ovaries

The lymphatic system is a secondary circulatory system made up of a complex network of vessels, nodes, lymph ducts, and certain organs. This system performs various filtering and transporting functions, including the return of excess tissue fluid, or lymph, and proteins to the bloodstream. (Most lymphatic drainage, as well as fat absorbed from the intestine, passes into the thoracic duct—the main lymphatic channel—which drains into a vein in the chest.) In addition, the lymphatic system plays an important role in immunity: Blood and lymph carry white blood cells called lymphocytes that help to defend the body against disease-causing agents, such as bacteria and viruses. (Lymphocytes are produced by the bone marrow and concentrated in the spleen, thymus, and lymph nodes.) The contraction of skeletal muscles moves lymph through the lymphatic vessels, while valves within the vessels help to prevent backflow.

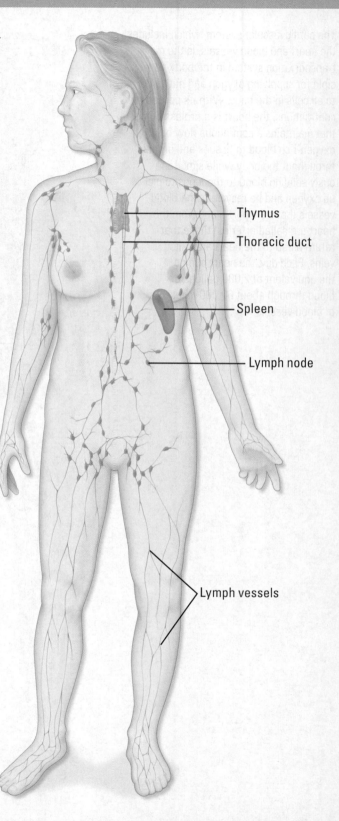

Thymus

Thoracic duct

Spleen

Lymph node

Lymph vessels

Body Atlas

The cardiovascular system, which includes the heart and blood vessels, is the main transportation system in the body, responsible for supplying oxygen and nutrients to all cells in the body. With its perpetual contractions, the heart is a tireless pump that maintains a continuous flow of oxygen-rich blood to tissues and organs throughout the body while simultaneously sending blood to the lungs to pick up oxygen and be recycled. The blood vessels that transport blood from the heart are called arteries; those that return blood to the heart are called veins. Each day, the heart pumps the equivalent of 2,000 gallons of blood through about 60,000 miles of blood vessels.

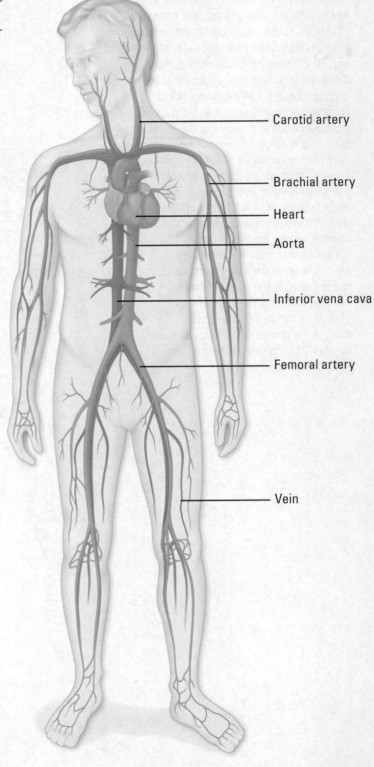

Carotid artery

Brachial artery

Heart

Aorta

Inferior vena cava

Femoral artery

Vein

The heart, which normally beats 60 to 80 times a minute, is a muscular organ with four chambers: the left and right atria and the left and right ventricles. With each contraction, the left side of the heart pumps oxygen-rich blood through the aorta, the body's largest artery, to smaller arteries throughout the body. These arteries, in turn, branch into even smaller vessels, called arterioles, and eventually into the microscopic capillaries that deliver oxygen and nutrients to every cell and pick up carbon dioxide and other waste products. Blood returns to the right side of the heart via the veins and is then sent through the pulmonary arteries to the lungs. Inside the lungs, carbon dioxide is removed, fresh oxygen is added, and the blood returns to the left chambers of the heart. The heart muscle itself is fed a continuous supply of oxygenated blood via the coronary arteries, which branch off at the root of the aorta.

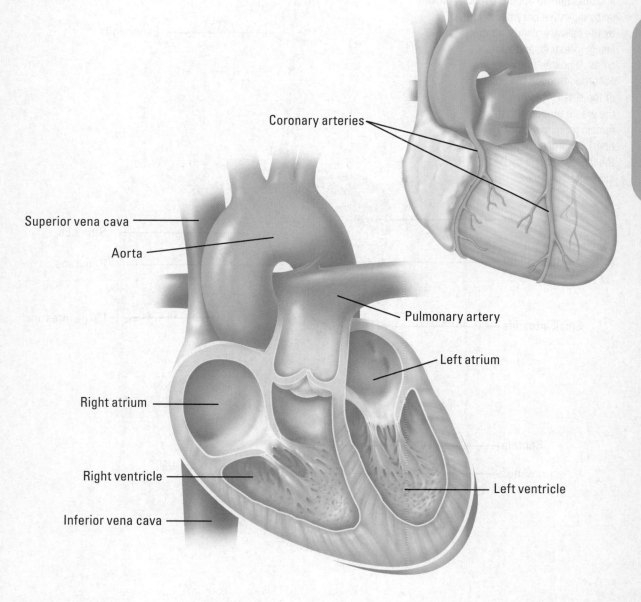

Coronary arteries

Superior vena cava

Aorta

Pulmonary artery

Left atrium

Right atrium

Right ventricle

Left ventricle

Inferior vena cava

The digestive (or gastrointestinal) system consists of a series of connected hollow organs and the organs and glands that secrete digestive juices into this tract. This system breaks down food into absorbable units that enter the bloodstream to nourish cells and provide energy. Food is crushed, mixed, and pushed forward with the wavelike muscular contractions, or peristalsis, of the esophagus, stomach, and intestine. In addition, food is broken up by digestive enzymes secreted by the salivary glands, stomach lining, intestine, and pancreas. Digested nutrients are absorbed through the walls of the small intestine; the waste products that remain (primarily plant fiber) are propelled into the large intestine and eliminated as feces.

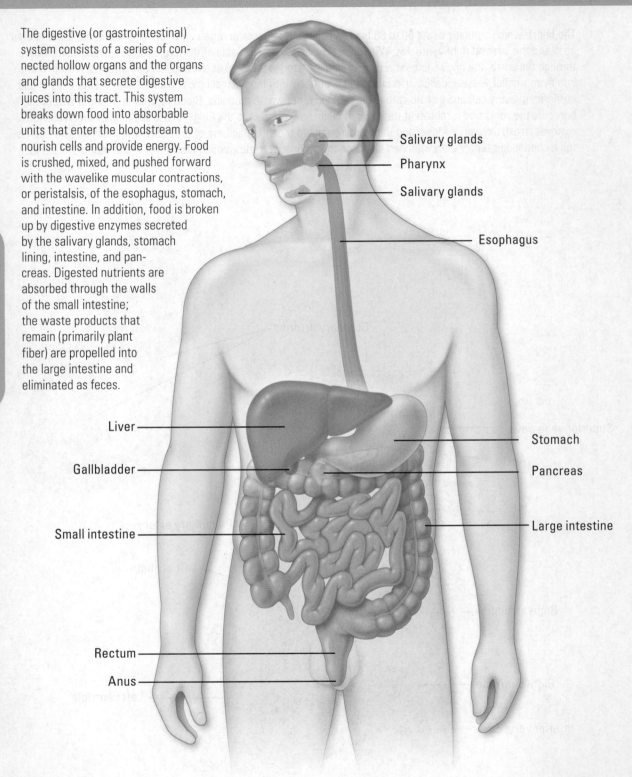

Salivary glands

Pharynx

Salivary glands

Esophagus

Liver

Gallbladder

Small intestine

Rectum

Anus

Stomach

Pancreas

Large intestine

More than 99 percent of digestion takes place in the small intestine (or small bowel), a coiled muscular tube ranging from 12 to 22 feet in length. This organ consists of three segments: the duodenum, jejunum, and ileum. In the duodenum, pancreatic enzymes and bile from the liver and gallbladder break food down into simple, absorbable components. Almost all the nutrients present in food are then absorbed into the bloodstream through the walls of the jejunum and ileum; the residue passes into the large intestine, a 5-foot tube also known as the colon or large bowel. Here, excess water and electrolytes are absorbed from the waste material, which is broken down further by intestinal bacteria and stored until it is excreted from the body. The large intestine is divided into the cecum, colon, rectum, and anal canal.

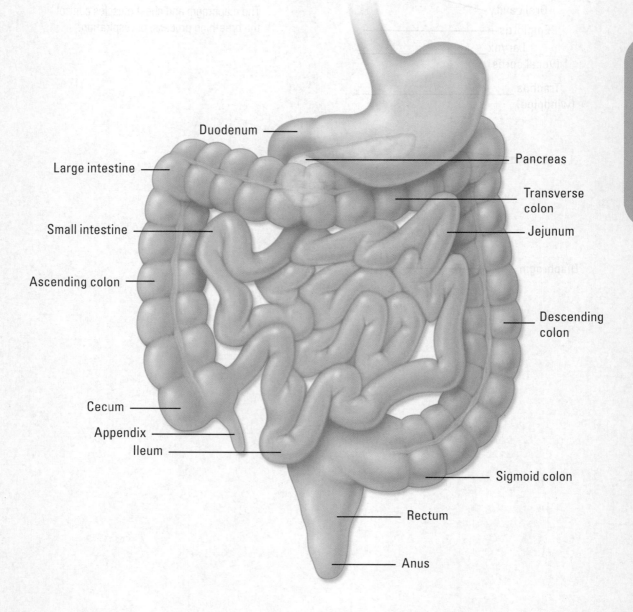

The respiratory system, made up of the lungs and air passages, provides the body with a continuous supply of oxygen and an efficient means of removing the cellular waste gas carbon dioxide. The oxygen we inhale with air passes from the lungs to the bloodstream, which carries it to cells throughout the body. At the same time, the blood picks up carbon dioxide and returns it to the lungs to be exhaled. The diaphragm and chest muscles control the breathing process, or respiration.

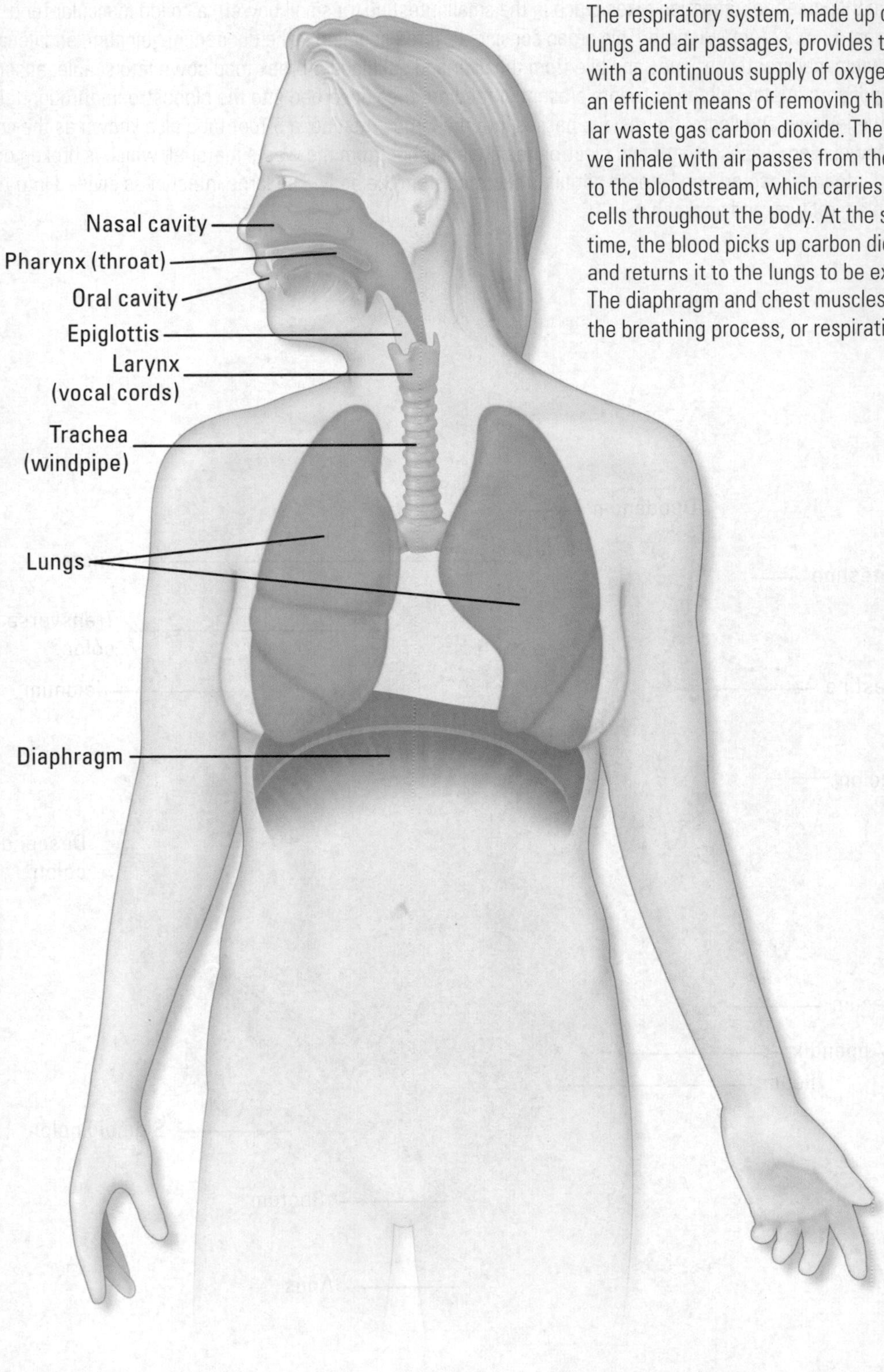

Nasal cavity

Pharynx (throat)

Oral cavity

Epiglottis

Larynx (vocal cords)

Trachea (windpipe)

Lungs

Diaphragm

The trachea, or windpipe, branches into two primary tubes, or bronchi, one leading into each lung. Each of these bronchi divides into progressively smaller bronchi, which branch into thousands of bronchioles, and finally culminate in some 300 million tiny air sacs, or alveoli. The grapelike clusters of alveoli are covered with a dense network of tiny blood vessels, or capillaries, where the exchange of oxygen and carbon dioxide occurs. The lung on the right side of the body has three lobes, while the left lung has only two. Both lungs are covered with a layer of moist membranes, called the pleura, which allows them to inflate and deflate smoothly.

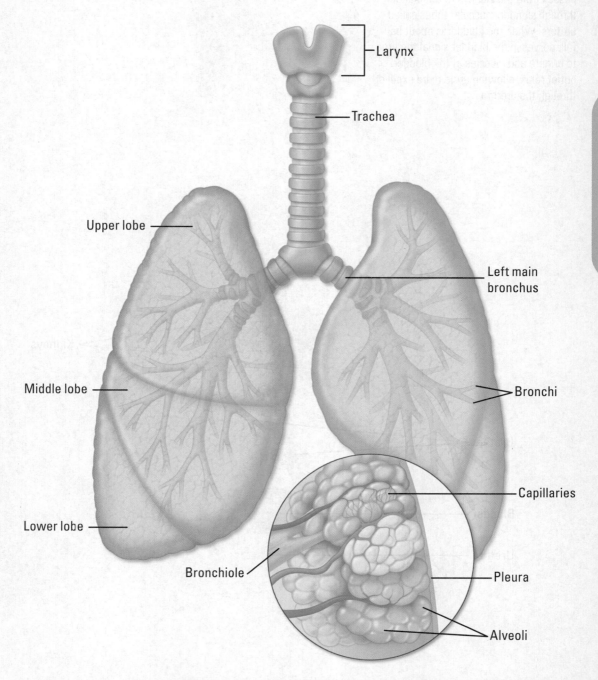

Larynx

Trachea

Upper lobe

Left main bronchus

Middle lobe

Bronchi

Lower lobe

Bronchiole

Capillaries

Pleura

Alveoli

The urinary system removes wastes from the body and helps to regulate body chemistry and fluid balance. The kidneys filter excess fluid, waste products, and drugs from the bloodstream to form urine for excretion from the body. Urine passes from the kidneys to the bladder through slender, muscular tubes called ureters. When the bladder is about half full, nerves in the bladder signal the urge to urinate and muscles at the bladder outlet relax, allowing urine to be expelled through the urethra.

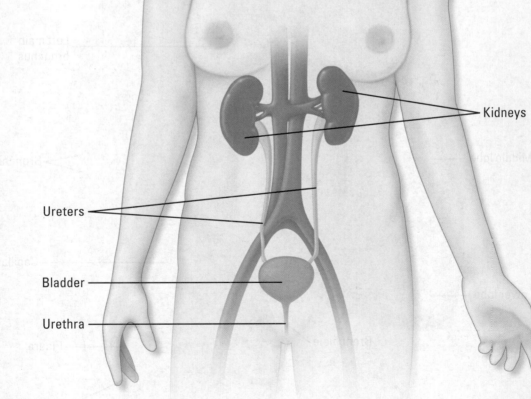

Kidneys

Ureters

Bladder

Urethra

Nearly one quarter of the volume of blood pumped with each heartbeat passes through the kidneys, where it is cleansed of waste products such as urea, uric acid, and excess salts. The outer part of the kidney is known as the cortex; the inner part is the medulla. Blood enters the kidney through the renal artery and then passes through a series of complex filtering units, called nephrons. Inside the one mill on nephrons in each kidney, water and other substances are filtered from the blood through tiny blood vessels, called glomeruli; the filtrate then enters small collecting tubes (renal tubules). As the filtrate passes through the renal tubules, urine formed from wastes and excess water eventually collects in the renal pelvis; from there, it is channeled through the ureter to the bladder. Filtered blood leaves the kidney via the renal vein and is recirculated.

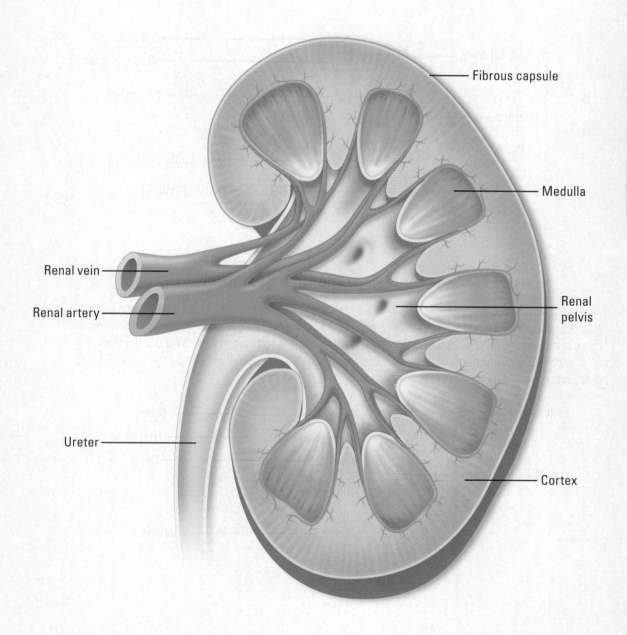

Male Reproductive System

The testes produce male sex hormones and sperm, the male reproductive cell. Sperm cells mature for two to four weeks in the epididymis, a tightly coiled tube on top of each testis. A thin, muscular tube called the vas deferens transports sperm from the testis to the ejaculatory duct, which empties into the urethra just inside of the prostate gland. Semen that is ejaculated through the urethra during sexual activity is made up of sperm cells mixed with fluids from the prostate and seminal vesicles.

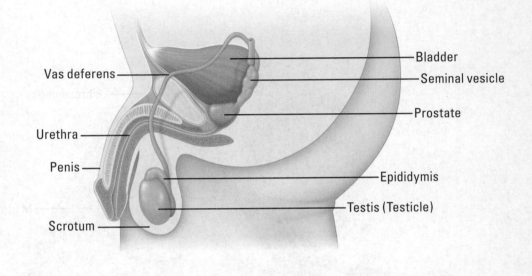

Female Reproductive System

The ovaries, which produce female sex hormones and the eggs needed for reproduction, are small oval organs located on either side of the uterus, a hollow organ with muscular walls. Eggs released during each menstrual cycle travel down the fallopian tubes to the uterus. When an egg is fertilized, it is implanted in the uterine lining, or endometrium. If fertilization does not occur, the endometrium is shed through the vaginal canal during menstruation.

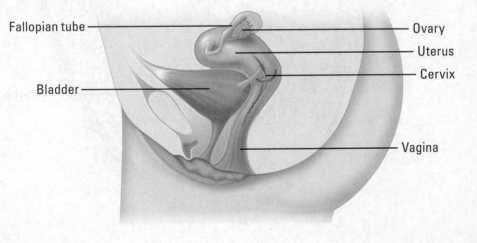

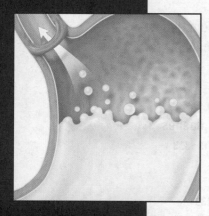

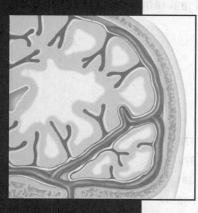

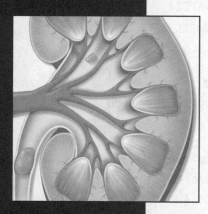

Disorders A–Z

Disorders A–Z

Disorders A–Z

A

Alzheimer's disease (AD) is the leading cause of dementia in the United States, affecting nearly 4 million older adults. (For more information about dementia, see pages 244 to 251.) AD is named after Dr. Alois Alzheimer, a German doctor who, while performing an autopsy in 1906, first noticed changes in the brain tissue of a woman who had died of an unusual mental illness. The plaques and tangles that he discovered in the brain are now considered hallmarks of AD.

A progressive disorder of the brain, AD is characterized by the deterioration of mental faculties due to the loss of nerve cells and the connections between them. AD is often accompanied by changes in behavior and personality. The course of the disease is relentless, although the rates of its progress and mental decline vary from person to person. Recent research suggests that, on average, a patient with AD survives 3 to 5 years after the initial diagnosis—a survival time much shorter than was previously reported.

Progression of Alzheimer's Disease

AD advances slowly in three general symptomatic stages, ranging from mild forgetfulness to severe dementia. Symptoms of the first stage—which include impaired memory of recent events, faulty judgment, and poor insight—appear most commonly after age 70. (However, in a small group of patients, symptoms may emerge as early as age 30 or 40.) In the first stage of the disease, people with AD may forget important appointments, recent family events, and highly publicized news items. Other symptoms include frequently losing

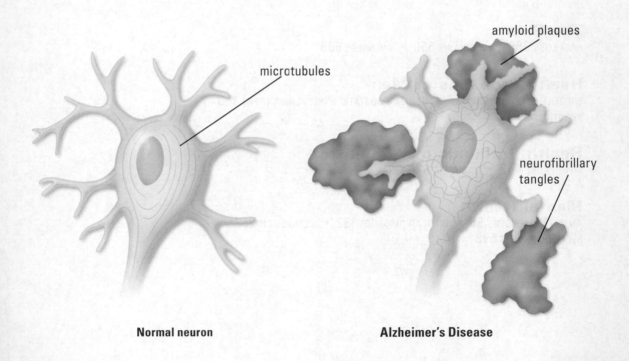

microtubules

amyloid plaques

neurofibrillary tangles

Normal neuron   **Alzheimer's Disease**

Amyloid plaques and neurofibrillary tangles (which arise from collapsed microtubules, the brain's internal transport system) are found at autopsy in virtually every patient with Alzheimer's disease.

Managing Behavior Problems in the Alzheimer's Patient

Behavioral changes are generally associated with Alzheimer's disease. Irritability, anxiousness, aggression and depression are common. Social skills also decline, and delusions, hallucinations, and wandering may become an issue. Here are some tips to manage problem behavior:

- During verbal exchanges, use simple, direct language, and give frequent reminders about the content of the conversation.
- Harmless behaviors, such as pacing and word repetition, should be accepted, though they may be annoying.
- Respond to disruptive behaviors, such as yelling, with reassurance or a distraction, such as a snack or a ride in the car.
- Ignore verbal abuse. People with AD often are unaware of what they're saying; responding may worsen the behavior.
- Be matter-of-fact, and don't encourage discussion about necessary activities. Simply say, "Now it's time to eat," or "Now I will help you with your bath.
- Minimize noise and visual distractions that might interfere with planned activities.
- Change the patient's routine only when absolutely necessary.
- Because behavior problems are often worse at night, schedule activities that the patient must do, but may not like, for daytime.
- Encourage independence by breaking down tasks into their component parts and using verbal, visual, or physical cues to prompt the patient to accomplish them.
- Lock doors; consider using childproof doorknobs and deadbolts, and see that the patient routinely wears identification. Register with the Alzheimer's Association's Safe Return program (888-572-8566). Since 1993 Safe Return has helped locate and return more than 6,400 individuals to their families and caregivers.

or misplacing possessions, repetition of questions or statements, and minor or occasional disorientation.

As the disease progresses into the second stage, memory problems grow worse and basic self-care skills begin to decline. AD patients may have trouble expressing themselves verbally or in writing, and be unable to perform everyday activities such as dressing, bathing, using a knife or fork, or brushing their teeth. They may also suffer from delusions or hallucinations.

In the third stage, people with AD lose almost all capacity for reasoning. They may end up completely dependent on others for their care. The disorder eventually becomes so debilitating that patients cannot walk or feed themselves and become susceptible to other diseases. Lung and urinary tract infections are common. Pneumonia is the most frequent cause of death.

Degenerative Changes in Alzheimer's Disease

In AD, nerve cells stop functioning, lose connections with each other, and ultimately die. The death of neurons in key parts of the brain causes those areas to shrink and results in substantial abnormalities of memory, thinking, and behavior.

Early in the disease, destruction of neurons is particularly widespread in parts of the brain controlling memory, especially the hippocampus (which is why memory impairment is often the first sign of AD). As nerve cells in the hippocampus break down, short-term memory fails and the ability to do familiar tasks begins to decline as well.

A

The disease also attacks the cerebral cortex, which controls thinking. The greatest damage occurs in the hippocampus and the areas of the cortex responsible for higher functions, such as language, reasoning, perception, and judgment. Thus, unwarranted emotional outbursts (known as catastrophic reactions), disturbing behaviors (such as wandering), and episodes of extreme agitation appear and become more frequent as the disease progresses.

Plaques and Tangles

Amyloid plaques and neurofibrillary tangles are the pathological hallmarks of AD. Although discovered only at autopsy, they are found in virtually every patient with AD. It remains unclear whether these abnormal brain deposits are the cause or a by-product of AD, but researchers have come to better understand how plaques and tangles are formed. This improved knowledge has spawned new attempts to block the underlying process that may lead to their buildup. The success of these strategies may ultimately form the basis of prevention or treatment if these plaques and tangles are the cause of AD.

Amyloid plaques develop in areas of the brain related to memory; they are a mixture of abnormal proteins and nerve cell fragments. Their main component is beta-amyloid, a protein that breaks off from the larger amyloid precursor protein. Beta-amyloid is formed when the amyloid precursor protein that is embedded in the cell membrane is broken down for disposal. Enzymes called secretases split the protein in two and form the beta-amyloid fragment.

Researchers recently identified beta-secretase as one of these "cleaving" enzymes. It cuts amyloid precursor protein in a place that causes beta-amyloid to become insoluble and form deposits in the brain. Investigators suspect that blocking beta-secretase activity may prevent production of undesirable forms of beta-amyloid, and experiments are currently under way to test this hypothesis. Still a mystery, however, is what happens to the beta-amyloid segment once it separates from amyloid precursor protein, and how it might cause AD.

Neurofibrillary tangles are the other pathologic characteristic of AD. Composed mostly of the protein tau, these twisted, hairlike threads are what remain after the collapse of the neuron's internal support structure, known as microtubules. In healthy neurons, microtubules act like train tracks to carry nutrients from one destination to another. Tau normally serves as the supporting "railroad ties," but in AD the protein becomes hopelessly twisted and disrupts the function of microtubules. This defect clogs communication within nerve cells, and eventually leads to their death.

Researchers are not sure why tau goes awry, but new findings suggest that the Pin1 enzyme may play an important role in keeping tau intact. When Pin1 binds to an altered tau in test tube experiments, the protein starts to function as it should and microtubule assembly is restored. Furthermore, researchers found substantially lower levels of Pin1 in the brains of AD patients than in healthy subjects. The significance of these findings remains uncertain, but the presence of an enzyme such as Pin1 may help maintain or restore the proper function of tau—and prevent the formation of tangles. This possibility raises the hope that therapies might be developed to keep tau functioning and prevent AD.

Neurotransmitters

Another characteristic of AD is a reduction in the levels of certain neurotransmitters that are necessary for healthy brain function. The cholinergic neurons in the brain produce acetylcholine, a neurotransmitter crucial to memory and learning. These neurons are plentiful in the hippocampus and the cerebral cortex—the two regions of the brain most ravaged by AD. (As is true for the plaques and tangles, it is not known whether neuronal loss in these parts of the brain is a cause or an effect of AD.)

As the disease progresses, acetylcholine levels drop dramatically and dementia becomes more pronounced. Levels of serotonin, norepinephrine, somatostatin, and GABA—neurotransmitters involved in many brain functions—are diminished in almost half of the patients with AD. Such imbalances may lead to insomnia, depression, aggression, and mood or personality changes.

Causes

Despite tremendous advances in the understanding of AD, scientists have yet to pinpoint a true cause for the disorder. Some patients may have a single underlying cause, but in others, a whole host of factors appear to interact in some way to bring on the disease. Old age is the strongest risk factor for AD; others are Down syndrome, a family history of dementia, and the presence of a specific form (e4) of the gene that makes a certain protein, called apolipoprotein E, or APOE.

A number of studies have focused on the specific form of the protein apolipoprotein E (APOE), called APOE e4, which appears to play a role in the formation of amyloid plaques. APOE e4 is linked with an increased risk or earlier onset of AD. A person with two copies of APOE e4 (approximately 3 percent of the white population) has a 50 percent chance of developing AD by age 80. Increased risk, however, does not guarantee illness, and the presence or absence of APOE e4 in a blood sample cannot predict who will get AD. A person can have APOE e4 and never get the disease.

Women may also be at higher risk for AD than men; and cardiovascular disorders such as high blood pressure and heart attack are also possible risk factors. Another possible risk factor is head injury. Other conditions that have been considered potential triggers of AD include immune system malfunctions, endocrine (hormonal) disorders, slow-acting viruses, and toxins.

Heredity plays a significant role in AD. Indeed, a handful of AD patients (fewer than 3 percent) have a strong genetic predisposition to the disease. In these families, AD is carried as a dominant trait (which means that half of the offspring will inherit the disorder) on one of three separate chromosomes—1, 14, and 21. However, in other families, genetic indicators are found both in AD patients and in their relatives who exhibit no AD symptoms. Therefore, environmental risk factors probably combine with a person's genetic makeup either to increase the chances that he or she will develop AD, or to cause the disease to begin earlier in life. In one study of identical twins, who share exactly the same genetic material, the age of onset of AD varied by as much as 15 years. By studying people from different ethnic, racial, and social groups, scientists may discover the full range of additional risk factors. These findings, in turn, could provide new insights into what triggers the disease.

Diagnosis

No available test can definitively detect the presence of AD, apart from autopsy after death. Instead, the current approach for establishing the cause of memory loss involves a process of elimination. Once other conditions—such as depression, Huntington disease, or hypothyroidism—have been ruled out as a cause for dementia, the diagnosis of AD is essentially made on the accumulation of data from the patient's history,

A

mental status exams, and interviews with the patient, family members, and friends over a period of several weeks. Diagnoses based on such clinical features are accurate about 90 percent of the time. Criteria for the diagnosis of AD from the *Diagnostic and Statistical Manual of Mental Disorders* require, among other things, that a combination of memory impairment and other cognitive deficits (such as difficulty communicating) is severe enough to affect social or job functioning, and that the decline is gradual.

Although less important than clinical features in making a diagnosis, laboratory and imaging studies can provide useful information in certain cases. Laboratory tests look for certain proteins or genes associated with AD, while imaging techniques examine the brain for shrinkage. No test is foolproof; having a genetic predisposition to AD does not mean that one will develop it, and many normal brains exhibit shrinkage.

Laboratory Tests

Recently, two new tests, called the ADmark Assays, became available. One of these assays measures beta-amyloid and tau protein in the spinal fluid (requiring a spinal tap).

The other assay bases the probability that a person's dementia is due to AD on whether the specific form of the gene that makes APOE—designated as e4—is present. Use of this test is also discouraged in asymptomatic individuals, however. According to a panel of experts assembled by the National Institutes of Health, testing for the APOE e4 gene should not be performed because there is presently no cure for AD and no recommended treatment to lower the risk of developing it. In addition, knowledge of the gene's presence could produce unnecessary anxiety in the individual and lead to discrimination by employers or health insurance companies.

Imaging Studies

Certain imaging studies may eventually aid in diagnosing AD before the onset of symptoms. Positron emission tomography (PET), single-photon emission computer tomography (SPECT), and magnetic resonance imaging (MRI) scans can all be used to examine brain structure or function. Currently, these scans are not routinely used to diagnose AD, though they can rule out other possible causes of mental impairment.

Treatment

As of yet, no treatment can prevent or halt the mental deterioration associated with AD. Many drugs have been tested, but most were abandoned when found ineffective or toxic. The search for an effective drug therapy has focused on preventing the destruction of neurons, with the ultimate goal of preserving cognitive function for as long as possible.

One theory driving research is that memory deficits in AD are due in part to a deficiency of the neurotransmitter acetylcholine. Scientists have sought ways to boost the amount of acetylcholine in the brain by administering substances containing it, by stimulating the brain to manufacture it in increased quantities, or by preventing the breakdown of the limited quantities of acetylcholine that the brain is able to make. Lecithin and choline, two substances that appear naturally in many foods, are used by the body to produce acetylcholine. Supplements of lecithin and choline have been given to AD patients in the hope of improving their mental function, but the results have been disappointing.

Cholinesterase Inhibitors

Drugs known as cholinesterase inhibitors were the first to be approved by the U.S. Food and Drug Administration (FDA) for the treatment of AD. These medications—which include tacrine (Cognex), donepezil (Aricept), rivastigmine (Exelon), and galantamine (Reminyl)—slow the breakdown of acetylcholine. While they may ease some mild symptoms associated with AD, they do not prevent or halt its progression. According to guidelines published by the American Academy of Neurology in 2001, these drugs are consistently better than placebo, but the average benefit is small and the disease continues to progress despite treatments.

Vitamin E

The antioxidant properties of vitamin E made it the focus of a well designed study published in *The New England Journal of Medicine* in 1997. Patients with moderately severe AD received a daily dose of 2,000 IU of vitamin E, 10 mg a day of selegiline (a medication used to treat Parkinson disease), both, or a placebo. Selegiline or vitamin E slowed the time to institutionalization and increased survival by about seven months. The number of people losing the ability to do daily activities, such as handling money or bathing, was cut by one-quarter. Combining vitamin E and selegilene did not further improve results.

Based on this study, the American Academy of Neurology concluded that good evidence exists for the use of vitamin E in an attempt to slow the progression of the disease. The evidence for selegilene is weaker, and there is no advantage to using selegilene if vitamin E is already being used.

Although vitamin E is generally safe, large doses have been associated with bleeding in some people.

Experimental Therapies

For reasons that are not entirely clear, enrollment in a clinical trial may delay progression of AD. This delay could have a number of explanations. For example, it may be due to a direct benefit from the drug being studied, or from improved coping skills that caregivers gained from additional contact with medical personnel during the study. In any case, enrollment in a clinical trial may be even more worthwhile for patients with AD than for those with other medical conditions, since there is no cure for AD.

A main focus of research on AD continues to be an effort to delay its onset. The following are currently being tested for their usefulness as preventive agents. They are still regarded as highly experimental and are by no means established as effective—but they do offer hope for the future.

Anti-inflammatory drugs. Among the more promising preventive therapies are nonsteroidal anti-inflammatory drugs (NSAIDs)—the class of drugs commonly used to treat rheumatoid arthritis. While it remains unclear how these drugs might be effective, researchers hypothesize that NSAIDs may provide protection against the inflammatory component of AD, or may exert their effect on the delivery of blood to the brain.

Estrogen. Evidence regarding whether estrogen may protect postmenopausal women against AD has been mixed. Some studies found a protective effect, others found no effect. It is possible that drugs that might prevent or delay the onset of AD are of no benefit after the disease has started. In addition, women who choose to take estrogen replacements tend to be of a higher socioeconomic status, better educated, and recipients of better healthcare; these factors—instead of estrogen itself—may have contributed to a lower rate of AD in some estrogen studies. Also, estrogen may have an effect on cognition only in the first weeks of treatment, and not over the long term.

A

Ginkgo biloba. How ginkgo biloba might work is unclear; however, some studies have found that patients taking this plant extract had a slower decline in mental function than patients who received a placebo. The American Academy of Neurology states that the evidence for ginkgo biloba is weak, but it is possible that it may benefit some patients with unspecified dementia (not AD). However, because it is considered a food supplement, ginkgo biloba is not regulated by the FDA. (It should also be noted that taking ginkgo biloba with aspirin may lead to an increased risk of bleeding.)

Other experimental therapies. Numerous other compounds are currently being tested for their effectiveness against AD. These include vitamin C; steroids such as prednisone; colchicine (commonly used to treat gout); and drugs designed to interfere with the formation of amyloid plaques and neurofibrillary tangles.

Alternative Measures

Some of the alternative treatments promoted for memory enhancement include choline, a building block for acetylcholine, which has not proven to be effective; dimethylaminoethanol (DMAE), a nutrient found in seafood; hydergine (ergoloid mesylates), which is approved for the treatment of noncognitive impairment and may be effective against vascular dementia; piracetam, which may improve the metabolism of acetylcholine; and vasopressin, a hormone produced by the hypothalamus.

Since no controlled studies have yet demonstrated that any of these substances improves memory, they cannot be recommended for use in the treatment of AD or any form of memory impairment. One potentially promising agent is huperzine A (hupA), which appears to work in a similar fashion to cholinesterase inhibitors. The results from a Chinese trial comparing hupA to a placebo are encouraging, but further studies are needed to prove effectiveness and safety, especially because the drug may cause many undesirable side effects.

Standard Care for Alzheimer's Disease

The amount of care necessary for a patient with AD changes over the course of the disorder. Cholinesterase inhibitors, possibly in conjunction with vitamin E, may be offered during the initial stages of mild AD. Other treatments can be instituted with the appearance of specific symptoms or associated disorders, such as depression or agitation.

According to the American Academy of Neurology, antipsychotic medications can be useful for the treatment of agitation and psychosis in dementia. Newer antipsychotic agents, such as risperidone (Risperdal), olanzepine (Zyprexa), and quetiapine (Seroquel), seem to be better tolerated than traditional antipsychotic agents such as haloperidol (Haldol).

The options for the treatment of depression are medication, psychotherapy, other therapeutic measures such as electroconvulsive therapy, or any combination of these. Treatment for depression is usually highly effective. The first antidepressant medication tried is successful in 60 percent to 70 percent of patients; psychotherapy alone works in about half of patients; and up to 70 percent of patients improve with electroconvulsive therapy. Examples of the most commonly used medications include sertraline (Zoloft), paroxetine (Paxil), citalopram (Celexa), bupropion (Wellbutrin), and venlafaxine (Effexor). The effectiveness of these drugs and their side effects vary from one individual to another. Some antidepressant drugs can themselves cause side effects that impair memory; therefore,

Caring for the Caregiver

Because Alzheimer's disease and other dementias can be debilitating, people with these conditions frequently require the help of a caregiver, especially in the later stages of the disease. Often, a spouse, child, or other family member takes on the role of caregiver. Providing constant care for a person with dementia can be physically, emotionally, and financially taxing, and caregivers frequently become overwhelmed by their situation.

Overly stressed caregivers may not attend to their own well-being, which puts them at risk for illness, alcohol or drug abuse, depression, and even death. Furthermore, people cared for by a stressed caregiver are more likely to be neglected, abused, or prematurely placed in an institution. Therefore, caregivers should periodically assess their own physical and mental health and seek help when appropriate. Here are some suggestions for managing the emotional demands of caregiving:

- Ask for assistance. You can't do everything alone. Set priorities and ask family members, friends, and neighbors for help. Explore the possibility of engaging a home health aide or utilizing respite services, such as adult day care.

- Acknowledge negative feelings. Disturbing emotions, such as guilt and resentment, are normal. Recognizing and accepting them are the first steps toward resolution. Share your feelings with loved ones and consider consulting a professional counselor.

- Take regular breaks. Continue to pursue some outside activities and social contacts. In the long run, maintaining such interests will help you be a better caregiver.

- Maintain your general health. Health affects your outlook and your ability to cope with all types of daily challenges. Be sure to eat well, exercise, and get enough rest.

- Join a support group. Such groups create an opportunity to share feelings and offer practical suggestions about how to cope with the demands of caregiving.

---

a patient's response to treatment must be carefully monitored. It can take as long as six to eight weeks before depression improves with medication or psychotherapy. Electroconvulsive therapy can work within a couple of weeks.

Coping with Caregiving

The daily challenges and frustrations of caring for an individual with AD can leave family members feeling physically exhausted and emotionally drained. Because they are often faced with overwhelming day-to-day responsibilities, most family caregivers tend to neglect their own physical and mental health. Caregivers must pay attention to their own well-being, however—for the ultimate benefit of both themselves and the person with AD.

Choosing a Nursing Home

As AD progresses, the patient's increasing dependency and need for supervision may make it more difficult for the family to provide all necessary care. Because such care often requires the skills of professionally trained people, nursing home placement may be in the best interest of the person with AD.

This decision, however, can be hard for the family to accept, and may be accompanied by feelings of guilt, sadness, and anger. You should keep in mind that many nursing homes provide excellent care; with some research, you should be able to find a suitable facility.

Before deciding on a nursing home, you may want to explore other residential care programs, such as assisted living facilities,

A

which provide a combination of housing, personalized assistance, and medical care. Whether such facilities—which vary in size, cost, services, location, and quality—are appropriate for a person with AD depends on the level of care needed.

If a nursing home proves the best option after discussions with the doctor and other members of your family, the first step toward finding a good one is to consult as many people as possible. Helpful information may come from the patient's physician, from friends and acquaintances who have resided in or have a family member in a home, and from the nursing home ombudsperson (who is responsible for investigating complaints). Also, the local chapter of the Alzheimer's Association may have a list of recommended homes or personal references. Remember, also, to visit any candidate nursing home several times before making a final decision.

Angina, which is short for angina pectoris, refers to episodes of chest pain precipitated by myocardial ischemia—a shortage of blood flow and oxygen to the heart muscle. Angina affects about 6.3 million Americans. It most often occurs when the heart requires more oxygen to meet its increased workload during physical activity, but the oxygen supply is limited by narrowing of one or more coronary arteries. Symptoms of ischemia rarely occur until an artery is at least 75 percent narrowed.

Causes

Angina is one of the complications of coronary heart disease (CHD)—a narrowing of the coronary arteries that restricts blood flow to the heart (see page 233 for more information on CHD).

The chest discomfort of angina is often triggered by walking. The distance that can be walked without pain tends to vary somewhat from day to day, but most people can predict what level of exertion is likely to produce angina for them.

Physical activity more often brings on angina early in the morning, after a meal, during cold weather, and when walking up an incline or into the wind. Activities involving use of the arms—such as shoveling, sweeping, scrubbing, or raking—may cause angina in some people. Sexual intercourse or a bowel movement also can be a trigger. Anger, fear, anxiety, and excitement also can cause anginal distress or reduce the amount of exertion required to produce angina.

Symptoms

A pressure sensation is the most common attribute of angina, but it may also produce a tightness, squeezing, burning, aching, heaviness, or choking. Rarely, the pain may be sharp. Angina is typically felt beneath the sternum (breastbone), but it may also begin at, or radiate to, any site above the waist, especially the left upper arm, forearm, and jaw. The intensity of angina usually increases steadily, reaches a plateau, and gradually diminishes with rest—all in a few minutes.

Symptoms in men and women. Women do not always experience angina in the same way as men; these differences are important since they can make diagnosis more difficult. While men often experience angina during exercise, women may experience it at rest. And they may feel angina as a pain in the jaw or as heartburn. Other vague symptoms common in women include breathlessness, nausea, and fatigue—which can be easily missed if they develop slowly.

Features suggesting that the pain is not due to angina are pain brought on by breathing or coughing, constant pain lasting for hours, episodes of pain lasting for a few seconds or less, and pain reproduced by moving or pressing on the chest wall or arms.

Diagnosis

The diagnosis of angina is based on a history of typical chest pain. The severity of angina is categorized by physicians using a system developed by the Canadian Cardiovascular Society (CCS), which is widely used in the United States as well. The four CCS classes range from Class I through Class IV.

In Class I, ordinary physical activity—such as walking or climbing stairs—does not cause angina. It occurs with strenuous, rapid, or prolonged exertion at work or recreation.

Class II is associated with some limitation of ordinary activity. Angina occurs when walking or climbing stairs rapidly; when walking uphill in the cold or into the wind; when walking or climbing stairs after meals; while under emotional stress; or only during the first few hours after awakening. Walking more than two level blocks or climbing more

A

than one flight of ordinary stairs at a normal pace brings on angina.

In Class III, there are marked limitations of ordinary physical activity. Angina occurs when walking one to two level blocks or climbing one flight of stairs at a normal pace.

In Class IV, there is an inability to perform any physical activity without discomfort. Anginal symptoms may even be present during rest.

Silent ischemia. Many people with CHD have myocardial ischemia without symptoms of angina. This condition is called silent ischemia. People with angina may have many episodes of silent ischemia in addition to their anginal pain.

Stable angina. The most common type of angina is referred to as stable angina, because a predictable amount of activity or stress triggers an attack; the amount and duration of the pain is similar in each attack; and the pain is promptly relieved by rest or by taking the drug nitroglycerin.

Unstable angina. Unstable angina, sometimes called crescendo angina, can be broadly defined as a condition intermediate in severity between stable angina and a heart attack. In unstable angina, increased demand for oxygen may not be responsible for the lack of oxygen to the heart. Instead, a blood clot or contraction (spasm) of a coronary artery decreases the supply of oxygen. As the opening (lumen) of the artery narrows, too little oxygen is delivered to the heart muscle and angina results.

There are three major characteristic features of unstable angina. First, angina occurs at rest and usually lasts for more than 20 minutes. Second, new onset of angina is severe enough to cause a marked limitation of ordinary activity (for example, pain when climbing one flight of stairs or walking two blocks at a normal pace). Finally, the pattern of stable angina changes so that the pain is distinctly more frequent, lasts longer, and is brought on by less physical activity (increased by at least one class in the CCS system, to at least class III severity).

Unstable angina is considered a preheart attack condition that often requires treatment in a hospital. The risk of heart attack or sudden death is increased in patients with unstable angina because an atherosclerotic plaque in the affected coronary artery can rupture and lead to a blood clot that may grow rapidly and cause a complete blockage.

Medications

Drugs can be used for short-term relief of angina symptoms and for long-term treatment to slow or halt progression of CHD.

Nitrates. These drugs dilate both arteries and veins. Dilation of the coronary arteries increases blood flow to the heart. Dilation of peripheral veins causes pooling of blood in the peripheral circulation. Because the heart then has to pump less blood, its workload and need for oxygen are reduced. Tablets of nitroglycerin, placed under the tongue during an attack of angina, generally bring relief within two to three minutes. If five minutes pass without a change in symptoms, a second dose may be taken. Typical doses range from 0.3 to 0.6 mg. Patients may experience headaches when first starting on nitrates, but these symptoms tend to diminish after a week or two.

Sublingual nitroglycerin may also prevent angina when taken shortly before beginning activities likely to provoke chest pain. Longer-acting nitrate tablets and transdermal patches, pastes, or ointments applied to the skin can provide longer protection against the onset of angina, although tolerance may develop. It is generally recommended that longer-acting nitrates be discontinued for four to six hours each day to prevent loss of their effectiveness. The longer and more frequently these nitrates are used, the less likely they are to relieve angina. Regular, long-term users often become resistant to the drug's effects.

Beta-blockers. These drugs control angina by slowing the heart rate and its force of contraction, thereby decreasing the heart's workload and oxygen consumption. Beta-blockers are often prescribed to help prevent a second heart attack.

Calcium channel blockers. Like nitrates and beta-blockers, calcium channel blockers reduce the heart's workload, allow more blood to flow through the coronary arteries, and decrease the oxygen requirements of the heart muscle. These drugs also alleviate angina by relieving coronary artery spasm (when this is the cause of angina). However, only the long-acting forms should be used.

Combination therapy. In some people, neither beta-blockers nor calcium channel blockers alone provide sufficient relief of angina. One study found that combining both types of drugs significantly lengthened the time patients could exercise before experiencing angina.

Revascularization Procedures
When medications for angina cannot be used because of coexisting medical problems, or the mediations do not control anginal pain, revascularization—angioplasty or bypass surgery—may become necessary.

Percutaneous Transluminal Coronary Angioplasty
Percutaneous transluminal coronary angioplasty, often called PTCA or angioplasty, does not remove plaque from the coronary arteries, but widens the channel for blood flow by inserting and inflating a balloon that breaks up the plaque on the lining of the artery wall and/or compresses it against the wall. More than half a million

First-Line Treatment
If angina is confirmed and CHD is the underlying cause, preventing disease progression is a primary goal of treatment. The first step is controlling the risk factors for heart disease—especially high blood cholesterol levels, high blood pressure, and excess weight—through lifestyle measures and medications (see pages 240–243). Cigarette smoking must stop. It's also important to avoid physical exertion that causes pain—but be certain to engage in regular, moderately paced exercise below the threshold of pain, guided by the advice of your doctor.

Americans undergo the procedure annually. About 90 percent of patients notice an immediate improvement in symptoms when the arterial lumen (opening) is at least 50 percent open after angioplasty. A stent (explained on page 92) is often placed in the artery at the time of angioplasty to help keep the vessel open. Other techniques include removing part of the plaque with a rotating blade (atherectomy) or a laser (laser ablation).

Performed in a cardiac catheterization laboratory, angioplasty generally takes one to two hours and does not require general anesthesia. The procedure usually requires no more than one night's stay in the hospital.

The risks associated with angioplasty are low. Fewer than 1 percent of patients die during the procedure. As might be expected, rates of complications are lower when angioplasty is performed by more experienced physicians. But the complication rate depends on many factors, and physicians who perform fewer angioplasties can still have low complication rates by focusing on simpler cases.

A

Women may run a greater risk of complications from angioplasty. Two studies indicate higher mortality in women than in men. It is possible, however, that these differences are due to more advanced age and more complicated illness among the women, or to their smaller coronary arteries (which are more easily damaged during angioplasty).

Stent implantation. Stent implantation is now used in conjunction with angioplasty in almost all patients. A stent is a mechanical device permanently inserted into a coronary artery to help keep it open. These devices are delivered with a catheter and expand within the lumen of the artery at a site just widened by angioplasty. Implantation of a stent during angioplasty is now standard procedure

Opening Arteries with Angioplasty

A blocked coronary artery causing angina pain can be dilated by means of coronary angioplasty, illustrated at right. The procedure, which takes one to two hours, is performed by a cardiologist, who makes a small incision in the patient's groin or an arm and introduces a plastic tube, called a sheath. A hollow catheter is inserted through the sheath into an artery. The catheter is about a yard long and is equipped with a balloon at its tip.

Guided by images on a television screen, the physician threads the catheter toward the heart and into the affected coronary artery (A). Using a guidewire, the catheter is positioned so that the plaque straddles the uninflated balloon. The physician then inflates the balloon several times, for 30 seconds to several minutes each time (B). The pressure squeezes the plaque against the arterial wall, stretches the artery, and widens the channel to allow more blood to flow (C).

Most patients also receive a stent—a wire mesh tube that is inserted while the balloon is inflated and is left inside the artery to help keep it open (D). After the catheter has been withdrawn, an angiogram—an x-ray of the artery—is performed to assess the results.

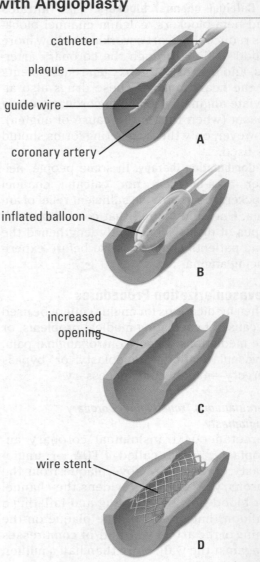

catheter

plaque

guide wire

coronary artery

A

inflated balloon

B

increased opening

C

wire stent

D

because it reduces the rate of restenosis (re-narrowing of the artery). A potential problem is the stimulation of clot formation on the stent. The use of new antiplatelet agents (see page 243) significantly decreases these events. Under study are stents coated with substances that decrease clotting or smooth muscle cell proliferation. Other possible ways to reduce restenosis are using slightly radioactive stents and irradiating the area around the stent.

Atherectomy. An atherectomy procedure utilizes a high-speed rotary blade or drill—delivered by a catheter to the site of arterial occlusion—to shave away portions of the plaque. A number of different atherectomy devices have been used. This technique is less likely to perforate the artery than laser ablation (see below). Atherectomy appears to be most successful when performed on large, straight arteries. Because it lessens stress on the healthy portion of the wall, the blade may be the device of choice for plaque deposits limited to one side of the artery wall, while the drill may yield better results than angioplasty for very long obstructions.

Laser ablation. The laser ablation technique, still an experimental procedure, resembles angioplasty except that the balloon is replaced with a probe that can be heated with a beam of laser light to cut through tissue occluding the coronary artery. A problem with laser ablation is the danger of creating a hole in the arterial wall, but the procedure may eventually prove successful in reopening completely blocked arteries, as well as for very long or calcified plaques that cannot be treated with angioplasty.

Coronary Artery Bypass Graft Surgery

Each year, about 300,000 patients undergo coronary artery bypass graft surgery (often called CABG or, simply, bypass surgery) in the United States. During bypass surgery, an artery from the chest or a portion of a vein from the patient's leg (venous graft) is used to channel blood around a narrowed segment of a coronary artery. When needed, five or more grafts can be constructed during a single operation.

The best vessel to use as a graft in most patients is the left internal mammary artery, or LIMA. This artery feeds the left side of the chest wall but can be explanted (removed) and used as a bypass graft because the corresponding artery on the right side of the chest is capable of supplying both sides of the chest. While venous grafts last about 10 years, the LIMA may last for 20 to 30 years. However, the LIMA may not be used in an emergency because it can take a longer time to be explanted.

When an internal mammary artery is used, it is sewn into the coronary artery beyond the blockage. To perform a venous graft, a piece of vein is removed from the leg, one end is sutured into a hole made in the aorta near the heart, and the other end is attached to the coronary artery beyond the occluded site.

Bypass surgery is quite arduous for the patient. It requires general anesthesia and four to six days of hospitalization. The operation is performed with the help of a heart-lung machine that maintains circulation while the heart is stopped. However, it is an extremely successful operation, even when the patient requires several grafts, has extensive heart disease, or is elderly. A 2000 study found that people age 80 and older had a higher in-hospital death rate after bypass surgery than those under 80 (8 percent vs. 3 percent), but the benefits may still outweigh the risks for many older patients.

About 90 percent of patients undergoing bypass experience relief of anginal symptoms after the procedure. Immediate complications after surgery are heart attack (2

A

Bypass Surgery vs. Angioplasty

About 90 percent of patients experience relief of anginal symptoms after bypass surgery or angioplasty. Which procedure to chose depends on a patient's general health, the location and extent of arterial blockage, and personal preference. Over the years, angioplasty has improved and doctors have become more proficient in performing it, so it is now used in patients with more extensive CHD. Recovery is also easier and quicker than with bypass surgery. However, angioplasty has some significant drawbacks, including early restenosis (recurrent blockage of an artery) and recurrence of angina, compared to bypass surgery (which has the disadvantages of longer hospital stays and rehabilitation).

Bypass surgery is generally the procedure of choice when one or more of the following conditions apply (exceptions are patients who are not surgical candidates owing to poor general health or other considerations):

Disease in the left main coronary artery. This vessel is the main artery supplying blood to the heart, and even a short period of blockage could deprive the heart of enough oxygen to produce serious damage or cause death.

Diffuse disease. Angioplasty cannot successfully treat multiple obstructions in several blood vessels.

Obstructions at an arterial branch. If the obstruction is at a point where one artery meets another, opening it might block the adjacent artery and deprive a part of the heart of its blood supply.

Diabetes. In the Bypass Angioplasty Revascularization Investigation (BARI) study, seven-year survival for people with diabetes was significantly better with bypass surgery (76 percent) than with angioplasty (56 percent).

Other factors. Other factors that make bypass surgery a better alternative include severe disease of all three major coronary arteries (especially in people with depressed left ventricular function) and a history of congestive heart failure.

Since neither angioplasty nor bypass surgery is a cure for atherosclerosis, blockages can re-form in treated arteries or new blockages can occur in the grafted or native coronary arteries. Therefore, it is essential to maintain dietary and other lifestyle measures, and often to use cholesterol-lowering or antihypertensive drugs, after angioplasty or bypass surgery.

percent to 5 percent); stroke, memory loss, or confusion (a combined rate of 6.1 percent, although same studies found a higher rate of cognitive decline); and infection. Deaths due to the procedure occur in less than 5 percent of cases, although the risk rises sharply when the patient's condition is more serious.

Women appear to be at higher risk from bypass surgery than men. While it had been thought that this difference existed because women were in worse health before the procedure, the risk remains greater even when adjusting for specific risk factors (such as diabetes). In a recent study, women had a 4.5 percent overall risk of postoperative death from bypass surgery vs. a 2.6 percent risk in men. The cause of the difference is unclear; until more is known, women should be aware of their CHD risk factors and seek prompt treatment. When needed, early surgery improves the likelihood of success in both genders.

Treatment of Unstable Angina
An episode of prolonged angina is an emergency situation often requiring hospitalization. At the hospital, the patient will likely be given intravenous heparin along with aspirin

to inhibit further clot formation. Intravenous nitroglycerin is also given to help relax the coronary vessels. Thrombolytic—or clot-busting—drug therapy is usually not used to treat unstable angina because the blood clots involved in this type of angina do not respond.

The next step is to determine how to manage unstable angina over the long term. The doctor makes this assessment based on the severity of the patient's condition and the response to initial treatment. Patients can be treated with medication if they respond to heparin and aspirin and are considered at relatively low risk for a heart attack. Medical treatment involves long-term aspirin to inhibit blood clotting, nitrates to widen blood vessels, and beta-blockers to decrease the workload of the heart.

Patients considered at intermediate or high risk for a heart attack will most likely undergo coronary angiography (see page 240) to determine the extent and location of the blockage(s). Patients are considered at high risk if they fail to respond to in-hospital medical treatment or have a history of angioplasty or bypass surgery, congestive heart failure, a low ejection fraction, or an abnormal ventricular arrhythmia. The angiography results will determine whether the patient can be managed with medical therapy or will require angioplasty or bypass surgery. Angioplasty or bypass surgery may also be performed if medical management fails to prevent subsequent episodes of unstable angina.

If drugs and surgery haven't provided sufficient relief from angina or are not appropriate for you, consider talking to your doctor about enhanced external counterpulsation (EECP). This non-invasive outpatient procedure entails lying on a table while wearing inflatable cuffs at three points on your legs. The cuffs are rapidly inflated in sequence and timed so that the heart muscle receives oxygenated blood when the heart is at rest—an action researchers think may stimulate the growth of tiny coronary blood vessels that "bypass" blocked vessels and increase blood flow to the heart. For patients who are suitable candidates for EECP (not everyone is), the procedure—which is covered by Medicare—may improve symptoms of angina as well as quality of life.

A

Anxiety is a common, normal, and sometimes useful response that may improve a person's performance when facing life's challenges and dangers. But in some people, anxiety spins out of control. Anxiety disorders are characterized by either recurrent or persistent psychological and physical symptoms that interfere with normal functioning, continue in the absence of obvious external stresses, or are excessive responses to these stresses. Anxiety disorders may result from hyperactivity in certain areas of the brain or decreased activity of a neurotransmitter (a chemical messenger) called gamma-aminobutyric acid (GABA), which suppresses the action of neurons.

Many forms of anxiety start during adolescence or early adulthood, though anxiety can also appear for the first time in the mature years. Up to 20 percent of those age 65 and older have symptoms of anxiety that prompt them to seek treatment.

Symptoms

Common psychological symptoms of anxiety include irritability, a "keyed-up" feeling, intense fear, worry, and difficulty concentrating. These symptoms may be accompanied by physical manifestations such as sweating, dry mouth, hot flashes or chills, dizziness, palpitations, muscle tension, trembling, or restlessness.

Some medical conditions and drugs can either cause anxiety or mimic its symptoms. These medical conditions include alcohol withdrawal, asthma, heart attack, overactive thyroid, and even deficiency in folate or vitamin B12. Drugs that might cause or mimic anxiety symptoms include bronchodilators, such as ephedrine (a dangerous component of many weight loss drugs) or epinephrine (Primatene Mist and others); psychostimulants, such as methylphenidate (Ritalin); and thyroid hormone.

Anxiety disorders are broken down into anxiety states (panic disorder, generalized anxiety disorder, obsessive-compulsive disorder, and post-traumatic stress disorder) and phobic disorders.

Panic Disorder

The cardinal features of panic disorder are short-lived, sudden attacks of terror and fear of losing control; attacks begin without warning during nonthreatening activities. Affected individuals often go to the emergency room or consult a cardiologist because their physical symptoms—severe difficulty in breathing; a pounding, rapid heart rate; and a choking sensation—may appear to be a heart attack. (Patients who suspect that they are having a heart attack should see a doctor immediately.) Panic attacks generally peak within 10 minutes and dissipate within 20 to 30 minutes. They are characterized by some combination of the following symptoms:

- Shortness of breath or hyperventilation;
- Heart palpitations or a racing pulse;
- Discomfort in the chest;
- Dizziness or feeling faint;
- Choking, nausea, or stomach pain;
- Sweating;
- Hot or cold flashes;
- Trembling or shaking;
- Sense of unreality; feeling detached from surroundings;
- Tingling or numbness;
- Fear of dying or losing one's mind.

Symptoms of depression and anxiety are common in persons with panic disorder and in members of their family. While both panic attacks and symptoms of depression or anxiety may respond to antidepressant medications for some patients, others may require different medications for the panic disorder and for the depression and anxiety. The prevalence of panic disorder is 1 percent to

Medication Overview

A

Several classes of medications are used to treat anxiety disorders. The most common are benzodiazepines, selective serotonin reuptake inhibitors (SSRIs) and tricyclics (both antidepressants), and the azaspirone buspirone. As with all medications, each has its advantages and drawbacks. (For more information on the treatment of specific anxiety disorders, see pages 98-101.)

Benzodiazepines. Benzodiazepines are thought to relieve anxiety by enhancing the effects of the inhibitory neurotransmitter GABA. However, their mechanisms of action are not completely understood. The side effects of benzodiazepines are generally minor, but two side effects—drowsiness and clumsiness—may increase the risk of accidents while driving.

The most troublesome features of the benzodiazepines are the development of tolerance (decreased effectiveness of a given dose with continued use) and both physical and psychological dependence, especially with long-term use of high doses. Tolerance may cause a person to request, and at times receive, increasingly larger doses to maintain benefits. Such patients benefit from switching to an SSRI or a tricyclic drug instead of higher doses of a benzodiazepine.

Antidepressants. Although benzodiazepines are still commonly used to treat anxiety, two classes of antidepressant drugs, SSRIs and tricyclics (see pages 257-258), have become the first line of treatment for anxiety in many people. These drugs are not habit forming and can be effective in low doses. Clearly, antidepressants are indicated when a person with anxiety is also depressed. Tricyclics and SSRIs take about two to three weeks to work, making them slower acting than benzodiazepines; but they do bring an early benefit to patients with anxiety by promoting better sleep, which quickly improves daily function. A third class of antidepressants, MAO inhibitors, are also sometimes used to treat panic disorders and phobias.

Buspirone. A newer drug, buspirone (BuSpar), has fewer adverse effects than benzodiazepines, but it may be less effective, in particular for panic disorder. Common side effects of buspirone are dizziness, headache, nervousness, and nausea. However, buspirone does not produce drowsiness, and abuse is unlikely because it does not cause tolerance or dependence. When switching from benzodiazepines to buspirone, patients may be able to minimize anxiety symptoms by starting immediately on buspirone while tapering the dose of a benzodiazepine.

2 percent in both men and women. Attacks commonly begin in the late teens or early 20s and often go undiagnosed and untreated. One study estimated that only one in four people with panic attacks receives appropriate care.

The most common complication of panic disorder is agoraphobia—fear of being in public places, especially when alone—which develops as a result of trying to avoid situations that have triggered panic attacks in the past. Left untreated, panic attacks and agoraphobia can markedly restrict an individual's lifestyle, since the person tends to avoid circumstances that might provoke another attack. Panic disorder is also associated with an increased frequency of major depression, alcohol and drug dependency, and suicide.

Treatment. Treatment of panic disorder often involves both psychotherapy and pharmacologic measures. Referral to a therapist experienced in treating panic disorder may be necessary. Growing evidence supports the effectiveness of cognitive and behavioral psychotherapy that involves graded exposure to situations that induce symptoms of anxiety.

A

The mainstay of drug treatment has been the tricyclic antidepressants or MAO inhibitors; both are 80 percent to 90 percent effective in blocking panic attacks but require 6 to 12 weeks to take effect. High doses of alprazolam (Xanax), one of the newer benzodiazepines, can be effective within a few days and cause fewer side effects than the antidepressants. Unfortunately, like other benzodiazepines, alprazolam can be addicting. A relapse of symptoms occurs in 30 percent to 60 percent of patients 6 to 12 months after drugs are discontinued.

In addition to these drugs, the SSRIs sertraline (Zoloft) and paroxetine (Paxil) have been approved by the FDA for the treatment of panic disorder. Beta-blockers, such as propranolol (Inderal) and atenolol (Tenormin), can halt the physical symptoms of panic attacks but do not prevent the fear or panic itself.

Lifestyle Measures to Treat Anxiety

Treatment of anxiety does not always require medication. The use of antianxiety drugs depends in part on whether patients can tolerate their symptoms while learning to manage them through measures such as becoming educated about the causes of anxiety; undergoing psychotherapy; or using techniques such as progressive muscle relaxation, biofeedback, or, less commonly, yoga, self-hypnosis, or meditation. In general, these nondrug approaches are designed to give people with anxiety a feeling of control over their symptoms.

Patients can also help themselves by getting enough sleep, exercising (which aids sleep and improves self-esteem), and avoiding caffeine and alcohol.

Generalized Anxiety Disorder

Generalized anxiety disorder (GAD) is characterized by recurrent, prolonged, and excessive anxiety or worrying. People with GAD typically agonize over everyday concerns, such as job responsibilities, finances, health, family well-being, or even such minor matters as household chores, car repairs, or personal appearance. The focus of anxiety may shift frequently from one concern to another, and sensations may vary from mild tension and nervousness to feelings of dread.

GAD affects 2 percent to 3 percent of the population. While people with GAD know that the intensity, duration, or frequency of their anxiety and worry are well out of proportion to the likelihood or impact of the feared event, they still have difficulty controlling their emotions. Perpetual anxiety may impair concentration, memory, and decision-making ability, decrease attention span, and lead to a loss of confidence. Normal activities, such as working, socializing with friends, or maintaining intimate relationships, may become difficult or impossible.

GAD may also produce a range of physical symptoms, including heart palpitations, sweating, headaches, and nausea. Some GAD sufferers, not realizing that GAD is a treatable illness, become accustomed to their condition and assume that it is normal to feel on edge all the time. But the constant anxiety can also lead to alcohol or drug abuse. The physical symptoms of GAD, along with alcohol or drug abuse, are often what finally compels a person to seek treatment.

Treatment. Despite its more chronic course, GAD responds better to treatment than does panic disorder. Psychotherapy benefits many people, either by itself or in combination with medication. In addition, relaxation techniques, such as deep breathing exercises or meditation, may relieve symptoms of GAD.

Venlafaxine (Effexor) and paroxetine have both received FDA approval for the treatment of GAD, but also used are other serotonin and norepinephrine reuptake inhibitors, SSRIs, tricyclics, buspirone, and benzodiazepines, such as alprazolam and diazepam (Valium).

Persistent GAD symptoms can lead to depression and abuse of alcohol and drugs—especially of benzodiazepines. Treatment with benzodiazepines should be limited to short (five- to seven-day) courses to avoid dependence. Buspirone and antidepressants may be better choices because they do not cause dependence or withdrawal symptoms.

Cutting back on caffeine may help ease the symptoms of GAD. One study found that the effects of caffeine on blood pressure, pulse rate, and brain activity were strongest in those with GAD. In addition, more subjects with GAD reported that caffeine heightened subjective symptoms of anxiety.

Obsessive-Compulsive Disorder

Obsessive-compulsive disorder (OCD) is marked by recurrent, repetitive thoughts (obsessions), behaviors (compulsions), or both that a person recognizes as unreasonable, unnecessary, or foolish yet are intrusive and cannot be resisted. People with OCD do not necessarily have both obsessions and compulsions, but either one often interferes with day-to-day activities and relationships with others.

Obsessions are recurring and persistent thoughts, ideas, images, or impulses, sometimes aggressive or violent, that seem to invade a person's consciousness. The sufferer tries to suppress or ignore these uncomfortable thoughts and often recognizes that they are unrealistic. Typical obsessions are fear of contamination from germs, thoughts of violent behavior (such as killing a family member), fear of making a mistake or harming oneself or others, and a constant need for reassurance.

Compulsions are ritualistic, repetitive, and purposeful behaviors that are performed according to certain rules or stereotypical patterns. The behavior, while clearly excessive, relieves tension and discomfort. Common compulsions are rechecking to be sure doors are locked, windows are closed, and the iron is unplugged; counting stairs while walking; excessive neatness; rearranging and straightening the contents of a desk; and repetitive hand washing that accompanies an obsession with dirt and germs.

OCD occurs in 2 percent to 3 percent of the population. It most often starts in the teens or the early 20s, however, studies demonstrate a high prevalence of OCD in those over age 65.

Embarrassed and upset by their behavior, most sufferers try to keep it secret; they often function with only minimal disruption of their daily activities. But obsessive thoughts or compulsive behaviors may be frequent or distressing enough to become incapacitating. Probably the most common complication is depression; others include alcoholism, abuse of sleeping pills or tranquilizers, and marked interference with normal social and occupational behaviors. While some people with OCD experience spontaneous remission, in most, the illness has an episodic course with periods of partial remission. In about 10 percent of sufferers, the course of OCD is chronic and unchanged.

A

Treatment. As with panic disorder, OCD may improve with a combination of medication and cognitive and behavioral psychotherapy. An important recent pharmacologic advance is the effective use of SSRIs, such as citalopram (Celexa), fluoxetine (Prozac), fluvoxamine (Luvox), paroxetine, and sertraline, in treating this illness. The FDA recently approved paroxetine and sertraline for the treatment of OCD (both have also been approved for panic disorder); fluvoxamine also has received approval. Improvements, which may take six to eight weeks of drug therapy, are more likely for compulsions than for obsessions.

Post-Traumatic Stress Disorder

A diagnosis of PTSD is made when a person experiences the following symptoms after witnessing or experiencing an event that involved actual or threatened serious physical injury or death, or after learning that this type of event happened to a family member or someone else close to them:

- Strong feelings of fear, horror, and helplessness because of the event;
- Reliving the traumatic event through intrusive, vivid, and painful memories, sometimes referred to as "flashbacks." This symptom may manifest itself as nightmares about the event;
- Steering clear of any situations or circumstances that remind the person of the trauma, and avoiding conversations about the traumatic event; and
- Behaving as if one is still in danger; typical behaviors include inappropriate anger, irritability, sleep difficulties, and an exaggerated startle response.

To diagnose PTSD, these symptoms must persist for longer than one month and seriously affect the person's social life, occupation, or other important functions.

In some people, symptoms of PTSD may not begin until months or even years after the trauma. This is called delayed-onset PTSD.

As many as 15 percent of the people involved in a major natural disaster may suffer enough distress to need treatment. Complications include anxiety, alcohol or drug abuse, depression, and marital or occupational problems.

Treatment. Successful treatment requires a combination of psychotherapy—aimed at desensitizing the individual to the traumatic experience—and medication. The FDA approved the SSRI sertraline (Zoloft) for the treatment of this condition in 1999. The tricyclics amitriptyline and desipramine (Norpramin) are commonly used to treat the mood disturbances and anxiety that accompany PTSD.

Phobic Disorders

The hallmarks of phobic disorders are persistent, irrational fears and avoidance of the specific things (for example, animals, heights, or closed spaces) or activities that induce these fears. The diagnosis of a phobic disorder is made only when the phobia significantly impairs the individual's social or occupational performance. National Institute of Mental Health statistics suggest that such extreme and irrational fears afflict one in ten people, and some research suggests that phobic disorders are among the most common psychiatric diagnoses in those over 65.

A common type of phobia is social phobia, which affects between 3 percent and 13 percent of the population. Social phobia is an undue fear of embarrassment in social situations. While most people feel some anxiety about being in a situation that forces them to meet and talk to new people, social phobia causes such an extreme reaction to this everyday aspect of life that it interferes with daily functioning.

A

Treatment. When treatment is needed, behavioral therapy may help desensitize the person to the thing or situation that causes the fear. The therapist can teach the patient to use relaxation techniques when overcome by fear.

Recent studies have shown that the antidepressants paroxetine (Paxil) and fluvoxamine (Luvox), both SSRIs, can relieve social phobia. MAO inhibitors and benzodiazepines are also used. Beta-blockers, such as propranolol (Inderal), may reduce the physical symptoms of performance anxiety but are not recommended for ongoing treatment.

Arrhythmias are disturbances in the heart's rhythm that affect 3.9 million Americans.

Each heartbeat begins with an electrical signal generated by cells in the sinus node—a region in the heart's right atrium (illustrated on page 67). The sinus node is the heart's natural pacemaker. Specialized cells constitute the conduction system, which spreads electrical impulses along specific pathways through the heart.

Normally, the sinus node fires 60 to 100 times a minute, depending on a person's activity level. The signals from the sinus node pass through the right and left atria, causing them to contract, and then pause briefly in the atrioventricular (AV) node—a cluster of cells near the center of the heart. This delay allows the atria to pump blood into the ventricles just before the ventricles themselves contract. Finally, the current travels through a network of pathways in the ventricles (the His-Purkinje system) and stimulates them to pump blood into the arteries.

Types of Arrhythmias

The various types of arrhythmias are distinguished by two features: their site of origin and their effect on heart rate. Arrhythmias, which can originate in the atria, the AV node, or the ventricles, can produce a heart rate that is either too slow (bradycardia) or too fast (tachycardia).

Atrial Fibrillation

One of the most common abnormal rhythms originating in the atria is atrial fibrillation, which is characterized by chaotic, extremely rapid impulses that lead to an uncoordinated quivering of the atria and a rapid, irregular ventricular pumping rate. A serious effect of atrial fibrillation is the formation of atrial blood clots, which may loosen and form emboli that can lodge in brain arteries and cause a stroke. The risk of atrial fibrillation is increased by age, cardiovascular disease (disease of the heart or circulatory system), heart valve abnormalities, or an overactive thyroid (hyperthyroidism).

Ventricular Arrhythmias

Arrhythmias that occur in the ventricles are potentially more serious than atrial arrhythmias. Ventricular arrhythmias—such as ventricular tachycardia or ventricular fibrillation—are often due to damage to the heart muscle and are initiated within the muscle mass of the ventricles. These rhythm disturbances often occur at the time of a heart attack, when dying heart muscle releases cellular products that interfere with normal electrical conduction. Later, ventricular arrhythmias can also originate in the areas of the heart where scar tissue formed as a result of the heart attack.

Although some patients can survive for hours—even days—with ventricular tachycardia, this arrhythmia is usually accompanied by severe symptoms, especially in those with significant heart damage. Decreased pumping can result in lightheadedness, severe weakness, loss of consciousness (syncope), congestive heart failure with pulmonary edema (fluid in the tissues of the lungs), heart attack, stroke, and, in the worst case scenario, sudden cardiac death. In ventricular fibrillation, pumping action is totally lost, and death occurs in a few minutes if resuscitation maneuvers are unsuccessful.

Milder Arrhythmias

Milder types of arrhythmia are usually due to problems with the electrical system of the atria or the specialized conduction system connecting the atria with the ventricles. People with premature ventricular contractions may notice "skipped" heartbeats, but no other symptoms. People with other arrhythmias may experience palpitations (fluttering, racing, or skipped beats) with irregular or very rapid rhythms. Extreme bradycardia (a heartbeat slower than 45 beats per minute) or tachycardia (a rapid heartbeat; more than 140 beats per minute) can be associated with lightheadedness or syncope. Angina, shortness of breath, or a heart attack may result from the inability of the coronary arteries to supply the oxygen needed to maintain the extra workload created by a very rapid heart rate.

Diagnosis

Arrhythmias can often be detected with an electrocardiogram, but electrophysiology studies may be needed to assess some arrhythmias. Because one of the objectives of electrophysiology testing may be to induce an abnormal heart rhythm, the procedure takes place under carefully controlled conditions in a cardiac catheterization laboratory.

A catheter that contains electrodes to record the heart's electrical activity is inserted into a vein in the groin and threaded up into the heart. The electrodes are also used to send pacing signals to the heart in an attempt to reproduce an abnormal rhythm. Different medications can then be tried to determine which ones prevent or suppress the arrhythmias. In spite of the seemingly dangerous character of this procedure, when performed by experts, the risk of complications is small.

Electrophysiology testing is much more accurate than an electrocardiogram (ECG) and allows doctors to pinpoint the exact origin of an abnormal heart rhythm and

characterize the abnormality. It is also useful in deciding which patients would best be treated with an automatic implantable cardioverter-defibrillator (see page 105). Not every patient with an arrhythmia needs to undergo electrophysiology testing. Most often it is used in those who have survived sudden cardiac arrest or who experience a significant rhythm disturbance, such as ventricular tachycardia.

Treatment

In many people, arrhythmias can be treated successfully with drugs, though these can have serious side effects. Other arrhythmias may require administration of an electrical stimulus to the heart. An increasing number of rhythm disturbances can be treated with a technique called radiofrequency ablation, which destroys the tissue producing an abnormal electrical circuit within the heart. In some cases, an implanted electrical device—such as a pacemaker or an automatic implantable cardioverter-defibrillator—is used instead of, or in addition to, drugs.

Medications

Aspirin or an anticoagulant, such as warfarin, is prescribed in patients with atrial fibrillation. Warfarin is preferred when the pumping chamber is weak and/or a heart valve is damaged. Atrial fibrillation increases the incidence of strokes from blood clots (emboli) that form within the atria, travel through the circulatory system, and become lodged in an artery supplying blood to the brain.

Digitalis is a first-line drug for the treatment of atrial fibrillation. By slowing the conduction of electrical impulses through the AV node, digitalis reduces the ventricular response to rapid atrial rhythms. Beta-blockers and calcium channel blockers, used for

A

What to Expect from an Implant

Pacemaker implantation is a minor surgical procedure that usually requires a day or two in the hospital (see page 105). Afterward, most people aren't even aware when the unit sends signals. Others may feel an occasional flutter or increase in their heart rate. Patients need to call a doctor only if they experience symptoms such as faintness or shortness of breath.

Implantation of an automatic implantable cardioverter-defibrillator (AICD) usually requires 2 to 3 days in the hospital and about a week at home for recovery. Shocks from an AICD are more disruptive than those generated by pacemakers, but they are usually needed less frequently. A mild shock may feel like a punch in the chest, while a strong one may feel like a sharp kick. If you receive such a shock, sit down, try to relax, and contact your doctor. If you have symptoms such as chest pain or shortness of breath, call 911. If you receive more than one shock a day, or three or more shocks in a week, a thorough evaluation is necessary.

An implantable cardiac device can lengthen life and improve the symptoms of an arrhythmia, but it's not a panacea. Nearly all recipients still have underlying heart disease and most require cardiac medications. Normal activities can usually resume a short time after implantation. After implantation, patients receive a card that should be carried in case of cardiac arrest or loss of consciousness. They should also wear a medical alert bracelet and keep a record of the implant manufacturer.

Generally speaking, there is no need for concern that a device will be affected by home appliances that generate electromagnetic fields, such as microwave ovens or electric blankets. Electronic anti-theft systems in stores are safe as long as you walk through them at a normal pace. Cell phones appear not to affect implantable devices, but to be safe, people wearing pacemakers should keep cell phones at least six inches away from the pacemaker.

All devices require periodic testing; the exact schedule depends on unit specifications, as well as how often the device fires and the strength of the impulse. In any case, most units have to be replaced within 4 to 10 years, depending on the lifespan of the battery.

treating hypertension, also inhibit conduction through the AV node. Another useful drug is the ibutilide (Corvert), which may quickly reverse abnormal atrial heart rhythms. Procainamide (Pronestyl and others) can help control cardiac arrhythmias through its direct action on heart muscle cells.

The drug most effective for controlling ventricular arrhythmias varies from one patient to another. Electrophysiology studies are often used to determine which drug to start. Drugs that suppress ventricular arrhythmias through a direct action on the ventricles include tocainide and mexiletine. Flecainide (Tambocor) and propafenone (Rythmol) not only affect the ventricles, but also slow AV conduction and can be used for either ventricular or supraventricular tachycardias (ones arising in the atria or AV node).

The two most potent antiarrhythmic drugs are sotalol (Betapace) and amiodarone (Cordarone), which can suppress almost any type of fast cardiac rhythm disturbance. Despite a high incidence of potentially serious side effects (for example, bradycardia or hypothyroidism with amiodarone), their effectiveness has made these the two medications most frequently used for arrhythmias.

A

Electrical Cardioversion

When drug measures fail, electrical cardioversion may be tried to return the heart rhythm to normal. This procedure is most commonly used for atrial fibrillation. After the patient receives a short-acting intravenous anesthetic, administration of an electrical stimulus to the heart stops its abnormal electrical activity and may allow the reinitiation of a normal rhythm.

Immediate electrical defibrillation (done without sedation) is an essential emergency measure in all cases of ventricular fibrillation, which rapidly causes cardiac arrest, loss of consciousness, and death if not corrected within a few minutes. Electrical defibrillation is the only effective treatment for ventricular fibrillation. The availability of new, portable external defibrillators can allow emergency personnel, or even the general public, to deliver life-saving electrical cardioversion when they are at the scene before an ambulance arrives.

Artificial Pacemakers

Artificial pacemakers are surgically implanted to provide regular electrical stimuli that control heart rate. Pacemakers are battery-driven units about the size of a cigarette lighter placed just under the skin in the upper chest. Their purpose is to provide a minimal safe heart rate in patients whose intrinsic rate is too slow or, in selected cases, too fast. Pacemaker implantation involves a minor surgical procedure performed under local anesthesia. Most patients are hospitalized one to two days for observation and can resume a normal schedule within two weeks. The pacemaker system must be tested periodically. When the battery runs out, the unit containing it is replaced in a minor operation, usually every seven to ten years.

Automatic Implantable Cardioverter-Defibrillators

People with life-threatening ventricular arrhythmias can have an automatic implantable cardioverter-defibrillator (AICD) implanted surgically in the abdomen. Sensing a rapid ventricular rate due to either ventricular tachycardia or fibrillation, the device automatically delivers an electrical shock to terminate the abnormal rhythm. After receiving a shock, patients should contact their physician or go to a hospital for evaluation. Some AICD models can also serve as a pacemaker, if necessary. Currently, most AICDs are implanted much like a pacemaker, so the recovery time is shorter than before. Regular follow-up visits to the doctor are still needed, and minor surgery is necessary every three to seven years to replace the unit.

Radiofrequency Catheter Ablation

A new method to suppress both supraventricular and ventricular arrhythmias, called radiofrequency catheter ablation, is becoming the treatment of choice when feasible. It involves an electrophysiology study to detect the area of the heart responsible for generating the abnormal rhythm. That area is then destroyed using the energy of a radiofrequency generator. The efficacy of this outpatient technique is high in appropriate patients, and the risk is minimal.

A

More than 20 million Americans suffer from asthma, a chronic, progressive respiratory condition that requires careful management. Over 10 percent—more than 2 million—are believed to be over age 65, and most of the 4,000-plus people who die of the disease each year are elderly. In older people, symptoms tend to occur more frequently, and coexisting medical conditions often complicate treatment, underscoring the importance of proper care. Over many years, repeated episodes may cause lung tissue to lose elasticity, which may lead to a gradual decline in lung function. During a very severe attack, the bronchi may collapse, and the patient may suffocate if he or she does not receive emergency care. Such episodes are rare with proper treatment.

Patients with asthma have a high incidence of heartburn (called gastroesophageal reflux disease, or GERD); chronic nasal inflammation (sinusitis and rhinitis); and nasal polyps, which can exacerbate the symptoms of asthma and increase the frequency of episodes.

A variety of medications are available to treat and manage asthma, but finding the best combination and optimal dosages always requires a good relationship with your doctor and, sometimes, the care of a specialist.

Causes

Asthma is an inflammatory disease that affects the lungs and the airways. Over the past decade, researchers have discovered that asthma results from an immune malfunction. Although the underlying cause of asthma is unknown, three key features have emerged:

Hyper-irritability. The bronchi (airway passages in the lungs) are unusually sensitive to specific irritants or allergens, such as cold air, pollen, animal dander, dust, cigarette smoke, and industrial fumes. Sometimes an infection is also involved.

Muscle spasm. When exposed to an irritant, the smooth muscle in the bronchial walls constricts and narrows the bronchial passages. This phenomenon is called "reversible airway obstruction" because the bronchial muscle maintains the capacity to relax. Bronchial muscle spasm causes wheezing, but the degree of wheezing is not related to the severity of disease. Some patients who wheeze severely are able to continue breathing fairly efficiently, while others who wheeze only mildly are seriously impaired.

Inflammation. Most patients with asthma have some degree of chronic bronchial inflammation (swelling and sometimes excess mucous production), even when symptoms are not apparent. Like muscle spasm, inflammation reduces the diameter of the bronchial airways and is probably initiated by exposure to an irritant. Bronchial inflammation causes cough.

When exposed to an irritant, some of the bronchi (which may already be somewhat inflamed and constricted) go into spasm and become more inflamed, significantly reducing the amount of air that can be expelled from the lungs. In an attempt to keep the bronchi open, the asthmatic tries to expand the lungs to a greater than normal capacity, placing great strain on the diaphragm and other breathing muscles.

When episodes are triggered by exposure to identifiable substances, the disorder is called extrinsic. This form of asthma usually begins before age 30 and may be associated with a family history of allergies. The many triggers that cause extrinsic asthma include not only allergens (such as pollen or dander) and irritants (such as dust or tobacco smoke), but also sinus and respiratory infections, certain medications (such as aspirin), foods

A

and food additives, and cold air. Physical exercise, especially a strenuous endurance activity such as long-distance running or cycling, also appears to be a major trigger of asthma attacks. If no triggers can be found, the disorder is known as intrinsic, nonallergic, or nonatopic asthma. Although intrinsic asthma can begin at any age, it usually develops in adulthood. Research indicates that most people who develop asthma late in life have the intrinsic (or nonallergic) form. However, recent evidence suggests that allergens may play a role in some cases.

If you have asthma, you might want to invest in a dehumidifier. Studies have shown that keeping indoor humidity levels low can reduce populations of household dust mites—a major source of allergens known to trigger asthma attacks. If showering or cooking raises humidity for several hours, reducing humidity during the rest of the day can compensate. The important thing is for relative humidity levels to average less than 50 percent over a 24-hour period.

Symptoms

Common signs of asthma are wheezing, shortness of breath, chest tightness (particularly in cold weather or during exercise), and recurrent coughing that may last more than a week after onset. Clear, sticky mucus is also typical. Episodes can last minutes or hours, and onset can be sudden or gradual.

Other possible signs of asthma include:
- Getting winded walking up a flight of stairs;
- Finding it difficult to perform any kind of physical exertion;
- Becoming short of breath or starting to cough while laughing.

See your doctor if any of these scenarios is familiar to you.

Diagnosis

Correct diagnosis is crucial to rule out other conditions that may cause similar symptoms. They include chronic obstructive pulmonary disease (chronic bronchitis and emphysema), cardiac asthma (wheezing due to fluid buildup in the lungs caused by failure of the heart to pump blood effectively), myocardial ischemia (insufficient blood flow to the heart), and pulmonary embolism (a blood clot in the lungs).

Mild cases of asthma can usually be diagnosed and treated by primary care doctors. But several studies have shown that people with moderate to severe asthma miss fewer days of work, require less hospital and emergency care, and have fewer episodes when treated by specialists—usually an allergist or pulmonologist. Symptoms that do not improve also call for specialist care. The evaluation usually includes a thorough medical history, analysis of nasal and mucus secretions, pulmonary function tests (breathing tests that measure airway obstruction), electrocardiography, and, sometimes, allergy tests. If asthma is confirmed, drug therapy is nearly always required.

Treatment

Medications to treat asthma are divided into two categories: short-term, which provide immediate relief during an asthma attack, and long-term, which help control persistent asthma.

Short-Term Therapy

Bronchodilators, which relax the muscles that surround the airways, are used to relieve and prevent acute symptoms. Taken before exercising, they can often prevent symptoms of exercise-induced asthma. Bronchodilators

A

Helpful Hints for Inhaler Users

If you use an inhaler, be sure to use it properly. About 60 percent of asthma patients do not take medication as directed, often owing to incorrect use of inhalers. Proper technique is important to ensure that you get the correct dosage of the medication. To use an inhaler properly often requires a special device such as a spacer, which helps get more of the medication deep into the lungs.

Also, keep a record of how many times you use your inhaler. The device may appear to function correctly after all the medicine is gone, but it is, in fact, delivering only propellant, which could exacerbate an asthma attack. Albuterol (Proventil), for example, is labeled to deliver 200 sprays, after which it should be discarded. Another option is a small, button-like device called the Doser. It sits atop most inhalers and records each use of the inhaler on a digital display counter, which shows how many inhalations you have taken on a particular day and how many are left in the canister. Ask your pharmacist or doctor about the Doser, which can be purchased in many drugstores and online.

are usually taken in aerosol form with an inhaler. However, liquid, tablet, capsule, and injectable preparations are also available. The primary categories are beta2 agonists (albuterol, bitolterol, metaproterenol, pirbuterol, salmeterol, and terbutaline), anticholinergics (atropine and ipratropium bromide), and methylxanthines (theophylline). Beta2 agonists are the quickest-acting and most often prescribed. They usually open airways in about five minutes or less and keep them open for up to six hours. Anticholinergics are primarily used to supplement beta2 agonists when more relief is necessary. Methylxanthines are an alternative for people who can't tolerate beta2 agonists.

Long-Term Therapy
Anti-inflammatory medications, which block production of certain substances involved in inflammation, are often prescribed if symptoms are not controlled by bronchodilators and episodes occur more than twice a week. Anti-inflammatories keep airways open by reducing or reversing swelling and lessening airway sensitivity. They must be used continually to be effective. Because several weeks of treatment may be necessary before the benefits of some anti-inflammatories become

apparent, some patients may discontinue their use prematurely.

Owing to their effectiveness, inhaled corticosteroids, which include beclomethasone dipropionate, budesonide, dexamethasone, flunisolide, fluticasone, and triamcinolone acetonide, are the first-line choice for long-term anti-inflammatory maintenance therapy. A recent study showed that people who used them were half as likely to be hospitalized as those who only used bronchodilators. When taken in oral (pill) form, corticosteroids provide fast, dramatic reversal of severe symptoms during acute episodes. But they should be used only to stabilize symptoms and for a limited time.

Other types of anti-inflammatories include mast cell stabilizers and leukotriene modifiers (also known as antileukotrienes or leukotriene antagonists). Mast cell stabilizers, such as cromolyn sodium (Intal), act on mast cells, which secrete substances that cause inflammation and swelling of the airways during an allergic reaction. Mast cell stabilizers are used primarily for mild to moderate symptoms in children and in adults with exercise-induced asthma. Approved by the Food and Drug Administration in 1996, leukotriene modifiers, such as montelukast (Singulair), are the first new class of asthma drugs in 20 years. They block the action of leukotrienes, which are potent chemicals that constrict airways and increase mucus production. They are used primarily for exercise- and aspirin-induced asthma and to supplement inhaled corticosteroids.

Side Effects of Medication

While asthma medications are extremely effective in controlling and managing the disease, side effects can be significant. Overuse of beta2 agonists can decrease their effectiveness and cause tremors or a racing heartbeat. Older people are especially susceptible to the side effects of theophylline, which can induce nausea and insomnia.

The most common side effects of inhaled corticosteroids are throat irritation and thrush (candidiasis), a yeast infection in the mouth and throat. These problems can be minimized by rinsing the mouth after inhalation, keeping the inhaler clean, and using a spacer device. Because long-term use of oral corticosteroids is associated with serious side effects (such as osteoporosis, diabetes, cataracts, fluid retention, weight gain, high blood pressure, adrenal gland impairment, and thinning of the skin), they must be taken at the lowest effective dose for the shortest amount of time possible—and only when other drugs cannot control symptoms. Adverse reactions to leukotriene modifiers include nausea, headache, and reversible liver problems. Mast cell stabilizers have few side effects.

See an ophthalmologist regularly if you take inhaled steroids for moderate to severe asthma. Taken for longer than three months, daily doses in excess of 1,500 to 1,600 micrograms may increase your risk of ocular hypertension (increased pressure in the eye) or glaucoma.

Drugs taken for other medical conditions, especially cardiovascular problems, can interact with asthma medications or worsen asthma symptoms. Beta-blockers and angiotensin-converting enzyme (ACE) inhibitors can cause coughing. Interactions with diuretics may increase the risk of cardiac arrhythmias—especially if digitalis is also taken. Sleeping pills, tranquilizers, and other sedative drugs can make breathing slower and more shallow. When these medications are necessary, careful management can ensure optimal treatment for all coexisting medical problems.

Monitoring Asthma

Another feature of asthma management is daily home monitoring of breathing efficiency by using a simple tool called a peak-flow meter. Peak flow is a measurement of the fastest rate at which a person can force air out of the lungs. The patient inhales fully and then exhales fully and forcefully into the flow meter. A simple scale registers a value for peak flow. By keeping a diary of the readings, a patient can maintain an accurate daily record of the illness, not unlike the diabetic who records blood-sugar values.

Peak flow measurements decrease dependence on symptoms as a measure of severity, and give the doctor an objective means of assessing lung function. A decrease of 25 percent from a patient's usual finding generally identifies a significant change in status. Taking appropriate treatment at this time may short-circuit a severe episode. A decrease of 50 percent is likely to mean that a severe episode requiring immediate emergency treatment is imminent. Studies show that monitoring peak flow and discussing their findings with a physician reduce the likelihood of a fatal episode.

Identifying and avoiding asthma triggers is also important. For example, if cold air

A

An Asthma Action Plan

Develop a plan for managing your asthma in consultation with your doctor. It should detail which drugs to take for specific symptoms, what to do for a pending episode, when to call the doctor, and where to go for treatment during a serious episode.

• Know the purpose of each medication. Lack of understanding most frequently leads to overuse of drugs that relieve symptoms (bronchodilators) and underuse of drugs that prevent future episodes (anti-inflammatories).

• Take medication properly. About 60 percent of asthma patients do not take medications as directed, often owing to incorrect use of inhalers. For tips on using an inhaler, see page 108.

• Make sure that each one of your doctors is aware of all the medications you take. This will reduce the possibility of side effects and drug interactions.

• Get a yearly flu shot and be sure you have been vaccinated against pneumonia. Respiratory infections are common asthma triggers.

• Lead a healthy life. Optimize lung function by not smoking, maintaining a healthy weight, and exercising regularly.

aggravates your condition, wear a scarf over your nose and mouth when you go outdoors in winter. Keeping a daily record of episodes and what immediately preceded them may help.

When irritants cannot be avoided, consider using a long-acting bronchodilator. In addition, treating the illnesses that are often associated with asthma (GERD, nasal infection, and nasal polyps) often helps to control symptoms.

B

After the common cold, back pain is the most frequent complaint that brings people to a doctor's office. Each day, 6.5 million Americans are plagued by persistent back pain, and every year back problems temporarily disable 17 percent of the U.S. work force. Four out of five Americans will have a significant backache at least once in their lifetime.

Most back pain is due to mechanical causes linked to the back's complicated, sophisticated structure. The spine, which supports the body and protects the delicate spinal cord, is made up of 33 bones called vertebrae (9 of them are fused vertebrae located in the coccyx). The vertebrae are stacked upon each other at a slight angle to form the spine's S-shaped curve. Together, the vertebrae, ligaments, and muscles (in the back and abdomen) help to maintain erect posture.

Between the vertebrae are flexible pads of tissue, called intervertebral disks, that cushion the vertebrae as the body moves, and prevent them from grinding against each other. The high water content of the disks makes them very elastic—they can expand and contract as the body bends and moves, and then return to their original shape. Thus, the disks, in conjunction with the interlocking facet joints formed between adjacent vertebrae, give the spine its tremendous flexibility. At the same time, our upright posture puts extra pressure on the vertebrae of the lower back, where the back curves most and pain is most likely to strike. Various body positions and activities that involve lifting, bending, and twisting place even greater demands on the spine.

Causes

Most of the time, the cause of back pain is not easily determined. Since about 90 percent of cases resolve on their own, it is not always important to find a precise cause.

People under age 60 tend to have acute backaches that are sudden and short-lived—most often resulting from a sprain, strain, muscle spasm, or, less frequently, a herniated or degenerated disk. In older people, chronic conditions are more commonly the source of back pain. These conditions are degenerative changes of the spinal bones and disks, spinal stenosis, vertebral compression fractures, and spinal deformities.

Though it may seem that back pain occurs suddenly—for example, when a person bends down to pick something up—it is precipitated by a number of factors, including normal aging, weak back and abdominal muscles, obesity, and poor posture. The frequency of sprains and strains tends to decline after age 60, in part because older adults are less likely to participate in the kind of vigorous activities that lead to these problems. Also, the disks between the vertebrae become less pliable in older adults and, as a result, are less likely to protrude and cause trouble. Such rigidity, however, leads to problems of its own, mostly due to degenerative changes in the vertebrae.

Sprains, Strains, and Spasms

Sprains, strains, and spasms usually result from activity or injury. The term sprain is used when a ligament is partly torn, while strain is applied when a muscle is overstretched.

The back is supported by overlapping layers of 140 muscles that help to hold the spine erect and allow it to bend and twist. Whenever the back is injured, these muscles tend to contract and cause pain—a phenomenon called muscle spasm. Although the pain may be intense, muscle spasm is ultimately a protective measure. The pain ensures that the injured area remains immobile, thus preventing further damage. A direct injury to a muscle can cause pain, but most muscle pain is a response to disk or joint injury.

Muscle pain can frustrate patients and their doctors. Unlike back pain due to the compression of a nerve, muscle pain cannot be confirmed by imaging technology, such as an x-ray or magnetic resonance imaging (MRI). One study found that people with muscle pain were less likely to report periods of relief than those in whom back pain was due to a herniated disk. The researchers who conducted the study suggested that patients with muscle pain feel frustrated by the inability to confirm the cause of their pain, or simply because their pain is more unrelenting.

Degenerative Changes

Degenerative changes in the lumbar spine, often referred to as degenerative osteoarthritis or spondylosis, are an inevitable consequence of aging. They usually begin at about age 20, but MRI studies have detected changes within the disks in teenagers. Degenerative changes, along with vertebral compression fractures and kyphosis (an abnormal curvature of the back), are responsible for the loss of height experienced by many people over 50.

As we age, lumbar disks wear out because they are subjected to such large loads. Depending on an individual's activities, pressure on the lumbar spine ranges from 1 to 11 times that of body weight. Standing erect places a load on a lumbar disk equivalent to one's body weight, and bending, twisting, and lifting increase the load in proportion to the activity and amount of weight lifted. Age-related loss of strength in the back muscles—which normally bear about one third of the load on the spine—also increases the stress on the disks and facet joints.

Over the years, the disk center (nucleus pulposus) slowly loses its water content and shrinks. This flattening of the disks leads to a narrowing of the space between the vertebrae. Also as a result of supporting heavy loads, the vertebrae may develop bone spurs (osteophytes) that can press on a spinal nerve and cause pain. Together, disk wear and vertebral changes can cause the facet joints to deteriorate—which, in and of itself, may cause pain.

In addition, arthritic changes—a gradual erosion of the cartilage that lines the facet joints—may cause pain and loss of the spine's coordinated smooth motion. Pain can also arise from irritation to nerves present in the outer portion of the disks.

Spinal Stenosis

Spinal stenosis, a common cause of low back pain, is a narrowing of the central canal of the spine or the lateral spinal canals. Spinal stenosis has many causes, but it often results from degenerative changes in the spine, such as those caused by osteoarthritis. For instance, as the body ages, gradual deterioration of the disks and facet joints in the spine causes the bones to rub together. This increased friction may eventually lead to the formation of osteophytes at the facet joints and around the rims of the vertebrae. Spinal stenosis occurs when these overgrowths of bone gradually narrow the central canal of the spine (central stenosis) or the bony canals through which nerves leave the spinal cord (lateral stenosis).

Although spinal stenosis can occur at any age, it usually affects people over age 50, and occurs more often in men than in

B

women. Symptoms of spinal stenosis usually start slowly and are mild at first. Central stenosis can cause back pain, but usually the pain radiates into both legs. The pain does not follow the distribution of specific nerves but rather seems to involve the buttocks, both thighs or calves, and, occasionally, even the entire length of both legs. The pain is cramping in nature and may be associated with weakness, a "rubbery" feeling, numbness, and a sensation of loss of power in the legs. As a result of this weakness, patients are often unable to walk on either their toes or heels, and they may sometimes fall. Because the nerves controlling the bladder emerge from the lower spine, spinal stenosis may also cause urinary incontinence. Lateral stenosis causes pain along the pathway of the nerve compressed as it exits the spinal cord. The pain of spinal stenosis is often not relieved by bed rest.

Vertebral Compression Fractures

A healthy vertebra will only break when subjected to a forceful injury, such as in a car accident. By contrast, even minor trauma—such as a sneeze—can cause a compression fracture of a vertebra weakened by cancer, osteoporosis, Paget's disease, or hyperparathyroidism. (Excessive secretion of parathyroid hormone by a benign tumor of the parathyroid gland weakens bones by promoting loss of bone calcium.)

The two most common factors precipitating a compression fracture in people with weakened vertebrae are falling and placing a load on outstretched arms—for example, raising a window or lifting a small child or bag of groceries. In a typical compression fracture, the front of a vertebral body collapses into a wedge shape, often causing immediate, intense pain in the area of the fracture. Sometimes, however, the fracture may be relatively painless.

As a person ages, the fibrous disks separating the vertebrae degenerate, causing them to lose moisture and become thinner. This allows facet joints, which contribute to spinal flexibility (as do the disks), to rub against one another (at right), and wear away their protective coating. A worn facet joint can rub directly against nerves to cause pain. Another painful problem occurs when pressure from surrounding vertebrae cause a disk to bulge, or herniate (far right). The bulging disk can impinge on a nerve and trigger intense radiating pain.

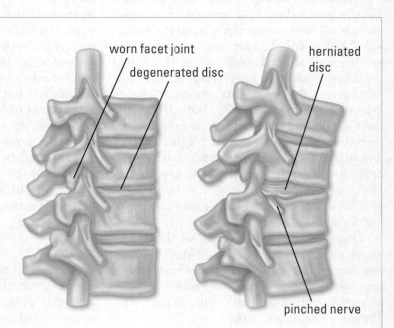

B

Before age 60, fractures are more common in men than in women, probably because men's lifestyles promote more trauma. But, because women rapidly lose bone mass during the first three to five years after a natural or surgical menopause—or any other cause of estrogen deficiency—osteoporosis and vertebral fractures are especially common in older women (see page 483). Estimates suggest that one quarter of American women over the age of 50 develop one or more compression fractures of their vertebrae.

Herniated Disk

At some point in their lives, 10 percent of people experience symptoms due to a herniated disk—which can occur when mild trauma, such as lifting an object or even sneezing, causes the gel-like center of the disk to bulge out through outer layers of tissue that have weakened with age.

Symptoms usually result from pressure by the protruding disk on one or more of the spinal nerves emerging from the spinal cord, but in some cases the disk may press on the spinal cord itself or on the cauda equina (a bundle of nerve roots at the base of the spinal cord). This pressure causes pain not only in the back, but also in the part of the body served by the compressed nerve. In some cases, disk fragments may break free, a condition referred to as sequestration. Although herniation can involve any disk, most cases occur in the two lowest lumbar disks because they carry the greatest weight.

The location and severity of the symptoms caused by a herniated disk depend on the extent and site of the rupture. In general, spasm of back muscles and difficulty in walking or standing straight indicate a herniated disk.

Pain from a herniated disk is usually sudden in onset. The patient may "feel something snap" before the start of pain, which may begin as a mild tingling or a "pins and needles" sensation before increasing in severity. If the herniated disk compresses the sciatic nerve, pain later radiates into a specific area of one leg (sciatica). A decrease in back pain may be accompanied by increasingly severe pain, numbness, and weakness in the legs, along with changes in reflexes. In fact, a herniated lumbar disk is the most common cause of sciatica. If a ruptured disk compresses nerves in the neck, pain may radiate down the arms and be accompanied by weakness and numbness in the arms and hands.

Spinal Deformities

The three basic types of spinal deformities are kyphosis, lordosis, and scoliosis. Kyphosis, an abnormal accentuation of the usual backward curvature of the thoracic spine, is commonly referred to as a humpback or hunchback. (It may, in rare instances, also occur in the neck or lower back.) In lordosis, or swayback, the abdomen is thrust too far forward and the buttocks too far to the rear. This condition is common in overweight people with weak abdominal muscles. Scoliosis, an abnormal lateral or sideways bend to the back, is caused by a twisting of the spine that gives the appearance of a side curvature. These conditions usually develop during childhood or adolescence and worsen with age, but they may occur in older individuals solely as the result of degenerative changes.

Sciatica

Sciatica, which affects 40 percent of adults over their lifetime, can occur when a herniated disk or lateral spinal stenosis irritates some part of either sciatic nerve. Each large sciatic nerve is formed by nerve roots that emerge from the lower spine, join together in the hip region, and run down the back of each thigh. Near the knee, the sciatic nerves branch into smaller nerves that extend into the calves, ankles, feet, and toes. Sciatica results from irritation of one of the nerve roots in the lower back. Pain or numbness develops along the path of the sciatic nerve; the precise location of symptoms depends on which spinal nerve root is affected.

Compression of the sciatic nerves can also diminish leg strength. After age 50, sciatica is more commonly caused by spinal stenosis than disk herniation. About 90 percent of the time, sciatica caused by a herniated disk resolves within six weeks with little or no treatment. Sciatica from spinal stenosis resolves by itself within a month in up to half of all cases, but one in four people may have pain for as long as four months.

Additional Causes of Low Back Pain

Other medical conditions affecting the spine and possibly leading to back pain include ankylosing spondylitis (a chronic inflammation of the facet joints and the sacroiliac joints, between the sacrum and the pelvis); osteomalacia (a softening of bone that results from a lack of the essential minerals calcium and phosphorus); spondylolisthesis (in which one of the vertebrae slips forward due to a vertebral defect); and vertebral osteomyelitis (a serious and increasingly common bacterial infection of the spine).

In rare instances, back pain is caused by cancer of the spine or by abnormalities in areas of the body close to the spine. Cancer can originate in the vertebrae—as in the case of multiple myeloma (cancer cells that move from the bone marrow to the bones at numerous sites)—or it can spread to the spine from other sites in the body, most often from the breast, prostate, lung, kidney, or thyroid gland.

Conditions such as pancreatitis (inflammation of the pancreas), an ulcer penetrating through the back wall of the duodenum (the first part of the small intestine), or an abdominal aortic aneurysm (a weak spot in the aorta, the body's largest artery, that balloons outward and may put pressure on the lower back) may also cause back pain. In addition, back pain may originate in, and be referred from, disorders at other body sites; such disorders include gallstones, kidney stones and infections, and endometriosis (a benign growth of endometrial tissue outside of the uterus).

Signs and Symptoms

Only about 2 percent of back pain episodes require immediate medical treatment. However, even though the vast majority of episodes are not serious, doctors routinely ask certain questions—for example, whether the pain is relieved by changing your position, or whether it continues at rest—in order to eliminate the possibility of dangerous conditions, such as infection, cancer, cauda equina syndrome, or an abdominal aortic aneurysm.

Since permanent damage to the nerves can result from untreated conditions, persons with a history of malignant disease and those experiencing any of the following symptoms should see their doctor immediately:

- Constant pain that is not relieved by changing position
- Pain that continues when resting, especially at night
- Fever
- Unexplained weight loss
- Impaired bowel or bladder function
- Muscle weakness in the arms, hands, legs, or feet

- Loss of sensation in buttocks and thighs
- Urinary retention

B

Compression of the cauda equina—a bundle of nerve roots in the lower spine—may result in the sudden onset of impaired bowel and bladder function (usually an inability to void or, conversely, overflow incontinence); loss of sensation in the groin, buttocks, and legs; and severe weakness or paralysis in the legs. These symptoms—known as cauda equina syndrome—indicate a surgical emergency. Patients who cannot reach their doctor quickly should go to a hospital emergency room.

Diagnosis

It is often difficult to pinpoint the exact cause of back pain because so many different structures can be affected. If back pain subsides on its own, it may not be necessary to determine the exact cause. If symptoms persist, your doctor will try to locate the anatomical cause with a physical examination, laboratory tests, and imaging studies—or any combination of these diagnostic techniques.

Back Pain History

Obtaining an accurate history and description of the back pain is a doctor's primary method of tracking down its cause and determining whether treatment is necessary. Topics a doctor will ask about include where the pain is located, the severity of pain, when it began, prior episodes of back pain, what kind of work the patient does, whether there are any other health problems, what relieves or worsens the pain, and if the patient is taking any medications.

Physical Examination

A physical examination typically focuses on the back and lower extremities. The doctor will look at a patient's posture and curvature of the spine; a hands-on examination of tender areas in the back may provide clues to the origin of the pain. To observe muscles and joints during movement, the doctor may ask patients to sit, stand, walk, walk on their toes or heels, bend over, twist, and bend sideways. A straight-leg-raise test is also important, since it can help the doctor determine whether disk herniation or other causes are responsible. And a neurological exam, including tests of sensation, strength, and reflexes, will be conducted as well. In some cases, a rectal examination may be done to assess nerve function of the anus, because its nerves also arise from the lower lumbar spine.

Laboratory Tests

Blood tests can help determine the cause of back problems in a few situations. Blood levels of alkaline phosphatase (an enzyme released by bone-forming cells called osteoblasts) are often extremely high in patients with active Paget's disease (which can cause spinal stenosis and vertebral compression fractures). Blood calcium levels are elevated in patients with hyperparathyroidism (which, along with osteoporosis, can lead to vertebral compression fractures). To eliminate the possibility that back pain is due to the spread of prostate cancer, men might receive a blood test for PSA (prostate-specific antigen), which is elevated in men with prostate cancer. Tests like erythrocyte sedimentation rate (which can reflect inflammation) and blood counts (which help measure the body's reaction to infection) may eliminate possible systemic disease as the cause of back pain.

Imaging Studies

Imaging studies provide a view of the bones and the soft tissues (muscles, ligaments, cartilage, tendons, and blood vessels). These studies are needed mainly for potential surgical candidates. (If osteoporosis is suspected, one or more tests to measure bone density may be carried out—see page 484.)

Conventional x-rays should be the first imaging study for chronic pain and for new-onset back pain lasting longer than four to six weeks. They are especially useful for detecting fractures and invasion of bone by multiple myeloma or other forms of cancer. X-rays are generally overused, but they may be needed for people over age 50 because these individuals have a greater risk of malignancy and vertebral fractures.

Computed tomography (CT or CAT) scans utilize multiple x-rays that are combined by a computer into a cross-sectional picture. CT scans are 10 to 20 times more sensitive than x-rays; they provide better soft tissue detail and good detail of the vertebrae.

Magnetic resonance imaging (MRI), which visualizes internal structures by means of a powerful magnet and radio waves, provides the best resolution of soft tissues. However, MRIs may not give a useful image of the vertebral bones and tend to be overused. Despite their sensitivity, studies have shown that MRIs should be reserved for pre-operative evaluation or when a herniated disk is suspected in patients whose back symptoms (including pain) do not respond to conservative treatment after four to six weeks.

CT myelograms involve a CT scan after the injection of a contrast material into the spinal canal. These scans offer the best detail of bone and soft tissue, but have side effects and carry a risk of infection. They are usually done only prior to surgery or after previous failed surgery.

Prevention of Low Back Pain

There is much that can be done to prevent back pain. Preventive measures that can reduce the risk of damage to the spine and related structures include paying close attention to your posture, engaging in regular exercise to strengthen the back and abdominal muscles, and changing your daily routines to protect the back. These are spelled out in more detail in the text box on page 118.

Treatment

In most cases, back pain resolves rather quickly, regardless of the type of treatment. Since about 90 percent of back pain episodes clear up within six weeks with little or no treatment, people suffering from low back pain can safely try self-treatment as long as they are not experiencing any of the significant symptoms listed on pages 115 to 116. Those with severe low back pain should visit a doctor if the pain is not relieved after a few days of bed rest, the pain recurs, or it is accompanied by pain, numbness, or tingling radiating into the buttocks or legs.

Self-Treatment

Back relaxation exercises—which involve gentle stretching to relax back muscles, lengthen the spine, and relieve compression of the vertebrae—are useful for alleviating stress and strain on the back. Ask your doctor for instructions or a referral to a physical therapist. In addition, several steps can be taken at home to help ease a backache.

Rest. Lying down takes pressure off the spine and usually lessens the pain. The best postures in bed are lying in the fetal

B

Prevention Strategies

Because back pain may recur, it's especially important to take preventive measures whenever there is a history of back problems.

Improve posture. Good posture allows the body to follow the natural S-shaped curve of the spine and helps prevent back problems like muscle strain.

Exercise to strengthen the back. Regular exercise tones and strengthens the muscles that hold the back in proper alignment. Just going for a walk is one of the best exercises for improving posture. Exercises that strength and stretch the back, abdominal, and buttock muscles also help prevent back pain.

Lift correctly. Always bend at the knees, and carry heavy objects close to the body. Holding objects at arm's length can increase the load on the lower spine by 15 times the object's weight.

Avoid activities that strain the back. Depending on the severity of the back problem, patients may need to avoid activities that require sudden twisting movements, including sports such as golf, bowling, football, basketball, baseball, weight lifting, and tennis and other racquet sports. With a physician's approval, it may only be necessary to improve or modify one's technique in these sports.

Maintain an ideal weight. Obesity not only places an extra burden on the lower back, it also increases the natural curve of the lumbar spine, which requires the vertebrae to bear weight at abnormal angles.

Don't smoke. Studies show that cigarette smoking speeds the degeneration of intervertebral disks.

Consider a back school. Back schools are usually directed by a physical therapist, sometimes with the aid of a physician. They provide a safe, inexpensive, and effective way to obtain a better understanding of how the back works and what can go wrong. The director can analyze how working conditions, daily activities, and sleeping habits may adversely affect your back. Back schools provide individualized exercise programs and may offer relaxation techniques.

position (with a pillow between the knees) or on the back with knees flexed (using two pillows to support the legs). Most experts, however, advise limiting bed rest to one or two days. The inactivity associated with longer periods of bed rest may do more harm than good by weakening muscles and prolonging the time to recovery. It is better to get out of bed and move around as soon as you can do so with reasonable comfort, even if some pain persists. Until the pain disappears, however, patients should avoid lifting, vigorous exercise, bending, or other activities that place stress on the back.

Ice. Immediate application of ice can alleviate pain after a sudden back injury that causes localized pain. In addition to relieving pain, ice reduces internal bleeding and swelling by decreasing blood flow. An ice bag, commercial ice pack, or even a package of frozen vegetables should be used for 10 to 20 minutes every two waking hours for 48 hours. To avoid frostbite, don't leave ice in place long enough to numb the skin.

Heat. It is best to wait for 48 hours after an acute back injury before applying heat. However, chronic back pain or a more widespread backache that starts some time after a back injury may be eased by relaxing muscles with a hot bath or shower, heating pad, heat lamp, or hot moist compresses.

Over-the-counter medications. Nonsteroidal anti-inflammatory drugs

(NSAIDs)—such as aspirin, ibuprofen (Advil, Motrin), naproxen (Aleve), or ketoprofen (Orudis)—or the pain reliever acetaminophen (Tylenol) may help alleviate discomfort. NSAIDs can also reduce inflammation.

Traction, corsets, and braces. Little evidence supports the use of traction or corsets, although temporary use of a corset with built-in supports may be helpful when recovering from surgery or to allow essential activities despite continued symptoms. Whether back braces help in treating low back pain is unclear, and seemingly contradictory results continue to be published. Industrial back supports for injury prevention are of little value, but they slightly restrict forward bending and may be of psychological value.

Alternative Therapies

A comprehensive study of alternative therapy use found that almost 60 percent of people who consulted a medical doctor for low back pain have also tried some sort of alternative therapy. When contemplating one of these options, it is important to remember that the treatments are considered alternative precisely because there is no scientific evidence proving that they work consistently. In addition, patients should be cautious about undertaking any treatments that are expensive and require repeated visits (i.e., more than half a dozen).

Some of the alternative methods frequently tried for low back pain are acupuncture, acupressure, massage, relaxation therapy, and biofeedback. Patients should be sure to tell their doctor if they are using any alternative therapies.

Medications

Regardless of the cause of the pain, a doctor will probably recommend the self-treatment techniques described above. In general, limiting both bed rest and pain medication for back pain has increasingly become the approach of choice among primary care physicians—a preference supported by current research.

Patients whose severe back pain lasts more than a few days, or whose mild back pain does not respond to self-treatment, should see their family doctor. A doctor might prescribe a prescription NSAID such as diflunisal (Dolobid) or meclofenamate (available in generic form).

Apart from the use of NSAIDs, a doctor may prescribe muscle relaxants for chronic pain (these drugs tend to cause more side effects in older adults). Potentially addicting drugs such as opiates (for example, morphine, codeine, or meperidine) should be used with great caution as a treatment for low back pain, and only after all else has failed. However, the use of opiates for chronic pain does not necessarily increase addiction and allows many people with such pain to function. Controlled-release formulations of oxycodone and morphine (OxyContin and MS Contin, respectively) are often used by people who need opiates for more than a few days. These long-acting drugs avoid the peaks and valleys that occur with standard, short-acting narcotics.

Spinal manipulation by a chiropractor or osteopath has also proven useful for treatment of short-term back pain. If symptoms do not improve after four weeks, however, use of manipulation should be reevaluated. Aerobic exercise also can be started during the first two weeks of symptoms if they are mild. After two weeks, exercises

Whether to Choose a Chiropractor

Chiropractic treatment—which primarily involves physical manipulation and adjustment of the spine, as well as massage, application of heat or cold, or electrical stimulation—may help some patients, but its long-term effectiveness has not been proven. Treatment can be a good choice for pain relief during the first month of symptoms, provided there is no evidence of radiating pain due to nerve damage. The chiropractor must be sure that back pain is not due to bone or joint disorders, since manipulating a spine damaged by osteoporosis, for example, could result in further, more serious injury. In addition, the procedure may be harmful if the cause of back pain is a herniated disk, a vertebral fracture, or a tumor. X-rays of the area are usually taken before spinal manipulation to rule out vertebral fractures.

Chiropractors should have a minimum of six years of college-level training in such fields as physiology, nutrition, biomechanics, and spinal manipulation, and should be licensed by the state. A thorough medical exam should precede any spinal manipulation. Serious complications of lower spine manipulations, including paralysis of the legs and even death, have been reported, but their occurrence is extremely low. (Complications are more common with manipulations of the cervical spine.)

Individuals who choose chiropractic treatment should be wary of chiropractors who prescribe or sell nutritional supplements or who claim that spinal manipulation will cure a wide variety of illnesses. It is also unwise to agree to full-spine or full-body x-rays, which offer little or no diagnostic value, are costly, and expose patients to unneeded radiation. Patients should tell their doctor if they are seeing a chiropractor.

to strengthen the back and abdominal muscles can be started slowly.

Prolonged bed rest (more than four days), spinal traction, lumbar corsets (except as a preventive measure by people who often lift heavy objects), support belts, and back machines are not recommended. Though still used sometimes, transcutaneous electrical nerve stimulation (TENS), the application of low-energy electrical radiation to "numb" the nerves, is not advised.

Surgery
In most cases, back pain can be relieved relatively quickly with conservative (nonsurgical) treatments such as rest, medication, or physical therapy. In fact, less than 5 percent of back pain sufferers are candidates for surgery. Each year, however, about 335,000 Americans undergo surgery

for low back problems. Most of them are suffering from pain caused by a herniated disk or spinal stenosis.

Surgical procedures for these conditions include diskectomy (used to take pressure off the pinched nerve from a herniated disk); laminectomy (which relieves pressure on the spinal cord by removing fragments of bone and other tissue responsible for spinal stenosis); spinal fusion (the grafting of bone to fuse two or more adjacent vertebrae together); or a combination of these procedures.

Surgery is a treatment of last resort, and it is appropriate only for certain types of low back pain. If your doctor cannot identify a structural cause for the pain—which is the case 85 percent of the time—back surgery will not be effective. But if such a cause of pain can be pinpointed, surgery may be an option.

Less often, back surgery is performed to remove a tumor, treat an infection, or correct a spinal deformity. In rare cases, emergency back surgery is required to treat a condition called cauda equina syndrome, which is caused by damage to nerves in the lower spine and can cause loss of bladder and bowel function (see page 116).

Deciding on Back Surgery

Because back surgery is rarely an emergency procedure, you have time to get a second opinion and to weigh carefully the benefits and risks of the procedure. Here are some things to consider:

- Even when patients are carefully selected, surgery is not always successful. Disk surgery eliminates both back pain and sciatica in about 70 percent of patients, and sciatica alone in 75 percent to 95 percent. Surgery for spinal stenosis significantly improves leg pain in 70 percent to 85 percent of patients. And spinal fusion is successful about 60 percent to 85 percent of the time. The best results are achieved in patients with less extensive disease and in those who have endured pain for less than a year.
- Surgery can result in complications such as nerve and muscle damage, infection, excessive bleeding, blood clots, scar tissue, and a weakened spine that is susceptible to degeneration. Fortunately, the risk of these complications is low.
- Even when back surgery is successful, pain can recur over the long term. Symptoms return in about 5 percent of people when a disk ruptures again after surgery for sciatica, and in 50 percent to 60 percent of people after a laminectomy. If back surgery needs to be repeated, the results are typically less favorable.
- Surgery for herniated disks usually relieves pain faster and allows people to regain normal function sooner. However, it appears to be no better than conservative treatment over the long term.
- Coexisting health conditions, such as heart disease or arthritis, can increase the risks of surgery and reduce the likelihood of a positive outcome. Smoking, old age, and poor nutrition can also increase the risk of surgical complications.
- Recovery from back surgery can take about six to eight weeks, and even longer following spinal fusion. During this time, you will be told to avoid driving, excessive sitting, lifting, and bending forward; to perform exercises daily; and to use proper posture when sitting, standing, and lifting.

Surgery for Spinal Deformity

Most spinal deformities in adults can be helped with flexibility exercises, posture maintenance, general fitness, and back-stretching exercises. Mild anti-inflammatory medication and, occasionally, a rigid brace may help, although many older people do not tolerate braces.

Not until the late 1960s did surgery in adults become more routine, and only in the last 15 years has it been used with increasing frequency in patients over age 50. Surgery for spinal deformity is indicated in an adult if the deformity is severe; if it will continue to progress in later adult life; if it is accompanied by associated neurological problems; or if pain is unresponsive to other measures. Surgery usually entails the application of internal implants fixed to the bone (which allow for partial correction of the deformity) together with a spinal fusion. Old age should not prevent patients from getting this surgery, provided they are in good general health. Results are satisfactory 85 percent of the time.

B

B

Acupuncture for Back Pain

Treatment with acupuncture, derived from a traditional form of Chinese medicine, generally entails a practitioner inserting 10 to 15 hair-like needles into specific body points. Sometimes the needles are stimulated with electricity or heat, or turned by hand. Acupuncture may relieve pain by triggering nerves to send out natural, pain-blocking chemicals (endorphins) within the body. Pain relief, while common, is usually temporary.

Although a panel convened by the National Institutes of Health (NIH) found few well-designed studies of the effects of acupuncture, they concluded that there was enough evidence of its value for

further research. They also stated that for certain situations, such as back pain, acupuncture "may be useful as an adjunct treatment or an acceptable alternative or be included in a comprehensive management program."

To find a reputable practitioner, contact the National Certification Commission for Acupuncture and Oriental Medicine (703-548-9004), the American Academy of Medical Acupuncture (323-937-5514), the American Association of Oriental Medicine (610-266-1433), or the National Acupuncture and Oriental Medicine Alliance (253-851-6896).

Managing Chronic Back Pain

For some people the pain becomes a constant problem that interferes with many important aspects of daily life. If ignored, chronic low back pain—generally defined as unremitting pain that lasts at least six months and is not relieved by standard treatments—can lead to depression, disturbed sleep, impaired balance, declining participation in physical and social activities, and decreased quality of life.

The first step to relieve chronic back pain is a careful medical evaluation by a doctor to assess the nature and degree of the pain and, if possible, to pinpoint the cause. If no specific cause for the pain can be identified (such as nerve entrapment that can be relieved by surgery), a variety of medications, along with other treatments discussed previously, may be tried. If these standard measures fail to relieve the pain, your doctor may advise enrolling in a pain treatment facility, where a variety of approaches are used to reduce or eliminate both pain and its effects on daily life. (See page 212 for more information on pain clinics.)

A t least half of all men over age 50 are bothered by benign prostatic hyperplasia (BPH), a gradual enlargement of the prostate (a small, walnut-shaped gland in men that surrounds the urethra—the tube that carries urine from the bladder to the penis). The prostate is composed of glandular and smooth muscle tissue encapsulated in a tough outer shell. The glandular tissue produces some of the substances found in semen. It also converts testosterone (the hormone responsible for fertility, sex drive, and secondary male sex characteristics) into dihydrotestosterone (DHT, the active form of testosterone). The smooth muscle periodically contracts to launch prostate secretions into the urethra, where they mix with semen.

Beginning around age 45, multiplication and expansion of glandular tissue in the prostate produces pressure outward against the exterior shell and inward against the urethra. Simultaneously, the smooth muscle tissue surrounding the urethra contracts and clenches the urethra like a fist. As a result, the urethra narrows and may become obstructed. These developments impede urine flow and may lead to urinary frequency, dribbling, and a weak urine stream.

BPH is the most common benign (noncancerous) tumor in men. Symptoms related to BPH are present in about one in four men by age 55, and in half of 75-year-old men. BPH occurs more often in Western than in Eastern countries, such as Japan and China,

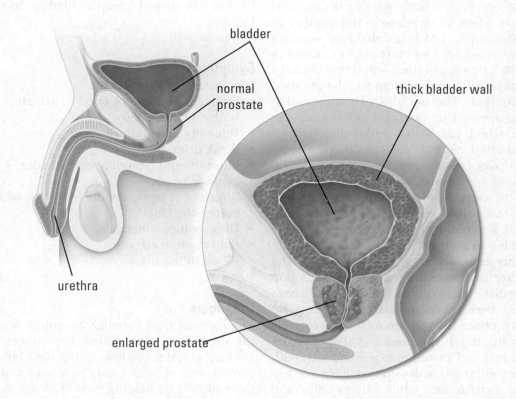

bladder

normal prostate

thick bladder wall

urethra

enlarged prostate

As the prostate enlarges, it may restrict urine flow, creating a frequent, urgent need to empty the bladder. Urine retention places excess demand upon the bladder wall, which can thicken as a result.

B

and may be more common among African Americans than in white men.

An enlarged prostate is not life threatening, nor is it cancer. In addition, there is no evidence that BPH leads to prostate cancer; however, symptoms of both disorders are similar, and it is possible to have BPH and prostate cancer at the same time.

Causes

Although the cause of BPH is not understood, normal levels of testosterone and aging are essential for the development of the condition. Studies in dogs suggest that the female sex hormone estrogen may also play a role in BPH.

The word hyperplasia refers to any abnormal accumulation of cells that causes enlargement of a body part or organ. BPH occurs when an increase in the number of prostate cells produces discrete nodules in the prostate. The increase in nodules is due to a slowing of the normal rate of death of these cells, rather than to a heightened production. The nodules are surrounded by a capsule that contains smooth muscle cells, which can also overdevelop.

Whether or not the resulting enlargement puts pressure on the urethra and increases resistance to urine flow depends on the location of the nodules. Although the transition zone accounts for only about 5 percent of the prostate mass, the nodules in men with BPH occur primarily in this region (rarely, it also affects the periurethral zone). Because the transition zone directly envelops the urethra, excess tissue then tends to obstruct urine flow. Contractions of the smooth muscle cells surrounding the nodules can also obstruct the urethra. Consequently, some men with a very enlarged prostate may have no urethral obstruction, while others with mild enlargement may have marked symptoms because a nodule is located where

it compresses the urethra, or because smooth muscles tighten.

To compensate for urethral narrowing, the muscular wall of the bladder contracts more strongly to expel urine. These stronger contractions lead to a thickened bladder wall, which decreases the bladder's capacity to store urine. Over time, the bladder holds smaller and smaller amounts of urine, resulting in a need to urinate more frequently. As the urethral obstruction worsens, the contractions can no longer empty the bladder completely. Urine retained in the bladder (residual urine) may then become infected or lead to the formation of bladder stones (calculi). Less often, the kidneys become damaged, either as a result of increased pressure on them from the overworked bladder or because an infection has spread from the bladder to the kidneys.

Symptoms

Symptoms of BPH include:
- Frequent and urgent need to urinate, both day and night
- Difficulty starting urination
- Weak urine flow
- Intermittent ("stopping and starting") urine flow
- A feeling of being unable to completely empty the bladder
- Urinary incontinence
- Pain upon urination
- Blood in the urine

Diagnosis

The International Prostate Symptom Score questionnaire, also called the American Urological Association Symptom Index, provides an objective way to assess symptoms of BPH by helping men evaluate their severity. This tool helps doctors and patients to decide on treatment. However, the

B

Acute Urinary Retention: Recognizing the Symptoms

At times, men with BPH may suddenly become unable to urinate at all, even though their condition is responding to treatment. This problem, called acute urinary retention, requires immediate medical attention. It is easily treated by passing a tube through the penis into the bladder (catheterization). Factors that may trigger acute urinary retention include an extended delay in urination; urinary tract infection; alcohol intake; and the use of certain drugs, such as antidepressants, decongestants, and tranquilizers. Acute urinary retention often occurs quite unexpectedly, and it is impossible to predict whether a man with only modest lower urinary tract symptoms will develop this condition. Although acute urinary retention usually leads to prostate surgery, one study found that one third of men who required catheterization for a bout of acute urinary retention were able to urinate normally after the catheter was removed.

questionnaire cannot be used for diagnosis, since other diseases can cause lower urinary tract symptoms similar to those of BPH.

Therefore, a careful medical history, physical examination, and laboratory tests are required to exclude other diseases. In fact, some reports indicate that as many as 30 percent of men who undergo prostate surgery following the usual evaluation show no evidence of urethral obstruction from BPH (their symptoms were due to another cause).

Medical History
A medical history often gives clues to conditions that can mimic BPH, such as urethral stricture, bladder cancer or stones, or abnormal bladder function (problems with holding or emptying urine) due to a neurological disorder (neurogenic bladder).

A thorough medical history should include questions about previous urinary tract infections or prostatitis. The physician will also ask whether any over-the-counter or prescription medications, supplements, or herbal remedies are being taken, because some of them can affect symptoms in men with BPH. Cold or sinus drugs, in particular, can worsen urinary symptoms.

Physical Examination
The physical examination may begin with the doctor observing urination to completion to detect any urinary irregularities. The doctor will manually examine the lower abdomen to check for the presence of a mass, which may indicate an enlarged bladder due to retained urine. In addition, a digital rectal exam is performed to assess the size, shape, and consistency of the prostate. This important examination, which involves the insertion of a gloved finger into the rectum, is mildly uncomfortable. If the history suggests possible neurological disease, the physical may also include an examination for abnormalities indicating that the urinary symptoms result from a neurogenic bladder.

Laboratory Tests
A urinalysis, which is obtained in all patients with lower urinary tract symptoms, may be the only laboratory test performed if symptoms are mild and no other abnormalities are suspected from the medical history and physical examination. A urine culture is added if a urinary infection is suspected. With more severe or chronic symptoms of BPH, blood creatinine or blood urea nitrogen and hemoglobin are measured to rule out kidney damage and anemia.

B

Measuring blood levels of prostate specific antigen (PSA) to screen for prostate cancer is optional unless the digital rectal exam suggests cancer. PSA values alone cannot determine whether symptoms are due to BPH or prostate cancer because both conditions can elevate PSA levels. However, a recent study found that knowing a man's PSA level is the best way to predict how rapidly his prostate will increase in size over time. PSA level was a better predictor than age or prostate volume of future prostate growth.

According to the Clinical Practice Guidelines on BPH from the Agency for Health Care Policy and Research (AHCPR), no further diagnostic tests are needed when the International Prostate Symptom Score is 0 to 7 and no abnormalities are found in the evaluation described above.

Special Diagnostic Tests

Men with moderate to severe symptoms (International Prostate Symptom Score of 8 or higher) may benefit from the following optional tests: uroflowmetry, which measures the speed of urine flow; pressure-flow urodynamic studies, which measure bladder pressure during voiding; and imaging studies, such as ultrasound or intravenous pyelogram (an x-ray of the urinary tract), which can detect structural abnormalities in the kidneys or bladder, and may be used to estimate the size of the prostate. In general, imaging studies are reserved for patients with blood in the urine, urinary tract infections, abnormal kidney function, previous surgery on the urinary tract, or a history of urinary tract stones. Cystoscopy—a procedure during which a small scope (cystoscope) is passed through the urethra into the bladder to provide direct visualization of the urethra and bladder—should be done only before surgery, not to make decisions

on the need for treatment. Another procedure, filling cystometry—a test that involves filling the bladder with fluid and assessing the sensation of urinary urgency felt by the patient—is considered useful only to evaluate bladder function in men who cannot urinate or in those with suspected neurological lesions.

Treatment

The course of BPH is not predictable in any individual. Symptoms and objective measurements of urethral obstruction can remain stable for many years, and may even improve over time in as many as one third of patients.

A progressive decrease in the size and force of the urinary stream and the feeling of incomplete emptying of the bladder are the symptoms most correlated with the eventual need for treatment. Although frequent nighttime urination (nocturia) is one of the most annoying symptoms of BPH, it does not predict the need for future intervention.

If worsening urethral obstruction is left untreated, possible complications are a thickened, irritable bladder with a reduced capacity to store urine, infected residual urine or bladder stones, and a backup of pressure that damages the kidneys.

Decisions regarding treatment are based on the severity of symptoms, the extent of urinary tract damage, and the man's age and overall health. In general, no treatment is needed in those who have only a few symptoms and are not bothered by them. Intervention—usually surgical—is required in the following situations: inadequate bladder emptying resulting in damage to the kidneys; inability to urinate after relief of acute urinary retention; incontinence due to overfilling or increased sensitivity of the bladder; bladder stones; infected residual urine; recurrent blood in the urine not responsive to medical therapy; and symptoms

Saw Palmetto for BPH

An herbal extract derived from the berries of the dwarf palm tree, saw palmetto may be an effective remedy for BPH. Though researchers are not sure exactly how saw palmetto might work, it is thought to contain certain compounds that may curb prostate cell growth. Saw palmetto also exhibits some anti-inflammatory properties.

In clinical trials, saw palmetto (alone or combined with other herbal therapies) was more effective than a placebo in improving symptoms of BPH, such as nocturia, peak urine flow, and average urine flow. In some studies, saw palmetto was as effective as finasteride in improving urinary tract symptoms and peak urine flow.

The adverse effects of saw palmetto were infrequent (fewer than with finasteride and similar to placebo); they included headache, dizziness, nausea, and mild abdominal pain.

Bear in mind that as with other dietary supplements, the FDA does not regulate saw palmetto or oversee the quality or content of its preparations. If you are diagnosed with BPH and choose to use saw palmetto, discuss this decision with your doctor.

that trouble the patient enough to diminish his quality of life.

Treatment decisions are most difficult for men with moderate symptoms. Each individual must determine whether the symptoms bother him enough, or interfere with his life enough, to merit treatment. When selecting a treatment, both patient and doctor must balance the effectiveness of different forms of therapy against their side effects and costs.

Currently, the main treatment options for BPH are watchful waiting, medication, surgery, and heat treatment. If medications prove ineffective in a man who would normally be a candidate for surgery but is unable to withstand its rigors, urethral obstruction and incontinence may be managed with intermittent catheterization or with an in-dwelling Foley catheter, which has an inflated balloon at its end to hold it in place in the bladder. A catheter can stay in place indefinitely but is usually changed monthly.

Watchful Waiting
Because the progress and complications of BPH are unpredictable, watchful waiting—meaning that no immediate treatment is attempted—is best for men whose minimal symptoms are not especially bothersome. Physician visits are needed about once a year to review the progress of symptoms, carry out an examination, and perform a few simple laboratory tests.

During watchful waiting, men should avoid tranquilizers and over-the-counter cold and sinus remedies that contain decongestants (these drugs can worsen obstructive symptoms). They should also avoid delaying urination and taking in large amounts of fluid, including alcohol, which can lead to rapid bladder filling. Limiting fluids at night may reduce nocturia.

Medications
Drug treatment of BPH is a relatively new development; data are still being gathered on the benefits and possible adverse effects of long-term therapy. Currently, two types of drugs—5-alpha-reductase inhibitors and alpha-1-adrenergic blockers—are used to treat BPH. Preliminary research suggests that these drugs improve symptoms in 30 to 60 percent of men taking them, but it is not yet possible to predict who will respond

B

to medical therapy, or which drug will work best for an individual patient.

5-alpha-reductase inhibitors. Finasteride (Proscar) blocks the conversion of testosterone to dihydrotestosterone, the major male sex hormone within the cells of the prostate. In some men, finasteride can relieve BPH symptoms, increase urinary flow rate, and shrink the size of the prostate, though the drug must be continued indefinitely to prevent recurrence of symptoms. It may take as long as six months, however, to achieve maximum benefits from finasteride.

Since finasteride shrinks the prostate, men with smaller glands are probably less likely to respond to the drug because their urinary symptoms typically result from causes other than physical obstruction (for example, smooth muscle constriction). One study specifically indicates that men with greater amounts of glandular tissue will benefit more from finasteride, since this tissue is more responsive to the drug. Finally, finasteride also reduces the risk of urinary retention and the need for surgery in men with BPH.

Finasteride causes relatively few side effects. Erectile dysfunction (the inability to achieve a full erection) occurs in 3 percent to 4 percent of men taking the drug. Finasteride may also decrease the volume of the ejaculate. In addition, a study from England found breast enlargement (gynecomastia) in 0.4 percent of patients taking the drug. Most men who developed gynecomastia had a partial or full remission of their breast enlargement when they stopped taking finasteride.

Finally, finasteride can lower PSA levels by about 50 percent. This change is not thought to limit the utility of PSA as a screening test for prostate cancer, but any increase in PSA while taking finasteride raises the possibility of prostate cancer.

The fall in PSA levels, and any adverse effects on sexual function, disappear when finasteride is stopped.

Alpha-1-adrenergic blockers. These drugs, originally used to treat high blood pressure, reduce the tension of smooth muscles in blood vessel walls and also relax smooth muscle tissue within the prostate. As a result, daily use of an alpha-blocker may increase urinary flow and relieve symptoms of urinary frequency, urinary urgency, and nocturia. Several alpha-blockers—doxazosin (Cardura), terazosin (Hytrin), and tamsulosin (Flomax)—have been approved by the U.S. Food and Drug Administration (FDA) for the treatment of BPH.

Possible side effects of alpha-blockers are: orthostatic hypotension (dizziness upon standing due to a drop in blood pressure), fatigue, insomnia, and headaches. For some, orthostatic hypotension can be mitigated by raising the dose of the drug slowly and by taking the daily dose in the evening. An advantage of alpha-blockers, compared with finasteride, is that they work to relieve symptoms almost immediately.

In men treated for high blood pressure, the doses of other antihypertensive drugs may need to be adjusted to account for the blood-pressure-lowering effects of an alpha-blocker. These drugs may also induce angina (chest pain due to an inadequate supply of oxygen to the heart) in men with coronary heart disease. A doctor will be able to determine which individuals are good candidates for alpha-blockers.

Tamsulosin is an alpha-blocker that primarily targets alpha receptors in the prostate. It has fewer side effects than the other alpha-blockers because it does not lower blood pressure as much. However, some men may benefit from lowering blood pressure and treating lower urinary tract symptoms at the same time.

Surgery

Surgery for BPH, known as a simple prostatectomy, typically involves removing only the inner portion of the prostate, and is performed either transurethrally (through the urethra) or by making an incision in the lower abdomen. A simple prostatectomy for BPH differs from a radical prostatectomy for prostate cancer, which involves removal of the entire prostate and the seminal vesicles.

Surgery offers the fastest, most certain way to improve BPH symptoms. Additionally, less than 10 percent of patients will require retreatment 5 to 10 years later. But surgery has a greater risk for long-term complications, such as erectile dysfunction, incontinence, and retrograde ejaculation, compared with other treatment options for BPH. (Retrograde ejaculation—ejaculation of semen into the bladder rather than through the penis—is not dangerous, but may cause infertility and anxiety.) The frequency of these complications varies with the type of surgical procedure.

Surgery is not performed until any urinary tract infection is successfully treated and kidney function is stabilized (if urinary retention has damaged the kidneys).

Now that medical therapy is available, fewer patients are opting for surgical procedures. In fact, the rates of transurethral prostatectomy (the most common type of simple prostatectomy) declined by about 50 percent between 1991 and 1997.

Transurethral prostatectomy (TURP). Transurethral prostatectomy, also called transurethral resection of the prostate (TURP), is considered the gold standard for BPH treatment—the one against which other therapeutic measures are compared. More than 90 percent of simple prostatectomies for BPH are performed transurethrally by TURP. This procedure is appropriate for patients with moderately enlarged prostates.

In this procedure, the inner portion of the prostate is removed with a long thin instrument (resectoscope) inserted into the urethra. The procedure is typically performed under general or spinal anesthesia and usually requires a one- to three-day hospital stay.

Most men experience little or no pain after a TURP procedure, and full recovery can be expected within three weeks.

Improvement in symptoms is noticeable almost immediately after surgery, and is greatest in those with the worst symptoms. Marked improvement occurs in about 93 percent of men with severe symptoms and in about 80 percent of those with moderate symptoms—a rate of improvement that is significantly better than is achieved with medication or watchful waiting. Further, more than 95 percent of men who undergo TURP require no further treatment over the next five years.

The most common complications immediately following TURP are bleeding, urinary tract infections, and urinary retention. Longer-term complications include erectile dysfunction, retrograde ejaculation, and incontinence. However, in men with bothersome symptoms, two randomized trials have shown that erectile dysfunction and incontinence occur no more frequently after TURP than with watchful waiting. Mortality from TURP is very low (0.1 percent).

Open prostatectomy. An open prostatectomy is the operation of choice when the prostate is so large (more than 80 to 100 g) that TURP cannot be performed safely. There are two types of open prostatectomy for BPH: suprapubic and retropubic. Both require an incision extending from below the navel to the pubic bone. The procedures are performed

B

under general or spinal anesthesia. As in TURP, tissue is checked for prostate cancer.

The hospital stay (five to seven days) and the recovery period (four to six weeks) are longer for open prostatectomy than for TURP.

Like TURP, an open prostatectomy is an effective way to relieve symptoms of BPH. But because complications are more common than with TURP—and, in some cases, the complications can be life-threatening—open prostatectomy is reserved for otherwise healthy men with the largest prostates. The most common complications immediately after open prostatectomy are excessive bleeding that may require a transfusion, and wound infection (usually superficial). Long-term complications, including erectile dysfunction, incontinence, and retrograde ejaculation, are slightly more frequent with open prostatectomy than with TURP.

Transurethral vaporization of the prostate (TVP). As in TURP, TVP involves inserting a resectoscope through the urethra. But instead of cutting away tissue with a wire loop, a powerful electrical current—delivered by a grooved roller at the end of the resectoscope—vaporizes prostate tissue with minimal bleeding.

TVP appears to be as effective as TURP. In addition to a reduced risk for bleeding, other advantages are its lower cost, fewer complications, and reduced hospital stay compared with TURP. Disadvantages of TVP include uncertainty about the long-term outcome of the procedure and the lack of a tissue sample to check for prostate cancer.

Laser therapy. Another transurethral method for treating BPH is laser therapy. There are four main types of laser therapy: holmium laser resection, contact laser vaporization, interstitial laser coagula-

tion (ILC), and visual laser ablation of the prostate (VLAP).

These techniques are all variations on the same concept: A laser fiber is passed through the urethra into the prostate, where bursts of laser energy shrink and destroy prostate tissue. These procedures require anesthesia and a hospital stay. Men undergoing laser therapy have minimal blood loss during the procedure and recover faster than with TURP. However, laser therapy has two disadvantages: It may only be effective in men with smaller prostates, and tissue samples are not available to test for prostate cancer.

Transurethral incision of the prostate (TUIP). TUIP is another transurethral procedure that involves making one or two small incisions in the prostate. These incisions alleviate the symptoms of BPH by decreasing the pressure exerted by prostate tissue on the urethra. TUIP takes less time than TURP, and can be performed on an outpatient basis under local anesthesia in most cases.

TUIP is effective only in men with small prostates (less than 40 grams). The degree of symptom improvement in these men is slightly less than that achieved with TURP, but the duration of symptom relief is similar. Since the incidence of retrograde ejaculation is lower than with TURP, TUIP is an option for men concerned about fertility.

Heat treatments. Symptoms may also be improved with two newer, minimally invasive treatments for BPH—transurethral microwave thermotherapy (TUMT) and transurethral needle ablation (TUNA). Like TURP, they eliminate some of the prostate tissue surrounding the urethra. But, instead of using an endoscope to remove the tissue, the surgeon treats the targeted area with heat. In TUNA, the heat is produced by radio waves; in TUMT, it's produced by microwaves.

After a few weeks, men undergoing TUMT or TUNA typically experience an improvement in BPH symptoms comparable to that achieved with TURP.

TUMT and TUNA generally cause no major complications or damage to sexual function, and nearly two thirds of men continue to experience relief of symptoms five years following one of these treatments. If BPH symptoms return after TUMT or TUNA, the procedure can be repeated. TUMT and TUNA do not prevent men from subsequently undergoing TURP, if necessary.

Treatments Under Investigation

A number of new treatment options for BPH are being investigated. These options tend to be less invasive and have fewer complications than simple prostatectomy.

Ultrasound. High-intensity, focused ultrasound (HIFU) destroys prostate tissue with heat from ultrasound waves. One benefit of HIFU is its ability to focus the ultrasound precisely and spare surrounding tissues. However, the duration of symptom relief over the long term has not been established. In addition, no tissue is available to test for prostate cancer.

Stents. Stents are plastic or metal devices placed in the urethra (via a catheter) to keep it open. This option is most often used in elderly men who have acute urinary retention and whose poor health makes them unable to withstand more aggressive treatments such as prostatectomy. The primary advantages of stents are that they can be placed quickly (in about 15 minutes) under regional anesthesia; the patients can leave the hospital either the same day or the next morning; and little convalescence is required. However, patients may experience bothersome voiding symptoms (urgency, frequency, or painful urination) for days to weeks after the operation. Another concern about these devices is the need for precise positioning within the urethra. Additionally, little is known about long-term effects of stents. If necessary, a stent can be removed, in most cases without damaging the urethra.

Bipolar disorder, also called manic depression, is characterized by mood swings from wild exuberance to severe depression. Treatment of the illness differs from that of the more common "unipolar" depression. But bipolar disorder is often misdiagnosed and mismanaged, particularly in older patients. General medical conditions that may alter function and personality, such as a stroke or Alzheimer's disease, should be ruled out in older patients who exhibit manic symptoms.

In bipolar disorder, about two thirds of those who recover completely from an acute episode have recurrent bouts of either depression or mania. Half of these recurrences tend to be manic, even when the first episode is depression. Bipolar disorder usually begins at an earlier age than depression. The median number of recurrences is four; episodes can be separated by weeks, months, or years. Over time, however, recurrences tend to become more frequent. Some patients with bipolar disorder cycle between depressive and manic episodes as often as four times a year (rapid mood cycling). Thus, there can be tremendous variability in the course of mood disorders from one individual to another.

Bipolar disorder often runs in families. The first manic episode typically appears before age 40, but they can also occur for the first time after 60; so bipolar disorder can't be ruled out because of a person's age.

Symptoms

The diagnosis of bipolar disorder is based on alternating periods of major depression and mania. Mania can occur on its own, but that is extremely rare. Intervals between manic episodes may be months or years, and vary from person to person.

During a manic episode, the person's mood is abnormally and persistently elevated, expansive, or irritable for at least one week. Episodes of milder manic symptoms are termed hypomania. Men tend to have more manic episodes; depressive episodes are more common in women.

The illness can begin with a bout of either depression or mania, but about two thirds of cases start with a manic episode, and mania tends to predominate. A manic episode is accompanied by at least three of the following seven symptoms:

- Feelings of grandeur or inflated self-esteem
- Diminished need for sleep
- Being extremely talkative
- Sensing that thoughts and ideas are racing
- Being easily distracted
- Increased productivity and/or activity at work, at school, or in social situations
- Excessive involvement in high-risk activities that are likely to have serious consequences

Mania is almost always followed by a crushing, debilitating depression.

Diagnosis

A survey found that patients with bipolar disorder sought help for an average of eight years, from at least three doctors, before getting the right diagnosis. Often, the condition is misdiagnosed as substance abuse, recklessness, and impulsivity—which indeed tend to accompany bipolar disorder. Nevertheless, a diagnosis can be made based on symptoms of the illness.

Treatment

As recently described by the American Psychiatric Association's *Practice Guideline for the Treatment of Patients with*

Bipolar Disorder, the goals of treatment are to reduce the frequency and severity of episodes as well as their social and psychological impact; and to improve the patient's ability to function socially and mentally between episodes. Because manic episodes can cause impaired judgment, people must be protected from engaging in self-destructive actions such as making unwise investments or other foolish business decisions, giving their money away, going on spending sprees, driving recklessly, or committing sexual indiscretions.

Treatment for this episodic, long-term illness must be continually monitored to match its somewhat unpredictable manifestations. Medication is critical for treating acute mania, for preventing future episodes, and to stabilize mood between bouts.

Medications

The drug of choice is lithium; it is the only drug proven to be effective for treatment of acute manic episodes, and for maintenance therapy. While 75 percent of those taking lithium have side effects such as weight gain and impaired memory, most of these adverse effects can be managed by reducing the dose. Monitoring of symptoms and blood levels of lithium is particularly important in older patients, who are more prone to toxic effects from lithium.

More recently, another medication, valproate (Depakote), has been prescribed as a first-choice treatment of acute manic episodes since it has fewer side effects than lithium. One recent study found that 48 percent of patients taking valproate for acute mania had at least a 50 percent reduction in manic symptoms—a rate similar to that for lithium. Thus far, it appears that valproate is equally effective for rapid mood cycling disorder and for more traditional forms of mania.

(Lithium generally does not work as well in rapid cycling cases.) Not established yet, however, is valproate's ability to prevent recurrences.

Other drugs, alone or in combination, may help in acute episodes. Carbamazepine appears to stabilize mood, but currently there are no data comparing it to lithium. This drug appears less effective than valproate for relieving symptoms of bipolar disorder and also has more dangerous long-term side effects (such as rare but serious bone marrow and liver abnormalities). Thus, it is used mainly in combination with lithium or on its own when other drugs fail.

Because it may take two to three weeks for mood-stabilizing drugs to take effect, many patients need additional medication to control psychotic symptoms during the acute phase of bipolar illness. Benzodiazepines or neuroleptics are used for this purpose. Benzodiazepines are usually safer, but neuroleptics may be needed when symptoms are severe. Three anticonvulsants, topiramate (Topamax), lamotrigine (Lamictal), and gabapentin (Neurontin), have also shown promise as mood stabilizers in small, preliminary studies.

Antidepressant medications, commonly taken by people who have depression without mania, are not usually used in manic forms of the illness because these drugs may prompt a swing to mania.

Electroconvulsive Therapy

Electroconvulsive therapy (ECT) has benefits comparable to lithium in treating both phases of bipolar disorder. A review of

B

studies of ECT found marked improvement in 80 percent of 589 patients with acute mania. While this treatment still elicits fear in many people, it is now considered extremely safe, though it's usually reserved for patients who don't respond well to medication.

Psychotherapy

Psychotherapy is often another important part of treatment. People with bipolar disorder have to confront a frightening loss of self-control. Therapy can help patients understand the illness and the need to take medication.

Support groups can provide information about bipolar disorder and its treatment. Patients often benefit from sharing their experiences with others struggling with common issues such as denial of the illness, the need for medications, and managing the side effects of medications.

B

The bladder is a hollow organ in the lower abdomen. It stores urine, the liquid waste produced by the kidneys. Urine passes from each kidney into the bladder through a tube called a ureter.

An outer layer of muscle surrounds the inner lining of the bladder. When the bladder is full, the muscles in the bladder wall can tighten to allow urination. Urine leaves the bladder through another tube, the urethra.

The wall of the bladder is lined with cells called transitional cells and squamous cells. More than 90 percent of bladder cancers begin in the transitional cells. This type of bladder cancer is called transitional cell carcinoma. About 8 percent of bladder cancer patients have squamous cell carcinomas.

Cancer that is only in cells in the lining of the bladder is called superficial bladder cancer. The doctor might call it carcinoma in situ. This type of bladder cancer often comes back after treatment. If this happens, the disease most often recurs as another superficial cancer in the bladder.

Cancer that begins as a superficial tumor may grow through the lining and into the muscular wall of the bladder. This is known as invasive cancer. Invasive cancer may extend through the bladder wall. It may grow into a nearby organ such as the uterus or vagina (in women) or the prostate gland (in men). It also may invade the wall of the abdomen.

When bladder cancer spreads outside the bladder, cancer cells are often found in nearby lymph nodes. If the cancer has reached these nodes, cancer cells may have spread to other lymph nodes or other organs, such as the lungs, liver, or bones.

When cancer spreads (metastasizes) from its original place to another part of the body, the new tumor has the same kind of abnormal cells and the same name as the primary tumor. For example, if bladder cancer spreads to the lungs, the cancer cells in the lungs are actually bladder cancer cells. The disease is metastatic bladder cancer, not lung cancer. It is treated as bladder cancer, not as lung

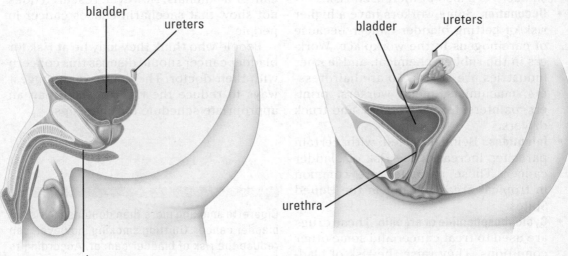

The bladder (essentially the same in both men and women) holds urine, which descends from the kidneys through two tubes called ureters. Urine is excreted from the bladder through another tube, the urethra.

B

cancer. Doctors sometimes call the new tumor "distant" disease.

Each year in the United States, bladder cancer is diagnosed in 38,000 men and 15,000 women. This is the fourth most common type of cancer in men and the eighth most common in women.

Who's at Risk?

People who get bladder cancer are more likely than other people to have certain risk factors. Still, most people with known risk factors do not get bladder cancer, and many who do get this disease have none of these factors. Doctors can seldom explain why one person gets this cancer and another does not.

Studies have found the following risk factors for bladder cancer:

- **Age.** The chance of getting bladder cancer goes up as people get older. People under 40 rarely get this disease.
- **Tobacco.** The use of tobacco is a major risk factor. Cigarette smokers are two to three times more likely than nonsmokers to get bladder cancer. Pipe and cigar smokers are also at increased risk.
- **Occupation.** Some workers have a higher risk of getting bladder cancer because of carcinogens in the workplace. Workers in the rubber, chemical, and leather industries are at risk. So are hairdressers, machinists, metal workers, printers, painters, textile workers, and truck drivers.
- **Infections.** Being infected with certain parasites increases the risk of bladder cancer. These parasites are common in tropical areas but not in the United States.
- **Cyclophosphamide or arsenic.** These drugs are used to treat cancer and some other conditions. They raise the risk of bladder cancer.
- **Race.** Whites get bladder cancer twice as often as African Americans and His-

panics. The lowest rates are among Asians.

- **Being a man.** Men are two to three times more likely than women to develop bladder cancer.
- **Family history.** People with family members who have bladder cancer are more likely to get the disease. Researchers are studying changes in certain genes that may increase the risk of bladder cancer.
- **Personal history of bladder cancer.** People who have had bladder cancer have an increased chance of getting the disease again.

Chlorine is added to water to make it safe to drink. It kills deadly bacteria. However, chlorine by-products can sometimes form in chlorinated water. Researchers have been studying chlorine by-products for more than 25 years. So far, there is no proof that chlorinated water causes bladder cancer in people. Studies continue to look at this question.

Some studies have found that saccharin, an artificial sweetener, causes bladder cancer in animals. However, research does not show that saccharin causes cancer in people.

People who think they may be at risk for bladder cancer should discuss this concern with their doctor. The doctor may suggest ways to reduce the risk and can plan an appropriate schedule for checkups.

Cigarette smoking more than doubles the risk of bladder cancer. Quitting smoking, however, can reduce the risk of bladder cancer. According to an article in the journal Cancer, risk was lowest after people were tobacco-free for at least 10 years.

Symptoms

Common symptoms of bladder cancer include:

- Blood in the urine (making the urine slightly rusty to deep red)
- Pain during urination
- Frequent urination, or feeling the need to urinate without results

These symptoms are not sure signs of bladder cancer. Infections, benign tumors, bladder stones, or other problems also can cause these symptoms. Anyone with these symptoms should see a doctor so that the doctor can diagnose and treat any problem as early as possible. People with symptoms like these may see their family doctor or a urologist, a doctor who specializes in diseases of the urinary system.

Diagnosis

If a patient has symptoms that suggest bladder cancer, the doctor may check general signs of health and may order lab tests. The person may have one or more of the following procedures:

- **Physical examination.** The doctor feels the abdomen and pelvis for tumors. The physical exam may include a rectal or vaginal exam.
- **Urine tests.** The laboratory checks the urine for blood, cancer cells, and other signs of disease.
- **Intravenous pyelogram.** The doctor injects dye into a blood vessel. The dye collects in the urine, making the bladder show up on x-rays.
- **Cystoscopy.** The doctor uses a thin, lighted tube (cystoscope) to look directly into the bladder. The doctor inserts the cystoscope into the bladder through the urethra to examine the lining of the bladder. The patient may need anesthesia for this procedure.

The doctor can remove samples of tissue with the cystoscope. A pathologist then examines the tissue under a microscope. The removal of tissue to look for cancer cells is called a biopsy. In many cases, performing a biopsy is the only sure way to tell whether cancer is present. For a small number of patients, the doctor removes the entire cancerous area during the biopsy. For these patients, bladder cancer is diagnosed and treated in a single procedure.

Staging

If bladder cancer is diagnosed, the doctor needs to know the stage, or extent, of the disease to plan the best treatment. Staging is a careful attempt to find out whether the cancer has invaded the bladder wall, whether the disease has spread, and, if so, to what parts of the body.

The doctor may determine the stage of bladder cancer at the time of diagnosis, or may need to give the patient more tests. Such tests may include imaging tests—CT scan, magnetic resonance imaging (MRI), sonogram, intravenous pyelogram, bone scan, or chest x-ray. Sometimes staging is not complete until the patient has surgery.

These are the main features of each stage of the disease:

- **Stage 0.** The cancer cells are found only on the surface of the inner lining of the bladder. The doctor may call this superficial cancer or carcinoma in situ.
- **Stage I.** The cancer cells are found deep in the inner lining of the bladder. They have not spread to the muscle of the bladder.
- **Stage II.** The cancer cells have spread to the muscle of the bladder.
- **Stage III.** The cancer cells have spread through the muscular wall of the bladder to the layer of tissue surrounding the bladder. The cancer cells may have spread to

B

the prostate (in men) or to the uterus or vagina (in women).

- **Stage IV.** The cancer extends to the wall of the abdomen or to the wall of the pelvis. The cancer cells may have spread to lymph nodes and other parts of the body far away from the bladder, such as the lungs.

Treatment

The doctor develops a treatment plan to fit each patient's needs. Treatment depends on the type of bladder cancer, the stage of the disease, and the grade of the tumor. (The grade tells how closely the cancer cells resemble normal cells. It suggests how fast the cancer is likely to grow. Low-grade cancers usually grow and spread more slowly than high-grade cancers.) The doctor also considers other factors, including the patient's age and general health.

People with bladder cancer have many treatment options. They may have surgery, radiation therapy, chemotherapy, or biological therapy. Some patients get a combination of therapies. A patient may want to talk to the doctor about taking part in a clinical trial, a research study of new treatment methods. Clinical trials are an important option for people with all stages of bladder cancer (see page 181). The doctor is the best person to describe treatment choices and discuss the expected results of treatment.

Surgery

Surgery is a common treatment for bladder cancer. The type of surgery depends largely on the stage and grade of the tumor. The doctor can explain each type of surgery and discuss which is most suitable for the patient:

Transurethral resection: The doctor may treat early (superficial) bladder cancer with transurethral resection (TUR). During TUR, the doctor inserts a cystoscope into the bladder through the urethra. The doctor then uses a tool with a small wire loop on the end to remove the cancer and to burn away any remaining cancer cells with an electric current; this is called fulguration. The patient may need to be in the hospital and may need anesthesia. After TUR, patients may also have chemotherapy or biological therapy.

Radical cystectomy: For invasive bladder cancer, the most common type of surgery is radical cystectomy. The doctor also chooses this type of surgery when superficial cancer involves a large part of the bladder. Radical cystectomy is the removal of the entire bladder, the nearby lymph nodes, part of the urethra, and the nearby organs that may contain cancer cells. In men, the nearby organs that are removed are the prostate, seminal vesicles, and part of the vas deferens. In women, the uterus, ovaries, fallopian tubes, and part of the vagina are removed.

Segmental cystectomy: In some cases, the doctor may remove only part of the bladder in a procedure called segmental cystectomy. The doctor chooses this type of surgery when a patient has a low-grade cancer that has invaded the bladder wall in just one area.

Sometimes, when the cancer has spread outside the bladder and cannot be completely removed, the surgeon removes the bladder but does not try to get rid of all the cancer. Or, the surgeon does not remove the bladder but makes another way for urine to leave the body. The goal of the surgery may be to relieve urinary blockage or other symptoms caused by the cancer.

When the entire bladder is removed, the surgeon makes another way to collect urine. The patient may wear a bag outside the body, or the surgeon may create a pouch inside the body with part of the intestine. The sections on "Side Effects of Treatment" and "Rehabilitation" on pages 140 to 142 have more information about these procedures.

B

Radiation

Radiation therapy (also called radiotherapy) uses high-energy rays to kill cancer cells. Like surgery, radiation therapy is local therapy. It affects cancer cells only in the treated area.

A small number of patients may have radiation therapy before surgery to shrink the tumor. Others may have it after surgery to kill cancer cells that may remain in the area. Sometimes, patients who cannot have surgery have radiation therapy instead.

Doctors use two types of radiation therapy to treat bladder cancer. Some patients with bladder cancer receive both kinds of radiation therapy.

External radiation: A large machine outside the body aims radiation at the tumor area. Most people receiving external radiation are treated five days a week for five to seven weeks as an outpatient. This schedule helps protect healthy cells and tissues by spreading out the total dose of radiation. Treatment may be shorter when external radiation is given along with radiation implants.

Internal radiation: The doctor places a small container of a radioactive substance in the bladder through the urethra or through an incision in the abdomen. The patient stays in the hospital for several days during this treatment. To protect others from radiation exposure, patients may not be able to have visitors or may have visitors for only a short period of time while the implant is in place. Once the implant is removed, no radioactivity is left in the body.

Chemotherapy

Chemotherapy uses drugs to kill cancer cells. The doctor may use one drug or a combination of drugs.

For patients with superficial bladder cancer, the doctor may use intravesical chemotherapy after removing the cancer with TUR. This is local therapy. The doctor inserts a tube (catheter) through the urethra and puts liquid drugs in the bladder through the catheter. The drugs remain in the bladder for several hours. They mainly affect the cells in the bladder. Usually, the patient has this treatment once a week for several weeks. Sometimes, the treatments continue once or several times a month for up to a year.

If the cancer has deeply invaded the bladder or spread to lymph nodes or other organs, the doctor may give drugs through a vein. This treatment is called intravenous chemotherapy. It is systemic therapy, meaning that the drugs flow through the bloodstream to nearly every part of the body. The drugs are usually given in cycles so that a recovery period follows every treatment period.

The patient may have chemotherapy alone or combined with surgery, radiation therapy, or both. Usually chemotherapy is an outpatient treatment given at the hospital, clinic, or at the doctor's office. However, depending on which drugs are given and the patient's general health, the patient may need a short hospital stay.

Biological Therapy

Biological therapy (also called immunotherapy) uses the body's natural ability (immune system) to fight cancer. Biological therapy is most often used after TUR for superficial bladder cancer. This helps prevent the cancer from coming back.

The doctor may use intravesical biological therapy with BCG solution. BCG solution contains live, weakened bacteria (bacille Calmette-Guerin). The bacteria stimulate the immune system to kill cancer cells in the bladder. The doctor uses a catheter to put the solution in the bladder. The patient must hold the solution in the bladder for about 2 hours. BCG treatment is usually done once a week for 6 weeks.

B

Side Effects of Treatment

Because cancer treatment may damage healthy cells and tissues, unwanted side effects sometimes occur. These side effects depend on many factors, including the type and extent of the treatment. Side effects may not be the same for each person, and they may even change from one treatment session to the next. Doctors and nurses will explain the possible side effects of treatment and how they will help the patient manage them.

Surgery

For a few days after TUR, patients may have some blood in their urine and difficulty or pain when urinating. Otherwise, TUR generally causes few problems.

After cystectomy, most patients are uncomfortable during the first few days. However, medicine can control the pain. Patients should feel free to discuss pain relief with the doctor or nurse. Also, it is common to feel tired or weak for a while. The length of time it takes to recover from an operation varies for each person.

After segmental cystectomy, patients may not be able to hold as much urine in their bladder as they used to, and they may need to urinate more often. In most cases, this problem is temporary, but some patients may have long-lasting changes in how much urine they can hold.

If the surgeon removes the bladder, the patient needs a new way to store and pass urine. In one common method, the surgeon uses a piece of the person's small intestine to form a new tube through which urine can pass. The surgeon attaches one end of the tube to the ureters and connects the other end to a new opening in the wall of the abdomen. This opening is called a stoma. A flat bag fits over the stoma to collect urine, and a special adhesive holds it in place. The operation to create the stoma is called a urostomy or an ostomy. (The section called "Rehabilitation" on page 142 has more information about how patients learn to care for the stoma.)

For some patients, the doctor is able to use a part of the small intestine to make a storage pouch (called a continent reservoir) inside the body. Urine collects in the pouch instead of going into a bag. The surgeon connects the pouch to the urethra or to a stoma. If the surgeon connects the pouch to a stoma, the patient uses a catheter to drain the urine.

Bladder cancer surgery may affect a person's sexual function. Because the surgeon removes the uterus and ovaries in a radical cystectomy, women are not able to get pregnant. Also, menopause occurs at once. Hot flashes and other symptoms of menopause caused by surgery may be more severe than those caused by natural menopause. Many women take hormone replacement therapy (HRT) to relieve these problems. If the surgeon removes part of the vagina during a radical cystectomy, sexual intercourse may be difficult.

In the past, nearly all men were impotent after radical cystectomy, but improvements in surgery have made it possible for some men to avoid this problem. Men who have had their prostate gland and seminal vesicles removed no longer produce semen, so they have dry orgasms. Men who wish to father children may consider sperm banking before surgery or sperm retrieval later on.

It is natural for a patient to worry about the effects of bladder cancer surgery on sexuality. Patients may want to talk with the doctor about possible side effects and how long these side effects are likely to last. Whatever the outlook, it may be helpful for patients and their partners to talk about their feelings and help one another find ways to share intimacy during and after treatment.

Radiation Therapy
The side effects of radiation therapy depend mainly on the treatment dose and the part of the body that is treated. Patients are likely to become very tired during radiation therapy, especially in the later weeks of treatment. Resting is important, but doctors usually advise patients to try to stay as active as they can.

External radiation may permanently darken or "bronze" the skin in the treated area. Patients commonly lose hair in the treated area and their skin may become red, dry, tender, and itchy. These problems are temporary, and the doctor can suggest ways to relieve them.

Radiation therapy to the abdomen may cause nausea, vomiting, diarrhea, or urinary discomfort. The doctor can suggest medicines to ease these problems.

Radiation therapy may also cause a decrease in the number of white blood cells, cells that help protect the body against infection. If the blood counts are low, the doctor or nurse may suggest ways to avoid getting an infection. Also, the patient may not get more radiation therapy until blood counts improve. The doctor will check the patient's blood counts regularly and change the treatment schedule if it is necessary.

For both men and women, radiation treatment for bladder cancer can affect sexuality. Women may experience vaginal dryness, and men may have difficulty with erections.

Although the side effects of radiation therapy can be distressing, the doctor can usually treat or control them. It also helps to know that, in most cases, the side effects are not permanent.

Chemotherapy
The side effects of chemotherapy depend mainly on the drugs and the doses the patient receives as well as how the drugs are given. In addition, as with other types of treatment, side effects vary from patient to patient.

Anticancer drugs that are placed in the bladder cause irritation, with some discomfort or bleeding that lasts for a few days after treatment. Some drugs may cause a rash when they come into contact with the skin or genitals.

Systemic chemotherapy affects rapidly dividing cells throughout the body, including blood cells. Blood cells fight infection, help the blood to clot, and carry oxygen to all parts of the body. When anticancer drugs damage blood cells, patients are more likely to get infections, may bruise or bleed easily, and may have less energy. Cells in hair roots and cells that line the digestive tract also divide rapidly. As a result, patients may lose their hair and may have other side effects such as poor appetite, nausea and vomiting, or mouth sores. Usually, these side effects go away gradually during the recovery periods between treatments or after treatment is over.

Certain drugs used in the treatment of bladder cancer also may cause kidney damage. To protect the kidneys, patients need a lot of fluid. The nurse may give the patient fluids by vein before and after treatment. Also, the patient may need to drink a lot of fluids during treatment with these drugs.

Certain anticancer drugs can also cause tingling in the fingers, ringing in the ears, or hearing loss. These problems may go away after treatment stops.

B

Biological Therapy

BCG therapy can irritate the bladder. Patients may feel an urgent need to urinate, and may need to urinate frequently. Patients also may have pain, especially when urinating. They may feel tired. Some patients may have blood in their urine, nausea, a low-grade fever, or chills.

Rehabilitation

Rehabilitation is an important part of cancer care. The health-care team makes every effort to help the patient return to normal activities as soon as possible.

Patients who have a stoma need to learn to care for it. Enterostomal therapists or nurses can help. These health-care specialists often visit patients before surgery to discuss what to expect. They teach patients how to care for themselves and their stomas after surgery. They talk with patients about lifestyle issues, including emotional, physical, and sexual concerns. Often they can provide information about resources and support groups.

Follow-up Care

Follow-up care after treatment for bladder cancer is important. Bladder cancer can return in the bladder or elsewhere in the body. Therefore, people who have had bladder cancer may wish to discuss the chance of recurrence with the doctor.

If the bladder was not removed, the doctor will perform cystoscopy and remove any new superficial tumors that are found. Patients also may have urine tests to check for signs of cancer. Follow-up care may also include blood tests, x-rays, or other tests.

People should not hesitate to discuss follow-up care with the doctor. Regular follow-up ensures that the doctor will notice changes so that any problems can be treated as soon as possible. Between checkups, people who have had bladder cancer should report any health problems as soon as they appear.

National Cancer Institute

Together, the brain and spinal cord form the central nervous system. This complex system is part of everything we do. It controls the things we choose to do—like walk and talk—and the things our body does automatically—like breathe and digest food. The central nervous system is also involved with our senses—seeing, hearing, touching, tasting, and smelling—as well as our emotions, thoughts, and memory.

The brain is a soft, spongy mass of nerve cells and supportive tissue. It has three major parts: the cerebrum, the cerebellum, and the brain stem. The parts work together, but each has special functions.

The cerebrum, the largest part of the brain, fills most of the upper skull. It has two halves called the left and right cerebral hemispheres. The cerebrum uses information from our senses to tell us what is going on around us and tells our body how to respond. The right hemisphere controls the muscles on the left side of the body, and the left hemisphere controls the muscles on the right side of the body. This part of the brain also controls speech and emotions as well as reading, thinking, and learning.

The cerebellum, under the cerebrum at the back of the brain, controls balance and complex actions like walking and talking.

The brain stem connects the brain with the spinal cord. It controls hunger and thirst and some basic body functions, such as body temperature, blood pressure, and breathing.

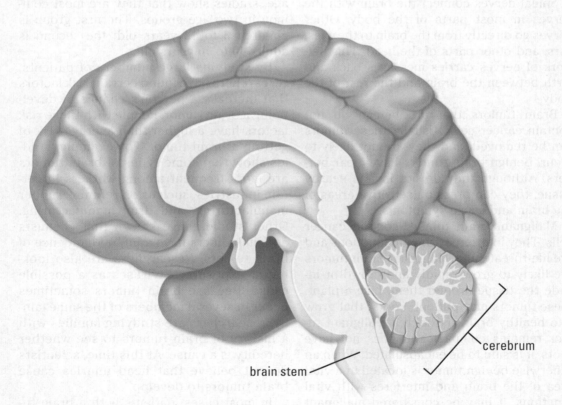

cerebrum

brain stem

Brain tumors can occur in any of the three major parts of the brain shown here. Each part of the brain controls different functions, as described in the text above.

B

The brain is protected by the bones of the skull and by a covering of three thin membranes called meninges. The brain is also cushioned and protected by cerebrospinal fluid. This watery fluid is produced by special cells in the four hollow spaces in the brain, called ventricles. It flows through the ventricles and in spaces between the meninges. Cerebrospinal fluid also brings nutrients from the blood to the brain and removes waste products from the brain.

The spinal cord is made up of bundles of nerve fibers. It runs down from the brain through a canal in the center of the bones of the spine. These bones protect the spinal cord. Like the brain, the spinal cord is covered by the meninges and cushioned by cerebrospinal fluid.

Spinal nerves connect the brain with the nerves in most parts of the body. Other nerves go directly from the brain to the eyes, ears, and other parts of the head. This network of nerves carries messages back and forth between the brain and the rest of the body.

Brain tumors that are benign do not contain cancer cells. Usually these tumors can be removed, and they are not likely to recur. Benign brain tumors have clear borders. Although they do not invade nearby tissue, they can press on sensitive areas of the brain and cause symptoms.

Malignant brain tumors contain cancer cells. They interfere with vital functions and are life-threatening. Malignant brain tumors are likely to grow rapidly and crowd or invade the tissue around them. Like a plant, these tumors may put out "roots" that grow into healthy brain tissue. If a malignant tumor remains compact and does not have roots, it is said to be encapsulated. When an otherwise benign tumor is located in a vital area of the brain and interferes with vital functions, it may be considered malignant (even though it contains no cancer cells).

Doctors refer to some brain tumors by grade—from low grade (grade I) to high grade (grade IV). The grade of a tumor refers to the way the cells look under a microscope. Cells from higher grade tumors are more abnormal looking and generally grow faster than cells from lower grade tumors; higher grade tumors are more malignant than lower grade tumors.

Possible Causes

The causes of brain tumors are not known. Researchers are trying to solve this problem. The more they can find out about the causes of brain tumors, the better the chances of finding ways to prevent them.

Although brain tumors can occur at any age, studies show that they are most common in two age groups. The first group is children 3 to 12 years old; the second is adults 40 to 70 years old.

By studying large numbers of patients, researchers have found certain risk factors that increase a person's chance of developing a brain tumor. People with these risk factors have a higher-than-average risk of getting a brain tumor. For example, studies show that some types of brain tumors are more frequent among workers in certain industries, such as oil refining, rubber manufacturing, and drug manufacturing. Other studies have shown that chemists and embalmers have a higher incidence of brain tumors. Researchers are also looking at exposure to viruses as a possible cause. Because brain tumors sometimes occur in several members of the same family, researchers are studying families with a history of brain tumors to see whether heredity is a cause. At this time, scientists do not believe that head injuries cause brain tumors to develop.

In most cases, patients with a brain tumor have no clear risk factors. The disease is probably the result of several factors acting together.

Primary Brain Tumors

Tumors that begin in brain tissue are known as primary brain tumors. (Secondary tumors that develop when cancer spreads to the brain are discussed in the Secondary Brain Tumors section.) Primary brain tumors are classified by the type of tissue in which they begin. The most common brain tumors are gliomas, which begin in the glial (supportive) tissue. There are several types of gliomas:

- **Astrocytomas** arise from small, star-shaped cells called astrocytes. They may grow anywhere in the brain or spinal cord. In adults, astrocytomas most often arise in the cerebrum. In children, they occur in the brain stem, the cerebrum, and the cerebellum. A grade III astrocytoma is sometimes called anaplastic astrocytoma. A grade IV astrocytoma is usually called glioblastoma multiforme.

- **Brain stem gliomas** occur in the lowest, stemlike part of the brain. The brain stem controls many vital functions. Tumors in this area generally cannot be removed. Most brain stem gliomas are high-grade astrocytomas.

- **Ependymomas** usually develop in the lining of the ventricles. They may also occur in the spinal cord. Although these tumors can develop at any age, they are most common in childhood and adolescence.

- **Oligodendrogliomas** arise in the cells that produce myelin, the fatty covering that protects nerves. These tumors usually arise in the cerebrum. They grow slowly and usually do not spread into surrounding brain tissue. Oligodendrogliomas are rare. They occur most often in middle-aged adults but have been found in people of all ages.

There are other types of brain tumors that do not begin in glial tissue. Some of the most common are described below:

- **Medulloblastomas** were once thought to develop from glial cells. However, recent research suggests that these tumors develop from primitive (developing) nerve cells that normally do not remain in the body after birth. For this reason, medulloblastomas are sometimes called primitive neuroectodermal tumors (PNET). Most medulloblastomas arise in the cerebellum; however, they may occur in other areas as well. These tumors occur most often in children and are more common in boys than in girls.

- **Meningiomas** grow from the meninges. They are usually benign. Because these tumors grow very slowly, the brain may be able to adjust to their presence; meningiomas often grow quite large before they cause symptoms. They occur most often in women between 30 and 50 years of age.

- **Schwannomas** are benign tumors that begin in Schwann cells, which produce the myelin that protects the acoustic nerve—the nerve of hearing. Acoustic neuromas are a type of schwannoma. They occur mainly in adults. These tumors affect women twice as often as men.

- **Craniopharyngiomas** develop in the region of the pituitary gland near the hypothalamus. They are usually benign; however, they are sometimes considered malignant because they can press on or damage the hypothalamus and affect vital functions. These tumors occur most often in children and adolescents.

- **Germ cell tumors** arise from primitive (developing) sex cells, or germ cells. The most frequent type of germ cell tumor in the brain is the germinoma.

B

- **Pineal region tumors** occur in or around the pineal gland, a tiny organ near the center of the brain. The tumor can be slow growing (pineocytoma) or fast growing (pineoblastoma). The pineal region is very difficult to reach, and these tumors often cannot be removed.

Secondary Brain Tumors

Metastasis is the spread of cancer. Cancer that begins in other parts of the body may spread to the brain and cause secondary tumors. These tumors are not the same as primary brain tumors. Cancer that spreads to the brain is the same disease and has the same name as the original (primary) cancer. For example, if lung cancer spreads to the brain, the disease is called metastatic lung cancer because the cells in the secondary tumor resemble abnormal lung cells, not abnormal brain cells.

Treatment for secondary brain tumors depends on where the cancer started and the extent of the spread as well as other factors, including the patient's age, general health, and response to previous treatment.

Symptoms

The symptoms of brain tumors depend mainly on their size and their location in the brain. Symptoms are caused by damage to vital tissue and by pressure on the brain as the tumor grows within the limited space inside the skull. They may also be caused by swelling and a buildup of fluid around the tumor, a condition called edema. Symptoms may also be due to hydrocephalus, which occurs when the tumor blocks the flow of cerebrospinal fluid and causes it to build up in the ventricles. If a brain tumor grows very slowly, its symptoms may appear so gradually that they are overlooked for a long time.

The most frequent symptoms of brain tumors include:

- Headaches that tend to be worse in the morning and ease during the day
- Seizures (convulsions)
- Nausea or vomiting
- Weakness or loss of feeling in the arms or legs
- Stumbling or lack of coordination in walking (ataxic gait)
- Abnormal eye movements or changes in vision
- Drowsiness
- Changes in personality or memory
- Changes in speech

These symptoms may be caused by brain tumors or by other problems. Only a doctor can make a diagnosis.

Diagnosis

To find the cause of a person's symptoms, the doctor asks about the patient's personal and family medical history and performs a complete physical examination. In addition to checking general signs of health, the doctor does a neurologic exam. This includes checks for alertness, muscle strength, coordination, reflexes, and response to pain. The doctor also examines the eyes to look for swelling caused by a tumor pressing on the nerve that connects the eye and the brain.

Depending on the results of the physical and neurologic examinations, the doctor may request one or both of the following:

- **A CT (or CAT) scan** is a series of detailed pictures of the brain. The pictures are created by a computer linked to an x-ray machine. In some cases, a special dye is injected into a vein before the scan. The dye helps to show differences in the tissues of the brain.
- **MRI (magnetic resonance imaging)** gives pictures of the brain, using a powerful

B

Where Should Patients Go for Treatment?

Brain and spinal cord tumors are often difficult to diagnose, and surgery to remove them demands great skill. Experience, therefore, is probably the most important factor in choosing among physicians. Brain and spinal cord tumors are also relatively rare. Many physicians see only a few patients with central nervous system (CNS) tumors each year. Others, however, have made treating brain and spinal cord tumors their specialty. Patients should consider how many patients a physician treats each year. Because many patients are understandably perplexed or frightened by a CNS tumor diagnosis, it is also important that they choose a physician who will answer questions and describe treatment options clearly and fully.

Patients should also learn what techniques and tools are available at the physician's hospital. Teaching hospitals affiliated with a medical college or university are more likely to be involved in research and, thus, have the equipment and specialists necessary to offer experimental treatments. Finally, if a patient is dissatisfied with a physician or a physician's recommendations, he or she may wish to seek another opinion.

magnet linked to a computer. MRI is especially useful in diagnosing brain tumors because it can "see" through the bones of the skull to the tissue underneath. A special dye may be used to enhance the likelihood of detecting a brain tumor.

The doctor may also request other tests such as:

- **A skull x-ray** can show changes in the bones of the skull caused by a tumor. It can also show calcium deposits, which are present in some types of brain tumors.
- **A brain scan** reveals areas of abnormal growth in the brain and records them on special film. A small amount of a radioactive material is injected into a vein. This dye is absorbed by the tumor, and the growth shows up on the film. (The radiation leaves the body within 6 hours and is not dangerous.)
- **An angiogram, or arteriogram,** is a series of x-rays taken after a special dye is injected into an artery (usually in the area where the abdomen joins the top of the leg). The dye, which flows through the blood vessels of the brain, can be seen on the x-rays. These x-rays can show the tumor and blood vessels that lead to it.

- **A myelogram** is an x-ray of the spine. A special dye is injected into the cerebrospinal fluid in the spine, and the patient is tilted to allow the dye to mix with the fluid. This test may be done when the doctor suspects a tumor in the spinal cord.

Treatment

Treatment for a brain tumor depends on a number of factors. Among these are the type, location, and size of the tumor, as well as the patient's age and general health. Treatment methods and schedules often vary for children and adults. The doctor develops a treatment plan to fit each patient's needs.

The patient's doctor may want to discuss the case with other doctors who treat brain tumors. Also, the patient may want to talk with the doctor about taking part in a research study of new treatment methods. Such studies, called clinical trials, are discussed in the Clinical Trials section.

Brain tumors are treated with surgery, radiation therapy, and chemotherapy. Depending on the patient's needs, several methods may be used. The patient may be referred to doctors who specialize in different kinds of treatment and work together as

B

a team. This medical team often includes a neurosurgeon, a medical oncologist, a radiation oncologist, a nurse, a dietitian, and a social worker. The patient may also work with a physical therapist, an occupational therapist, and a speech therapist.

Before treatment begins, most patients are given steroids, to relieve swelling (edema). They may also be given anticonvulsant medicine to prevent or control seizures. If hydrocephalus is present, the patient may need a shunt to drain the cerebrospinal fluid. A shunt is a long, thin tube placed in a ventricle of the brain and then threaded under the skin to another part of the body, usually the abdomen. It works like a drainpipe: Excess fluid is carried away from the brain and is absorbed in the abdomen. (In some cases, the fluid is drained into the heart.)

Surgery is the usual treatment for most brain tumors. To remove a brain tumor, a neurosurgeon makes an opening in the skull. This operation is called a craniotomy.

Whenever possible, the surgeon attempts to remove the entire tumor. However, if the tumor cannot be completely removed without damaging vital brain tissue, the doctor removes as much of the tumor as possible. Partial removal helps to relieve symptoms by reducing pressure on the brain and reduces the amount of tumor to be treated by radiation therapy or chemotherapy.

Some tumors cannot be removed. In such cases, the doctor may do only a biopsy. A small piece of the tumor is removed so that a pathologist can examine it under a microscope to determine the type of cells it contains. This helps the doctor decide which treatment to use.

Sometimes, a biopsy is performed with a needle. Doctors use a special headframe (like a halo) and CT scans or MRI to pinpoint the exact location of the tumor. The surgeon makes a small hole in the skull and then guides a needle to the tumor. (Using this technique to do a biopsy or for treatment is called stereotaxis.)

Radiation therapy (also called radiotherapy) is the use of high-powered rays to damage cancer cells and stop them from growing. This form of treatment is often used to destroy tumor tissue that cannot be removed with surgery or to kill cancer cells that may remain after surgery. Radiation therapy is also used when surgery is not possible.

Radiation therapy may be given in two ways. External radiation comes from a large machine. Generally, external radiation treatments are given five days a week for several weeks. The treatment schedule depends on the type and size of the tumor and the age of the patient. Giving the total dose of radiation over an extended period helps to protect healthy tissue in the area of the tumor.

Radiation can also come from radioactive material placed directly in the tumor (implant radiation therapy). Depending on the material used, the implant may be left in the brain for a short time or permanently. Implants lose a little radioactivity each day. The patient stays in the hospital for several days while the radiation is most active.

External radiation may be directed just to the tumor and the tissue close to it or, less often, to the entire brain. (Sometimes the radiation is also directed to the spinal cord.) When the whole brain is treated, the patient often receives an extra dose of radiation to the area of the tumor. This boost can come from external radiation or from an implant.

Stereotactic radiosurgery is another way to treat brain tumors. Doctors use the techniques described in the Surgery section to pinpoint the exact location of the tumor. Treatment is given in just one session; high-energy rays are aimed at the tumor from many angles. In this way, a high dose of radiation reaches the tumor without damaging other brain tissue. (This use of radiation therapy is sometimes called the gamma knife.)

Chemotherapy is the use of drugs to kill cancer cells. The doctor may use just one drug or a combination, usually giving the drugs by mouth or by injection into a blood vessel or muscle. Intrathecal chemotherapy involves injecting the drugs into the cerebrospinal fluid.

Chemotherapy is usually given in cycles: a treatment period followed by a recovery period, then another treatment period, and so on. Patients often do not need to stay in the hospital for treatment. Most drugs can be given in the doctor's office or the outpatient clinic of a hospital. However, depending on the drugs used, the way they are given, and the patient's general health, a short hospital stay may be necessary.

Side Effects of Treatment

Cancer treatment often causes side effects. These side effects occur because treatment to destroy cancer cells damages some healthy cells as well.

The side effects of cancer treatment vary. They depend on the type of treatment used and on the area being treated. Also, each person reacts differently. Doctors try to plan the patient's therapy to keep side effects to a minimum. They also watch patients very carefully so they can help with any problems that occur.

Surgery

A craniotomy is a major operation. The surgery may damage normal brain tissue, and edema may occur. Weakness, coordination problems, personality changes, and difficulty in speaking and thinking may result. Patients may also have seizures. In fact, for a short time after surgery, symptoms may be worse than before. Most of the side effects of surgery lessen or disappear with time.

Radiation

Most of the side effects of radiation therapy go away soon after treatment is over. However, some side effects may occur or persist long after treatment is complete.

Some patients have nausea for several hours after treatment. Patients receiving radiation therapy may become very tired as treatment continues. Resting is important, but doctors usually advise their patients to try to stay reasonably active. Radiation therapy to the scalp causes most patients to lose their hair. When it grows back, the new hair is sometimes softer and may be a slightly different color. In some cases, the hair loss is permanent.

Skin reactions in the treated area are common. The scalp and ears may be red, itchy, or dark; these areas may look and feel sunburned. The treated area should be exposed to the air as much as possible but should be protected from the sun. Patients should not wear anything on the head that might cause irritation. Good skin care is important at this time. The doctor may suggest certain kinds of soap or ointment, and patients should not use any other lotions or creams on the scalp without the doctor's advice.

Sometimes brain cells killed by radiation form a mass in the brain. The mass may look like a tumor and may cause similar symptoms, such as headaches, memory loss, or seizures. Doctors may suggest surgery or steroids to relieve these problems. About 4 to 8 weeks after radiation therapy, patients may become quite sleepy or lose their appetite. These symptoms may last several

B

B

weeks, but they usually go away on their own. Still, patients should notify the doctor if they occur.

Children who have had radiation therapy for a brain tumor may have learning problems or partial loss of eyesight. If the pituitary gland is damaged, children may not grow or develop normally.

Chemotherapy

The side effects of chemotherapy depend on the drugs that are given. In general, anticancer drugs affect rapidly growing cells, such as blood cells that fight infection, cells that line the digestive tract, and cells in hair follicles. As a result, patients may have a lower resistance to infection, loss of appetite, nausea, vomiting, or mouth sores. Patients may also have less energy and may lose their hair. These side effects usually go away gradually after treatment stops.

Some anticancer drugs can cause infertility. Women taking certain anticancer drugs may have symptoms of menopause (hot flashes and vaginal dryness; periods may be irregular or stop). Some drugs used to treat children and teenagers may affect their ability to have children later in life.

Certain drugs used in the treatment of brain tumors may cause kidney damage. Patients are given large amounts of fluid while taking these drugs. Patients may also have tingling in the fingers, ringing in the ears, or difficulty hearing. These problems may not clear up after treatment stops.

Treatment with steroids to reduce swelling in the brain may cause increased appetite and weight gain. Swelling of the face and feet is common. Steroids can also cause restlessness, mood swings, burning indigestion, and acne. However, patients should not stop using steroids or change their dose without consulting the doctor.

The use of steroids must be stopped gradually to allow the body to adjust to the change.

Loss of appetite can be a problem for patients during therapy. People may not feel hungry when they are uncomfortable or tired. Some of the common side effects of cancer treatment, such as nausea and vomiting, can also make it hard to eat. Yet good nutrition is important because patients who eat well generally feel better and have more energy. Eating well means getting enough calories and protein to help prevent weight loss, regain strength, and rebuild normal tissues. Many patients find that eating several small meals and snacks during the day works better than trying to have three large meals.

Patients being treated for a brain tumor may develop a blood clot and inflammation in a vein, most often in the leg. This is called thrombophlebitis. A patient who notices swelling in the leg, leg pain, and/or redness in the leg should notify the doctor right away.

Rehabilitation

Rehabilitation is a very important part of the treatment plan. The goals of rehabilitation depend on the patient's needs and how the tumor has affected his or her daily activities. The medical team makes every effort to help patients return to their normal activities as soon as possible.

Patients and their families may need to work with an occupational therapist to overcome any difficulty in activities of daily living, such as eating, dressing, bathing, and using the toilet. If an arm or leg is weak or paralyzed, or if a patient has problems with balance, physical therapy may be necessary. Speech therapy may be helpful for individuals having trouble speaking or expressing their thoughts. Speech therapists

B

also work with patients who have difficulty swallowing.

If special arrangements are necessary for school-age children, they should be made as soon as possible. Sometimes, children have tutors in the hospital or after they go home from the hospital. Children who have problems learning may need tutors or special classes when they return to school.

Follow-up Care

Regular follow-up is very important after treatment for a brain tumor. The doctor will check closely to make sure that the tumor has not returned. Checkups usually include general physical and neurologic exams. From time to time, the patient will have CT scans or MRIs.

Patients who receive radiation therapy to large areas of the brain or certain anti-cancer drugs may have an increased risk of developing leukemia or a second tumor at a later time. Also, radiation that affects the eyes may lead to the development of cataracts. Patients should carefully follow their doctor's advice on health care and checkups. If any unusual health problem occurs, they should report it to the doctor as soon as it appears.

National Cancer Institute

O ther than skin cancer, breast cancer is the most common type of cancer among women in the United States. More than 180,000 women are diagnosed with breast cancer each year.

Breast cancer also affects more than 1,000 men in this country each year. Much of the information on symptoms, diagnosis, treatment, and living with the disease applies to men as well. However, the "Early Detection" section on page 154 does not apply to men. Experts do not recommend routine screening for men.

Each breast has 15 to 20 sections called lobes. Within each lobe are many smaller lobules. Lobules end in dozens of tiny bulbs that can produce milk. The lobes, lobules, and bulbs are all linked by thin tubes called ducts. These ducts lead to the nipple in the center of a dark area of skin called the areola. Fat surrounds the lobules and ducts. There are no muscles in the breast, but muscles lie under each breast and cover the ribs.

Each breast also contains blood vessels and lymph vessels. The lymph vessels carry colorless fluid called lymph, and lead to small bean-shaped organs called lymph nodes. Clusters of lymph nodes are found near the breast in the axilla (under the arm), above the collarbone, and in the chest. Lymph nodes are also found in many other parts of the body.

When cancer arises in breast tissue and spreads (metastasizes) outside the breast, cancer cells are often found in the lymph nodes under the arm (axillary lymph nodes). If the cancer has reached these nodes, it means that cancer cells may have spread to other parts of the body—other lymph nodes and other organs, such as the bones, liver, or lungs. When cancer spreads from its original location to another part of the body, the new tumor has the same kind of abnormal cells and the same name as the primary tumor. For example, if breast cancer spreads to the brain, the cancer cells in the brain are actually breast cancer cells. The disease is called metastatic breast cancer. (It is not brain cancer.) Doctors sometimes call this "distant" disease.

Who's at Risk?

The exact causes of breast cancer are not known. However, studies show that the risk of breast cancer increases as a woman gets older. This disease is very uncommon in women under the age of 35. Most breast cancers occur in women over the age of 50, and the risk is especially high for women

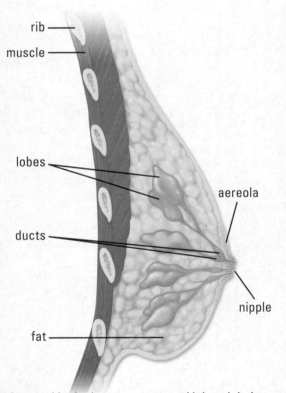

rib
muscle
lobes
aereola
ducts
nipple
fat

Located in the breast are several lobes, lobules, milk-producing bulbs, and connecting ducts. Most breast cancers begin in the ducts or lobules.

Prophylactic Mastectomy

Women at particularly high risk for breast cancer might choose bilateral prophylactic mastectomy (surgical removal of both breasts) to reduce their risk substantially. Such women might include those with a strong family history, who carry cancer susceptibility genes such as BRCA1 or BRCA2, or those who have been diagnosed with lobular carcinoma in situ. A Mayo Clinic study of 639 women who had a strong family history of breast cancer and underwent bilateral prophylactic mastectomy between 1960 and 1993 indicated that the procedure cut the risk of breast cancer by at least 90 percent.

However, the procedure does not totally eliminate the risk of breast cancer because the disease can still arise in the breast tissue left behind at the time of surgery. In addition, it is unclear whether prophylactic mastectomy saves lives. With early detection and treatment, the majority of women in this study would have survived without the procedure, or never even developed breast cancer in the first place. In addition, the emphasis of surgical treatment for women with early-stage breast cancer is to spare as much of the breast as possible.

Although most women who have a bilateral prophylactic mastectomy report long-term satisfaction with the results, including decreased emotional concern about developing cancer, some have expressed regrets. A doctor can discuss the risks and benefits of this procedure. *The Editors*

over age 60. Also, breast cancer occurs more often in white women than African-American or Asian women.

Research has shown that the following conditions increase a woman's chances of getting breast cancer:

Personal history of breast cancer. Women who have had breast cancer face an increased risk of getting breast cancer in their other breast.

Family history. A woman's risk for developing breast cancer increases if her mother, sister, or daughter had breast cancer, especially at a young age.

Certain breast changes. Having a diagnosis of atypical hyperplasia or lobular carcinoma in situ (LCIS) may increase a woman's risk for developing cancer.

Genetic alterations. Changes in certain genes (BRCA1, BRCA2, and others) increase the risk of breast cancer. In families in which many women have had the disease, gene testing can sometimes show the presence of specific genetic changes that increase the risk of breast cancer. Doctors may suggest ways to try to delay or prevent breast cancer, or to improve the detection of this disease in women who have these changes in their genes. (For more information, see "Possible Causes and Prevention" on page 166.)

Other factors associated with an increased risk for breast cancer include:

Estrogen. Evidence suggests that the longer a woman is exposed to estrogen (estrogen made by the body, taken as a drug, or delivered by a patch), the more likely she is to develop breast cancer. For example, the risk is somewhat increased among women who began menstruation at an early age (before age 12), experienced menopause late (after age 55), never had children, or took hormone replacement therapy for long periods of time. Each of these factors increases the amount of time a woman's body is exposed to estrogen.

B

DES (diethylstilbestrol). DES is a synthetic form of estrogen that was used between the early 1940s and 1971. Women who took DES during pregnancy to prevent certain complications are at a slightly higher risk for breast cancer. This does not appear to be the case for their daughters who were exposed to DES before birth. However, more studies are needed as these daughters enter the age range when breast cancer is more common.

Late childbearing. Women who have their first child late (after about age 30) have a greater chance of developing breast cancer than women who have a child at a younger age.

Breast density. Breasts that have a high proportion of lobular and ductal tissue appear dense on mammograms. Breast cancers nearly always develop in lobular or ductal tissue (not fatty tissue). That's why cancer is more likely to occur in breasts that have a lot of lobular and ductal tissue (that is, dense tissue) than in breasts with a lot of fatty tissue. In addition, when breasts are dense, it is more difficult for doctors to see abnormal areas on a mammogram.

Radiation therapy. Women whose breasts were exposed to radiation during radiation therapy before age 30, especially those who were treated with radiation for Hodgkin's disease, are at an increased risk for developing breast cancer. Studies show that the younger a woman was when she received her treatment, the higher her risk for developing breast cancer later in life.

Alcohol. Some studies suggest a slightly higher risk of breast cancer among women who drink alcohol.

Most women who develop breast cancer have none of the risk factors listed above, other than the risk that comes with growing older. Scientists are conducting research into the causes of breast cancer to learn more about risk factors and ways of preventing this disease.

The statistic that one in nine women will get breast cancer is well publicized, yet somewhat misleading. It refers to the cumulative lifetime risk for women who live past age 85. But the risk in any single decade of life never approaches one in nine. The average woman in her 40s has a 1 in 77 chance. Risk increases with age, but in no decade does it ever exceed 1 in 34.

Early Detection

Women should talk with their doctor about factors that can increase their chance of getting breast cancer. Women of any age who are at higher risk for developing this disease should ask their doctor when to start and how often to be checked for breast cancer. Breast cancer screening has been shown to decrease the risk of dying from breast cancer.

Women can take an active part in the early detection of breast cancer by having regularly scheduled screening mammograms and clinical breast exams (breast exams performed by health professionals). Some women also perform breast self-exams.

A screening mammogram is the best tool available for finding breast cancer early, before symptoms appear. A mammogram is a special kind of x-ray. Screening mammograms are used to look for breast changes in women who have no signs of breast cancer.

Mammograms can often detect a breast lump before it can be felt. Also, a mammogram can show small deposits of calcium in the breast. Although most calcium deposits are benign, a cluster of very tiny specks of

Breast Self-Exam

All women should make breast self-examination (BSE) part of their monthly routine, since consistency is the key to catching breast cancer in its early and treatable stages. The more familiar you are with the normal texture and appearance of your breasts, the more easily you will recognize small changes that could signal cancer. Perform BSE at the same time each month, since breasts change with the monthly hormonal cycle. (The best time is 2 or 3 days after menstruation ends, when breasts tend to be least swollen. Postmenopausal women should choose an easy-to-remember day, such as the first of the month.) The following are some common guidelines for BSE; some doctors recommend different variations (such as performing the palpation exam in the shower). Report any unusual findings to your doctor.

Visual Exam

1. Stand in front of a mirror, arms at your sides. Observe each breast in turn, including the areola and nipple. Keep an eye out for any difference in appearance of the skin, such as swelling, dimpling, or puckering; changes in contour; skin discoloration; scaling; rash; or nipple discharge.
2. Clasp your hands behind your head and press them forward. Again inspect each breast as in step 1.
3. Lean slightly toward the mirror with your hands on your hips, and shoulders and elbows pulled forward. Repeat the inspection as in step 1.

Palpation Exam

1. Raise your left arm over your head. Using 3 or 4 fingers of your right hand, examine your left breast for any unusual lump or mass. Beginning at the outside edge, press down firmly and carefully with the flat pads of your fingers (not the fingertips), moving in small circles. Rotate these circles along the outer edge, and then make a slow, gradual spiral toward the nipple (see illustration below). After inspecting the entire breast thoroughly, examine the area between the breast and underarm and the underarm itself.
2. Squeeze the nipple gently, checking for any type of discharge. Repeat steps 1 and 2 to examine the right breast with the left hand.
3. Repeat step 1 on the left breast while lying down with your left arm extended over your head and a small pillow or rolled towel placed under your left shoulder; then extend your right arm with the pillow or towel under your right shoulder, and check your right breast. *The Editors*

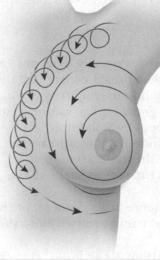

A breast self-exam involves pressing your fingers in a circular motion, beginning with small circles at the outer edge of the breast.

B

calcium (called microcalcifications) may be an early sign of cancer.

If an area of the breast looks suspicious on the screening mammogram, additional (diagnostic) mammograms may be needed. Depending on the results, the doctor may advise the woman to have a biopsy.

Although mammograms are the best way to find breast abnormalities early, they do have some limitations. A mammogram may miss some cancers that are present (false negative) or may find things that turn out not to be cancer (false positive). And detecting a tumor early does not guarantee that a woman's life will be saved. Some fast-growing breast cancers may already have spread to other parts of the body before being detected.

Nevertheless, studies show that mammograms reduce the risk of dying from breast cancer. Most doctors recommend that women in their forties and older have mammograms regularly, every one to two years.

Symptoms

Early breast cancer usually does not cause pain. In fact, when breast cancer first develops, there may be no symptoms at all. But as the cancer grows, it can cause changes that women should watch for:

- A lump or thickening in or near the breast or in the underarm area;
- A change in the size or shape of the breast;
- Nipple discharge or tenderness, or the nipple pulled back (inverted) into the breast;
- Ridges or pitting of the breast (the skin looks like the skin of an orange); or
- A change in the way the skin of the breast, areola, or nipple looks or feels (for example, warm, swollen, red, or scaly).

A woman should see her doctor about any symptoms like these. Most often, they are not cancer, but it's important to check with the doctor so that any problems can be diagnosed and treated as early as possible.

Diagnosis

To help find the cause of any sign or symptom, a doctor does a careful physical exam and asks about personal and family medical history. In addition, the doctor may do one or more breast exams:

- **Clinical breast exam.** The doctor can tell a lot about a lump by carefully feeling it and the tissue around it. Benign lumps often feel different from cancerous ones. The doctor can examine the size and texture of the lump and determine whether the lump moves easily.
- **Mammography.** X-rays of the breast can give the doctor important information about a breast lump.
- **Ultrasonography.** Using high-frequency sound waves, ultrasonography can often show whether a lump is a fluid-filled cyst (not cancer) or a solid mass (which may or may not be cancer). This exam may be used along with mammography.

Based on these exams, the doctor may decide that no further tests are needed and no treatment is necessary. In such cases, the doctor may need to check the woman regularly to watch for any changes.

Biopsy

Often, fluid or tissue must be removed from the breast so the doctor can make a diagnosis. A woman's doctor may refer her for further evaluation to a surgeon or other health- care professional who has experience with breast diseases. These doctors may perform:

- **Fine-needle aspiration.** A thin needle is used to remove fluid and/or cells from a breast lump. If the fluid is clear, it may not need to be checked by a lab.

Sentinel Node Biopsy

One of the first places where breast cancer spreads (metastasizes) is to nearby lymph nodes, which filter out waste products, bacteria, and other substances draining from cells.

Surgeons have typically performed an axillary node dissection—removal of most or all of the lymph nodes located under the arm—during a mastectomy or lumpectomy to check for evidence of metastatic breast cancer. However, this procedure may result in major complications such as lymphedema, a buildup of fluid that causes an uncomfortable, chronic swelling and stiffness of the arm. Also, since no cancer is found in the nodes of up to 80 percent of patients who have a complete lymph node dissection, many patients have undergone the procedure unnecessarily.

Fortunately, a new, less invasive procedure called sentinel node biopsy has been developed and may replace extensive dissection of lymph nodes as the standard way to determine whether cancer has spread. Metastatic cancer cells are usually found in the lymph nodes nearest to the primary tumor, and the so-called sentinel lymph node is the first one to receive lymphatic fluid draining from the cancer site. Examining this node alone should therefore indicate whether breast cancer has spread.

In fact, sentinel node biopsy allows surgeons to predict whether cancer is likely to be found in the rest of the lymphatic system without removing all of the nearby nodes. If the sentinel node contains no cancer cells, the other lymph nodes are also likely to be clear, and a complete lymph node dissection may be unnecessary. If the sentinel node tests positive for cancer, however, all other nodes must be removed.

During sentinel node mapping, a radioactive tracer, a blue dye, or a combination of the two is injected into the skin at the site of the primary tumor or, if the tumor has been removed, at the biopsy site. When these substances enter the lymph duct system, they flow from the tumor and drain into the nearest, or sentinel, node. Surgeons can then pinpoint the node and remove it for analysis.

Several clinical studies have shown that sentinel node biopsy is as effective as axillary dissection for staging breast cancer. Nevertheless, further research is needed to determine which patients can benefit most from the procedure, and whether sentinel node biopsy will substantially decrease the risk of lymphedema or other risks of standard lymph node sampling. *The Editors*

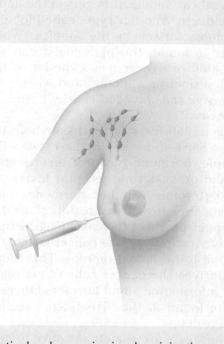

Sentinel node mapping involves injecting a radioactive tracer, a blue dye, or a combination of the two at the primary tumor or biopsy site.

B

- **Needle biopsy.** Using special techniques, tissue can be removed with a needle from an area that looks suspicious on a mammogram but cannot be felt. Tissue removed in a needle biopsy goes to a lab to be checked by a pathologist for cancer cells.
- **Surgical biopsy.** In an incisional biopsy, the surgeon cuts out a sample of a lump or suspicious area. In an excisional biopsy, the surgeon removes all of a lump or suspicious area and an area of healthy tissue around the edges. A pathologist then examines the tissue under a microscope to check for cancer cells.

When Cancer Is Found

The most common type of breast cancer is ductal carcinoma. It begins in the lining of the ducts. Another type, called lobular carcinoma, arises in the lobules. When cancer is found, the pathologist can tell what kind of cancer it is (whether it began in a duct or a lobule) and whether it is invasive (has invaded nearby tissues in the breast).

Special lab tests of the tissue help the doctor learn more about the cancer. For example, hormone receptor tests (estrogen and progesterone receptor tests) can help determine whether hormones help the cancer to grow. If test results show that hormones do affect the cancer's growth (a positive test result), the cancer is likely to respond to hormonal therapy. This therapy deprives the cancer cells of estrogen. More information about hormonal therapy can be found in the "Treatment" section on page 160.

Other tests are sometimes done to help the doctor predict whether the cancer is likely to progress. For example, the doctor may order x-rays and lab tests. Sometimes a sample of breast tissue is checked for a gene (the human epidermal growth factor receptor-2 or HER-2 gene) that is associated with a higher risk that the breast cancer will come back. The doctor may also order special exams of the bones, liver, or lungs because breast cancer may spread to these areas.

Staging

A woman's treatment options depend on a number of factors. These factors include her age and menopausal status; her general health; the size and location of the tumor and the stage of the cancer; the results of lab tests; and the size of her breast. Certain features of the tumor cells (such as whether they depend on hormones to grow) are also considered. In most cases, the most important factor is the stage of the disease. The stage is based on the size of the tumor and whether the cancer has spread. The following are brief descriptions of the stages of breast cancer and the treatments most often used for each stage. (Other treatments may sometimes be appropriate.)

Stage 0 is sometimes called noninvasive carcinoma or carcinoma in situ.

Lobular carcinoma in situ (LCIS) refers to abnormal cells in the lining of a lobule. These abnormal cells seldom become invasive cancer. However, their presence is a sign that a woman has an increased risk of developing breast cancer. This risk of cancer is increased for both breasts. Some women with LCIS may take a drug called tamoxifen, which can reduce the risk of developing breast cancer. Others may take part in studies of other promising new preventive treatments. Some women may choose not to have treatment, but to return to the doctor regularly for checkups. And, occasionally, women with LCIS may decide to have surgery to remove both breasts to try to prevent cancer from developing. (In most cases, removal of underarm lymph nodes is not necessary.)

B

Ductal carcinoma in situ (DCIS) refers to abnormal cells in the lining of a duct. DCIS is also called intraductal carcinoma. The abnormal cells have not spread beyond the duct to invade the surrounding breast tissue. However, women with DCIS are at an increased risk of getting invasive breast cancer. Some women with DCIS have breast-sparing surgery followed by radiation therapy. Or they may choose to have a mastectomy, with or without breast reconstruction (plastic surgery) to rebuild the breast. Underarm lymph nodes are not usually removed. Also, women with DCIS may want to talk with their doctor about tamoxifen to reduce the risk of developing invasive breast cancer.

Stage I and stage II are early stages of breast cancer in which the cancer has spread beyond the lobe or duct and invaded nearby tissue. Stage I means that the tumor is no more than about an inch across and cancer cells have not spread beyond the breast. Stage II means one of the following: the tumor in the breast is less than 1 inch across and the cancer has spread to the lymph nodes under the arm; or the tumor is between 1 and 2 inches (with or without spread to the lymph nodes under the arm); or the tumor is larger than 2 inches but has not spread to the lymph nodes under the arm.

Women with early stage breast cancer may have breast-sparing surgery followed by radiation therapy to the breast, or they may have a mastectomy, with or without breast reconstruction to rebuild the breast. These approaches are equally effective in treating early stage breast cancer. (Sometimes radiation therapy is also given after mastectomy.)

The choice of breast-sparing surgery or mastectomy depends mostly on the size and location of the tumor, the size of the woman's breast, certain features of the cancer, and how the woman feels about preserving her breast. With either approach, lymph nodes under the arm usually are removed.

Many women with stage I and most with stage II breast cancer have chemotherapy and/or hormonal therapy after primary treatment with surgery or surgery and radiation therapy. This added treatment is called adjuvant therapy. If the systemic therapy is given to shrink the tumor before surgery, this is called neoadjuvant therapy. Systemic treatment is given to try to destroy any remaining cancer cells and prevent the cancer from recurring, or coming back, in the breast or elsewhere.

Stage III is also called locally advanced cancer. In this stage, the tumor in the breast is large (more than 2 inches across) and the cancer has spread to the underarm lymph nodes; or the cancer is extensive in the underarm lymph nodes; or the cancer has spread to lymph nodes near the breastbone or to other tissues near the breast.

Inflammatory breast cancer is a type of locally advanced breast cancer. In this type of cancer the breast looks red and swollen (or inflamed) because cancer cells block the lymph vessels in the skin of the breast.

Patients with stage III breast cancer usually have both local treatment to remove or destroy the cancer in the breast and systemic treatment to stop the disease from spreading. The local treatment may be surgery and/or radiation therapy to the breast and underarm. The systemic treatment may be chemotherapy, hormonal therapy, or both. Systemic therapy may be given before local therapy to shrink the tumor or afterward to prevent the disease from recurring.

Stage IV is metastatic cancer. The cancer has spread beyond the breast and underarm lymph nodes to other parts of the body.

B

Surgery: Questions for Your Doctor

Here are some questions a woman may want to ask her doctor before having surgery:

- What kinds of surgery can I consider? Is breast-sparing surgery an option for me? Which operation do you recommend for me? What are the risks of surgery?
- Should I store some of my own blood in case I need a transfusion?
- Do I need my lymph nodes removed? How many? Why? What special precautions will I need to take if lymph nodes are removed?
- How will I feel after the operation?

- Will I need to learn how to do special things to take care of myself or my incision when I get home?
- Where will the scars be? What will they look like?
- If I decide to have plastic surgery to rebuild my breast, how and when can that be done? Can you suggest a plastic surgeon to contact?
- Will I have to do special exercises?
- When can I get back to my normal activities?
- Is there someone I can talk with who has had the same treatment I'll be having?

Women who have stage IV breast cancer receive chemotherapy and/or hormonal therapy to destroy cancer cells and control the disease. They may have surgery or radiation therapy to control the cancer in the breast. Radiation may also be useful to control tumors in other parts of the body.

Recurrent cancer means the disease has come back in spite of the initial treatment. Even when a tumor in the breast seems to have been completely removed or destroyed, the disease sometimes returns because undetected cancer cells remained somewhere in the body after treatment. Most recurrences appear within two or three years after treatment, but breast cancer can recur many years later.

Cancer that returns only in the area of the surgery is called a local recurrence. If the disease returns in another part of the body, the distant recurrence is called metastatic breast cancer. The patient may have one type of treatment or a combination of treatments for recurrent cancer.

Treatment

Women with breast cancer now have many treatment options. Breast cancer may be treated with local or systemic therapy, and usually begins within a few weeks after the diagnosis. Some patients have both kinds of treatment.

Local therapy is used to remove or destroy breast cancer in a specific area. Surgery and radiation therapy are considered local treatments. They are used to treat the disease in the breast. When breast cancer has spread to other parts of the body, local therapy may be used to control cancer in those specific areas, such as in the lung or bone.

Systemic treatments are used to destroy or control cancer throughout the body. Chemotherapy, hormonal therapy, and biological therapy are systemic treatments. Some patients have systemic therapy to shrink the tumor before local therapy. Others have systemic therapy to prevent the cancer from coming back, or to treat cancer that has spread.

The doctor is the best person to answer questions about treatment for a particular patient: what her treatment choices are and how successful her treatment is expected to be. Most patients also want to know how they will look after treatment and whether they will have to change their normal activities. A woman should not feel that she needs to ask all her questions or understand all the answers at once. She will have many chances to ask the doctor to explain things that are not clear and to ask for more information.

A woman may want to talk with her doctor about taking part in a clinical trial, a research study of new treatment methods. Clinical trials are an important option for women with all stages of breast cancer.

Surgery is the most common treatment for breast cancer, and there are several types of surgery. The doctor can explain each type, discuss and compare their benefits and risks, and describe how each will affect the patient's appearance.

- An operation to remove the cancer but not the breast is called breast-sparing surgery or breast-conserving surgery. Lumpectomy and segmental mastectomy (also called partial mastectomy) are types of breast-sparing surgery. After breast-sparing surgery, most women receive radiation therapy to destroy cancer cells that remain in the area.
- An operation to remove the breast (or as much of the breast as possible) is a mastectomy. Breast reconstruction is often an option at the same time as the mastectomy, or later on.
- In most cases, the surgeon also removes lymph nodes under the arm to help determine whether cancer cells have entered the lymphatic system. This is called an axillary lymph node dissection.

In lumpectomy, the surgeon removes the breast cancer and some normal tissue around it. (Sometimes an excisional biopsy serves as a lumpectomy.) Often, some of the lymph nodes under the arm are removed.

In segmental mastectomy, the surgeon removes the cancer and a larger area of normal breast tissue around it. Occasionally, some of the lining over the chest muscles below the tumor is removed as well. Some lymph nodes under the arm may also be removed.

In total (simple) mastectomy, the surgeon removes the whole breast. Some lymph nodes under the arm may also be removed.

In modified radical mastectomy, the surgeon removes the whole breast, most of the lymph nodes under the arm, and, often, the lining over the chest muscles. The smaller of the two chest muscles also may be taken out to help in removing the lymph nodes.

In radical mastectomy (also called Halsted radical mastectomy), the surgeon removes the breast, both chest muscles, all of the lymph nodes under the arm, and some additional fat and skin. For many years, this operation was considered the standard one for women with breast cancer, but it is almost never used today. In rare cases, radical mastectomy may be suggested if the cancer has spread to the chest muscles.

Breast reconstruction (surgery to rebuild the shape of a breast) is often an option after mastectomy. Women considering reconstruction should discuss this with a plastic surgeon before having a mastectomy.

Radiation therapy (radiotherapy) is the use of high-energy rays to kill cancer cells. The radiation may be directed at the breast by a machine (external radiation). The radiation can also come from radioactive material placed in thin plastic tubes that are placed directly in the breast (implant radiation). Some women have both kinds of therapy.

For external radiation therapy, the patient goes to the hospital or clinic, generally five days a week for several weeks. For implant

B

radiation, a patient stays in the hospital. The implants remain in place for several days. They are removed before the woman goes home.

Sometimes, depending on the size of the tumor and other factors, radiation therapy is used after surgery, especially after breast-sparing surgery. The radiation destroys any breast cancer cells that may remain in the area.

Before surgery, radiation therapy, alone or with chemotherapy or hormonal therapy, is sometimes used to destroy cancer cells and shrink tumors. This approach is most often used in cases in which the breast tumor is large or not easily removed by surgery.

Chemotherapy is the use of drugs to kill cancer cells. Chemotherapy for breast cancer is usually a combination of drugs. The drugs may be given in a pill or by injection. Either way, the drugs enter the bloodstream and travel throughout the body.

Most patients have chemotherapy in an outpatient part of the hospital, at the doctor's office, or at home. Depending on which drugs are given and her general health, however, a woman may need to stay in the hospital during her treatment.

Hormonal therapy keeps cancer cells from getting the hormones they need to grow. This treatment may include the use of drugs that change the way hormones work, or surgery to remove the ovaries, which make female hormones. Like chemotherapy, hormonal therapy can affect cancer cells throughout the body.

Biological therapy is a treatment designed to enhance the body's natural defenses against cancer. For example, Herceptin (trastuzumab) is a monoclonal antibody that targets breast cancer cells that have too much of a protein known as human epidermal growth factor receptor-2 (HER-2). By blocking HER-2, Herceptin slows or stops the growth of these cells. Herceptin may be given by itself or along with chemotherapy.

A woman's treatment options depend on a number of factors. These factors include her age and menopausal status; her general health; the size and location of the tumor and the stage of the cancer; the results of lab tests; and the size of her breast. Certain features of the tumor cells (such as whether they depend on hormones to grow) are also considered. In most cases, the most important factor is the stage of the disease.

Side Effects of Treatment

It is hard to protect healthy cells from the harmful effects of breast cancer treatment. Because treatment does damage healthy cells and tissues, it causes side effects. The side effects of cancer treatment depend mainly on the type and extent of the treatment. Also, the effects may not be the same for each person, and they may be different from one treatment to the next. An important part of the treatment plan is the management of side effects.

A patient's reaction to treatment is closely monitored by physical exams, blood tests, and other tests. Doctors and nurses will explain the possible side effects and they can suggest ways to deal with problems that may occur during and after treatment.

Surgery

Surgery causes short-term pain and tenderness in the area of the operation, so women may need to talk with their doctor about pain management. Any kind of surgery also carries a risk of infection, poor wound healing, bleeding, or a reaction to the anesthesia used during surgery. Women who experience any of these problems should tell their doctor or nurse right away.

Removal of a breast can cause a woman's weight to be out of balance—especially if she has large breasts. This imbalance can cause discomfort in her neck and back. Also, the skin in the area where the breast was removed may be tight, and the muscles of the arm and shoulder may feel stiff. After a mastectomy, some women have some permanent loss of strength in these muscles, but for most women, reduced strength and limited movement are temporary. The doctor, nurse, or physical therapist can recommend exercises to help a woman regain movement and strength in her arm and shoulder.

Because nerves may be injured or cut during surgery, a woman may have numbness and tingling in the chest, underarm, shoulder, and upper arm. These feelings usually go away within a few weeks or months, but some women have permanent numbness.

Removing the lymph nodes under the arm slows the flow of lymph. In some women, this fluid builds up in the arm and hand and causes swelling (lymphedema). Women need to protect the arm and hand on the treated side from injury or pressure, even long after surgery. They should ask the doctor how to handle any cuts, scratches, insect bites, or other injuries to the arm or hand. Also, they should contact the doctor if an infection develops in that arm or hand.

Radiation Therapy

During radiation therapy, patients may become extremely tired, especially after several treatments. This feeling may continue for a while after treatment is over. Resting is important, but doctors usually advise their patients to try to stay reasonably active, matching their activities to their energy level. It is also common for the skin in the treated area to become red, dry, tender, and itchy. The breast may feel heavy and hard, but these conditions will clear up with time. Toward the end of treatment, the skin may become moist and "weepy." Exposing this area to air as much as possible will help the skin heal. Because bras and some types of clothing may rub the skin and cause irritation, patients may want to wear loose-fitting cotton clothes. Gentle skin care is important at this time, and patients should check with their doctor before using any deodorants, lotions, or creams on the treated area. These effects of radiation therapy on the skin are temporary, and the area gradually heals once treatment is over. However, there may be a permanent change in the color of the skin.

Chemotherapy

As with radiation, chemotherapy affects normal as well as cancer cells. The side effects of chemotherapy depend mainly on the specific drugs and the dose. In general, anticancer drugs affect rapidly dividing cells. These include blood cells, which fight infection, help the blood to clot, and carry oxygen to all parts of the body. When blood cells are affected, patients are more likely to get infections, may bruise or bleed easily, and may feel very weak and tired. Rapidly dividing cells in hair roots and cells that line the digestive tract may also be affected. As a result, side effects may include loss of hair, poor appetite, nausea and vomiting, diarrhea, or mouth sores. Many of these side effects can now be controlled with new or improved drugs. Side effects generally are short-term and they gradually go away. Hair will grow back, but may be different in color and texture.

Some anticancer drugs can damage the ovaries. If the ovaries fail to produce hormones, the woman may have symptoms of menopause, such as hot flashes and vaginal dryness. Her periods may become irregular

B

or may stop, and she may not be able to become pregnant. Other long-term side effects are quite rare, but there have been cases in which the heart is weakened, and second cancers such as leukemia (cancer of the blood cells) have occurred.

Women who are still menstruating may still be able to get pregnant during treatment. Because the effects of chemotherapy on an unborn child are not known, it is important for a woman to talk with her doctor about birth control before treatment begins. After treatment, some women regain their ability to become pregnant, but in women over the age of 35, infertility is likely to be permanent.

Hormonal Therapy

The side effects of hormonal therapy depend largely on the specific drug or type of treatment. Tamoxifen is the most common hormonal treatment. This drug blocks the cancer cells' use of estrogen but does not stop estrogen production. Tamoxifen may cause hot flashes, vaginal discharge or irritation, nausea, and irregular periods. Women who are still menstruating and having irregular periods may become pregnant more easily when taking tamoxifen. They should discuss birth control methods with their doctor.

Serious side effects of tamoxifen are rare. It can cause blood clots in the veins, especially in the legs and in the lungs, and in a small number of women, it can slightly increase the risk of stroke. Also, tamoxifen can cause cancer of the lining of the uterus. Any unusual vaginal bleeding should be reported to the doctor. The doctor may do a pelvic exam, as well as a biopsy of the lining of the uterus, or other tests. (This does not apply to women who have had a hysterectomy, surgery to remove the uterus.)

Young women whose ovaries are removed to deprive the cancer cells of estrogen experience menopause immediately. Their symptoms are likely to be more severe than symptoms associated with natural menopause.

Biological Therapy

The side effects of biological therapy differ with the types of substances used, and from patient to patient. Rashes or swelling where the biological therapy is injected are common. Flu-like symptoms also may occur.

Herceptin may cause these and other side effects, but these effects generally become less severe after the first treatment. Less commonly, Herceptin can also cause damage to the heart that can lead to heart failure. It can also affect the lungs, causing breathing problems that require immediate medical attention. For these reasons, women are checked carefully for heart and lung problems before taking Herceptin. Patients who do take it are watched carefully during treatment.

Breast Reconstruction

After a mastectomy, some women decide to wear a breast form (prosthesis). Others prefer to have breast reconstruction, either at the same time as the mastectomy or later on. Each option has its pros and cons, and what is right for one woman may not be right for another. What is important is that nearly every woman treated for breast cancer has choices. It is best to consult with a plastic surgeon before the mastectomy, even if reconstruction will be considered later on.

Various procedures are used to reconstruct the breast. Some use implants (either saline or silicone); others use tissue moved from another part of the woman's body. The safety of silicone breast implants has been under review by the Food and Drug Administration (FDA) for several years. Women interested in having silicone implants should talk with their doctor about the FDA's findings and the availability of silicone implants. Which type of reconstruction is best depends on a woman's age, body type, and the type of surgery she had. A woman should ask the plastic surgeon to explain the risks and benefits of each type of reconstruction.

Rehabilitation

Rehabilitation is a very important part of breast cancer treatment. The health-care team makes every effort to help women return to their normal activities as soon as possible. Recovery will be different for each woman, depending on the extent of the disease, the type of treatment, and other factors.

Exercising the arm and shoulder after surgery can help a woman regain motion and strength in these areas. It can also reduce pain and stiffness in her neck and back. Carefully planned exercises should be started as soon as the doctor says the woman is ready, often within a day or so after surgery. Exercising begins slowly and gently and can even be done in bed. Gradually, exercising can be more active, and regular exercise becomes part of a woman's normal routine. (Women who have a mastectomy and immediate breast reconstruction need special exercises, which the doctor or nurse will explain.)

Often, lymphedema after surgery can be prevented or reduced with certain exercises and by resting with the arm propped up on a pillow. If lymphedema occurs, the doctor may suggest exercises and other ways to deal with this problem. For example, some women with lymphedema wear an elastic sleeve or use an elastic cuff to improve lymph circulation. The doctor also may suggest other approaches, such as medication, manual lymph drainage (massage), or use of a machine that gently compresses the arm. The woman may be referred to a physical therapist or another specialist.

Follow-up Care

Regular follow-up exams are important after breast cancer treatment. Regular checkups ensure that changes in health are noticed. Follow-up exams usually include examination of the breasts, chest, neck, and underarm areas, as well as periodic mammograms. If a woman has a breast implant, special mammogram techniques can be used. Sometimes the doctor may order other imaging procedures or lab tests.

A woman who has had cancer in one breast should report any changes in the treated area or in the other breast to her doctor right away. Because a woman who has had breast cancer is at risk of getting cancer in the other breast, mammograms are an important part of follow-up care.

Also, a woman who has had breast cancer should tell her doctor about other physical problems, such as pain, loss of appetite or weight, changes in menstrual cycles, unusual vaginal bleeding, or blurred vision. She should also report headaches, dizziness, shortness of breath, coughing or hoarseness, backaches, or digestive problems that seem unusual or that don't go away. These symptoms may be a sign that the cancer has returned, but they can also be signs of various other problems. It's important to share these concerns with a doctor.

The Promise of Cancer Research
Possible Causes and Prevention

Scientists are trying to learn more about factors that increase the risk of developing this disease. For example, they are looking

B

at whether the risk of breast cancer might be affected by environmental factors. So far, scientists do not have enough information to know whether any factors in the environment increase the risk of this disease. (The main known risk factors are listed in "Who's At Risk," page 152.)

Some aspects of a woman's lifestyle may affect her chances of developing breast cancer. For example, recent studies suggest that regular exercise may decrease the risk in younger women. Also, some evidence suggests a link between diet and breast cancer. Ongoing studies are looking at ways to prevent breast cancer through changes in diet or with dietary supplements. However, it is not yet known whether specific dietary changes will actually prevent breast cancer. These are active areas of research.

Scientists are trying to learn whether having a miscarriage or an abortion increases the risk of breast cancer. Thus far, studies have produced conflicting results, and this question is still unresolved.

Research has led to the identification of changes (mutations) in certain genes that increase the risk of developing breast cancer. Women with a strong family history of breast cancer may choose to have a blood test to see if they have inherited a change in the BRCA1 or BRCA2 gene. Women who are concerned about an inherited risk for breast cancer should talk to their doctor. The doctor may suggest seeing a health professional trained in genetics. Genetic counseling can help a woman decide whether testing would be appropriate for her. Also, counseling before and after testing helps women understand and deal with the possible results of a genetic test. Counseling can also help with concerns about employment or about health, life, and disability insurance.

Scientists are looking for drugs that may prevent the development of breast cancer.

In one large study, the drug tamoxifen reduced the number of new cases of breast cancer among women at an increased risk for the disease. Doctors are now studying how another drug called raloxifene compares to tamoxifen. This study is called STAR (Study of Tamoxifen and Raloxifene). (For more information about clinical trials, see page 181.)

Detection and Diagnosis

At present, mammograms are the most effective tool we have to detect breast cancer. Researchers are looking for ways to make mammography more accurate, such as using computers to read mammograms (digital mammography). They are also exploring other techniques, such as magnetic resonance imaging (MRI), breast ultrasonography, and positron emission tomography (PET), to produce detailed pictures of the tissues in the breast.

In addition, researchers are studying tumor markers. These are substances that may be present in abnormal amounts in people with cancer. Tumor markers may be found in blood or urine, or in fluid from the breast (nipple aspirate). Some of these markers may be used to check women who have already been diagnosed with breast cancer. At this time, however, no tumor marker test is reliable enough to be used routinely to detect breast cancer.

Treatment

Through research, doctors try to find new, more effective ways to treat cancer. Many studies of new approaches for patients with breast cancer are under way. When laboratory research shows that a new treatment method has promise, cancer patients receive the new approach in treatment clinical

B

trials. These studies are designed to answer important questions and to find out whether the new approach is safe and effective. Often, clinical trials compare a new treatment with a standard approach.

Researchers are testing new anticancer drugs, doses, and treatment schedules. They are working with various drugs and drug combinations, as well as with several types of hormonal therapy. They also are looking at the effectiveness of using chemotherapy before surgery (called neoadjuvant chemotherapy) and at new ways of combining treatments, such as adding hormonal therapy or radiation therapy to chemotherapy.

New biological approaches are also under study. For example, several cancer vaccines have been designed to stimulate the immune system to mount a response against breast cancer cells. Combinations of biological treatments with other agents are also undergoing clinical study.

Researchers are exploring ways to reduce the side effects of treatment (such as lymphedema from surgery), improve the quality of patients' lives, and reduce pain. One procedure under study is called sentinel lymph node biopsy. Researchers are trying to learn whether this procedure may reduce the number of lymph nodes that must be removed during breast cancer surgery. Before surgery, the doctor injects a radioactive substance near the tumor. The substance flows through the lymphatic system to the first lymph node or nodes where cancer cells are likely to have spread (the "sentinel" node or nodes). The doctor uses a scanner to locate the radioactive substance in the sentinel nodes. Sometimes the doctor also injects a blue dye near the tumor. The dye travels through the lymphatic system to collect in the sentinel nodes. The surgeon makes a small incision and removes only the nodes with radioactive substance or blue dye. A pathologist checks the sentinel lymph nodes for cancer cells. If no cancer cells are detected, it may not be necessary to remove additional nodes. If sentinel lymph node biopsy proves to be as effective as the standard axillary lymph node dissection, the new procedure could prevent lymphedema.

Chemotherapy can reduce the ability of bone marrow to make blood cells. That is why researchers are studying ways to help the blood cells recover so that high doses of chemotherapy can be given. These studies use biological therapies (which are known as colony-stimulating factors), autologous bone marrow transplants, or peripheral stem cell transplants.

National Cancer Institute

B

Bronchitis occurs when an irritant or infection causes inflammation and swelling of the lining of the bronchial tubes. These tubes, the bronchi, are the major air passages that lead from the trachea into the lungs. When cells lining the airways are irritated beyond a certain point, the tiny cilia (hairs) that normally trap and eliminate foreign matter stop working properly. The buildup of irritants leads to the production of excess mucus, which clogs air passages further and produces the characteristic heavy cough of bronchitis.

Bronchitis occurs in two forms—acute and chronic. While both types of bronchitis produce a persistent cough, most cases of acute bronchitis clear up in about two weeks; chronic bronchitis may persist for a number of years. Between January and March, the number of doctor visits for bronchitis peaks at about 10 million to 12 million cases a year. Proper treatment can speed recovery and prevent complications, especially in those who smoke.

Causes

Contrary to popular belief, acute bronchitis is usually caused by a virus. Bronchitis generally develops when a virus invades the air passages of the lungs (bronchi) in the aftermath of an upper respiratory infection, also known as the common cold. The virus stimulates an immune response, which causes the bronchial lining to become inflamed. As a result, the air passages narrow and, in

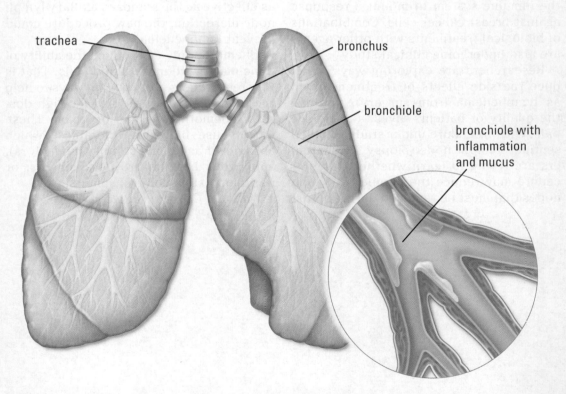

trachea

bronchus

bronchiole

bronchiole with inflammation and mucus

Chronic bronchitis is characterized by recurrent inflammation of the lining of the bronchi or bronchioles (branches of the trachea through which inhaled air and exhaled gas pass).

about half of patients, the bronchi become more responsive (hypersensitive) to dust and other irritants.

Bacterial infection is suspected only when acute bronchitis persists for more than two weeks, or when there is a change in the symptoms of chronic bronchitis, such as a worsening cough, a fever above 101° F, or a change in the color, quantity, or consistency of phlegm.

While most people recover from acute bronchitis within a couple of weeks, sometimes symptoms persist or recur frequently. Chronic bronchitis is diagnosed when symptoms have lasted for at least three months of the year for more than two years in a row.

About 90 percent of those who develop chronic bronchitis are smokers. Such irritation leads to inflammation and scarring of the bronchial lining. Eventually, air flow becomes obstructed.

Symptoms

Acute bronchitis is characterized by reduced air flow, coughing spells, increased mucus production, and sometimes bronchial spasms (sudden contractions of bronchial muscles).

The hallmark of chronic bronchitis is a mucus-producing cough. Typically, the cough first appears during the winter months. Gradually, over a number of years, the cough may become continuous. As the condition worsens, relapses become more frequent and breathing may become difficult. Over time, the illness may become permanent and lung tissue may be irreversibly damaged.

Treatment

Most cases of acute infectious bronchitis clear up in about two weeks with rest, increased fluid intake, and over-the-counter cough medicines that contain the expectorant guaifenesin. In the past, acute bronchitis was also treated with antibiotics. However, treatment strategies have evolved since research has shown that bronchodilators—medications that are routinely prescribed for asthma—may be effective for acute cases that linger longer than two weeks. Research also proves that antibiotics should not be prescribed routinely. Inappropriate use of antibiotics is a serious problem because it may render the medications less effective when needed for a legitimate purpose. The problem, which has received considerable media attention, is known as antibiotic resistance.

In general, if antibiotics are useful in treating bronchitis, they should be prescribed for acute bronchitis only when symptoms last longer than two weeks, and for chronic bronchitis only when there is a change in symptoms that may indicate the presence of a bacterial infection. However, antibiotics may be used sooner in smokers, the elderly, those with asthma or emphysema, and others at increased risk for respiratory complications.

A doctor should be consulted anytime symptoms of acute bronchitis linger for more than two weeks. However, if you are a smoker or elderly, have been diagnosed with heart or lung disease, have a fever higher than 101° F, experience chest pain or tightness, or notice blood in your phlegm, you should see a doctor. State-of-the-art care involves pulmonary function testing, a simple office procedure that measures the volume of exhaled air before and after taking a bronchodilator to determine if you are experiencing bronchospasms. If the test is positive, a bronchodilator such as

B

ipratropium (Atrovent) can be prescribed to relieve symptoms and possibly speed recovery by a day or two.

The best way to prevent chronic symptoms is to give up cigarettes and to treat acute bronchitis properly, should it occur. Even after chronic bronchitis has developed, you may eliminate symptoms and prevent lung damage by not smoking. Other important steps include adequate fluid intake, exercise (especially walking at a brisk but comfortable pace for a minimum of 30 minutes, at least three times a week), bronchodilators as needed, and supplementary oxygen for advanced cases. Because bronchitis makes sufferers vulnerable to infection, patients with the chronic form should also limit contact with people who have colds, the flu, pneumonia, and other infectious illnesses. A yearly influenza vaccination and a one-time pneumonia vaccination are also recommended.

A pproximately 150 small, fluid-filled sacs called bursae are situated throughout the body. These bursae (from the Greek for wineskins) act to cushion joint components and allow shoulders, knees, and elbows easy mobility. More specifically, they protect muscles and tendons from irritation produced by coming into direct contact with bones. Bursitis, an inflammation of one or more of these small sacs—most commonly in the shoulders, elbows, hips, knees, and feet—results in swelling and pain that can be debilitating.

While bursitis may produce some of the same symptoms as arthritis, it affects the tissues surrounding the joint rather than the joint itself. Bursitis is not chronic (most cases resolve on their own within a few days to two weeks); but it can recur unless

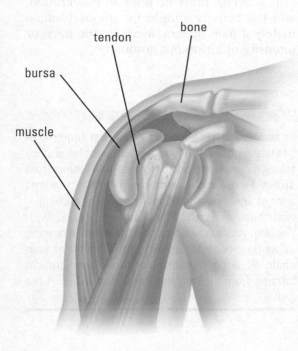

Bursitis is an inflammation of a small, fluid-filled bursa inside a joint. The shoulder (shown here) is one of the sites most commonly affected.

preventive measures are adopted, and subsequent flare-ups often take longer to respond to treatment.

Causes

Joint overuse from repetitive motion is a common cause of bursitis, as is any activity that puts constant pressure on a bursa (such as kneeling). Other causes include:

- Repetitive movement coupled with excessive strain (such as serving a tennis ball);
- Trauma to a bursa from a bump or blow;
- Foot problems that cause improper leg alignment, irritating bursae in the hips;
- Ill-fitting or uncomfortable shoes that cause bunions, which are actually an inflammation of the bursa near the joint of the big toe;
- Inflammation from arthritis or gout.

People with arthritis are at greater risk for bursitis because they may try to compensate for sore joints with awkward or exaggerated movements that lead to improper body mechanics. As a result, everyday activities may irritate the bursae.

Symptoms

The primary symptom of bursitis is pain in the affected area. In most cases, the pain is dull and persistent and increases with movement, but it can be severe enough to awaken the individual at night. Though localized, the pain may radiate down an arm or leg. The bursa may be swollen and tender. Redness and warmth indicate the bursa has become infected. In addition to pain, movement in the affected area may be restricted.

Bursitis can be mistaken for several other disorders, such as tendinitis (inflammation of a tendon) or arthritis. But, while bursitis is characterized by a dull ache that gets worse when the affected area is in use, tendinitis typically causes sharp pain, and arthritis

B

involves the joint, whereas bursitis involves the soft tissues that surround the joint.

Diagnosis

A physical exam that includes inspection of the joints and surrounding tissues is the primary diagnostic method. The doctor will probably ask when the pain began; what makes the pain worse; if the onset of pain was related to any activity (particularly a new activity) or injury; if similar pain occurred in the past; and if any pain medications are being taken. Bursitis is not visible on x-rays, but sometimes an x-ray is taken to see if pain is caused by joint inflammation or some other cause.

Treatment

A suspected case of bursitis can be safely treated at home. The first step is to rest the affected area until the pain is gone, by eliminating or cutting back on the activity that brought on the problem. Apply ice packs to the affected area for 20 minutes every 1 to 2 hours to help reduce pain and swelling. (Applying ice for more than 20 minutes at a time can lead to frostbite.) After 48 hours, use heat to stimulate blood flow and help ease the pain. Over-the-counter non-steroidal anti-inflammatory drugs (NSAIDs), such as aspirin or ibuprofen (Motrin), can alleviate pain; acetaminophen is not effective for bursitis because it does not relieve inflammation.

After the pain subsides, do gentle stretching exercises and gradually build up to your accustomed level of activity. Do not massage the area; it will only further irritate the bursa. Liniments (topical pain relievers) are not usually recommended, as they do not repair the damage. Most often, they contain an ingredient that irritates the nerve endings in the skin and so "confuses" the nervous system into feeling less intense pain.

If pain is disabling or does not subside after three or four days, consult a physician. In some instances, cortisone injections into the bursa or removal of fluid from the bursa with a needle and syringe can help reduce swelling and inflammation. In rare cases, surgery may be required to remove the troublesome bursa.

Prevention

The best way to prevent bursitis is to avoid activities that require repetitive motions, although this is not always possible. Staying in shape helps prevent bursitis, since well-conditioned muscles are less susceptible to overuse injuries than tight or weak muscles. Still, exercise must be done in moderation, and the activity should be stopped immediately if pain occurs. Increase the pace or intensity of a workout gradually.

In addition to avoiding activities that require repetitive motions, you can help prevent bursitis by taking measures to protect susceptible joints from stress. For example, for any activity that requires a lot of kneeling—waxing a floor or gardening— wear knee pads and take frequent breaks. Or, if you lean your elbows on a hard desk while reading or writing, consider adjusting the height of your chair. Wearing comfortable shoes can prevent bursitis from striking the heels and sides of the feet.

C ancer is a group of many related diseases that begin in cells, the body's basic unit of life. To understand cancer, it is helpful to know what happens when normal cells become cancerous.

The body is made up of many types of cells. Normally, cells grow and divide to produce more cells only when the body needs them. This orderly process helps keep the body healthy. Sometimes,

however, cells keep dividing when new cells are not needed. These extra cells form a mass of tissue, called a growth or tumor.

Tumors can be benign or malignant.

- Benign tumors are not cancer. They can often be removed and, in most cases, they do not come back. Cells from benign tumors do not spread to other parts of the body. Most important, benign tumors are rarely a threat to life.

- Malignant tumors are cancer. Cells in these tumors are abnormal and divide without control or order. They can invade and damage nearby tissues and organs. Also, cancer cells can break away from a malignant tumor and enter the bloodstream or the lymphatic system. That is how cancer spreads from the original cancer site to form new tumors in other organs. The spread of cancer is called metastasis.

Leukemia and lymphoma are cancers that arise in blood-forming cells. The abnormal cells circulate in the bloodstream and lymphatic system. They may also invade (infiltrate) body organs and form tumors.

Most cancers are named for the organ or type of cell in which they begin. For example, cancer that begins in the lung is lung cancer, and cancer that begins in cells in the skin known as melanocytes is called melanoma.

When cancer spreads (metastasizes), cancer cells are often found in nearby or regional lymph nodes (sometimes called lymph glands). If the cancer has reached these nodes, it means that cancer cells may have spread to other organs, such as the liver, bones, or brain. When cancer spreads from its original location to another part of the body, the new tumor has the same kind of abnormal cells and the same name as the primary tumor. For example, if lung cancer spreads to the brain, the cancer

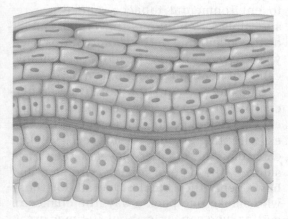

normal cells

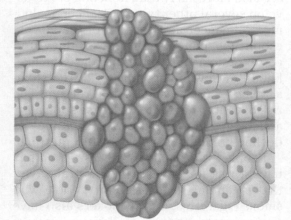

cancerous cells

Normal cells grow and divide only when the body needs them. Cancer cells divide in an uncontrolled way to form a mass, or tumor.

cells in the brain are actually lung cancer cells. The disease is called metastatic lung cancer (it is not brain cancer).

Possible Causes and Prevention of Cancer

The more we can learn about what causes cancer, the more likely we are to find ways to prevent it. In the laboratory, scientists explore possible causes of cancer and try to determine exactly what happens in cells when they become cancerous. Researchers also study patterns of cancer in the population to look for risk factors, conditions that increase the chance that cancer might occur. They also look for protective factors, things that decrease the risk.

Even though doctors can seldom explain why one person gets cancer and another does not, it is clear that cancer is not caused by an injury, such as a bump or bruise. And although being infected with certain viruses may increase the risk of some types of cancer, cancer is not contagious; no one can "catch" cancer from another person.

Cancer develops over time. It is a result of a complex mix of factors related to lifestyle, heredity, and environment. A number of factors that increase a person's chance of developing cancer have been identified. Many types of cancer are related to the use of tobacco, what people eat and drink, exposure to ultraviolet (UV) radiation from the sun, and, to a lesser extent, exposure to cancer-causing agents (carcinogens) in the environment and the workplace. Some people are more sensitive than others to factors that can cause cancer.

Still, most people who get cancer have none of the known risk factors. And most people who do have risk factors do not get the disease.

Some cancer risk factors can be avoided. Others, such as inherited factors, are unavoidable, but it may be helpful to be aware of them. People can help protect themselves by avoiding known risk factors whenever possible. They can also talk with their doctor about regular checkups and about whether cancer screening tests could be of benefit.

These are some of the factors that increase the likelihood of cancer:

Tobacco. Smoking tobacco, using smokeless tobacco, and being regularly exposed to environmental tobacco smoke are responsible for about one-third of all cancer deaths occurring in the United States each year. Tobacco use is the most preventable cause of death in this country.

Smoking accounts for more than 85 percent of all lung cancer deaths. For smokers, the risk of getting lung cancer increases with the amount of tobacco smoked each day, the number of years they have smoked, the type of tobacco product, and how deeply they inhale. Overall, for those who smoke one pack a day, the chance of getting lung cancer is about 10 times greater than for nonsmokers. Cigarette smokers are also more likely than nonsmokers to develop several other types of cancer, including oral cancer and cancers of the larynx, esophagus, pancreas, bladder, kidney, and cervix. Smoking may also increase the likelihood of developing cancers of the stomach, liver, prostate, colon, and rectum. The risk of cancer begins to decrease soon after a smoker quits, and the risk continues to decline gradually each year after quitting.

People who smoke cigars or pipes have a risk for cancers of the oral cavity that is similar to the risk for people who smoke cigarettes. Cigar smokers also have an increased chance of developing cancers of the lung, larynx, esophagus, and pancreas.

The use of smokeless tobacco (chewing tobacco and snuff) causes cancer of the mouth and throat. Precancerous conditions, tissue changes that may lead to cancer, often begin to go away after a person stops using smokeless tobacco.

Studies suggest that exposure to environmental tobacco smoke, also called secondhand smoke, increases the risk of lung cancer for nonsmokers.

People who use tobacco in any form and need help quitting may want to talk with their doctor, dentist, or other health professional, or join a smoking cessation group sponsored by a local hospital or voluntary organization.

Diet. Researchers are exploring how dietary factors play a role in the development of cancer. Some evidence suggests a link between a high-fat diet and certain cancers, such as cancers of the colon, uterus, and prostate. Being seriously overweight may be linked to breast cancer among older women and to cancers of the prostate, pancreas, uterus, colon, and ovary. On the other hand, some studies suggest that foods containing fiber and certain nutrients may help protect against some types of cancer.

People may be able to reduce their cancer risk by making healthy food choices. A well-balanced diet includes generous amounts of foods that are high in fiber, vitamins, and minerals, and low in fat. This includes eating lots of fruits and vegetables and more whole-grain breads and cereals every day, fewer eggs, and not as much high-fat meat, high-fat dairy products (such as whole milk, butter, and most cheeses), salad dressing, margarine, and cooking oil.

Most scientists think that making healthy food choices is more beneficial than taking vitamin and mineral supplements.

Ultraviolet (UV) radiation. UV radiation from the sun causes premature aging of the skin and skin damage that can lead to skin cancer. Artificial sources of UV radiation, such as sunlamps and tanning booths, can also cause skin damage and probably an increased risk of skin cancer.

To help reduce the risk of skin cancer caused by UV radiation, it is best to reduce exposure to the midday sun (from 10 A.M. to 3 P.M.). Another simple rule is to avoid the sun when your shadow is shorter than you are.

Wearing a broad-brimmed hat, UV-absorbing sunglasses, long pants, and long sleeves offers protection. Many doctors believe that in addition to avoiding the sun and wearing protective clothing, wearing a sunscreen (especially one that reflects, absorbs, and/or scatters both types of ultraviolet radiation) may help prevent some forms of skin cancer. Sunscreens are rated in strength according to a sun protection factor (SPF). The higher the SPF, the more sunburn protection is provided. Sunscreens with an SPF of 12 through 29 are adequate for most people, but sunscreens are not a substitute for avoiding the sun and wearing protective clothing.

Alcohol. Heavy drinkers have an increased risk of cancers of the mouth, throat, esophagus, larynx, and liver. (People who smoke cigarettes and drink heavily have an especially high risk of getting these cancers.) Some studies suggest that even moderate drinking may slightly increase the risk of breast cancer.

Ionizing radiation. Cells may be damaged by ionizing radiation from x-ray procedures, radioactive substances, rays that enter the Earth's atmosphere from outer space, and other sources. In very high doses, ionizing radiation may cause cancer and other diseases. Studies of survivors of the atomic bomb in Japan show that ionizing radiation increases the risk of developing leukemia and cancers of the breast, thyroid, lung, stomach, and other organs.

Before 1950, x-rays were used to treat noncancerous conditions (such as an enlarged thymus, enlarged tonsils and adenoids, ringworm of the scalp, and acne) in children and young adults. Those who have received radiation therapy to the head and neck have a higher-than-average risk of developing thyroid cancer years later. People with a history of such treatments should report it to their doctor.

Radiation that patients receive as therapy for cancer can also damage normal cells. Patients may want to talk with their doctor about the effect of radiation treatment on their risk of a second cancer. This risk can depend on the patient's age at the time of treatment as well as on the part of the body that was treated.

X-rays used for diagnosis expose people to lower levels of radiation than x-rays used for therapy. The benefits nearly always outweigh the risks. However, repeated exposure could be harmful, so it is a good idea for people to talk with their doctor about the need for each x-ray and to ask about the use of shields to protect other parts of the body.

Chemicals and other substances. Being exposed to substances such as certain chemicals, metals, or pesticides can increase the risk of cancer. Asbestos, nickel, cadmium, uranium, radon, vinyl chloride, benzidene, and benzene are examples of well-known carcinogens. These may act alone or along with another carcinogen, such as cigarette smoke, to increase the risk of cancer. For example, inhaling asbestos fibers increases the risk of lung diseases, including cancer, and the cancer risk is especially high for asbestos workers who smoke. It is important to follow work and safety rules to avoid or minimize contact with dangerous materials.

Hormone replacement therapy (HRT). Doctors may recommend HRT, using either estrogen alone or estrogen in combination with progesterone, to control symptoms (such as hot flashes and vaginal dryness) that may occur during menopause. Studies have shown that the use of estrogen alone increases the risk of cancer of the uterus. Therefore, most doctors prescribe HRT that includes progesterone along with low doses of estrogen. Progesterone counteracts estrogen's harmful effect on the uterus by preventing overgrowth of the lining of the uterus; this overgrowth is associated with taking estrogen alone. (Estrogen alone may be prescribed for women who have had a hysterectomy—surgery to remove the uterus—and are, therefore, not at risk for cancer of the uterus.) Other studies show an increased risk of breast cancer among women who have used estrogen for a long time; and some research suggests that the risk might be higher among those who have used estrogen and progesterone together.

Researchers are still learning about the risks and benefits of taking HRT. A woman considering HRT should discuss these issues with her doctor.

Diethylstilbestrol (DES). DES is a synthetic form of estrogen that was used between the early 1940s and 1971. Some women took DES during pregnancy to prevent certain complications. Their DES-exposed daughters have an increased chance of developing abnormal cells (dysplasia) in the cervix and vagina. In addition, a rare type of vaginal and cervical cancer can occur in DES-exposed daughters. DES daughters should tell their doctor about their exposure. They should also have pelvic exams by a doctor familiar with conditions related to DES.

Women who took DES during pregnancy may have a slightly higher risk for developing breast cancer. These women should tell their doctor about their exposure. At this time, there does not appear to be an increased risk of breast cancer for daughters who were exposed to DES before birth. However, more studies are needed as these daughters enter the age range when breast cancer is more common.

There is evidence that DES-exposed sons may have testicular abnormalities, such as undescended or abnormally small testicles. The possible risk for testicular cancer in these men is under study.

Close relatives with certain types of cancer. Some types of cancer (including melanoma and cancers of the breast, ovary, prostate, and colon) tend to occur more often in some families than in the rest of the population. It is often unclear whether a pattern of cancer in a family is primarily due to heredity, factors in the family's environment or lifestyle, or just a matter of chance.

Researchers have learned that cancer is caused by changes (called mutations or alterations) in genes that control normal cell growth and cell death. Most cancer-causing gene changes are the result of factors in lifestyle or the environment. However, some alterations that may lead to cancer are inherited; that is, they are passed from parent to child. But having such an inherited gene alteration does not mean that the person is certain to develop cancer; it means that the risk of cancer is increased.

People who have any of the cancer risk factors listed above should talk with their doctor. The doctor may be able to suggest ways to reduce the risk and can recommend an appropriate schedule of checkups.

Screening and Early Detection
Sometimes, cancer can be found before the disease causes symptoms. Checking for cancer (or for conditions that may lead to cancer) in a person who does not have any symptoms of the disease is called screening.

For more information about cancer screening, see pages 49-54 as well as entries on specific types of cancer.

Symptoms of Cancer
Cancer can cause a variety of symptoms. These are some of them:
- Thickening or lump in the breast or any other part of the body
- Obvious change in a wart or mole
- A sore that does not heal
- Nagging cough or hoarseness
- Changes in bowel or bladder habits
- Indigestion or difficulty swallowing
- Unexplained changes in weight
- Unusual bleeding or discharge

When these or other symptoms occur, they are not always caused by cancer. They may also be caused by infections, benign tumors, or other problems. It is important to see the doctor about any of these symptoms or about other physical changes. Only a doctor can make a diagnosis. One should not wait to feel pain: Early cancer usually does not cause pain.

Diagnosis
If symptoms are present, the doctor asks about the person's medical history and performs a physical exam. In addition to checking general signs of health, the doctor may order various tests and exams. These may include laboratory tests and imaging procedures. A biopsy is usually necessary to determine whether cancer is present.

C

Laboratory Tests

Blood and urine tests can give the doctor important information about a person's health. In some cases, special tests are used to measure the amount of certain substances, called tumor markers, in the blood, urine, or certain tissues. Tumor marker levels may be abnormal if certain types of cancer are present. However, lab tests alone cannot be used to diagnose cancer.

Imaging

Images (pictures) of areas inside the body help the doctor see whether a tumor is present. These pictures can be made in several ways.

X-rays are the most common way to view organs and bones inside the body. A computed tomography (CT or CAT) scan is a special kind of imaging that uses a computer linked to an x-ray machine to make a series of pictures.

In radionuclide scanning, the patient swallows or receives an injection of a radioactive substance. A machine (scanner) measures radioactivity levels in certain organs and prints a picture on paper or film. The doctor can detect abnormal areas by looking at the amount of radioactivity in the organs. The radioactive substance is quickly eliminated by the patient's body after the test is done.

Ultrasonography is another procedure for viewing areas inside the body. High-frequency sound waves that cannot be heard by humans enter the body and bounce back. Their echoes produce a picture called a sonogram. These pictures are shown on a monitor like a TV screen and can be printed on paper.

In magnetic resonance imaging (MRI), a powerful magnet linked to a computer is used to make detailed pictures of areas in

---

Biopsy: Questions for Your Doctor

A patient who needs a biopsy may want to ask the doctor some of the following questions:

- Why do I need to have a biopsy?
- How long will it take? Will I be awake? Will it hurt?
- How soon will I know the results?
- Are there any risks? What are the chances of infection or bleeding after the biopsy?
- If I do have cancer, who will talk with me about treatment? When?

---

the body. These pictures are viewed on a monitor and can also be printed.

Biopsy

A biopsy is almost always necessary to help the doctor make a diagnosis of cancer. In a biopsy, tissue is removed for examination under a microscope by a pathologist. Tissue may be removed in three ways: endoscopy, needle biopsy, or surgical biopsy.

During an endoscopy, the doctor can look at areas inside the body through a thin, lighted tube. Endoscopy allows the doctor to see what's going on inside the body, take pictures, and remove tissue or cells for examination, if necessary.

In a needle biopsy, the doctor takes a small tissue sample by inserting a needle into the abnormal (suspicious) area.

A surgical biopsy may be excisional or incisional. In an excisional biopsy, the surgeon removes the entire tumor, often with some surrounding normal tissue. In an incisional biopsy, the doctor removes just a portion of the tumor. If cancer is present, the entire tumor may be removed immediately or during another operation.

Patients sometimes worry that having a biopsy (or any other type of surgery for

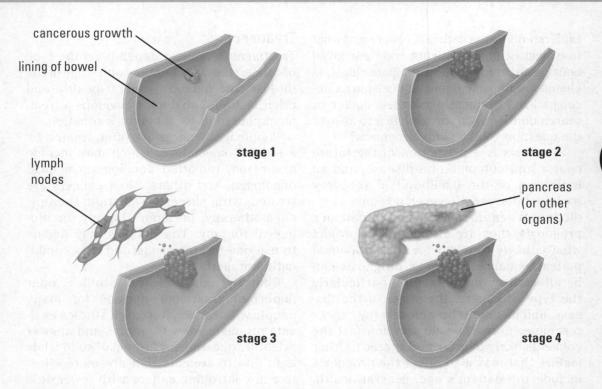

cancerous growth

lining of bowel

stage 1

stage 2

lymph nodes

pancreas (or other organs)

stage 3

stage 4

Stage 1 cancer refers to a small growth on the lining of an organ; stage 2 cancer has invaded the tissue, but hasn't spread; stage 3 cancer has spread to the lymph nodes; stage 4 cancer has spread to other sites.

cancer) will spread the disease. This is a very rare occurrence. Surgeons use special techniques and take many precautions to prevent cancer from spreading during surgery. For example, if tissue samples must be removed from more than one site, they use different instruments for each one. Also, a margin of normal tissue is often removed along with the tumor. Such efforts reduce the chance that cancer cells will spread into healthy tissue.

Some people may be concerned that exposing cancer to air during surgery will cause the disease to spread. This is not true. Exposure to air does not cause the cancer to spread.

Patients should discuss their concerns about the biopsy or other surgery with their doctor.

Staging

When cancer is diagnosed, the doctor will want to learn the stage, or extent, of the disease. Staging is a careful attempt to find out whether the cancer has spread and, if so, to which parts of the body. Treatment decisions depend on the results of staging. The doctor may order more laboratory tests and imaging studies or additional biopsies to find out whether the cancer has spread. An operation called a laparotomy can help the doctor find out whether cancer has spread within the abdomen. During this operation, a surgeon makes an incision into the abdomen and removes samples of tissue.

Handling the Diagnosis

It is natural for anyone facing cancer to be concerned about what the future holds.

Understanding the nature of cancer and what to expect can help patients and their loved ones plan treatment, anticipate lifestyle changes, and make financial decisions. Cancer patients frequently ask their doctor or search on their own for statistics to answer the question, "What is my prognosis?"

Prognosis is a prediction of the future course and outcome of a disease, and an indication of the likelihood of recovery from that disease. However, it is only a prediction. When doctors discuss a patient's prognosis, they are attempting to project what is likely to occur for that individual patient. A cancer patient's prognosis can be affected by many factors, particularly the type of cancer, the stage of the disease, and its grade (how closely the cancer resembles normal tissue and how fast the cancer is likely to grow and spread). Other factors that may also affect the prognosis include the patient's age, general health, and response to treatment. As these factors change over time, a patient's prognosis is also likely to change.

Sometimes people use statistics to try to figure out their chances of being cured. However, for individual patients and their families, statistics are seldom helpful because they reflect the experience of a large group of patients. Statistics cannot predict what will happen to a particular patient because no two patients are alike; treatment and responses vary greatly.

Prognosis should be discussed with a doctor. The doctor who is most familiar with a patient's situation is in the best position to help interpret statistics and discuss prognosis. But even the doctor may not be able to describe exactly what to expect.

Seeking information about prognosis and statistics can help some people reduce their fears. How much information to seek and how to deal with it are personal matters.

Treatment

Treatment for cancer depends on the type of cancer; the size, location, and stage of the disease; the person's general health; and other factors. The doctor develops a treatment plan to fit each person's situation.

People with cancer are often treated by a team of specialists, which may include a surgeon, radiation oncologist, medical oncologist, and others. Most cancers are treated with surgery, radiation therapy, chemotherapy, hormone therapy, or biological therapy. The doctors may decide to use one treatment method or a combination of methods.

Clinical trials (research studies) offer important treatment options for many people with cancer. Research studies evaluate promising new therapies and answer scientific questions. The goal of such trials is to find treatments that are more effective in controlling cancer with fewer side effects.

Getting a Second Opinion

Before starting treatment, the patient may want to have a second opinion from another doctor about the diagnosis and the treatment plan. Some insurance companies require a second opinion; others may cover a second opinion if the patient requests it.

There are a number of ways to find a doctor who can give a second opinion:
- The patient's doctor may be able to suggest specialists to consult;
- The Cancer Information Service, at 1-800-4-CANCER, can tell callers about cancer treatment facilities all over the country, including cancer centers and other programs supported by the National Cancer Institute;
- Patients can get the names of doctors from their local medical society, a nearby hospital, or a medical school;

Should You Enroll in a Clinical Trial?

Clinical trials are structured research studies designed to test the safety and effectiveness of medical treatments. The trials include studies of ways to prevent, detect, diagnose, and treat cancer; studies of the psychological effects of the disease; and studies of ways to improve comfort and quality of life.

Participants in a clinical trial are randomly assigned to receive either the investigational treatment or a placebo (an inactive treatment that looks like the real drug). If patients could be harmed by not receiving an active treatment, investigators will often compare the investigational drug to a standard one.

Typically, patients are blinded, meaning they are not told which treatment they are receiving. Many studies are double-blinded, so that neither the patient nor the doctors know what treatment the patient receives. This procedure minimizes the chances that a treatment will work only because of the expectations or biases of those involved.

A complete clinical trial has four phases.

- **Phase I** evaluates the safety of the medication in 20 to 80 healthy people, determines the appropriate dosage, and identifies side effects.
- **Phase II** focuses on whether the treatment works in people who have the relevant medical condition.
- **Phase III** examines the effect of the treatment in a large number of patients, often over a longer period of time, to assure the drug's long-term safety and efficacy. Researchers may compare the new treatment to a standard one in this phase.
- **Phase IV** occurs once the drug is on the market. Manufacturers often compare the efficacy, side effects, and cost effectiveness of the treatment with others on the market.

Trial participants reap substantial personal rewards. They receive the latest medications and therapies provided by top specialists at leading healthcare facilities. For some terminally ill patients, clinical trials may offer the only source of hope. Often, this care is provided free, and sometimes people are paid to participate. Plus, participants are making important contributions to medical science.

On the downside, subjects might receive only a standard treatment rather than the investigational one. The investigational treatment may be ineffective, or have unanticipated side effects that could be serious or life-threatening. Furthermore, patients will likely be asked to keep detailed records and follow strict medication schedules. The research may also entail frequent trips to the trial site and repeated blood samples. In some cases, costs not covered by the researchers might not be covered by insurance, either. Despite these potential drawbacks, many patients enjoy taking part in clinical trials and benefit from them.

Listings of current clinical trials can be found at the Web sites www.clinicaltrials.gov and www.centerwatch.com. *The Editors*

- The Official ABMS Directory of Board Certified Medical Specialists lists doctors' names along with their specialty and their educational background. This resource, produced by the American Board of Medical Specialties (ABMS), is available in most public libraries. The ABMS also provides an online service to help people locate doctors (http://www.certifieddoctor.org).

Preparing for Treatment

Many people with cancer want to take an active part in decisions about their medical care. They want to learn all they can about their disease and their treatment choices. However, the shock and stress that people often feel after a diagnosis of cancer can make it hard for them to think of everything they want to ask the doctor.

C

Questions for Your Doctor

These are some questions a patient may want to ask the doctor before treatment begins:

- What is my diagnosis?
- Is there any evidence the cancer has spread? What is the stage of the disease?
- What are my treatment choices? Which do you recommend for me? Why?
- What new treatments are being studied? Would a clinical trial be appropriate for me?
- What are the expected benefits of each kind of treatment?

- What are the risks and possible side effects of each treatment?
- Is infertility a side effect of cancer treatment? Can anything be done about it?
- What can I do to prepare for treatment?
- How often will I have treatments?
- How long will treatment last?
- Will I have to change my normal activities? If so, for how long?
- What is the treatment likely to cost?

Often it is helpful to prepare a list of questions in advance. To help remember what the doctor says, patients may take notes or ask whether they may use a tape recorder. Some people also want to have a family member or friend with them when they talk to the doctor—to take part in the discussion, to take notes, or just to listen.

Patients do not need to ask all their questions or remember all the answers at one time. They will have many opportunities to ask the doctor to explain things and to get more information.

Methods of Treatment and Their Side Effects

Treatment for cancer can be either local or systemic. Local treatments affect cancer cells in the tumor and the area near it. Systemic treatments travel through the bloodstream, reaching cancer cells all over the body. Surgery and radiation therapy are types of local treatment. Chemotherapy, hormone therapy, and biological therapy are examples of systemic treatment.

It is hard to protect healthy cells from the harmful effects of cancer treatment.

Because treatment does damage healthy cells and tissues, it often causes side effects. The side effects of cancer treatment depend mainly on the type and extent of the treatment. Also, the effects may not be the same for each person, and they may change for a person from one treatment to the next. A patient's reaction to treatment is closely monitored by physical exams, blood tests, and other tests. Doctors and nurses can explain the possible side effects of treatment, and they can suggest ways to reduce or eliminate problems that may occur during and after treatment.

Surgery

Surgery is therapy to remove the cancer; the surgeon may also remove some of the surrounding tissue and lymph nodes near the tumor. Sometimes surgery for cancer is done on an outpatient basis, or the patient may have to stay in the hospital. This decision depends mainly on the type of surgery and the type of anesthesia.

The side effects of surgery depend on many factors, including the size and location of the tumor, the type of operation, and the patient's general health. Although patients are often uncomfortable during the first few days after surgery, this pain can be controlled with medicine. Patients should feel free to discuss ways of relieving pain with the doctor or nurse. (More information about pain control is in the "Pain Control" section on page 187.) It is also common for patients to feel tired or weak for a while after surgery. The length of time it takes to recover from an operation varies among patients.

Some patients have concerns that cancer will spread during surgery. This subject is discussed in the section on "Biopsy" (page 178).

Radiation

Radiation therapy (also called radiotherapy) uses high-energy rays to kill cancer cells. For some types of cancer, radiation therapy may be used instead of surgery as the primary treatment. Radiation therapy may also be given before surgery (neoadjuvant therapy) to shrink a tumor so that it is easier to remove. In other cases, radiation therapy is given after surgery (adjuvant therapy) to destroy any cancer cells that may remain in the area. Radiation may also be used alone, or along with other types of treatment, to relieve pain or other problems if the tumor cannot be removed.

Radiation therapy can be in either of two forms: external or internal. Some patients receive both.

External radiation comes from a machine that aims the rays at a specific area of the body. Most often, this treatment is given on an outpatient basis in a hospital or clinic. There is no radioactivity left in the body after the treatment.

With internal radiation (also called implant radiation, interstitial radiation, or brachytherapy), the radiation comes from radioactive material that is sealed in needles, "seeds," wires, or catheters and placed directly in or near the tumor. Patients may stay in the hospital while the level of radiation is highest. They may not be able to have visitors during the hospital stay or may have visitors for only a short time. The implant may be permanent or temporary. The amount of radiation in a permanent implant goes down to a safe level before the person leaves the hospital. The doctor will advise the patient if any special precautions should be taken at home. With a temporary implant, there is no radioactivity left in the body after the implant is removed.

The side effects of radiation therapy depend on the treatment dose and the part of the body that is treated. Patients are likely to become extremely tired during radiation therapy, especially in the later weeks of treatment. Extra rest is often necessary, but doctors usually encourage patients to try to stay as active as they can between rest periods.

With external radiation, there may be permanent darkening or "bronzing" of the skin in the treated area. In addition, it is common to have temporary hair loss in the treated area and for the skin to become red, dry, tender, and itchy. Radiation therapy may also cause a decrease in the number of white blood cells, cells that help protect against infection.

Although radiation therapy can cause side effects, these can usually be treated or controlled. Most side effects are temporary, but some may be persistent or occur months to years later.

Chemotherapy

Chemotherapy is the use of drugs to kill cancer cells. The doctor may use one drug or a combination of drugs. Chemotherapy may be

C

the only kind of treatment a patient needs, or it may be combined with other forms of treatment. Neoadjuvant chemotherapy refers to drugs given before surgery to shrink a tumor; adjuvant chemotherapy refers to drugs given after surgery to help prevent the cancer from recurring. Chemotherapy may also be used (alone or along with other forms of treatment) to relieve symptoms of the disease.

Chemotherapy is usually given in cycles: a treatment period (one or more days when treatment is given) followed by a recovery period (several days or weeks), then another treatment period, and so on. Most anticancer drugs are given by injection into a vein (IV); some are injected into a muscle or under the skin; and some are given by mouth.

Often, patients who need many doses of IV chemotherapy receive the drugs through a catheter (a thin, flexible tube) that stays in place until treatment is over. One end of the catheter is placed in a large vein in the arm or the chest; the other end remains outside the body. Anticancer drugs are given through the catheter. Patients who have catheters avoid the discomfort of having a needle inserted into a vein for each treatment. Patients and their families learn how to care for the catheter and keep it clean.

Sometimes the anticancer drugs are given in other ways. For example, in an approach called intraperitoneal chemotherapy, anticancer drugs are placed directly into the abdomen through a catheter. To reach cancer cells in the central nervous system (CNS), the patient may receive intrathecal chemotherapy. In this type of treatment, the anticancer drugs enter the cerebrospinal fluid through a needle placed in the spinal column or a device placed under the scalp.

Usually a patient has chemotherapy as an outpatient (at the hospital, at the doctor's office, or at home). However,

depending on which drugs are given, the dose, how they are given, and the patient's general health, a short hospital stay may be needed.

The side effects of chemotherapy depend mainly on the drugs and the doses the patient receives. As with other types of treatment, side effects vary from person to person. Generally, anticancer drugs affect cells that divide rapidly. In addition to cancer cells, these include blood cells, which fight infection, help the blood to clot, and carry oxygen to all parts of the body. When blood cells are affected, patients are more likely to get infections, may bruise or bleed easily, and may feel unusually weak and very tired. Rapidly dividing cells in hair roots and in the cells that line the digestive tract may also be affected. As a result, side effects may include loss of hair, poor appetite, nausea and vomiting, diarrhea, or mouth and lip sores.

Hair loss is a major concern for many people with cancer. Some anticancer drugs only cause the hair to thin, while others may result in the loss of all body hair. Patients may cope better if they prepare for hair loss before starting treatment (for example, by buying a wig or hat). Most side effects go away gradually during the recovery periods between treatments, and hair grows back after treatment is over.

Some anticancer drugs can cause long-term side effects such as loss of fertility (the ability to produce children). Loss of fertility may be temporary or permanent, depending on the drugs used and the patient's age and sex. For men, sperm banking before treatment may be an option. Women's menstrual periods may stop, and they may have hot flashes and vaginal dryness. Periods are more likely to return in young women.

Hormone Therapy
Hormone therapy is used against certain cancers that depend on hormones for their

The Role of Alternative Therapies

Although studies show that about a third of cancer patients use alternative remedies, many doctors estimate that the percentage is much higher—and climbing. Alternative remedies are unproven treatments for which there is little or no scientific evidence. In contrast, conventional treatments are based on sound scientific research. When used to complement conventional cancer treatments, some alternative remedies may be helpful. However, when used instead of conventional treatment, they may delay lifesaving care. In addition, some alternative remedies can be harmful, and some may interfere with conventional care or worsen its side effects.

To provide safe and effective treatment, doctors must be aware of the alternative remedies their patients are using. Yet many patients keep this information to themselves—perhaps, as one survey of breast cancer patients indicated, out of concern that doctors may respond negatively or that they may not have adequate training in alternative remedies.

Although these assumptions may have been reasonable in the past, doctors have begun to recognize the need for a frank and open discussion about alternative remedies.

"Complementary" Therapies

When used to complement conventional treatment, some alternative remedies may enhance general well-being, improve the quality of life, build strength, promote relaxation, relieve pain, and lessen the side effects of conventional cancer treatments. Although herbs are popular, many other remedies may be safer and more effective.

- **Massage,** which has become widely accepted, may be useful for relieving pain, reducing stress, and promoting relaxation. As a massage therapist works the muscles, blood vessels dilate, increasing blood flow and delivering more oxygen to body tissues.

- **Hydrotherapy** (water treatment) used externally in various forms is also frequently soothing. Cold compresses can reduce swelling and hot ones can relieve pain after swelling abates; whirlpool baths and hot tubs can ease muscle pain and reduce stress; and exercising in a swimming pool reduces the risk of bone or muscle injury.

- **Acupuncture** entails placing hair-thin needles into the skin. There is some evidence that this ancient Chinese art is effective for the nausea associated with chemotherapy.

- **Prayer and meditation** can reduce stress and promote a positive outlook. Behavorial and psychological approaches, which include support groups, individual counseling, hypnosis, and biofeedback, may also be helpful.

- **A healthy diet** is an indisputable component of good cancer care. Researchers are currently investigating whether any vitamins may either promote or delay cancer growth.

Ensuring Safety

Alternative remedies should never be used in lieu of conventional care. Be sure to talk to your doctor about any alternative remedies you may consider using. Herbs are a particular concern. Some may have to be stopped during conventional treatment because they magnify side effects or could lead to complications. For example, St. John's wort (which may ease mild depression) increases sensitivity to radiation treatments, while ginkgo (which is promoted as a memory aid) can prolong clotting time and cause excessive bleeding. And some herbal remedies should be avoided altogether because of potentially serious side effects of their own.
The Editors

growth. Hormone therapy keeps cancer cells from getting or using the hormones they need. This treatment may include the use of drugs that stop the production of certain hormones or that change the way they work. Another type of hormone therapy is surgery to remove organs (such as the ovaries or testicles) that make hormones.

Hormone therapy can cause a number of side effects. Patients may feel tired, have fluid retention, weight gain, hot flashes, nausea and vomiting, changes in appetite, and, in some cases, blood clots. In women, hormone therapy may cause interrupted menstrual periods and vaginal dryness. Hormone therapy in women may also cause either a loss of or an increase in fertility; women taking hormone therapy should talk with their doctor about contraception during treatment. In men, hormone therapy may cause impotence, loss of sexual desire, or loss of fertility. Depending on the drug used, these changes may be temporary, long-lasting, or permanent. Patients may want to talk with their doctor about these and other side effects.

Biological Therapy

Biological therapy (also called immunotherapy) helps the body's natural ability (immune system) to fight disease or protects the body from some of the side effects of cancer treatment. Monoclonal antibodies, interferon, interleukin-2, and colony-stimulating factors are some types of biological therapy.

The side effects caused by biological therapy vary with the specific treatment. In general, these treatments tend to cause flu-like symptoms, such as chills, fever, muscle aches, weakness, loss of appetite, nausea, vomiting, and diarrhea. Patients may also bleed or bruise easily, get a skin rash, or have swelling. These problems can be severe, but they go away after the treatment stops.

Bone Marrow and Peripheral Stem Cell Transplantation

Bone marrow transplantation (BMT) or peripheral stem cell transplantation (PSCT) may also be used in cancer treatment. The transplant may be autologous (the person's own cells that were saved earlier), allogeneic (cells donated by another person), or syngeneic (cells donated by an identical twin). Both BMT and PSCT provide the patient with healthy stem cells (very immature cells that mature into blood cells). These replace stem cells that have been damaged or destroyed by very high doses of chemotherapy and/or radiation treatment.

Patients who have a BMT or PSCT face an increased risk of infection, bleeding, and other side effects due to the high doses of chemotherapy and/or radiation they receive. The most common side effects associated with the transplant itself are nausea and vomiting during the transplant, and chills and fever during the first day or so. In addition, graft-versus-host disease (GVHD) may occur in patients who receive bone marrow from a donor. In GVHD, the donated marrow (the graft) reacts against the patient's (the host's) tissues (most often the liver, the skin, and the digestive tract). GVHD can be mild or very severe. It can occur any time after the transplant (even years later). Drugs may be given to reduce the risk of GVHD and to treat the problem if it occurs.

Nutrition During Cancer Treatment

Eating well during cancer treatment means getting enough calories and protein to help prevent weight loss and maintain strength. Eating well often helps people feel better and have more energy.

Some people with cancer find it hard to eat because they lose their appetite. In addition, common side effects of treatment, such as nausea, vomiting, or mouth and lip sores, can make eating difficult. Often, foods taste different. Also, people being treated for cancer may not feel like eating when they are uncomfortable or tired.

Doctors, nurses, and dietitians can offer advice on how to get enough calories and protein during cancer treatment.

Pain Control

Pain is a common problem for people with some types of cancer, especially when the cancer grows and presses against other organs and nerves. Pain may also be a side effect of treatment. However, pain can generally be relieved or reduced with prescription medicines or over-the-counter drugs as recommended by the doctor. Other ways to reduce pain, such as relaxation exercises, may also be useful. It is important for patients to report pain so that steps can be taken to help relieve it.

Rehabilitation

Rehabilitation is an important part of the overall cancer treatment process. The goal of rehabilitation is to improve a person's quality of life. The medical team, which may include doctors, nurses, a physical therapist, an occupational therapist, or a social worker, develops a rehabilitation plan to meet each patient's physical and emotional needs, helping the patient return to normal activities as soon as possible.

Patients and their families may need to work with an occupational therapist to overcome any difficulty in eating, dressing, bathing, using the toilet, or other activities. Physical therapy may be needed to regain strength in muscles and to prevent stiffness and swelling. Physical therapy

may also be necessary if an arm or leg is weak or paralyzed, or if a patient has trouble with balance.

Follow-up Care

It is important for people who have had cancer to continue to have examinations regularly after their treatment is over. Follow-up care ensures that any changes in health are identified, and if the cancer recurs, it can be treated as soon as possible. Checkups may include a careful physical exam, imaging procedures, endoscopy, or lab tests.

Between scheduled appointments, people who have had cancer should report any health problems to their doctor as soon as they appear.

Support for People with Cancer

Living with a serious disease is not easy. People with cancer and those who care about them face many problems and challenges. Having helpful information and support services can make it easier to cope with these problems.

Friends and relatives can be very supportive. Also, it helps many patients to discuss their concerns with others who have cancer. People with cancer often get together in support groups, where they can share what they have learned about coping with their disease and the effects of their treatment. It is important to keep in mind, however, that each person is different. Treatments and ways of dealing with cancer that work for one person may not be right for another—even if they both have the same kind of cancer. It is always a good idea to discuss the advice of friends and family members with the doctor.

People living with cancer may worry about caring for their families, keeping their jobs, or continuing daily activities.

C

Concerns about tests, treatments, hospital stays, and medical bills are also common. Doctors, nurses, and other members of the health-care team can answer questions about treatment, working, or other activities. Meeting with a social worker, counselor, or member of the clergy can be helpful to people who want to talk about their feelings or discuss their concerns. Often, a social worker can suggest resources for help with rehabilitation, emotional support, financial aid, transportation, or home care.

National Cancer Institute

Carpal tunnel syndrome (CTS) is an often debilitating condition that causes numbness and pain in the hand and wrist. Derived from the Greek word "karpos," meaning wrist, the carpal tunnel is a passageway into the hand for the median nerve (which provides sensory and motor function to the thumb, index, and middle fingers, and the side of the ring finger toward the thumb) and for nine tendons (which flex the fingers). As the fingers move, the tendons that control them ordinarily slide back and forth beside the bones and ligaments that form the corridor. CTS develops when the membrane that lubricates the tendons (the tendon sheath) becomes inflamed and swollen, thus pressing the median nerve against the carpal bones. Often both hands are affected.

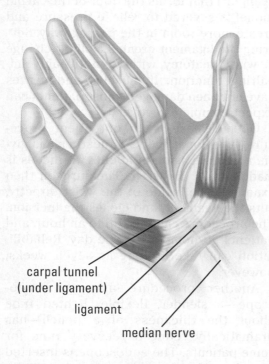

carpal tunnel
(under ligament)

ligament

median nerve

Carpal tunnel syndrome results from repeated pressure on the median nerve, which passes through a "tunnel" of bones and ligaments.

The disorder occurs most often among women between the ages of 30 and 60. A study showing an increased incidence of CTS among pregnant and menopausal women suggests that hormonal factors may play a role. Rheumatoid arthritis, which causes joint inflammation and deformity, is another commonly reported factor, as are diabetes mellitus and thyroid disease, among others.

Perhaps the most stressful actions implicated in CTS are wringing motions and the movements associated with playing a musical instrument, knitting, using power tools that vibrate, typing, using a computer mouse, and tightly gripping a steering wheel for long periods. Fortunately, using your hands wisely can help to prevent CTS. Furthermore, if CTS does occur, early diagnosis and treatment can generally ensure relief and full recovery.

Symptoms

Symptoms usually begin with tingling or numbness in the hand, often the dominant one, and are often first noticed at night. Pain, burning, weakness, and stiffness sometimes follow. All fingers except the pinky may be affected. You may find yourself shaking your hands and fingers frequently because they feel as if they are asleep, or you may notice yourself dropping things.

If you have any of these symptoms, rest your hands until they subside. You should also see your physician. Left untreated, CTS can lead to muscle atrophy and permanent nerve damage, and may cause pain throughout the length of the arm.

Diagnosis

If your physician suspects CTS, you may be referred to a specialist, who will perform tests to assess the extent of your sensory and motor loss. A nerve conduction velocity test pinpoints how much the median nerve is

C

Preventing CTS

If you use your hands for prolonged, repetitive tasks, or if you have sprained your wrist, have arthritis, or are menopausal, you may be at increased risk of developing carpal tunnel syndrome (CTS). The following tips may help reduce this risk:

- If your hand hurts during a repetitive activity, give it a rest. Even if hand pain hasn't occurred, take short preventive breaks from hand-intensive work every half hour or so.
- Lift objects with your whole hand and all your fingers, not just your thumb and index finger.

- Don't hold your hands in the same position or keep your wrists flexed for long periods of time.
- Don't prop your head on your hands when you are sleeping.
- When typing, use a light stroke and do not rest your wrists on the keyboard or desk. Your fingers should be lower than your wrists; a pad on which to rest your wrists can be useful.
- When driving, hold the steering wheel gently.

pinched; electromyography (EMG) assesses motor control; x-rays may be taken to rule out a bone fracture or arthritis as the cause of your symptoms.

Treatment

The goal of initial treatment is to decrease the inflammation in the carpal tunnel through rest or drug therapy. The wrist may be immobilized with a lightweight plastic splint that still permits use of the hand for most daily tasks. Your physician will probably recommend wearing the splint all day. However, some patients get relief just by wearing the splint at night.

Nonsteroidal anti-inflammatory drugs (NSAIDS), such as aspirin and ibuprofen, may also ease pain. If this approach is unhelpful, injection of a corticosteroid drug into the carpal tunnel may decrease swelling. Results of these injections are often dramatic, but the duration of relief is limited.

Surgery

If these measures fail and symptoms persist for several months, you may need to undergo surgery—especially if muscle and nerve fibers have deteriorated. In the

standard practice, called open release, the thick, fibrous band of tissue (transverse ligament) that forms the floor of the carpal tunnel is severed to relieve pressure and create more room in the passageway. Severing the ligament creates a slight change in wrist anatomy without noticeably impairing function. If muscles and nerves have not been damaged, most patients can expect complete recovery.

Open release is an outpatient procedure. A regional or local anesthesia is given, and an incision of about two inches is made across the wrist. The surgeon then examines the inside of the wrist directly, cuts the ligament, and closes the incision. The procedure can take up to an hour, and patients go home the same day. Rehabilitation can take as long as seven weeks, however.

Another procedure using an endoscope—a slender, flexible, lighted tube about the thickness of a pencil—has dramatically reduced recovery time for some patients. The endoscope is inserted into the wrist through an incision slightly larger than the instrument. A miniaturized camera and knife are then inserted into the carpal tunnel through or alongside the endoscope. The surgeon examines and severs the ligament while controlling the knife from outside the wrist and watching the procedure on a video monitor that receives an image from the camera.

Endoscopy, an outpatient procedure that lasts about an hour, can be performed under general or a regional anesthetic. Its chief advantage is that less tissue is disturbed, cutting recuperation time in half.

Endoscopy is not for everyone with CTS, however. People with arthritis or limited wrist mobility should have the traditional open-release procedure because these conditions require maximum visibility for the surgeon.

Complications from both techniques include the possibility of an incompletely severed transverse ligament and damage to nerves and arteries. The risk of these complications is less than 1 percent with open release, but rises to between 2 and 8 percent with endoscopy. The method you select depends on how much time you have for recovery, what margin of risk you are comfortable with, and which procedure your physician favors.

C

C

A cataract is a cloudy area in the lens. Located in the front of the eye behind the pupil, the lens is ordinarily clear. Under normal circumstances, light passes through it and converges on the retina, which senses the light and passes electrical information down the optic nerve in the back of the eye to the brain.

Once a cataract forms and begins to progress, the lens becomes increasingly opaque. The more opaque it becomes, the more the cataract interferes with the transmission and convergence of light. Light rays are no longer precisely focused but instead are scattered before reaching the retina. As a result, the ability to perceive fine detail gradually declines. Eventually, symptoms may become highly disabling.

Cataracts can occur at any age but are most common later in life. They are present in 50 percent of people age 65 to 74 and in 70 percent of those age 75 and older. However, not all cataracts affect vision significantly or require treatment. The severity and exact nature of symptoms depend on the type and density of the cataract.

Types of Cataracts

The three common types of cataracts are defined by their location in the lens:

- A cataract in the central part of the lens, the nucleus, is a nuclear cataract.
- A cortical cataract is located in the cortex, which surrounds the center of the lens.
- A posterior subcapsular cataract is located at the back of the lens in the rear of the lens capsule.

More than one type is often present in the same eye. Posterior subcapsular cataracts are most likely to occur in younger people and may be associated with prolonged use of corticosteroids (such as prednisone), inflammation, or trauma.

The extent of visual damage and how quickly vision is impaired depend not only on the size and density of the cataract, but also its location in the lens. For example, a cataract in the periphery of the cortex has little effect on vision because it does not interfere with the passage of light through

normal eye

eye with cataract

poorly focused light

cataract in lens

A normal clear lens (top) allows light to pass through unobstructed. When a cataract forms, the clouded lens (middle) diffuses incoming light (bottom), and results in blurred vision.

the center of the lens, while a dense nuclear cataract causes severe blurring of vision.

Causes

The cause of most cataracts is unknown, but at least two factors associated with aging contribute to their development. Clumping (aggregation) of lens proteins leads to scattering of light and a decrease in the transparency of the lens. In addition, clouding of the lens results from the accumulation of a yellow-brown pigment caused by the breakdown of lens proteins.

Certain chemical changes also take place. These include a reduced uptake of oxygen in the lens and alterations in its water content. Amounts of calcium and sodium increase, while potassium, vitamin C, and protein levels decrease. Lenses with cataracts appear to be deficient in glutathione, an antioxidant. (Studies of medications or vitamins to alter the levels of these substances in the lens have not produced promising results, however.) Currently, there is no effective drug therapy to prevent cataract formation.

In addition, cigarette smoking, medications such as steroids, eye injuries, sunlight, diabetes, and even obesity and excessive sodium intake, can increase the risk of cataracts.

Symptoms

The most common symptom of cataracts is a painless blurring of vision. Everything becomes dimmer, as if glasses always need cleaning. Most often, both eyes are affected, though one eye is usually more compromised than the other. The impairment usually progresses at a similar rate in the two eyes. Changes can occur in a matter of months or almost imperceptibly over many years. Occasionally, double vision occurs because of differences in the degree of opacity in one part of the lens, as compared with another. Other possible symptoms of cataracts are the need for increasingly frequent changes in prescriptions for glasses and noting a yellowish tinge to objects.

As a nuclear cataract develops, some people who previously needed reading glasses for presbyopia are able to read without them, a change referred to as second sight. Over time, however, progression of the cataract generally impairs vision further.

Individuals with cortical or posterior subcapsular cataracts often have worse vision in bright light. They may have problems with night driving because of the glare of oncoming headlights.

Prevention

It is not yet certain whether cataracts can be prevented. Wearing UV-light-blocking sunglasses and a hat with a wide brim will help reduce exposure of the eyes to UV radiation. The American National Standards Institute (ANSI) sets standards for sunglasses. Sunglasses that are labeled "special purpose" or "meets ANSI UV requirements" block at least 99 percent of all types of UV light. Alternately, people should look for a statement that glasses absorb "99 percent to 100 percent of all UV light" or "UV absorption up to 400 nm," which is equivalent to 100 percent UV light absorption.

Since smoking may be responsible for 20 percent of cataracts, smoking cessation is a vital step in cataract prevention.

Whether consuming particular foods or vitamin supplements, or taking medications, reduces the risk of cataracts is the subject of considerable debate. Trials of medications, such as aspirin or estrogen replacement therapy, showed no benefit or gave unclear results. However, antioxidant vitamins may help prevent cataracts. This possibility is based on the fact that normal chemical reactions in the eye produce unstable oxygen molecules, called free radicals, which over

C

Whether to Have Cataract Surgery

Immediate removal of a cataract is rarely necessary. Instead, deciding when to have the surgery almost always rests with the patient and is based on the effect of the cataract on daily living; the balance between the operation's benefits and risks; and the presence of other medical conditions that might affect the outcome.

Answers to the following questions may suggest a cataract is interfering with daily life, and that surgery might be beneficial.

- Am I having trouble performing my job duties because I cannot see clearly? Do I have to strain to read computer screens?
- Am I constantly squinting?

- Do visual limitations inhibit my participation in activities I enjoy—such as reading, watching TV, or going out at night with friends?
- Does glare from the sun or car headlights interfere with or prevent me from driving?
- Am I fearful of bumping into something or falling because of my eyesight?
- Do I need help performing daily activities because of my vision? Could I be more independent if my vision were improved?
- Am I becoming increasingly nearsighted? Despite frequent prescription changes, do I still have trouble seeing with my glasses?
- Does my eyesight bother me all the time? In addition, you should discuss the possible benefits and risks of surgery with your physician.

time can damage various components of the lens. Protection against these free radicals by antioxidants may prevent their harmful effects. Abundant in fruits and vegetables, antioxidants include beta-carotene, vitamin C, and selenium. Some studies have found that high intakes of antioxidants may reduce the incidence of cataracts; however, more evidence is needed before a recommendation can be made.

Nonsurgical Treatment

Currently, no nonsurgical treatment cures or slows the development of cataracts. Some nonsurgical treatments may improve vision in the short term, however. One option is mydriatic eye drops to dilate the pupil and allow more light to reach the retina, but the resultant glare may be unacceptable. Glasses, contact lenses, strong bifocals, or magnifying lenses may improve vision in the early stages of cataracts. (Frequent changes in prescriptions for glasses also may help.)

Fortunately, fewer than 15 percent of people with cataracts have visual problems severe enough to require surgery.

Surgical Treatment

Cataract surgery involves removing the clouded lens and inserting an artificial lens implant, known as an intraocular lens (IOL). The IOL restores the ability of the eye to focus light on the retina accurately, thus minimizing problems with image size, glare, and depth perception. Surgical removal of a cataract, along with implantation of an intraocular lens, is the most frequently performed surgery in people over age 65. Cataract surgery is considered by many doctors to be the most effective surgical procedure in all of medicine—and one of the safest.

About 90 percent of cataract operations are now performed with a local anesthetic on an outpatient basis. The operation usually takes less than an hour. If both eyes are affected, in almost all cases they are operated on one at a time, with at least several weeks—and more often months—separating the two operations. There are several reasons for the delay. First, it gives the first eye time to recover. Second, should any complications become evident, the surgeon might do the second operation differently. Finally, since the goal of a cataract operation is to reduce visual limitations, the delay allows the patient and surgeon to determine whether the results with the first eye are good enough to eliminate the need for a second operation.

If the eye is normal except for the cataract, surgery will improve vision in about 95 percent of cases; 85 percent of patients undergoing cataract surgery attain vision of at least 20/40—good enough to drive a car—one year after the operation. Significant postsurgical complications occur in only 1 percent to 2 percent of operations (page 196).

Proper preparation before surgery will ease recovery after cataract removal. Patients should review what to expect with their ophthalmologist, including how to protect the eye, what medications are needed, what activities are permitted, when to return for follow-up visits, the signs of complications, and how to seek emergency care. Specific written instructions should be provided.

Types of Cataract Surgery

Three different surgical techniques are used to treat cataracts. In rare instances, such as in patients who also suffer from glaucoma, a fourth procedure—intracapsular cataract surgery—is used.

Extracapsular surgery. In extracapsular surgery, the surgeon removes the opacified portion of the lens. The posterior capsule is left intact. Extracapsular surgery is now by far the most common type of cataract operation, because it minimizes trauma to the eye and is associated with fewer postoperative complications than intracapsular procedures.

Phacoemulsification. This type of extracapsular surgery is performed with an ultrasonic device that nearly liquifies the nucleus and cortex so that they can be removed by suction through a tube. Phacoemulsification surgery permits an even smaller incision than the other techniques, which facilitates healing of the surgical wound. Like standard extracapsular surgery, this procedure leaves the posterior capsule intact and is associated with a lower rate of postoperative complications than intracapsular surgery.

Laser surgery. The Food and Drug Administration (FDA) has approved a new laser device as an alternative to phacoemulsification for the removal of cataracts. The *Dodick Laser PhotoLysis System* allows surgeons to remove cataracts using an incision approximately half the size of the one needed for phacoemulsification.

Lens Replacement

In order to see clearly, the refractive power of the lens must be replaced so that light can focus onto the retina. The three most common replacement options are intraocular lens implants, glasses, and contact lenses.

Intraocular lenses. By far the most frequent approach to lens replacement is an intraocular lens implant at the time of cataract surgery. Plastic lens implants are placed either just in front of the iris (anterior implants) or just behind it (posterior implants); most of the many current brands of implants are posterior ones. These rest against the back wall of the lens capsule, with plastic loops jutting out to hold the implant in position behind the iris. Posterior implants are typically used only in conjunction with extracapsular surgery. Intraocular lens implants have been in wide use since 1977, and most ophthalmologists consider them to be very safe.

Lens implantation may not be possible in individuals with certain eye diseases; some

C

active cases of proliferative diabetic retinopathy; and rubeosis iridis (new blood vessel growth on the iris, usually in people with diabetes). Most patients with open-angle glaucoma or elevated intraocular pressure can receive an artificial lens; for those who can, posterior implants are usually preferred.

Types of lens implants. The most common type of lens implant is the single-focus lens. Unlike the natural lens of the eye, a single-focus lens cannot alter its shape to bring objects at different distances into focus. As a result, the surgeon generally selects a lens that will provide good distance vision, and the person wears reading glasses for near vision. Alternately, the surgeon can correct one eye for distance and the other for near vision; this is called monovision.

The first multifocal lens implant, which provides both distance and near vision, was approved by the U.S. Food and Drug Administration (FDA) several years ago. Multifocal lenses contain several concentric rings, each of which permits the user to see at a different distance. Although these lenses reduce the need for eyeglasses, many people still have to wear glasses for certain tasks. In addition, multifocal lenses can cause visual side effects such as glare and halos.

The newest type of lens implant, called an accommodating lens, contains a hinge that allows for both distance and near vision.

Many of the single-focus and all of the multifocal lens implants available today are foldable. Foldable implants, which have been available since the early 1990s, are made from silicone, acrylic, or hydrogel, and can be inserted into a smaller surgical opening than that required for other types of implants. The smaller opening may cause less trauma to the eye and lead to quicker recovery.

Once inserted, lens implants require no care of any kind. Like any device, however, complications can occur. The most common complication is glare or reduced vision when the lens is not aligned with the pupil.

Glasses. Although glasses are effective, the ones needed for lens replacement are heavy and awkward. They magnify objects by about 25 percent, causing them to appear closer than they actually are—a somewhat disorienting sensation. Because of the thickness and curvature of their lenses, cataract glasses also magnify objects unequally and so have a distorting effect. In addition, they tend to limit peripheral vision. Given these problems, cataract glasses are practical only in people who have had lenses removed from both eyes or will have surgery on the second eye relatively soon. Since the glasses are not fitted until four to eight weeks after surgery, patients who choose this option must purchase a temporary pair of glasses or borrow a pair from the ophthalmologist's office.

Contact lenses. Contact lenses provide patients with almost normal vision. Their major drawback is that some people have difficulty handling, removing, and cleaning them. The frequent handling of contact lenses may also increase the long-term risk of eye infections. Because the patient must be able to see when the contacts are not in place, a pair of cataract glasses is also necessary. Both the contacts and glasses can be prescribed four to eight weeks after surgery.

Possible Complications of Surgery
Though cataract surgery is associated with a low rate of complications, problems may arise, especially in older adults or in those with general health problems. Patients should contact their doctor if any of the following symptoms develop during recovery:
- Swelling
- Unusual pain or aching
- Persistent redness
- Bleeding
- Excessive tearing or discharge

What to Expect After Surgery

Vision is initially blurry following cataract surgery; however, as the eye heals, vision gradually improves. In addition, most patients have minimal discomfort after the surgery. Some redness, scratchiness, or slight morning discharge (which can be gently wiped away with a warm washcloth) may be present during the first few days after surgery. It is also common to see a few black spots or shapes (floaters) drifting through the field of vision. Most people must wear a protective patch over the eye for 24 hours. Then, glasses are worn during the day to avoid eye trauma. For several days to a few weeks, an eye shield is used at night to prevent accidentally rubbing or poking the eye while asleep. Because the eye that has been operated on may be more sensitive to sunlight, patients should initially wear sunglasses while outside during the day.

- Any sudden visual change
- Seeing many bright flashes of light
- Nausea, vomiting, or excessive coughing

In up to 20 percent of extracapsular surgeries, the posterior capsule of the lens subsequently becomes cloudy and causes visual difficulties similar to those created by the original cataract. Laser treatment can correct this problem but increases the risk of macular edema and retinal detachment (risk of the latter rises fourfold).

A small minority of patients develop an infection of the vitreous humor (the gel-like substance that fills the back of the eyeball behind the lens)—called endophthalmitis—following surgery. Patients who notice an increasingly red eye, blurred vision, and pain should see their ophthalmologist promptly. Typically, this condition can be treated with antibiotics and removal of some of the vitreous humor. A chronic low-grade endophthalmitis can also occur long after surgery but, fortunately, is very uncommon.

Full recovery is considered to be the point when the eye is completely healed and vision has stabilized.

Laser Treatment Following Surgery

A YAG (yttrium, aluminum, and garnet) laser is used if vision is blurred by clouding of the remaining (posterior) portion of the lens capsule following extracapsular surgery. The YAG laser creates a hole in the posterior capsule by focusing a burst of energy on it. Vision clears promptly if the blurring is related to capsular opacification. The procedure may be associated with increased rates of complications after cataract surgery. So, just as the initial decision to have cataract surgery is based on balancing possible risks and benefits, similar issues are weighed prior to treatment with YAG.

C

The cervix is the lower, narrow part of the uterus (womb). The uterus, a hollow, pear-shaped organ, is located in a woman's lower abdomen, between the bladder and the rectum. The cervix forms a canal that opens into the vagina, which leads to the outside of the body.

Cancer of the cervix also may be called cervical cancer. Like most cancers, it is named for the part of the body in which it begins. Cancers of the cervix also are named for the type of cell in which they begin. Most cervical cancers are squamous cell carcinomas. Squamous cells are thin, flat cells that form the surface of the cervix.

When cancer spreads to another part of the body, the new tumor has the same kind of abnormal cells and the same name as the original (primary) cancer. For example, if cervical cancer spreads to the bones, the cancer cells in the bones are cervical cancer cells. The disease is called metastatic cervical cancer (it is not bone cancer).

Cancer of the cervix is different from cancer that begins in other parts of the uterus and requires different treatment. The most common type of cancer of the uterus begins in the endometrium, the lining of the organ.

Precancerous Conditions and Cancer of the Cervix

Cells on the surface of the cervix sometimes appear abnormal but not cancerous. Scientists believe that some abnormal changes in cells on the cervix are the first step in a

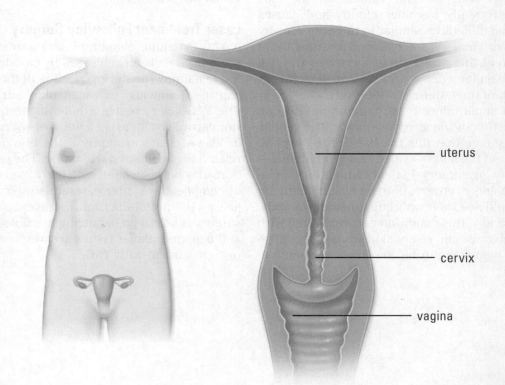

uterus

cervix

vagina

The cervix, at the far end of the vaginal canal, marks the opening of the uterus. Most cervical cancers are squamous cell carcinomas that form on the surface of the cervix.

series of slow changes that can lead to cancer years later. That is, some abnormal changes are precancerous; they may become cancerous with time.

Over the years, doctors have used different terms to refer to abnormal changes in the cells on the surface of the cervix. One term now used is squamous intraepithelial lesion (SIL). (The word lesion refers to an area of abnormal tissue; intraepithelial means that the abnormal cells are present only in the surface layer of cells.) Changes in these cells can be divided into two categories:

- **Low-grade SIL** refers to early changes in the size, shape, and number of cells that form the surface of the cervix. Some low-grade lesions go away on their own. However, with time, others may grow larger or become more abnormal, forming a high-grade lesion. Precancerous low-grade lesions also may be called mild dysplasia or cervical intraepithelial neoplasia 1 (CIN 1). Such early changes in the cervix most often occur in women between the ages of 25 and 35 but can appear in other age groups as well.
- **High-grade SIL** means there is a large number of precancerous cells; they look very different from normal cells. Like low-grade SIL, these precancerous changes involve only cells on the surface of the cervix. The cells will not become cancerous and invade deeper layers of the cervix for many months, perhaps years. High-grade lesions may also be called moderate or severe dysplasia, CIN 2 or 3, or carcinoma in situ. They develop most often in women between the ages of 30 and 40 but can occur at other ages as well.

If abnormal cells spread deeper into the cervix or to other tissues or organs, the disease is then called cervical cancer, or invasive cervical cancer. It occurs most often in women over the age of 40.

Cause and Prevention

By studying large numbers of women all over the world, researchers have identified certain risk factors that increase the chance that cells in the cervix will become abnormal or cancerous. They believe that, in many cases, cervical cancer develops when two or more risk factors act together.

Research has shown that women who began having sexual intercourse before age 18 and women who have had many sexual partners have an increased risk of developing cervical cancer. Women are also at increased risk if their partners began having sexual intercourse at a young age, have had many sexual partners, or were previously married to women who had cervical cancer.

Scientists do not know exactly why the sexual practices of women and their partners affect the risk of developing cervical cancer. However, research suggests that some sexually transmitted viruses can cause cells in the cervix to begin the series of changes that can lead to cancer. Women who have had many sexual partners or whose partners have had many sexual partners may have an increased risk for cervical cancer at least in part because they are more likely to get a sexually transmitted virus.

Scientists are studying the effects of sexually transmitted human papillomaviruses (HPVs). Some sexually transmitted HPVs cause genital warts (condylomata acuminata). In addition, scientists believe that some of these viruses may cause the growth of abnormal cells in the cervix and may play a role in cancer development. They have found that women who have HPV or whose partners have HPV have a higher-than-average risk of developing cervical cancer. However, most women who are infected with HPV do not develop cervical cancer, and the virus is not present in

C

all women who have this disease. For these reasons, scientists believe that other factors act together with HPVs. For example, the genital herpes virus also may play a role. Further research is needed to learn the exact role of these viruses and how they act together with other factors in the development of cervical cancer.

Smoking also increases the risk of cancer of the cervix, although it is not clear exactly how or why. The risk appears to increase with the number of cigarettes a woman smokes each day and with the number of years she has smoked.

Women whose mothers were given the drug diethylstilbestrol (DES) during pregnancy to prevent miscarriage are also at increased risk. (This drug was used for this purpose from about 1940 to 1970.) A rare type of vaginal and cervical cancer has been found in a small number of women whose mothers used DES.

Several reports suggest that women whose immune systems are weakened are more likely than others to develop cervical cancer. For example, women who have the human immunodeficiency virus (HIV), which causes AIDS, are at increased risk. Also, organ transplant patients, who receive drugs that suppress the immune system to prevent rejection of the new organ, are more likely than others to develop precancerous lesions.

Some researchers believe that there is an increased risk of cervical cancer in women who use oral contraceptives (the pill). However, scientists have not found that the pill directly causes cancer of the cervix. This relationship is hard to prove because the two main risk factors for cervical cancer—intercourse at an early age and multiple sex partners—may be more common among women who use the pill than among those who do not. Still, oral contraceptive labels warn of this possible

risk and advise women who use them to have yearly Pap tests.

Some research has shown that vitamin A may play a role in stopping or preventing cancerous changes in cells like those on the surface of the cervix. Further research with forms of vitamin A may help scientists learn more about preventing cancer of the cervix.

At present, early detection and treatment of precancerous tissue remain the most effective ways of preventing cervical cancer. Women should talk with their doctors about an appropriate schedule of checkups. The doctor's advice will be based on such factors as the women's age, medical history, and risk factors.

Early Detection

If all women had pelvic exams and Pap tests regularly, most precancerous conditions would be detected and treated before cancer develops. That way, most invasive cancers could be prevented. Any invasive cancer that does occur would likely be found at an early, curable stage.

In a pelvic exam, the doctor checks the uterus, vagina, ovaries, fallopian tubes, bladder, and rectum. The doctor feels these organs for any abnormality in their shape or size. A speculum is used to widen the vagina so that the doctor can see the upper part of the vagina and the cervix.

The Pap test is a simple, painless test to detect abnormal cells in and around the cervix. A woman should have this test when she is not menstruating; the best time is between 10 and 20 days after the first day of her menstrual period. For about 2 days before a Pap test, she should avoid douching or using spermicidal foams, creams, or jellies or vaginal medicines (except as directed by a physician), which may wash away or hide any abnormal cells.

Screening for Cervical Cancer

All women over age 50 should have a Pap smear every 1 to 3 years. Many women believe that cervical cancer only occurs in young women, but it may develop at any age, and regular Pap smears are an important tool for catching the disease in its early, treatable stages. (The test may also occasionally help to detect vaginal or endometrial cancer.) While some experts advise that women over 65 who have had three normal Pap results in a row can be tested every three years, we recommend annual screening for most women. Three-year intervals may be appropriate, however, for those who have had a hysterectomy (surgical removal of the uterus, including the cervix). Testing should be more frequent if the hysterectomy was performed due to a precancerous condition or for cancer, or if the woman has a family history of uterine or endometrial cancer. In addition, a Pap smear is essential whenever unexplained vaginal bleeding occurs, especially after menopause.

The Editors

A Pap test can be done in a doctor's office or a health clinic. A wooden scraper (spatula) and/or a small brush is used to collect a sample of cells from the cervix and upper vagina. The cells are placed on a glass slide and sent to a medical laboratory to be checked for abnormal changes.

The way of describing Pap test results is changing. The newest method is the Bethesda System. Changes are described as low-grade or high-grade SIL. Many doctors believe that the Bethesda System provides more useful information than an older system, which uses numbers ranging from class 1 to class 5. (In class 1, the cells in the sample are normal, while class 5 refers to invasive cancer.) Women should ask their doctor to explain the system used for their Pap test.

Women should have regular checkups, including a pelvic exam and a Pap test, if they are or have been sexually active or if they are age 18 or older. Those who are at increased risk of developing cancer of the cervix should be especially careful to follow their doctor's advice about checkups. (For a discussion of risk factors for cervical cancer see the "Cause and Prevention" section on page 199.) Women who have had a hysterectomy (surgery to remove the uterus, including the cervix) should ask their doctor's advice about having pelvic exams and Pap tests.

Women ages 65 and older account for nearly 25 percent of all cervical cancer cases and 41 percent of cervical cancer deaths in the United States, but they have much lower screening rates than younger women. In a 1994 government survey, 57.3 percent of women ages 65 and older said that they had had a Pap test in the past three years, compared to 81.1 percent of younger women.

Symptoms

Precancerous changes of the cervix usually do not cause pain. In fact, they generally do not cause any symptoms and are not detected unless a woman has a pelvic exam and a Pap test.

Symptoms usually do not appear until abnormal cervical cells become cancerous and invade nearby tissue. When this happens, the most common symptom is abnormal bleeding. Bleeding may start and stop between regular menstrual periods, or it may occur after sexual intercourse, douching, or

C

a pelvic exam. Menstrual bleeding may last longer and be heavier than usual. Bleeding after menopause also may be a symptom of cervical cancer. Increased vaginal discharge is another symptom of cervical cancer.

These symptoms may be caused by cancer or by other health problems. Only a doctor can tell for sure. It is important for a woman to see her doctor if she is having any of these symptoms.

Diagnosis

The pelvic exam and Pap test allow the doctor to detect abnormal changes in the cervix. If these exams show that an infection is present, the doctor treats the infection and then repeats the Pap test at a later time. If the exam or Pap test suggests something other than an infection, the doctor may repeat the Pap test and do other tests to find out what the problem is.

Colposcopy is a widely used method to check the cervix for abnormal areas. The doctor applies a vinegar-like solution to the cervix and then uses an instrument much like a microscope (called a colposcope) to look closely at the cervix. The doctor may then coat the cervix with an iodine solution (a procedure called the Schiller test). Healthy cells turn brown; abnormal cells turn white or yellow. These procedures may be done in the doctor's office.

The doctor may remove a small amount of cervical tissue for examination by a pathologist. This procedure is called a biopsy. In one type of biopsy, the doctor uses an instrument to pinch off small pieces of cervical tissue. Another method used to do a biopsy is called loop electrosurgical excision procedure (LEEP). In this procedure, the doctor uses an electric wire loop to slice off a thin piece of tissue. These types of biopsies may be done in the doctor's office using local anesthesia.

The doctor may also want to check inside the opening of the cervix, an area that cannot be seen during colposcopy. In a procedure called endocervical curettage (ECC), the doctor uses a curette (a small, spoon-shaped instrument) to scrape tissue from inside the cervical opening.

These procedures for removing tissue may cause some bleeding or other discharge. However, healing usually occurs quickly. Women also often experience some pain similar to menstrual cramping, which can be relieved with medicine.

These tests may not show for sure whether the abnormal cells are present only on the surface of the cervix. In that case, the doctor will then remove a larger, cone-shaped sample of tissue. This procedure, called conization or cone biopsy, allows the pathologist to see whether the abnormal cells have invaded tissue beneath the surface of the cervix. Conization also may be used as treatment for a precancerous lesion if the entire abnormal area can be removed. This procedure requires either local or general anesthesia and may be done in the doctor's office or in the hospital.

In a few cases, it may not be clear whether an abnormal Pap test or a woman's symptoms are caused by problems in the cervix or in the endometrium (the lining of the uterus). In this situation, the doctor may do dilation and curettage (D and C). The doctor stretches the cervical opening and uses a curette to scrape tissue from the lining of the uterus as well as from the cervical canal. Like conization, this procedure requires local or general anesthesia and may be done in the doctor's office or in the hospital.

Treating Precancerous Conditions

Treatment for a precancerous lesion of the cervix depends on a number of factors. These factors include whether the lesion is low or high grade, whether the woman wants to have children in the future, the woman's age and general health, and the preference of the woman and her doctor. A woman with a low-grade lesion may not need further treatment, especially if the abnormal area was completely removed during biopsy, but she should have a Pap test and pelvic exam regularly. When a precancerous lesion requires treatment, the doctor may use cryosurgery (freezing), cauterization (burning, also called diathermy), or laser surgery to destroy the abnormal area without harming nearby healthy tissue. The doctor also can remove the abnormal tissue by LEEP or conization. Treatment for precancerous lesions may cause cramping or other pain, bleeding, or a watery discharge.

In some cases, a woman may have a hysterectomy, particularly if abnormal cells are found inside the opening of the cervix. This surgery is more likely to be done when the woman does not want to have children in the future.

Staging

The choice of treatment for cervical cancer depends on the location and size of the tumor, the stage (extent) of the disease, the woman's age and general health, and other factors.

Staging is a careful attempt to find out whether the cancer has spread and, if so, what parts of the body are affected. Blood and urine tests are usually done. The doctor may also do a thorough pelvic exam in the operating room with the patient under anesthesia. During this exam, the doctor may do procedures called cystoscopy and proctosigmoidoscopy. In cystoscopy, the doctor looks inside the bladder with a thin, lighted instrument. Proctosigmoidoscopy is a procedure in which a lighted instrument is used to check the rectum and the lower part of the large intestine. Because cervical cancer may spread to the bladder, rectum, lymph nodes, or lungs, the doctor may also order x-rays or tests to check these areas. For example, the woman may have a series of x-rays of the kidneys and bladder, called an intravenous pyelogram. The doctor may also check the intestines and rectum using a barium enema. To look for lymph nodes that may be enlarged because they contain cancer cells, the doctor may order a CT or CAT scan, a series of x-rays put together by a computer to make detailed pictures of areas inside the body. Other procedures that may be used to check organs inside the body are ultrasonography and MRI.

Treatment

Most often, treatment for cervical cancer involves surgery and radiation therapy. Sometimes, chemotherapy or biological therapy is used. Patients are often treated by a team of specialists. The team may include gynecologic oncologists and radiation oncologists. The doctors may decide to use one treatment method or a combination of methods. Some patients take part in a clinical trial (research study) using new treatment methods. Such studies are designed to improve cancer treatment (see page 181).

Surgery is local therapy to remove abnormal tissue in or near the cervix. If the cancer is only on the surface of the cervix, the doctor may destroy the cancerous cells in ways similar to the methods used to treat precancerous lesions. If the disease has invaded deeper layers of the cervix but has not spread beyond the cervix, the doctor may perform an operation to remove the tumor but leave the uterus and the ovaries. In other cases, however, a woman may need to have a hysterectomy or may choose to have this surgery, especially if she is not planning to have children in the future. In this procedure, the doctor removes the entire uterus, including the cervix; sometimes the ovaries and fallopian tubes also are removed. In addition, the doctor may remove lymph nodes near the uterus to learn whether the cancer has spread to these organs.

Radiation therapy (or radiotherapy) uses high-energy rays to damage cancer cells and stop them from growing. Like surgery, radiation therapy is local therapy; the radiation can affect cancer cells only in the treated area. The radiation may come from a large machine (external radiation) or from radioactive materials placed directly into the cervix (implant radiation). Some patients receive both types of radiation therapy.

A woman receiving external radiation therapy goes to the hospital or clinic each day for treatment. Usually treatments are given five days a week for five to six weeks. At the end of that time, the tumor site very often gets an extra "boost" of radiation.

For internal or implant radiation, a capsule containing radioactive material is placed directly in the cervix. The implant puts cancer-killing rays close to the tumor while sparing most of the healthy tissue around it. It is usually left in place for one to three days, and the treatment may be repeated several times over the course of one to two weeks. The patient stays in the hospital while the implants are in place.

Chemotherapy is the use of drugs to kill cancer cells. It is most often used when cervical cancer has spread to other parts of the body. The doctor may use just one drug or a combination of drugs.

Anticancer drugs used to treat cervical cancer may be given by injection into a vein or by mouth. Either way, chemotherapy is systemic treatment, meaning that the drugs flow through the body in the bloodstream.

Chemotherapy is given in cycles: a treatment period followed by a recovery period, then another treatment period, and so on. Most patients have chemotherapy as an outpatient (at the hospital, at the doctor's office, or at home). Depending on which drugs are given and the woman's general health, however, she may need to stay in the hospital during her treatment.

Biological therapy is treatment using substances to improve the way the body's immune system fights disease. It may be used to treat cancer that has spread from the cervix to other parts of the body. Interferon is the most common form of biological therapy for this disease; it may be used in combination with chemotherapy. Most patients who receive interferon are treated as outpatients.

Side Effects of Treatment

It is hard to limit the effects of therapy so that only cancer cells are removed or destroyed. Because treatment also damages healthy cells and tissues, it often causes unpleasant side effects. The side effects of cancer treatment depend mainly on the type and extent of the treatment. Also, each patient reacts differently. Doctors and nurses can explain the possible side effects of treatment, and they can help relieve symptoms that may occur during and after treatment. It is important to let the doctor know if any side effects occur.

Surgery

Methods for removing or destroying small cancers on the surface of the cervix are similar to those used to treat precancerous lesions. Treatment may cause cramping or other pain, bleeding, or a watery discharge.

Hysterectomy is major surgery. For a few days after the operation, the woman may have pain in her lower abdomen. The doctor can order medicine to control the pain. A woman may have difficulty emptying her bladder and may need to have a catheter

Questions for Your Doctor

Here are some questions a woman may want to ask the doctor before surgery:

- What kind of operation will it be?
- How will I feel after the operation?
- If I have pain, how will you help me?
- When can I return to my normal activities?
- How will this treatment affect my sex life?

inserted into the bladder to drain the urine for a few days after surgery. She may also have trouble having normal bowel movements. For a period of time after the surgery, the woman's activities should be limited to allow healing to take place. Normal activities, including sexual intercourse, usually can be resumed in four to eight weeks.

Women who have had their uterus removed no longer have menstrual periods. However, sexual desire and the ability to have intercourse usually are not affected by hysterectomy. On the other hand, many women have an emotionally difficult time after this surgery. A woman's view of her own sexuality may change, and she may feel an emotional loss because she is no longer able to have children. An understanding partner is important at this time. Women may want to discuss these issues with their doctor, nurse, medical social worker, or member of the clergy.

Radiation Therapy
Patients are likely to become very tired during radiation therapy, especially in the later weeks of treatment. Resting is important, but doctors usually advise patients to try to stay as active as they can.

With external radiation, it is common to lose hair in the treated area and for the skin to become red, dry, tender, and itchy. There may be permanent darkening or "bronzing" of the skin in the treated area. This area should be exposed to the air when possible but protected from the sun, and patients should avoid wearing clothes that rub the treated area. Patients will be shown how to keep the area clean. They should not use any lotion or cream on their skin without the doctor's advice.

Usually, women are told not to have intercourse during radiation therapy or while an implant is in place. However, most women can have sexual relations within a few weeks after treatment ends. Sometimes, after radiation treatment, the vagina becomes narrower and less flexible, and intercourse may be painful. Patients may be taught how to use a dilator as well as a water-based lubricant to help minimize these problems.

Patients who receive external or internal radiation therapy may also have diarrhea and frequent, uncomfortable urination. The doctor can make suggestions or order medicines to control these problems.

Chemotherapy
The side effects of chemotherapy depend mainly on the drugs and the doses the patient receives. In addition, as with other types of treatment, side effects vary from person to person. Generally, anticancer drugs affect cells that divide rapidly. These include blood cells, which fight infection, help the blood to clot, or carry oxygen to all parts of the body. When blood cells are affected by anticancer drugs, patients are more likely to get infections, may bruise or bleed easily, and may have less energy. Cells in hair roots and cells that line the digestive tract also divide rapidly. When chemotherapy affects these cells, patients may lose their hair and may have other side effects, such as poor appetite, nausea, vomiting, or mouth sores. The

C

doctor may be able to give medicine to help with side effects. Side effects gradually go away during the recovery periods between treatments or after treatment is over.

Biological Therapy

The side effects caused by biological therapies vary with the type of treatment the patient receives. These treatments may cause flu-like symptoms such as chills, fever, muscle aches, weakness, loss of appetite, nausea, vomiting, and diarrhea. Sometimes patients get a rash, and they may bleed or bruise easily. These problems can be severe, but they gradually go away after the treatment stops.

Follow-up Care

Regular follow-up exams—including a pelvic exam, a Pap test, and other laboratory tests—are very important for any woman who has been treated for precancerous changes or for cancer of the cervix. The doctor will do these tests and exams frequently for several years to check for any sign that the condition has returned.

Cancer treatment may cause side effects many years later. For this reason, patients should continue to have regular checkups and should report any health problems that appear.

National Cancer Institute

Every day, the average person takes a minimum of 17,000 breaths—with virtually no effort. But 11 percent of Americans have chronic obstructive pulmonary disease (COPD), a progressive lung disorder that interferes with breathing.

COPD is an umbrella term used for both chronic bronchitis and emphysema, two conditions that interfere with gas exchange by blocking air flow. Although these conditions can occur alone, most people with COPD have both. Chronic, unremitting asthma may also be included under the COPD umbrella.

COPD is the fourth leading cause of death in the United States. Nearly everyone who develops the condition is—or has been—a long-term cigarette smoker. Although COPD is not curable, lifestyle measures and medication can slow disease progression and help sufferers breathe more easily.

Causes

The lungs take in oxygen, which the body requires for chemical reactions, and expels carbon dioxide, a waste product of these reactions. This exchange of gases takes place across membranes that line millions of tiny air sacs (alveoli) in the lungs. The alveoli are connected to the wind pipe (trachea) via successively smaller and smaller air passages called bronchi and bronchioli.

Chronic bronchitis is characterized by inflammation and scarring of the bronchial lining. The inflammation impedes air flow to and from the lungs and increases mucus production. Obstruction increases the work of breathing, which causes shortness of breath, while increased mucus production leads to coughing and frequent throat clearing.

Chronic bronchitis is more enduring than acute bronchitis. The diagnosis is made when a mucus-producing cough has been present most days of the month, for three months in each of two successive years, without any other explanation for the cough. There are more than 9 million cases of chronic bronchitis a year in the United States and more than 1,000 deaths. Chronic bronchitis is more prevalent in women than in men.

Emphysema develops when the loss of elasticity in the walls between air sacs causes them to weaken and break. This deterioration permits stale air to get trapped inside the sacs. When this happens, the lungs are unable to exchange the trapped air for fresh air effectively, and breathing becomes labored. About two million Americans have emphysema.

COPD is nearly always caused by exposure to environmental irritants, especially cigarette smoke. But industrial dust and workplace fumes may also play a role—especially when combined with smoking. In some people, heredity is a contributing factor.

When to See Your Doctor

Flare-ups require a visit to the doctor. Symptoms to watch for include:

- Any change in the amount, color, thickness, or stickiness of mucus
- Increased shortness of breath, coughing, or wheezing
- A general feeling of ill health
- Ankle swelling
- Forgetfulness, confusion, or slurring of speech
- Sleepiness, difficulty sleeping, or propping oneself up with pillows or sleeping in a chair to avoid shortness of breath
- Unexplained weight changes
- Morning headaches, dizzy spells, or restlessness

C

C

Symptoms

Signs of emphysema include shortness of breath, coughing, and wheezing. A mucus-producing cough and shortness of breath that persist for three months of the year during two years indicates chronic bronchitis.

At first, COPD symptoms may be apparent only during exertion. But eventually, they may develop even at rest. Sufferers have high rates of depression, malnutrition, and respiratory failure, and are susceptible to pneumonia, congestive heart failure, and pulmonary embolism (a blood clot carried to the lungs). Severe hot or cold air temperatures and poor air quality typically worsen symptoms.

Treatment

Treatment can prolong life, maintain independence, and make patients more comfortable. The goal is to promote general health, strengthen muscles (including those used for breathing), and reduce airway irritation and constriction. Lifestyle measures are the most important aspect of therapy. Everyone with COPD should stop smoking and reduce exposure to airborne toxins whenever possible.

Also key are pulmonary exercises to strengthen the muscles used for breathing and conventional exercises to condition the rest of the body. But patients should rest when they get tired and avoid exerting themselves when it's very hot, very cold, or very humid, or when air quality is poor. Certain breathing techniques can also ease symptoms and increase endurance (see text box on page 209).

Diet is another important aspect of care. Many sufferers find that eating is tiresome and that several small meals are more enjoyable than a few large ones. It may also be wise to include a liquid protein supplement in patients' daily meal plans. Also important is drinking plenty of fluids, especially water, to prevent dehydration.

Medications

Drug therapy includes taking bronchodilators to relax and open constricted airways. An anticholinergic such as ipratropium bromide (Atrovent) is generally tried first. If symptoms don't improve adequately, a beta2-agonist such as albuterol (Proventil, Ventolin), pirbuterol (Maxair), or salmeterol (Serevent) may be added. When inflammation or extreme sensitivity to irritants is a problem, a corticosteroid such as prednisone, beclomethasone (Beclovent, Vanceril), or flunisolide (AeroBid) may be tried. Theophylline is another option.

Although some of these medications can be taken orally, they are usually inhaled as aerosol spray through a device called a metered dose inhaler (MDI). MDIs deliver a highly concentrated amount of medication directly to the tissues that need it most. They also reduce the likelihood of systemic side effects. But proper technique is important, and up to 40 percent of older adults use their MDIs incorrectly. People who find it difficult to use an MDI can opt for a spacer, an attachment that eliminates the need to release the medication and breathe in simultaneously. But spacers are bulky and difficult for some people to hold. Another option is a device called a nebulizer, which vaporizes the medication. However, nebulizers are not portable and can only be used at home.

In addition to slowing disease progression and preserving lung function, proper treatment helps prevent flare-ups that can lead to further lung damage and functional decline. Such exacerbations usually occur in the winter and are generally caused by bacterial or viral infections. Flu and pneumonia vaccinations are recommended as preventive

Tips for Easier Breathing

Breath training helps control respiration rate, decreases the amount of energy required for breathing, and improves the position and function of respiratory muscles. A respiratory therapist can help sufferers practice these and other helpful techniques.

Diaphragmatic breathing. People who breathe properly use the diaphragm (the sheet of muscle between the lungs and the abdominal cavity) to breathe, while people with COPD typically use the muscles in the rib cage. Practice using the diaphragm: Lie on your back; place your hand on your abdomen and breathe. Your hand should move up on inhalation and down on exhalation. Practice for 20 minutes twice daily. Once you have mastered this skill while lying down, try to do it sitting up.

Forward-bending posture. Breathing while bending slightly forward from the waist relieves symptoms for some patients with severe COPD, possibly because the diaphragm has more room to expand.

Another helpful technique is pursed-lip breathing, which is described on page 303.

---

measures, and people with COPD should try to avoid others who have colds or the flu.

Oxygen Therapy

Supplemental oxygen is beneficial for people with severely impaired lung function and an abnormally low blood oxygen concentration. Using it typically improves sleep and mood, increases mental alertness and stamina, and allows users to carry out normal functions more efficiently. It also prevents heart failure, a frequent complication of severe COPD, and has been shown to prolong life.

Home oxygen can be taken in three ways—as compressed gas, as a liquid, or extracted from room air. Liquid oxygen is often used by active people because it is more portable than compressed gas, as larger amounts can be stored in smaller, more convenient containers. However, unlike gas, liquid oxygen evaporates, has a limited shelf life, and is expensive.

Oxygen can also be extracted from the environment using an electric device called an oxygen concentrator. About the size of an end table, the device isolates oxygen from the air and eliminates other gases. Oxygen concentration is less expensive and easier to maintain than other forms of oxygen. But concentrated oxygen is not for everyone. It is not portable, some units emit heat and noise, and the oxygen is too dilute for some patients. A backup method is necessary in case of power failure.

Surgery

Two types of surgery—lung volume reduction and lung transplantation—are available, but only for carefully selected patients. Lung volume reduction surgery removes the diseased portion of the lung. The procedure appears to prolong life in people who have emphysema that predominantly affects the upper lobes and low exercise capacity.

Lung transplantation is recommended only for certain patients with very severe, late-stage COPD.

C hronic pain afflicts an estimated 50 million Americans. Over time, such pain can cause a destructive physiologic response marked by fatigue, mood disorders, brain hormone abnormalities, muscle pain, and other physical and mental impairments. Like a grating noise that grows increasingly jarring with each repetition, chronic pain can set off a vicious cycle of stress and disability that ultimately raises a person's sensitivity to pain. Uncontrolled chronic pain can disrupt family life, result in the loss of employment and income, and lead to depression, isolation, and anxiety. It can even deprive some people of their sense of self. The key to breaking this damaging cycle is to treat pain early and effectively.

Types of Pain

Acute pain is caused by tissue damage, and its source is obvious, perhaps a bee sting or a burn. Although acute pain may be severe, it is typically short-lived. The natural healing powers of the body eventually repair the damage, and the pain fades away. Sometimes, a person may take a painkiller for a short period to relieve the pain until the healing and repair process is complete.

In contrast, chronic pain is persistent, and the nervous system continues to transmit pain impulses for months, even years. Inflammation or musculoskeletal injury lies at the root of some forms of chronic pain. Other people may have an ongoing source of pain, such as rheumatoid arthritis, cancer, or coronary artery disease. But in many cases, the original cause, perhaps a herniated disk or a tumor, has been successfully treated—yet the pain remains or even grows worse. This type of chronic pain, which is often out of proportion to the initial injury, arises from nerve damage, and is termed neuropathic pain.

Neuropathic pain can occur whenever nerves have been damaged. Until fairly recently, the term neuropathic pain was applied to only a few specific pain syndromes—postherpetic neuralgia, the intense pain that sometimes follows shingles; tic douloureux (trigeminal neuralgia), a condition marked by searing jolts of facial pain; and diabetic peripheral neuropathy, a form of nerve damage that leads to numbness and pain in the hands, feet, and legs. Now, it's clear that a much broader range of conditions come under the umbrella of neuropathic pain. Pain syndromes associated with amputation, mastectomy, spinal cord injury, migraine, multiple sclerosis, and Parkinson's disease are now thought to be examples of neuropathic pain. In addition, some scientists think that many cases of persistent low back pain may have a neuropathic component.

Chronic pain, whatever the source, triggers the release of cortisol and other hormones that can have negative effects on a person's immune system and psychological well-being. Recent research has also pinpointed some of the changes underlying chronic neuropathic pain. Apparently, our nervous systems are highly plastic; the nerve circuits that transmit pain impulses can "rewire" themselves after a nerve injury and lead to persistent pain. If the pain remains untreated, these wiring changes can become permanent and result in progressively more severe and widespread chronic pain.

Treatment

Chronic pain of an inflammatory or musculoskeletal origin can often be treated successfully with analgesics such as nonsteroidal anti-inflammatory drugs (NSAIDs) or opioids, perhaps combined with physical therapy or corrective surgery. For example, specific regimens have been developed to relieve the chronic pain of rheumatoid arthritis, an autoimmune inflammatory disorder, and severe osteoarthritis, a musculoskeletal disorder with some associated inflammation.

Neuropathic pain requires its own unique drug regimen. The following medications are primarily used to treat neuropathic pain:

Tricyclic antidepressants such as nortriptyline (Pamelor) and desipramine (Norpramin) can relieve neuropathic pain such as that caused by trigeminal neuralgia and postherpetic neuralgia. The antidepressants are effective even in absence of depression. It appears that the neurotransmitters serotonin and norepinephrine play a critical role in a pain-controlling pathway, and antidepressants evidently relieve pain by boosting serotonin and norepinephrine levels. Recent research also indicates that antidepressants can enhance the pain-relieving effects of opioids, permitting their use at lower doses.

Antiseizure drugs quell the pain signals discharged from injured sensory nerves in patients with neuropathic pain. Gabapentin (Neurontin) and lamotrigine (Lamictal) have proved effective in alleviating the pain associated with diabetic neuropathy, postherpetic neuralgia, and trigeminal neuralgia.

Opioids such as oxycodone (OxyContin), fentanyl (Duragesic), or morphine (MS Contin) are also used for neuropathic pain, often in combination with an antidepressant or antiseizure drug. Opioids may cause such side effects as drowsiness, respiratory depression, nausea, and constipation. When opioids are given in combination with antidepressants or antiseizure drugs, their dose can often be lowered and potential side effects minimized.

Many patients are wary of the potential for abuse with opioids. Despite the potential for abuse, drug addiction among chronic pain patients is very rare (less than one percent in people without a previous history of addiction). Addiction is probably uncommon in such patients because the opioids provide relief from pain and are given in a form that supplies a steady amount of medication throughout the day and doesn't produce euphoria.

Nondrug Treatments

Sometimes, the need for analgesics can be reduced with nondrug treatments. Exercise is by far the most effective measure. It helps keep joints and connective tissue strong and limber, improves sleep, fights depression, and maintains endurance. The greatest benefit is achieved from a comfortable level of regular, consistent activity.

Hot and cold applications are often effective, too. Cold packs can be applied to the painful area for 10 to 20 minutes at a time. Heat packs should actually be warm, not hot, and should not be used if inflammation is present. Alternating heat and cold treatments can be highly soothing. Always wrap packs in a towel or other protective layer and decrease the application time if you experience discomfort. People with diabetes or circulation problems should be extremely cautious and should not apply heat to the feet because of the possibility of injury.

Nontraditional therapies are another nondrug treatment option. Nontraditional techniques may be offered at comprehensive pain centers, or in a variety of other reputable settings, from senior centers to community hospitals. After reviewing the available literature, the National Institutes of Health (NIH) found some evidence in support of the following techniques:

Chiropractic manipulation: Manipulation may help relieve back and neck pain, especially if performed soon after symptoms arise. Manipulation should not be used on people with osteoporosis, disc herniation, rheumatoid arthritis, fractures, or cervical arthritis because of the possibility of injury.

Relaxation techniques: Certain techniques, such as guided meditation and deep breathing, may decrease the muscle tension that amplifies pain.

Transcutaneous electrical stimulation (TENS): Although results are variable and studies inconclusive, many patients report relief from TENS (brief pulses of electricity applied to the skin).

Biofeedback: Results are mixed, but biofeedback (using visual or auditory cues to help patients learn to influence their physical response to pain) may be most appropriate for headaches and low back pain.

Acupuncture: May be beneficial for osteoarthritis, headache, and low back pain. Based on the ancient Chinese procedure, acupuncture involves inserting fine needles into the skin at key points.

Cognitive and behavior therapy and group counseling: Sessions provide support and teach coping skills that may help relieve the anxiety that frequently accompanies pain.

Pain Clinics

Most pain can be relieved or greatly eased with proper management. Pain clinics offer the possibility of more effective pain control and improved quality of life for patients with inadequately controlled chronic pain. A multidisciplinary pain program is the best approach. Such programs typically involve the participation of psychiatrists, psychologists, anesthesiologists, neurosurgeons, neurologists, experts in physical rehabilitation and occupational therapy, orthopedic surgeons, and obstetrician/gynecologists.

Comprehensive pain management programs, such as those at major medical centers, have many components. In addition to drugs specifically targeted at pain relief, the medical management of people with chronic pain may include medications to promote better sleep, muscle relaxants to relieve muscle spasms, and antidepressants to relieve depression. Psychotherapy may also be employed to ease the depression, anxiety, diminished self-esteem, and isolation that often accompany intractable pain. Depending on the patient's specific problem, various other pain-relieving techniques may also be employed, such as spinal cord stimulation, nerve blocks, implantable pumps to deliver pain-relieving drugs directly into the spinal fluid, transcutaneous electrical nerve stimulation (TENS), and acupuncture.

Most pain clinics also offer various stress management techniques, such as relaxation therapy, biofeedback, and self-hypnosis, to help patients exert some control over their pain and its associated symptoms. Physical therapists may also evaluate patients for muscle and movement problems that contribute to the pain and develop exercise programs that can help ease their pain and increase their activity level.

Your doctor may be able to recommend a facility, or you can call the Commission on Accreditation of Rehabilitation Facilities (520-325-1044), which will provide a list of accredited programs near you. The American Pain Society (www.ampainsoc.org) can also provide information.

The liver, the largest internal organ in the body, is essential in keeping the body functioning properly. It removes or neutralizes poisons from the blood, produces immune agents to control infection, and removes germs and bacteria from the blood. It makes proteins that regulate blood clotting and produces bile to help absorb fats and fat-soluble vitamins. You cannot live without a functioning liver.

In cirrhosis of the liver, scar tissue replaces normal, healthy tissue, blocking the flow of blood through the organ and preventing it from working as it should. In the U. S., cirrhosis is the eighth leading cause of death by disease, killing about 25,000 people each year. Also, the cost of cirrhosis in terms of human suffering, hospital costs, and lost productivity is high.

Causes

Cirrhosis has many causes. In the United States, chronic alcoholism and hepatitis C are the most common causes.

Alcoholic liver disease. To many people, cirrhosis of the liver is synonymous with chronic alcoholism, but in fact, alcoholism is only one of the causes. Alcoholic cirrhosis usually develops after more than a decade of heavy drinking. The amount of alcohol that can injure the liver varies greatly from person to person. In women, as few as two to three drinks per day have been linked with cirrhosis and in men, as few as three to four drinks per day. Alcohol seems to injure the liver by blocking the normal metabolism of protein, fats, and carbohydrates.

Chronic hepatitis C. The hepatitis C virus ranks with alcohol as the major cause of

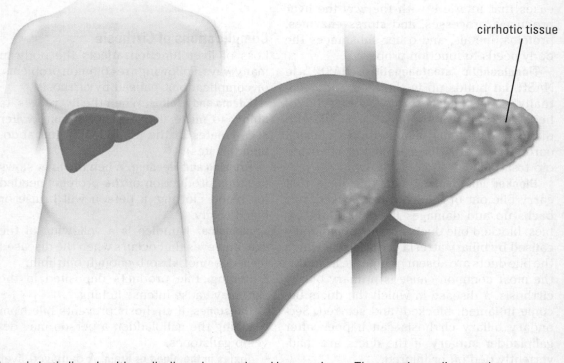

cirrhotic tissue

In a cirrhotic liver, healthy cells die and are replaced by scar tissue. The scar tissue disrupts the structure of the liver, which interferes with blood flow and the processing of nutrients, hormones, and toxins.

C

chronic liver disease and cirrhosis in the United States. Infection causes inflammation of and low grade damage to the liver that over several decades can lead to cirrhosis.

Chronic hepatitis B and D. The hepatitis B virus is probably the most common cause of cirrhosis worldwide, but in the United States and Western world it is less common. Hepatitis B, like hepatitis C, causes liver inflammation and injury that over several decades can lead to cirrhosis. The hepatitis D virus is another virus that infects the liver, but only in people who already have hepatitis B.

Autoimmune hepatitis. This type of hepatitis is caused by a problem with the immune system.

Inherited diseases. Alpha-1 antitrypsin deficiency, hemochromatosis, Wilson's disease, galactosemia, and glycogen storage diseases are among the inherited diseases that interfere with the way the liver produces, processes, and stores enzymes, proteins, metals, and other substances the body needs to function properly.

Nonalcoholic steatohepatitis (NASH). In NASH, fat builds up in the liver and eventually causes scar tissue. This type of hepatitis appears to be associated with diabetes, protein malnutrition, obesity, coronary artery disease, and corticosteroid treatment.

Blocked bile ducts. When the ducts that carry bile out of the liver are blocked, bile backs up and damages liver tissue. In babies, blocked bile ducts are most commonly caused by biliary atresia, a disease in which the bile ducts are absent or injured. In adults, the most common cause is primary biliary cirrhosis, a disease in which the ducts become inflamed, blocked, and scarred. Secondary biliary cirrhosis can happen after gallbladder surgery, if the ducts are inadvertently tied off or injured.

Drugs, toxins, and infections. Severe reactions to prescription drugs, prolonged exposure to environmental toxins, the parasitic infection schistosomiasis, and repeated bouts of heart failure with liver congestion can each lead to cirrhosis.

Symptoms

Many people with cirrhosis have no symptoms in the early stages of the disease. However, as scar tissue replaces healthy cells, liver function starts to fail and a person may experience the following symptoms:

- Exhaustion
- Fatigue
- Loss of appetite
- Nausea
- Weakness
- Weight loss

As the disease progresses, complications may develop. In some people, these may be the first signs of the disease.

Complications of Cirrhosis

Loss of liver function affects the body in many ways. Following are common problems, or complications, caused by cirrhosis.

Edema and ascites. When the liver loses its ability to make the protein albumin, water accumulates in the leg (edema) and abdomen (ascites).

Bruising and bleeding. When the liver slows or stops production of the proteins needed for blood clotting, a person will bruise or bleed easily.

Jaundice. Jaundice is a yellowing of the skin and eyes that occurs when the diseased liver does not absorb enough bilirubin.

Itching. Bile products deposited in the skin may cause intense itching.

Gallstones. If cirrhosis prevents bile from reaching the gallbladder, a person may develop gallstones.

Toxins in the blood or brain. A damaged liver cannot remove toxins from the blood, causing them to accumulate in the blood and eventually the brain. There, toxins can dull mental functioning and cause personality changes, coma, and even death. Signs of the buildup of toxins in the brain include neglect of personal appearance, unresponsiveness, forgetfulness, trouble concentrating, or changes in sleep habits.

Sensitivity to medication. Cirrhosis slows the liver's ability to filter medications from the blood. Because the liver does not remove drugs from the blood at the usual rate, they act longer than expected and build up in the body. This causes a person to be more sensitive to medications and their side effects.

Portal hypertension. Normally, blood from the intestines and spleen is carried to the liver through the portal vein. But cirrhosis slows the normal flow of blood through the portal vein, which increases the pressure inside it. This condition is called portal hypertension.

Varices. When blood flow through the portal vein slows, blood from the intestines and spleen backs up into blood vessels in the stomach and esophagus. These blood vessels may become enlarged because they are not meant to carry this much blood. The enlarged blood vessels, called varices, have thin walls and carry high pressure, and thus are more likely to burst. If they do burst, the result is a serious bleeding problem in the upper stomach or esophagus that requires immediate medical attention.

Problems in other organs. Cirrhosis can cause immune system dysfunction, leading to infection. Ascites (fluid) in the abdomen may become infected with bacteria normally present in the intestines, and cirrhosis can also lead to kidney dysfunction and failure.

Diagnosis

The doctor may diagnose cirrhosis on the basis of symptoms, laboratory tests, the patient's medical history, and a physical examination. For example, during a physical examination, the doctor may notice that the liver feels harder or larger than usual and order blood tests that can show whether liver disease is present.

If looking at the liver is necessary to check for signs of disease, the doctor might order a computerized axial tomography (CAT) scan, ultrasound, or a scan of the liver using a radioisotope (a harmless radioactive substance that highlights the liver). Or the doctor might look at the liver using a laparoscope, an instrument inserted through the abdomen that relays pictures back to a computer screen.

A liver biopsy will confirm the diagnosis. For a biopsy, the doctor uses a needle to take a small sample of tissue from the liver, then examines it for signs of disease.

Treatment

Liver damage from cirrhosis cannot be reversed, but treatment can stop or delay further progression and reduce complications. Treatment depends on the cause of cirrhosis and any complications a person is experiencing. For example, cirrhosis caused by alcohol abuse is treated by abstaining from alcohol. Treatment for hepatitis-related cirrhosis involves medications used to treat the different types of hepatitis, such as interferon for viral hepatitis and corticosteroids for autoimmune hepatitis. Cirrhosis caused by Wilson's disease, in which copper builds up in organs, is treated with medications to remove the copper. These are just a few examples—treatment for cirrhosis resulting from other diseases will depend on the underlying cause. In all cases, regardless of the cause, following a healthy diet and avoiding alcohol are essential because the body needs all the nutrients it can get, and alcohol will only lead to more liver damage.

C

Treatment will also include remedies for complications. For example, for ascites and edema, the doctor may recommend a low-sodium diet or the use of diuretics (drugs that remove fluid from the body). Antibiotics will be prescribed for infections, and various medications can help with itching. Protein causes toxins to form in the digestive tract, so eating less protein will help decrease the buildup of toxins in the blood and brain. The doctor may also prescribe laxatives to help absorb the toxins and remove them from the intestines.

For portal hypertension, the doctor may prescribe blood pressure medication such as a beta-blocker. If varices bleed, the doctor may either inject them with a clotting agent or perform a rubber-band ligation, which uses a special device to compress the varices and stop the bleeding.

When complications cannot be controlled or when the liver becomes so damaged from scarring that it completely stops functioning, a liver transplant is necessary. In liver transplantation surgery, a diseased liver is removed and replaced with a healthy one from an organ donor. About 80 to 90 percent of people survive liver transplantation. Survival rates have improved over the past several years because of drugs such as cyclosporine and tacrolimus, which suppress the immune system and keep it from attacking and damaging the new liver.

National Institute of Diabetes and Digestive and Kidney Diseases

The colon and rectum are parts of the body's digestive system, which removes nutrients from food and stores waste until it passes out of the body. Together, the colon and rectum form a long, muscular tube called the large intestine (also called the large bowel). The colon is the first six feet of the large intestine, and the rectum is the last eight to ten inches.

Cancer that begins in the colon is called colon cancer, and cancer that begins in the rectum is called rectal cancer. Cancers affecting either of these organs may also be called colorectal cancer.

Who's at Risk?

The exact causes of colorectal cancer are not known. However, studies show that the following risk factors increase a person's chances of developing colorectal cancer:

- **Age.** Colorectal cancer is more likely to occur as people get older. This disease is more common in people over the age of 50. However, colorectal cancer can occur at younger ages, even, in rare cases, in the teens.
- **Diet.** Colorectal cancer seems to be associated with diets that are high in fat and calories and low in fiber. Researchers are exploring how these and other dietary factors play a role in the development of colorectal cancer.

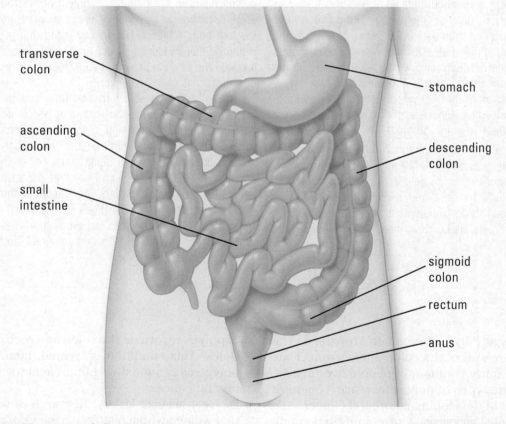

transverse colon

ascending colon

small intestine

stomach

descending colon

sigmoid colon

rectum

anus

About 75 percent of all colorectal cancers and polyps occur in the rectum or in the sigmoid portion of the colon—the segments that are easiest to examine and treat.

Can Fiber Prevent Colon Cancer?

The idea that fiber protects against colon cancer was first proposed many years ago when researchers found that Africans who ate high fiber diets had a low incidence of colon cancer. Since then dozens of studies have supported the protective role of fiber. There are plenty of reasons it might lower cancer risk: Fiber increases fecal bulk and may dilute potential cancer-causing substances; it reduces the time the stool spends in the intestine, which might limit the colon's exposure to carcinogens. It may also alter the intestinal environment in other beneficial ways. Yet, several recent studies have cast doubt on the theory that fiber protects against colon cancer.

- The well-known Nurses Health Study tracked more than 88,500 female nurses over a 16-year period, dividing the women into five groups based on their estimated intake of fiber. By the end of the study, 787 new cases of colon cancer occurred. Surprisingly, the women who ate the most fiber—nearly 25 grams per day—were just as likely to develop colon cancer and precancerous tumors as those who ate the least (about 10 grams per day).

- In a study published in 2000, researchers randomly assigned 1,429 men and women with a history of colon polyps (a pre-cancerous condition) to eat either a high-fiber or low-fiber wheat-bran supplement in addition to their ordinary diet. After three years, researchers found at least one polyp in about 50 percent of the participants in each group.

- In a well-designed study published in *The New England Journal of Medicine*, 2,079 people with a history of polyps were randomly assigned to eat either a low-fat, high-fiber diet (consisting largely of fruits and vegetables) or a low-fiber diet. After four years, a similar number of people in each group—about 39 percent—developed at least one recurrent polyp.

Indeed, such results are confusing, but realize they're far from definitive. First, the amount of fiber may have been insufficient to exert an effect. Subjects in the randomized studies may not have been followed long enough to detect whether the polyps found in the high-fiber subjects have the same potential for malignancy as the polyps from the low-fiber subjects. It's also possible that introducing dietary changes, such as increased fiber intake, later in adult life may be ineffective at reducing the risk of colon cancer.

While the relationship between fiber and colon cancer is unclear, a fiber-rich diet has other definite benefits. A diet high in soluble fiber can reduce elevated cholesterol levels, and fiber-rich foods can smooth out blood sugar spikes in people with diabetes. A high-fiber diet can also aid in preventing constipation, which reduces the risk of diverticulitis. Finally, foods rich in fiber—fruits, vegetables, legumes, and whole grains—are important sources of vitamins, minerals, and phytochemicals. *The Editors*

- **Polyps.** Polyps are benign growths on the inner wall of the colon and rectum. They are fairly common in people over age 50. Some types of polyps increase a person's risk of developing colorectal cancer.
- **Familial polyposis.** A rare, inherited condition, familial polyposis causes hundreds of polyps to form in the colon and rectum. Unless this condition is treated, familial polyposis is almost certain to lead to colorectal cancer.
- **Personal medical history.** Research shows that women with a history of cancer of the ovary, uterus, or breast have a somewhat

increased chance of developing colorectal cancer. Also, a person who has already had colorectal cancer may develop this disease a second time.

- **Family medical history.** First-degree relatives (parents, siblings, children) of a person who has had colorectal cancer are somewhat more likely to develop this type of cancer themselves, especially if the relative had the cancer at a young age. If many family members have had colorectal cancer, the chances increase even more.
- **Ulcerative colitis.** Ulcerative colitis is a condition in which the lining of the colon becomes inflamed. Having this condition increases a person's chance of developing colorectal cancer.

Having one or more of these risk factors does not guarantee that a person will develop colorectal cancer. It just increases the chances. People may want to talk with a doctor about these risk factors. The doctor may be able to suggest ways to reduce the chance of developing colorectal cancer and can plan an appropriate schedule for checkups.

Reducing the Risk

The National Cancer Institute supports and conducts research on the causes and prevention of colorectal cancer. Research shows that colorectal cancer develops gradually from benign polyps. Early detection and removal of polyps may help to prevent colorectal cancer. Studies are looking at smoking cessation, use of dietary supplements, use of aspirin or similar medicines, decreased alcohol consumption, and increased physical activity to see if these approaches can prevent colorectal cancer. Some studies suggest that a diet low in fat and calories and high in fiber can help prevent colorectal cancer.

Researchers have discovered that changes in certain genes (basic units of heredity) raise the risk of colorectal cancer. Individuals in families with several cases of colorectal cancer may find it helpful to talk with a genetic counselor. The genetic counselor can discuss the availability of a special blood test to check for a genetic change that may increase the chance of developing colorectal cancer. Although having such a genetic change does not mean that a person is sure to develop colorectal cancer, those who have the change may want to talk with their doctor about what can be done to prevent the disease or detect it early.

Early Detection

People who have any of the risk factors described under "Colorectal Cancer: Who's at Risk?" (page 217) should ask a doctor when to begin checking for colorectal cancer, what tests to have, and how often to have them. The doctor may suggest one or more of the tests listed below. These tests are used to detect polyps, cancer, or other abnormalities, even when a person does not have symptoms. Your health-care provider can explain more about each test.

- **A fecal occult blood test (FOBT)** is a test used to check for hidden blood in the stool. Sometimes cancers or polyps can bleed, and FOBT is used to detect small amounts of bleeding.
- **A sigmoidoscopy** is an examination of the rectum and lower colon (sigmoid colon) using a flexible, lighted instrument called a sigmoidoscope.
- **A colonoscopy** is an examination of the rectum and entire colon using a lighted instrument called a colonoscope.
- **A double contrast barium enema (DCBE)** is a series of x-rays of the colon and rectum. The patient is given an enema with a solution that contains barium, which outlines the colon and rectum on the x-rays.

C

Screening for Colorectal Cancer

Using some combination of screening tests at regular intervals can greatly enhance the likelihood that colorectal abnormalities will be detected before they cause symptoms or become life-threatening. According to guidelines endorsed by the U.S. Preventive Services Task Force, the American Cancer Society, the American Gastroenterological Association, and several other groups, screening should begin at age 50 with an annual fecal occult blood test (FOBT); a colonoscopy should be performed at that time and every five years to ten years thereafter. Other screening options include yearly FOB testing and a flexible sigmoidoscopy every five years or a barium enema every five to ten years. Which option you choose depends on your preferences as well as your doctor's, and the procedures available in your area.

People at increased risk for colorectal cancer should be screened at an earlier age (which varies depending on your particular medical history) and at more frequent intervals.

Finally, all patients with a positive DRE or FOBT should be thoroughly evaluated, preferably with colonoscopy. Any unexplained gastrointestinal symptoms—such as abdominal discomfort, bleeding, a change in bowel habits, weight loss, or decreased appetite—should be brought to a doctor's attention so that appropriate tests can be performed. *The Editors*

- **A digital rectal exam (DRE)** is an exam in which the doctor inserts a lubricated, gloved finger into the rectum to feel for abnormal areas.

Symptoms
Common signs and symptoms of colorectal cancer include:
- A change in bowel habits
- Diarrhea, constipation, or feeling that the bowel does not empty completely
- Blood (either bright red or very dark) in the stool
- Stools that are narrower than usual
- General abdominal discomfort (frequent gas pains, bloating, fullness, and/or cramps)
- Weight loss with no known reason
- Constant tiredness
- Vomiting

These symptoms may be caused by colorectal cancer or by other conditions. It is important to check with a doctor.

Diagnosis
To help find the cause of symptoms, the doctor evaluates a person's medical history. The doctor also performs a physical exam and may order one or more diagnostic tests.
- X-rays of the large intestine, such as the DCBE, can reveal polyps or other changes.
- A sigmoidoscopy lets the doctor see inside the rectum and the lower colon and remove polyps or other abnormal tissue for examination under a microscope.
- A colonoscopy lets the doctor see inside the rectum and the entire colon and remove polyps or other abnormal tissue for examination under a microscope.
- A polypectomy is the removal of a polyp during a sigmoidoscopy or colonoscopy.
- A biopsy is the removal of a tissue sample for examination under a microscope by a pathologist to make a diagnosis.

Staging

If the diagnosis is cancer, the doctor needs to learn the stage (or extent) of disease. Staging is a careful attempt to find out whether the cancer has spread and, if so, to what parts of the body. More tests may be performed to help determine the stage. Knowing the stage of the disease helps the doctor plan treatment. Listed below are descriptions of the various stages of colorectal cancer.

- **Stage 0.** The cancer is very early. It is found only in the innermost lining of the colon or rectum.
- **Stage I.** The cancer involves more of the inner wall of the colon or rectum.
- **Stage II.** The cancer has spread outside the colon or rectum to nearby tissue, but not to the lymph nodes. (Lymph nodes are small, bean-shaped structures that are part of the body's immune system.)
- **Stage III.** The cancer has spread to nearby lymph nodes, but not to other parts of the body.
- **Stage IV.** The cancer has spread to other parts of the body. Colorectal cancer tends to spread to the liver and/or lungs.
- **Recurrent.** Recurrent cancer means the cancer has come back after treatment. The disease may recur in the colon or rectum or in another part of the body.

Treatment

Treatment depends mainly on the size, location, and extent of the tumor, and on the patient's general health. Patients are often treated by a team of specialists, which may include a gastroenterologist, surgeon, medical oncologist, and radiation oncologist. Several different types of treatment are used to treat colorectal cancer. Sometimes different treatments are combined. Clinical trials (research studies) to evaluate new ways to treat cancer are an appropriate option for many patients with colorectal cancer.

Surgery to remove the tumor is the most common treatment for colorectal cancer. Generally, the surgeon removes the tumor along with part of the healthy colon or rectum and nearby lymph nodes. In most cases, the doctor is able to reconnect the healthy portions of the colon or rectum. When the surgeon cannot reconnect the healthy portions, a temporary or permanent colostomy is necessary. Colostomy, a surgical opening (stoma) through the wall of the abdomen into the colon, provides a new path for waste material to leave the body. After a colostomy, the patient wears a special bag to collect body waste. Some patients need a temporary colostomy to allow the lower colon or rectum to heal after surgery. About 15 percent of colorectal cancer patients require a permanent colostomy.

Chemotherapy is the use of anticancer drugs to kill cancer cells. Chemotherapy may be given to destroy any cancerous cells that may remain in the body after surgery, to control tumor growth, or to relieve symptoms of the disease. Chemotherapy is a systemic therapy, meaning that the drugs enter the bloodstream and travel through the body. Most anticancer drugs are given by injection directly into a vein (IV) or by means of a catheter, a thin tube that is placed into a large vein and remains there as long as it is needed. Some anticancer drugs are given in the form of a pill.

Radiation therapy, also called radiotherapy, involves the use of high-energy x-rays to kill cancer cells. Radiation therapy is a local therapy, meaning that it affects the cancer cells only in the treated area. Most often it is used in patients whose cancer is in the rectum. Doctors may use radiation therapy before surgery (to shrink a tumor so that

C

Managing the Discomfort of Colonoscopy

Whether colonoscopy is painful depends on how difficult it is to negotiate the curves of the colon. The colon is a long tube that folds around itself. If there are a lot of curves, your doctor has to get through them by dispensing air into the colon, which in some patients causes cramping and pain. (Air dilates the area so your doctor can negotiate the curves.)

Because doctors can't tell the shape of the colon before the procedure is done, it is difficult to predict who will experience pain. Every patient is given an intravenous mixture of a sedative and pain reliever before the procedure. If you've had a painful previous colonoscopy, your doctor may be able to give you a higher dose of sedative. Adequate preparation to clear the bowel in the days leading to the procedure also is important. Finally, expecting some degree of discomfort, or even pain, during colonoscopy may help better prepare you psychologically. *The Editors*

it is easier to remove) or after surgery (to destroy any cancer cells that remain in the treated area). Radiation therapy is also used to relieve symptoms. The radiation may come from a machine (external radiation) or from an implant (a small container of radioactive material) placed directly into or near the tumor (internal radiation). Some patients have both kinds of radiation therapy.

Biological therapy, also called immunotherapy, uses the body's immune system to fight cancer. The immune system finds cancer cells in the body and works to destroy them. Biological therapies are used to repair, stimulate, or enhance the immune system's natural anticancer function. Biological therapy may be given after surgery, either alone or in combination with chemotherapy or radiation treatment. Most biological treatments are given by injection into a vein (IV).

Clinical trials (research studies) to evaluate new ways to treat cancer are an appropriate option for many patients with colorectal cancer. In some studies, all patients receive the new treatment. In others, doctors compare different therapies by giving the promising new treatment to one group of patients and the usual (standard) therapy to another group. Research has led to many advances in the treatment of colorectal cancer. Through research, doctors explore new ways to treat cancer that may be more effective than the standard therapy.

Side Effects of Treatment

The side effects of cancer treatment depend on the type of treatment and may be different for each person. Most often the side effects are temporary. Doctors and nurses can explain the possible side effects of treatment. Patients should report severe side effects to their doctor. Doctors can suggest ways to help relieve symptoms that may occur during and after treatment.

Surgery causes short-term pain and tenderness in the area of the operation. Surgery for colorectal cancer may also cause temporary constipation or diarrhea. Patients who have a colostomy may have irritation of the skin around the stoma. The doctor, nurse, or enterostomal therapist can teach the patient how to clean the area and prevent irritation and infection.

Chemotherapy affects normal as well as cancer cells. Side effects depend largely on the specific drugs and the dose (amount of drug given). Common side effects of chemotherapy include nausea and vomiting, hair loss, mouth sores, diarrhea, and fatigue. Less often, serious side effects may occur, such as infection or bleeding.

Radiation therapy, like chemotherapy, affects normal as well as cancer cells. Side effects of radiation therapy depend mainly on the treatment dose and the part of the body that is treated. Common side effects of radiation therapy are fatigue, skin changes at the site where the treatment is given, loss of appetite, nausea, and diarrhea. Sometimes, radiation therapy can cause bleeding through the rectum (bloody stools).

Biological therapy may cause side effects that vary with the specific type of treatment. Often, treatments cause flu-like symptoms, such as chills, fever, weakness, and nausea.

Follow-up Care

Follow-up care after treatment for colorectal cancer is important. Regular checkups ensure that changes in health are noticed. If the cancer returns or a new cancer develops, it can be treated as soon as possible. Checkups may include a physical exam, a fecal occult blood test, a colonoscopy, chest x-rays, and lab tests. Between scheduled checkups, a person who has had colorectal cancer should report any health problems to the doctor as soon as they appear.

National Cancer Institute

C

Damage to heart muscle impairs its pumping ability and can lead to heart failure, also called congestive heart failure (CHF). The condition affects 4.7 million Americans; about 550,000 new cases of CHF are diagnosed each year.

Causes

The condition is most often due to atherosclerosis (page 234), a heart attack (page 376), or untreated high blood pressure (page 384). Other common causes include abnormalities in the heart valves and a virus-induced inflammatory process.

Symptoms

In most cases, initial symptoms are mild—for example, feeling overly tired after exertion—but eventually, even slight activity becomes exhausting. One of the common symptoms of CHF, shortness of breath (dyspnea), can even interfere with sleep. When lying down, fluid settling in the lungs may cause extreme shortness of breath and awaken an individual at night (paroxysmal nocturnal dyspnea). Sitting up relieves symptoms.

Severe shortness of breath, often accompanied by wheezing, coughing, and production of blood-tinged sputum, is a manifestation of pulmonary edema (marked buildup of fluid in the lungs), which generally requires immediate medical treatment. Older patients may experience lightheadedness or confusion.

The symptoms of CHF can come on quickly or gradually. Acute CHF may begin with sudden, unexpected, severe shortness of breath or even pulmonary edema.

Alternatively, the onset may begin slowly with unexplained fatigue, mild fluid retention (edema), slight shortness of breath, and excessive urination at night (nocturia).

The following system, developed by the New York Heart Association, is widely used to classify the severity of CHF:

Class I. Symptoms with greater than ordinary activity; no symptoms associated with ordinary activity;

Class II. Patient comfortable at rest; some limitation of activity;

Class III. Patient comfortable at rest; marked limitation of activity; and

Class IV. Discomfort with any physical activity; symptoms of CHF may be present at rest.

Diagnosis

The diagnosis of congestive heart failure is usually made from the combination of typical symptoms—such as fatigue and shortness of breath—and abnormal findings during a physical examination. Abnormal findings include:

- Crackling noises (rales) heard over the lungs with a stethoscope during inhalation (caused by excess fluid in the lungs)
- An enlarged heart in association with one or two extra heart sounds
- Engorgement of the neck veins; momentary indentation (pitting) of the skin over the ankles or sacrum (a bone in the pelvis) due to edema
- An accumulation of fluid in the chest (pleural effusion) or abdominal cavity (ascites)
- An enlarged liver

A chest x-ray can confirm the presence of an enlarged heart and pleural effusion and possibly show a cloudy area in the lungs from fluid buildup.

The capacity of the heart muscle to contract and its effectiveness as a pump are often assessed by measuring the ejection fraction, defined as the percentage of the blood in the left ventricle that is pumped out with each contraction. In a healthy individual, the ejection fraction ranges from 50 to 65 percent. A fall in the ejection fraction over time indicates a decline in the heart's contractility and pumping capability. The ejection fraction is most commonly measured with ultrasound, using a technique called echocardiography.

Echocardiography
Echocardiography is a noninvasive, painless exam that uses the reflection of ultrasonic waves to determine the motion and ejection fraction of the left ventricle and to identify the presence of ventricular aneurysms and regions of abnormal heart function. The procedure, which can also detect other abnormalities, is carried out with a transducer, an instrument that transmits the ultrasonic waves and receives the reflected echoes, which are recorded for analysis. The transducer is placed on various areas of the chest to create an image of the heart that is transmitted to a television screen for inspection.

Treatment
The first steps in the treatment of acute CHF (signaled by a a buildup of fluid in the lungs denoting pulmonary edema) are bed rest, oxygen supplementation, and intravenous administration of morphine, nitrates, and diuretics until the condition has stabilized.

Angioplasty or bypass surgery (see pages 91-95) may be performed if the patient does not respond to treatment, the CHF is due to low blood flow to the heart, and greater blood flow would improve the function of the heart muscle. Sometimes a poor response is due to damage to the mitral valve (the valve that prevents blood from flowing back to the left atrium and lung) or its supporting structures, causing blood to back up into the lungs. Correction of this condition may require surgical repair of the valve or its replacement with an artificial one.

Chronic CHF
Guidelines developed by the Agency for Health Care Policy and Research for managing chronic CHF are as follows:

- Left ventricular function should be measured in all patients who have symptoms strongly suggestive of CHF;
- Patients with moderately or severely reduced left ventricular function should be treated with an ACE inhibitor even if they have no symptoms of CHF. Most patients with established CHF should also be treated with ACE inhibitors, diuretics, and, sometimes, digoxin. ACE inhibitors tend to be underused and underdosed, possibly because of concerns over their side effects;
- Those with angina or a previous heart attack should be assessed to determine whether they would benefit from angioplasty or bypass surgery;
- Sodium intake should be restricted to 2,000 mg or less per day to help limit accumulation of fluid;
- Alcohol intake should be avoided;
- Regular exercise may help stabilize CHF. Patients should ask their doctor about an exercise program;
- Patients should report to their doctor a weight gain of more than three pounds per week (rapid weight gain may indicate excess fluid retention) as well as any new symptoms or a worsening of previous symptoms; and
- Patients with severe chronic CHF should limit their activities and plan periodic rest sessions.

Additional Treatment Options
A variety of medications can be prescribed for CHF. Daily Spironolactone (Aldactone) has been shown to substantially reduce CHF symptoms, hospitalizations for CHF, and

overall mortality over a 24-month period in patients with severe CHF.

Diuretics and digitalis have been used to treat CHF for many years, and the addition of a beta-blocker to the standard drug treatment is successful in many patients. In a meta-analysis of 17 studies, mortality from all causes was 31 percent lower in CHF patients treated with beta-blockers than in those not receiving a beta-blocker.

Patients with class IV CHF may require heart transplantation if other treatments prove ineffective. Donor hearts are in short supply, however, and individuals may have a long wait before one becomes available. During this period, a special machine called a left ventricular assist device can help the patient's heart pump more effectively.

The outcome for CHF patients who do receive heart transplants has improved significantly over the past decade as a result of advances in surgical techniques and immunosuppressive measures. About 85 percent of patients are now alive after one year, and 65 percent survive for at least five years. The improvement is primarily due to refinements in the prevention and early recognition of graft rejection—an attack by the immune system that attempts to destroy the "foreign" donated heart.

Constipation is passage of small amounts of hard, dry bowel movements, usually fewer than three times a week. People who are constipated may find it difficult and painful to have a bowel movement. Other symptoms of constipation include feeling bloated, uncomfortable, and sluggish.

Many people think they are constipated when, in fact, their bowel movements are regular. For example, some people believe they are constipated, or irregular, if they do not have a bowel movement every day. However, there is no right number of daily or weekly bowel movements. Normal may be three times a day or three times a week depending on the person. In addition, some people naturally have firmer stools than others.

At one time or another almost everyone gets constipated. Poor diet and lack of exercise are usually the causes. In most cases, constipation is temporary and not serious. Understanding causes, prevention, and treatment will help most people find relief.

Who Gets Constipated?

According to a National Health Interview Survey, about 4.5 million people in the United States say they are constipated most or all of the time. Those reporting constipation most often are women, children, and adults age 65 and over. Pregnant women also complain of constipation, and it is a common problem following childbirth or surgery.

Constipation is the most common gastrointestinal complaint in the United States, resulting in about 2 million annual visits to the doctor. However, most people treat themselves without seeking medical help, as is evident from the $725 million Americans spend on laxatives each year.

What Causes Constipation?

To understand constipation, it helps to know how the colon (large intestine) works. As food moves through it, the colon absorbs water while forming waste products, or stool. Muscle contractions in the colon push the stool toward the rectum. By the time stool reaches the rectum, it is solid because most of the water has been absorbed.

The hard and dry stools of constipation occur when the colon absorbs too much water. This happens because the colon's muscle contractions are slow or sluggish, causing the stool to move through the colon too slowly.

Diet. The most common cause of constipation is a diet low in fiber (found in vegetables, fruits, and whole grains) and high in fats (found in cheese, eggs, and meats). People who eat plenty of high-fiber foods are less likely to become constipated.

Fiber—soluble and insoluble—is the part of fruits, vegetables, and grains that the body cannot digest. Soluble fiber dissolves easily in water and takes on a soft, gel-like texture in the intestines. Insoluble fiber passes almost unchanged through the intestines. The bulk and soft texture of fiber help prevent hard, dry stools that are difficult to pass.

On average, Americans eat about 5 to 20 grams of fiber daily, short of the 20 to 35 grams recommended by the American Dietetic Association. Both children and adults eat too many refined and processed foods from which the natural fiber has been removed.

A low-fiber diet also plays a key role in constipation among older adults. They often lack interest in eating and may choose fast foods low in fiber. In addition, loss of teeth may force older people to eat soft foods that are processed and low in fiber.

Not enough liquids. Liquids like water and juice add fluid to the colon and bulk to stools, making bowel movements softer and easier to pass. People who have problems with constipation should drink enough of these liquids every day, about eight 8-ounce glasses. Other liquids, like coffee and soft

C

Bowel Regularity: What Is Normal?

Some people have two bowel movements a day, others, two a week. Both patterns are normal, provided there is no discomfort. Regularity, as well as the color and texture of the stool, are more important than frequency. The number of bowel movements you have should be consistent from week to week. Stool should be light to medium brown, and it should be solid enough to have a shape but soft enough to pass without straining.

If changes in the pattern, color, or texture of bowel movements persist for more than about a week; if bowel movements are painful; or if stool, undergarments, or toilet paper appears bloody, see your doctor. Bloody stools can be a symptom of many gastrointestinal problems, from the relatively benign (such as hemorrhoids) to the serious (such as colorectal cancer). *The Editors*

drinks, that contain caffeine seem to have a dehydrating effect.

Lack of exercise. Lack of exercise can lead to constipation, although doctors do not know precisely why. For example, constipation often occurs after an accident or during an illness when one must stay in bed and cannot exercise.

Medications. Pain-relieving medications (especially narcotics), antacids that contain aluminum, antispasmodics, antidepressants, iron supplements, diuretics, and anticonvulsants for epilepsy can slow passage of bowel movements.

Irritable bowel syndrome (IBS). Some people with IBS, also known as spastic colon, have spasms in the colon that affect bowel movements. Constipation and diarrhea often alternate, and abdominal cramping, gassiness, and bloating are other common complaints. Although IBS can produce lifelong symptoms, it is not a life-threatening condition. It often worsens with stress, but there is no specific cause or anything unusual that the doctor can see in the colon.

Changes in life or routine. During pregnancy, women may be constipated because of hormonal changes or because the heavy uterus compresses the intestine. Aging may also affect bowel regularity because a slower metabolism results in less intestinal activity and muscle tone. In addition, people often become constipated when they are traveling because their normal diet and daily routines are disrupted.

Abuse of laxatives. Myths about constipation have led to a serious abuse of laxatives. This is especially common among older adults who are preoccupied with having a daily bowel movement.

Laxatives are not usually necessary and can be habit-forming. The colon begins to rely on laxatives to bring on bowel movements. Over time, laxatives can damage nerve cells in the colon and interfere with the colon's natural ability to contract. For the same reason, regular use of enemas can also lead to a loss of normal bowel function.

Ignoring the urge to have a bowel movement. People who ignore the urge to have a bowel movement may eventually stop feeling the urge, which can lead to constipation. Some people delay having a bowel movement because they do not want to use toilets outside the home. Others ignore the urge because of emotional stress or because they are too busy. Children may postpone having a bowel movement because of stressful toilet training or because they do not want to interrupt their play.

Specific diseases. Diseases that cause constipation include neurological disorders, metabolic and endocrine disorders, and systemic conditions that affect organ systems. These disorders can slow the movement of stool through the colon, rectum, or anus.

Problems with the colon and rectum. Intestinal obstruction, scar tissue (adhesions), diverticulosis, tumors, colorectal stricture, Hirschsprung's disease, or cancer can compress, squeeze, or narrow the intestine and rectum and cause constipation.

Problems with intestinal function (chronic idiopathic constipation). Also known as functional constipation, chronic idiopathic (of unknown origin) constipation is rare. However, some people are chronically constipated and do not respond to standard treatment. This chronic constipation may be related to multiple problems with hormonal control or with nerves and muscles in the colon, rectum, or anus. Functional constipation occurs in both children and adults and is most common in women.

Colonic inertia and delayed transit are two types of functional constipation caused by decreased muscle activity in the colon. These syndromes may affect the entire colon or may be confined to the left or lower (sigmoid) colon.

Functional constipation that stems from abnormalities in the structure of the anus and rectum is known as anorectal dysfunction, or anismus. These abnormalities result in an inability to relax the rectal and anal muscles that allow stool to exit.

What Diagnostic Tests Are Used?

Most people do not need extensive testing and can be treated with changes in diet and exercise. For example, in young people with mild symptoms, a medical history and physical examination may be all the doctor needs to suggest successful treatment. The tests the doctor performs depends on the duration and severity of the constipation, the person's age, and whether there is blood in stools, recent changes in bowel movements, or weight loss.

Medical History

The doctor may ask a patient to describe the constipation, including duration of symptoms, frequency of bowel movements, consistency of stools, presence of blood in the stool, and toilet habits (how often and where one has bowel movements). Recording eating habits, medication, and level of physical activity or exercise also helps the doctor determine the cause of constipation.

Physical Examination

A physical exam may include a digital rectal exam with a gloved, lubricated finger to evaluate the tone of the muscle that closes off the anus (anal sphincter) and to detect tenderness, obstruction, or blood. In some cases, blood and thyroid tests may be necessary.

Extensive testing is usually reserved for people with severe symptoms, for those with sudden changes in number and consistency of bowel movements or blood in the stool, and for older adults. Because of an increased risk of colorectal cancer in older adults, the doctor may use one or more of the following tests to rule out a diagnosis of cancer:

Barium enema x-ray. A barium enema x-ray involves viewing the rectum, colon, and lower part of the small intestine to locate any problems. This part of the digestive tract is known as the bowel. This test may show intestinal obstruction and Hirschsprung's disease, a lack of nerves within the colon.

The night before the test, bowel cleansing, also called bowel prep, is necessary to clear the lower digestive tract. The patient drinks 8 ounces of a special liquid every 15 minutes for about 4 hours. This liquid flushes out the bowel. A clean bowel is important, because even a small amount of stool in the colon can hide details and result in an inaccurate exam.

Because the colon does not show up well on an x-ray, the doctor fills the bowel with a barium enema, a chalky liquid to make the area visible. Once the mixture coats the organs, x-rays are taken that reveal their shape and condition. The patient may feel some abdominal cramping when the barium fills the colon, but usually feels little discomfort after the procedure. Stools may be a whitish color for a few days after the exam.

Sigmoidoscopy or colonoscopy. An examination of the rectum and lower colon (sigmoid) is called a sigmoidoscopy. An examination of the rectum and entire colon is called a colonoscopy.

The night before a sigmoidoscopy, the patient usually has a liquid dinner and takes an enema in the early morning. A light breakfast and a cleansing enema an hour before the test may also be necessary.

To perform a sigmoidoscopy, the doctor uses a long, flexible tube with a light on the end, called a sigmoidoscope, to view the rectum and lower colon. First, the doctor examines the rectum with a gloved, lubricated finger. Then, the sigmoidoscope is inserted through the anus into the rectum and lower colon. The procedure may cause a mild sensation of wanting to move the bowels, and abdominal pressure. Sometimes the doctor fills the organs with air to get a better view. The air may cause mild cramping.

To perform a colonoscopy, the doctor uses a flexible tube with a light on the end, called a colonoscope, to view the entire colon. This tube is longer than a sigmoidoscope. The same bowel cleansing used for the barium x-ray is needed to clear the bowel of waste. The patient is lightly sedated before the exam. During the exam, the patient lies on his or her side and the doctor inserts the tube through the anus and rectum into the colon. If an abnormality is seen, the doctor can use the colonoscope to remove a small piece of tissue for examination (biopsy). The patient may feel gassy and bloated after the procedure.

Colorectal transit study. This test, reserved for those with chronic constipation, shows how well food moves through the colon. The patient swallows capsules containing small markers, which are visible on x-ray. The movement of the markers through the colon is monitored with abdominal x-rays taken several times three to seven days after the capsule is swallowed. The patient follows a high-fiber diet during the course of this test.

Anorectal function tests. These tests are used to diagnose constipation caused by abnormal functioning of the anus or rectum (anorectal function). Anorectal manometry evaluates anal sphincter muscle function. A catheter or air-filled balloon is inserted into the anus and then slowly pulled back through the sphincter muscle to measure muscle tone and contractions.

Defecography is an x-ray of the anorectal area that evaluates completeness of stool elimination, identifies anorectal abnormalities, and evaluates rectal muscle contractions and relaxation. During the exam, the doctor fills the rectum with a soft paste that is the same consistency as stool. The patient sits on a toilet positioned inside an x-ray machine and then relaxes and squeezes the anus and expels the solution. The doctor studies the x-rays for anorectal problems that occurred while the patient emptied the paste.

How Is Constipation Treated?
Although treatment depends on the cause, severity, and duration, in most cases dietary and lifestyle changes will help relieve symptoms and help prevent constipation.

Diet

A diet with enough fiber (20 to 35 grams each day) helps form soft, bulky stool. A doctor or dietitian can help plan an appropriate diet. High-fiber foods include beans; whole grains and bran cereals; fresh fruits; and vegetables such as asparagus, brussels sprouts, cabbage, and carrots. For people prone to constipation, limiting foods that have little or no fiber, such as ice cream, cheese, meat, and processed foods is also important.

Lifestyle Changes

Other changes that can help treat and prevent constipation include drinking enough water and other liquids such as fruit and vegetable juices and clear soup, engaging in daily exercise, and reserving enough time to have a bowel movement. In addition, the urge to have a bowel movement should not be ignored.

Laxatives

Most people who are mildly constipated do not need laxatives. However, for those who have made lifestyle changes and are still constipated, doctors may recommend laxatives or enemas for a limited time. These treatments can help retrain a chronically sluggish bowel. For children, short-term treatment with laxatives, along with retraining to establish regular bowel habits, also helps prevent constipation.

A doctor should determine when a patient needs a laxative and which form is best. Laxatives taken by mouth are available in liquid, tablet, gum, powder, and granule forms. They work in various ways:

- **Bulk-forming laxatives** are generally considered the safest but can interfere with absorption of some medicines. These laxatives, also known as fiber supplements, are taken with water. They absorb water in the intestine and make the stool softer.

Brand names include Metamucil, Citrucel, Konsyl, and Serutan.
- **Stimulants** cause rhythmic muscle contractions in the intestines. Brand names include Correctol, Dulcolax, Purge, Feen-A-Mint, and Senokot. Studies suggest that phenolphthalein, an ingredient in some stimulant laxatives, might increase a person's risk for cancer. The Food and Drug Administration has proposed a ban on all over-the-counter products containing phenolphthalein. Most laxative makers have replaced or plan to replace phenolphthalein with a safer ingredient.
- **Stool softeners** provide moisture to the stool and prevent dehydration. These laxatives are often recommended after childbirth or surgery. Products include Colace, Dialose, and Surfak.
- **Lubricants** grease the stool enabling it to move through the intestine more easily. Mineral oil is the most common lubricant.
- **Saline laxatives** act like a sponge to draw water into the colon for easier passage of stool. Laxatives in this group include Milk of Magnesia, Citrate of Magnesia, and Haley's M-O.

People who are dependent on laxatives need to slowly stop using the medications. A doctor can assist in this process. In most people, this restores the colon's natural ability to contract.

Other Treatment

Treatment may be directed at a specific cause. For example, the doctor may recommend discontinuing medication or performing surgery to correct an anorectal problem such as rectal prolapse.

People with chronic constipation caused by anorectal dysfunction can use biofeedback to retrain the muscles that control release of bowel movements. Biofeedback

C

involves using a sensor to monitor muscle activity that at the same time can be displayed on a computer screen allowing for an accurate assessment of body functions. A health-care professional uses this information to help the patient learn how to use these muscles.

Surgical removal of the colon may be an option for people with severe symptoms caused by colonic inertia. However, the benefits of this surgery must be weighed against possible complications, which include abdominal pain and diarrhea.

Can Constipation Be Serious?

Sometimes constipation can lead to complications. These complications include hemorrhoids caused by straining to have a bowel movement or anal fissures (tears in the skin around the anus) caused when hard stool stretches the sphincter muscle. As a result, there may be rectal bleeding that appears as bright red streaks on the surface of the stool. Treatment for hemorrhoids may include warm tub baths, ice packs, and application of a cream to the affected area. Treatment for anal fissure may include stretching the sphincter muscle or surgical removal of tissue or skin in the affected area.

Sometimes straining causes a small amount of intestinal lining to push out from the anal opening. This condition is known as rectal prolapse and may lead to secretion of mucus from the anus. Usually, eliminating the cause of the prolapse, such as straining or coughing, is the only treatment necessary. Severe or chronic prolapse requires surgery to strengthen and tighten the anal sphincter muscle or to repair the prolapsed lining.

Constipation may also cause hard stool to pack the intestine and rectum so tightly that the normal pushing action of the colon is not enough to expel the stool. This condition, called fecal impaction, occurs most often in children and older adults. An impaction can be softened with mineral oil taken by mouth and an enema. After softening the impaction, the doctor may break up and remove part of the hardened stool by inserting one or two fingers in the anus.

National Institute of Diabetes and Digestive and Kidney Diseases

The heart is a muscular organ that pumps oxygen- and nutrient-rich blood to all the body's tissues. To function properly, the heart also requires a supply of oxygenated blood from the coronary arteries, which encircle the top of the heart like a crown (a "corona").

In coronary heart disease (CHD), sometimes called coronary artery disease, narrowing of the coronary arteries jeopardizes their ability to provide adequate blood to the heart. CHD is the single largest killer in the United States, responsible for one of five deaths—nearly half a million a year.

In the United States, the underlying causes of CHD are so widespread that one survey of over 90,000 adults found that only 18 percent reported having no risk factors for the disorder. Identifying and controlling CHD risk factors can prevent or delay the development of the disease. When preventive efforts are not enough, CHD can usually be managed and controlled through lifestyle measures, medications, surgical procedures, or a combination of all three.

This entry focuses on the causes of CHD, the measures that can be taken to reduce the risk factors associated with it, and basic treatment options. Typically, CHD gives rise to complications tied to the site and the severity of blockage in a coronary artery. Treatment of CHD is usually aimed at one

C

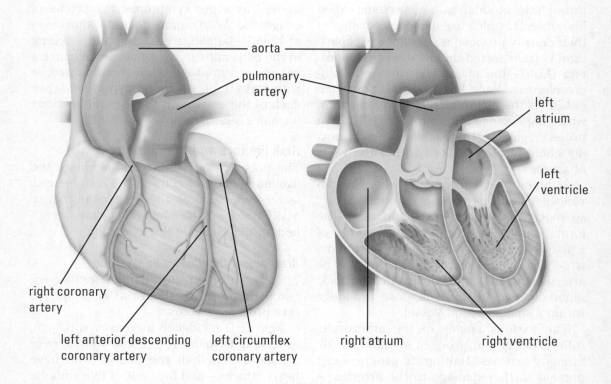

aorta

pulmonary artery

left atrium

left ventricle

right coronary artery

left anterior descending coronary artery

left circumflex coronary artery

right atrium

right ventricle

The heart has four chambers—two ventricles and two atria—that contract in sequence to pump blood to the lungs and to all the body's tissues. Blood that has been oxygenated in the lungs is carried through the aorta to smaller arteries throughout the body. In coronary heart disease, partial or complete blockage of one or more coronary arteries interferes with the blood supply to the heart.

C

of these complications, which are covered in detail elsewhere in this book. They include angina (page 89), heart attack (page 376), congestive heart failure (page 224), and arrhythmias (page 102).

Causes

The underlying cause of CHD is atherosclerosis—narrowing of large arteries by deposits called plaques. Plaques are composed of cholesterol-laden foam cells, smooth muscle cells, fibrous proteins, and calcium. The accumulation of cholesterol in the arterial wall initiates and plays a continuing central role in the atherosclerotic process.

Cholesterol and triglycerides are lipids (fats) found in the blood. They are carried through the bloodstream on proteins called lipoproteins, which are named according to their density properties. Most of the cholesterol is transported on low density lipoprotein (LDL)—the major contributor to atherosclerosis. Very low density lipoprotein (VLDL) is the major carrier of triglycerides, while high density lipoprotein (HDL) can protect against atherosclerosis by removing cholesterol deposited within the walls of arteries.

Symptoms of CHD result when an advanced plaque narrows a coronary artery so much that it hinders blood flow. The formation of a blood clot on the exterior of a plaque—which is particularly likely to occur if the plaque ruptures—may block the artery completely and cause a heart attack. Blood clots can also break loose and lodge within a smaller blood vessel.

The various stages of the atherosclerotic process can proceed simultaneously in many arteries. Halting its progress can prevent further damage to the arteries. A key step in this process is the accumulation of oxidized LDL within the arterial walls. If there were little LDL to accumulate, or

if oxidation could be prevented, plaque buildup would slow or possibly reverse. HDL cholesterol is often called "good" cholesterol because HDL can remove cholesterol from the arterial wall and return it to the liver for disposal. This action, as well as HDL's believed ability to slow LDL oxidation, explains why high levels of HDL protect against CHD.

Symptoms

Atherosclerosis seldom produces any symptoms until it has produced a significant blockage of one or more arteries, which usually develops over years. When symptoms do appear, they result from a specific complication of atherosclerosis. *Angina* and *heart attack* produce chest pain as well as other symptoms. Symptoms of *congestive heart failure* include shortness of breath, fatigue, weakness, and swelling in the extremities. *Arrhythmias* can cause a variety of symptoms, though some people with arrhythmias have no symptoms. (See each of the entries on these complications for more information.)

Risk Factors and Prevention

The presence of risk factors increases the likelihood of developing CHD. The more risk factors a person has, the greater the chance of CHD. Some of the many risk factors identified for CHD include the following.

Risk Factors That Cannot Be Changed

The following risk factors cannot be changed, but their presence should alert people to take preventive steps.

Age. CHD incidence increases with age, especially in men over 45 and women over 55. More than half the people who have heart attacks—and four out of five who die of a heart attack—are over 65.

Gender. CHD is more common in young men than young women.

Evaluating Blood Lipid Levels

Cholesterol and triglycerides are the two principal lipids, or fats, in the blood. Because they cannot dissolve in the blood, special proteins, called lipoproteins, carry them through the bloodstream. The cholesterol carried on low-density lipoproteins (LDL) is often called "bad" cholesterol because it contributes to CHD risk. On the other hand, high-density lipoproteins (HDL) carry so-called "good" cholesterol because high HDL levels protect against CHD.

The chart here shows risk classifications for levels of blood lipids and lipoproteins (in milligrams per deciliter, or mg/dL) when measured according to guidelines from the National Cholesterol Education Program (see page 236). These classifications apply to people without CHD. If you have CHD or more than one risk factor for CHD, a desirable LDL level may be lower than 100 mg/dL. Because everyone's situation is different, ask your doctor for help in interpreting the test results for cholesterol and triglycerides.

Total Cholesterol
Desirable................. <200 mg/dL
Borderline-high .... 200–239 mg/dL
Increased Risk .... ≥240 mg/dL

LDL Cholesterol
Optimal*................. <100 mg/dL
Desirable................ 100–129 mg/dL
Borderline............... 130–159 mg/dL
Increased Risk .... ≥160 mg/dL

HDL Cholesterol
Desirable................ ≥60 mg/dL
Borderline............... 40–59 mg/dL
Increased Risk .... <40 mg/dL

Triglycerides
Desirable................ <150 mg/dL
Borderline............... 150–199 mg/dL
Increased Risk .... 200–499 mg/dL

* For people with diabetes, peripheral arterial disease, history of stroke or aortic aneurysm, or known CHD, and for some people with two or more CHD risk factors, a target of LDL <70 mg/dL should be considered.

Heredity. People who have a male first-degree relative (parent, sibling, or child) with a manifestation of CHD before age 55 or a female first-degree relative with CHD before age 65 are at increased risk for CHD.

Postmenopausal status in women. CHD is by far the major cause of death among women after menopause, when low levels of estrogen lead to an increase in LDL cholesterol and a drop in HDL cholesterol. Younger women who undergo premature menopause due to surgical removal of the ovaries or spontaneous ovarian failure at an early age, have a risk of CHD similar to that of postmenopausal women.

Risk Factors That Can Be Changed

The following risk factors can be modified to some extent, if not completely. Some of them (smoking, hypertension, and abnormal cholesterol levels) are better established than others (for example, lack of exercise, stress, and homocysteine).

Cigarette smoking. Cigarette smoking is a dangerous risk factor for CHD, as well as for lung cancer and many other disorders. Fortunately, much can be gained by stopping smoking. Even after many years of smoking, the risk of CHD events (such as heart attacks) returns to that of a nonsmoker within five years of quitting smoking.

Hypertension. High blood pressure (hypertension) causes the left ventricle of the heart to enlarge so that the heart muscle requires

Guidelines for Cholesterol Testing and Treatment

The government-sponsored National Cholesterol Education Program (NCEP) issued updated guidelines in 2001 for the detection, evaluation, and treatment of high blood cholesterol levels. In 2004, an expert NCEP panel issued revised guidelines—based on evidence from several new clinical trials—that call for even more aggressive lipid-lowering therapy for people at high risk of a heart attack.

Key Recommendations:

- Everyone age 20 and older should obtain a lipid profile (sometimes called a lipoprotein profile) after a 12-hour fast. This test measures total cholesterol, LDL cholesterol, HDL cholesterol, and triglycerides .

- If you are healthy, your results are all in the desirable range (see page 235), and you have no other major risk factors for CHD—which include older age, smoking, hypertension, diabetes, HDL cholesterol below 40 mg/dL, and/or a history of premature CHD in a first-degree relative (parent, sibling, or child)—then you should be retested in five years.

- The target for people with one CHD risk factor is an LDL level of less than 160 mg/dL. In most individuals who do not have diabetes or known vascular disease, but have two or more risk factors, LDL levels should be kept below 130 mg/dL.

- In patients with any form of known cardiovascular disease (who are considered at high risk of a heart attack), the NCEP guidelines recommend that LDL cholesterol be lowered to less than 100 mg/dL. This target also applies to individuals with diabetes, which is now designated as a "CHD equivalent" rather than simply another risk factor for CHD. The newest guidelines suggest an LDL target level of less than 70 mg/dL for these high risk individuals—and recommend that patients consider drug therapy even if LDL cholesterol levels are below 100 mg/dL.

- A high level of HDL cholesterol (60 mg/dL or higher) is considered protective against CHD. A high HDL level cancels out the effects of one other CHD risk factor when determining the total number of risk factors.

- The NCEP guidelines emphasize the dangers of metabolic syndrome, which is largely related to obesity and inactivity. High blood pressure, low HDL cholesterol, high triglycerides, high blood sugar, and abdominal obesity are among the diagnostic features.

- Based on your test results and an assessment of your risk factors, your doctor will decide on treatment, usually beginning with lifestyle changes (see page 240). When lifestyle measures do not lower LDL levels sufficiently, your doctor may also recommend a cholesterol-lowering medication (page 241).

more blood. At the same time, it increases the rate of atherosclerosis, thus limiting the heart's blood supply.

People with a blood pressure that is consistently 120 to 139 mm Hg systolic (the higher number in a blood pressure reading) or 80 to 89 mm Hg diastolic (the lower number) are considered to have prehypertension. These individuals are more likely to develop high blood pressure and have a greater risk of cardiovascular events (for example, heart attacks and strokes) than those with lower blood pressures. High blood pressure is defined as a systolic blood pressure of 140 mm Hg or more or a diastolic blood pressure of 90 mm Hg or more.

Lowering blood pressure in people with prehypertension or high blood pressure reduces the likelihood of heart attacks, lowers the risk of heart failure and strokes, and slows the progression of kidney disease. (For more information on causes and diagnosis of hypertension, see page 384.)

Abnormal levels of blood lipids and lipoproteins. High levels of total and LDL cholesterol and a low HDL cholesterol are risk factors for CHD. Recent research indicates that elevated blood triglycerides are also a risk factor. Medical knowledge of the effects of abnormalities in lipids and lipoproteins has grown rapidly. In response to this new knowledge, the National Cholesterol Education Program (NCEP) recently updated its guidelines (see the text box on page 236).

Elevations in lipoprotein(a)—a lipoprotein with a structure similar to LDL—are another risk factor for CHD, though no benefits of lowering lipoprotein(a) are proven.

Size and density of LDL particles also can affect CHD risk. LDL particles vary in size and density in a way that produces two different patient profiles, called patterns A and B. Pattern A patients have mostly large LDL particles, while pattern B denotes a predominance of small, dense particles. Pattern B patients have a higher risk of CHD than those with pattern A. Men are more likely than women to have pattern B, which may be genetic in origin or develop as a result of hypertriglyceridemia or diabetes.

Some researchers, however, have questioned whether the density of LDL particles matters as much as the number of particles. It is possible that pattern B patients have a higher risk profile because their LDL particles, being smaller, are also more numerous than those in pattern A patients, not because the particles have greater density.

Obesity. Being significantly overweight or obese is a risk factor for CHD. Abdominal obesity is particularly dangerous because it leads to resistance to the actions of insulin, which in turn elevates blood levels of insulin and is associated with high triglycerides, low HDL cholesterol, high blood pressure, and an increased CHD risk. A waist circumference (measured with a tape wrapped around the waist so that it crosses the top of the hips) greater than 40 inches in men or 35 inches in women indicates abdominal obesity and a heightened risk. (See page 458 for more information on assessing obesity.)

Physical inactivity. A large body of research shows that regular physical activity and physical fitness help prevent a first heart attack, and the American Heart Association cites physical inactivity as an important risk factor for CHD. Nonetheless, the role of exercise in preventing CHD remains controversial, because the studies show only an association between exercise and reduced heart disease, not proof that exercise directly lowers risk. Still, most experts and health-care workers recommend regular exercise, which helps to control weight, lower blood pressure, and produce a more favorable lipid profile.

Stress. Over the past 30 years, studies by many investigators have shown a relationship between mental stress and various aspects of CHD. Nonetheless, stress is not generally accepted as a risk factor for CHD, partly because it is so difficult to quantify the amount of stress in the life of an individual.

But if the coronary arteries are already narrowed, the combination of reduced supply and greater demand for blood triggered by a stressful event can cause myocardial ischemia—an inadequate supply of blood to the heart muscle—that is either "silent" (asymptomatic) or accompanied by angina. If the blockage of the artery is nearly total, these physiological responses can cause a heart attack.

Blood-clotting factors (platelets, fibrinogen, factor VII). Although the formation of an intravascular blood clot is the most common cause of a heart attack, efforts to find

C

a consistent clotting abnormality in people prone to heart attacks have been unsuccessful. Studies have found that an elevation in blood levels of fibrinogen or factor VII, two of the clotting proteins, or an over-responsiveness of platelets (circulating particles involved in blood clotting) to certain stimuli is associated with an increased risk of a heart attack.

PLA2. Platelets play a critical role in the formation of blood clots. A variation in PLA2, one of the proteins involved in platelet aggregation, was the first inherited platelet abnormality identified as a risk factor for CHD. A study conducted by a team of Johns Hopkins researchers found that heart attacks occurred more often in patients who had the PLA2 genotype than in those who did not.

Homocysteine. The amino acid homocysteine may be linked with cardiovascular disease. It is not known how homocysteine adversely affects the arteries, but high levels may promote atherosclerosis by damaging the endothelium and stimulating the growth of smooth muscle cells.

C-reactive protein (CRP). This protein is produced by the liver in response to tissue inflammation or infection, and elevated levels predict heart attacks and strokes many years before they occur. People with even small elevations of CRP appear to be at increased risk for CHD and its complications, regardless of their age, gender, general health, or the presence of other CHD risk factors. It is not known whether reducing CRP levels reduces the risk of CHD.

Disorders Associated with CHD

The following disorders confer an increased risk of CHD:

Diabetes. Elevated triglycerides, low HDL cholesterol, hypertension, and obesity are more common in people with diabetes, but the diabetic state itself imparts another, as-yet-unidentified mechanism for greatly increasing the risk of CHD. Even careful control of blood glucose levels with dietary and drug therapy does not eliminate the increased risk of CHD associated with diabetes. Therefore, it is particularly important for people with diabetes or prediabetes (see page 264) to control other risk factors for CHD, such as smoking, abnormal blood lipid levels, and hypertension.

Metabolic syndrome. A person is considered to have metabolic syndrome if he or she has at least three of the following findings: abdominal obesity (as stated on page 237, a waist measurement of greater than 40 inches in men and 35 inches in women), high triglycerides, low HDL cholesterol, high blood pressure, and high blood glucose.

Cerebrovascular or peripheral arterial disease. CHD is the most likely cause of death in people with either of these disorders. Reduced blood pressure at the ankles; muscle pains in the legs upon exertion; or evidence of thickened carotid arteries, which supply the brain, are all associated with increased deaths from CHD, even in people who have no symptoms of CHD. (See Stroke, page 592 and Peripheral Arterial Disease, page 527.)

Aortic valve sclerosis. The aortic valve controls the flow of blood from the left ventricle to the aorta. Aortic valve sclerosis is hardening and thickening of this valve. In a study of nearly 6,000 adults age 65 or older, aortic valve sclerosis was associated with a 50% increased risk of a heart attack or CHD-related death. This is because aortic valve sclerosis results from the same process that causes atherosclerosis in the coronary arteries.

Diagnosis

The diagnosis of angina is based on a history of typical chest pain (see page 89). Special tests, usually beginning with an electrocardiogram (ECG), are carried out to substantiate the presence of CHD and to help identify which arteries are affected. An ECG uses small metal sensors (electrodes) applied to the skin to detect and then record electrical impulses from the heart. This test is especially valuable in detecting abnormal heart rhythms and new heart attacks; it also allows recognition of areas of previously damaged heart muscle. Additional relevant findings obtained with an ECG include signs of left ventricular hypertrophy and defects in the electrical conduction from the atria to the ventricles.

A normal resting ECG does not eliminate the possibility of ischemia, which may occur and cause chest pain only during increased physical activity. Silent or asymptomatic ischemia can be detected by a Holter monitor (also called an ambulatory electrocardiogram), which records the heart's electrical activity over a 24-hour period.

Exercise Stress Test

If a resting ECG is normal but angina is still suspected as the cause of chest pain, the next step is often an exercise stress test. This test involves recording the ECG while an individual walks on a treadmill or pedals a stationary bicycle to create a possible mismatch between the demand for and the supply of oxygen to the myocardium. The amount of work is gradually increased by raising the angle and speed of the treadmill or increasing the resistance to pedaling. Results show how well the heart functions as it is required to work harder. Findings can be used to confirm CHD, establish a safe level of exercise when CHD is diagnosed, or help direct treatment of stabilized patients who have experienced a heart attack or unstable angina (see page 90).

While a stress test is useful to support the clinical diagnosis of CHD in patients with clear symptoms, it may be less helpful in asymptomatic people unless they are at increased risk for CHD. Stress tests are often falsely positive in people at low risk for CHD, especially women.

If results from a stress test are unclear or negative, and chest pain remains unexplained, a nuclear medicine stress test—which tracks the distribution of a radioactive substance in the heart muscles after it is injected into the blood—may yield more precise results.

Echocardiography

Echocardiography uses ultrasonic waves to determine the motion and ejection fraction of the left ventricle and to identify the presence of ventricular aneurysms and regions of abnormal heart function. The ejection fraction is the fraction of the blood in the left ventricle that is pumped out with each contraction. In a healthy individual, the ejection fraction ranges from 50% to 65%. This noninvasive painless procedure may also be used to detect defects in the walls dividing the chambers of the heart, valve disease, and blood clots within the chambers.

In stress echocardiography, ultrasonic waves are used to image the heart at rest and then immediately following exercise. The technique can detect abnormalities in the motion of the heart wall. Abnormal motion at rest and during exercise indicates heart damage due to a prior heart attack. Normal motion at rest but abnormal motion during exercise indicates myocardial ischemia.

C

Coronary Angiography

At the present time, coronary angiography is the "gold standard" method for delineating the status of the coronary arteries. It is most often performed when significant CHD is highly likely based on symptoms and the results of other tests. In addition to identifying the affected arteries, it can be used to determine whether bypass surgery or angioplasty (see page 91) is necessary.

The doctor threads a catheter slowly from an artery in the groin into one of the coronary arteries (guided by images projected on a television screen). Injection of contrast material into the vessel allows the detection of abnormalities in the coronary arteries on x-ray film. If angioplasty is required, it is often performed immediately after the angiogram.

Angiography confers some risk from the effects of the injected contrast material and possible damage to the arteries from the catheter. But the risk is small: In a patient who is stable and not in an emergency situation, the risk of a heart attack or death from this procedure is about 1 in 1,000.

Lifestyle Measures for Prevention and Treatment

Lifestyle measures can have a greater impact on CHD than on practically any other disease. The same interventions that are used to prevent CHD are also effective in treating established CHD.

CHD is a progressive disorder: Once CHD develops, it can be controlled but not cured. As a result, a heart-healthy lifestyle is necessary even for those who are taking medication to lower cholesterol levels, reduce blood pressure, or control angina, and in those who have undergone bypass surgery or angioplasty. For example, even when lifestyle changes do not lower blood pressure to acceptable levels, they can reduce the amount of antihypertensive medication needed and thus lower the risk of side effects.

Three lifestyle measures are most effective: quitting smoking, dietary changes (limiting fat and sodium intake and increasing the amount of dietary fiber, fruits, and vegetables), and engaging in regular physical activity.

Other measures that can help reduce the risk of developing CHD include maintaining a healthy weight, managing daily stress, and—for some people—consuming moderate amounts of alcohol.

You can find more information on the benefits of these measures, along with advice on how to incorporate them into your life, in the section on disease prevention (page 14).

For both prevention and treatment of CHD, it's important to know your blood lipid (cholesterol and triglyceride) levels and, if necessary, take steps to keep them within the levels recommended in the chart on page 236. If lipid levels do not respond sufficiently to fat reduction and other dietary measures, then medication may be required, as outlined below. The benefits of reducing total and LDL cholesterol levels with both diet and medication have been clearly demonstrated by a number of well designed studies.

Medications

Lifestyle changes may be all that are needed to control blood lipid levels and hypertension, but when they fail to do so, a wide array of medications is available. Drugs can also relieve angina and reduce the clotting ability of the blood. (Medications for angina, heart attack, congestive heart failure, and arrythmias are discussed in the individual entries for those conditions.)

Lipid-Lowering Medications

If three to six months of a low-fat, low-cholesterol diet fail to adequately lower cholesterol levels, drugs may also be prescribed.

Cholesterol-lowering medications often should be prescribed after a heart attack—and yet are greatly underprescribed. No more than 30 to 50 percent of such patients who should be on lipid-lowering therapy actually receive it. Moreover, studies have shown that as many as half of patients discontinue the medication after one year.

Five classes of lipid-lowering drugs are available: HMG-CoA reductase inhibitors (statins); bile acid sequestrants; nicotinic acid, or niacin; fibrates; and cholesterol absorption inhibitors.

HMG-CoA reductase inhibitors. Known as statins, these medications are well tolerated and are the most effective agents for lowering total and LDL cholesterol. They can produce a 25 to 55 percent reduction in LDL cholesterol levels, a 5 to 15 percent increase in HDL levels, and a 10 to 25 percent reduction in triglyceride levels. The statins include atorvastatin (Lipitor), fluvastatin (Lescol), lovastatin (Mevacor), pravastatin (Pravachol), rosuvastatin (Crestor), and simvastatin (Zocor).

In addition to their positive effects on blood lipid levels, the statins also appear to improve the function of the endothelium that lines the arteries. Specifically, they help arteries to regain at least some of their normal ability to widen and permit increased blood flow during exercise. Statins also reduce the risk of plaque rupture by decreasing inflammation within the walls of arteries.

Bile-acid sequestrants. The sequestrants, cholestyramine (Questran), colesevelam, (WelChol), and colestipol (Colestid), have proven long-term safety and effectiveness. Combinations of sequestrants with statins or niacin are especially effective in lowering LDL cholesterol levels. A number of studies have shown that such combinations slow the progression, or even cause regression, of plaques.

Niacin. Large doses of this B vitamin are the most effective therapy to raise HDL cholesterol. Nicotinic acid also can lower triglycerides and LDL cholesterol.

Nicotinic acid frequently causes adverse effects. Skin flushing and itching are common but not dangerous. More serious side effects include liver toxicity, peptic ulcers (ulcers in the stomach or upper intestine), gout, and a rise in blood glucose levels. Nicotinic acid should not be taken by those with current or past peptic ulcers, liver disease, or gout. It should be used with caution in people with diabetes or pre-diabetes.

Extended-release niacin (Niaspan) is associated with less flushing than immediate-release niacin (Niacor) and has the added advantage of once-a-day dosing at bedtime, rather than three times a day with meals. Older, sustained-release niacin preparations increase the risk of liver toxicity and should be avoided. Although niacin is available over the counter, all preparations should be used under a doctor's supervision.

Fibrates. The fibrates, gemfibrozil (Lopid) and fenofibrate (Tricor), are the treatment of choice for those with markedly high triglycerides, but any fall in triglycerides may be accompanied by a rise in total and LDL cholesterol. When this problem occurs, the addition of a statin can improve LDL cholesterol levels but may cause muscle inflammation (myositis) in about 1 percent of patients. Myositis is reversible, but both drugs

C

Hormone Replacement Therapy and CHD

Replacing the female hormone estrogen is effective in relieving menopausal symptoms such as hot flashes and vaginal dryness. Most postmenopausal women who take estrogen also take progestin (synthetic progesterone), because progestin negates the risk of uterine cancer in women taking estrogen alone. This combination is called hormone replacement therapy (HRT); it usually consists of 0.625 mg Premarin plus 2.5 mg medroxyprogstrone, taken separately or in a single pill.

Estrogen improves both LDL and HDL cholesterol levels, so it was hoped that taking estrogen might reduce the incidence of CHD. Until recently, research suggested that HRT reduced the incidence of CHD events by as much as 50 percent in postmenopausal women.

These early findings were based on observational studies, which did not directly compare the effects of taking estrogen versus not taking it in two otherwise identical groups of women. Then a randomized controlled study called the Heart and Estrogen/Progestin Replacement Study (HERS) found that the rates of heart attack or death due to CHD were the same whether or not the women took these hormones.

More recently, an even larger randomized, controlled trial called the Women's Health Initiative found that after five years, women taking HRT (the study used Prempro) had a slightly increased risk of heart attacks, strokes, breast cancer, and blood clots in the lungs, compared with those taking a placebo. As a result, the HRT portion of the Women's Health Initiative was halted in July 2002.

Women who have had a hysterectomy can take estrogen without progestin; this is called estrogen replacement therapy (ERT). A smaller portion of the Women's Health Initiative involved assigning women to either estrogen alone or a placebo. This portion of the study was halted in February 2004, when researchers discovered that estrogen alone did not reduce the risk of heart attacks and in fact increased the risk of stroke.

Consequently, HRT and ERT should not be used for the prevention of heart attack or stroke, and when used to reduce the symptoms of menopause should be taken for the shortest possible time at the smallest effective dose.

Women who have had breast cancer or have a family history of early breast cancer (a mother or sister who developed the disease before age 40) should be especially cautious about using HRT or ERT for any period of time. These women may want to ask their doctor about tamoxifen (Nolvadex), which has beneficial effects on LDL and HDL cholesterol levels similar to those of estrogen.

must be promptly discontinued since severe myositis can cause kidney damage.

Cholesterol absorption inhibitors. As their name implies, these recently introduced drugs work by blocking the absorption of cholesterol from the small intestine. Ezetimibe (Zetia) is the first drug to be approved in this class. Studies show that ezetimibe lowers total and LDL cholesterol by about 10% to 15%, and lowers cholesterol even more when combined with a statin. A pill containing simvastatin and ezetimibe (Vytorin) is available.

Stanols and sterols. These substances have been added to margarines (Benecol, Take Control, SmartBalance OmegaPlus) and orange juice (Minute Maid Premium Heart Wise). The margarines can reduce LDL cholesterol levels by 7% to 14% when used daily for a year or longer in combination with a low-saturated fat, low-cholesterol diet and regular exercise.

In a recent study, sterol-fortified orange juice reduced LDL cholesterol by 12% when participants drank two 8-oz. glasses daily with meals for eight weeks. Note: Stanol- and sterol-fortified foods contain calories and can cause weight gain when consumed in large quantities or in addition to the usual diet.

Antihypertensive Medications
Five classes of drugs, used individually or in combination, are most frequently prescribed for the treatment of hypertension: diuretics, beta-blockers, ACE inhibitors, angiotensin II receptor blockers, and calcium channel blockers. Some have other benefits as well: Beta-blockers and calcium channel blockers can alleviate the symptoms of angina, and ACE inhibitors are quite effective in the treatment of congestive heart failure. For information on these medications, see pages 391-393.

Antiplatelet and Anticoagulant Drugs
Antiplatelet drugs include aspirin, clopidogrel (Plavix), abciximab (ReoPro), eptifibatide (Integrilin), and tirofiban (Aggrastat), while warfarin (Coumadin) is an anticoagulant drug.

Aspirin decreases the formation of blood clots by preventing platelets from clumping together. Long-term aspirin therapy reduces the risk of death, heart attack, and stroke in people with CHD. Aspirin is routinely prescribed for patients who have had a heart attack to reduce the risk of a second one.

In addition, immediate aspirin use increases the chances of survival when a heart attack does occur. One study found that heart attack victims treated with aspirin had a 25 percent lower risk of death from CHD than those who did not take aspirin. Individuals with a history of gastrointestinal bleeding or those who take anticoagulant drugs should take aspirin with caution or not at all.

Clopidogrel is mainly used for two to four weeks after angioplasty with stent placement. Three new antiplatelet agents—abciximab, eptifibatide, and tirofiban—are administered intravenously in patients undergoing angioplasty and in those with unstable angina.

The drug warfarin is used in heart attack patients with evidence of a blood clot inside the heart, and in those with markedly impaired heart function. Patients with atrial fibrillation are also treated with warfarin, especially if they have other risk factors for a stroke. The risk of bleeding, the most common side effect of warfarin, can be minimized with periodic blood tests.

Dementia refers to a cluster of symptoms caused by changes in brain function. Memory loss is the hallmark of dementia, but personality and behavior changes are also common. Nearly everyone experiences memory lapses as they age, but dementia interferes with a person's ability to carry out daily activities.

Dementia is caused by many disorders; only a few of them are reversible. In these instances, patients may have a physical or psychological condition, such as a high fever, depression, or a minor head injury, that can improve or be cured with treatment. Most forms of dementia are not reversible. They include Alzheimer's disease (AD), the most common cause of dementia. (For more information on Alzheimer's disease, see pages 80 to 88.)

Diagnosis

According to guidelines published by the Agency for Health Care Policy and Research, a person who has difficulties with one or more of the following activities should be evaluated for dementia:

- **Learning and retaining new information.** The person regularly misplaces objects, has trouble remembering appointments or recent conversations, or is repetitive in conversation.
- **Handling complex tasks.** The individual has trouble with previously familiar activities, like balancing a checkbook, cooking a meal, or other tasks that involve a complex train of thought.
- **Ability to reason.** The person finds it difficult to respond appropriately to everyday problems, such as a flat tire. Or, a previously responsible, well-adjusted person may display poor judgement about social or financial matters.
- **Spatial ability and orientation.** Driving and finding one's way in familiar surroundings become difficult or impossible, and the person may have problems recognizing known objects and landmarks.
- **Language.** The ability to speak or comprehend seems impaired, and the person may have problems following or participating in conversations.
- **Behavior.** Personality changes emerge. For example, the person appears more passive and less responsive than usual, or more suspicious and irritable. Visual or auditory stimuli may be misinterpreted.

Differentiating between age-associated memory impairment and dementia due to a medical condition involves a process of systematic elimination. Doctors often start by looking for conditions that are correctable. If these possibilities can be eliminated, then more serious, irreversible dementias—such as AD—are considered. In addition, the presence of reversible disorders can complicate the irreversible forms of dementia. In these cases, diagnosing and treating concurrent depression, for example, makes it possible to gain a clearer view of any conditions that may persist.

The first step in diagnosis is a thorough medical history and physical examination to identify any vision, hearing, cardiovascular, or other disorders. While checking for these conditions might seem unnecessary, they often go unrecognized in older adults and can have an important effect on memory.

For example, congestive heart failure (a decreased pumping ability of the heart) may impede mental function by reducing the amount of blood circulating to the brain. Bypass surgery for coronary artery disease or recovering from cardiac arrest can also affect memory. A complete medical history is necessary to account for any pre-existing conditions, such as psychiatric disorders, head trauma, or alcohol abuse.

Tests of mental status—for example, the Mini-Mental State Examination or the Short

Diagnosis via Autopsy

Although the clinical tests for dementia are accurate about 85 percent to 90 percent of the time, the only way to confirm a diagnosis of dementia is to examine the brain after the patient has died. Only this examination makes it possible to know for certain if one type of dementia was misdiagnosed as another, or if a disorder that mimics dementia was wrongly diagnosed.

An additional benefit of autopsy is the knowledge that as a surviving relative, you may be at risk for Alzheimer's disease or another form of dementia. Although no effective measures are currently available to prevent or treat dementia, the information may be useful when such measures are discovered. Furthermore, an autopsy can reveal otherwise unrecognized disorders.

To make a postmortem diagnosis of dementia, only the brain needs to be examined. A pathologist makes an incision along the back of the head, opens the skull, and removes the brain; the head is then stitched closed. A wake or viewing can still be open-casket, since the autopsy leaves no visible scars.

If you wish to have an autopsy performed on a loved one, you should make plans well in advance. Discuss and coordinate your plans with family members, doctors, the institution that will perform the autopsy, the funeral home, and, as much as possible, the person with dementia. If the person is in a hospital or long-term care facility, you should also inform the staff of your decision.

Test of Mental Status—are also given to check for any basic cognitive impairment. These tests, which take between 5 and 15 minutes to complete, offer a baseline for comparison should further testing be necessary.

A second critical part of the history is an interview with a family member or close friend. Someone close to the patient knows the level of his or her former functioning, and therefore is able to help the physician determine whether deterioration has occurred.

The American Academy of Neurology recently came out with guidelines on dementia. In them, they recommend the following tests in the routine evaluation of a patient:

- Complete blood cell count
- Serum electrolytes (potassium, sodium, and chloride)
- Blood glucose (sugar), blood urea nitrogen, and creatinine
- Serum vitamin B12 levels
- Depression screening
- Liver function and thyroid function tests

- A brain scan such as computed tomography (CT) or magnetic resonance imaging (MRI)

A routine evaluation would not include single-photon emission computer tomography (SPECT), genetic testing, or apoliprotein E (APOE) genotyping. Screening for syphilis and lumbar puncture should be performed only in special circumstances.

The usefulness of positron emission tomography (PET), testing for other genetic markers for AD, markers for AD in the cerebrospinal fluid, and AD gene mutations in patients with frontotemporal dementia, is unknown at this time, according to the American Academy of Neurology.

Memory and Reversible Dementia
Memory loss can result from causes that can be controlled by the patient or physician. Medication side effects, depression, and certain medical conditions are important areas of concern.

D

Memory Loss Due to Medication

Although older adults make up only 12 percent of the population, they receive about 30 percent of all prescriptions written in the United States. Unfortunately, as people age, natural changes within the body make adverse effects more likely from any medication: The kidneys may not remove drugs from the bloodstream as quickly as in younger adults; drug metabolism in the liver may be slowed; and a greater ratio of fat to muscle increases the time it takes to eliminate some drugs from the body. Equally important, however, is the fact that older adults take an average of more than five prescription drugs and three over-the-counter drugs at the same time. In geriatric clinics, about 5 percent to 10 percent of the patients seen for memory impairment have reversible dementia due to medication.

Some of the medications that may cause memory impairment include the anti-inflammatory drug prednisone (Deltasone, for example); heartburn drugs such as cimetidine (Tagamet), famotidine (Pepcid), and ranitidine (Zantac); anti-anxiety/sedative drugs, such as triazolam (Halcion), alprazolam (Xanax), or diazepam (Valium); or even insulin—too high a dose can cause low blood sugar (hypoglycemia) leading to abnormal mental function. Other possibilities are some medications for cancer, heart disease, high blood pressure, pain, nausea, Parkinson disease, allergies, and colds. Alcohol is the most prevalent intoxicant implicated in dementia. Fortunately, as is often the case with other drugs, the negative effects of alcohol on intellectual abilities can be reversed with abstinence, though chronic abuse may lead to permanent damage.

Memory impairment caused by medications can often be reversed or minimized by changing drugs or lowering the dose (which should be done only under a doctor's supervision). Other strategies to prevent adverse memory effects from medications are to avoid use of multiple drugs, verify that each drug is carefully monitored (preferably by a single primary care physician), and use drug-free periods as a way to determine whether adverse memory effects are due to a medication. The best way to monitor drug use with a doctor is the "brown bag" review—patients bring all of their prescription and nonprescription medications to the doctor's office. In this way, the patient eliminates the chance of forgetting to mention any of the drugs or confusing drug names and doses.

Memory Loss Due to Depression

Because the cognitive changes of dementia—impairment of memory, learning, attention, and concentration—can occur in people who are depressed, the diagnosis of dementia can be more difficult. In fact, depression and cognitive decline often occur together.

A person is more likely to be suffering from depression if there is a history of psychiatric illness, a sudden onset of cognitive symptoms, difficulties with sleep, or precipitation of symptoms by an emotional event. In addition, depressed patients often complain that they're unable to concentrate or remember things, while individuals with dementia are generally unaware of any mental problems. For example, when depressed persons are asked a question, they are likely to say "I don't know the answer." By contrast, someone with AD might attempt to answer, but be unable to do so correctly. Because depression and dementia are difficult to distinguish, it may be necessary to start antidepressant therapy, and later reassess the patient for the presence of dementia.

Age-Associated Memory Impairment

A certain amount of forgetfulness is to be expected with age. The difference between normal forgetfulness that increases with age—known clinically as age-associated memory impairment (AAMI)—and serious dementia is that the former is not disabling.

The memory lapses associated with AAMI are most likely to occur when a person is tired, sick, distracted, or under stress. Under better, less stressful circumstances, the same person is usually able to remember the necessary information with ease. Indeed, studies repeatedly show that older people who do poorly on timed tests actually do as well as or better than their college-age counterparts when permitted to work at their own pace.

Worrying about memory loss, in fact, makes it much more likely that no serious conditions are responsible for the lapse: People with serious memory impairment tend to be unaware of their lapses, don't worry about them, or attribute them to other causes. However, if the memory lapses interfere with normal daily functioning, or if close friends and relatives of the individual believe that the lapses are serious, some more complex cause may be at fault.

Although AAMI is common and is not a sign of a serious neurologic disorder, it can be frustrating and socially embarrassing. While there is no way to eliminate completely the minor memory lapses that occur with age-associated memory impairment, a number of strategies can improve overall memory ability at any age.

- **Relax.** Individuals are more likely to remember things when they are calm and relaxed, and less likely to remember when they are anxious and tense.
- **Exercise.** Even a brisk walk for 20 minutes, several times a week, may help improve mental function.
- **Stay mentally active.** Intellectually curious people—for example, those who take classes, learn a new language, play chess, or do brain-teasing puzzles—are more likely to remain mentally agile into their 70s and 80s.
- **Organize.** Making a simple "to do" list will serve as a reminder, and the mere act of writing lists reinforces memory.
- **Use memory aids.** A pocket notepad, personal digital assistant, or voice recorder may help you keep track of information.
- **Avoid excessive alcohol consumption.** Alcohol can significantly hasten the destruction of brain cells. Men should drink no more than the equivalent of one or two glasses of wine a day; women should limit themselves to one glass daily.
- **Take stock of mental health.** Depression, stress, grief, and anxiety make it difficult to concentrate, learn, and remember. If such conditions persist, seek treatment.
- **Use mnemonic devices.** Mnemonics, the art of improving memory, depends on strong visual imagery and meaningful associations. Also helpful are making up rhymes (for instance, "I before E, except after C"). In addition, repetition or rehearsal of new facts is always useful.

Memory Loss Due to Medical Conditions

A number of medical conditions can lead to memory problems, and in some cases, treatment of the underlying illness can reverse or reduce the memory deficit. These conditions include hormonal imbalances—due to thyroid disease or Cushing's disease (overproduction of steroid hormones by the adrenal gland); infectious diseases, including acquired immune deficiency syndrome (AIDS), neurosyphilis, and chronic meningitis resulting from fungal infections or tuberculosis; tumors of the frontal or temporal lobe of the cerebral cortex; subdural hematomas (a collection of blood between the skull and the brain); normal pressure hydrocephalus (caused by excess fluid in the brain); and vitamin deficiencies (vitamin B12 and niacin).

Memory and Irreversible Dementia

After eliminating treatable causes of memory loss, physicians will consider irreversible dementias as a possible diagnosis. These include well-known conditions, such as AD, stroke, and other vascular abnormalities, dementia with Lewy bodies, and Parkinson disease, as well as less common disorders, such as frontotemporal dementia (for example, Pick disease) and Huntington's disease. Other causes include infectious diseases such as Creutzfeldt-Jakob disease and AIDS.

Vascular Dementia

After AD, the most common cause of memory loss is vascular dementia—a disorder often resulting from a series of tiny strokes (known as infarcts) that destroy brain cells. Each infarct may be so small that it is inconsequential alone; however, the cumulative effect of many infarcts can destroy enough brain tissue to impair a person's memory, language, and other intellectual abilities.

Symptoms of vascular dementia can also involve other brain functions: loss of bladder or bowel control (incontinence); a mask-like facial expression; and weakness or paralysis on one side of the body are thought to be noncognitive hallmarks of vascular dementia. Patients who survive a cardiac arrest can also suffer from memory deficits. Rare causes of vascular dementia include lupus erythematosus and other collagen-vascular diseases (these may be at least partially reversible), as well as a major stroke. Vascular causes account for 10 percent to 20 percent of dementia cases.

Many people suffer from vascular dementia as a long-term result of chronic high blood pressure, diabetes, or coronary heart disease (CHD, narrowing of the coronary arteries that supply blood to the heart). Preventive measures can help forestall the development of dementia and prevent further deterioration. Weight control, exercise, and a low-salt diet can reduce blood pressure; a lower-fat diet can decrease the risk of CHD. Medications can lower blood pressure or cholesterol when necessary, and a daily aspirin may be prescribed to prevent blood clots from forming in the arteries feeding the brain or heart. In some cases, a procedure known as a carotid endarterectomy may be performed to remove a blockage from the main arteries that lead to the brain. People can reduce their risk of developing diabetes by controlling their weight with diet and exercise.

According to results from what is referred to as the "nun study," the same measures used to lower stroke risk may also reduce the risk of dementia related to AD. In this study, 102 elderly nuns (average age 83) were evaluated for Alzheimer's- and stroke-related symptoms while they were alive, and careful examinations of their brains were made after death. Among the nuns who had the brain lesions of AD, those who also had evidence of infarcts due to vascular disease were 11 times more likely to have shown signs of dementia when they were alive.

Dementia with Lewy Bodies

Dementia with Lewy bodies, which sometimes occurs simultaneously with AD or Parkinson disease, may account for 5 to 15 percent of cases of dementia. An individual with this form of dementia experiences episodes of confusion, falls, and repetitive hallucinations (such as always seeing the same person sitting on a particular chair), and also

Placing a Relative in Residential Care

The progression of dementia does not follow a uniform path, but is unique in each individual with the disease. It is difficult, therefore, to establish a specific timeline to determine when someone with dementia can still be cared for at home and when an assisted-living situation is appropriate.

In addition, families and caregivers may feel guilty about placing a relative with dementia in residential care, and often resist doing so—frequently at the expense of the caregiver's mental and physical health. However, it is not always safe to keep the person at home, especially when the individual has poor safety awareness.

Families of people with dementia should have a meeting soon after the diagnosis is made to discuss who will be responsible for caregiving, how to handle finances, and what roles each family member will assume. They should also discuss when they will begin seeking assisted living for the person with dementia. Each family has different financial, emotional, and time limitations that determine how long the person can stay at home. It is important to decide the timeline early in the disease, since later, the decision is more likely to be clouded by guilt and caregiver burnout.

The following signs may indicate that a person with dementia can no longer be cared for at home, and that their needs will be better addressed in a residential facility:

- **Wandering.** In particular, families should note whether the wandering is predictable—does it occur at the same time or place, or does it appear to be aimless?

- **Neglecting safety practices.** Forgetting common safety practices, such as turning off a stove or iron, can place the person with dementia—and others—at risk.

- **Agitation.** Problem behaviors such as shouting, moaning, fidgeting, pacing, and aggression can result from being left alone all day or from psychological or physical problems such as depression or headaches. These behaviors can prevent the caregiver from delivering care and may put the both the caregiver and receiver at physical risk.

- **Forgetting medication schedules.** People with dementia may have trouble recalling if and when they took their medications. As a result, they could skip doses of medications and/or end up taking extra doses.

- **Poor judgment.** As AD progresses, patients may begin to engage in behaviors that put them (and others) at great risk. For instance, they may continue to drive despite warnings.

- **Rejecting outside help in the home.** A rejection of outside help—like Meals on Wheels or a visiting nurse—is often a sign that a person with dementia can no longer be cared for at home.

- **Caregiver burnout.** A caregiver who is overburdened will likely be unable to provide effective care for a person with dementia.

has signs of parkinsonism (such as shuffling gait, rigid, stooped posture, poor balance, and slowness) early in the disease. The disease is characterized by cortical Lewy bodies—abnormal structures within brain cells that are distributed throughout the brain. Lewy body dementia progresses over several years. Risk factors for developing the disease have yet to be identified. While there are no current treatments, the depression and hallucinations that accompany the disease may be improved with medication.

Frontotemporal Dementias

Diseases causing frontotemporal dementia are much less frequent than AD, and account for 5 percent of cases of dementia. Pick disease is responsible for approximately one third of cases of frontotemporal dementia. Symptoms associated with Pick disease include impaired initiation of plans and goal setting, personality changes, unawareness of any loss of mental function, and language difficulties (aphasia). Palilalia—compulsive repetition of a word or phrase with increasing rapidity—sometimes occurs later in the illness. The course of the disease can vary from 2 to 10 years, but its final result is death.

Huntington's Disease

Huntington's disease is a rare hereditary disorder of the central nervous system characterized by uncontrollable movement and dementia. (In the past, the disease was called Huntington's chorea, from the Greek word meaning "dance.") The illness begins gradually, usually between the ages of 30 and 40, and can last for up to 20 years. Early signs of Huntington's disease include changes in behavior and unusual, fidgety movements. Symptoms may be mild enough for the disease to go unnoticed for many years. Eventually, however, twisting and jerking movements spread to the entire body and are followed by memory loss, confusion, and hallucinations.

Huntington's disease directly affects the parts of the brain that control coordination. Studies have shown a striking decrease in brain levels of the neurotransmitter gamma-amino butyric acid (GABA), but it is unclear whether this change plays a role in the disease. In 1993, scientists identified the gene defect believed to cause Huntington's disease. The gene is dominant, meaning that children with a parent who carries the defective gene have a 50 percent chance of developing Huntington's disease. (Genetic tests can determine whether these children have the gene responsible for Huntington's disease.) The discovery raises the possibility that a therapy may be developed to correct the defective gene, though currently no treatment is available.

Creutzfeldt-Jakob Disease

Creutzfeldt-Jakob disease (CJD) is a rare, fatal brain disorder that causes a rapidly progressing dementia. The disease affects approximately 1 in 1 million people worldwide each year, including 250 to 300 Americans. It can be transmitted through infected tissue (usually transplants), be inherited, or occur with no known explanation. It typically strikes people between the ages of 50 and 70 and leads to death within a few months.

A disorder with similar symptoms appeared in England in the mid-1990s, approximately 10 years after an outbreak of bovine spongiform encephalopathy (mad cow disease) in cattle that was linked to feed that included infected animal tissue. The disorder in humans was named new variant CJD (vCJD). It has been reported in about 150 people worldwide, most of whom have been younger than age 30. All are thought to have eaten tainted beef in Europe during the epidemic of mad cow disease. The disorder progresses more slowly than classic CJD (about 14 months) but inevitably leads to death. To date no cases of vCJD have been acquired in the United States.

No treatments exist for either classic CJD or vCJD. Yet the number of cases of vCJD has declined drastically since laws have been passed banning the inclusion of animal remains in cattle feed. If a family member dies of CJD or vCJD, however, an autopsy should be performed to definitively determine the cause of death.

Amnestic Syndrome (Amnesia)

Patients with amnestic syndrome (amnesia) demonstrate severe memory loss while retaining normal intelligence. The exotic nature of the disorder—memories become hidden due to a head injury, stroke, or encephalitis—has long fascinated scientists.

The first direct evidence that structures in the medial temporal lobe (where the hippocampus is located) play an important role in memory was provided by research on a patient with amnesia. Injury to the temporal lobe, due to an accident, severe alcoholism, prolonged low blood pressure, or viral inflammation of the brain, for example, can cause amnesia. Brain damage from such injuries usually results in anterograde amnesia, an inability to remember anything occurring after the injury. Retrograde amnesia, a loss of memory from a time prior to the accident—such as during childhood—is uncommon.

D

D

Sadness may be caused by a setback or a loss, and is often appropriate and transitory. But if sadness persists or begins to impair daily life, a mood disorder may be present. Major hallmarks of depression are a persistently low or sad mood, decreased or absent interest in almost all activities, loss of self-confidence, and a sense of worthlessness. Usually depression is episodic—that is, bouts of illness are separated by periods of full recovery.

Some 18 million Americans suffer from depression, the world's leading cause of chronic disability. Mood disorders most often surface between ages 20 and 30, but they can occur at any age. The duration of an untreated episode of major depression is usually eight to nine months. This period can be shortened considerably with proper diagnosis and treatment, which leads to a more rapid remission of symptoms in up to 80 percent of cases.

Causes

The specific cause of depression is unknown in most cases, but the disorder appears to result from some combination of genetic predisposition and psychological and medical factors.

Changes in the Brain

Chemical changes occur in the brain during depression, and researchers believe that these changes are linked to the symptoms of depression.

The brain is composed of distinct regions—each with particular functions—made up of networks of nerve cells, or neurons. Messages pass from one neuron to another. One region thought to be involved in depression is the limbic system, which is concerned with emotional behavior. An area within this system called the hypothalamus regulates the pituitary

gland and may be involved in the hormonal imbalances sometimes associated with depression.

Because individual neurons are separated from others by small gaps (synaptic clefts) at each end, chemicals called neurotransmitters are needed to bridge the synaptic cleft and pass messages from one neuron to the next. Of particular concern in depression are the neurotransmitters norepinephrine, serotonin, and dopamine. Imbalances in the amounts of these substances in the brain appear to contribute to depression or bipolar disorder.

Genetic Factors

Genetic factors are clearly important in the development of depression. Research shows that when one identical twin has a mood disorder, there is about a 50 percent chance that the other will develop the illness at some time. Genetics also plays a role in treatment. Some evidence shows that patients have a better chance of responding to the same antidepressant medication that a depressed first-degree relative (a parent, sibling, or child) has responded to.

For these reasons, it is important to be aware of any family history of depression. Still, while genetic factors may make a person more susceptible to mood disorders, a trigger such as another medical condition or psychological stress is often required for a mood disorder to develop.

Other Causes

In about 10 percent to 15 percent of cases, mood disorders are caused by medication, illegal drugs, or neurological or medical abnormalities. For example, depression can result from the chronic use of beta-blockers, reserpine derivatives (for high blood pressure), steroid medications such as prednisone (Deltasone), benzodiazepines (for anxiety), or anti-cancer drugs. Withdrawal from central nervous system stimulants, like amphetamines or cocaine, can also precipitate depression.

Patients with dementing brain disorders, such as Alzheimer's disease and Huntington's disease, are prone to depression. Depression can also be a consequence of stroke, affecting about 25 percent of people who have had a stroke in the left frontal area of the brain. In addition, an underactive thyroid can lead to depression. Overproduction of the steroid hormone cortisol by the adrenal gland (Cushing Syndrome) can cause either depression or mania in some patients.

Deficiencies in folic acid, vitamin B_6, or vitamin B_{12} may also cause depression. In one study of 700 women published in 2000, those who had a vitamin B_{12} deficiency were two times more likely to be severely depressed than women who did not have a vitamin B_{12} deficiency.

Some people experience episodes of depression only during certain times of the year, usually beginning in November, when there is less sunlight—hence the name "winter depression," or seasonal affective disorder (SAD). Typically, depressive symptoms peak between the fall and the spring. One theory is that the relative lack of sunlight during these times may alter brain levels of certain mood-controlling substances, for example, increasing levels of the hormone melatonin.

Symptoms

Although severe depression is readily recognized (see below), it can be difficult to distinguish the milder (and more common) forms of depression from the emotional changes that are part of everyday life. The dominant form of depression is major depression, which clinicians distinguish from other forms of the disorder, such as dysthymia (page 260), grief (page 262), and atypical depression (page 254).

Unlike most medical disorders, depression is not associated with any characteristic laboratory changes or tissue abnormalities that can be used to confirm a diagnosis.

The American Psychiatric Association has established diagnostic classification systems to allow consistent diagnoses of major depression. These criteria are contained in the fourth edition of the *Diagnostic and Statistical Manual of Mental Disorders (DSM-IV)*.

Major Depression

According to the DSM-IV, a person is suffering from a major depressive episode if he or she exhibits either the first or second of the following nine symptoms, along with four others, continually for more than two weeks:

- Depressed mood with overwhelming feelings of sadness and grief
- Loss of interest and pleasure in activities formerly enjoyed
- Insomnia, early-morning waking, or oversleeping nearly every day
- Decreased energy; fatigue
- Noticeable changes in appetite and weight (significant loss or gain)
- Inability to concentrate; indecisiveness
- Physical symptoms of restlessness or being slowed down
- Feelings of guilt, worthlessness, and helplessness
- Recurrent thoughts of death and suicide; suicide attempts

The diagnosis is more certain when these criteria are supplemented by either a positive family history, a prior episode of depression or mania, or the presence of a precipitating factor such as a recent stroke or the

D

Atypical Depression

Patients with major depression are generally perceived as being sad or having a depressed mood, but sometimes they do not exhibit either the sadness or some of the other symptoms normally associated with the disorder. Although such cases are quite common, comprising 29 percent to 42 percent of depressed outpatients, this kind of depression is known as atypical depression. The disorder is just as debilitating as major depression, despite the apparent lack of sadness. In fact, during a 13-year follow-up of 1,612 participants in one study, patients over age 50 who had atypical depression were significantly more likely to die than persons with major depression or no depression. Older individuals are less likely than younger ones to report sadness as a primary symptom of depression.

use of medications known to cause mood disorders.

Other symptoms of depression include disorganized thinking and delusions. In addition to these disturbances in mood and cognition (thinking), patients with major depression may have abnormalities in body functions such as constipation or decreased sexual drive.

Episodes of major depression range from mild to severe. In mild episodes, symptoms barely meet the requirements for a diagnosis and the associated functional impairment is minor. Severe episodes are characterized by several debilitating symptoms, including a marked decline in mood and interference with social and job-related functions. Severely afflicted individuals have difficulty with almost every activity—going to work, socializing, and even getting up in the morning. They may be unable to feed and dress themselves or to maintain personal hygiene.

Suicide

Suicide—the 11th leading cause of death in the United States—is a major complication of depression. About 1 in 16 people diagnosed with depression die by suicide, and two thirds of people who die by suicide are depressed.

In the United States, the risk of suicide is highest in older white males and in those who live alone, have made prior suicide attempts, refuse psychiatric evaluation, or abuse alcohol or drugs. Although women attempt suicide three to four times more often than men, men are three to four times more likely to be successful.

Up to three quarters of people who die of suicide have visited their medical doctor in the prior month. This suggests that these people "knew" something was wrong, but that neither they nor their doctor identified depression as the problem. Although it is impossible to predict accurately who will attempt suicide, there are warning signs that a severely depressed person may make an attempt. All too often, friends and family of people who commit suicide are unaware of the seriousness of these signs until it is too late.

The most important step in preventing suicide is recognizing the risk factors and warning signs and facilitating appropriate treatment of the underlying psychiatric illness. Signs include:

- Social isolation that may be self-imposed
- Drastic mood swings or overall personality changes
- Neglecting home, finances, or pets

- Exaggerated complaints of aches or pains
- Recent psychological trauma, such as a divorce, death of a loved one, or job loss (which may trigger suicidal thinking in an already depressed person)
- Giving away cherished belongings to loved ones; putting one's affairs in order
- Sudden calm or cheerfulness after a period of depression
- Frequent use of alcohol or other drugs
- Buying a gun
- Verbal threats of suicide or statements that suggest a desire to die
- Family history of suicide or previous suicide attempts

Not all people who commit suicide have these risk factors, however, and most people who do have them are not suicidal.

Treatment

Treatment of depression has three goals. In order of importance, they are to relieve the symptoms of depression; to return patients to their previous ability to function socially and in the workplace; and to reduce the likelihood of a recurrence.

Treatment goals are accomplished over three stages: acute, continuation, and maintenance. Acute treatment focuses on immediate relief from symptoms and restoration of function. Once symptoms respond to acute treatment, continuation treatment is begun to prevent a relapse. If a patient has no symptoms for four to nine months after an episode, he or she is considered recovered. At this point, maintenance treatment is initiated to prevent a new episode; it can last from one year to a lifetime, depending on the individual. Depression recurs in about half of cases within two years of stopping treatment, so timing must be carefully considered when stopping medications. The longer a person remains on treatment, the smaller the likelihood of recurrence.

The four treatment options for dealing with depression are antidepressant medications; psychotherapy; other treatments, such as electroconvulsive therapy or light therapy; and any combination of these. Exercise and a healthy diet also play a role in improving mood and self-image. It is important to start treatment as soon as possible, since the disorder becomes more difficult to treat the longer it lasts. Because response to any particular treatment varies from one patient to another, a person who does not improve with the first treatment may respond to a different one. Medications are probably the most common form of therapy, and any given antidepressant has up to a 70 percent chance of working in a particular individual.

Psychotherapy alone helps a significant number of mildly to moderately depressed persons. It has fewer side effects than medication and may be more acceptable than medication to some people. Combination therapy (both medication and psychotherapy) is more effective than either one alone for mild to moderate depression. This option may be beneficial if either treatment alone produces only partial results; if the depression is chronic; or if an evaluation suggests several discrete aspects of a disorder that are each best treated by different means, such as medication for depressive symptoms and psychotherapy for job-related problems.

The more severe cases of depression are best treated with medication. Up to 90% of extremely depressed people improve with electroconvulsive therapy when it it used as first-line treatment. It is usually used only when several other therapies have failed, however, in which case the response rate drops to 50% to 60%.

Alcoholism makes recovery from depression more difficult. A recent study compared 176 men and women who fit the criteria for both alcoholism and major depression with 412 people who had major depression alone. Subjects who were never alcoholics or who no longer drank were two times more likely to recover from an episode of major depression than the active alcoholics. However, active alcoholism did not increase the chance of having recurrent episodes of major depression, suggesting that depression is triggered by other factors.

Psychotherapy

An advantage of psychotherapy is that it produces few physiologic side effects—an especially important consideration for older adults who are often taking more than one type of medication. Psychotherapy may also help patients learn to cope with, or avoid factors contributing to, a recurrence of depression, and offers the possibility of effective treatment for patients who have not responded to drugs. On the downside, it may take longer to achieve any benefit using psychotherapy—six to eight weeks or longer, as compared with four to six weeks for medication. Also, psychotherapy alone is not effective in patients with severe depression.

Based on the severity of the illness and factors specific to each patient, therapists select a combination of different approaches from a range of psychotherapeutic techniques, such as interpersonal therapy, behavioral therapy, or cognitive therapy. Essential to all psychotherapy is the establishment of a trusting relationship with the therapist that enables the patient to share confidences, life experiences, and problems. As a result, patients unable to communicate owing to severe physical debilitation or delusions caused by depression may not benefit from psychotherapy until medications or other treatments improve the depression.

If psychotherapy alone produces no response by 6 weeks, or only a partial response by 12 weeks, medication should be strongly considered.

Medications

There are several advantages to treating depression with medications: They are effective against mild, moderate, and severe forms of major depression; patients usually respond more quickly to them than to psychotherapy; they are easy to administer; and they require little time from the patient. In addition, patients should be assured that antidepressants are not addictive and, when properly administered, are rarely dangerous. However, drug treatment can cause unwanted side effects; it requires strict adherence to a medication schedule and repeated medical visits to monitor response; and as many as 10 percent to 30 percent of patients fail to complete treatment. Older people and those with chronic illnesses are more susceptible to the adverse effects of antidepressants.

Although researchers believe that these drugs work by affecting levels of neurotransmitters (chemical messengers that communicate between nerve cells) in the brain, physicians cannot determine which medication will be most effective in any particular individual. Therefore, drug selection remains largely a process of educated guesses. Family history can also determine which drug is most likely to be effective, as well as which is most likely to cause side effects. In most cases, older patients are started on lower doses than younger patients in order to reduce the risk of side effects. Typically about 60 percent to 70 percent of patients have some response to the first antidepressant they try.

By themselves, antidepressant drugs usually produce a significant improvement by four to six weeks, although it may take up to eight weeks to see the full benefit.

When a drug proves ineffective, another one is often selected from a different class of medications, since drugs in the same class tend to work similarly. In 20 percent to 50 percent of patients, adding the drug lithium can help augment the action of an antidepressant. However, this combination increases the risk of side effects and adverse drug interactions. (For this reason, lithium should be prescribed only by a physician knowledgeable in its use.) If a drug from one class is producing good results but unacceptable side effects, changing to a different drug from the same class may help. If maintenance treatment is no longer required, drugs are discontinued slowly to avoid withdrawal symptoms. Relapses are most common during the first two months after stopping an antidepressant. Therefore, individuals should remain in contact with their physician during this period. (Should a relapse occur, the same drug that was used successfully the first time often proves effective again.)

Antidepressants must be used with caution by depressed people who are suicidal; important precautions include frequent follow-up visits and prescriptions for a relatively small number of pills at a time. Suicide attempts or suicidal thoughts are common symptoms of depression, and the risk of suicide may increase as depression begins to respond to treatment, because patients might regain just enough energy and motivation to follow through on a suicidal urge.

Selective serotonin reputake inhibitors (SS-RIs). These drugs, which include citalopram (Celexa), escitalopram (Lexapro), fluoxetine (Prozac), fluvoxamine (Luvox), paroxetine (Paxil), and sertraline (Zoloft), inhibit the reuptake of serotonin and thereby raise its concentration in the synaptic cleft. All of the SSRIs are equally effective and have similar rates and types of side effects, although it is possible that an individual might respond better or have fewer side effects with one medication. Side effects are not always a reason to change medications. For example, paroxetine can produce a sedative effect in some people, but this may be beneficial to people with combined anxiety and depression.

Because SSRIs have milder side effects than most other antidepressants, they are now favored by most physicians as the first-line drug treatment for depression. Studies have demonstrated that SSRIs are as effective as tricyclics; about half of patients taking an SSRI achieve a complete resolution of all their depressive symptoms. Advantages of SSRIs over the tricyclics include a lower risk of fatal overdoses and serious heart rhythm disturbances in people with cardiac disease.

Side effects of SSRIs include insomnia, drowsiness, nausea, anxiety, and weight loss. Another troublesome side effect is sexual dysfunction—for example, diminished sexual desire, changes in the sensations of arousal, and orgasmic disturbances—which may occur in about 37% of both men and women taking these drugs. Any of these side effects usually develop within the first week of starting an SSRI, though they may arise more slowly as blood levels of the medication build up. Ways to combat sexual dysfunction include choosing a medication with a low rate of sexual side effects (such as bupropion), waiting to see if sexual side effects abate, changing the time you take the medication (possibly to nighttime), reducing the dosage, taking drug holidays (for example, not taking the medication on the weekend), or adding another medication, such as sildenafil (Viagra). (Do not change any aspect of your medication regimen without first consulting your doctor.)

Recently, it was recognized that SSRIs may produce neurological side effects—symptoms like those of Parkinson disease, such as impaired muscle tone, tremors, and spasms, or feelings of restlessness that can become so severe that patients are unable to sit still—however, these side effects are rare.

Tricyclics. Named for their chemical structure—a chain of three rings—these drugs raise brain concentrations of the neurotransmitters norepinephrine and serotonin by blocking their reabsorption by the nerve cells (neurons) that release them. A puzzling feature of tricyclics is that their effect on neurotransmitters is rapid, but it takes weeks before depression improves. Tricyclics are used mainly to treat moderate to severe depression. About 60 percent of tricyclic users experience significant improvement within four to six weeks. Each of the tricyclics is believed to be equally effective, but side effects may differ.

Six to eight weeks of treatment may be needed before deciding whether a tricyclic is working. Failure to improve may be due to ineffectiveness of the medication or lack of compliance by the patient. About one third of patients stop taking tricyclics because of side effects, and about two thirds of older patients miss 25 percent to 50 percent of their doses. Poor compliance leads to fluctuating blood levels of the drug and an unfavorable response. The most prominent side effects of tricyclics are drowsiness, orthostatic hypotension (dizziness on standing due to a drop in blood pressure), a fine tremor of the hands, nausea and vomiting, blurred vision, dry mouth, rapid heart rate, difficulty urinating, and constipation.

Tetracyclics. The action, efficacy, and side effects of maprotiline (Ludiomil) and mirtazapine (Remeron) are similar to those of the tricyclics. However, maprotiline is more likely to cause seizures than most other antidepressants. A version of mirtazapine that dissolves on the tongue and does not need to be chewed or swallowed whole became available in early 2001.

Dopamine reuptake inhibitors. Bupropion (Wellbutrin) decreases the reuptake of dopamine, a neurotransmitter and a precursor of other neurotransmitters. This drug causes less drowsiness and other side effects than the tricyclics, but on rare occasions, it can cause seizures, particularly at higher doses.

Monoamine oxidase (MAO) inhibitors. Like tricyclics, MAO inhibitors increase brain levels of norepinephrine, serotonin, and dopamine, in this case by blocking the action of the enzyme MAO, which normally inactivates these three neurotransmitters. MAO inhibitors are effective in many depressed patients, especially those whose depression is accompanied by marked anxiety, panic attacks, heightened appetite, or excessive sleeping. The results of one small study suggest that the MAO inhibitor selegiline (Eldepryl), a drug commonly used to treat Parkinson disease, may help older adults whose depression has not responded to other drugs or to electroconvulsive therapy.

MAO inhibitors can cause some of the same side effects as the tricyclics (see left). These drugs should not be used by patients with active alcoholism, congestive heart failure, or severe impairment of liver or kidney function, or by those who are taking multiple medications for high blood pressure. In addition, MAO inhibitors have the unique potential for causing a sudden, extreme elevation in blood pressure (a hypertensive crisis) when people using them take certain drugs or consume foods or beverages containing tyramine. Tyramine is found in nasal decongestants, cold or allergy medicines, very ripe bananas, beer, and aged or smoked meats, among other things. (Patients taking an MAO inhibitor must get a complete list of restricted foods and drugs from their doctor.)

Serotonin and norepinephrine reuptake inhibitors. Trazodone (Desyrel) and venlafaxine (Effexor) are serotonin and norepinephrine reuptake inhibitors. Like the tricyclics, these drugs work by raising brain concentrations of the neurotransmitters serotonin and norepinephrine. They are often the most effective drugs for older patients. Possible side effects include nausea, dry mouth, dizziness, and drowsiness. Venlafaxine may increase blood pressure in some people, so monitoring blood pressure is important for anyone taking this drug.

Alternative treatments. Despite the availability of a full arsenal of medications proven to be effective for treating depression, some people are turning to alternative treatments for this condition. Most of these alternative treatments—including St. John's wort and S-adenosylmethionine (SAM-e)—are considered dietary supplements in the United States and therefore have not been tested or approved by the U.S. Food and Drug Administration (FDA). No one is sure how well they work or how they may interact with prescription medications. In addition, one concern with alternative treatments is that individuals tend to medicate themselves instead of being evaluated and monitored by a health professional. As a result, they may not recognize worsening symptoms.

St. John's wort, which is extracted from a yellow flowered plant called *Hypericum perforatum*, is the best known of the supplements purported to be natural antidepressants. The American College of Physicians and the American Society of Internal Medicine recently included it in their guidelines as a treatment option for mild depression, but two large studies published in the *Journal of the American Medical Association* in 2000 and 2001 found that St. John's wort was no more effective than a placebo for treating major depression. Thus, the authors recommend that people with major depression not take St. John's wort until well-designed studies support its use. People with mild to moderate depression would be wise to follow the same advice.

Recent reports have illustrated that St. John's wort may not be as benign as it appears. St. John's wort lowers blood levels of indinavir (Crixivan), a drug prescribed for HIV (human immunodeficiency virus) infection, as well as cyclosporine (Sandimmune), a drug given to prevent organ rejection in transplant patients. Physicians suspect that St. John's wort might interfere with a range of medications, including those prescribed to treat depression, heart disease, seizures, and some cancers. The supplement may also cause increased sensitivity to the sun.

Another supplement widely touted for the treatment of depression is S-adenosylmethionine, better known as SAM-e. But results of published studies that purport to show the benefits of SAM-e are not at all convincing.

Electroconvulsive Therapy

Electroconvulsive therapy (ECT) is a relatively painless procedure that is effective in treating major depression.

People with depression typically first receive psychotherapy, antidepressant medication, or a combination of the two. These treatments, though often effective, take time to work. This delay can be dangerous for patients whose depression is accompanied by delusions or intense suicidal thoughts. ECT can work much more quickly than antidepressants and is useful when patients are at immediate risk for self-injury or suicide.

D

Dysthymia

Dysthymia is a chronic form of depression that is milder than major depression. It is characterized by the presence of depressed mood for most of the day, for more days than not, over a period of at least two years. It may be intermittent, with periods of feeling normal, but the duration of the relief lasts for no more than two months. Because the onset of symptoms is insidious, the disorder often goes unnoticed. On average, symptoms, which can wax and wane, last 16 years before a diagnosis is made.

Dysthymia is twice as common in women as in men, but older patients are as likely to be men as women. Some medical conditions, including neurological disorders (such as multiple sclerosis and stroke), hypothyroidism, fibromyalgia, and chronic fatigue syndrome, are associated with dysthymia. Severe psychological stress, such as death of a spouse or caring for a chronically ill loved one, can also trigger dysthymia. In particular, older patients who have been free from psychiatric disorders often develop dysthymia after such life stresses.

Symptoms

In addition to depressed mood, symptoms include two or more of the following:

- Poor appetite or overeating
- Insomnia or hypersomnia
- Low energy or fatigue
- Low self-esteem
- Poor concentration
- Difficulty making decisions
- Feelings of hopelessness

About 10 percent of people with dysthymia also have recurrent episodes of major depression, a condition known as double depression. Symptoms that accompany dysthymia during major depressive episodes include:

- Feelings of worthlessness; low self-esteem
- Noticeable changes in appetite and weight (significant loss or gain)
- Noticeable changes in sleep patterns (such as insomnia, early-morning awakening, or oversleeping)
- Decreased energy; fatigue
- Inability to concentrate or think; indecisiveness
- Persistent feelings of hopelessness

Treatment

Many of the treatments used for major depression can also treat dysthymia effectively, particularly the selective serotonin reuptake inhibitors, or SSRIs (see page 257).

If the drugs provide relief, they should be continued for at least two years, and lifetime use may be warranted. Psychotherapy may also be beneficial. In addition, steps should be taken to provide support during periods of ongoing stress, such as illness.

ECT can help other patients as well. It may be prescribed when antidepressant medications have not worked. It can be useful for older patients who are unable to tolerate antidepressants and for pregnant women in whom medication might damage the fetus.

ECT is performed under general anesthesia (along with a muscle relaxant) in an inpatient or outpatient setting. Because patients are under anesthesia and have taken muscle relaxants, they neither convulse nor feel the current. Patients awaken about five to ten minutes after the end of the treatment, and most are oriented and alert within a half hour.

Typically, ECT is given 2 to 3 times a week for a total of 6 to 12 sessions. These sessions improve depression in 50 percent to 70 percent of patients, a response rate similar to that of antidepressant drugs.

Yet the benefits of ECT are short-lived. Within a year, between 50 percent and 60 percent of patients relapse. Patients may have to continue receiving ECT periodically or take antidepressant medication to prevent relapse.

The immediate side effects of the procedure can be headaches, nausea, muscle aches and soreness, disorientation, and confusion lasting about an hour. Patients may also develop memory problems, including difficulty recalling newly acquired information, though this problem should end in the weeks following a course of treatment. Patients can also lose memories that were formed up to six months before the procedure. Usually, learning and memory return to normal within a few months of the last treatment. Patients may never recover memories of events immediately surrounding an ECT session.

No one is sure how ECT helps certain mental disorders. It may flood the brain with neurotransmitters such as serotonin and dopamine, which are known to be involved in depression. ECT may also help regulate hormones that play a role in these disorders.

Depression in Older Adults

Although increasing age alone does not put a person at greater risk for depression, the incidence of depression is higher in older adults. A survey of Californians, age 50 to 95, found that factors such as chronic illness, physical disabilities, and social isolation—which often coincide with increasing age—were more predictive of depression than age. As a result, depression in older adults is a serious problem. The National Institute of Mental Health's Epidemiologic Catchment Area Study estimated that at least 1 million of the nation's 31 million people age 65 and older suffer from major depression,

and an additional 5 million have depressive symptoms that are severe enough to require treatment.

Unfortunately, the disease is often misdiagnosed and left untreated in the elderly. According to *Diagnosis and Treatment of Depression in Late Life*, a consensus report from the National Institutes of Health (NIH): "What makes depression in the elderly so insidious is that neither the victim nor the health-care provider may recognize its symptoms in the context of the multiple physical problems of many elderly people."

Many older persons who live alone have inadequate support mechanisms and are confused by the multitude of systems available to provide medical care, social services, and financial assistance for their medical needs. Older adults also tend to be embarrassed and reluctant to seek professional help for emotional problems, partly because the stigma of psychiatric illness is especially strong among people in this age group. In addition, friends and family often fail to perceive signs of distress. Older depressed patients are more likely to tell their primary care physician about physical complaints than about subjective feelings of depressed mood. For example, they may report loss of appetite, insomnia, lack of energy, or loss of interest and enjoyment in daily activities. Unfortunately, both doctor and patient often consider these symptoms a "normal part of aging" that accompanies the physical, social, and economic problems faced by many older adults.

Depression is sometimes left undiagnosed because of life circumstances that are common in later years. The elderly are typically subjected to numerous stressful life situations: loss of a spouse, family members, or friends by death or geographic relocation; retirement, which may be accompanied by a loss of status and self-identity; diminished financial resources; fears of death or loss of

Grief vs. Depression

The loss of a loved one can cause intense mental anguish. Occasionally, this anguish triggers a major depressive episode, but few people in mourning experience true clinical depression. If acute symptoms of grief—such as sadness accompanied by sleeping difficulties or weight loss—do not show signs of subsiding within two months of the loss, the person may have unresolved grief and may develop major depression. According to the American Psychiatric Association's Diagnostic and Statistical Manual of Mental Disorders, symptoms indicative of major depression, but not of normal grief, include:

- Excessive guilt (unrelated to things done or not done at the time of the death)
- Excessive thoughts of death
- Excessive feelings of worthlessness
- A slowing of one's actions or movements (psychomotor retardation)
- Impaired ability to perform functions of daily life
- Hallucinations (other than brief episodes of hearing or seeing the deceased person)

Major depression can also be distinguished from grief by the timing of the symptoms. Unlike grief, during which a person can have good and bad days, depression is experienced persistently throughout (or at specific times) every day. Other indications that a person may have major depression are the presence of suicidal thoughts or physical complaints that cannot be explained; trouble sleeping or early-morning awakenings that last over six weeks; or loss of more than 15 pounds. People with unresolved grief may also experience apathy or panic attacks, or they may feel as if they are developing the symptoms suffered by the deceased person.

Treatment. If you feel that a loss has left you with unresolved grief and depression, you should seek help. A bereavement support group might be useful for some people. Other people may prefer individual counseling sessions to address both the issues surrounding the loss and the related depression. In some cases, antidepressant medication may be needed to help a person return to daily functioning while working through the grief and depression. Exercising regularly can also be helpful in dealing with depression and stress.

---

independence and self-sufficiency; social isolation; and medical problems. Any of these factors may trigger symptoms of depression that are attributed to life stresses and not recognized as a true depressive illness.

In addition, the higher prevalence of concurrent medical conditions and a greater use of medications in older people further complicate the diagnosis. While the depression may be a primary disorder, it may also result from some underlying organic cause such as cancer, stroke, or a reaction to a prescription drug. The possibility of dementia adds further difficulties: Symptoms of major depression can mimic symptoms (for example, disorientation, distractibility, or memory loss) of a dementing disease such as Alzheimer's disease. Thus, doctors need to perform a careful mental status evaluation, as well as a medical history and physical exam, to find the primary cause of the psychological symptoms.

Treatment. Older people are more susceptible to adverse side effects than younger ones, so drug therapy must be approached carefully. Older people may require smaller dosages as well as closer monitoring for toxic reactions and to see whether the drugs are being taken as prescribed. Moreover, the elderly use prescription drugs approximately three times more often than the general population and are therefore at greater risk for adverse interactions between these drugs and antidepressants. Treatment can also be difficult in reluctant patients and in those lacking a social support system to help them with practical considerations such as costs and transportation for visits to a doctor.

Despite all of these obstacles, treatment for depression in older patients is generally effective; even partial success can lead to improved quality of life and productivity. Some studies even suggest that treatment with medications is more effective in older patients than in younger ones.

D

Diabetes mellitus is a metabolic disorder characterized by abnormally high levels of blood glucose, the sugar that all cells in the body need for energy. The manufacture of glucose by the liver, and the use of glucose in cells, are regulated primarily by insulin, a hormone produced in the pancreas. In a person who has diabetes, either the pancreas isn't producing enough insulin (type 1 diabetes) or the cells are resistant to the actions of insulin (type 2 diabetes). In either case, the result is abnormally high blood levels of glucose, or hyperglycemia, and an accompanying spillover of excess glucose into the urine. The passage of large amounts of sugar-laden urine is a key manifestation of diabetes and gives the disorder its name: diabetes is the Greek word for "siphon" and mellitus is the Latin word for "honey-sweet."

In the United States about 18 million people have diabetes—though more than one third of them do not yet know they have the disorder because symptoms of type 2 diabetes often develop gradually. A large portion of people with diabetes, some 9 million, are age 65 or older. Since 1997, the number of people diagnosed with diabetes in the United States has more than tripled, rising from less than 5 percent of the population to almost 7 percent today.

Diabetes can be detected before symptoms appear, and it can also be controlled and in some cases prevented. When it is not controlled, however, there are dangers from the immediate complications of high blood glucose levels and long-term complications affecting the eyes, nerves, kidneys, and large blood vessels.

Types of Diabetes

Type 1 diabetes usually emerges before age 30 and tends to come on suddenly. Type 2 diabetes is far more common—about 90 percent of people with diabetes have type 2. It usually starts later in life, after age 40. The onset tends to be more gradual, and blood glucose levels are more stable. Most patients with type 2 disease are obese.

Type 1 diabetes was once called insulin-dependent or juvenile diabetes, while type 2 diabetes was formerly called non-insulin dependent or adult diabetes. These terms are no longer used because some people with type 2 diabetes eventually require insulin, and there is a growing epidemic of type 2 disease in children.

Prediabetes

Prediabetes is a relatively new term for a medical condition in which blood glucose levels are between 100 and 125 mg/dL—higher than normal but not high enough to be diagnostic of diabetes. Previous names for the condition were impaired fasting glucose and impaired glucose tolerance. About 41 million Americans have prediabetes. Without treatment, most of them will develop type 2 diabetes within 10 years.

Like people with diabetes, those with prediabetes have an increased risk of coronary heart disease (CHD). Individuals with prediabetes should attain a healthy body weight, check for signs of diabetes, and try to modify other risk factors for CHD (such as cigarette smoking, high blood pressure, and elevated cholesterol levels).

Causes

Type 1 diabetes is an autoimmune disease: For reasons that aren't clear, the body produces antibodies that attack and damage the pancreatic beta cells that secrete insulin. At first, the ability of the beta cells to secrete insulin is merely impaired, but eventually (usually in less than a year) they produce little or no insulin. Fortunately, body tissues respond normally to insulin delivered by injection, and so people with type 1 diabetes can compensate by injecting insulin regularly. Although heredity plays some role in type 1 diabetes, most patients have no known family history of diabetes.

In type 2 diabetes, the body's tissues (primarily the liver and muscles) become less sensitive to insulin action. In order for cells to get the glucose they need, the pancreas must increase its production of insulin. Diabetes results when the pancreas is unable to secrete enough extra insulin to overcome the tissue resistance. (Although the majority of patients with type 2 diabetes can be treated with lifestyle measures [diet and exercise] or oral drugs, about 30 percent need insulin injections to achieve adequate control of their blood glucose.)

Heredity plays an important role in type 2 diabetes, but obesity is a major contributing factor for the disorder. For example, insulin resistance is a common feature of both obesity and type 2 diabetes, and 80 percent to 90 percent of people with type 2 diabetes are obese. The risk of type 2 diabetes increases as a person's weight increases. And people who store extra body fat in their abdominal region have a higher risk of developing diabetes than those whose fat is mainly in their hips and thighs. In addition, type 2 diabetes is more common in certain races, such as African Americans, Native Americans and Hispanic Americans.

Though much less common, diabetes can sometimes develop because of some other disorder. For example, diabetes can result from diseases that destroy the pancreas—such as hemochromatosis (an excessive absorption and storage of iron) or chronic pancreatitis (inflammation of the pancreas)—or from surgical removal of the pancreas for cancer. Diabetes is also associated with other endocrine disorders, such as Cushing's disease (overproduction of glucocorticoid, by the adrenal gland), or the administration of glucocorticoids, such as prednisone, to treat disorders like asthma.

Prevention

Prevention of diabetes is, of course, preferable to its treatment. Efforts to prevent type 2 diabetes are especially important for individuals at highest risk for developing the disease—those who have impaired glucose tolerance, are overweight, have a family history of the disorder, belong to a high-risk ethnic group (such as African Americans, Hispanics, or Native Americans), or have a history of diabetes during pregnancy (gestational diabetes).

The main strategy for prevention is a combination of diet and exercise. Both help to achieve and maintain weight loss; and exercise improves insulin resistance by making muscles and other tissues more sensitive to insulin. In addition, there is some evidence that a high-fiber diet may decrease the risk of developing type 2 diabetes.

The Diabetes Prevention Program study—a nationwide study conducted at 27 medical centers—found that people with prediabetes can take steps to prevent type 2 diabetes. In the study, participants who followed a low-calorie, low-fat diet; exercised 30 minutes a day; and lost an average of 15 lbs. were 58% less likely to develop type 2 diabetes over a three-year period than people who did not make these lifestyle changes. In addition, people who took the diabetes drug metformin (Glucophage) reduced their risk of type 2 diabetes by 31%, compared with people who received a placebo. In another study, the Heart Outcomes Prevention Evaluation (HOPE), people taking the ACE inhibitor ramipril (Altace) were 30% less likely to develop diabetes than those taking a placebo.

In addition, a high-fiber diet may decrease the risk of developing type 2 diabetes. An

Insulin Defects in Type 1 and Type 2 Diabetes

After a meal, carbohydrates from food are converted to glucose (sugar) and enter the bloodstream. In response to the rise in blood glucose levels, the pancreas—a small, elongated gland located below and behind the stomach—produces the hormone insulin and secretes it into the bloodstream. Insulin allows glucose to enter cells, where it is used for energy or converted to a storage form for future use. Insulin also inhibits the release of glucose by the liver.

Insulin works similarly to a key in a lock. Specifically, insulin interacts with structures (called receptors) on the surface of cells to open small passageways through which glucose can enter cells. As a result, blood glucose levels fall and insulin production stops (see illustration A).

This process of moving glucose from the bloodstream into cells is disrupted in people with diabetes. In type 1 diabetes, damage to the pancreas by an abnormal autoimmune reaction reduces insulin production, so that little or no insulin is available to help get glucose into cells. The result is abnormally high levels of glucose in the blood, a condition called hyperglycemia (see illustration B). In type 2 diabetes, cells are less responsive to the actions of insulin. In other words, insulin interacts with the structures on the cell surfaces but has difficulty opening the small passageways, and insufficient glucose enters the cells. The pancreas compensates by producing more insulin, but over time it cannot produce enough to overcome the cells' reduced response. As in type 1 diabetes, the result is hyperglycemia (see illustration C). In addition, as type 2 diabetes progresses, the ability of the pancreas to produce insulin may also become impaired, making it even more difficult to remove glucose from the bloodstream.

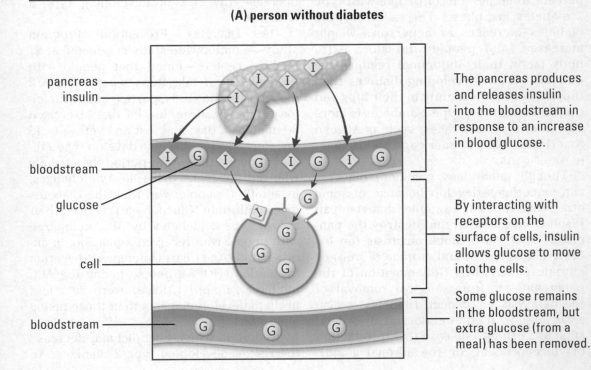

(A) person without diabetes

pancreas

insulin

The pancreas produces and releases insulin into the bloodstream in response to an increase in blood glucose.

bloodstream

glucose

By interacting with receptors on the surface of cells, insulin allows glucose to move into the cells.

cell

Some glucose remains in the bloodstream, but extra glucose (from a meal) has been removed.

bloodstream

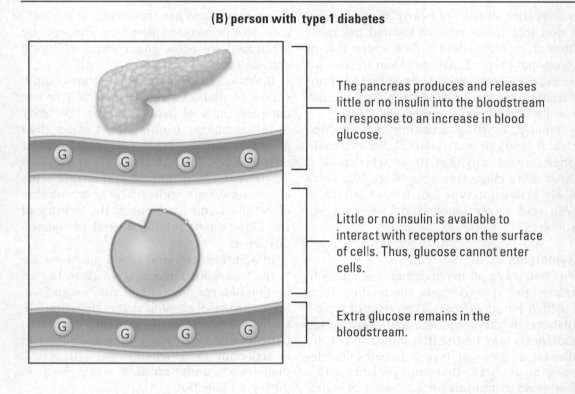

(B) person with type 1 diabetes

The pancreas produces and releases little or no insulin into the bloodstream in response to an increase in blood glucose.

Little or no insulin is available to interact with receptors on the surface of cells. Thus, glucose cannot enter cells.

Extra glucose remains in the bloodstream.

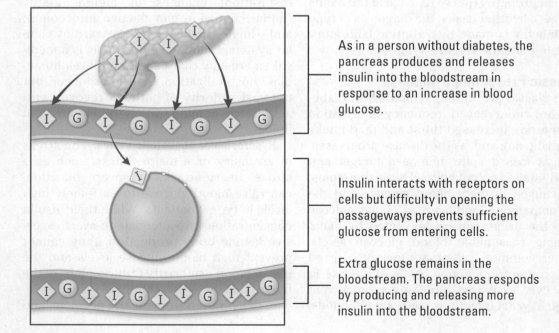

(C) person with type 2 diabetes

As in a person without diabetes, the pancreas produces and releases insulin into the bloodstream in response to an increase in blood glucose.

Insulin interacts with receptors on cells but difficulty in opening the passageways prevents sufficient glucose from entering cells.

Extra glucose remains in the bloodstream. The pancreas responds by producing and releasing more insulin into the bloodstream.

D

observational study of nearly 36,000 women found that those who consumed the most fiber from cereal had a 36% lower risk of developing type 2 diabetes than those consuming the least fiber from cereal. A more recent study from Finland reported similar results in men and women.

Finally, quitting smoking may reduce risk. A study of more than 21,000 U.S. male physicians found that those who smoked 20 or more cigarettes a day were 70% more likely to develop type 2 diabetes than those who had never smoked or were former smokers.

Symptoms

The initial symptoms of diabetes are usually related to hyperglycemia, the medical term for high blood glucose. The onset of type 1 diabetes is often sudden, and diabetic ketoacidosis may be the first indication of the disease. In contrast, type 2 diabetes may develop so gradually that some patients notice few or no symptoms for a number of years. They may initially complain of symptoms from chronic complications, such as peripheral neuropathy (nerve damage in the hands or feet). In other cases, the diagnosis of type 2 diabetes is made by a routine laboratory test in patients who are symptom-free.

Classic Presenting Symptoms

The classic presenting symptoms of diabetes are an increased frequency of urination (polyuria), increased thirst and fluid intake (polydipsia), and, as the disease progresses, weight loss despite increased hunger and food intake (polyphagia). These symptoms, all caused by high blood glucose and the accompanying "spillover" of excess glucose into the urine, can be prevented by maintaining reasonable blood glucose levels. Other common symptoms include blurred vision due to changing levels of glucose in the eye; weakness and fatigue; recurrent vaginal yeast infections; and skin infections.

These symptoms are transient, do not indicate any permanent damage, and can be eliminated by achieving control of blood glucose levels.

Diabetic ketoacidosis. This acute complication of diabetes results when a nearly complete lack of insulin forces the body to utilize energy from sources other than glucose—namely, acids released from fat tissue stores. These fatty acids are broken down by the liver into several strong acids known as ketone bodies. The accumulation of ketone bodies increases the acidity of the blood (metabolic acidosis) to dangerous levels.

In addition, elevated blood glucose (due to the lack of insulin action) leads to the excretion of large amounts of glucose and water in the urine, causing severe dehydration. Diabetic ketoacidosis is generally limited to patients who have type 1 diabetes, but it can occasionally occur when those with type 2 diabetes are under physical stress, such as during an infection.

Symptoms of ketoacidosis include fruity breath; nausea and vomiting; slow, deep respiration; changes in mental status (initial confusion can deepen into coma); and—finally—collapse of the cardiovascular system. Diabetic ketoacidosis is a medical emergency that usually requires immediate hospitalization. Death can occur, but the vast majority of patients recover with aggressive administration of insulin and fluids.

Hyperosmolar nonketotic states. The stress of an injury or a major illness, such as a stroke, heart attack, or severe infection, can raise blood glucose to extremely high levels in type 2 patients. While their insulin concentrations are adequate to avert excessive ketone body production, they cannot prevent high blood glucose levels and the rise in blood osmolarity ("thickening" of the blood) that gives this condition its name. Severe dehydration worsens the problem, and

The Diabetes Health-Care Team

Because even basic health care is rendered more complicated by diabetes, it is best if people with the disorder work with a team of professionals who can provide the necessary specialized medical knowledge. Members of the health care team with the initials C.D.E. after their names (for certified diabetes educator) have passed a special certification exam on patient education. The ADA can provide the names of certified diabetes educators in various localities. (See page 648 to contact the ADA.)

Some key members of a diabetes team include diabetes nurse educators, registered nurses who specialize in providing instruction and advice on issues related to the day-to-day management of diabetes; diabetes specialists, medical doctors such as diabetologists and endocrinologists; primary care physicians; nutritionists; registered dietitians; exercise physiologists to help people with diabetes create an individualized exercise program; mental health professionals; ophthalmologists; and podiatrists.

patients develop lethargy, prostration, confusion, and, in extreme cases, coma.

In about a third of patients with this condition, it is the first indication of their diabetes. Like ketoacidosis, hyperosmolar states can be fatal if not rapidly treated with insulin and large amounts of fluids. People experiencing the above-mentioned symptoms should contact their doctor. If unconsciousness occurs, an ambulance should be called.

Diagnosis and Follow-up

Symptoms may suggest the presence of diabetes, but laboratory tests are needed to make a definitive diagnosis. In an effort to promote the early detection of diabetes, and thus help reduce the risk of its complications, the American Diabetes Association (ADA) recommends that individuals age 45 and older be tested every three years.

The presence of certain factors that heighten the risk for developing diabetes should prompt earlier and more frequent testing. These factors are:
- Obesity
- Having a parent or sibling with diabetes
- Being in a high-risk ethnic group (including African American, Hispanic American, and Native American)

- Delivering a baby weighing more than 9 pounds or being diagnosed with gestational diabetes
- High blood pressure (140/90 mm Hg or higher, also called hypertension)
- Low HDL cholesterol levels (less than 40 mg/dL)
- High triglycerides (150 mg/dL or higher)
- Prediabetes

If diabetes is diagnosed, the progress of the disease is monitored through regular physical examinations and laboratory tests.

Laboratory Tests

Prediabetes and diabetes are diagnosed by measuring blood glucose levels. The diagnosis of diabetes is made when a blood glucose level greater than 200 mg/dL in any blood sample is associated with the classic symptoms of high blood glucose—thirst, frequent urination, and weight loss. A diagnosis of diabetes is most often made when a fasting blood glucose level is above 125 mg/dL on at least two tests. Fasting blood glucose values between 100 and 125 mg/dL indicate prediabetes. A normal fasting blood glucose level is less than 100 mg/dL.

Oral glucose tolerance test. An oral glucose tolerance test may also be used to diagnose diabetes, but it is not necessary when either of the above criteria for diabetes is satisfied. In this test, an individual ingests a drink containing 75 g of glucose. The diagnosis of diabetes is made if two hours later the blood glucose level is 200 mg/dL or more. A diagnosis of prediabetes is made if the two-hour glucose levels are between 140 and 199 mg/dL. Glucose levels below 140 mg/dL at two hours are normal.

Hemoglobin A1c test. The HbA1c test is used in people already diagnosed with diabetes. It measures the amount of glucose attached to hemoglobin—the oxygen-carrying protein in red blood cells that gives blood its color. As blood glucose levels rise, so does the amount of glucose attached to hemoglobin. Since hemoglobin circulates in the blood until the red blood cells die (half of red blood cells are replaced every 120 days), the HbA1c test is useful for measuring average blood glucose levels over the previous two to three months.

People with diabetes should have a HbA1c test every three to six months; they should aim to keep their HbA1c levels below 7%.

Other tests. In addition to measures of blood glucose and HbA1c, initial and subsequent doctor visits may include tests of blood urea nitrogen (BUN), blood creatinine, and protein (albumin) in the urine to check for kidney damage, as well as measurements of blood triglycerides, total cholesterol, low-density lipoprotein (LDL, or "bad") cholesterol, and high-density lipoprotein (HDL, or "good") cholesterol to assess risk factors for CHD.

Medical History and Physical Examination

Certain features of the patient's medical history and physical examination are particularly important in people with diabetes. The history should cover time and circumstances of the diagnosis; dietary habits; weight history; use of oral blood glucose-lowering drugs; insulin use, including amounts and time of administration; symptoms of long-term diabetic complications; effectiveness of blood glucose control (symptoms of high blood glucose, blood glucose values, and HbA1C values); frequency and timing of symptoms of hypoglycemia (low blood glucose); history of diabetic ketoacidosis; alcohol and tobacco use; exercise habits; family history of diabetes, CHD, and stroke; and other medications taken.

A physical examination should emphasize weight; blood pressure; examination of the eyes with dilated pupils (by an ophthalmologist, a medical doctor who specializes in diseases of the eye); inspection of the feet for ulcers, infection, cuts, blisters, or calluses; and neurological testing for reflexes and loss of sensation.

Long-Term Complications

Chronic, or long-term, complications can occur in both types of diabetes and in many cases are directly related to elevated blood glucose levels. Long-term complications include microvascular disease (abnormalities of small blood vessels), neuropathy (nerve damage), changes to the skin, gums, and teeth, and macrovascular disease (abnormalities of large blood vessels). They typically appear only after years or decades of the disease, and their development is not inevitable.

There is definitive evidence that good control of blood glucose and control of other risk factors, such as high blood pressure, can eliminate or postpone diabetic complications, and may reduce their severity if complications do occur. However, improved glucose control may not reverse these complications once they appear. Treatments for long-term complications of diabetes are covered on page 283.

Microvascular Disease

Microvascular disease due to diabetes affects the eyes and kidneys.

Retinopathy. Diabetic retinopathy, the most common diabetic eye complication and the leading cause of blindness among U.S. adults, is damage to the retina (the light-sensitive nerve tissue at the back of the eye that transmits visual images to the brain). This damage is caused by changes in the tiny blood vessels that supply the retina.

In the early stages of retinopathy—called nonproliferative retinopathy—the retinal vessels weaken and develop bulges (microaneurysms) that may leak blood (hemorrhage) or fluid (exudate) into the surrounding tissue. Vision is rarely affected during this stage of retinopathy, but annual eye examinations should be performed by an ophthalmologist to ensure that the condition does not progress. Later on, however, patients can develop proliferative retinopathy, when fragile new blood vessels begin to grow on the retina and into the vitreous humor (the jelly-like substance inside the back of the eye). These abnormal vessels

D

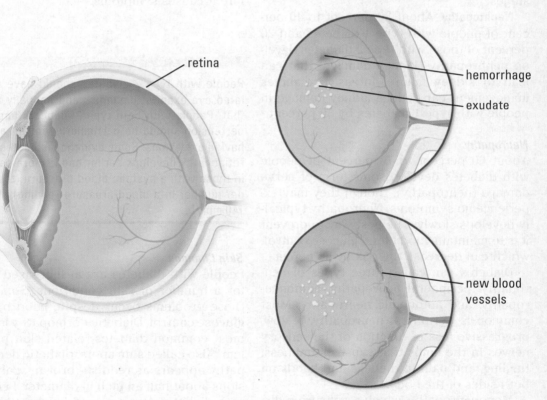

nonproliferative diabetic retinopathy

retina

hemorrhage

exudate

new blood vessels

proliferative diabetic retinopathy

In nonproliferative retinopathy, blood vessels in the retina develop weak spots that may hemorrhage into the retina. When the condition worsens (proliferative retinopathy), new blood vessels grow on the retina.

are prone to rupture and bleed into the vitreous humor, causing blurred vision or temporary blindness.

Research studies show that maintaining good blood sugar control can reduce both the incidence and progression of retinopathy. However, if proliferative retinopathy ensues, it can be treated with laser surgery and vision can be preserved if it is detected early. About half of those with untreated proliferative retinopathy will become blind within five years, compared to just 5 percent of those who receive laser treatment. Regular eye exams offer the best chance of detecting retinopathy in its treatable stages.

Nephropathy. About 30 percent to 40 percent of people with type 1 diabetes and 20 percent of those with type 2 diabetes develop nephropathy (kidney damage) that can lead to kidney failure. Intensive diabetes management can reduce kidney damage in people with type 1 diabetes by 50 percent.

Neuropathy

About 60 percent to 70 percent of people with diabetes develop some form of nerve damage (neuropathy), though they may experience no symptoms. Neuropathy typically develops slowly. The best way to prevent it is to maintain good blood glucose control, which can decrease the risk by 60 percent.

Diabetes can cause three types of neuropathy: peripheral neuropathy, mononeuropathy, and autonomic neuropathy. Most common is peripheral neuropathy, a slow, progressive loss of function of the sensory nerves in the limbs that causes numbness, tingling, and pain in the legs and hands on both sides of the body.

Mononeuropathy, which results from disruption of the blood supply to one or more nerves, leads to the sudden onset of pain or weakness in the area of the body served by the affected nerve.

Autonomic neuropathy damages nerves to the digestive tract, bladder, heart, and other internal organs.

Glaucoma and Cataracts

These two treatable eye conditions occur with increased frequency in people with diabetes. There is some evidence that an elevated level of sorbitol, a sugar formed from glucose, within the lens of the eye enhances cataract formation in people with diabetes. While cataracts are usually treated only when they begin to interfere with vision, it is important to be tested regularly for glaucoma, since serious damage may occur before it causes symptoms.

People with type 2 diabetes should have a dilated eye exam at diagnosis and annually after that. People with both type 2 diabetes and hypertension should be particularly vigilant about having eye exams: Some evidence indicates that retinopathy develops earlier and is more severe in those with a systolic blood pressure (the upper number in a blood pressure reading) above 140 mm Hg.

Skin Changes

People with diabetes are at increased risk for a number of skin conditions. Some of these problems occur despite good blood glucose control. Diabetic dermopathy is the most common diabetes-related skin problem. Also called shin spots, diabetic dermopathy appears as reddish- brown, scaly lesions about half an inch in diameter. People with diabetes also are more susceptible to skin infections. Unlike shin spots, which are harmless and require no treatment, infections can be serious and require medical attention.

If you develop a diabetic skin ulcer, ask your doctor about the prescription gel becaplermin (Regranex). The medicine is a growth factor that contains a combination of proteins which help summon regenerative cells to the injury site, stimulating new tissue growth. Although not a cure, studies show that when used as part of a treatment regimen that includes keeping the ulcer clean and free of pressure, the gel stimulates healing faster than standard wound care.

Dental Changes

Diabetes can lead to complications affecting the teeth and gums; dry mouth is also common. Because saliva normally protects against bacterial growth in the mouth, and insufficient saliva permits dental plaque and food particles to accumulate, people with poorly controlled diabetes are more likely to develop cavities. As a result of excess plaque formation, two gum disorders, gingivitis and the more serious periodontitis, are also more common in people with diabetes. On the other hand, people who control their diabetes well may reduce their chance of cavities by selecting a diet that is lower in simple sugars (which can encourage cavity formation) and by following an oral health regimen carefully. Another dental complication, a burning sensation in the mouth and tongue, can result from dry mouth or diabetic neuropathy.

Macrovascular Disease

Diabetic patients are highly susceptible to the atherosclerotic narrowing of large blood vessels that causes such complications as heart attacks, strokes, and poor circulation to the legs (peripheral arterial disease).

Metabolic syndrome. Elevated blood glucose levels, high blood pressure, abdominal obesity, high blood triglyceride levels, and low HDL cholesterol levels occur together in some people. This cluster of risk factors, known as metabolic syndrome, increases the risk of diabetes, coronary heart disease (CHD), and stroke. The incidence of metabolic syndrome increases with age so that nearly half of Americans over the age of 50 have this condition.

At least three of the following five factors must be present for a diagnosis of metabolic syndrome:

- abdominal obesity (a waist circumference greater than 40 inches in men or 35 inches in women);
- triglyceride levels of 150 mg/dL or greater;
- HDL cholesterol levels less than 40 mg/dL in men or 50 mg/dL in women;
- blood pressure of 130/85 mm Hg or higher, or taking antihypertensive medication;
- fasting blood glucose levels of 100 mg/dL or greater.

The features and risks of metabolic syndrome can be avoided by controlling body weight (preferably through a combination of diet and exercise), blood pressure, and blood lipids (cholesterol and triglycerides) and by quitting smoking.

Coronary heart disease (CHD). People with diabetes have a two to four times greater likelihood of developing CHD, narrowing of the coronary arteries by atherosclerosis. The incidence of heart attacks is particularly increased in women with diabetes.

Other research has shown that diabetes decreases the normal tendency of the coronary arteries to widen—and thereby increase blood flow to the heart—during exercise. As a result, people with diabetes are at greater risk for angina and heart attacks. The Framingham Heart Study (an ongoing study in Massachusetts) and many others have shown that diabetes adds significantly to conventional risk factors such as smoking, high blood pressure, and elevated LDL or low HDL cholesterol levels. In fact, one study found that even when people with type 2 diabetes have no prior history of heart disease, they have the same risk of a heart attack as those without diabetes who have already had a heart attack. These data underscore the fact that people with diabetes should be especially attentive to all risk factors in guarding against CHD.

Lifestyle changes can lower the risk of cardiovascular complications. For instance, results from the analysis of several intervention trials indicate that a 45-year-old man with diabetes would gain an average of one year of life expectancy with prophylactic aspirin treatment (to help prevent CHD) or with lower blood pressure, and gain over three years by quitting smoking.

Stroke. People with diabetes are two to four times more likely to suffer a stroke than those without diabetes. A stroke occurs when a clot blocks blood flow through an artery that leads to the brain. Experts suspect that high blood glucose increases the risk of stroke by promoting atherosclerosis and clots. In addition, high blood pressure—one of the most important risk factors for stroke—is twice as common in people with diabetes as in those without the disease.

Peripheral arterial disease. Peripheral arterial disease is a narrowing of the arteries in the legs due to atherosclerosis. The characteristic symptom of the condition is intermittent claudication—pain in the thighs, calves, and, sometimes, the buttocks—that is brought on by exercise and subsides promptly with rest.

In most people, pain occurs after a predictable amount of physical activity.

Symptoms of peripheral arterial disease usually progress slowly. Eventually the pain can interfere with normal activities and may even occur at rest if blood vessels are severely narrowed. The poor blood flow in the legs can result in slow healing of foot blisters and other skin injuries and may lead to chronic ulcers on the feet and legs.

Diabetes doubles the risk of peripheral arterial disease. Preventive measures are the same as those for CHD and stroke: HbA1c levels less than 7%, blood pressure below 130/80 mm Hg, and LDL cholesterol levels lower than 100 or 70 mg/dL in certain cases. Smoking cessation is absolutely essential.

Diabetes Foot Problems

People with diabetes need to pay special attention to their feet for a number of reasons. Diabetes-related nerve damage can reduce feeling in the feet, making it difficult to detect a foot injury. Diabetes can also impair blood circulation and wound healing by narrowing the arteries supplying blood to the legs. A wound on the foot that does not heal can turn into an ulcer (deep sore) that may become infected and possibly even require an amputation if untreated. The risk of these complications can be reduced by keeping diabetes well controlled, having a foot inspection performed regularly by a medical professional, and taking care of the feet as described in the text box above.

Treatment

The goals in the treatment of diabetes are to prevent its acute manifestations (high blood glucose and its symptoms of excessive thirst, frequent urination, and weight loss; hypoglycemia; diabetic ketoacidosis; and hyperosmolar coma) and long-term complications associated with the disorder (such as retinopathy,

Good Foot Care

Everyone with diabetes, but especially those with established neuropathy or poor circulation, should make a routine of good foot care. This routine involves inspecting each foot daily and carefully treating and monitoring even the most trivial cut or abrasion. When they occur, abrasions should be washed with warm water and soap, cleaned with a mild antiseptic (for example, Bactine), and then covered with a dry, sterile dressing and paper tape. Ulcers are extremely serious and must be brought to the attention of a doctor immediately. Toenails should be neatly trimmed, cut straight across rather than rounded at the corners. And at least twice a year, each foot should be examined by a physician or podiatrist.

Here are some additional suggestions for foot care.

Do the following:

- Bathe feet daily in warm, soapy water and pat them dry.
- Keep feet warm and dry. Wear warm socks in the winter; keep feet cool in the summer.
- Take off shoes and put feet up from time to time during the day.
- Get regular exercise: It will help keep feet in good condition and may improve circulation somewhat.
- Tell the doctor of any unusual feelings of cold, numbness, tingling, burning, or fatigue in the feet or legs.

Do not do the following:

- Put hot-water bottles or electric heating pads on the feet—they may cause unnoticed burns.
- Sit with legs crossed, or expose feet and legs to cold or heat (for example, prolonged exposure to sunlight).
- Soak the feet—unless soaking is recommended by a doctor.
- Wear garters or tight-fitting socks, stockings, or shoes.
- Smoke—smoking reduces circulation to the feet.
- Put off seeing a physician or podiatrist if any problems develop, however minor.

nephropathy, neuropathy, and macrovascular disease).

People with type 1 diabetes, whose diabetes results from a lack of insulin production, require daily injections of insulin. The management of type 2 diabetes is more complex. Eating a healthful diet and exercising regularly are the first steps in treating type 2 diabetes, but some form of pharmacological treatment is often needed as well.

Control of Cardiovascular Disease Risk Factors

The high incidence of narrowing of the arteries (atherosclerosis) in people with diabetes demands strict attention to treatable risk factors: cigarette smoking; high blood pressure; high levels of LDL cholesterol, total cholesterol, and triglycerides; and low levels of HDL cholesterol. Several risk factors—including obesity, high blood pressure, high triglycerides, and low HDL cholesterol—are more common in people with diabetes than in the general population.

People with diabetes should strive for LDL cholesterol levels below 100 mg/dL, and HDL levels of 40 mg/dL or higher. Diet and, if necessary, drug therapy may be indicated in some cases to reach these levels. In addition, prophylactic aspirin treatment may be recommended to help prevent CHD.

High triglycerides (greater than 150 mg/dL) are best managed by weight loss and good control of diabetes, but drug treatment may be needed if patients fail to lose weight or if their triglycerides remain high despite weight loss and control of blood glucose.

D

Purchasing a Glucose Monitor

Several factors should be considered when purchasing a glucose monitor. Take into account whether the numbers on the readout can be read easily, how difficult the meter is to use, and whether the meter has advanced memory features that could simplify record keeping. Monitors that can download meter results and print out summaries are particularly useful. The test strips required by the meter should also be considered. Since the strips are perishable, they come packaged either in a vial or individually wrapped in foil, which might be difficult to handle for people with arthritis.

Over time the cost of the strips is far greater than the cost of the meter, which can cost from $30 to about $300. Some insurance companies reimburse for certain meters and strips, and this should be investigated before making a purchase.

Self-Monitoring of Blood Glucose Control

Currently, the best method to assess diabetic control is self-testing of blood glucose. (Testing for the presence of glucose in the urine is far less useful.) Results from recent long-term studies indicate that people with diabetes must be aggressive in their daily monitoring of blood glucose levels. This means not only making more frequent measurements, but also adjusting diet, exercise, and doses of insulin or oral diabetes drugs according to the results.

Along with regularly measuring blood glucose levels, people with diabetes should keep a log of their readings. (A log book is often included with the purchase of a blood glucose meter.) This record allows more accurate tracking of progress and can help point out the source of difficulties in controlling diabetes. Thus, if high or low blood glucose levels follow a trend—occurring several days in a row at the same time each day—reviewing the log with a doctor can lead to suggestions on changing medication, or adjusting the timing or dose of insulin. In some cases, unexpected fluctuations in blood glucose readings can be traced to simple changes in routine, for example, eating unusually large or small meals, variations in exercise, or even psychological stress.

People with diabetes—whether they have type 1 or type 2—should strive for the best blood glucose control that is safely possible. No guidelines have been set for tight control, but the intensive-treatment group in the Diabetes Control and Complications Trial achieved an average blood glucose level of around 155 mg/dL, which is equivalent to an HbA1c level of about 7%. While tight control always involves blood glucose monitoring, it may not require insulin injections in people with type 2 diabetes: A carefully constructed program of diet, exercise, and oral drugs (if needed) may be sufficient.

Blood glucose testing. The development of simple and accurate tests to measure blood glucose, which allow people with diabetes to make rapid changes in their diet and medication, has made home glucose monitoring the backbone of diabetic management. Most blood tests require only a single drop of blood, which can be withdrawn by a special lancet or by the meter itself in some cases. (A wide variety of devices can make drawing blood as painless and simple as possible; some are spring-loaded and adjustable to give a shallow stick while still drawing blood.)

The blood is then placed on a reagent strip impregnated with an enzyme called glucose oxidase. The blood glucose level is determined by inserting the strip into a meter, which provides a digital readout. (The older method of visually comparing the color of the strip to a chart is far less accurate.) The meters take from 15 to 45 seconds to give a result. Recommendations for the frequency and timing of glucose monitoring vary from once a day or less in patients with very stable, well controlled type 2 diabetes to multiple times daily in type 1 patients.

There are many different types of glucose monitors with a large number of features. A doctor or diabetes educator can provide information on the type of monitor best suited to individual needs.

Urine glucose testing. Testing urine for the presence of glucose is far less accurate than blood glucose monitoring and is rarely used.

Ketone testing. Ketone bodies in the urine can be measured easily by placing a test strip or tablet in urine and examining it for a color change. Typically, only people with type 1 diabetes need to perform this test. A person should check for ketones if blood glucose levels are over 250 mg/dL and symptoms such as fruity breath, nausea, vomiting, or difficulties in concentration suggest ketoacidosis. If the test is strongly positive, a doctor should be called immediately.

Dietary Measures

The right diet may not only keep glucose levels in check but also help to control a number of other factors, such as elevated blood lipids, obesity, and high blood pressure, that affect the risk of developing complications from diabetes.

Most experts recommend that people with diabetes eat a high-carbohydrate/low-fat diet. According to this school of thought, 50 percent to 60 percent of calories should come from carbohydrates and 25 to 35 percent from fat, as long as saturated and trans fatty acid intake is kept low. The primary goal of this diet is to keep blood lipid levels low—so as to reduce the risk of macrovascular disease—without adversely affecting blood glucose levels. Most people do best when they consume a relatively stable amount of carbohydrates at each meal, rather than trying to eliminate carbohydrates, which increases the amount of fat in the diet.

In addition to following basic guidelines for a healthy diet (see pages 30-36), people with diabetes should also pay special attention to their intake of sugar and alcohol.

Sugar. As long as sugar replaces other carbohydrates gram for gram (calorie for calorie) and is not simply added to the diet, it is safe for people with diabetes to consume foods that contain sugar. Remember, however, that sugary foods often contain empty calories, whereas starchy foods also supply vitamins, minerals, and fiber. Therefore, for overall health it is preferable for people with diabetes to limit sugar-containing foods. (Artificial sweeteners approved by the FDA, such as saccharin, aspartame, acesulfame potassium, and sucralose are not restricted.)

Alcohol. People with well controlled diabetes can drink alcoholic beverages in moderation and with food. The ADA recommends that men drink no more than two alcoholic drinks per day, and women no more than one. Alcohol should not be consumed on an empty stomach by people who take insulin or oral blood glucose-lowering drugs. People with additional medical problems, such as pancreatitis (inflammation of the pancreas) or elevated triglyceride levels, should abstain from alcohol altogether.

The calories from alcohol should be exchanged for those that would normally be allotted to fat servings. Drinks that contain smaller amounts of sugar, such as light beers and dry wines, are preferable to mixed drinks that are high in sugar.

Heavy drinking should be avoided, and those who drink should be aware that alcohol can cause weight gain (because of its high caloric content), hypoglycemia, elevated triglycerides, and flushing or nausea in some people taking oral diabetes drugs, especially chlorpropamide (Diabinese).

Exercise

While it is likely that exercise helps to prevent diabetes, it is certain that regular exercise benefits those who already have the disorder. Exercise burns calories and thus helps control weight, and can also lower blood glucose levels by enhancing insulin action. In addition, exercise may postpone or eliminate the long-term complications of the disease. For example, exercise can lower blood pressure and triglycerides while raising levels of HDL cholesterol.

Though physical activity can be increased by changing everyday habits, such as taking the stairs rather than an elevator, it is more effective to set aside time for exercise (even a simple program of brisk walks) on a regular basis. Exercise may be limited by arthritis, CHD, or peripheral arterial disease, and those with peripheral neuropathy may need to modify their type of workout to avoid foot trauma (for example, they can replace running with swimming).

Exercise requires careful planning and monitoring, particularly for people who take oral medication or insulin to control their diabetes. These individuals need to check their blood glucose levels before and after exercising and may need to make adjustments to their medication or food intake to prevent blood glucose levels that are too low or too high during exercise. Always be sure to talk to your doctor before beginning an exercise program or making any changes to your medication or diet.

Oral Agents to Lower Blood Glucose

Diet and exercise may suffice to control blood glucose levels in some patients with type 2 diabetes; but when the response to these measures is inadequate, oral agents are generally started.

Six classes of oral drugs are available to treat type 2 diabetes; each acts on different sites in the body and through different mechanisms to control blood glucose levels (see chart on pages 280-281).

These drugs should be used in conjunction with diet and exercise and are only effective if the pancreas produces insulin (making them ineffective for people with type 1 diabetes). They may be prescribed individually or in combination, or, as the disease progresses, with insulin.

Insulin

More than a third of patients with type 2 diabetes eventually require treatment with insulin to control blood glucose levels as the severity of diabetes worsens and oral drugs lose their effectiveness. Some oral medications—the sulfonylureas, metformin, and the thiazolidinediones—are also being prescribed with increasing frequency in combination with insulin.

Types of insulin. All insulins were isolated from beef or pork pancreases until 1982, when techniques became available to produce human insulin. Only human insulin and its biosynthetic modifications are manufactured today. Four types of insulin are available: rapid-acting, very rapid-acting, intermediate-acting, and long-acting. Insulin mixtures are also available.

Typically, a combination of insulin types is used to treat diabetes. The dose and mixture

Alternative Treatments for Diabetes

In recent years, a growing interest and market has emerged for the use of "alternative" therapies to manage diabetes. Several natural remedies and nutritional supplements—including chromium, gymnea sylvestre, and vanadium—reportedly reduce blood glucose levels; others—for example, alpha-lipoic acid, evening primrose oil, ginkgo biloba, and chelation therapy—purport to treat or prevent the major complications of diabetes.

There is little or no hard medical evidence that any of these alternatives are effective in controlling blood glucose or preventing complications. Patients wishing to try one of these options should do so in addition to, not instead of, their prescribed treatment regimen. And they should do so only with their doctor's knowledge.

of insulin used, as well as the frequency and timing of injections, vary from patient to patient based on such factors as age, weight, eating habits, exercise, and blood glucose levels. Insulin schedules will continue to be adjusted, when necessary, throughout life; for example, less insulin may be needed when a person begins an exercise program, and more during periods of psychological stress.

Modes of insulin administration. To be effective, insulin must be injected. It cannot be swallowed, because digestive enzymes would destroy the insulin before it reached the bloodstream. Injections are given subcutaneously (under the skin) at any site where there is fatty tissue, for example the abdomen or the front and outer side of the thigh.

A needle and syringe are most often used for insulin injection; other methods include insulin pens and jet injectors. Another option for insulin administration is continuous subcutaneous insulin infusion (CSII), which involves the continuous infusion of insulin by an external pump, usually worn on a belt. The insulin passes through tubing (a cannula) and is delivered beneath the skin of the abdomen via a needle, which is changed by the patient every few days. The continuous insulin infusion, supplemented

with additional doses of insulin through the pump with each meal, promotes excellent control of type 1 diabetes while limiting the number of needle sticks to one every two to four days. Some people with type 2 diabetes that is hard to control may also benefit from the device.

Adverse effects of insulin. Patients taking insulin are susceptible to hypoglycemia when they administer too much insulin, delay or miss a meal, or exercise without first eating a snack. Consequently, insulin treatment requires careful attention to the timing of meals, exercise, and alcohol intake. Frequent tests of blood glucose at home, and periodic hemoglobin A1c tests by a physician, are necessary to determine the doses of insulin needed to give good control and limit bouts of hypoglycemia.

Other adverse effects of insulin are loss or overgrowth of fat tissue at the injection sites, allergic reactions, and insulin resistance. Alterations in fat tissue, less common with the types of insulin used today, can be further minimized by rotating injection sites. Allergic reactions, also now rare, are managed with a desensitization procedure that involves beginning with injections of small doses of insulin and gradually increasing the dose. Insulin resistance, most often caused by the

Oral Blood Glucose-Lowering Agents

Drug Type	Generic Name	Brand Name
Sulfonylureas	chlorpropamide	Diabinese
	glimepiride	Amaryl
	glipizide	Glucotrol
	glipizide, extended-release	Glucotrol XL
	glyburide	DiaBeta Glynase Micronase
Biguanides	metformin	Glucophage
	metformin, extended-release	Glucophage XR
Combination agent	glipizide/metformin glyburide/metformin rosiglitazone/metformin	Metaglip Glucovance Avandamet
Thiazolidinediones	pioglitazone rosiglitazone	Actos Avandia
Meglitinide	repaglinide	Prandin
D-phenylalanine derivative	nateglinide	Starlix
Alpha-glucosidase inhibitors	acarbose miglitol	Precose Glyset

D

Mechanism of Action	Comments
Stimulate the pancreas to produce more insulin.	Hypoglycemia is the most worrying side effect (particularly in the elderly, debilitated, or malnourished). May cause water retention, constipation, diarrhea, dizziness, headache, heartburn, increased or decreased appetite, or stomach pain/discomfort. Drinking alcohol while taking chlorpropamide can cause abdominal cramps, nausea, flushing, or headaches.
	Generally more expensive than the first-generation agent, chlorpropamide. A lower dosage is required. Side effects are similar to those listed for chlorpropamide.
Decrease glucose levels in the blood primarily by lowering glucose production in the liver; also increases uptake of glucose by muscle cells.	May be used alone or with sulfonylureas, acarbose, or insulin. Also helps lower cholesterol and triglycerides, and may help with weight control. Does not produce hypoglycemia when used alone. May cause nausea, diarrhea, bloating, or, very rarely, a fatal buildup of lactic acid in the blood.
	See separate entries for glipizide, glyburide, rosiglitazone, and metformin.
Heighten the sensitivity of muscle and fat cells to insulin, increasing the body's response to the insulin produced in the pancreas.	May be used alone or with insulin. Side effects are uncommon, but include swelling of the hands and feet. Liver tests are advised. Insulin dose may need to be decreased to avoid hypoglycemia. Full effects may require 2 to 8 weeks of treatment.
Stimulates the pancrease to produce more insulin.	Hypoglycemia, the most frequent side effect, is less common than with sulfonylureas.
Stimulates rapid insulin secretion to reduce increases in blood glucose levels that occur soon after eating.	May be used alone or with metformin.
Inhibit intestinal enzymes, thereby delaying the digestion of complex carbohydrates and sucrose (table sugar), and blunting the peak levels of blood glucose and insulin after a meal.	May be used alone or with sulfonylureas or metformin. May cause gas, soft stools, diarrhea, or abdominal discomfort, which tend to lessen with time.

formation of antibodies against insulin, is treated by increasing the insulin dose.

Treatment of Hypoglycemia

Hypoglycemia, which refers to low blood glucose, is a potential side effect of insulin, as well as of several oral drugs. There are two types of hypoglycemic symptoms: adrenergic and neurologic. Adrenergic symptoms—typically sweating, palpitations, nervousness, hunger, faintness, weakness, and numbness in the fingers and around the mouth—result when low blood glucose levels trigger the release of the hormone epinephrine into the blood. This response helps return glucose levels to normal, as does the release of glucagon from the pancreas.

These protective actions—particularly the release of glucagon—are often lost after 5 to 10 years of diabetes. Though unpleasant, adrenergic symptoms alert people with diabetes that they need to eat some sugar-containing food or drink some juice to raise their blood glucose levels rapidly. However, the symptoms of hypoglycemia may be diminished or absent in patients who are taking beta-blockers or in those who have nerve damage after many years of diabetes.

Neurologic symptoms—headache, lack of coordination, double vision, inappropriate behavior, confusion—are a greater danger because people may become confused before they can treat themselves (and thus need another person's assistance). Extreme hypoglycemia can cause seizures, coma, or, in rare cases, permanent brain damage and death.

Certain foods and liquids are especially helpful for treating hypoglycemia. For example, 4 to 6 oz. of apple or orange juice, five to seven hard candies, or glucose tablets can raise blood glucose quickly. People with diabetes should always have one of these on hand. Avoid using foods like chocolate or nuts, which do contain carbohydrates, but take longer to digest because they also contain fat. Glucagon injections can rapidly raise blood glucose levels. Some people with diabetes keep glucagon in the refrigerator. Someone else can be trained to inject glucagon, in case the person with diabetes experiences a severe episode of hypoglycemia and is not alert enough to eat anything.

Treatment of Diabetic Complications

If diabetic complications develop, they must be treated along with the diabetes itself.

Retinopathy

Laser photocoagulation halts or retards the decline in vision from diabetic retinopathy in most patients, and it must be carried out before too much damage has occurred. The procedure is done on an outpatient basis, often over several visits. The ophthalmologist dilates the pupil with eye drops and then targets a series of spots on the retina with a sharp burst of laser light, causing tiny scars to form. The procedure prevents the small vessels from rupturing and bleeding into the vitreous humor.

Laser treatment reduces the chance of blindness by half in those with proliferative retinopathy. Though extensive photocoagulation usually diminishes peripheral vision and may decrease night vision, its success in preserving visual acuity makes it worthwhile despite these side effects. Laser treatment also helps preserve vision when used to treat what is called "clinically significant macular edema." Only a qualified ophthalmologist can determine when laser treatment is needed.

If the extent or location of the damage makes photocoagulation ineffective, or if the vitreous humor is too clouded with blood, vision may be improved with a vitrectomy, a surgical procedure that removes the vitreous humor and replaces it with a saline solution. Roughly 70 percent of people who have vitrectomies notice an improvement or stabilization of their sight, and some recover enough vision to resume reading as well as driving.

Because photocoagulation works so remarkably well if done in time, and because even advanced retinopathy can be asymptomatic, it is crucial for people with type 2 diabetes to begin seeing an ophthalmologist for annual eye examinations when diabetes is first diagnosed. For people with type 1 diabetes, annual eye examinations should start no later than five years after diagnosis.

Nephropathy

Four strategies are used to prevent nephropathy or slow its progression:

Tight glucose control is one method (see page 276). Treating high blood pressure, common in diabetes, is extremely important. High blood pressure damages the kidneys, which in turn raises blood pressure further. Restricting dietary protein is another way to delay the course of kidney disease. The fourth and most recent strategy is treatment with angiotensin-converting enzyme (ACE) inhibitors, a class of drugs commonly prescribed to treat high blood pressure. The benefit of ACE inhibitors in slowing the progression of kidney disease is independent of their effects on blood pressure.

Once kidney failure occurs, treatment is directed toward slowing the accumulation of waste products in the blood. Limitation of protein intake is necessary to decrease a buildup of the breakdown products of ingested proteins; at the same time the diet must contain enough protein to prevent malnutrition. Antacids, such as aluminum hydroxide, are given to bind dietary phosphate in the intestine. This prevents marked increases in levels of blood phosphate that

can, in turn, lower blood calcium levels. Calcium supplements may be necessary to raise blood calcium levels and prevent loss of bone minerals. Tablets containing sodium bicarbonate are often needed to counteract the acidic condition of the blood in kidney failure.

Anemia, with associated weakness and fatigue, invariably accompanies chronic kidney failure; it can be improved with the use of erythropoietin, a hormone that stimulates the production of red blood cells. Many common medications are normally excreted by the kidneys. In kidney failure, the doses of such drugs must be decreased to avoid their buildup to toxic levels. Kidney dialysis is usually initiated when kidney function deteriorates to less than 10 percent of normal—a condition called end-stage kidney disease.

Neuropathy

It is often difficult to treat symptoms that result from diabetic neuropathy. Improved control of blood glucose levels is the first step in prevention and treatment.

Amitriptyline (Amitid, Amitril, Elavil, Emitrip, Endep, Enovil, Vanatrip), usually used as an antidepressant, is often the most effective medication for relieving the symptoms of symmetrical peripheral neuropathy.

Gabapentin (Neurontin) is another option, either alone or in combination with amitriptyline. An anticonvulsant approved for epilepsy in 1994, gabapentin is generally well tolerated.

The symptoms of autonomic neuropathy depend on which organ is involved, and include heartburn, alternating bouts of diarrhea and constipation, and urinary retention or incontinence. Treatment can alleviate these and other symptoms of autonomic neuropathy. For instance, eating small, frequent meals may help improve heartburn symptoms, while eating foods high in fiber

D

may relieve constipation. When bladder control is the problem, visiting the bathroom at regular intervals may be helpful.

Macrovascular Disease

With few exceptions, preventive measures and treatment of macrovascular disease are the same in people with diabetes as in others. High levels of blood cholesterol and high blood pressure—major risk factors for macrovascular disease—are initially treated with diet and lifestyle modifications in an effort to bring these conditions under control without medication. In fact, many of these lifestyle measures—such as a low-fat, high-carbohydrate diet, weight loss, and exercise—are the same as the ones recommended by the ADA for patients with diabetes. Medication is generally needed if elevated cholesterol or blood pressure persists despite strict adherence to these measures.

Diarrhea—loose, watery stools occurring more than three times in one day—is a common problem that usually lasts a day or two and goes away on its own without any special treatment. However, prolonged diarrhea can be a sign of other problems.

Diarrhea can cause dehydration, which means the body lacks enough fluid to function properly. Dehydration is particularly dangerous in children and the elderly, and it must be treated promptly to avoid serious health problems. Dehydration is discussed below (pages 286-287).

People of all ages can get diarrhea. The average adult has a bout of diarrhea about four times a year.

What Causes Diarrhea?

Diarrhea may be caused by a temporary problem, such as an infection, or a chronic problem, such as an intestinal disease. A few of the more common causes of diarrhea are:

- **Bacterial infections.** Several types of bacteria, consumed through contaminated food or water, can cause diarrhea. Common culprits include *Campylobacter*, *Salmonella*, *Shigella*, and *Escherichia coli*.
- **Viral infections.** Many viruses cause diarrhea, including rotavirus, Norwalk virus, cytomegalovirus, herpes simplex virus, and viral hepatitis.
- **Food intolerances.** Some people are unable to digest a component of food, such as lactose, the sugar found in milk.
- **Parasites.** Parasites can enter the body through food or water and settle in the digestive system. Parasites that cause diarrhea include *Giardia lamblia*, *Entamoeba histolytica*, and *Cryptosporidium*.
- **Reaction to medicines,** such as antibiotics, blood pressure medications, and antacids containing magnesium.

- **Intestinal diseases,** such as inflammatory bowel disease or celiac disease.
- **Functional bowel disorders,** such as irritable bowel syndrome, in which the intestines do not work normally.

Some people develop diarrhea after stomach surgery or removal of the gallbladder. The reason may be a change in how quickly food moves through the digestive system after stomach surgery or an increase in bile in the colon that can occur after gallbladder surgery.

In many cases, the cause of diarrhea cannot be found. As long as diarrhea goes away on its own, an extensive search for the cause is not usually necessary.

People who visit foreign countries are at risk for traveler's diarrhea, which is caused by eating food or drinking water contaminated with bacteria, viruses, or, sometimes, parasites. Traveler's diarrhea is a particular problem for people visiting developing countries. Visitors to the United States, Canada, most European countries, Japan, Australia, and New Zealand do not face much risk for traveler's diarrhea.

What Are the Symptoms?

Diarrhea may be accompanied by cramping abdominal pain, bloating, nausea, or an urgent need to use the bathroom. Depending on the cause, a person may have a fever or bloody stools.

Diarrhea can be either acute or chronic. The acute form, which lasts less than three weeks, is usually related to a bacterial, viral, or parasitic infection. Chronic diarrhea lasts more than three weeks and is usually related to functional disorders such as irritable bowel syndrome or diseases such as celiac disease or inflammatory bowel disease.

Diarrhea in Children

Children can have acute (short-term) or chronic (long-term) forms of diarrhea. Causes include bacteria, viruses, parasites, medications, functional disorders, and food sensitivities. Infection with the rotavirus is the most common cause of acute childhood diarrhea. Rotavirus diarrhea usually resolves in five to eight days.

Medications to treat diarrhea in adults can be dangerous to children and should be given only under a doctor's guidance.

Diarrhea can be dangerous in newborns and infants. In small children, severe diarrhea lasting just a day or two can lead to dehydration. Because a child can die from dehydration within a few days, the main treatment for diarrhea in children is rehydration. Rehydration is discussed below.

Take your child to the doctor if any of the following symptoms appear:

- Stools containing blood or pus, or black stools
- Temperature above 101.4° F
- No improvement after 24 hours
- Signs of dehydration (see text box at right)

When Should a Doctor Be Consulted?

Although usually not harmful, diarrhea can become dangerous or signal a more serious problem. You should see the doctor if

- you have diarrhea for more than three days;
- you have severe pain in the abdomen or rectum;
- you have a fever of 102°F or higher;
- you see blood in your stool or have black, tarry stools;
- you have signs of dehydration.

If your child has diarrhea, do not hesitate to call the doctor for advice. Diarrhea can be dangerous in children if too much fluid is lost and not replaced quickly.

What Is Dehydration?

General signs of dehydration include:

- Thirst
- Less frequent urination
- Dry skin
- Fatigue
- Lightheadedness
- Dark-colored urine

Signs of dehydration in children include:

- Dry mouth and tongue
- No tears when crying
- No wet diapers for three hours or more
- Sunken abdomen, eyes, or cheeks
- High fever
- Listlessness or irritability
- Skin that does not flatten when pinched and released

If you suspect that you or your child is dehydrated, call the doctor immediately. Severe dehydration may require hospitalization.

What Tests Might the Doctor Do?

Diagnostic tests to find the cause of diarrhea include the following:

- **Medical history and physical examination.** The doctor will need to know about your eating habits and medication use and will examine you for signs of illness.
- **Stool culture.** Lab technicians analyze a stool sample to check for bacteria, parasites, or other signs of disease or infection.
- **Blood tests.** Blood tests can be helpful in ruling out certain diseases.
- **Fasting tests.** To find out if a food intolerance or allergy is causing the diarrhea, the doctor may ask you to avoid lactose (found in milk products), carbohydrates, wheat, or other foods to see whether the diarrhea responds to a change in diet.

- **Sigmoidoscopy.** For this test, the doctor uses a special instrument to look at the inside of the rectum and lower part of the colon.
- **Colonoscopy.** This test is similar to sigmoidoscopy, but the doctor looks at the entire colon.

What Is the Treatment?

In most cases, replacing lost fluid to prevent dehydration is the only treatment necessary. (See "Preventing Dehydration" at right) Medicines that stop diarrhea may be helpful in some cases, but they are not recommended for people whose diarrhea is from a bacterial infection or parasite—stopping the diarrhea traps the organism in the intestines, prolonging the problem. Instead, doctors usually prescribe antibiotics. Viral causes are either treated with medication or left to run their course, depending on the severity and type of the virus.

In addition to drinking plenty of fluids (which combat dehydration), diarrhea sufferers can take antidiarrhea agents, such as bismuth subsalicylate (Pepto-Bismol, Bismatrol), attapulgite (Kaopectate), and kaolin/pectin (Kao-Spen, Kapectolin), to solidify the stool. Some antidiarrhea medications, such as loperamide (Imodium A-D) or diphenoxylate/atropine (Lomotil), slow the movement of feces. These medications should be avoided by people with acute infectious diarrhea (related to bacteria or a parasite).

Preventing Dehydration

Dehydration occurs when the body has lost too much fluid and electrolytes (the minerals potassium and sodium). The fluid and electrolytes lost during diarrhea need to be replaced promptly—the body cannot function properly without them. Dehydration is particularly dangerous for children, who can die from it within a matter of days.

Although water is extremely important in preventing dehydration, it does not contain electrolytes. To maintain electrolyte levels, you could have broth or soups, which contain sodium, and fruit juices, soft fruits, or vegetables, which contain potassium.

For children, doctors often recommend a special rehydration solution that contains the nutrients they need. You can buy this solution in the grocery store without a prescription. Examples include Pedialyte and Infalyte.

Tips about Food

Until diarrhea subsides, try to avoid milk products and foods that are greasy, high-fiber, or very sweet. These foods tend to aggravate diarrhea.

As you improve, you can add soft, bland foods to your diet, including bananas, plain rice, boiled potatoes, toast, crackers, cooked carrots, and baked chicken without the skin or fat. For children, the pediatrician may recommend what is called the BRAT diet: bananas, rice, applesauce, and toast.

Preventing Traveler's Diarrhea

Traveler's diarrhea occurs when you consume food or water contaminated with bacteria, viruses, or parasites. You can take the following precautions to prevent traveler's diarrhea when you go abroad:

- Do not drink any tap water, not even when brushing your teeth.
- Do not drink unpasteurized milk or dairy products.
- Do not use ice made from tap water.
- Avoid all raw fruits and vegetables (including lettuce and fruit salad) unless they can be peeled and you peel them yourself.

D

- Do not eat raw or rare meat and fish.
- Do not eat meat or shellfish that is not hot when served to you.
- Do not eat food from street vendors.

You can safely drink bottled water (if you are the one to break the seal), carbonated soft drinks, and hot drinks such as coffee and tea.

Depending on where you are going and how long you are staying, your doctor may recommend that you take antibiotics before leaving to protect you from possible infection.

National Institute of Diabetes and Digestive and Kidney Diseases

M ost people have in their colons small pouches that bulge outward through weak spots, like an inner tube that pokes through weak places in a tire. Each pouch is called a diverticulum. Pouches are diverticula. The condition of having diverticula is called diverticulosis. About half of all Americans age 60 to 80, and almost everyone over age 80, have diverticulosis.

When the pouches become infected or inflamed, the condition is called diverticulitis. This happens in 10 percent to 25 percent of people with diverticulosis. Diverticulosis and diverticulitis are also known as diverticular disease.

What Causes Diverticular Disease?

Doctors believe a low-fiber diet is the main cause of diverticular disease. The disease was first noticed in the United States in the early 1900s. At about the same time, processed foods were introduced to the American diet. Many processed foods contain refined, low-fiber flour. Unlike whole-wheat flour, refined flour has no wheat bran.

Diverticular disease is common in developed or industrialized countries-—particularly the United States, England, and Australia—where low-fiber diets are common. The disease is rare in countries of Asia and Africa, where people eat high-fiber vegetable diets.

Fiber is the part of fruits, vegetables, and grains that the body cannot digest. Some fiber dissolves easily in water (soluble fiber). It takes on a soft, jelly-like texture in the intestines. Some fiber passes almost unchanged through the intestines (insoluble fiber). Both kinds of fiber help make stools soft and easy to pass. Fiber also helps prevent constipation.

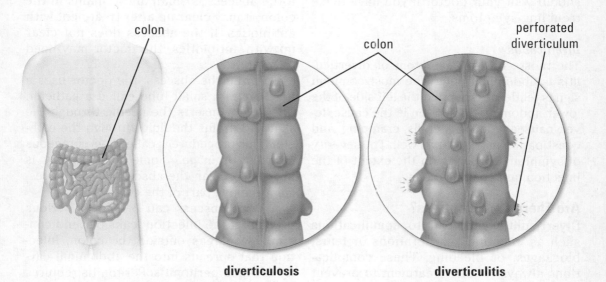

diverticulosis   diverticulitis

In diverticulosis, small pouches (diverticula) form in weakened areas in the wall of the colon. In diverticulitis, these pouches become infected and may perforate, which can allow pus to leak outside of the colon.

Constipation makes the muscles strain to move stool that is too hard. It is the main cause of increased pressure in the colon. The excess pressure causes the weak spots in the colon to bulge out and become diverticula.

Diverticulitis occurs when diverticula become infected or inflamed. Doctors are not certain what causes the infection. It may begin when stool or bacteria are caught in the diverticula. An attack of diverticulitis can develop suddenly and without warning.

What Are the Symptoms?
Diverticulosis
Most people with diverticulosis do not have any discomfort or symptoms. However, symptoms may include mild cramps, bloating, and constipation. Other diseases such as irritable bowel syndrome (IBS) and stomach ulcers cause similar problems, so these symptoms do not always mean a person has diverticulosis. You should visit your doctor if you have these troubling symptoms.

Diverticulitis
The most common symptom of diverticulitis is abdominal pain. The most common sign is tenderness around the left side of the lower abdomen. If infection is the cause, fever, nausea, vomiting, chills, cramping, and constipation may occur as well. The severity of symptoms depends on the extent of the infection and complications.

Are There Complications?
Diverticulitis can lead to complications such as infections, perforations or tears, blockages, or bleeding. These complications always require treatment to prevent them from progressing and causing serious illness.

Bleeding
Bleeding from diverticula is rare. When diverticula bleed, blood may appear in the toilet or in your stool. Bleeding can be severe, but it may stop by itself and not require treatment. Doctors believe bleeding diverticula are caused by a small blood vessel in a diverticulum that weakens and finally bursts. If you have bleeding from the rectum, you should see your doctor. If the bleeding does not stop, surgery may be necessary.

Abscess, Perforation, and Peritonitis
The infection causing diverticulitis often clears up after a few days of treatment with antibiotics. If the condition gets worse, an abscess may form in the colon.

An abscess is an infected area with pus that may cause swelling and destroy tissue. Sometimes, the infected diverticula may develop small holes, called perforations. These perforations allow pus to leak out of the colon into the abdominal area. If the abscess is small and remains in the colon, it may clear up after treatment with antibiotics. If the abscess does not clear up with antibiotics, the doctor may need to drain it.

To drain the abscess, the doctor uses a needle and a small tube called a catheter. The doctor inserts the needle through the skin and drains the fluid through the catheter. This procedure is called "percutaneous catheter drainage." Sometimes surgery is needed to clean the abscess and, if necessary, remove part of the colon.

A large abscess can become a serious problem if the infection leaks out and contaminates areas outside the colon. Infection that spreads into the abdominal cavity is called peritonitis. Peritonitis requires immediate surgery to clean the abdominal cavity and remove the damaged part of the colon. Without surgery, peritonitis can be fatal.

Fistula

A fistula is an abnormal connection of tissue between two organs or between an organ and the skin. When damaged tissues come into contact with each other during infection, they sometimes stick together. If they heal that way, a fistula forms. When diverticulitis-related infection spreads outside the colon, the colon's tissue may stick to nearby tissues. The most common organs involved are the urinary bladder, small intestine, and skin.

The most common type of fistula occurs between the bladder and the colon. It affects men more than women. This type of fistula can result in a severe, long-lasting infection of the urinary tract. The problem can be corrected with surgery to remove the fistula and the affected part of the colon.

Intestinal Obstruction

The scarring caused by infection may cause partial or total blockage of the large intestine. When this happens, the colon is unable to move bowel contents normally. When the obstruction totally blocks the intestine, emergency surgery is necessary. Partial blockage is not an emergency, so the surgery to correct it can be planned.

How Is Diverticular Disease Diagnosed?

To diagnose diverticular disease, the doctor asks about medical history, does a physical exam, and may perform one or more diagnostic tests. Because most people do not have symptoms, diverticulosis is often found through tests ordered for another ailment.

Medical History and Physical Exam

When taking a medical history, the doctor may ask about bowel habits, symptoms, pain, diet, and medications. The physical exam usually involves a digital rectal exam. To perform this test, the doctor inserts a gloved, lubricated finger into the rectum to detect tenderness, blockage, or blood. The doctor may check stool for signs of bleeding and test blood for signs of infection. The doctor may also order x-rays or other tests.

What Is the Treatment for Diverticular Disease?

A high-fiber diet and, occasionally, mild pain medications will help relieve symptoms in most cases. Sometimes an attack of diverticulitis is serious enough to require a hospital stay and possibly surgery.

Diverticulosis

Increasing the amount of fiber in the diet may reduce symptoms of diverticulosis and prevent complications such as diverticulitis. Fiber keeps stool soft and lowers pressure inside the colon so that bowel contents can move through easily. The American Dietetic Association recommends 20 to 35 grams of fiber each day.

The doctor may also recommend drinking a fiber product such as Citrucel or Metamucil once a day. These products are mixed with water and provide about 4 to 6 grams of fiber per glass.

Until recently, many doctors suggested avoiding foods with small seeds such as tomatoes or strawberries because they believed that particles could lodge in the diverticula and cause inflammation. However, this is now a controversial point and no evidence supports this recommendation.

If cramps, bloating, and constipation are problems, the doctor may prescribe a short course of pain-relieving medication. However, many medications affect emptying of the colon, an undesirable side effect for people with diverticulosis.

People with diverticulosis and diverticulitis need to pay attention to their fiber intake. Whole grains, legumes, fruits, and vegetables generally contain the most fiber. However, if you are experiencing an acute attack of diverticulitis, speak to your doctor or dietitian about your diet; a low-fiber diet may be recommended until you feel better.

Diverticulitis

Treatment for diverticulitis focuses on clearing up the infection and inflammation, resting the colon, and preventing or minimizing complications. An attack of diverticulitis without complications may respond to antibiotics within a few days if treated early.

To help the colon rest, the doctor may recommend bed rest and a liquid diet, along with a pain reliever or a drug such as propantheline (Pro-Banthine) to control muscle spasms in the colon.

An acute attack with severe pain or severe infection may require a hospital stay. Most acute cases of diverticulitis are treated with antibiotics and a liquid diet. The antibiotics are given by injection into a vein. In some cases, however, surgery may be necessary.

When Is Surgery Necessary?

If attacks are severe or frequent, the doctor may advise surgery. The surgeon opens the abdomen and removes the affected part of the colon. The remaining sections of the colon are rejoined. This type of surgery, called colon resection, aims to keep attacks from recurring and to prevent complications. The doctor may also recommend surgery for complications of a fistula or intestinal obstruction.

If antibiotics do not correct the attack, emergency surgery may be required. Other reasons for emergency surgery include a large abscess, perforation, peritonitis, or continued bleeding.

Emergency surgery usually involves two operations. The first surgery will clear the infected abdominal cavity and remove part of the colon. Because of infection and sometimes obstruction, it is not safe to rejoin the colon during the first operation. The surgeon creates a temporary hole, or stoma, in the abdomen during the first operation. The end of the colon is connected to the hole, a procedure called a colostomy, to allow normal eating and bowel movement. The stool goes into a bag attached to the opening in the abdomen. In the second operation, the surgeon rejoins the ends of the colon.

National Institute of Diabetes and Digestive and Kidney Diseases

Dizziness, a catch-all word for feeling lightheaded, faint, and unsteady, is the third most common reason patients over age 65 see a doctor and the single most frequent physical complaint among people over age 75. Not only can dizziness be profoundly disturbing, but it can also lead to debilitating falls and may be a symptom of many medical problems.

The sense of balance is complex and depends on messages received from many predictable sources such as the eyes, muscles, and joints. Also involved, although less obvious, are pressure receptors in the feet and tiny hair cells in the inner ear. All of these structures send signals to the brain. If any part of the system is damaged or fails to function properly; if the messages are contradictory; or if the brain fails to properly coordinate the information it receives, a person feels dizzy.

Dizziness can be caused by something as simple as an incorrect prescription for corrective lenses. Other likely, treatable possibilities include atherosclerosis, anemia, head trauma, transient ischemic attacks, depression, anxiety, motion sickness, excess alcohol consumption, ear infection, and certain drugs (see text box on page 294). In most cases, however, the culprit is

D

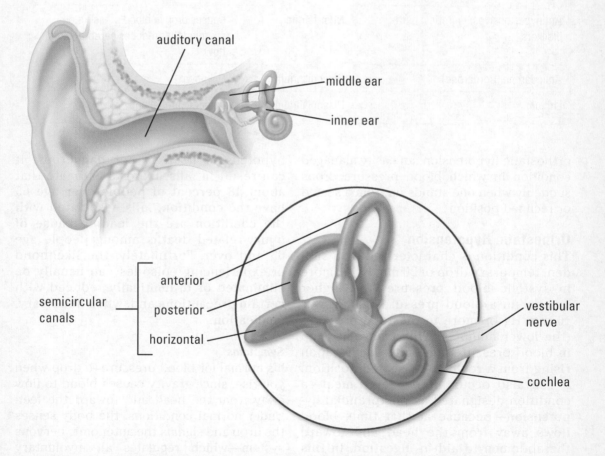

The semicircular canals and vestibule of the inner ear contain a fluid called endolymph that moves in response to head movement, triggering nerve signals to the brain that help maintain balance.

D

Medications That May Cause Dizziness

Drug	Type of Dizziness	Mechanism
Aminoglycosides such as streptomycin, neomycin, and gentamicin; cisplatin (Platinol)	Disequilibrium, oscillopsia (visual impairment when head is moving)	Damages vestibular hair cells
Antiepileptics such as carbamazepine (Atretol, Tegretol); phenytoin (Dilantin); primidone (Mysoline)	Disequilibrium	Interferes with activity in the cerebellum, an area of the brain that helps with posture
Tranquilizers; barbiturates; antihistamines; tricyclic antidepressants; sleeping pills; anxiolytics such as diazepam (Valium, Vazepalm)	Disequilibrium	Alters brain activity
Antihypertensives; diuretics; beta-blockers	Near-fainting	Causes drop in blood pressure on standing that reduces cerebral blood flow
Amiodarone (Cordarone)	Disequilibrium	Unknown
Lithium	Disequilibrium	Affects cerebellum

orthostatic hypotension, an easily managed condition in which blood pressure drops suddenly when one stands up from a seated or reclined position.

Orthostatic Hypotension

This condition is characterized by a sudden, temporary drop of 20 mm Hg or more in systolic blood pressure (the higher number in a blood pressure reading) or 10 mm Hg or more in diastolic pressure (the lower number). This transient drop in blood pressure generally occurs upon rising from a reclined or seated position. It can also occur after a large meal—a condition designated as postprandial hypotension—because at that time, blood flows away from the head and toward the abdomen to aid in digestion. In this case, dizziness can develop up to 30 minutes after eating. While orthostatic hypotension itself is not dangerous, it can result in falls. Experts estimate that about 18 percent of people over age 65 have the condition; falls associated with the condition are the leading cause of injury-related deaths among people age 65 and over. Fortunately, the likelihood of experiencing episodes can usually be eliminated or dramatically reduced with certain precautions and, when necessary, medication.

Symptoms

It's normal for blood pressure to drop when you rise, since gravity causes blood to flow away from the head and toward the feet. Under normal conditions, the body senses the drop and signals the autonomic nervous system—which regulates all involuntary muscles (including the heart) and glands—to constrict blood vessels in the lower part of the body. This action increases the amount of blood that is returned to the heart and then pumped to the brain.

When the autonomic response is slowed and the brain briefly receives inadequate blood flow, dizziness or faintness may result. Light-headedness, blurred vision, weakness, fatigue, nausea, difficulty thinking clearly, trembling, and head and/ or neck ache are other common symptoms. The symptoms usually stop after a few minutes or after sitting or lying down again.

Causes
Orthostatic hypotension can have many different causes. Medications are responsible for a large percentage of episodes. Other possible causes include diabetic neuropathy (nerve damage due to diabetes), Parkinson's disease, excessive alcohol consumption, and severe dehydration. Dehydration is a factor because it results in lower overall blood volume, which makes it harder for the heart to pump blood to the brain when the body is upright. Although some experts believe age is a contributing factor, research indicates that only about 6 percent of people over age 65 experience orthostatic hypotension in the absence of medical problems or medications.

Treatment
Treatment focuses on preventing symptoms. Often helpful are medication adjustments, including changing the dosage or the time of day the medication is taken, made in consultation with a doctor. Lifestyle changes can also help (see text box on page 296.)

If these measures do not provide relief, medication may be prescribed to specifically address the problem. One drug—midodrine (ProAmatine)—is approved specifically for orthostatic hypotension. It raises blood pressure by constricting blood vessels, which helps return blood to the heart. Doses can be timed to produce this effect during the day, when it is most needed.

Vertigo
In some instances, dizziness involves another troubling sensation called vertigo, the disturbing feeling that the body or the environment is spinning in space. With proper diagnosis and treatment, vertigo can nearly always be controlled if not cured.

When vertigo occurs, the malfunction can usually be traced to a chamber in the inner ear called the vestibule. Located behind the eardrum, the vestibule contains two tiny structures (the utricle and the saccule, known collectively as the otoliths) and three semicircular canals called the vestibular labyrinths. The labyrinths are filled with a gel-like fluid called endolymph, which moves in response to head movements. Minute calcium stones called otoconia float in the endolymph. When the head tilts, gravity pulls on these stones and bends tiny, slender, hairlike fibers that grow in the otolith. The bending of the hair cells sends nerve signals to the brain, conveying a complex and precise sense of orientation.

When one of these structures is disturbed, the brain may think the head is rotating or tilted even though signals coming from other balance mechanisms indicate otherwise. This confusion may induce nystagmus—frantic, involuntary back-and-forth eye movements. Nystagmus is the direct precursor of vertigo. In most instances, the underlying cause is one of two inner ear disturbances: Ménière's disease (about 10 percent of cases) or benign paroxysmal positional vertigo (which accounts for most of the remainder).

Vertigo may also be caused by many other problems, including labyrinthitis (an

D

D

Preventing Orthostatic Hypotension

Orthostatic hypotension (OH) is a condition in which blood pressure drops suddenly when one stands up from a seated or reclined position. OH is a frequent cause of dizziness. The following tips are helpful in the management of OH.

- **Avoid sudden changes in posture.** Before sitting or standing, encourage blood flow by flexing your feet or raising your arms over your head. Stand up slowly, hold onto a sturdy object for support, and wait a few minutes before walking; rocking or walking in place may improve blood flow. If dizziness occurs when you first get up in the morning, sit up in bed for a few minutes before standing.

- **Avoid overexertion early in the morning,** when orthostatic hypotension is usually more severe.

- **Eat smaller, more frequent meals.** Consuming fewer carbohydrates and more protein and drinking more beverages with caffeine (a stimulant that constricts blood vessels) at mealtime may be beneficial, as well. A recent study found that two cups of coffee with meals reduced postprandial hypotension by up to 50 percent.

- **Drink about 64 oz. of fluid daily.** Even mild dehydration lowers blood volume. Increased salt intake, which promotes fluid retention, may help maintain blood volume. However, if you have high blood pressure, your doctor may recommend limiting salt intake.

- **Reduce nighttime urination,** which can lower morning blood pressure. Limit fluid intake close to bedtime and elevate the head of your bed by 5 to 20 degrees. Heavy blood flow to the heart stimulates urination; a slight head elevation reduces this flow.

- **Keep cool.** Take cool baths and showers and avoid exercising in hot weather. Overheating causes bloods vessels to expand, leading to drops in blood pressure; excessive sweating may lead to dehydration.

infection in the labyrinth), vestibular neuritis (inflammation in vestibular nerve tissue), a blow to the head, excessive use of aspirin, epilepsy, and anxiety.

Ménière's Disease

In Ménière's disease, an increase in the amount of fluid in the labyrinth raises the pressure in the inner ear. Although its cause is poorly understood, researchers suspect that viral infection and a malfunction of the immune system may play a role. Whatever the reason, increased pressure induces nystagmus and ultimately vertigo. Certain hair cells may also be damaged, leading to hearing loss.

Although Ménière's disease can develop at any age, most patients are in their 50s. Patients usually experience a feeling of fullness in the ears and gradual hearing loss along with tinnitus (ringing in the ears) and episodes of vertigo. Symptoms can be so severe that all normal activities must be curtailed. Episodes can occur as often as every few weeks or as infrequently as every few years.

In some patients, the disease disappears spontaneously, while in others, it continues and may worsen. Although some permanent hearing loss may occur, deafness is rare. A mild sedative, an antinausea drug, and several days of rest nearly always bring relief, since most patients can find a position that lessens symptoms. In more severe cases, diuretics and salt restriction to reduce fluid retention sometimes produce excellent results, though no controlled studies have been conducted to support their use.

About 5 percent to 10 percent of patients continue to have debilitating episodes despite treatment. Such patients have two options: surgery or injections of a drug called gentamicin. Surgery severs the vestibular portion of the nerve that transmits orientation signals from the affected ear. Consequently, the brain no longer receives messages contradicting the correct information it obtains from other balance mechanisms. Thus, nystagmus and vertigo are eliminated.

Gentamicin, one of a powerful group of drugs called aminoglycosides, is ordinarily administered intravenously for serious bacterial infections. However, to treat Ménière's disease, it is introduced into the ear by injection in order to destroy nerve tissue. A recent study indicates that two or three small injections given once a week is the best approach. Surgery and gentamicin treatment are recommended when only one ear is affected because of the possibility of complications, such as deafness. However, when used for one ear, the treatments are 95 percent effective, and much of the hearing is usually preserved in the treated ear.

Benign Paroxysmal Positional Vertigo

Benign paroxysmal positional vertigo (BPPV) appears to be caused by debris that lodges in the semicircular canals. The debris, probably composed of tiny pieces of calcium that have broken away from the otoconia due to normal wear and tear, interferes with nerve transmission. In susceptible people, tilting the head up and down forces these particles into the vestibular canals. As a result, the brain receives messages that contradict the information arriving from other balance mechanisms, which leads to nystagmus and vertigo. Many sufferers find that ordinary movements, such as rolling over in bed, sitting up, or looking up to find something on a high shelf, bring on severe vertigo, loss of balance, nausea, or vomiting, while side-to-side head movement poses no problems.

Onset of symptoms is typically sudden and brief, with episodes lasting no more than half a minute. However, many patients experience several episodes a day, and symptoms frequently awaken sufferers from sleep. Consequently, they often make many unusual adjustments to avoid bouts. Some sleep with several pillows to avoid lying flat, for example, and at least one patient has reported tying his hand to the bedpost to keep from rolling over. Hearing loss, if present, is generally unrelated.

Treatment involves a series of safe, simple maneuvers that can be performed in a doctor's office. The maneuvers use gravity to move debris out of the affected area and into a part of the ear where it can do no harm. The procedure can be done by any doctor familiar with it. First, vertigo is induced by moving the head in a manner known to cause symptoms. The head is held there for a few moments and then quickly turned 90 degrees, where it is again held in place. After a few moments, the patient can sit up and go home. Eventually, the repositioned debris probably dissolves.

For the maneuver to be effective, the patient must keep the head elevated at least 45 degrees for two days after treatment. This means that it's necessary to sleep sitting up with the aid of pillows and a soft support collar. Some patients require one or two more treatments to completely eliminate symptoms. If the problem returns after that, as occasionally happens, patients can be taught to perform the maneuver themselves, and further professional treatment is not usually necessary. Experience suggests that this approach is effective in at least 90 percent of cases. When the maneuver fails, surgery on the affected canal may be an option.

When to See a Doctor

Severe, recurrent, unexplained, or prolonged dizziness requires a visit to the doctor for a thorough evaluation. You should also see a doctor if you experience vertigo or dizziness accompanied by headache, loss of hearing, weakness in the arms or legs, blurred vision, difficulty speaking, loss of consciousness, falling, or numbness or tingling in any part of the body.

During the examination, be sure to describe the exact nature of your symptoms (such as whether you experience vertigo, lightheadedness, faintness, or instability) and mention any accompanying symptoms (such as nausea, vomiting, or a feeling of fullness in the ears). Also, be prepared to explain how long episodes last, how often they occur, and what brings them on (such as rising from a chair, a specific head movement, or a loud noise). Your medical history is also important. Conditions such as thyroid disease, diabetes, certain autoimmune disorders, and cardiac arrhythmias can exacerbate dizziness.

If a vestibular disorder is suspected, it can usually be confirmed without expensive imaging studies. Referral to an ear, nose, and throat specialist or one of the 50 vestibular rehabilitation centers across the United States may be advised. For simple lightheadedness, common sense measures apply. If you become dizzy, sit or lie down, take a few deep breaths, and have a short rest. It's also important to avoid circumstances—such as rising too quickly to get out of bed—that cause episodes.

Everyone has a dry mouth once in a while—if they are nervous, upset or under stress.

But if you have a dry mouth all or most of the time, it can be uncomfortable and can lead to serious health problems.

Dry mouth

- can cause difficulties in tasting, chewing, swallowing, and speaking;
- can increase your chance of developing dental decay and other infections in the mouth;
- can be a sign of certain diseases and conditions;
- can be caused by certain medications or medical treatments.

Dry mouth is not a normal part of aging. So if you think you have dry mouth, see your dentist or physician—there are things you can do to get relief.

What Is Dry Mouth?

Dry mouth is the condition of not having enough saliva, or spit, to keep your mouth wet. The technical term for dry mouth is xerostomia (ZEER-oh-STOH-mee-ah)

Symptoms include:

- A sticky, dry feeling in the mouth
- Trouble chewing, swallowing, tasting, or speaking
- A burning feeling in the mouth
- A dry feeling in the throat
- Cracked lips
- A dry, tough tongue
- Mouth sores
- An infection in the mouth

Why Is Saliva So Important?

Saliva does more than keep the mouth wet.

- It helps digest food.
- It protects teeth from decay.
- It prevents infection by controlling bacteria and fungi in the mouth.

- It makes it possible for you to chew and swallow.

Without enough saliva you can develop tooth decay or other infections in the mouth. You also might not get the nutrients you need if you cannot chew and swallow certain foods.

Some people feel they have a dry mouth even if their salivary glands are working correctly. People with certain disorders, such as Alzheimer's disease, or those who have suffered a stroke, may not be able to feel wetness in their mouth and may think their mouth is dry even though it is not.

What Causes Dry Mouth?

People get dry mouth when the glands in the mouth that make saliva are not working properly. Because of this, there might not be enough saliva to keep your mouth wet. There are several reasons why these glands (called salivary glands) might not work right.

- Side effects of some medicines. More than 400 medicines can cause the salivary glands to make less saliva. Medicines for high blood pressure and depression often cause dry mouth.
- Disease. Some diseases affect the salivary glands. Sjögren's syndrome, HIV/AIDS, diabetes, and Parkinson's disease can all cause dry mouth.
- Radiation therapy. The salivary glands can be damaged if they are exposed to radiation during cancer treatment.
- Chemotherapy. Drugs used to treat cancer can make saliva thicker, causing the mouth to feel dry.
- Nerve damage. Injury to the head or neck can damage the nerves that tell salivary glands to make saliva.

D

What Can Be Done About Dry Mouth?

Dry mouth treatment will depend on what is causing the problem. If you think you have dry mouth, see your dentist or physician. He or she can try to determine what is causing the condition.

- If your dry mouth is caused by medicine, your physician might change your medicine or adjust the dosage.
- If your salivary glands are not working right but can still produce some saliva, your physician or dentist might give you a medicine that helps the glands work better.
- Your physician or dentist might suggest that you use artificial saliva to keep your mouth wet.

What Can I Do?

- Sip water or sugarless drinks often.
- Avoid drinks with caffeine, such as coffee, tea, and some sodas. Caffeine can dry out the mouth.
- Sip water or a sugarless drink during meals. This will make chewing and swallowing easier. It may also improve the taste of food.
- Chew sugarless gum or suck on sugarless hard candy to stimulate saliva flow; citrus, cinnamon or mint-flavored candies are good choices.
- Don't use tobacco or alcohol. They dry out the mouth.
- Be aware that spicy or salty foods may cause pain in a dry mouth.
- Use a humidifier at night.

Tips for Keeping Your Teeth Healthy

Remember, if you have dry mouth, you need to be extra careful to keep your teeth healthy. Make sure you do the following:

- Gently brush your teeth at least twice a day.
- Floss your teeth every day.
- Use toothpaste with fluoride in it. Most toothpastes sold at grocery and drug stores have fluoride in them.
- Avoid sticky, sugary foods. If you do eat them, brush immediately afterwards.
- Visit your dentist for a check-up at least twice a year. Your dentist might give you a special fluoride solution that you can rinse with to help keep your teeth healthy.

National Institute of Dental and Craniofacial Research

More than 3 million Americans have difficulty walking up stairs, carrying groceries, and performing other simple tasks because of emphysema, a chronic lung disease that damages lung tissue and causes 65,000 deaths each year. Nearly 80 percent of cases occur in long-time cigarette smokers, who are also at increased risk for lung cancer.

Once lung tissue is damaged, it cannot be repaired. But exercise, drug therapy, and supplemental oxygen, along with giving up smoking cigarettes, can relieve symptoms and possibly slow the progression of disease, or sometimes even halt it. When these measures fail or become ineffective, surgery may be considered.

Causes

The lungs contain more than 200 million tiny air sacs (alveoli) made of thin, elastic tissue. With every breath, the alveoli deliver oxygen to and remove carbon dioxide from the blood. In emphysema, the alveoli enlarge and lose their elasticity. As a result, the lungs become less efficient and the respiratory muscles must work harder to sustain breathing.

Cigarette smoking causes emphysema because the irritants in tobacco, which inflame the air passages in the lungs, lead to an increase in disease-fighting enzymes called proteases. In an effort to reverse the inflammation, the proteases destroy healthy lung tissue as if it were invading bacteria or viruses. Tobacco irritants block the effects of alpha-1-antitrypsin (AAT), a protein that protects lungs from the ill effects of the proteases, and also inhibit the action of cilia (tiny hairlike structures that help propel mucus and other unwanted materials out of the lungs). Why such irritants lead to emphysema or cancer in some people and not in others remains unknown, although heredity and environment are probably key factors.

Other causes of emphysema include prolonged exposure to industrial fumes and dusts (such as those found in coal mines and rock quarries). An inherited AAT deficiency usually causes the rare cases of emphysema that occur before age 50.

Symptoms

The symptoms of emphysema most often appear when patients are in their 50s or 60s. But lung damage begins much earlier. By the time symptoms become obvious, 50 percent to 70 percent of lung tissue may already be damaged.

The hallmark symptoms of emphysema include shortness of breath, fatigue, weight loss, a barrel-chested appearance, and

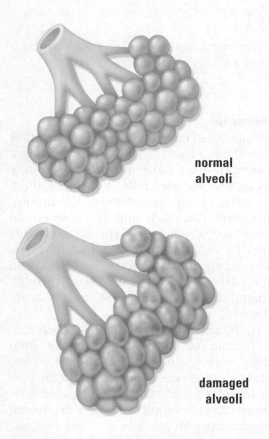

normal alveoli

damaged alveoli

Alveoli are air sacs that deliver oxygen to and remove carbon dioxide from the blood. In emphysema, alveoli enlarge and become less efficient.

E

Getting the Most from Your Medication

Older adults sometimes have difficulty using an inhaler because of arthritis or other medical problems that impair hand/breath coordination. At best, only 10 percent to 20 percent of the medication gets to the right place, so proper technique is important. The following tips from the National Emphysema Foundation can help:

- Control and slow your rate of respiration by using pursed-lip breathing.
- Remove the cap from the mouthpiece of the inhaler.
- Shake the unit for 5 to 10 seconds.
- Place the mouthpiece in one of three acceptable positions—in your mouth with your tongue and teeth out of the way, resting on your lower lip with your mouth wide open, or 1 to 1.5 inches in front of your wide open mouth.
- Begin to inhale as you press the inhaler.
- If possible, inhale slowly for 5 to 6 seconds; this helps the medication to get deep into your lungs (Inhaling too quickly deposits most of the medication on the back of the throat.)
- At the end of the inhalation, hold your breath for about 10 seconds.
- Exhale through pursed lips.
- If more than one puff is prescribed, wait a few minutes before taking your second puff.
- After your last puff, rinse your mouth and throat with mouthwash or water.
- Rinse the mouthpiece with warm water at least once a day and let it dry before storage.

overdeveloped neck and shoulder muscles owing to the increased demand on these muscles that aid respiration. Many people with emphysema also have chronic bronchitis (an inflammation of the alveoli and other bronchial passages), a chronic cough, repeated respiratory infections, asthma, and heart disease. (For more information on chronic bronchitis, see pages 168-170.)

Treatment

The best treatment for emphysema—indeed, the best way to prevent it—is to stop smoking. Second-hand smoke and other respiratory irritants should also be avoided whenever possible. Studies show that lung function improves slightly once the patient stops smoking, even after symptoms develop. Thereafter, lung function continues to decline at about the same rate as in people of comparable age who have never smoked.

Exercise, which improves breathing, is beneficial during all stages of the disease.

Medications

Though the symptoms of emphysema differ from those of asthma, its drug treatment is similar. Most patients with moderately advanced disease take a bronchodilating drug, such as albuterol (Ventolin), pirbuterol (Maxair), and metaproterenol (Alupent), which keeps the air passages open by relaxing the bronchial muscles. They come in two forms: aerosols and pills. Aerosols, which are taken through a metered-dose inhaler, are usually more effective.

To reduce inflammation, 20 percent to 30 percent of patients also benefit from taking systemic or inhaled corticosteroids, such as prednisone (Deltasone) or flunisolide (AeroBid). Long-term use of steroids requires calcium supplementation to prevent osteoporosis. All patients with emphysema, especially those who also have chronic bronchitis, must take special care to avoid respiratory infections. If infections do occur, they should be treated promptly. Antibiotics

---

Breathing Exercise

Athletes have long used a technique called pursed-lip breathing to improve their performance. Patients with emphysema can use the same method during ordinary activities. Start by doing the following exercise for about ten minutes a day while lying on your back with your head on a pillow. As you become more comfortable with the technique, do it while sitting up, walking, and climbing stairs or a hill:

• Breathe in through your nose.

• Tighten your abdominal muscles so they push upward on the lungs.

• Exhale through your mouth, pursing your lips so that you hear a hissing sound and feel pressure in your windpipe and chest. This pressure keeps the bronchial tubes open so that the lungs expel air more completely. Exhaling should take twice as long as inhaling.

---

may be prescribed, and annual influenza and one-time pneumonia vaccinations are recommended. (The pneumonia vaccine may require a booster every five years, especially for people who were first vaccinated before age 65.)

When the blood oxygen level is low, supplementary oxygen can be used intermittently or continuously as necessary. Many different types of units are available; some are portable enough to fit in the car or be carried over the shoulder.

Surgery

When other treatments fail, there are two surgical alternatives: lung transplantation, which replaces one or both lungs, and lung-volume reduction (LVR), which removes diseased portions of the lung so that remaining tissue can function more efficiently. Both surgeries are expensive, and costs can rise as a result of complications.

Lung transplantation. Over the past 20 years, the number of patients undergoing surgery for emphysema has skyrocketed. In 1985, only two lung transplants were performed; today more than 1,000 are performed annually. The procedure is limited, however, by the availability of donors. The cutoff age for recipients is 64, and patients must be in good general health except for their emphysema. Postsurgical care requires lifelong drug therapy to prevent rejection. The five-year survival rate is 50 percent.

Lung-volume reduction. Though LVR has been available since the early 1990s, it is still considered an experimental approach, and remains under evaluation. Although early successes have led to widespread use, the exact indications for LVR, and the best techniques, remain unknown. Mortality rates range from 4 to 10 percent with experienced surgeons; complication rates can be even higher, depending on the technique used, the condition of the patient, and the experience of the surgeon.

Epilepsy is a brain disorder in which clusters of nerve cells, or neurons, in the brain sometimes signal abnormally. Neurons normally generate electrochemical impulses that act on other neurons, glands, and muscles to produce human thoughts, feelings, and actions. In epilepsy, the normal pattern of neuronal activity becomes disturbed, causing strange sensations, emotions, and behavior, or sometimes convulsions, muscle spasms, and loss of consciousness. During a seizure, neurons may fire as many as 500 times a second, much faster than the normal rate of about 80 times a second. In some people, this happens only occasionally; for others, it may happen up to hundreds of times a day.

More than 2 million people in the United States—about 1 in 100—have experienced an unprovoked seizure or been diagnosed with epilepsy. For about 80 percent of those diagnosed with epilepsy, seizures can be controlled with modern medicines and surgical techniques. However, about 20 percent of people with epilepsy will continue to experience seizures even with the best available treatment. Doctors call this situation intractable epilepsy. Having a seizure does not necessarily mean that a person has epilepsy. Only when a person has had two or more seizures is he or she considered to have epilepsy.

Epilepsy is not contagious and is not caused by mental illness or mental retardation. Some people with mental retardation may experience seizures, but seizures do not necessarily mean the person has or will develop mental impairment. Many people with epilepsy have normal or above-average intelligence. Famous people who are known or rumored to have had epilepsy include the Russian writer Dostoyevsky, the philosopher Socrates, the military general Napoleon, and the inventor of dynamite, Alfred Nobel, who established the Nobel prize. Several Olympic medalists and other athletes have also had epilepsy. Seizures sometimes do cause brain damage, particularly if they are severe. However, most seizures do not seem to have a detrimental effect on the brain. Any changes that do occur are usually subtle, and it is often unclear whether these changes are caused by the seizures themselves or by the underlying problem that caused the seizures.

While epilepsy cannot currently be cured, for some people it does eventually go away. One study found that children with idiopathic epilepsy, or epilepsy with an unknown cause, had a 68 percent to 92 percent chance of becoming seizure-free by 20 years after their diagnosis. The odds of becoming seizure-free are not as good for adults, or for children with severe epilepsy syndromes, but it is nonetheless possible that seizures may decrease or even stop over time. This is more likely if the epilepsy has been well-controlled by medication or if the person has had epilepsy surgery.

What Causes Epilepsy?

Epilepsy is a disorder with many possible causes. Anything that disturbs the normal pattern of neuron activity—from illness to brain damage to abnormal brain development—can lead to seizures.

Epilepsy may develop because of an abnormality in brain wiring, an imbalance of nerve-signaling chemicals called neurotransmitters, or some combination of these factors. Researchers believe that some people with epilepsy have an abnormally high level of excitatory neurotransmitters that increase neuronal activity, while others have an abnormally low level of inhibitory neurotransmitters that decrease neuronal activity in the brain. Either situation can result in too much neuronal activity and cause epilepsy.

If you see someone having a seizure with convulsions and/or loss of consciousness, here's how you can help:

1. Roll the person on his or her side to prevent choking on any fluids or vomit.
2. Cushion the person's head.
3. Loosen any tight clothing around the neck.
4. Keep the person's airway open. If necessary, grip the person's jaw gently and tilt his or her head back.
5. Do NOT restrict the person from moving unless he or she is in danger.
6. Do NOT put anything into the person's mouth, not even medicine or liquid. These can cause choking or damage to the person's jaw, tongue, or teeth. Contrary to widespread belief, people cannot swallow their tongues during a seizure (or any other time).
7. Remove any sharp or solid objects that the person might hit during the seizure.
8. Note how long the seizure lasts and what symptoms occurred so you can tell a doctor or emergency personnel if necessary.
9. Stay with the person until the seizure ends.

Call 911 if:

- The person is pregnant or has diabetes.
- The seizure happened in water.
- The seizure lasts longer than 5 minutes.

- The person does not begin breathing again and return to consciousness after the seizure stops.
- Another seizure starts before the person regains consciousness.
- The person injures himself or herself during the seizure.
- This is a first seizure or you think it might be. If in doubt. check to see if the person has a medical identification card or jewelry stating that he or she has epilepsy or a seizure disorder.

After the seizure ends, the person will probably be groggy and tired. He or she may also have a headache and be confused or embarrassed. Be patient with the person and try to help him or her find a place to rest if he or she is tired or doesn't feel well. If necessary, offer to call a taxi, a friend, or a relative to help the person get home safely.

If you see someone having a non-convulsive seizure, remember that the person's behavior is not intentional. The person may wander aimlessly or make alarming or unusual gestures. You can help by following these guidelines:

- Remove any dangerous objects from the area around the person or in his or her path.
- Don't try to stop the person from wandering unless he or she is in danger.
- Don't shake the person or shout.
- Stay with the person until he or she is completely alert.

One of the most-studied neurotransmitters that plays a role in epilepsy is GABA, or gamma-aminobutyric acid, which is an inhibitory neurotransmitter. Research on GABA has led to drugs that alter the amount of this neurotransmitter in the brain or change how the brain responds to it. Researchers also are studying excitatory neurotransmitters such as glutamate.

In some cases, the brain's attempts to repair itself after a head injury, stroke, or other problem may inadvertently generate abnormal nerve connections that lead to epilepsy. Abnormalities in brain "wiring" that occur during brain development may also disturb neuronal activity and lead to epilepsy.

Research has shown that the cell membrane that surrounds each neuron plays an important role in epilepsy. Cell membranes are crucial for neurons to generate electrical impulses. For this reason, researchers are studying details of the membrane structure, how molecules move in and out of membranes, and how the cell nourishes and repairs the membrane. A disruption in any of these processes may lead to epilepsy. Studies in animals have shown that, because the brain continually adapts to changes in stimuli, a small change in neuronal activity, if repeated, may eventually lead to full-blown epilepsy. Researchers are investigating whether this phenomenon, called kindling, may also occur in humans.

In some cases, epilepsy may result from changes in non-neuronal brain cells called glia. These cells regulate concentrations of chemicals in the brain that can affect neuronal signaling.

About half of all seizures have no known cause. However, in other cases, the seizures are clearly linked to infection, trauma, or other identifiable problems.

Genetic Factors

Research suggests that genetic abnormalities may be some of the most important factors contributing to epilepsy. Some types of epilepsy have been traced to an abnormality in a specific gene. Many other types of epilepsy tend to run in families, which suggests that genes influence epilepsy. Some researchers estimate that more than 500 genes could play a role in this disorder. However, it is increasingly clear that, for many forms of epilepsy, genetic abnormalities play only a partial role, perhaps by increasing a person's susceptibility to seizures that are triggered by an environmental factor.

Several types of epilepsy have now been linked to defective genes for ion channels, the "gates" that control the flow of ions in and out of cells and regulate neuron signaling. Another gene, which is missing in people with progressive myoclonus epilepsy, codes for a protein called cystatin B. This protein regulates enzymes that break down other proteins. Another gene, which is altered in a severe form of epilepsy called LaFora disease, has been linked to a gene that helps to break down carbohydrates.

While abnormal genes sometimes cause epilepsy, they may also influence the disorder in subtler ways. For example, one study showed that many people with epilepsy have an abnormally active version of a gene that increases resistance to drugs. This may help explain why anticonvulsant drugs do not work for some people. Genes may also control other aspects of the body's response to medications and each person's susceptibility to seizures, or seizure threshold. Abnormalities in the genes that control neuronal migration—a critical step in brain development— can lead to areas of misplaced or abnormally formed neurons, or dysplasia, in the brain that can cause epilepsy. In some cases, genes may contribute to development of epilepsy even in people with no family history of the disorder. These people may have a newly developed abnormality, or mutation, in an epilepsy-related gene.

Other Disorders

In many cases, epilepsy develops as a result of brain damage from other disorders. For example, brain tumors, alcoholism, and Alzheimer's disease frequently lead to epilepsy because they alter the normal workings of the brain. Strokes, heart attacks, and other conditions that deprive the brain of oxygen can also cause epilepsy in some cases. About 32 percent of all newly developed epilepsy in elderly people appears to be due to cerebrovascular disease, which reduces the supply of oxygen to brain cells. Meningitis, AIDS, viral encephalitis, and other infectious diseases can lead to epilepsy, as can hydrocephalus—a condition in which excess fluid builds up in the brain. Epilepsy can also result from intolerance to wheat gluten (known as celiac disease), or from a parasitic infection of the brain called neurocysticercosis. Seizures may stop once these disorders are treated successfully. However, the odds of becoming seizure-free after the primary disorder is treated are uncertain and vary depending on the type of disorder, the brain region that is affected, and how much brain damage occurred prior to treatment.

Epilepsy is associated with a variety of developmental and metabolic disorders, including cerebral palsy, neurofibromatosis, pyruvate deficiency, tuberous sclerosis, Landau-Kleffner syndrome, and autism. Epilepsy is just one of a set of symptoms commonly found in people with these disorders.

Head Injury. In some cases, head injury can lead to seizures or epilepsy. Safety measures such as wearing seat belts in cars and using helmets when riding a motorcycle or playing competitive sports can protect people from epilepsy and other problems that result from head injury.

Prenatal Injury and Developmental Problems. The developing brain is susceptible to many kinds of injury. Maternal infections, poor nutrition, and oxygen deficiencies are just some of the conditions that may take a toll on the brain of a developing baby. These conditions may lead to cerebral palsy, which often is associated with epilepsy, or they may cause epilepsy that is unrelated to any other disorders. About 20 percent of seizures in children are due to cerebral palsy or other neurological abnormalities. Abnormalities in genes that control development may also contribute to epilepsy. Advanced brain imaging has revealed that some cases of epilepsy that occur with no obvious cause may be associated with areas of dysplasia in the brain that probably develop before birth.

Poisoning. Seizures can result from exposure to lead, carbon monoxide, and many other poisons. They can also result from exposure to street drugs and from overdoses of antidepressants and other medications.

Seizures are often triggered by factors such as lack of sleep, alcohol consumption, stress, or hormonal changes associated with the menstrual cycle. These seizure triggers do not cause epilepsy but can provoke first seizures or cause breakthrough seizures in people who otherwise experience good seizure control with their medication. Sleep deprivation in particular is a universal and powerful trigger of seizures. For this reason, people with epilepsy should make sure to get enough sleep and should try to stay on a regular sleep schedule as much as possible. For some people, light flashing at a certain speed or the flicker of a computer monitor can trigger a seizure; this problem is called photosensitive epilepsy. Smoking cigarettes can also trigger seizures. The nicotine in cigarettes acts on receptors for the excitatory neurotransmitter acetylcholine in the brain, which increases neuronal firing. Seizures are not triggered by sexual activity except in very rare instances.

What Are the Different Kinds of Seizures?

Doctors have described more than 30 different types of seizures. Seizures are divided into two major categories—partial seizures and generalized seizures. However, there are many different types of seizures in each of these categories.

Partial Seizures

Partial seizures occur in just one part of the brain. About 60 percent of people with epilepsy have partial seizures. These seizures are frequently described by the area of the brain in which they originate. For example, someone might be diagnosed with partial frontal lobe seizures.

In a simple partial seizure, the person will remain conscious but may experience unusual feelings or sensations that can take many forms. The person may experience sudden and unexplainable feelings of joy, anger, sadness, or nausea. He or she also may hear, smell, taste, see, or feel things that are not real.

In a complex partial seizure, the person has a change in or loss of consciousness. His or her consciousness may be altered, producing a dreamlike experience. People having a complex partial seizure may display strange, repetitious behaviors such as blinks, twitches, mouth movements, or even walking in a circle. These repetitious movements are called automatisms. They may also fling objects across the room or strike out at walls or furniture as though they are angry or afraid. These seizures usually last just a few seconds.

Some people with partial seizures, especially complex partial seizures, may experience auras—unusual sensations that warn of an impending seizure. These auras are actually simple partial seizures in which the person maintains consciousness. The symptoms an individual person has, and the progression of those symptoms, tends to be stereotyped, or similar every time.

The symptoms of partial seizures can easily be confused with other disorders. For instance, the dreamlike perceptions associated with a complex partial seizure may be misdiagnosed as migraine headaches, which can also cause a dreamlike state. The strange behavior and sensations caused by partial seizures can also be mistaken for symptoms of narcolepsy, fainting, or even mental illness. It may take many tests and careful monitoring by a knowledgeable physician to tell the difference between epilepsy and other diseases and disorders.

Generalized Seizures

Generalized seizures are a result of abnormal neuronal activity in many parts of the brain. These seizures may cause loss of consciousness, falls, or massive muscle spasms.

There are many kinds of generalized seizures.

- In absence seizures, the person may appear to be staring into space and/or have jerking or twitching muscles. These seizures are sometimes referred to as petit mal seizures, which is an older term.
- Tonic seizures cause stiffening of muscles of the body, generally those in the back, legs, and arms.
- Clonic seizures cause repeated jerking movements of muscles on both sides of the body.
- Myoclonic seizures cause jerks or twitches of the upper body, arms, or legs.
- Atonic seizures cause a loss of normal muscle tone. The affected person will fall down or may nod his or her head involuntarily.
- Tonic-clonic seizures cause a mixture of symptoms, including stiffening of the body and repeated jerks of the arms and/or legs as well as loss of consciousness. Tonic-clonic seizures are sometimes referred to by an older term: grand mal seizures.

Not all seizures can be easily defined as either partial or generalized. Some people have seizures that begin as partial seizures but then spread to the entire brain. Other people may have both types of seizures but with no clear pattern.

Society's lack of understanding about the many different types of seizures is one of the biggest problems for people with epilepsy. People who witness a non-convulsive seizure often find it difficult to understand that behavior that looks deliberate is not under the person's control. In some cases, this has led to the affected person being arrested, sued, or placed in a mental institution. To combat these problems, people everywhere need to understand the many different types of seizures and how they may appear.

How Is Epilepsy Diagnosed?

Doctors have developed a number of different tests to determine whether a person has epilepsy and, if so, what kind of seizures the person has. In some cases, people may have symptoms that look very much like a seizure but in fact are nonepileptic events caused by other disorders. Even doctors may not be able to tell the difference between these disorders and epilepsy without close observation and intensive testing.

EEG Monitoring

An EEG records brain waves detected by electrodes placed on the scalp. This is the most common diagnostic test for epilepsy and can detect abnormalities in the brain's electrical activity. People with epilepsy frequently have changes in their normal pattern of brain waves, even when they are not experiencing a seizure. While this type of test can be very useful in diagnosing epilepsy, it is not foolproof. Some people continue to show normal brain wave patterns even after they have experienced a seizure. In other cases, the unusual brain waves are generated deep in the brain where the EEG

is unable to detect them. Many people who do not have epilepsy also show some unusual brain activity on an EEG. Whenever possible, an EEG should be performed within 24 hours of a patient's first seizure. Ideally, EEGs should be performed while the patient is sleeping as well as when he or she is awake, because brain activity during sleep is often quite different than at other times.

Video monitoring is often used in conjunction with EEG to determine the nature of a person's seizures. It can also be used in some cases to rule out other disorders, such as cardiac arrhythmia or narcolepsy, that may look like epilepsy.

In some cases, doctors may use an experimental diagnostic technique called a magnetoencephalogram, or MEG. MEG detects the magnetic signals generated by neurons to allow doctors to monitor brain activity at different points in the brain over time, revealing different brain functions. While MEG is similar in concept to EEG, it does not require electrodes and it can detect signals from deeper in the brain than an EEG.

Brain Scans

One of the most important ways of diagnosing epilepsy is through the use of brain scans. The most commonly used brain scans include CT (computed tomography), PET (positron emission tomography) and MRI (magnetic resonance imaging). CT and MRI scans reveal the structure of the brain, which can be useful for identifying brain tumors, cysts, and other structural abnormalities. PET and an adapted kind of MRI called functional MRI (fMRI) can be used to monitor the brain's activity and detect abnormalities in how it works. SPECT (single photon emission computed tomography) is a relatively new kind of brain scan that is sometimes used to locate seizure foci in the brain. Doctors are also experimenting with brain scans called magnetic resonance spectroscopy (MRS) that can detect abnormalities in the brain's biochemical processes, and with near-infrared spectroscopy, a technique that can detect oxygen levels in brain tissue.

Medical History

Taking a detailed medical history, including symptoms and duration of the seizures, is still one of the best methods available to determine if a person has epilepsy and what kind of seizures they have. The doctor will ask questions about the seizures and any past illnesses or other symptoms a person may have had. Since people who have suffered a seizure often do not remember what happened, caregivers' accounts of the seizure are vital to this evaluation.

Blood Tests

Doctors often take blood samples for testing, particularly when they are examining a child. These blood samples are often screened for metabolic or genetic disorders that may be associated with the seizures. They may also be used to check for underlying problems such as infections, lead poisoning, anemia, and diabetes that may be causing or triggering the seizures.

Developmental, Neurological, and Behavioral Tests

Doctors often use tests devised to measure motor abilities, behavior, and intellectual capacity as a way to determine how the epilepsy is affecting that person. These tests can also provide clues about what kind of epilepsy the person has.

Can Epilepsy Be Prevented?

Many cases of epilepsy can be prevented by wearing seatbelts and bicycle helmets, putting children in car seats, and other measures that prevent head injury and other trauma. Prescribing medication after first or second seizures or febrile seizures may also help prevent epilepsy in some cases. Good prenatal care, including treatment of high blood pressure and infections during pregnancy, can prevent brain damage in the developing baby that may lead to epilepsy and other neurological problems later. Treating cardiovascular disease, high blood pressure, infections, and other disorders that can affect the brain during adulthood and aging also may prevent many cases of epilepsy. Finally, identifying the genes for many neurological disorders can provide opportunities for genetic screening and prenatal diagnosis that may ultimately prevent many cases of epilepsy.

How Can Epilepsy Be Treated?

Accurate diagnosis of the type of epilepsy a person has is crucial for finding an effective treatment. There are many different ways to treat epilepsy. Currently available treatments can control seizures at least some of the time in about 80 percent of people with epilepsy. However, another 20 percent—about 600,000 people with epilepsy in the United States—have intractable seizures, and another 400,000 feel they get inadequate relief from available treatments. These statistics make it clear that improved treatments are desperately needed.

Doctors who treat epilepsy come from many different fields of medicine. They include neurologists, pediatricians, pediatric neurologists, internists, and family physicians, as well as neurosurgeons and doctors called epileptologists who specialize in treating epilepsy. People who need specialized or intensive care for epilepsy may be treated at large medical centers and neurology clinics at hospitals, or by neurologists in private practice. Many epilepsy treatment centers are associated with university hospitals that perform research in addition to providing medical care.

Once epilepsy is diagnosed, it is important to begin treatment as soon as possible. Research suggests that medication and other treatments may be less successful in treating epilepsy once seizures and their consequences become established.

Medications

By far the most common approach to treating epilepsy is to prescribe antiepileptic drugs. The first effective antiepileptic drugs were bromides, introduced by an English physician named Sir Charles Locock in 1857. He noticed that bromides had a sedative effect and seemed to reduce seizures in some patients. More than 20 different antiepileptic drugs are now on the market, all with different benefits and side effects. The choice of which drug to prescribe, and at what dosage, depends on many different factors, including the type of seizures a person has, the person's lifestyle and age, how frequently the seizures occur, and, for a woman, the likelihood that she will become pregnant. People with epilepsy should follow their doctor's advice and share any concerns they may have regarding their medication.

Doctors seeing a patient with newly developed epilepsy often prescribe carbamazapine, valproate, or phenytoin first, unless the epilepsy is a type that is known to require a different kind of treatment. For absence seizures, ethosuximide is often the primary treatment. Other commonly prescribed drugs include clonazepam, phenobarbital, and primidone. In recent years, a number of new drugs have become available. These include tiagabine, lamotrigine, gabapentin, topiramate, levetiracetam, felbamate, and zonisamide, as well as oxcarbazepine, a drug that is similar to carbamazapine but has fewer side effects. These new drugs may have advantages for many patients.

Other drugs are used in combination with one of the standard drugs or for intractable seizures that do not respond to other medications. A few drugs, such as fosphenytoin, are approved for use only in hospital settings to treat specific problems such as status epilepticus (see "Are There Special Risks Associated With Epilepsy?" on page 315). For people with stereotyped recurrent severe seizures that can be easily recognized by the person's family, the drug diazepam is now available as a gel that can be administered rectally by a family member. This method of drug delivery may be able to stop prolonged seizures before they develop into status epilepticus.

Using Antiepileptic Drugs

For most people with epilepsy, seizures can be controlled with just one drug at the optimal dosage. Combining medications usually amplifies side effects such as fatigue and decreased appetite, so doctors usually prescribe monotherapy, or the use of just one drug, whenever possible. Combinations of drugs are sometimes prescribed if monotherapy fails to effectively control a patient's seizures.

The number of times a person needs to take medication each day is usually determined by the drug's half-life, or the time it takes for half the drug dose to be metabolized or broken down into other substances in the body. Some drugs, such as phenytoin and phenobarbital, need to be taken only once a day, while others such as valproate must be taken more frequently.

Side Effects of Medications

Most side effects of antiepileptic drugs are relatively minor, such as fatigue, dizziness, or weight gain. However, severe and life-threatening side effects such as allergic reactions can occur. Epilepsy medication may also predispose people to developing depression or psychoses. People with epilepsy should consult a doctor immediately if they develop any kind of rash while on medication, or if they find themselves depressed or otherwise unable to think in a rational manner. Other danger signs that should be discussed with a doctor immediately are extreme fatigue, staggering or other movement problems, and slurring of words. People with epilepsy should be aware that their epilepsy medication can interact with many other drugs in potentially harmful ways. For this reason, people with epilepsy should always tell doctors who treat them which medications they are taking. Women should also be aware that some antiepileptic medications can interfere with the effectiveness of oral contraceptives, and they should discuss this possibility with their doctors.

Since people can become more sensitive to medications as they age, they should have their blood levels of medication checked occasionally to see if the dose needs to be adjusted. The effects of a particular medication also sometimes wear off over time, leading to an increase in seizures if the dose is not adjusted. People should know that some citrus fruit, in particular grapefruit juice, may interfere with breakdown of many drugs. This can cause too much of the drug to build up in their bodies, often worsening the side effects.

Tailoring the Dosage of Antiepileptic Drugs

When a person starts a new epilepsy drug, it is important to tailor the dosage to achieve the best results. People's bodies react to medications in very different and sometimes unpredictable ways, so it may take some time to find the right drug at the right dose to provide optimal control of seizures while minimizing side effects. A drug that has no effect or very bad side effects at one dose may work very well at another dose. Doctors will usually prescribe a low dose of the new drug initially and monitor blood levels of the drug to determine when the best possible dose has been reached.

Generic versions are available for many antiepileptic drugs. The chemicals in generic drugs are exactly the same as in the brand-name drugs, but they may be absorbed or processed differently in the body because of the way they are prepared. Therefore, patients should always check with their doctors before switching to a generic version of their medication.

Surgery

When seizures cannot be adequately controlled by medications, doctors may recommend that the person be evaluated for surgery. Most surgery for epilepsy is performed by teams of doctors at medical centers. To decide if a person may benefit from surgery, doctors consider the type or types of seizures he or she has. They also take into account the brain region involved and how important that region is for everyday behavior. Surgeons usually avoid operating in areas of the brain that are necessary for speech, language, hearing, or other important abilities. Doctors may perform tests such as a Wada

Surgery for Epilepsy

The most common type of surgery for epilepsy is removal of a seizure focus, or small area of the brain where seizures originate. This type of surgery, which doctors may refer to as a lobectomy or lesionectomy, is appropriate only for partial seizures that originate in just one area of the brain. In general, people have a better chance of becoming seizure-free after surgery if they have a small, well-defined seizure focus.

Lobectomies have a 55 percent to 70 percent success rate when the type of epilepsy and the seizure focus are well-defined. The most common type of lobectomy is a temporal lobe resection, which is performed for people with temporal lobe epilepsy. Temporal lobe resection leads to a significant reduction or complete cessation of seizures about 70 percent to 90 percent of the time.

test (administration of the drug amobarbitol into the carotid artery) to find areas of the brain that control speech and memory. They often monitor the patient intensively prior to surgery in order to pinpoint the exact location in the brain where seizures begin. They may also use implanted electrodes to record brain activity from the surface of the brain. This yields better information than an external EEG.

A 1990 National Institutes of Health consensus conference on surgery for epilepsy concluded that there are three broad categories of epilepsy that can be treated successfully with surgery. These include partial seizures, seizures that begin as partial seizures before spreading to the rest of the brain, and unilateral multifocal epilepsy with infantile hemiplegia (such as Rasmussen's encephalitis). Doctors generally recommend surgery only after patients have tried two or three different medications without success, or if there is an identifiable brain lesion believed to cause the seizures.

If a person is considered a good candidate for surgery and has seizures that cannot be controlled with available medication, experts generally agree that surgery should be performed as early as possible. It can be difficult for a person who has had years of seizures to fully re-adapt to a seizure-free life if the surgery is successful. The person may never have had an opportunity to develop independence and he or she may have had difficulties with school and work that could have been avoided with earlier treatment. Surgery should always be performed with support from rehabilitation specialists and counselors who can help the person deal with the many psychological, social, and employment issues he or she may face.

While surgery can significantly reduce or even halt seizures for some people, it is important to remember that any kind of surgery carries some amount of risk (usually small). Surgery for epilepsy does not always successfully reduce seizures and it can result in cognitive or personality changes, even in people who are excellent candidates for surgery. Patients should ask their surgeon about his or her experience, success rates, and complication rates with the procedure they are considering.

Even when surgery completely ends a person's seizures, it is important to continue taking seizure medication for some time to give the brain time to re-adapt. Doctors generally recommend medication for two years after a successful operation to avoid new seizures.

E

Devices

The vagus nerve stimulator was approved by the U.S. Food and Drug Administration (FDA) in 1997 for use in people with seizures that are not well-controlled by medication. The vagus nerve stimulator is a battery-powered device that is surgically implanted under the skin of the chest, much like a pacemaker, and is attached to the vagus nerve in the lower neck. This device delivers short bursts of electrical energy to the brain via the vagus nerve. On average, this stimulation reduces seizures by about 20 percent to 40 percent. Patients usually cannot stop taking epilepsy medication because of the stimulator, but they often experience fewer seizures and they may be able to reduce the dose of their medication. Side effects of the vagus nerve stimulator are generally mild, but may include ear pain, a sore throat, or nausea. Adjusting the amount of stimulation can usually eliminate these side effects. The batteries in the vagus nerve stimulator need to be replaced about once every five years; this requires a minor operation that can usually be performed as an outpatient procedure.

Several new devices may become available for epilepsy in the future. Researchers are studying whether transcranial magnetic stimulation, a procedure that uses a strong magnet held outside the head to influence brain activity, may reduce seizures. They also hope to develop implantable devices that can deliver drugs to specific parts of the brain.

Diet

Studies have shown that, in some cases, children may experience fewer seizures if they maintain a strict diet rich in fats and low in carbohydrates. This unusual diet, called the ketogenic diet, causes the body to break down fats instead of carbohydrates to survive. This condition is called ketosis. One study of 150 children whose seizures were poorly controlled by medication found that about one-fourth of the children had a 90 percent or better decrease in seizures with the ketogenic diet, and another half of the group had a 50 percent or better decrease in their seizures. Moreover, some children can discontinue the ketogenic diet after several years and remain seizure-free. The ketogenic diet is not easy to maintain, as it requires strict adherence to an unusual and limited range of foods. Possible side effects include retarded growth due to nutritional deficiency and a buildup of uric acid in the blood, which can lead to kidney stones. People who try the ketogenic diet should seek the guidance of a dietitian to ensure that it does not lead to serious nutritional deficiency.

Researchers are not sure how ketosis inhibits seizures. One study showed that a byproduct of ketosis called beta-hydroxybutyrate (BHB) inhibits seizures in animals. If BHB also works in humans, researchers may eventually be able to develop drugs that mimic the seizure-inhibiting effects of the ketogenic diet.

Other Treatment Strategies

Researchers are studying whether biofeedback—a strategy in which individuals learn to control their own brain waves—may be useful in controlling seizures. However, this type of therapy is controversial and most studies have shown discouraging results. Taking large doses of vitamins generally does not help a person's seizures and may even be harmful in some cases. However, a good diet and some vitamin supplements, particularly folic acid, may help reduce some birth defects and medication-related nutritional deficiencies. Use of non-vitamin supplements such as melatonin is controversial and can be risky. One study showed that melatonin may reduce seizures in some children, while another found that the risk of seizures increased measurably with melatonin. Most non-vitamin supplements such as those found in health food stores are not regulated by the FDA, so their true effects and their interactions with other drugs are largely unknown.

How Does Epilepsy Affect Daily Life?

Most people with epilepsy lead outwardly normal lives. Approximately 80 percent can be significantly helped by modern therapies, and some may go months or years between seizures. However, epilepsy can and does affect daily life for people with epilepsy, their families, and their friends. People with severe seizures that resist treatment have, on average, a shorter life expectancy and an increased risk of cognitive impairment, particularly if the seizures developed in early childhood. These impairments may be related to the underlying conditions that cause epilepsy or to epilepsy treatment rather than the epilepsy itself.

Are There Special Risks Associated With Epilepsy?

Although most people with epilepsy lead full, active lives, they are at special risk for two life-threatening conditions: status epilepticus and sudden unexplained death.

Status Epilepticus

Status epilepticus is a severe, life-threatening condition in which a person either has prolonged seizures or does not fully regain consciousness between seizures. The amount of time in a prolonged seizure that must pass before a person should be diagnosed with status epilepticus is a subject of debate. Many doctors now diagnose status epilepticus if a person has been in a prolonged seizure for 5 minutes. However, other doctors use more conservative definitions of this condition and may not diagnose status epilepticus unless the person has had a prolonged seizure of 10 minutes or even 30 minutes.

Status epilepticus affects about 195,000 people each year in the United States and results in about 42,000 deaths. While people with epilepsy are at an increased risk for status epilepticus, about 60 percent of people who develop this condition have no previous seizure history. These cases often result from tumors, trauma, or other medical problems that affect the brain and may themselves be life-threatening.

While most seizures do not require emergency medical treatment, someone with a prolonged seizure lasting more than 5 minutes may be in status epilepticus and should be taken to an emergency room immediately. It is important to treat a person with status epilepticus as soon as possible. One study showed that 80 percent of people in status epilepticus who received medication within 30 minutes of seizure onset eventually stopped having seizures, whereas only 40 percent recovered if 2 hours had passed before they received medication. Doctors in a hospital setting can treat status epilepticus with several different drugs and can undertake emergency life-saving measures, such as administering oxygen, if necessary.

People in status epilepticus do not always have severe convulsive seizures. Instead, they may have repeated or prolonged nonconvulsive seizures. This type of status epilepticus may appear as a sustained episode of confusion or agitation in someone who does not ordinarily have that kind of mental impairment. While this type of episode may not seem as severe as convulsive status epilepticus, it should still be treated as an emergency.

Sudden Unexplained Death

For reasons that are poorly understood, people with epilepsy have an increased risk of dying suddenly for no discernible reason. This condition, called sudden unexplained death, can occur in people without epilepsy, but epilepsy increases the risk about two-fold. Researchers are still unsure why sudden unexplained death occurs. One study suggested that use of more than two anticonvulsant drugs may be a risk factor. However, it is not clear whether the use of multiple drugs causes the sudden death, or whether people who use multiple anticonvulsants have a greater risk of death because they have more severe types of epilepsy.

National Institute of Neurological Disorders and Stroke

E

An estimated 20 million American men suffer from some degree of erectile dysfunction (ED). Commonly called impotence, ED is the persistent inability to achieve and sustain an erection sufficient for intercourse. ED does not affect libido or the ability to have an orgasm. (Ejaculation may also be possible). The incidence of ED rises sharply with age, and as many as a third of men over 60 have the condition.

Causes

An erection occurs when arteries in the penis widen and veins narrow to prevent blood outflow. As a result, blood rushes into the penis, becomes trapped, and produces an erection. Impotence occurs when something interferes with this process.

Blood flow has to increase to about six times its normal rate to fill the penis and cause an erection.

Up to 75 percent of all cases of ED can be traced to underlying medical conditions. The main causes are: nerve disorders, vascular problems, and medications.

Nerve disorders. The nerves are signal-carriers that relay information from the brain to penile tissues, causing the blood vessels to open and blood to rush into the penis. If there is a problem with these nerves, the messages aren't transmitted correctly and the ability to have or maintain an erection can become impaired.

The major cause of penile nerve problems is diabetes mellitus, which often damages nerves and prevents nerve impulses from reaching the penis. In some cases, diabetes delivers a double threat: in addition to damaging nerves, it also encourages atherosclerosis in the arteries, which causes blockages that interrupt blood flow to the penis.

It is now estimated that 35 percent to 75 percent of men with diabetes suffer from ED.

Other nerve-related disorders include multiple sclerosis and Parkinson's disease. Nerve disruptions can also result from back surgery or disc herniation in the lower back; surgery to remove cancer from the prostate, lower rectum, or colon; and radiation therapy to the pelvic area.

Vascular problems. The major vascular cause of erectile difficulties typically originates from problems with the two, deep cavernosal arteries, or the larger arteries that feed blood to these cavernosal vessels. The culprit is atherosclerotic narrowing, which diminishes blood flow through the arteries. This arterial narrowing begins when men are in their 20s, and is mostly due to cigarette smoking, high blood pressure, a genetic predisposition, high cholesterol, or a combination of these four factors. As the blockage slowly progresses over the years, the arteries are unable to widen enough to permit increased blood flow to the penis.

Medications. ED is a common side effect of many prescription drugs. The most common offenders are medications for high blood pressure, heart ailments, and allergies. Other culprits are medications prescribed to combat depression—especially the serotonin reuptake inhibitors (SSRIs), such as Prozac, Zoloft, and Paxil.

Other causes. Other causes of ED include excessive alcohol consumption, smoking (which impedes blood flow), and low levels of testosterone, the male sex hormone.

E

Less commonly, psychological factors such as fatigue, tension, stress, anger, or depression can cause ED. However psychological problems are rarely the sole cause of ED.

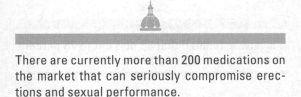

There are currently more than 200 medications on the market that can seriously compromise erections and sexual performance.

Treatment

IF ED stems from a medical problem or a medication, treating the underlying condition or fine-tuning a prescription may be all that is needed. If there is reason to believe ED is caused by smoking or excessive alcohol use, the remedy is apparent—cutting out smoking and drinking will often cure the problem. In addition, obesity—while not a direct cause of ED—is linked with hypertension, diabetes, and atherosclerosis, which are associated with ED. Therefore, losing weight may have an impact on ED. If ED persists, most people can restore potency with other treatment options.

However, no convincing evidence supports the use of yohimbine, a heart drug available in different formulations with or without prescription, or the nonprescription herbal products that are so often advertised as a remedy for ED.

Oral Drugs

Oral drugs are the newest advance in the treatment of erectile dysfunction. Sildenafil (Viagra), the first oral medication for this condition, became available in 1998. Since then, two additional ED drugs have been approved: vardenafil (Levitra) and tadalafil (Cialis). All three belong to a class of drugs known as phosphodiesterase type 5 inhibitors. Unlike other therapies for erectile dysfunction, these drugs do not produce erections in the absence of sexual stimulation.

Normally, sexual arousal increases levels of a substance called cyclic guanosine monophosphate (cGMP) in the penis. Higher levels of cGMP relax smooth muscles in the penis and allow blood to flow into its two inner chambers. Sildenafil, vardenafil, and tadalafil work by blocking the actions of an enzyme called phosphodiesterase type 5, which is found primarily in the penis. This enzyme causes erections to subside by breaking down cGMP. By maintaining increased cGMP levels, the drugs enhance both relaxation of smooth muscles in the corpora cavernosa and engorgement of these chambers with blood. As a result, men with erectile dysfunction can respond naturally to sexual arousal.

No studies have directly compared one PDE5 inhibitor with another, but all three drugs seem to work equally well for mild to moderate ED. Although data suggest that all three become effective in about 20 minutes, individual patient response varies widely. Some research suggests that higher doses of Levitra may "peak" faster. Faster peaking time means a faster effect.

Viagra and Levitra typically improve erections for about four hours, and they cannot be taken more than once daily. By contrast, Cialis is effective for 24 to 36 hours, meaning you can take a pill Friday night, for example, and have it last for much of the weekend.

Common side effects include headache, indigestion, and facial flushing. Cialis can cause muscle aches, and at high doses, Viagra may make objects appear tinged with blue. Not all men experience these problems, and when such side effects do occur, they often lessen with repeated use.

However, PDE5 inhibitors are not suitable for everyone. All three drugs can enhance the action of alpha-blocker medications (frequently prescribed for benign prostatic hyperplasia) and of nitrates, such as nitroglycerin, which are used to treat angina. In both instances, these interactions can cause potentially dangerous decreases in blood pressure (hypotension). Therefore, PDE5 inhibitors should not be taken by men who use nitrates of any kind or alpha-blockers. Nor should they be taken by men who have had a heart attack, stroke, or life-threatening arrhythmia during the previous six months.

Liver or kidney impairment may also preclude taking a PDE5 inhibitor or affect the dosage. Other medications that require special consideration include erythromycin (an antibiotic), ketoconazole (an antifungal drug), and ritonavir and saquinavir, protease inhibitors used to treat HIV infection.

At the request of the the Food and Drug Administration, all three drugs carry warnings about the risk of a rare form of blindness associated with taking the drugs (though it is not clear if the drugs caused the reported cases of blindness). Those most at risk for the vision loss are patients older than 50 who have diabetes, heart disease, and elevated cholesterol levels.

Vacuum Device

Nearly all forms of impotence can be treated with a special vacuum device. An acrylic tube is placed around the penis and the air is pumped out of the tube. The resultant vacuum causes blood to flow into the penis; an erection is produced in three to five minutes. The device is then removed and a constricting ring is slipped onto the base of the penis to keep the blood from flowing out, and so hold the penis erect for a half hour. The nerves that convey the sensation of intercourse and ejaculation

Exercise and Erectile Dysfunction

Exercise may reduce the risk of erectile dysfunction (ED) according to a recent study. In nearly 600 men who initially reported no problems with ED, information was gathered on ED risk factors such as smoking, alcohol consumption, obesity, and activity level. After eight years of follow-up, there was clear evidence that the men who exercised were less likely to develop ED than those who were sedentary—even if exercise was not started until midlife. Regular exercise improves cardiovascular function and may improve blood flow to the penis and other organs.

E

are not affected by the device, although using it may initially seem cumbersome and embarrassing. But, with practice, the vacuum device is effective, and those who have used it generally report very high levels of sexual satisfaction.

Vasodilators

Erections can be produced directly by vasodilators—drugs that widen the arteries and allow the penis to become engorged with blood. Injection of one of several vasodilators—such as papaverine, phentolamine, or prostaglandin E-1—directly into the base of the penis can artificially induce a normal erection. The most common vasodilator is alprostadil. Alprostadil can be self-injected (with instructions from your physician) using a tiny syringe and needle; it can also be inserted into the urethra as a pellet through a delivery system called MUSE. By dilating the blood vessels, these drugs cause an erection that lasts for 30 to 45 minutes.

Vasodilators, however, have drawbacks. Injections can cause pain, scarring, and prolonged erections (priapism)—for as long as four to five hours—which can require immediate treatment to prevent permanent damage to the penis. And MUSE can cause urethral burning. Low doses should minimize the risk of such side effects.

Surgery

Surgical implants may also be considered to cure ED, though usually as a last resort. One approach implants a semi-rigid device in the corpora cavernosa as a substitute for the effect of blood flowing into these areas of spongy muscle. The rods are flexible and can be manually straightened to be erect, or bent to remain close to the body.

Other implants are more complex, inflatable devices, which are implanted along with fluid reservoirs and a tiny pump that are operated manually to move the fluid from the reservoir into the device and so make the prosthesis enlarge and stiffen. Penile implants are reliable, although—as with any mechanical device—they may break down, and surgery is required to make the repair.

In general, surgical implants can require a long recovery period—up to six weeks. Urination is unaffected, but a natural, unassisted erection is never again possible. As with any surgery, there is a small risk of infection, scarring, or bleeding. Occasionally, the surgical implant may slip and protrude from underneath the skin, or the device may malfunction (perhaps inflating by itself at an inopportune moment). Additional surgery can correct these problems.

Vascular Surgery

Some physicians may recommend vascular surgery to enhance blood flow through the arteries into the corpora cavernosa. However, the results of this type of surgery have generally been unsatisfactory when tried in men over the age of 50, especially when there is widespread blockage of the arteries that supply blood to the penis.

Future Treatments

Erectile dysfunction is an expanding field of research, with new treatments on the horizon. One experimental drug called apomorphine (Uprima) targets mechanisms in the brain to stimulate an erection. It may be available within the next year or two. Although apomorphine may not be as effective as sildenafil, vardenafil, or tadalafil, it may provide another option for men who cannot take these oral medications.

A topical preparation of alprostadil (Topiglan) has shown some promise for men with erectile dysfunction. This preparation is applied to the head of the penis. Further research is necessary, but absorption will likely be a problem with this approach. An ointment is easier to use than alprostadil injections or the MUSE delivery system, and it would be associated with fewer side effects; but it is difficult to achieve efficient absorption of the drug through the skin.

The esophagus is a hollow tube that carries food and liquids from the throat to the stomach. When a person swallows, the muscular walls of the esophagus contract to push food down into the stomach. Glands in the lining of the esophagus produce mucus, which keeps the passageway moist and makes swallowing easier. The esophagus is located just behind the trachea (windpipe). In an adult, the esophagus is about 10 inches long.

Cancer that begins in the esophagus (also called esophageal cancer) is divided into two major types, squamous cell carcinoma and adenocarcinoma, depending on the type of cells that are malignant. Squamous cell carcinomas arise in squamous cells that line the esophagus. These cancers usually occur in the upper and middle part of the esophagus. Adenocarcinomas usually develop in the glandular tissue in the lower part of the esophagus. The treatment is similar for both types of esophageal cancer.

If the cancer spreads outside the esophagus, it often goes to the lymph nodes first. (Lymph nodes are small, bean-shaped structures that are part of the body's immune system.) Esophageal cancer can also spread to almost any other part of the body, including the liver, lungs, brain, and bones.

Causes and Prevention

The exact causes of cancer of the esophagus are not known. However, studies show that any of the following factors can increase the risk of developing esophageal cancer:

- **Age.** Esophageal cancer is more likely to occur as people get older; most people who develop esophageal cancer are over age 60.
- **Sex.** Cancer of the esophagus is more common in men than in women.
- **Tobacco use.** Smoking cigarettes or using smokeless tobacco is one of the major risk factors for esophageal cancer.
- **Alcohol use.** Chronic and/or heavy use of alcohol is another major risk factor for esophageal cancer. People who use both alcohol and tobacco have an especially high risk of esophageal cancer. Scientists believe that these substances increase each other's harmful effects.
- **Barrett's esophagus.** Long-term irritation can increase the risk of esophageal cancer. Tissues at the bottom of the esophagus can become irritated if stomach acid frequently "backs up" into the esophagus—a problem called gastric reflux. Over time, cells in the irritated part of the esophagus may change and begin to resemble the cells that line the stomach. This condition, known as Barrett's esophagus, is a premalignant condition that may develop into adenocarcinoma of the esophagus.
- **Other types of irritation.** Other causes of significant irritation or damage to the lining of the esophagus, such as swallowing lye or other caustic substances, can increase the risk of developing esophageal cancer.
- **Medical history.** Patients who have had other head and neck cancers have an increased chance of developing a second cancer in the head and neck area, including esophageal cancer.

Having any of these risk factors increases the likelihood that a person will develop esophageal cancer. Still, most people with one or even several of these factors do not get the disease. And most people who do get esophageal cancer have none of the known risk factors.

Identifying factors that increase a person's chances of developing esophageal cancer is the first step toward preventing the disease. We already know that the best ways to prevent this type of cancer are to quit (or never start) smoking cigarettes or using smokeless tobacco and to drink alcohol only in moderation. Researchers continue to study the causes of esophageal cancer and to search for other ways to prevent it. For example, they are exploring the possibility that increasing one's intake of fruits and vegetables, especially raw ones, may reduce the risk of this disease.

Researchers are also studying ways to reduce the risk of esophageal cancer for people with Barrett's esophagus.

Symptoms

Early esophageal cancer usually does not cause symptoms. However, as the cancer grows, symptoms may include:

- Difficult or painful swallowing
- Severe weight loss
- Pain in the throat or back, behind the breastbone or between the shoulder blades
- Hoarseness or chronic cough
- Vomiting
- Coughing up blood

These symptoms may be caused by esophageal cancer or by other conditions. It is important to check with a doctor.

Diagnosis

To help find the cause of symptoms, the doctor evaluates a person's medical history and performs a physical exam. The doctor usually orders a chest x-ray and other diagnostic tests. These tests may include the following:

- **A barium swallow** (also called an esophagram) is a series of x-rays of the esophagus. The patient drinks a liquid containing barium, which coats the inside of the esophagus. The barium makes any changes in the shape of the esophagus show up on the x-rays.

- **Esophagoscopy** (also called endoscopy) is an examination of the inside of the esophagus using a thin lighted tube called an endoscope. An anesthetic (substance that causes loss of feeling or awareness) is usually used during this procedure. If an abnormal area is found, the doctor can collect cells and tissue through the endoscope for examination under a microscope. This is called a biopsy. A biopsy can show cancer, tissue changes that may lead to cancer, or other conditions.

Staging

If the diagnosis is esophageal cancer, the doctor needs to learn the stage (or extent) of disease. Staging is a careful attempt to find out whether the cancer has spread and, if so, to what parts of the body. Knowing the stage of the disease helps the doctor plan treatment. Listed below are descriptions of the four stages of esophageal cancer.

- **Stage I**. The cancer is found only in the top layers of cells lining the esophagus.
- **Stage II**. The cancer involves deeper layers of the lining of the esophagus, or it has spread to nearby lymph nodes. The cancer has not spread to other parts of the body.
- **Stage III**. The cancer has invaded more deeply into the wall of the esophagus or has spread to tissues or lymph nodes near the esophagus. It has not spread to other parts of the body.
- **Stage IV**. The cancer has spread to other parts of the body. Esophageal cancer can spread almost anywhere in the body, including the liver, lungs, brain, and bones.

Some tests used to determine whether the cancer has spread include:

- **CAT (or CT) scan** (computed tomography). A computer linked to an x-ray machine creates a series of detailed pictures of areas inside the body.

- **Bone scan.** This technique, which creates images of bones on a computer screen or on film, can show whether cancer has spread to the bones. A small amount of radioactive substance is injected into a vein; it travels through the bloodstream, and collects in the bones, especially in areas of abnormal bone growth. An instrument called a scanner measures the radioactivity levels in these areas.
- **Bronchoscopy.** The doctor puts a bronchoscope (a thin, lighted tube) into the mouth or nose and down through the windpipe to look into the breathing passages.

Treatment

Treatment for esophageal cancer depends on a number of factors, including the size, location, and extent of the tumor, and the general health of the patient. Patients are often treated by a team of specialists, which may include a gastroenterologist (a doctor who specializes in diagnosing and treating disorders of the digestive system), surgeon (a doctor who specializes in removing or repairing parts of the body), medical oncologist (a doctor who specializes in treating cancer), and radiation oncologist (a doctor who specializes in using radiation to treat cancer). Because cancer treatment may make the mouth sensitive and at risk for infection, doctors often advise patients with esophageal cancer to see a dentist for a dental exam and treatment before cancer treatment begins.

Many different treatments and combinations of treatments may be used to control the cancer and/or to improve the patient's quality of life by reducing symptoms.

Surgery is the most common treatment for esophageal cancer. Usually, the surgeon removes the tumor along with all or a portion of the esophagus, nearby lymph nodes, and other tissue in the area. (An operation

> ## Questions for Your Doctor
>
> - After treatment, how often do I need to be checked? What type of follow-up care should I have?
> - What type of nutritional support will I need? Where can I get it?
> - Will I eventually be able to resume my normal activities?

to remove the esophagus is called an esophagectomy.) The surgeon connects the remaining healthy part of the esophagus to the stomach so the patient is still able to swallow. Sometimes, a plastic tube or part of the intestine is used to make the connection. The surgeon may also widen the opening between the stomach and the small intestine to allow stomach contents to pass more easily into the small intestine. Sometimes surgery is done after other treatment is finished.

Radiation therapy, also called radiotherapy, involves the use of high-energy rays to kill cancer cells. Radiation therapy affects cancer cells in the treated area only. The radiation may come from a machine outside the body (external radiation) or from radioactive materials placed in or near the tumor (internal radiation). A plastic tube may be inserted into the esophagus to keep it open during radiation therapy. This procedure is called intraluminal intubation and dilation. Radiation therapy may be used alone or combined with chemotherapy as primary treatment instead of surgery, especially if the size or location of the tumor would make an operation difficult. Doctors may also combine radiation therapy with chemotherapy to shrink the tumor before surgery. Even if the tumor cannot be removed by surgery or destroyed entirely by radiation therapy, radiation therapy can

E

E

often help relieve pain and make swallowing easier.

Chemotherapy is the use of anticancer drugs to kill cancer cells. The anticancer drugs used to treat esophageal cancer travel throughout the body. Anticancer drugs used to treat esophageal cancer are usually given by injection into a vein (IV). Chemotherapy may be combined with radiation therapy as primary treatment (instead of surgery) or to shrink the tumor before surgery.

Laser therapy is the use of high-intensity light to destroy tumor cells. Laser therapy affects the cells only in the treated area. The doctor may use laser therapy to destroy cancerous tissue and relieve a blockage in the esophagus when the cancer cannot be removed by surgery. The relief of a blockage can help to reduce symptoms, especially swallowing problems.

Photodynamic therapy (PDT), a type of laser therapy, involves the use of drugs that are absorbed by cancer cells; when exposed to a special light, the drugs become active and destroy the cancer cells. The doctor may use PDT to relieve symptoms of esophageal cancer such as difficulty swallowing.

Side Effects of Treatment

Side effects depend on the type of treatment and may be different for each person. Doctors and nurses can explain the possible side effects of treatment, and they can suggest ways to help relieve symptoms that may occur during and after treatment.

Surgery for esophageal cancer may cause short-term pain and tenderness in the area of the operation, but this discomfort or pain can be controlled with medicine. Patients are taught special breathing and coughing exercises to keep their lungs clear.

Radiation therapy affects normal as well as cancerous cells. Side effects of radiation therapy depend mainly on the dose and the part of the body that is treated. Common side effects of radiation therapy to the esophagus are a dry, sore mouth and throat; difficulty swallowing; swelling of the mouth and gums; dental cavities; fatigue; skin changes at the site of treatment; and loss of appetite.

Chemotherapy, like radiation therapy, affects normal as well as cancerous cells. Side effects depend largely on the specific drugs and the dose (amount of drug administered). Common side effects of chemotherapy include nausea and vomiting, poor appetite, hair loss, skin rash and itching, mouth and lip sores, diarrhea, and fatigue. These side effects generally go away gradually during the recovery periods between treatments or after treatment is over.

Laser therapy can cause short-term pain where the treatment was given, but this discomfort can be controlled with medicine.

Photodynamic therapy makes the skin and eyes highly sensitive to light for six weeks or more after treatment. Other temporary side effects of PDT may include coughing, trouble swallowing, abdominal pain, and painful breathing or shortness of breath.

Nutrition for Cancer Patients

Eating well during cancer treatment means getting enough calories and protein to control weight loss and maintain strength. Eating well often helps people with cancer feel better and have more energy.

However, many people with esophageal cancer find it hard to eat well because they have difficulty swallowing. Patients may not feel like eating if they are uncomfortable or tired. Also, the common side effects of treatment, such as poor appetite, nausea, vomiting, dry mouth, or mouth sores, can make eating difficult. Foods may taste different.

After surgery, patients may receive nutrients directly into a vein. (This way of getting nourishment into the body is called an IV.) Some may need a feeding tube (a flexible plastic tube that is passed through the nose to the stomach or through the mouth to the stomach) until they are able to eat on their own.

Patients with esophageal cancer are usually encouraged to eat several small meals and snacks throughout the day, rather than try to eat three large meals. When swallowing is difficult, many patients can still manage soft, bland foods moistened with sauces or gravies. Puddings, ice cream, and soups are nourishing and are usually easy to swallow. It may be helpful to use a blender to process solid foods. The doctor, dietitian, nutritionist, or other health-care provider can advise patients about these and other ways to maintain a healthy diet.

The Importance of Follow-up Care

Follow-up care after treatment for esophageal cancer is important to ensure that any changes in health are found. If the cancer returns or progresses or if a new cancer develops, it can be treated as soon as possible. Checkups may include physical exams, x-rays, or lab tests. Between scheduled appointments, patients should report any health problems to their doctor as soon as they appear.

National Cancer Institute

E

F

ibromyalgia syndrome is a chronic disorder characterized by fatigue and widespread pain in the fibrous tissues of the body—the ligaments, tendons, and muscles. (A syndrome is a set of symptoms and physical findings that together characterize a particular disorder.) The name fibromyalgia describes the disorder: "fibro" refers to fibrous tissues, "my" to muscles, and "algia" means pain. People with fibromyalgia tend to feel achy and stiff all over the body.

The distinguishing feature of fibromyalgia, however, is localized pain from various tender sites ("trigger points"), particularly in the neck, spine, shoulders, and hips. These trigger points can cause excruciating pain when pressure is applied to them, but otherwise may not hurt. The other main characteristic of fibromyalgia

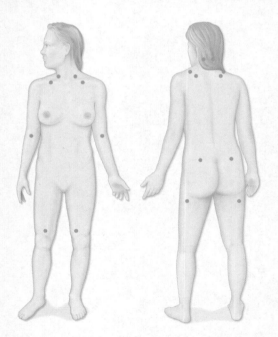

The dots indicate locations of "tender points" common to fibromyalgia. Patients experience undue soreness when pressure is applied to these regions.

is chronic fatigue, possibly related to disturbed sleep patterns. Sufferers often complain of waking up as tired as when they went to sleep and remaining fatigued throughout the day.

Unlike arthritis, fibromyalgia does not affect the joints, nor does it cause inflammation—the hallmark of rheumatoid arthritis. The pain produced by fibromyalgia, while severe, does not damage or deform connective tissues or muscles. The absence of physical abnormalities makes it difficult to diagnose fibromyalgia syndrome. Yet, according to one estimate, 2 percent of Americans, or about 3.7 million people (including many older women), may have the disorder, making it the second most common rheumatic problem in the United States.

Fibromyalgia primarily affects women—up to 90 percent of patients visiting a doctor with symptoms of this disorder are women—and the disorder usually first occurs between the ages of 20 and 60. Because this syndrome is poorly understood and difficult to recognize, it is not unusual for many years to elapse between the onset of symptoms and a diagnosis. Fortunately, more doctors have recently become aware of the collection of symptoms that characterize fibromyalgia.

Fibromyalgia, while not life-threatening, cannot be cured, but the symptoms can be managed so that patients can experience significant improvement once they are accurately diagnosed and treated.

Causes
The cause of fibromyalgia is not known, but there are several theories. Fibromyalgia may develop following a bout of flu or another illness or after extreme physical or emotional stress. Some researchers believe that fibromyalgia results when microtrauma to the muscles decreases their blood flow and causes weakness and fatigue.

Another theory is that the sleep disturbance associated with fibromyalgia is the underlying cause of the syndrome. The deepest, restorative stage of sleep—called delta-wave sleep—is somehow disrupted in people with fibromyalgia. When healthy volunteers were deprived of delta-wave sleep, they developed tenderness in the trigger point areas for fibromyalgia, as well as other symptoms of the disorder.

Other potential causes include an abnormality in the central nervous system; low levels of somatomedin C—a substance formed in the liver upon stimulation by growth hormone, which is secreted by the pituitary gland in greatest amounts during sleep; and low blood pressure.

Because clusters of fibromyalgia sometimes occur in families, a genetic link is also suspected. Women develop the condition 10 times more often than men, and 20 percent of those with rheumatoid arthritis also have fibromyalgia. Most patients are diagnosed around age 50.

Symptoms

Pain is the primary symptom of fibromyalgia. It usually starts in one area, such as the neck or lower back, but later spreads to other parts of the body. Most often, people with fibromyalgia complain of widespread aches and pains, similar to the symptoms associated with a bad bout of the flu. Sometimes the pain is described as gnawing or burning. People often feel stiffer and achier in the morning than at other times of the day. The severity of pain may vary from day to day, but most people with fibromyalgia report that some level of pain is always present. Exercise, physical or emotional stress, poor sleep, or even bad weather may increase the intensity of pain.

Numbness, tingling, and the sensation of swelling of the hands are other common complaints. Fibromyalgia is also accompanied by moderate to severe fatigue. Sufferers often feel that they do not have the energy to do the things they used to do. They may be unable to walk as far or exercise as much without becoming tired.

People with fibromyalgia also have a greater incidence of certain other symptoms. For example, some patients report increased allergic-type reactions to medications and substances in the environment. These reactions are not necessarily true allergies but may be due to an overly reactive central nervous system. Also, tension headaches and migraines occur more often in fibromyalgia patients.

Depression has been linked to fibromyalgia, but it isn't clear whether depression causes the syndrome or is a consequence of it. Many people with fibromyalgia have a history of depression, but only about 20 percent to 30 percent are clinically depressed at any given time. However, over a lifetime, 50 percent experience major depression. Other research has shown that depression occurs with about the same frequency in people with fibromyalgia as in those with other chronic conditions. Certainly, long-term pain and fatigue can cause depression. Nevertheless, some researchers believe that the mechanisms that underlie depression may be similar to those involved in fibromyalgia.

In addition, anxiety occurs in about half of fibromyalgia patients. About one third to one half of people with fibromyalgia also have irritable bowel syndrome, a gastrointestinal disorder of unknown cause. It is characterized by abdominal distention, bloating, and pain, as well as alternating bouts of constipation and diarrhea. And restless leg syndrome (a condition marked by an unpleasant aching in the legs at bedtime, with an overpowering urge to walk around for relief) may affect three quarters of fibromyalgia patients.

F

Diagnosis

Fibromyalgia is difficult to diagnose because it produces no objective physical changes that can be used to identify the syndrome. X-rays, biopsy tissue samples from tender areas, and blood tests reveal no characteristic abnormalities. Until recently, the lack of physical evidence had led many doctors to suspect a psychological basis for the symptoms. Despite the absence of any physical or laboratory evidence, fibromyalgia is a physical disorder. Fortunately, more doctors are now aware of the symptoms of fibromyalgia and are better able to diagnose the condition.

Trigger Points

In 1990, the American College of Rheumatology (ACR) developed a set of criteria to diagnose fibromyalgia. Widespread pain, present for at least three months, must be located on both sides of the body, both above and below the waist. Pressure of about 9 lbs. applied to at least 11 of 18 trigger points must produce pain. To apply the same amount of pressure at each point tested, the doctor may use an instrument called a dolorimeter to measure and control the pressure. In most cases the pain is not just mild discomfort but acute pain that may cause a person to flinch or cry out. Although the diagnosis can sometimes be made when fewer tender points are involved, both types of pain are necessary for a definitive finding.

It was once thought that pressure on areas as little as one inch away from the trigger points would not cause pain in people with fibromyalgia, and that this specificity of location would help to confirm the diagnosis. However, recent research has not supported this belief. While not part of the ACR criteria, reports of fatigue and, particularly, of nonrestorative sleep help confirm the diagnosis.

Laboratory Tests

Because the symptoms of fibromyalgia are similar to those of many other disorders, several tests may be done to rule out other problems. The doctor may perform blood tests to check for an underactive thyroid, rheumatoid arthritis, lupus, Lyme disease, and polymyalgia rheumatica. Imaging tests such as magnetic resonance imaging (MRI) should not be used initially, since they are expensive and sometimes associated with misleading results in diagnosing fibromyalgia.

Fibromyalgia, nonetheless, is not a disorder of exclusion, meaning that the diagnosis is not made simply by ruling out other diseases. Instead, the diagnosis must be based on the criteria described above. Fibromyalgia can, of course, coexist with other illnesses. For example, up to 10 percent of rheumatoid arthritis patients also have fibromyalgia. If fibromyalgia-like symptoms disappear when the other disorder is treated, it can be assumed that the symptoms were caused by the other condition.

People who suspect they have fibromyalgia should consult a doctor who has experience with this syndrome. Some doctors are still not familiar with the diagnostic criteria for fibromyalgia and others may apply too little or too much pressure when examining the trigger points. Often, a rheumatologist is the best type of doctor to see.

Treatment

Despite the lack of a definitive cause, fibromyalgia symptoms can be significantly improved with a multifaceted approach. The goals are to lessen pain and improve sleep. Much of the success of treatment lies with the patient, and many people report improvement simply because a diagnosis has been made. It is reassuring for patients to know that the disorder is not deforming or life-threatening and that they are able to take control of their situation.

People with fibromyalgia may find that home remedies, such as warm baths and applied heat, help relieve pain. Sufferers can also take advantage of mechanical aids, such as telephone headsets, jar openers, and voice-activated computer software. In some cases, people may need to make changes at the workplace to improve symptoms. When fibromyalgia patients were surveyed to determine which job-related activities aggravated their symptoms, the most troublesome were tasks that were prolonged or repetitive, and ones that required working under adverse conditions, such as at night or in the cold. To help prevent a symptom flare-up, people with fibromyalgia should not overdo any activity. Frequent changes in the types of tasks performed are a good way to keep occupational activities from aggravating symptoms.

Exercise

Getting people with fibromyalgia up and moving is key to improving their condition. A lack of activity worsens symptoms because unconditioned muscles are more sensitive to pain. Although exercising is the last thing people with fibromyalgia may want to do when they are achy and tired, studies have shown that symptoms improve after six to eight weeks of moderate aerobic exercise.

It is important not to overdo it, however. Start slowly, with perhaps 5 or 10 minutes of brisk walking a day. Gradually increase the exercise time to 30 to 40 minutes of aerobic activity at least three times a week. Patients whose pain is exacerbated by the jarring movements of weight-bearing exercise (such as walking or jogging) may instead try swimming or riding a stationary bicycle. Stretching exercises can help to prevent injury by keeping muscles flexible.

Improving Sleep Patterns

Many doctors recommend that patients with fibromyalgia try to establish a regular sleep schedule that involves the following measures: going to bed and getting up at the same time every day; getting at least eight hours of sleep; avoiding alcohol, caffeine, and smoking (all of which are chemical stimulants) in the evening; and eliminating daytime naps. This approach may not work for everyone, and some people may require medication. There has been some success with low doses of tricyclic antidepressants at bedtime; apparently these drugs enhance the action of neurotransmitters involved in the regulation of deep sleep.

Physical Therapy

Doctors may refer some patients with fibromyalgia to a physical therapist, either to design an exercise program or to treat particularly painful flare-ups. In one pain relief technique, called "spray and stretch," a physical therapist sprays the sore region with ethyl chloride to anesthetize it before stretching the patient's muscles.

Improving Body Mechanics

Day-to-day activities can cause fatigue and exacerbate pain if not done properly. Fibromyalgia patients may benefit from appropriate exercises and improved posture. In addition, people whose jobs or hobbies require repetitive movements that cause pain—for example, typing, needlepoint, working on an assembly line, golf, or tennis—must learn to perform them correctly. A physical therapist or lessons from a professional can help achieve this goal.

Psychological Counseling

Talking to a psychologist or a therapist may help to manage the emotional stress that can exacerbate symptoms and may even help

F

reduce their severity. Some people with fibromyalgia are depressed by their efforts to cope with a disorder that causes chronic pain. Others may have major depression that requires the use of antidepressant medication. The need for psychological counseling is not a sign of weakness or mental instability. It doesn't mean that a patient's symptoms are all "in their head." Rather, counseling can be valuable in helping someone to manage a chronic illness.

Medications

Drug therapy for fibromyalgia can relieve pain and improve sleep. Since inflammation is not a part of this syndrome, neither corticosteroids nor high doses of NSAIDs are prescribed. However, judicious use of NSAIDs or acetaminophen may provide pain relief during flare-ups.

Abnormal sleep patterns and accompanying depression are typically treated with low doses of tricyclic antidepressants, such as amitriptyline (Elavil or Endep), or with the muscle relaxant cyclobenzaprine (Flexeril). Doctors start patients on a dose of about 10 mg of the tricyclic, taken one to two hours before bedtime, and slowly raise the dose. It may take some time before the optimal dose is reached.

Antidepressant drugs called selective serotonin reuptake inhibitors, such as fluoxetine (Prozac) and sertraline (Zoloft), are another option. Patients should keep in mind that it can take as long as four to six weeks to respond to drug therapy. Side effects, though often temporary and rarely severe, may include vivid dreams, daytime drowsiness, constipation, dry mouth, and increased appetite.

If patients have severe pain in a specific area, injection of an anesthetic (usually procaine) can provide relief. Benefits are felt within five days and can last from two to four months. A three-month wait is then required before another injection can be given.

Nearly everyone experiences visual floaters or flashes from time to time. In most cases, floaters and flashes are a harmless, passing experience. Sometimes, however, they can signal a detachment, tear, or other problem involving the retina. People who experience a sudden shower of floaters, along with quick, lightning-like flashes, should be examined by an ophthalmologist promptly.

Floaters

Floaters are black or gray dots, lines, cobwebs, or other shapes that drift in the visual field. They are caused by small clumps of material within the vitreous humor. By blocking light passing through the vitreous, these clumps cast shadows on the retina that are perceived as floating spots in front of the eye.

Floaters that remain relatively constant for many years are typically of little

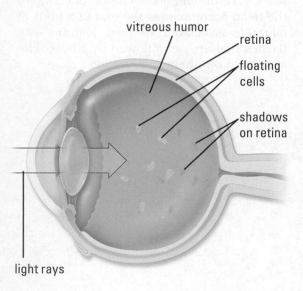

vitreous humor
retina
floating cells
shadows on retina
light rays

Tiny clumps of protein, or "floaters," may drift around in the vitreous humor and create shadows on the retina.

medical concern, and most people eventually become accustomed to them. But some floaters result from a condition in which the the vitreous humor (which is connected to the retina at several points) detaches from the retina. This can produce a sudden flurry of new floaters. Such a posterior vitreous detachment (PVD), as it is known, can result from a head injury; it is also more common in middle age and in people who are nearsighted, have a history of inflammation inside the eye, have undergone YAG laser surgery of the eye, or who have had cataract surgery. PVD develops in 10 percent of adults by age 50 and in two thirds of those aged 70 and over.

Posterior vitreous detachments do not require treatment unless the retina has been detached or torn (see page 332). Floaters that result from clumps of vitreous material are benign, and there is not much you can do to get rid of them. If they are bothersome, closing the eyes and gently looking up and down (to stir contents in the vitreous humor) may help them become less noticeable.

Flashes

Flashes are visual sensations of light that are not caused by light sources in the environment. They may appear as quick bursts of light or streaks of lightening that are similar to what happens when one is hit in the eye and sees stars. Flashes, which result when the vitreous pulls on, rubs on, or tears away from the retina, are more common in older people. Flashes occur only in one eye at a time and tend to last only a second or so, though bouts of flashes often recur over a period of weeks or months. Even though most of these bouts end without treatment, it is important to contact your doctor when flashes occur.

Some flashes are associated with migraine headaches rather than problems involving

Detached Retina

People who experience a sudden onset of new floaters or flashes should call their ophthalmologist immediately, even if the symptoms disappear on their own. If floaters or flashes are caused by a posterior vitreous detachment (PVD) that produced a tear in the retina, it can lead to permanent vision loss if left untreated. Another sign of PVD that warrants immediate medical attention is the appearance of a dark curtain or cloud over the visual field. (If an ophthalmologist is not available, go to a hospital emergency room.)

To diagnose PVD, an ophthalmologist uses eyedrops to dilate the pupils and then views the vitreous and retina with specialized equipment. (This procedure makes the eyes sensitive to light for several hours, so the person may have to arrange to be driven or accompanied home.)

Both retinal tears and detachments require treatment. (PVD that does not result in a detached or torn retina does not warrant treatment.) Five common procedures are used to treat retinal tearing and detachment, depending on their extent and location. In certain cases, small holes in the retina may require no treatment. In others, combinations of more than one surgical approach may be required. All are generally performed on an outpatient basis. The amount of vision restored and preserved with all procedures is greater if the macula (the small area at the center of the retina that is responsible for central and fine-detail vision) is still attached—but even if the prognosis is poor, treatment is usually still advisable.

the retina. Flashes associated with migraines are distinguished by their unique pattern: They appear as shimmering, jagged lines in both eyes and last between 10 and 20 minutes. These flashes usually begin in the middle of the visual field and gradually move outward. Often, but not always, a throbbing headache on one side of the head accompanies the end of a bout of migraine-associated flashes. Migraine-like flashes that are not followed by a headache are called ophthalmic migraines.

The stress and tension of your daily life are, literally, borne by your feet. The 56 bones (a quarter of the bones in the entire body) and 200 ligaments of your feet must serve as a sturdy foundation for your upright body every time you take a step, jump, dance, or kick. They also flex on all types of surfaces to move you forward with powerful thrusts. Then, too, they have to softly brake each of the 5,000 to 10,000 footsteps you take on an average day.

With such demands, it is not surprising that so many people have sore or painful feet. Every year, roughly 59 million people—the vast majority of them over 50—lodge foot complaints, and 15 million seek medical attention. Many of the most common foot problems develop from years of neglect and abuse. Ill-fitting or poorly designed shoes and inappropriate, overly stressful exercise are common causes of foot maladies. So is aging, which affects the foot just as it does the rest of the body. For example, the skin thins and loses elasticity; ligaments becomes less elastic; muscle strength diminishes; and the protective fat pads on the bottom and sides of the foot erode. These changes tend to widen the front of the foot and make foot tissues more vulnerable to irritation and injury. Medical problems, such as obesity, arthritis, and poor circulation, may worsen the situation.

The following are among the most common foot ailments of people over 50. Three affect the bones and tendons; the rest affect the skin and nails. Most of these problems respond favorably to self-care measures. If foot discomfort or pain is severe or doesn't improve over time, you may need the advice and care of a physician or a podiatrist (see the text box on page 337).

Foot ailments can be dangerous if you have a history of diabetes or circulatory disease; in these cases, you should be cared for by your physician. Also contact your physician if, despite self-treatment, your foot or any toe shows reddening, swelling, or pus—each a sign of infection—or if you experience severe or increasing pain.

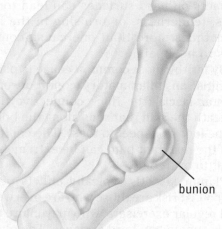

bunion

A bunion forms when outward protrusion of the bone forces the toe to point inward. The result is an inflamed joint and irritated skin.

Bunion

A bunion, from the Greek word for turnip, is an unsightly thickening of the bone around the "big" toe that not only disfigures, but also causes pain. Although the tendency to develop bunions may be hereditary, poorly fitting shoes, especially high heels and narrow-toe models, are the worst offenders. When you have a bunion, the shape of the foot begins to change; instead of pointing straight ahead, the big toe bends toward the second toe. Tissue soon develops around the bony protrusion at the toe joint to protect it from being rubbed by the inside of a shoe. That tissue can then become thick, rough, inflamed, and extremely painful. Since bunions change foot shape, shoes will no longer fit properly. Bunions can seriously interfere with standing and walking if neglected over the years.

Remedies for bunions. You cannot reverse the deformity caused by a bunion, but wearing properly fitted, soft leather shoes with low heels and ample toe room can help reduce pressure and pain. Wearing an over-the-counter bunion pad can also ease pain by decreasing pressure and reducing friction on the joint. Bunion surgery is seldom necessary. Before deciding on surgery, be sure you have exhausted all self-care options and, as with any surgery, get a second opinion.

Hammertoe

Hammertoe is a painful toe deformity that causes the toe to bend unnaturally and become claw-like. It occurs when abnormal contractions of the tendons of the toe force the toe to bend downward while its middle joint protrudes upward. Although any toe may be affected, hammertoe usually affects the second toe. Because of the constant rubbing of the affected toe when wearing shoes, a callus on the sole of the foot or a corn on top of the toe may develop and make walking especially painful.

Hammertoe can also develop from wearing shoes that are too narrow or short, which probably explains why women are far more prone to the condition than men. Another cause is diabetes mellitus, which damages nerves in the feet.

Remedies for hammertoe. As long as hammertoe causes no pain or any change in your gait, it isn't harmful and doesn't require treatment. If hammertoe is bothersome, mild cases can be treated with the corn pads or felt pads available in most pharmacies. Toe caps (small, padded sleeves that fit around the tip of the toe) may help relieve the pain. Changing your shoes may help as well. Wear wide shoes with resilient soles; avoid shoes with pointed toes.

Contact your physician or podiatrist if you experience continuous pain because of a hammertoe, or if it interferes with your everyday activities. Surgery may be needed to correct severe cases.

Heel Pain

About 2 million Americans suffer from heel pain, the most common complaint in foot clinics. Common sources of heel pain include a fracture of the heel bone, tendinitis or bursitis (inflammation of the tendons or bursae), and arthritis. In addition, inflammation around a heel spur (a hook of bony overgrowth at the bottom of the heel bone) or the stress of multiple impacts on hard surfaces can lead to redness, tenderness, or bruising in the heel. Sometimes more than one cause contributes to heel pain.

By far the most common cause is plantar fasciitis, an inflammatory condition of the plantar fascia (the thick connective tissue beneath the skin that runs along the bottom of the foot from heel to toes). The condition and the resultant pain can be extremely difficult to overcome.

Plantar fasciitis typically afflicts people over 50. At risk are those who are overweight and regular exercisers, who may injure their heels running on hard surfaces. The plantar fascia is protected by a pad of fat lying beneath it. But since the heel bears the brunt of large forces, the pad's shock-absorbing ability literally wears thin. Repeated stress on the heel often leads to microscopic tears where the plantar fascia connects to the heel bone; the result is inflammation and pain. The chief symptoms include a dull ache or intermittent pain that is felt directly under or to the side of the heel. If left untreated, over time the ache turns into an unrelenting burning pain that usually diminishes during sleep. Often, the heel is especially painful upon awakening and after sitting for an extended period of time.

Remedies for heel pain. Rest is the first line of defense, regardless of the cause. Limit your activities for a few days until the pain lessens. Take over-the-counter anti-inflammatories, such aspirin or ibuprofen. A good remedy is to massage your heel daily with ice, or to roll your heel over an ice-filled plastic jar or a container of frozen juice. Another relatively inexpensive but effective treatment is to place either a cushioned heel pad or rubber heel cup in your shoes. Both are available over-the-counter.

Once pain diminishes, slowly return to your previous level of physical activity. Reduce your activity if pain returns. Be patient. It can take months for pain to go away. Fortunately, nearly everyone recovers fully.

Contact your doctor or podiatrist if heel pain is severe, it lasts for four to six weeks, or you still experience pain or stiffness after trying the self-help measures. Your doctor may x-ray your foot to check for a bone problem and to rule out other causes of heel pain, such as a fracture or arthritis.

If plantar fasciitis is the cause, physical therapy sessions may be recommended. A simple calf stretch may also help: Place your hands on a wall from a distance of about two feet; step forward with one foot, keeping the other heel flat on the ground; hold the stretch for about 10 seconds, then switch feet. To help reduce pressure, your doctor may demonstrate how to tape your heel. A cortisone-type injection may also help relieve symptoms. Should these measures fail to bring relief, the foot may be placed in a cast for several weeks to immobilize the heel

F

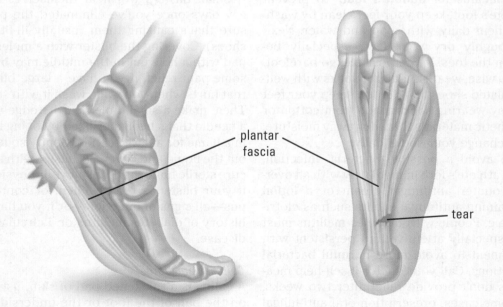

plantar fascia

tear

The plantar fascia runs from a bone at the heel to the underside of the toes. Pain occurs when this fibrous band is torn where it connects to the heel.

completely. In rare instances, when pain persists for about a year, a physician may suggest surgery.

Athlete's Foot

Athlete's foot is the most common of all skin infections, and, though typically harmless, can be unusually persistent and itchy. Other symptoms include blisters on your toes, soles, or sides of your feet, and scaling, peeling and cracking of the skin in these areas and between your toes. The name falsely implies that this condition only afflicts athletes. On the contrary, even sedentary people can contract athlete's foot.

Trichophyton—the most common group of fungi that causes athlete's foot—thrive best in warm, moist, enclosed environments, such as gym showers and locker rooms. Snug, non-leather shoes and damp, sweaty socks provide warm climates and ideal breeding grounds. Typically, the fungus is spread by shed fragments of affected skin.

Remedies for athlete's foot. To prevent athlete's foot, keep your feet clean by washing them daily with soap and water. Next, thoroughly dry your feet, especially between the toes. When possible, go barefoot. Otherwise, wear sandals, or socks with well-ventilated shoes. In addition, keep your feet dry by wearing socks made from cotton or synthetic materials that wick away moisture, and change your socks daily.

To avoid a possible bacterial infection, treat athlete's foot immediately with an over-the-counter antifungal cream or a lotion containing antifungal agents such as clotrimazole. People with diabetes mellitus must be especially attentive and persistent with treatment to avoid more harmful bacterial infections. Call your doctor if self-help measures don't provide relief after two weeks. In some cases, prescription oral anti-fungal medications may be required.

Blisters

A blister is a small and sometimes painful bubble of fluid under the skin, most commonly caused by irritation due to friction from ill-fitting shoes. In hot weather, when feet tend to become swollen and sweaty, blisters can result from going without socks or stockings, even in normally well-fitting shoes.

Remedies for blisters. To prevent blisters, make sure that you buy shoes in your size that are comfortable and provide ample room. It is helpful to shop towards the end of the normal day since your feet swell as the day progresses. A shoe that fits well should provide one-half inch of space between the end of your big toe and the tip of the shoe, should fit comfortably in the widest part of your foot, and, while standing on your tiptoes, should bend where your foot bends. To keep feet dry, wear socks made of cotton or synthetic fibers (such as polyproplylene) that cushion your feet and wick away moisture.

Small blisters will heal themselves in a few days once you've eliminated the pressure that's causing them (usually ill-fitting shoes). Covering the blister with a moleskin pad with a hole cut in the middle may bring some pain relief. If you have a large blister that hurts when you walk, wash it with soap. Then, make a small hole near its edge with a needle that's been sterilized by being held in a flame for a few seconds. Gently squeeze out the liquid and cover the blister with a secure sterile bandage. Consult your physician if your blister is red, swollen, or contains pus—all signs of infection—or if you have a history of diabetes mellitus or a circulatory disease.

Calluses and Corns

A callus is a thickened pad of skin, usually on the ball of the foot or the underside of the big toe, that results from chafing and

Foot Specialists

When foot problems don't respond to home treatment, you should see a professional. Primary-care physicians treat most foot complaints. But almost 40 percent of patients choose a podiatrist and 15 percent see an orthopedist.

Both of these specialists treat foot problems, but their area of expertise and their training differ. Podiatrists are foot and ankle experts. Though not medical doctors, they attend a four-year podiatric college, studying medicine and learning minor surgical procedures, with a major focus on the foot and ankle. The graduate becomes a doctor of podiatric medicine (D.P.M.). About 60 percent of podiatrists complete a hospital residency. Some podiatrists spend four more years as residents to become specialists in foot and ankle surgery.

Orthopedists deal with feet as well as musculoskeletal injuries that occur above the ankle bone. They attend four years of medical school and graduate with a medical degree (M.D.). All orthopedists serve a one-year surgical internship, followed by four years of hospital residency, to become trained surgeons who can operate on the entire skeletal system. Approximately 25 percent of training is devoted to foot and leg surgery; those physicians who wish to specialize in the foot and ankle spend an additional year of training in those areas.

Depending on your diagnosis, a specialist may recommend any of several options, including medication, special exercises, taping and strapping of the heel, orthotic devices (special foot supports that fit in your shoes), and possibly surgery. No matter which type of practitioner you choose, be sure to discuss how often the person takes care of your particular problem and the results you can expect from the recommended treatment.

---

pressure. A corn is a highly concentrated callus that occurs at a pressure point such as the top of the toe or under a toe joint. Either can become more painful when it presses on sensitive nerves in the surrounding skin, which typically becomes red and inflamed. After eliminating ill-fitting footwear (which usually causes the problem), calluses and corns generally clear up within four weeks.

Remedies for calluses and corns. The best way to treat corns and calluses at home is to soak the foot in warm (never hot) water until the hardened skin softens, then gently use a pumice stone or callus file; but don't rub the area raw. It may take several treatments before you see results. Until full healing is achieved, protect the area by using a light pad or bandage. Do not use over-the-counter chemical corn remedies. Many contain salicylic acid, which not only can remove the corn, but can also damage the surrounding healthy skin and result in more discomfort.

Ingrown Toenail

If you trim the nail of the big toe improperly, or wear tight shoes, socks, and stockings that press the nail into the tissue, you risk developing this common toe ailment. When pressure is exerted on the toe, the sides or upper corners of the nail may curl down and cut into the soft toe tissue, causing pain, swelling, and redness.

Remedies for ingrown toenail. Soak the toe in warm water for 15 to 25 minutes to soften the nail and help drain out any pus beneath it. If the nail is not extremely painful or infected, use tweezers to raise the nail and press a few strands of absorbent cotton under the nail to keep it from further cutting the skin. Repeat this process daily, until the nail finally grows out. For mild inflammation or infection, apply an over-the-counter antibacterial cream and cover the nail with a bandage. In rare instances, the infection may cause severe pain and discharge. In this case, your doctor can trim away the part of the nail that is growing into your flesh and prescribe antibiotics.

To prevent ingrown toenails, always cut nails straight across (keeping toe nails square instead of rounded) and wear wide, roomy shoes.

Toenail Fungus

A small white or yellow spot on your toenail may be all that heralds this common nail problem (in rare instances, it may affect fingernails). But left untreated, your whole nail may be infected by the fungus in a matter of months. In extreme cases, the nail becomes brittle and can crack, sometimes breaking away completely from the nail bed. The cause of nail fungus is not entirely understood, but may be due to trauma to the nail.

Remedies for toenail fungus. To prevent fungal infections, keep nails clipped, using one pair of clippers for infected nails and another for healthy nails. Disinfect clippers with an alcohol swab or cotton ball soaked in alcohol after each use. Also, keep your feet clean and dry since moist environments encourage the spread of these infections. In addition, it may be helpful to use an antifungal foot powder. (Avoid cornstarch-based powder because it encourages fungal growth).

Nonprescription topical treatments do not work for this ailment. The best way to treat it successfully is with one of several oral prescription medications, such as itraconazole (Sporanox), fluconazole (Diflucan), or terbinafine (Lamisil). Because of the high cost of these medications (from $700 to $1,200 for a course of itraconazole) and a 20 percent chance of recurrence after treatment, many people choose to live with toenail fungus, which, although unsightly, is rarely painful or disabling.

The gallbladder is a pear-shaped sac located under the right lobe of the liver. Between meals, it stores and concentrates bile, which is produced at a constant rate by the liver. After meals, the gallbladder releases bile into the duodenum. Bile salts emulsify dietary fats and prepare them for absorption following the action of digestive enzymes released by the pancreas and intestinal mucosal cells. The gallbladder neck leads into the cystic duct, which carries bile from the gallbladder to the common bile duct.

In many people, pebble-like solid debris forms from some of the components of bile. Gallstones may be as small as a grain of sand or as large as an egg, and there may be many or just one. Between 70 percent and 80 percent of these "stones" are composed primarily of cholesterol; the remaining stones are pigment stones, which form in people with hemolytic anemia (anemia caused by a rapid destruction of red blood cells), or when bacterial infection is present inside the bile ducts.

It is difficult to estimate the true incidence of gallstones because most affected individuals experience no symptoms. Approximately 20 million Americans have gallstones. Women are two to three times more likely to have gallstones than men of the same age. The estimated prevalence of gallstones in adult women is between 10 percent and 30 percent.

Risk Factors

Why only some people develop gallstones is poorly understood. Excessive weight, the ability of the gallbladder to contract, and diet are possible contributing factors.

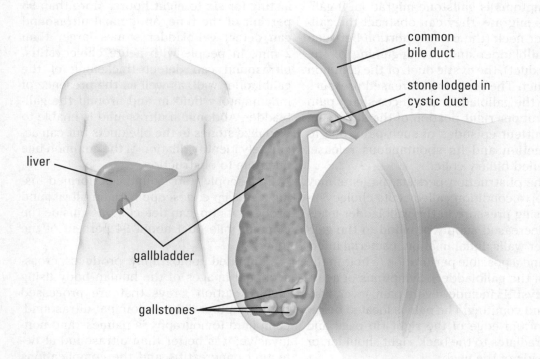

common bile duct

stone lodged in cystic duct

liver

gallbladder

gallstones

Between 70 percent and 80 percent of gallstones produce no symptoms. However, sharp abdominal pain results if gallstones move from the gallbladder to obstruct the cystic duct or the common bile duct.

Other risk factors include: genetic predisposition (especially in people of Pima Indian or Scandinavian ancestry); being over age 50; obesity; pregnancy; use of medications such as estrogen, oral contraceptives, or the antibiotic ceftriaxone (Rocephin); prolonged total intravenous nutrition; rapid weight loss; and diseases of the terminal ileum. (The terminal ileum, the last portion of the small intestine, is responsible for reabsorption of bile acids from the bowel into the blood.)

Symptoms

Between 70 percent and 80 percent of gallbladder stones produce no symptoms and are discovered incidentally during imaging studies or postmortem examinations. Asymptomatic people have an estimated 1 percent to 4 percent risk per year of developing symptoms. One possible cause of symptoms is gallstone migration. If gallstones migrate, they can obstruct the gallbladder neck (the narrow portion between the gallbladder and the beginning of the cystic duct), the cystic duct, or the common bile duct. The resulting increased pressure inside the gallbladder produces sharp pain in the upper right portion of the abdomen. Intermittent episodes of such pain, due to obstruction and its spontaneous release, are called biliary colic.

If the obstruction persists, patients may develop a condition called acute cholecystitis. Rising pressure in the gallbladder leads to a decreased supply of blood to the gallbladder walls, inflammation, bacterial infection, and a possible perforation (a hole in the wall of the gallbladder). Symptoms of acute cholecystitis include severe pain, fever, nausea, and vomiting. The pain is located below the bottom edge of the right rib cage and often radiates to the back, right shoulder, or right side of the neck.

When stones move from the gallbladder into the common bile duct, they cause partial or complete obstruction of bile flow. Signs and symptoms of bile duct obstruction include intermittent abdominal pain, jaundice (yellow discoloration of the skin and eyes), and cholangitis (inflammation of the bile ducts). Gallstones impacted in the major duodenal papilla can cause acute pancreatitis (inflammation of the pancreas) with abdominal pain, nausea, and vomiting.

Diagnosis

Multiple tests are available to evaluate people with suspected gallstones. The best way to diagnose stones inside the gallbladder is with abdominal ultrasound, performed by placing an acoustic probe on the abdominal wall. This noninvasive, totally painless test requires no special preparation aside from fasting for six to eight hours. More than 95 percent of the time, abdominal ultrasound can detect gallbladder stones larger than 2 mm. In people with acute cholecystitis, ultrasound can detect thickening of the gallbladder wall, as well as the presence of inflammatory fluid in and around the gallbladder. Abdominal ultrasound is unable to visualize stones in the bile ducts but can accurately identify dilation of the common bile duct due to obstruction.

Endoscopic ultrasound, performed using a special endoscope with an ultrasound probe at its tip, can detect stones inside the common bile duct about 94 percent of the time.

Computed tomography produces cross-sectional images of the human body using high-resolution x-rays that are processed by a computer. Like abdominal ultrasound, computed tomography is painless and noninvasive; it is better than ultrasound at detecting pancreatitis and the complications of acute cholecystitis, such as perforation of

When Surgery Is Warranted

Many people discover they have gallstones when they undergo an imaging study for another medical reason. If the stones have never caused symptoms, surgery is inappropriate because most "silent" stones never lead to a painful episode. There is one exception: Silent stones should always be eliminated through surgical removal of the gallbladder when the risk of gallbladder cancer is elevated. Patients at increased risk include those with a calcified gallbladder (a rare condition) and members of certain Native American tribes (who are genetically predisposed). Patients with large stones (more than 3 cm) and gallbladder polyps are also more likely to develop gallbladder cancer.

Mild or infrequent symptoms require monitoring to see if they worsen before moving forward with surgery. A wait-and-see approach is also appropriate after a single, full-blown attack of gallstone pain. One third of patients will never experience another attack, and dangerous complications rarely follow a first episode. However, severe or chronic episodes are another matter. Under these circumstances, surgery is advisable if ultrasound imaging has confirmed that stones are present. Surgery is the ultimate cure because, when the gallbladder is removed, direct drainage of bile from the liver into the intestine eliminates the opportunity for stone formation.

the gallbladder or bile ducts, and the formation of an abscess (a localized accumulation of pus).

Hepatobiliary scintigraphy can evaluate the passage of bile through the bile ducts and gallbladder, and detect obstruction of the cystic duct, which is a highly sensitive and specific sign of acute cholecystitis. This procedure is safe and subjects the patient to only small amounts of radioactivity.

Endoscopic retrograde cholangiopancreatography (ERCP) allows the physician to study the anatomy of the ductal systems and identify possible defects or blockages caused by stones, strictures, or masses. Currently the best way to diagnose stones in the bile ducts, this test is accurate more than 95 percent of the time.

Treatment
People who have gallstones but no symptoms require no treatment. Those with frequent, recurrent episodes of biliary colic, however, may elect to have their gallbladder removed, an operation called cholecystectomy. Nearly all cholecystectomies are now performed by laparoscopy, which decreases the amount of postoperative pain and discomfort and allows more rapid recovery than open surgery. Other approaches are to dissolve the gallstones or break them up using ultrasonic shock waves, but these techniques are not very effective and frequently lead to recurrence of stones.

People with acute cholecystitis usually require hospitalization. Fluids and nutrients are given intravenously to let the bowels rest completely, and antibiotics are administered. If complications develop, the gallbladder is removed unless the patient is unable to undergo surgery. In such cases, the gallbladder can be drained by passing a tube into the gallbladder through a small incision in the abdomen. Ultrasound or computed tomography is used to guide the placement of the draining tube.

In certain patients, pressure within the gallbladder can be relieved by using ERCP to place a small tube (stent) into the gallbladder to keep it open. In addition, stones

G

from the bile ducts can be removed during ERCP. The physician can use a special device called a sphincterotome to cut the duodenal sphincter (endoscopic sphincterotomy) and then extract the stones from the bile duct with a special endoscopic basket or balloon. These procedures are easily tolerated by most people, have a low complication rate, and are usually done on an outpatient basis.

Gastroesophageal refers to the stomach and esophagus. Reflux means to flow back or return. Therefore, gastroesophageal reflux is the return of the stomach's contents back up into the esophagus.

In normal digestion, the lower esophageal sphincter (LES) opens to allow food to pass into the stomach and closes to prevent food and acidic stomach juices from flowing back into the esophagus. Gastroesophageal reflux disease (GERD) occurs when the LES is weak or relaxes inappropriately allowing the stomach's contents to flow up into the esophagus.

The severity of GERD depends on LES dysfunction as well as the type and amount of fluid brought up from the stomach and the neutralizing effect of saliva.

Many people, including pregnant women, suffer from heartburn or acid indigestion caused by GERD. Doctors believe that some people suffer from GERD due to a condition called hiatal hernia. In most cases, heartburn can be relieved through diet and lifestyle changes; however, some people may require medication or surgery.

What Is the Role of Hiatal Hernia?

Some doctors believe a hiatal hernia may weaken the LES and cause reflux. Hiatal hernia occurs when the upper part of the stomach moves up into the chest through a small opening in the diaphragm (diaphragmatic

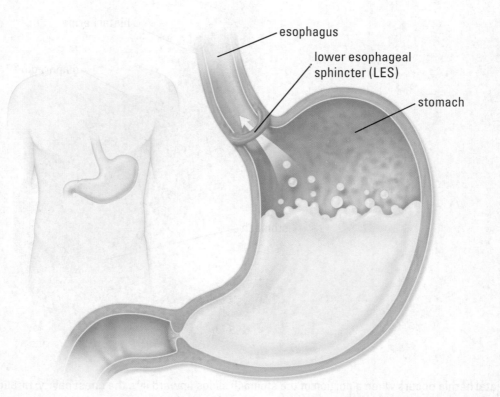

esophagus

lower esophageal
sphincter (LES)

stomach

A weak lower esophageal sphincter (LES) or inappropriate relaxation of the LES allows stomach acid to escape into the esophagus and cause heartburn.

hiatus). The diaphragm is the muscle separating the stomach from the chest (see illustration below). Recent studies show that the opening in the diaphragm acts as an additional sphincter around the lower end of the esophagus. Studies also show that hiatal hernia results in retention of acid and other contents above this opening. These substances can easily reflux into the esophagus.

Coughing, vomiting, straining, or sudden physical exertion can cause increased pressure in the abdomen resulting in hiatal hernia. Obesity and pregnancy also contribute to this condition. Many otherwise healthy people age 50 and over have a small hiatal

hernia. Although considered a condition of middle age, hiatal hernias affect people of all ages.

Hiatal hernias usually do not require treatment. However, treatment may be necessary if the hernia is in danger of becoming strangulated (twisted in a way that cuts off blood supply, i.e., paraesophageal hernia) or is complicated by severe GERD or esophagitis (inflammation of the esophagus). The doctor may perform surgery to reduce the size of the hernia or to prevent strangulation.

What Other Factors Contribute To GERD?

Dietary and lifestyle choices may contribute to GERD. Certain foods and beverages,

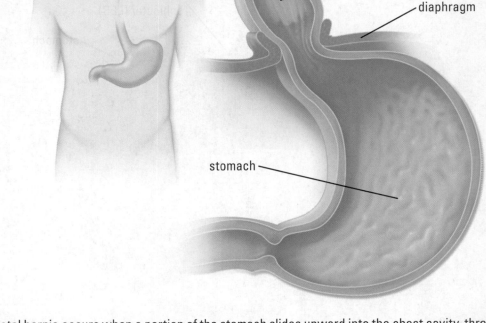

esophagus

hiatal hernia

diaphragm

stomach

A hiatal hernia occurs when a portion of the stomach slides upward into the chest cavity, through a hiatus (opening) in the diaphragm.

Is it Heartburn or a Heart Attack?

Of the millions of people each year who show up at U.S. emergency departments with concerns that their chest pain is due to a heart attack, some 10 percent or more may be suffering from an intense episode of heartburn. Because heartburn and a heart attack can both cause chest pain, it is easy to see how these two conditions might be confused. A key difference is the location of the chest pain: a heart attack causes pain that radiates into the shoulder arm, or jaw, particularly on the left side of the body; heartburn causes a burning feeling behind the breastbone or ribs that may travel into the neck and throat.

If you believe you may be having a heart attack (see page 377), seek medical attention immediately. Much of the damage of a heart attack occurs in the first hour, so waiting to see if chest pain is due to heartburn could prove fatal.

The Editors

including chocolate, peppermint, fried or fatty foods, coffee, or alcoholic beverages, may weaken the LES causing reflux and heartburn. Studies show that cigarette smoking relaxes the LES. Obesity and pregnancy can also cause GERD.

What Does Heartburn Feel Like?

Heartburn, also called acid indigestion, is the most common symptom of GERD and usually feels like a burning chest pain beginning behind the breastbone and moving upward to the neck and throat. Many people say it feels like food is coming back into the mouth leaving an acid or bitter taste.

The burning, pressure, or pain of heartburn can last as long as two hours and is often worse after eating. Lying down or bending over can also result in heartburn. Many people obtain relief by standing upright or by taking an antacid that clears acid out of the esophagus.

Heartburn pain can be mistaken for the pain associated with heart disease or a heart attack, but there are differences. Exercise may aggravate pain resulting from heart disease, and rest may relieve the pain. Heartburn pain is less likely to be associated with physical activity.

How Common Is Heartburn?

More than 60 million American adults experience GERD and heartburn at least once a month, and about 25 million adults suffer daily from heartburn. Twenty-five percent of pregnant women experience daily heartburn, and more than 50 percent have occasional distress. Recent studies show that GERD in infants and children is more common than previously recognized and may produce recurrent vomiting, coughing and other respiratory problems, or failure to thrive.

What Is the Treatment for GERD?

Doctors recommend lifestyle and dietary changes for most people with GERD. Treatment aims at decreasing the amount of reflux or reducing damage to the lining of the esophagus from refluxed materials.

Avoiding foods and beverages that can weaken the LES is recommended. These foods include chocolate, peppermint, fatty foods, coffee, and alcoholic beverages. Foods and beverages that can irritate a damaged esophageal lining, such as citrus fruits and juices, tomato products, and pepper, should also be avoided.

Decreasing the size of portions at mealtime may also help control symptoms. Eating

G

Guide to Prescription Medication

If you still experience discomfort from GERD despite attempting lifestyle measures and taking OTC medications, or if you have symptoms more than twice a week without medication, you should see a doctor. Treatment may involve taking a prescription-strength H2-blocker, proton-pump inhibitor (PPI), or a PPI along with a prokinetic agent. High-dose H2-blocker therapy with ranitidine (Zantac), famotidine (Pepcid), cimetidine (Tagamet) or nizatidine (Axid) is successful in at least 60 percent of cases and is usually tried first.

PPI therapy with either omeprazole (Prilosec), lansoprazole (Prevacid), rabeprazole (Aciphex), pantoprazole (Protonix), or esomeprazole (Nexium), is appropriate and nearly always successful for advanced GERD or severe symptoms when H2-blockers have failed. Like H2-blockers, PPIs decrease the production of stomach acid, although by a different chemical mechanism and to a greater degree. Many patients require daily maintenance therapy.

The effects of proton-pump inhibitors can be augmented by the administration of a prokinetic agent. Prokinetic agents, which include bethanechol (Urecholine) and metoclopramide (Reglan), increase clearance of acid from the esophagus, raise pressure of the lower esophageal sphincter, and speed up the emptying of the stomach.

The Editors

G

meals at least two to three hours before bedtime may lessen reflux by allowing the acid in the stomach to decrease and the stomach to empty partially. In addition, being overweight often worsens symptoms. Many overweight people find relief when they lose weight.

Cigarette smoking weakens the LES. Therefore, stopping smoking is important to reduce GERD symptoms.

Elevating the head of the bed on 6-inch blocks or sleeping on a specially designed wedge reduces heartburn by allowing gravity to minimize reflux of stomach contents into the esophagus.

Antacids taken regularly can neutralize acid in the esophagus and stomach and stop heartburn. Many people find that nonprescription antacids provide temporary or partial relief. An antacid combined with a foaming agent such as alginic acid helps some people. These compounds are believed to form a foam barrier on top of the stomach that prevents acid reflux from occurring.

Long-term use of antacids, however, can result in side effects, including diarrhea, altered calcium metabolism (a change in the way the body breaks down and uses calcium), and buildup of magnesium in the body. Too much magnesium can be serious for patients with kidney disease. If antacids are needed for more than three weeks, a doctor should be consulted.

For chronic reflux and heartburn, the doctor may prescribe medications to reduce acid in the stomach. These medicines include H2- blockers, which inhibit acid secretion in the stomach. Currently, four H2-blockers are available: cimetidine, famotidine, nizatidine, and ranitidine. Another type of drug, the proton-pump (or acid-pump) inhibitor omeprazole inhibits an enzyme (a protein in the acid-producing cells of the stomach) necessary for acid secretion. The acid-pump inhibitor lansoprazole is currently under investigation as a new treatment for GERD.

Other approaches to therapy will increase the strength of the LES and quicken emptying of stomach contents with motility drugs that act on the upper gastrointestinal (GI) tract. These drugs include bethanechol and metoclopramide.

What If Symptoms Persist?

People with severe, chronic esophageal reflux or with symptoms not relieved by the treatment described above may need more complete diagnostic evaluation. Doctors use a variety of tests and procedures to examine a patient with chronic heartburn.

An upper GI series may be performed during the early phase of testing. This test is a special x-ray that shows the esophagus, stomach, and duodenum (the upper part of the small intestine). While an upper GI series provides limited information about possible reflux, it is used to rule out other diagnoses, such as peptic ulcers.

Endoscopy is an important procedure for individuals with chronic GERD. By placing a small lighted tube with a tiny video camera on the end (endoscope) into the esophagus, the doctor may see inflammation or irritation of the tissue lining the esophagus (esophagitis). If the findings of the endoscopy are abnormal or questionable, biopsy (removing a small sample of tissue) from the lining of the esophagus may be helpful.

The Bernstein test (dripping a mild acid through a tube placed in the mid-esophagus) is often performed as part of a complete evaluation. This test attempts to confirm that the symptoms result from acid in the esophagus. Esophageal manometric studies—pressure measurements of the esophagus—occasionally help identify critically low pressure in the LES or abnormalities in esophageal muscle contraction.

For patients in whom diagnosis is difficult, doctors may measure the acid levels inside the esophagus through pH testing. Testing pH monitors the acidity level of the esophagus and symptoms during meals, activity, and sleep. Newer techniques of long-term pH monitoring are improving diagnostic capability in this area.

Does GERD Require Surgery?

A small number of people with GERD may need surgery because of severe reflux and poor response to medical treatment. Fundoplication is a surgical procedure that increases pressure in the lower esophagus. However, surgery should not be considered until all other measures have been tried.

What Are the Complications of Long-Term GERD?

Sometimes GERD results in serious complications. Esophagitis can occur as a result of too much stomach acid in the esophagus. Esophagitis may cause esophageal bleeding or ulcers. In addition, a narrowing or stricture of the esophagus may occur from chronic scarring. Some people develop a condition known as Barrett's esophagus, which is severe damage to the skin-like lining of the esophagus. Doctors believe this condition may be a precursor to esophageal cancer.

Although GERD can limit daily activities and productivity, it is rarely life-threatening. With an understanding of the causes and proper treatment most people will find relief.

National Institute of Diabetes and Digestive and Kidney Diseases

Glaucoma refers to a pair of eye disorders that initially lead to blind spots in the peripheral field of vision. Loss of vision—caused by damage to the optic nerve usually owing to intraocular pressure (IOP) that is too high—occurs gradually, and sometimes without warning. In fact, half of the 3 million Americans with glaucoma don't know they have it since early stages of the disease are often symptomless. Glaucoma is the second leading cause of adult blindness in the United States after age-related macular degeneration. Between 5 and 10 million people are at increased risk for glaucoma due to elevated IOP that has not yet caused optic nerve damage.

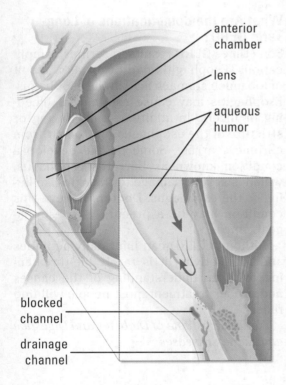

anterior chamber

lens

aqueous humor

blocked channel

drainage channel

Normally, aqueous humor flows in and out of the eye. In glaucoma, the outward flow is blocked and pressure builds up within the eye.

Types of Glaucoma

The two principal forms of glaucoma are closed angle and open angle. About 20 percent of people with closed-angle glaucoma experience acute symptoms: severe eye pain, nausea, or rapid loss of vision. The other 80 percent have no symptoms. Closed-angle glaucoma is relatively uncommon among whites and African Americans but is equal in frequency to open-angle glaucoma among people of Chinese descent and some other Asian groups.

Open-angle glaucoma, which accounts for 90 percent of all glaucoma cases in the United States, is a slow, progressive disease that produces no obvious symptoms until its late stages. Both types of glaucoma can lead to blindness by damaging the optic nerve. Some glaucoma patients have normal IOP but still suffer damage to the optic nerve, since susceptibility to IOP level varies from individual to individual, and risk factors other than IOP play a role. Early detection and treatment can usually control IOP and prevent optic nerve damage.

The occurrence of glaucoma rises with age. The likelihood of having open-angle glaucoma is equal in men and women, but closed-angle glaucoma is more common in women.

Causes

Each day, the eye produces about one teaspoon of aqueous humor—a clear fluid that provides nutrients to, and carries waste products away from, the lens and cornea. (In other tissues, these functions are carried out by the blood, but the lens and cornea are the only parts of the body that have no blood supply.) The ciliary body (which surrounds the lens) produces the aqueous humor. It flows from behind the iris through the pupil and into the anterior (front) chamber of the eye. Aqueous humor then drains from the eye through a spongy network of connective tissue, called the trabecular meshwork, and ultimately enters the bloodstream. An alternate drainage system, the uveoscleral pathway, is located behind the trabecular meshwork. Ordinarily, fluid production and drainage are in balance, and IOP is between 10 and 20 mm Hg (millimeters of mercury).

In those with high IOP open-angle glaucoma, ophthalmologists suspect that a partial blockage of the trabecular meshwork traps the aqueous humor. Exactly how this happens is unclear. The blockage causes an increase of IOP as more aqueous humor is formed than is removed, but IOP does not climb high enough in its early stages to cause discomfort or any easily perceived visual changes. When IOP remains elevated or continues to rise, however, fibers in the optic nerve are compressed and die, leading to a gradual loss of vision over a period of several years. In some people, even the normal level of IOP is sufficient to damage the optic nerve.

Cardiovascular disease, diabetes, and high degrees of myopia (nearsightedness) appear to increase the risk of nerve damage from glaucoma. African Americans are at increased risk for open-angle glaucoma.

Also, mutations causing glaucoma have been identified in the chromosome 1 open-angle glaucoma gene (GLC1A), which directs the production of myocilin, a protein that is involved in some unknown function of the eye.

Inhaled steroids—commonly used to treat asthma—or nasal sprays with steroids appear to raise IOP and the risk of open-angle glaucoma, possibly by inhibiting the outflow of aqueous humor. Oral steroids (glucocorticoids) may have the same effect. Patients who must use these drugs (for asthma, arthritis, sinusitis, or chronic bronchitis, for example) should have their IOP and vision monitored regularly.

Closed-angle glaucoma is caused by a blockage of aqueous humour at the pupil, leading to a bowing forward of the iris that prevents aqueous humor from reaching the trabecular meshwork. The sudden occlusion of the outflow of aqueous humor induces a rapid buildup of extremely high IOP that can produce severe, permanent visual damage within a day or two. The exact cause of closed-angle glaucoma is unknown.

Symptoms

Open-angle glaucoma generally involves both eyes, although the changes in IOP and the extent of optic nerve damage often differs between them. Optic nerve damage is uncommon before age 50 in whites but can occur as many as 10 years earlier in African Americans.

The first nerve fibers damaged are those necessary for peripheral vision, the ability to see objects at the edges of the visual field. People with advanced open-angle glaucoma can have 20/20 vision when looking straight ahead but may have blind spots (scotomas) for images located to the sides, above, or below the central visual field. The damage is often undetected by visual field tests until as much as 40 percent of the optic nerve fibers are destroyed. Eventually, the fibers needed for central vision may be lost as well.

Unlike the open-angle form, closed-angle glaucoma sometimes occurs as acute attacks, as IOP rises rapidly to a dangerous level. Symptoms of an attack include severe pain in the eye, nausea and vomiting, blurred vision, and seeing rainbow-colored halos around lights. The disorder usually affects both eyes, although attacks rarely occur in both eyes at the same time; after an initial attack, there is a 40 percent to 80 percent chance of a similar attack occurring in the other eye within the next 5 to 10 years.

Diagnosis

While glaucoma cannot be prevented, early detection by IOP measurement, optic disc exam and visual field testing allow treatment that may prevent damage to the optic nerve. A common recommendation is an examination every two years after age 50 in whites and after age 40 in African Americans.

IOP alone cannot be used to diagnose glaucoma; some people with elevated IOP do not develop optic nerve damage, while others develop glaucoma despite normal IOP. A high IOP raises the index of suspicion, but other tests are needed to confirm a diagnosis.

Ophthalmologists now use three types of tests or examinations to screen people at risk for glaucoma, to make the diagnosis, and to follow patients during treatment: tonometry to measure IOP; ophthalmoscopy to inspect the optic nerve; and perimetry to test the visual fields. A high IOP warrants consideration of further testing, but the final diagnosis is made by finding evidence of optic nerve damage typical of glaucoma on inspection of the optic nerve or by identifying characteristic defects in the visual fields. The distinction between open- and closed-angle glaucoma is made by examining the front part of the eye to check the angle where the iris meets the cornea, using a special technique known as gonioscopy.

Treatment

Glaucoma is a chronic disorder that cannot be cured. Open-angle glaucoma can often be treated safely and effectively with medication or surgery, though lifelong therapy is almost always necessary. Decisions on when to start treatment are based on evidence of optic nerve damage, visual field loss, and risk factors—not just IOP. Acute closed-angle glaucoma is an ophthalmic emergency. Patients with the symptoms of closed-angle glaucoma (see page 349) should contact their ophthalmologist immediately.

The overall aim in the treatment of any form of glaucoma is to prevent damage to the optic nerve by lowering IOP and maintaining it consistently within a range that is unlikely to cause further nerve damage. The proper target for IOP is generally 25 pe rcent below the baseline IOP at the time of diagnosis. In the few patients with extremely high pressure (above 35 mm Hg), the percent decrease in the target is substantially more. Once the target pressure is achieved, patients are monitored to confirm stability of the optic nerve. If progressive damage is detected at the target pressure, a new, lower target pressure is selected. Unfortunately, treatment cannot reverse optic nerve damage or restore visual loss.

The choice among therapies is dictated by an effort to achieve the greatest benefits at the lowest risk, cost, and inconvenience. Both medical and surgical treatments are available; each has its own complications and possible side effects. Laser or traditional surgery can be successful even early in the course of treatment. Complications such as the development of cataracts are rare, and are lower with laser surgery than with traditional surgery.

Although medications are frequently used first, the American Academy of Ophthalmology states that, in some cases, medications and surgery (including laser surgery) are each reasonable first options.

Medications

Periodic follow-up examinations to monitor IOP, the appearance of the optic nerve, visual fields, and side effects are essential during medical therapy. Follow-up visits may be as frequent as daily or weekly during the

How to Use Eye Drops

For best results when using eye drops, patients should follow these steps:

- While lying down, pull down your lower eyelid with your finger to create a pocket.
- Place the drops—one at a time—in the center of this pocket.
- After placing each drop, close your eye and press down gently on the inside corner of the eyelid near your nose. (This prevents the medication from escaping through the nasal ducts to the rest of the body, ensuring that it remains in the eye where it is needed.)
- If more than one type of drop at a time has been prescribed, wait one minute before applying the next drop.

initiation or adjustment of therapy for those with severe nerve damage or extreme elevations of IOP, or every three to six months for patients with stable IOP and minimal optic nerve damage.

Some people tend not to adhere to their glaucoma treatment, in part because the medication may need to be taken more than twice a day. Other patients stop taking the medication on their own because of cost or side effects. Failure to comply with the medication regimen may result in progression of visual field loss if the target IOP is not achieved. Patients must understand the need to take their glaucoma medication, how often it should be administered, and possible side effects. And they should consult their ophthalmologist before they stop taking a glaucoma medication.

Eye drops. Eye drops are the most common medical treatment for glaucoma because they have fewer systemic effects (effects other than on the eye) than oral medications. There are five classes of eye drops used to treat glaucoma: beta-blockers, adrenergic agonists, miotics, carbonic anhydrase inhibitors, and topical prostaglandins. The drops work by decreasing the production of aqueous humor, increasing its drainage, or both.

In general, eye drops are applied one to four times a day, regularly and on schedule.

Drops can cause local side effects, such as burning, stinging, tearing, itching, or redness in the eye. Because some amount of the drug is quickly absorbed into the body, systemic side effects may occur. For example, beta-blocker drops taken for glaucoma can lower blood pressure at the same time they lower IOP. (Conversely, a beta-blocker tablet taken for high blood pressure may also lower IOP.) Obviously, physicians must tailor therapy to the individual needs of each patient, taking into account the presence of such conditions as high blood pressure.

Oral medications. Carbonic anhydrase inhibitor pills are the only glaucoma medication that is taken orally. Their side effects generally limit their use to when optic nerve damage continues or seems likely to continue despite the use of eye drops at the greatest tolerable dose. The pills initially lower IOP by 20 percent to 30 percent, on average, but significant systemic side effects, such as numbness or tingling in the extremities, malaise, and loss of appetite, and occasional serious complications (such as depression, kidney stones, diarrhea, and damage to blood cells) can limit their utility.

Surgery

Presently, about 10 percent of patients with open-angle glaucoma undergo surgery. They choose surgery either by preference or because they experience serious side effects from medications; do not comply with or respond adequately to drug treatment; are unable to take their medications properly; or have medical conditions or allergies that do not permit maximal drug therapy. While surgery cannot restore lost vision, the two most common surgical procedures—laser trabecular surgery and filtration surgery—can reduce IOP by improving the drainage of aqueous humor.

Laser trabecular surgery. In this procedure, 80 to 100 tiny laser burns are made in the area of the trabecular meshwork. The procedure increases the drainage of aqueous humor, possibly by stimulating the metabolic activity of trabecular cells. The procedure takes about 15 minutes and is performed on an outpatient basis using eye drops for anesthesia. IOP must be tested one hour after surgery because it may rise as a result of the treatment. Postoperative inflammation, blurred vision, and minimal discomfort usually last for only about 24 hours.

It takes up to six weeks to determine whether the procedure has been effective. Complications are minimal and include eye inflammation and pain. Laser surgery may allow medications to be continued at lower doses if the procedure reduced IOP. As with many treatments, however, the effect of surgery diminishes in some people with time. About 40 percent of patients treated with lasers need additional medical treatment or some other form of surgery within five years.

Filtration surgery. Filtration surgery (trabeculectomy) uses conventional surgical instruments to open a passage through the trabecular meshwork, so that aqueous humor can drain into surrounding tissues. The outpatient operation takes about 20 to 60 minutes, is performed under local anesthesia, and is relatively safe and long-

lasting. Recovery time varies from person to person, but most can walk immediately after surgery. In general, a protective eye patch must be worn for one day, and patients are advised to avoid driving, bending over, and any type of strenuous activity for at least a week. If necessary, the drainage flap can be loosened or tightened after the surgery with a new laser procedure, called suture lysis, or with special adjustable sutures.

About half of patients can discontinue glaucoma medications completely after filtration surgery; 35 percent to 40 percent still need some medications; and 10 percent to 15 percent will need some additional type of surgery, such as cyclodestructive or shunt surgery (see below and page 353). Filtration surgery poses more risk of infection and bleeding in the eye than laser surgery and requires a longer period for recovery. About one third of patients experience worsening of cataracts within five years. It is not clear whether the surgery itself causes the cataracts or whether they would have occurred anyway, but they can be surgically removed when necessary.

Shunts. If filtration surgery is unsuccessful, one alternative is the creation of a new passage to drain excess aqueous humor using a shunt of plastic tubing. The effectiveness of shunts is being studied widely. In one study, a shunt called the Baerveldt implant lowered IOP in 72 percent of patients with previously uncontrolled glaucoma.

Cyclodestructive surgery. This form of surgery destroys the ciliary body (which produces aqueous humor) using a laser. Patients may experience some pain and inflammation after surgery; recovery time depends on the type and extent of surgery. This procedure does not require an incision, so normal activity can be resumed earlier than after some filtration operations. Visual recovery, however, may be slower than with the other types of surgery. Cyclodestructive surgery is generally used only when other measures have failed because it has a less predictable outcome and poses a greater risk to the eye (for example, inflammation, cataracts, or IOP that is too low for a prolonged time).

Treatment of Closed-Angle Glaucoma

During an acute attack of closed-angle glaucoma, the IOP may be high enough to damage the optic nerve or obstruct one of the blood vessels feeding the retina. Unless the pressure is relieved promptly, blindness can occur within a day or two. The goals of treatment are to protect the optic nerve by rapidly stopping the attack; to protect the other eye; and to carry out definitive treatment—making a hole in the iris (iridotomy) or, much more rarely, a surgical filtering operation to allow a path for the flow of aqueous humor. These procedures are effective for acute cases, and repeat treatment is rarely necessary. A preventive iridotomy in the other eye is always recommended because of the high likelihood that it will be involved in a future acute attack. In some patients, a chronic form of closed-angle glaucoma may require eye drops or filtration surgery.

Gout is a form of arthritis characterized by high levels of uric acid (one of the body's waste products) in the blood and crystals in the joints. These crystals irritate the joints and surrounding tissue. The crystals trigger an inflammatory response and the affected joint becomes red, warm, swollen, and extremely painful. Most commonly, the first attack is in the joint of the big toe. Other vulnerable sites include the knee, wrist, heel, instep, and Achilles tendon.

The initial attack may resolve on its own within a few days. Subsequent attacks often require treatment. If neglected, the condition may eventually affect other joints. Repeated attacks generally strike without warning and occur with increasing frequency. They may eventually erode bone and cause permanent loss of mobility and joint deformity.

Gout affects about 2.1 million Americans. The disorder occurs much more frequently in men, most often starting after age 30. In women, attacks of gout usually don't begin until after menopause. Obesity increases the risk of developing gout; about half of patients with gout are 15 percent or more above ideal weight.

Causes

Normally, your body processes uric acid and excretes it with the urine. Gout occurs when there is an excessive formation of uric acid, or when your kidneys are not functioning properly and cannot eliminate it.

There are two types of gout. Primary gout, which is inherited, results from an increased production of uric acid, a reduced excretion of uric acid in the urine, or some combination of the two. In secondary gout, high uric acid levels are caused by certain medications, such as diuretics, chronic kidney failure, or a massive release of the chemical precursors of uric acid that occurs during the rapid destruction of cells (for instance, during cancer chemotherapy).

Acute gouty arthritis is initiated by the deposition of sodium urate crystals into a joint and its synovial membrane. White blood cells (specifically, polymorphonuclear cells) enter the joint, engulf the urate crystals, and release a number of substances that trigger inflammation and an acute attack of arthritis. Urate crystals can also accumulate in many other sites, such as the kidneys, tendons, bones, and subcutaneous tissues. Accumulations of urate create characteristic lesions called tophi—uric acid crystals surrounded by cells that amass to defend against the deposited "foreign body." Chronic gouty arthritis results when a joint is damaged by the formation of tophi within and around the joint; osteoarthritis often complicates chronic gout.

A high blood level of uric acid (hyperuricemia) is a consistent finding in patients with gout, but many people with persistent hyperuricemia never develop gout. In some cases, urate crystals build up for 10 to 20 years before the first episode of gout strikes. In addition, it appears that a rapid drop—as well as a rapid rise—in blood uric acid levels can precipitate attacks of acute gout.

Pseudogout

Pseudogout, which also causes inflammation, is due to the accumulation of calcium pyrophosphate crystals (rather than uric acid) within a joint. (Blood uric acid levels are usually normal in individuals with pseudogout.) The disorder is often first suspected from x-rays that show calcification in the cartilage (chondrocalcinosis). Diagnosis is confirmed when microscopic examination of fluid taken from the affected joint reveals the typical calcium pyrophosphate crystals.

The disorder can lead to recurrent attacks of acute arthritis, generally involving large joints such as the knee and wrist. It occurs most often in people over age 60, and symptoms are limited to the joints. Pseudogout is frequently associated with some underlying metabolic abnormality, such as diabetes, an underactive thyroid, an overactive parathyroid, excessive tissue deposits of iron (hemochromatosis) or copper (Wilson's disease), and even true gout.

No known medication can prevent pseudogout by stopping the formation of joint crystals. Treatment is limited to easing the pain with aspirin or other NSAIDs. When swelling and pain persist, removal of fluid from the joint may provide relief.

Symptoms

Acute attacks of gout usually occur without warning, often at night. Gouty arthritis of the big toe (podagra) is particularly common; the big toe is eventually affected in 75 percent of people with gout. However, gout can affect other joints simultaneously.

The symptoms are consistent with inflammation: moderate fever, pain, which is progressive and sometimes excruciating, extreme tenderness and swelling of the affected joint, and warmth and redness of the skin overlying the joint. Relief is obtained quickly with drugs. If left untreated, however, an acute attack can last for days.

Each attack may be followed by months or years free from further episodes, but these pain-free intervals tend to become shorter over time. Progression of the disease is particularly rapid when gout begins before age 50. Unless treated, gout often advances to its chronic stage, with loss of function and deformity of joints.

Uric acid kidney stones occur in 10 to 20 percent of gout sufferers. The stones result from the excessive excretion of uric acid in the urine; deposition of urates in the kidneys can eventually lead to kidney damage and failure. Patients with gout also have an increased incidence of high blood pressure, diabetes, and atherosclerosis (a buildup of plaques in the arteries that can lead to a heart attack or stroke).

Diagnosis

A diagnosis of gout is strongly suspected from the typical symptoms and appearance of an affected joint. After patients have suffered several attacks of gouty arthritis, a physical exam may reveal tophi in the earlobes, hands, feet, or around the elbows. Blood tests show an increased level of uric acid and, during an acute attack, an elevated sedimentation rate ("sed" rate—a nonspecific indicator of inflammation) and white blood cell count. The diagnosis is confirmed by the presence of urate crystals in a microscopic examination of fluid removed from an affected joint. X-rays usually appear normal at first, but later in the course of the disease the presence of tophi may produce "punched-out," or eroded, areas in bones.

Treatment

Prevention of acute attacks of gouty arthritis is the cornerstone of treatment. Fortunately, much is known about preventing flare-ups. Another important goal is preventing urate kidney stones and kidney damage due to the deposition of urate in the kidneys.

Diet

Many foods contain purines, which can be converted to uric acid in the body. It was formerly thought that attacks of gout were provoked by eating large amounts of purine-rich foods, such as liver, anchovies, kidneys, and sweetbreads (calf's thymus or pancreas). However, avoidance of such foods has little impact on blood uric acid levels, and therefore is no longer recommended. Currently recommended dietary measures are weight control (however, patients should avoid fasting, which can raise uric acid levels), avoidance of excessive alcohol, and consumption of enough fluid to maintain a urine output of at least two liters daily (to minimize formation of uric acid stones and deposition of urate in the kidneys).

Drugs That Cause Hyperuricemia

Patients predisposed to gout should avoid certain medications to prevent an attack. They are: Hydrochlorothiazide (Esidrix, HydroDiuril), cyclosporine (an immunosuppressant used to treat RA and prevent rejection of transplanted organs), furosemide (Lasix), and high dosages of aspirin. All of these medications decrease uric acid excretion by the kidneys. Niacin should also be avoided.

Drugs to Lower Uric Acid Levels

Two types of medications can lower blood uric acid levels: allopurinol (Zyloprim) and uricosuric agents, such as probenecid (Benemid, Probalan) and sulfinpyrazone (Anturane). Uricosuric agents increase excretion of uric acid by the kidneys, while allopurinol partly inhibits the enzyme xanthine oxidase, which produces uric acid in the body. Measuring the amount of uric acid in the urine helps to determine which drug will be most effective.

Uricosuric drugs are chosen for patients with small amounts of uric acid in the urine (which indicates excretion is insufficient); allopurinol is most useful in people whose urine contains large amounts of uric acid (indicating its excessive formation). These drugs are not helpful during acute attacks of gout. In fact, drugs to lower uric acid should never be started when a patient is suffering from a flare-up, because they may cause further attacks. Moreover, neither class of

drug should be used by people who have hyperuricemia, but no symptoms, or have infrequent attacks of gout.

Uricosuric agents. One of the uricosuric drugs is given daily when the frequency or severity of arthritis increases. Neither drug is effective in patients with poor kidney function. About 10 percent of patients experience adverse gastrointestinal effects; about 5 percent develop a fever or rash. The greatest risk from taking uricosuric drugs is the development of uric acid kidney stones and kidney damage from the deposition of urate crystals in the kidneys.

Allopurinol. By rapidly lowering uric acid in the blood and urine, daily doses of allopurinol can promote the removal of urates from tophi and lessen the likelihood of uric acid kidney stones. Although used to decrease the incidence of arthritis in those not responding to the uricosuric agents, allopurinol can precipitate an acute attack of gout. But such attacks can be prevented by giving colchicine for a short period before allopurinol is started. Another common adverse effect is an itchy rash that may (rarely) turn into a potentially fatal skin disorder. (After allopurinol is started, patients should report any new rashes to their doctor.) Other side effects include hepatitis and inflammation of small blood vessels.

Colchicine

Colchicine reduces the frequency of attacks of acute gouty arthritis without lowering blood uric acid levels. Long-term colchicine treatment is most likely to benefit those who have frequent attacks and especially high levels of uric acid.

When colchicine is used to prevent acute attacks, allopurinol or a uricosuric agent should also be taken to avoid the buildup of tophi (which might not be noticed without arthritic attacks to serve as a warning sign). Colchicine may also prevent acute arthritis, which is provoked when initial drug therapy rapidly lowers uric acid levels.

The most common side effects from colchicine are diarrhea, vomiting, nausea, and stomach pain. Other side effects include allergic reactions, such as rash or hives; muscle aching or weakness; and signs of anemia or immune suppression, such as fever, fatigue, and chills. While such reactions are rare, they can be life-threatening and tend to occur more frequently at higher dosages.

Since the dosing plan for an individual patient can be complicated (depending on whether the drug is used to prevent attacks or for treatment of an acute attack), some patients find it helpful to carry a schedule of when to take the medication.

Treatment of Acute Attacks

When attacks of gout occur, early treatment provides rapid pain relief. The following measures are used to treat acute gouty arthritis.

- **Bed rest.** To lessen the likelihood of recurrence, patients should remain in bed for about 24 hours after symptoms abate since movement can induce inflammation and trigger another attack.
- **Nonsteroidal anti-inflammatory drugs.** NSAIDs have replaced colchicine as the treatment of choice for acute gout.

All types appear equally effective in general, but some individuals tend to respond better to one or another of the various NSAIDs.

- **Colchicine.** Colchicine can be effective when used early in the course of an acute gout attack. The drug is taken orally each hour until the pain stops, a specific maximal dose is reached, or the patient experiences nausea, vomiting, abdominal cramping, or diarrhea. Unfortunately, side effects occur in more than 80 percent of patients who take it in this manner.
- **Corticosteroids.** Oral corticosteroids are effective but are generally used only in people who do not tolerate NSAIDs. In some cases, corticosteroids are injected directly into an affected joint.
- **Analgesics.** Although not commonly needed, codeine or meperidine can provide rapid relief of severe pain while the patient is waiting for the previously mentioned drugs to take effect. Intramuscular injections of ketorolac (Toradol) may also provide relief of acute gout pain.

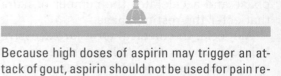

Because high doses of aspirin may trigger an attack of gout, aspirin should not be used for pain relief. However, low-dose aspirin therapy to reduce the risk of a heart attack—a half an aspirin or one baby aspirin daily—can be safely continued.

The average person loses between 50 and 100 scalp hairs each day. As long as growth keeps up with loss, hair remains abundant. But this balance gradually shifts over time. By age 50, some degree of baldness affects about half of all men and at least a quarter of all women. Medical or surgical treatment can help restore thinning hair.

Causes

The average human scalp is covered with roughly 100,000 hairs; each emerges from a small pouch-like sac called a follicle. A complete hair cycle includes two major phases: the growth phase, which lasts four to six years, and a resting phase, which lasts two to three months. After completing the cycle, the hair falls out.

The hair cycle is mediated by an enzyme called 5 alpha-reductase type 2, which converts testosterone (a male sex hormone present in both women and men) into dihydrotestosterone (DHT). Over several hair cycles, DHT causes hairs to become finer and shorter. It also truncates the growth phase and accelerates the number of hairs that enter the resting phase.

Alopecia, the medical term for excessive hair loss, occurs when hair loss exceeds new hair growth. Androgenetic alopecia, or male-pattern baldness, is the most common type of alopecia. An inherited, hormone-linked condition, it affects about 40 million American men and 20 million American women. A quarter of the men begin losing their hair by age 30; the remaining two thirds start balding by age 60.

Because women have much lower blood levels of testosterone than men, as well as a different pattern of hormone receptors and enzymes on the scalp, they generally begin to lose hair later in life. The decrease in estrogen production associated with menopause does not appear to play a significant role in the process.

Excessive hair loss can also be caused by medical problems, such as alopecia areata (a non-hormone-related immune disorder that affects about 2 percent of the population) and thyroid disorders. Hair loss can also be a side effect of some medical treatments, especially chemotherapy for cancer. Malnutrition or very rapid weight loss can also cause hair to thin. Unlike androgenetic alopecia, however, these other types of hair loss may correct themselves spontaneously or when the underlying problem is treated.

Treatment

Two medications have been approved by the Food and Drug Administration (FDA) for treating hair loss—one topical, one oral. Minoxidil was originally used as an antihypertensive agent, but was also found to promote hair growth. A topical solution that must be applied to the scalp twice daily, minoxidil is available over-the-counter. Studies indicate it helps regrow hair in 20 percent to 40 percent of those who use it. But its real advantage lies in its ability to slow hair loss in up to 90 percent of users. It does this by enlarging follicles, prolonging the growth phase, and stimulating resting hairs to grow. But the exact mechanism remains a mystery.

Common side effects of minoxidil include itchiness, burning, tingling, and flaking of the scalp.

Finasteride (Propecia) is the oral treatment for hair loss. Finasteride was first approved, under the name Proscar, to treat prostate enlargement in men . But like minoxidil, finasteride proved to encourage hair growth. Proscar and Propecia are the same agent, but the dose of Propecia is smaller. Proscar contains 5 mg per pill; Propecia contains 1 mg. Finasteride blocks the enzyme that converts testosterone to DHT. Three clinical trials that included men with mild to moderate androgenetic alopecia demonstrated the drug's ability to reverse or slow balding. In two of the studies, the men who took it grew, on average, about 100 more hairs in a 1-inch area on top of the head than those who took a placebo. After two years of treatment, approximately two thirds of the men had more scalp coverage, one third had the same amount of hair they started with, and only a fraction of the group lost hair. However, older men did not experience as dramatic a response as their younger counterparts.

There are no common side effects associated with the use of finasteride.

Minoxidil is approved for both men and women. Finasteride is approved for use in men only, mostly because it might feminize a male fetus in a pregnant woman. In addition one year-long trial found the drug was not helpful in post-menopausal women. Minoxidil costs about $30 a month and sometimes causes an itchy scalp; finasteride costs about $50 a month and can cause erectile dysfunction (but this is rare and reversible). Although finasteride is a prescription medication, insurance usually does not cover the cost.

Also note that neither drug works in every case, and hair that does regrow is usually fine and fuzzy. Once drug treatment stops, new growth falls out and balding resumes. Six months of treatment is often needed before results are apparent.

Surgical Options

Surgery is the only way to permanently restore lost hair. The most popular approach is grafting, which uses microsurgical techniques to take donor follicles from a hair-bearing portion of the scalp and insert them into bald areas. The procedure involves harvesting and using thousands of individual hairs to achieve a completely natural look.

Other surgical options include a flap procedure, which moves hair-bearing areas of the scalp to the top of the head, and scalp reduction, which removes bald scalp and brings the hair-bearing scalp closer together. Local anesthesia and sedation are used for all three outpatient procedures.

Of the three procedures, hair grafting is preferred since the recovery is much simpler, there are no postoperative bandages, patients can shampoo their hair within 48 hours, and crusting from the surgery is gone within 10 days. The cost of one grafting session is about $5,000, and patients usually require two sessions. Side effects, though rare in the hands of an experienced surgeon (usually a plastic surgeon or a dermatologist), include infection and scarring.

Even with surgery, a full head of hair may be unattainable if there isn't a lot of hair to begin with—since the patient is his or her own donor. Therefore, the first goal is to frame the face with a natural hairline and frontal coverage. But surgeons may one day be able to harvest hair from other donors. A British team recently transplanted some hair follicles from a man's head to a woman's forearm. Within weeks, new hairs sprouted at the transplant site, and there were no signs of tissue rejection. Much more research is necessary, however, to determine if this approach is viable and can be applied to the scalp. Until then, drug therapy and traditional surgical methods remain the only proven options for increasing hair density.

H

An estimated 45 million Americans experience chronic headaches. For at least half of these people, the problem is severe and sometimes disabling. It can also be costly: headache sufferers make over 8 million visits a year to doctor's offices. Migraine victims alone lose over 157 million workdays because of headache pain.

Why Does it Hurt?

What hurts when you have a headache? The bones of the skull and tissues of the brain itself never hurt, because they lack pain-sensitive nerve fibers. Several areas of the head can hurt, including a network of nerves that extends over the scalp and certain nerves in the face, mouth, and throat. Also sensitive to pain, because they contain delicate nerve fibers, are the muscles of the head and blood vessels found along the surface and at the base of the brain.

The ends of these pain-sensitive nerves, called nociceptors, can be stimulated by stress, muscular tension, dilated blood vessels, and other triggers of headache. Once stimulated, a nociceptor sends a message up the length of the nerve fiber to the nerve cells in the brain, signaling that a part of the body hurts. The message is determined by the location of the nociceptor. A person who suddenly realizes "My toe hurts," is responding to nociceptors in the foot that have been stimulated by the stubbing of a toe.

A number of chemicals help transmit pain-related information to the brain. Some of these chemicals are natural painkilling proteins called endorphins, Greek for "the morphine within." One theory suggests that

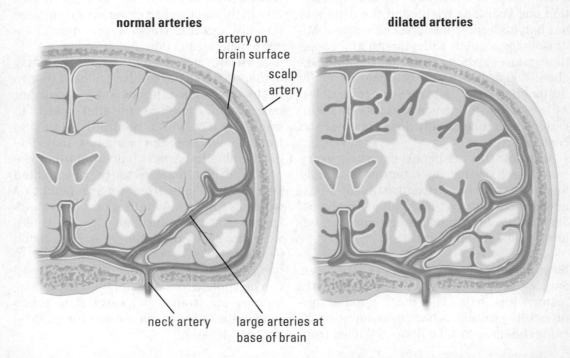

normal arteries

artery on brain surface
scalp artery

neck artery   large arteries at base of brain

dilated arteries

Migraines may begin when a spasm in arteries at the base of the brain reduces its blood supply. The brain's arteries then dilate to meet its energy needs, but this action triggers a release of pain-causing chemicals.

When to See a Physician

Headaches can nearly always be controlled by reducing exposure to avoidable triggers, such as certain medications. But if you do experience a headache, over-the-counter analgesics, such as acetaminophen, aspirin, or ibuprofen, can bring relief. Some types of headache, however, call for prompt medical attention. Warning signs include:

- Sudden, severe headache
- Sudden, severe headache associated with a stiff neck
- Headache associated with fever
- Headache associated with convulsions
- Headache associated with pain in the eye or ear

- Headache accompanied by confusion or loss of consciousness
- Headache following a blow on the head
- Persistent headache in a person who was previously headache free
- Recurring headache in children
- Headache that interferes with normal life

These warning signs raise the possibility of a serious disorder and may require investigation. Possible causes include brain aneurysm, brain tumor, stroke, meningitis, and encephalitis.

The Editors

---

people who suffer from severe headache and other types of chronic pain have lower levels of endorphins than people who are generally pain free.

Diagnosing a Headache

Diagnosing a headache is like playing Twenty Questions. Experts agree that a detailed question-and-answer session with a patient can often produce enough information for a diagnosis. Many types of headaches have clear-cut symptoms that fall into an easily recognizable pattern.

Patients may be asked: How often do you have headaches? Where is the pain? How long do the headaches last? When did you first develop headaches? The patient's sleep habits and family and work situations may also be probed.

Most physicians will also obtain a full medical history from the patient, inquiring about past head trauma or surgery, eye strain, sinus problems, dental problems, difficulties with opening and closing of the jaw, and the use of medications. This may be

enough to suggest strongly that the patient has migraine or cluster headaches. A complete and careful physical and neurological examination will exclude many possibilities and the suspicion of aneurysm, meningitis, or certain brain tumors. A blood test may be ordered to screen for thyroid disease, anemia, or infections that might cause a headache.

A test called an electroencephalogram (EEG) may be given to measure brain activity. EEGs can indicate a malfunction in the brain, but they cannot usually pinpoint a problem that might be causing a headache. A physician may suggest that a patient with unusual headaches undergo a computed tomographic (CT) scan and/or a magnetic resonance imaging (MRI) scan. The scans enable the physician to distinguish, for example, between a bleeding blood vessel in the brain and a brain tumor, and are important diagnostic tools in cases of headache associated with brain lesions or other serious disease. CT scans produce x-ray images of the brain that show structures or variations in the density of different types of tissue. MRI scans use magnetic fields and radio waves to produce an image that provides information about the structure and biochemistry of the brain.

If an aneurysm—an abnormal ballooning of a blood vessel—is suspected, a physician may order a CT scan to examine for blood and then an angiogram. In this test, a special fluid, which can be seen on an x-ray, is injected into the patient and carried in the bloodstream to the brain to reveal any abnormalities in the blood vessels there.

A physician analyzes the results of all these diagnostic tests along with a patient's medical history and examination in order to arrive at a diagnosis.

Headaches are diagnosed as
• Vascular
• Muscle contraction (tension)
• Traction
• Inflammatory

Vascular headaches—a group that includes the well-known migraine—are so named because they are thought to involve abnormal function of the brain's blood vessels or vascular system. Muscle contraction headaches appear to involve the tightening or tensing of facial and neck muscles. Traction and inflammatory headaches are symptoms of other disorders, ranging from stroke to sinus infection. Some people have more than one type of headache.

Migraine Headaches

The most common type of vascular headache is migraine. Migraine headaches are usually characterized by severe pain on one or both sides of the head, an upset stomach, and, at times, disturbed vision.

Symptoms of Migraine

Sensitivity to light is a standard symptom of the two most prevalent types of migraine-caused headache: classic and common.

The major difference between the two types is the appearance of neurological symptoms 10 to 30 minutes before a classic migraine attack. These symptoms are called an aura. The person may see flashing lights or zigzag lines, or may temporarily lose vision. Other classic symptoms include speech difficulty, weakness of an arm or leg, tingling of the face or hands, and confusion.

The pain of a classic migraine headache may be described as intense, throbbing, or pounding and is felt in the forehead, temple, ear, jaw, or around the eye. Classic migraine starts on one side of the head but may eventually spread to the other side. An attack lasts one to two pain-wracked days.

Common migraine—a term that reflects the disorder's greater occurrence in the general population—is not preceded by an aura. But some people experience a variety of vague symptoms beforehand, including mental fuzziness, mood changes, fatigue, and unusual retention of fluids. During the headache phase of a common migraine, a person may have diarrhea and increased urination, as well as nausea and vomiting. Common migraine pain can last three or four days.

Both classic and common migraine can strike as often as several times a week, or as rarely as once every few years. Both types can occur at any time. Some people, however, experience migraines at predictable times—for example, near the days of menstruation or every Saturday morning after a stressful week of work.

The Migraine Process

Research scientists are unclear about the precise cause of migraine headaches. There seems to be general agreement, however, that a key element is blood flow changes in the brain. People who get migraine headaches appear to have blood vessels that overreact to various triggers.

Scientists have devised one theory of migraine that explains these blood flow changes and also certain biochemical changes that may be involved in the headache process. According to this theory, the nervous system responds to a trigger such as stress by causing a spasm of the nerve-rich arteries at the base of the brain. The spasm closes down or constricts several arteries supplying blood to the brain, including the scalp artery and the carotid or neck arteries.

As these arteries constrict, the flow of blood to the brain is reduced. At the same time, blood-clotting particles called platelets clump together—a process that is believed to release a neurotransmitter called serotonin. Serotonin acts as a powerful constrictor of arteries, further reducing the blood supply to the brain.

Reduced blood flow decreases the brain's supply of oxygen. Symptoms signaling a headache, such as distorted vision or speech, may then result, similar to symptoms of stroke.

Reacting to the reduced oxygen supply, certain arteries within the brain open wider to meet the brain's energy needs. This widening or dilation spreads, finally affecting the neck and scalp arteries. The dilation of these arteries triggers the release of pain-producing substances called prostaglandins from various tissues and blood cells. Chemicals that cause inflammation and swelling, and substances that increase sensitivity to pain, are also released. The circulation of these chemicals and the dilation of the scalp arteries stimulate the pain-sensitive nociceptors. The result, according to this theory: a throbbing pain in the head.

Women and Migraine

Although both males and females seem to be equally affected by migraine, the condition is more common in adult women. Both sexes may develop migraine in infancy, but most often the disorder begins between the ages of 5 and 35.

The relationship between female hormones and migraine is still unclear. Women may have "menstrual migraine"— headaches around the time of their menstrual period—which may disappear during pregnancy. Other women develop migraine for the first time when they are pregnant. Some are first affected after menopause.

The effect of oral contraceptives on headaches is perplexing. Scientists report that some women with migraine who take birth control pills experience more frequent and severe attacks. However, a small percentage of women have fewer and less severe migraine headaches when they take birth control pills. And women who do not suffer from headaches may develop migraines as a side effect when they use oral contraceptives. Investigators around the world are studying hormonal changes in women with migraine in the hope of identifying the specific ways these naturally occurring chemicals cause headaches.

Triggers of Headache

Although many sufferers have a family history of migraine, the exact hereditary nature of this condition is still unknown. People who get migraines are thought to have an inherited abnormality in the regulation of blood vessels. "It's like a cocked gun with a hair trigger," explains one specialist. "A person is born with a potential for migraine and the headache is triggered by things that are really not so terrible."

These triggers include stress and other normal emotions, as well as biological and environmental conditions. Fatigue, glaring or flickering lights, changes in the weather, and certain foods can set off migraine. It may seem hard to believe that eating such seemingly harmless foods as yogurt, nuts, and lima beans can result in a painful migraine headache. However, some scientists believe that these foods and several others contain chemical substances, such as tyramine, that constrict arteries—the first step of the migraine process. Other scientists believe that foods cause headaches by setting off an allergic reaction in susceptible people.

While a food-triggered migraine usually occurs soon after eating, other triggers may not cause immediate pain. Scientists report that people can develop migraine not only during a period of stress but also afterwards when their vascular systems are still reacting. For example, migraines that wake people up in the middle of the night are believed to result from a delayed reaction to stress.

Other Forms of Migraine
In addition to classic and common, migraine headache can take several other forms:

Hemiplegic migraine patients have temporary paralysis on one side of the body, a condition known as hemiplegia. Some people may experience vision problems and vertigo—a feeling that the world is spinning. These symptoms begin 10 to 90 minutes before the onset of headache pain.

Ophthalmoplegic migraine is characterized by pain around the eye and is associated with a droopy eyelid, double vision, and other problems with vision.

Basilar artery migraine involves a disturbance of a major brain artery at the base of the brain. Preheadache symptoms include vertigo, double vision, and poor muscular coordination. This type of migraine occurs primarily in adolescent and young adult women and is often associated with the menstrual cycle.

Benign exertional headache is brought on by running, lifting, coughing, sneezing, or bending. The headache begins at the onset of activity, and pain rarely lasts more than several minutes.

Status migrainosus is a rare and severe type of migraine that can last 72 hours or longer. The pain and nausea are so intense that people who have this type of headache must be hospitalized. The use of certain drugs can trigger status migrainosus. Neurologists report that many of their status migrainosus patients were depressed and anxious before they experienced headache attacks.

Headache-free migraine is characterized by such migraine symptoms as visual problems, nausea, vomiting, constipation, or diarrhea. Patients, however, do not experience head pain. Headache specialists have suggested that unexplained pain in a particular part of the body, fever, and dizziness could also be possible types of headache-free migraine.

Treating Migraine Headache
During the Stone Age, pieces of a headache sufferer's skull were cut away with flint instruments in an effort to relieve pain. Another unpleasant remedy used in the British Isles around the ninth century

involved drinking "the juice of elderseed, cow's brain, and goat's dung dissolved in vinegar." Fortunately, today's headache patients are spared such drastic (and ineffective) measures.

Drug therapy, biofeedback training, stress reduction, and elimination of certain foods from the diet are the most common methods of preventing and controlling migraine and other vascular headaches.

Regular exercise, such as swimming or vigorous walking, can also reduce the frequency and severity of migraine headaches.

During a migraine headache, temporary relief can sometimes be obtained by applying cold packs to the head or by pressing on the bulging artery found in front of the ear on the painful side of the head.

Medications

There are two ways to approach the treatment of migraine headache with drugs: prevent the attacks, or relieve symptoms after the headache occurs.

For infrequent migraine, drugs can be taken at the first sign of a headache in order to stop it or to at least ease the pain. People who get occasional mild migraine may benefit by taking aspirin or acetaminophen at the start of an attack. Aspirin raises a person's tolerance to pain and also discourages clumping of blood platelets. Small amounts of caffeine may be useful if taken in the early stages of migraine. But for most migraine sufferers who get moderate to severe headaches, and for all cluster headache patients (see page 368), stronger drugs may be necessary to control the pain.

Several drugs for the prevention of migraine have been developed in recent years, including serotonin agonists which mimic the action of this key brain chemical. One of the most commonly used drugs for the relief of classic and common migraine symptoms is sumatriptan, which binds to serotonin receptors. For optimal benefit, the drug is taken during the early stages of an attack. If a migraine has been in progress for about an hour after the drug is taken, a repeat dose can be given.

Physicians caution that sumatriptan should not be taken by people who have angina pectoris, basilar migraine, severe hypertension, or vascular or liver disease.

Another migraine drug is ergotamine tartrate, a vasoconstrictor that helps counteract the painful dilation stage of the headache. Other drugs that constrict dilated blood vessels or help reduce blood vessel inflammation also are available.

For headaches that occur three or more times a month, preventive treatment is usually recommended. Drugs used to prevent classic and common migraine include methysergide maleate, which counteracts blood vessel constriction; propranolol hydrochloride, which stops blood vessel dilation; amitriptyline, an antidepressant; valproic acid, an anticonvulsant; and verapamil, a calcium channel blocker.

Antidepressants called MAO inhibitors also prevent migraine. These drugs block an enzyme called monoamine oxidase which normally helps nerve cells absorb the artery-constricting brain chemical, serotonin. MAO inhibitors can have potentially serious side effects—particularly if taken while ingesting foods or beverages that contain tyramine, a substance that constricts arteries.

Many antimigraine drugs can have adverse side effects. But like most medicines they are relatively safe when used carefully and under a physician's supervision. To avoid long-term side effects of preventive medications, headache specialists advise patients to reduce the dosage of these drugs and then stop taking them as soon as possible.

Biofeedback and Relaxation Training

Drug therapy for migraine is often combined with biofeedback and relaxation training. Biofeedback refers to a technique that can give people better control over such body function indicators as blood pressure, heart rate, temperature, muscle tension, and brain waves. Thermal biofeedback allows a patient to consciously raise hand temperature. Some patients who are able to increase hand temperature can reduce the number and intensity of migraines. The mechanisms underlying these self-regulation treatments are being studied by research scientists.

"To succeed in biofeedback," says a headache specialist, "you must be able to concentrate and you must be motivated to get well."

A patient learning thermal biofeedback wears a device which transmits the temperature of an index finger or hand to a monitor. While the patient tries to warm his hands, the monitor provides feedback either on a gauge that shows the temperature reading or by emitting a sound or beep that increases in intensity as the temperature increases. The patient is not told how to raise hand temperature, but is given suggestions such as "Imagine your hands feel very warm and heavy."

In another type of biofeedback called electromyographic or EMG training, the patient learns to control muscle tension in the face, neck, and shoulders.

Either kind of biofeedback may be combined with relaxation training, during which patients learn to relax the mind and body.

Biofeedback can be practiced at home with a portable monitor. But the ultimate goal of treatment is to wean the patient from the machine. The patient can then use biofeedback anywhere at the first sign of a headache.

The Antimigraine Diet

Scientists estimate that a small percentage of migraine sufferers will benefit from a treatment program focused solely on eliminating headache-provoking foods and beverages.

Other migraine patients may be helped by a diet to prevent low blood sugar. Low blood sugar, or hypoglycemia, can cause headache. This condition can occur after a period without food: overnight, for example, or when a meal is skipped. People who wake up in the morning with a headache may be reacting to the low blood sugar caused by the lack of food overnight.

Treatment for headaches that are caused by low blood sugar consists of scheduling smaller, more frequent meals for the patient. A special diet designed to stabilize the body's sugar-regulating system is sometimes recommended.

For the same reason, many specialists also recommend that migraine patients avoid oversleeping on weekends. Sleeping late can change the body's normal blood sugar level and lead to a headache.

Other Vascular Headaches

After migraine, the most common type of vascular headache is the toxic headache produced by fever. Pneumonia, measles, mumps, and tonsillitis are among the diseases that can cause severe toxic vascular headaches. Toxic headaches can also result from the presence of foreign chemicals in the body. Other kinds of vascular headaches include "clusters," which cause repeated episodes of intense pain, and headaches resulting from a rise in blood pressure.

Foods and Beverages That May Trigger a Migraine

Many foods contain chemicals that can trigger migraine. But dietary triggers can be difficult to recognize for several reasons:

- They may not prompt symptoms for a day or two after ingestion;
- Because they are mixed with each other and with nondietary triggers, the role of individual dietary triggers may be obscured;
- Caffeine (one of the most common dietary culprits) is a paradox—at first, it constricts blood vessels, which may seem to ease headache pain; however, when caffeine wears off, it causes rebound swelling of blood vessels and ultimately worsens pain.

To determine which foods and beverages may be causing your headaches, eliminate the following items until symptoms diminish: all cheeses except cottage, cream, and American; alcoholic beverages; aspartame (the artificial sweetener in NutraSweet); avocados; chicken livers; chocolate; cured meats (including bacon, bologna, hot dogs, salami, and pepperoni); coffee and tea (ideally even decaffeinated varieties, because they still contain other chemical triggers); certain fruits and juices (bananas, canned figs, grapefruits, lemons, limes, and oranges); herring; lima beans; monosodium glutamate (a flavor enhancer); nuts; onions; and yogurt.

After headaches are controlled, foods can be added back gradually, one at a time. If symptoms return after consuming a particular food or beverage, it should be avoided. As you reintroduce items, remember that the impact of dietary triggers may be delayed for a day or two. Furthermore, your tolerance of any given dietary trigger will depend on the level of other triggers, such as stress or falling barometric pressure, around that time period. *The Editors*

Chemical Culprits

Repeated exposure to nitrite compounds can result in a dull, pounding headache that may be accompanied by a flushed face. Nitrite, which dilates blood vessels, is found in such products as heart medicine and dynamite, but is also used as a chemical to preserve meat. Hot dogs and other processed meats containing sodium nitrite can cause headaches.

Eating foods prepared with monosodium glutamate (MSG) can result in headache. Soy sauce, meat tenderizer, and a variety of packaged foods contain this chemical, which is touted as a flavor enhancer.

Headache can also result from exposure to poisons, even common household varieties such as insecticides, carbon tetrachloride, and lead. Children who ingest flakes of lead paint may develop headaches. So may anyone who has contact with lead batteries or lead-glazed pottery.

Artists and industrial workers may experience headaches after exposure to materials that contain chemical solvents. These solvents, like benzene, are found in turpentine, spray adhesives, rubber cement, and inks.

Drugs such as amphetamines can cause headaches as a side effect. Another type of drug-related headache occurs during withdrawal from long-term therapy with the antimigraine drug ergotamine tartrate.

Jokes are often made about alcohol hangovers but the headache associated with "the morning after" is no laughing matter. Fortunately, there are several suggested treatments for the pain. The hangover headache may also be reduced by taking honey, which speeds alcohol metabolism, or caffeine, a constrictor of dilated arteries. Caffeine,

Temporal Arteritis

Older adults who experience sudden or unexplained severe headaches, tenderness of the scalp, muscle aches, fatigue, fever, unexplained weight loss, jaw pain when eating, or visual disturbances may be suffering from temporal arteritis (TA). Left untreated, TA—an immune disorder characterized by inflammation in the arteries of the head, neck, and sometimes the aortic arch—may lead to blindness and, occasionally, to a stroke, heart attack, or aortic dissection (a tear in the aorta). Aggressive treatment with anti-inflammatory medications, such as corticosteroids, can relieve symptoms and prevent complications. For those who experience symptoms of TA, seeking treatment early on can ensure that the condition resolves without causing serious discomfort or permanent disability. *The Editors*

however, can cause headaches as well as cure them. Heavy coffee drinkers often get headaches when they try to break the caffeine habit.

Over-the-counter pain relievers that contain caffeine (such as some forms of Anacin and Excedrin) can worsen headaches by causing blood vessels to swell as their effects wear off (a phenomenon called rebound). To avoid this problem, do not take combination products more than twice a month. Single-ingredient analgesics, such as acetaminophen, aspirin, and ibuprofen, are not associated with rebound.

Cluster Headaches

Cluster headaches, named for their repeated occurrence over weeks or months at roughly the same time of day or night in clusters, begin as a minor pain around one eye, eventually spreading to that side of the face. The pain quickly intensifies, compelling the victim to pace the floor or rock in a chair. "You can't lie down, you're fidgety," explains a cluster patient. "The pain is unbearable." Other symptoms include a stuffed and runny nose and a droopy eyelid over a red and tearing eye.

Cluster headaches last between 30 and 45 minutes. But the relief people feel at the end of an attack is usually mixed with dread as they await a recurrence. Clusters may mysteriously disappear for months or years. Many people have cluster bouts during the spring and fall. At their worst, chronic cluster headaches can last continuously for years.

Cluster attacks can strike at any age but usually start between the ages of 20 and 40. Unlike migraine, cluster headaches are more common in men and do not run in families.

Studies of cluster patients show that they are likely to have hazel eyes and that they tend to be heavy smokers and drinkers. Paradoxically, both nicotine, which constricts arteries, and alcohol, which dilates them, trigger cluster headaches. The exact connection between these substances and cluster attacks is not known.

Despite a cluster headache's distinguishing characteristics, its relative infrequency and similarity to such disorders as sinusitis can lead to misdiagnosis. Some cluster patients have had tooth extractions, sinus surgery, or psychiatric treatment in futile efforts to cure their pain.

Research studies have turned up several clues as to the cause of cluster headache, but no answers. One clue is found in the thermograms of untreated cluster patients, which show a "cold spot" of reduced blood flow above the eye.

The sudden start and brief duration of cluster headaches can make them difficult to treat; however, research scientists have identified several effective drugs for these headaches. The antimigraine drug sumatriptan can subdue a cluster, if taken at the first sign of an attack. Injections of dihydroergotamine, a form of ergotamine tartrate, are sometimes used to treat clusters. Corticosteroids also can be used, either orally or by intramuscular injection.

Some cluster patients can prevent attacks by taking propranolol, methysergide, valproic acid, verapamil, or lithium carbonate.

Another option that works for some cluster patients is rapid inhalation of pure oxygen through a mask for 5 to 15 minutes. The oxygen seems to ease the pain of cluster headache by reducing blood flow to the brain.

In chronic cases of cluster headache, certain facial nerves may be surgically cut or destroyed to provide relief. These procedures have had limited success. Some cluster patients have had facial nerves cut only to have them regenerate years later.

Painful Pressure

Chronic high blood pressure can cause headache, as can rapid rises in blood pressure such as those experienced during anger, vigorous exercise, or sexual excitement.

The severe "orgasmic headache" occurs right before orgasm and is believed to be a vascular headache. Since sudden rupture of a cerebral blood vessel can occur, this type of headache should be evaluated by a doctor.

Muscle-Contraction Headaches

Tension headache is named not only for the role of stress in triggering the pain, but also for the contraction of neck, face, and scalp muscles brought on by stressful events. Tension headache is a severe but temporary form of muscle-contraction headache. The pain is mild to moderate and feels like pressure is being applied to the head or neck. The headache usually disappears after the period of stress is over. Ninety percent of all headaches are classified as tension/muscle contraction headaches.

By contrast, chronic muscle-contraction headaches can last for weeks, months, and sometimes years. The pain of these headaches is often described as a tight band around the head or a feeling that the head and neck are in a cast. "It feels like somebody is tightening a giant vise around my head," says one patient. The pain is steady, and is usually felt on both sides of the head. Chronic muscle-contraction headaches can cause sore scalps—even combing one's hair can be painful.

Causes of Muscle-Contraction Headaches

In the past, many scientists believed that the primary cause of the pain of muscle-contraction headache was sustained muscle tension. However, a growing number of authorities now believe that a far more complex mechanism is responsible.

Occasionally, muscle-contraction headaches will be accompanied by nausea, vomiting, and blurred vision, but there is no preheadache syndrome as with migraine. Muscle-contraction headaches have not been linked to hormones or foods, as has migraine, nor is there a strong hereditary connection.

Research has shown that for many people, chronic muscle-contraction headaches are caused by depression and anxiety. These people tend to get their headaches in the early morning or evening when conflicts in the office or home are anticipated.

Emotional factors are not the only triggers of muscle-contraction headaches. Certain physical postures that tense head and neck muscles—such as holding one's chin down while reading—can lead to head and neck pain. So can prolonged writing under poor light, or holding a phone between the shoulder and ear, or even gum-chewing.

More serious problems that can cause muscle-contraction headaches include degenerative arthritis of the neck and temporomandibular joint dysfunction, or TMD. TMD is a disorder of the joint between the temporal bone (above the ear) and the mandible or lower jaw bone. The disorder results from poor bite and jaw clenching.

Treating Muscle-Contraction Headaches

Treatment for muscle-contraction headache varies. The first consideration is to treat any specific disorder or disease that may be causing the headache. For example, arthritis of the neck is treated with anti-inflammatory medication and TMD may be helped by corrective devices for the mouth and jaw.

Acute tension headaches not associated with a disease are treated with analgesics such as aspirin and acetaminophen. Stronger analgesics, such as propoxyphene and codeine, are sometimes prescribed. As prolonged use of these drugs can lead to dependence, patients taking them should have periodic medical check-ups and follow their physicians' instructions carefully.

If your headaches are severe enough for you to take the maximum dosage of acetaminophen or an NSAID more than twice a week, or if you notice worsening of the frequency, duration, or intensity of your symptoms, you should consult your doctor.

Nondrug therapy for chronic muscle-contraction headaches includes biofeedback, relaxation training, and counseling. A technique called cognitive restructuring teaches people to change their attitudes and responses to stress. Patients might be encouraged, for example, to imagine that they are coping successfully with a stressful situation. In progressive relaxation therapy, patients are taught to first tense and then relax individual muscle groups. Finally, the patient tries to relax his or her whole body. Many people imagine a peaceful scene—such as lying on the beach or by a beautiful lake. Passive relaxation does not involve tensing of muscles. Instead, patients are encouraged to focus on different muscles, suggesting that they relax. Some people might think to themselves, "Relax," or "My muscles feel warm."

People with chronic muscle-contraction headaches my also be helped by taking antidepressants or MAO inhibitors. Mixed muscle-contraction and migraine headaches are sometimes treated with barbiturate compounds, which slow down nerve function in the brain and spinal cord.

People who suffer infrequent muscle-contraction headaches may benefit from a hot shower or moist heat applied to the back of the neck. Cervical collars are sometimes recommended as an aid to good posture. Physical therapy, massage, and gentle exercise of the neck may also be helpful.

Conclusion

If you suffer from headaches and none of the standard treatments help, do not despair. Some people find that their headaches disappear once they deal with a troubled marriage, pass their certifying board exams, or resolve some other stressful problem. Others find that if they control their psychological reaction to stress, the headaches disappear.

For those who cannot say no, or who get headaches anyway, today's headache research offers hope. The work of NINDS-supported scientists around the world promises to improve our understanding of this complex disorder and provide better tools to treat it.

National Institute of Neurological Disorders and Stroke

As the first generation exposed to live concerts with excessive amplification, many people over age 50 are now experiencing premature hearing loss. And as people move into their 60s and 70s, nearly everyone experiences some degree of age-related hearing loss, or presbycusis, which gradually affects hearing in both ears, especially for high-pitched sounds. Among older adults, hearing loss is the third leading chronic medical complaint, after arthritis and high blood pressure.

The first symptom is usually difficulty hearing such high frequency sounds as the voices of women and children, or the trill of a bird's song. Loss of high frequencies can also distort speech, making words difficult to understand even though they can be heard. In the United States, hearing impairment affects 28 million people, including one third of those between ages 56 and 74, and half of those over age 85.

The Mechanics of Sound

All sources of sound generate vibrations (sound waves) that move through the air. Hearing depends on a series of mechanical events that convert the energy contained in these waves into electrical impulses that are transmitted to the brain. This process takes

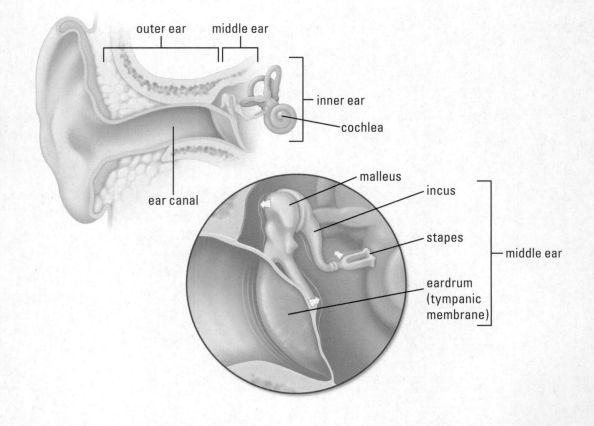

As we age, structures in the middle and inner ear deteriorate. Hearing loss (presbycusis) results when the auditory nerve is not properly stimulated and nerve impulses don't reach the brain.

place in the ear, which is divided into three distinct regions: the outer, visible portion of the ear; the middle ear, a complex system of membranes and tiny bones; and the inner ear, where the energy conversion takes place.

The outer ear receives sound waves and directs them through a narrow passage (the auditory canal) to a thin, skin-covered membrane known as the eardrum, or the tympanic membrane, which separates the outer ear from the middle ear. When sound waves strike the eardrum, it begins to vibrate. These vibrations stimulate three tiny bones (the ossicles) in the middle ear to amplify the vibrations and convey them to the inner ear.

The inner ear contains fluid and a snail-shaped structure called the cochlea. The area at the center of the cochlea is called the organ of Corti, which is lined with specialized hair cells. These cells are fringed with very fine hairs that stick out into the inner ear fluid. When this fluid responds to the movement of the ossicles, the hair cells begin to vibrate and trigger internal changes that produce electrical impulses. The auditory nerve transmits these impulses to the brain, where they are perceived as sound. Because sounds of different pitches and intensities move the hair cells in an infinite number of ways, the brain perceives sounds as having different pitches (tones) and levels of intensity (loudness).

Pitch, which corresponds to the frequency of a sound wave, is measured in cycles per second (Hertz, abbreviated Hz). The pitch of human speech ranges from 300 Hz for very low tones to 4,000 Hz for very high tones. Young children, who have the best hearing, can often hear sounds between 20 Hz (corresponding to the lowest note on a large pipe organ) to 20,000 Hz (corresponding to the high shrill of a dog whistle).

Sound intensity, which corresponds to the amplitude of a sound wave, is measured in decibels (db). The decibel scale runs from 0 db (the faintest sounds detectable by the human ear) to more than 180 db (the noise of a rocket launch). Because decibels are measured logarithmically, a small increase in decibels indicates a substantial increase in intensity. Thus, a 10-db increase indicates a sound that's 10 times louder. For example, 20 db is 10 times louder than 10 db, and 30 db is 100 times louder than 10 db.

Causes

Each day 20 million Americans are exposed to noises that can harm hearing. Such noises are the leading cause of hearing loss among adults, resulting in one-third of all hearing deficits.

Over time, normal wear and tear damage the delicate middle and inner ear structures—especially the hair cells in the cochlea. When these structures deteriorate, the auditory nerve is not properly stimulated, and nerve impulses do not reach the brain. Also called nerve deafness, presbycusis (which literally means "old hearing") is commonly caused by repeated exposure to loud noises—the whirring sound of a power tool, loud music, and honking horns.

Damage to hair cells and other sensory structures can also be caused by certain medications (such as too much aspirin or certain antibiotics), genetic predisposition, and cardiovascular problems such as stroke. Less common reasons for hearing impairment include conductive hearing loss and central auditory dysfunction. Conductive hearing loss occurs when ear wax, fluid buildup in the middle ear, or abnormal bone growth or infection in the inner ear blocks sound wave transmission to the inner ear. Central auditory dysfunction is a rare disorder resulting

H

from damage to auditory nerve centers in the brain. Causes include extended illness with high fever, head injuries, vascular problems, or tumors.

Symptoms

The following problems may indicate hearing impairment:

- Difficulty hearing over the phone
- Trouble following a conversation when two or more people are talking at the same time
- Listening to a TV at a volume too high for others
- Straining to understand a conversation, asking people to repeat themselves, or misunderstanding what people say
- Trouble hearing in a noisy background
- Trouble understanding the speech of women and children
- Difficulty distinguishing the sounds S, F, SH, CH, H and soft C sounds (which are in a higher frequency range than vowel and other consonant sounds.)

Diagnosis

Ignored or untreated hearing problems frequently worsen. If you experience the symptoms listed above, see your family doctor for possible referral to a physician who specializes in hearing problems (an otologist, otolaryngologist, or otorhinolaryngologist) or an audiologist (a professional who specializes in measuring hearing loss and rehabilitation).

Prevention and Treatment

Although presbycusis is permanent and generally occurs in both ears, it rarely leads to total deafness. Hearing aids can help compensate for any hearing loss that does occur, and protecting the ears from potentially damaging noise can often prevent further deterioration in hearing.

As a general rule, a noise may be harmful if you have to shout over it to be heard; if the noise hurts your ears or makes your ears ring; or if you're slightly deaf for several hours after the noise stops. The longer you're exposed and the closer you are to the source of the noise, the greater the potential for harm. Many experts agree that continuous exposure to noises of more than 85 db can be dangerous. Heavy traffic and lawn mowers produce about this level of noise.

Earplugs and earmuffs. If you work in a noisy environment or use power tools or noisy yard equipment, you should protect your hearing with earplugs or earmuffs. These devices decrease the intensity of the sound that reaches the eardrum by blocking the auditory canal. Earplugs are available in a variety of standard shapes and sizes, or they can be custom-made. To be effective, they must totally block the auditory canal with an airtight seal. Earmuffs fit over the entire outer ear and are held in place by a headband. By forming an air seal around the entire circumference of the outer ear, they block the auditory canal, but they won't seal around eyeglasses or long hair.

Properly fitted devices can reduce noise levels by 15 to 30 db. Simultaneous use of both usually adds 10 to 15 db more protection. The American Academy of Otolaryngology-Head and Neck Surgery recommends combined use as a must when the noise level exceeds 105 db, roughly the equivalent of the noise produced by a power saw. Earplugs and muffs can be purchased at some pharmacies and from many medical, gun, power tool, and heavy equipment suppliers.

Hearing aids. If your evaluation indicates hearing loss, your doctor may suggest using a hearing aid. In most instances, having two devices—one for each ear—works best. Hearing aids augment whatever hearing remains by enhancing sound (see text box

Hearing Aids

Hearing aids, which artificially boost sound, cannot restore hearing that has been lost—but they can augment whatever hearing remains. There are many kinds of hearing aids. Working with your physician, an audiologist will recommend one based on your hearing level, ability to understand speech, comfort in using hearing-aid controls, and concern about how the device will look in your ear. Some models fit inside the ear canal and can barely be seen. Others are slightly larger and either fit into the contours of the outer ear or behind it. Some have different settings for various situations, such as multi-person conversation or music. Prices range from $800 to $3,000.

The three basic types of hearing aids are:

Conventional. Based on analog circuitry, these units have manually adjusted volume controls that uniformly amplify low- and high-frequency sound waves.

Programmable. Also based on analog circuitry, these units are customized by computer to accommodate individual patterns of hearing loss. They adjust volume automatically and provide many options, such as different settings for music, one-on-one conversation, and background noise reduction.

Digital. Based on digital technology, these units offer clearer, crisper sound. They also adjust volume, suppress background noise, and amplify speech automatically. Options include directional microphones that allow amplification to be redirected at the touch of a button.

All three types are available in four sizes. Ranging from the largest to the smallest, they are: behind the ear, in the outer ear, partially in the ear canal, and completely in the ear canal. Smaller units are more expensive. Which type and size is right for you depends on many factors, including the size and shape of the ear canal, the degree of hearing loss, manual dexterity, and listening needs.

Although Medicare and other insurance plans usually cover the cost of hearing tests, they generally do not cover the cost of hearing aids.

Bear in mind that no hearing aid will capture sound as well as your own ear, so you'll need patience and practice to learn how to use the one you choose. People using a hearing aid for the first time require a period of adaptation and learning. It may take weeks to get used to an aid. Most models are capable of a wide variety of electroacoustic adjustments, but these cannot be made unless the user works closely with the audiologist and explains particular problems and needs. This partnership is a preeminent consideration in ensuring optimal usage. Consider finding an audiologist who will allow you to try the hearing aid for 30 to 60 days before concluding the sale.

on page 375). They can help users identify words and are especially helpful for difficult-to-hear consonant sounds, although at first it may be difficult to distinguish conversation from background noise.

Implants. There are also implant options for some hearing loss sufferers but they are more expensive than hearing aids. A surgically implanted, bone-anchored hearing aid (which amplifies sound using a titanium bolt to vibrate bone) can help some people who cannot tolerate an external device. Cochlear implants (which bypass nonfunctioning inner ear structures and transmit electrical impulses directly to the auditory nerve) may be a possibility for some people whose severe hearing loss is not helped by external units.

H

A heart attack, technically known as a myocardial infarction, occurs when one of the coronary arteries becomes completely blocked. The result is tissue death (infarction) due to an insufficient blood supply to portions of the heart muscle (the myocardium). About 1.2 million Americans have a heart attack each year.

Causes and Prevention

Most often, the blockage that ultimately triggers a heart attack is caused by a blood clot that forms at a site where a coronary artery is narrowed by atherosclerosis, the underlying cause of coronary heart disease. Atherosclerosis, in turn, occurs through a series of changes that are associated with a host of risk factors that include smoking, a family history of early heart attack, high blood pressure, a poor lipid profile, and diabetes. Many of these risk factors can be modified through lifestyle measures and/or medical therapy, as explained in the entry on Coronary Heart Disease on pages 233-243.

Symptoms

Many heart attack victims have a history of angina and may experience more frequent or more severe anginal pain in the days preceding the attack. Others may have ill-defined warning symptoms. In many cases, however, a heart attack strikes suddenly and without any warning.

The following are warning symptoms of a heart attack:

- Uncomfortable pressure, fullness, squeezing, or pain in the center of the chest that lasts more than 10 minutes
- Pain spreading to the jaw, neck, shoulders, arms (especially the left arm), back, or upper abdomen
- Chest discomfort accompanied by lightheadedness, sweating, nausea, shortness of breath, and/or fainting

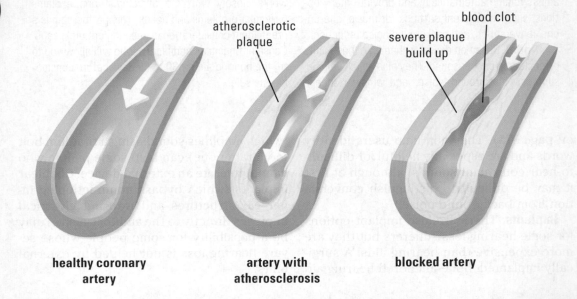

A healthy coronary artery can narrow due to atherosclerosis, a buildup of plaque. A heart attack most often occurs when a blood clot forms in the narrowed artery and blocks blood flow to part of the heart.

It is essential to get immediate medical help when symptoms suggest a heart attack (dial 911 in most areas of the United States). Half of the deaths from heart attacks occur within the first hour, before the victim gets to a hospital, where the chances of survival are greatly improved.

If it is clear that an ambulance will not be available for an extended period (30 minutes or more), another person should drive the patient to the nearest emergency department. Under no circumstances should the person experiencing the symptoms drive himself or herself to the hospital. In addition, the person suffering the symptoms should immediately chew an aspirin—which may help the blood clot to dissolve before stronger drugs can be administered. (The emergency personnel will need to know that an aspirin has been taken.)

Women and heart attacks. As is true for angina (see page 89), women may not experience the same symptoms as men. Instead (or in addition to the above symptoms) women may have more vague symptoms, such as a mild chest pain, breathlessness, dizziness, heartburn, or nausea. Unfortunately, the nonspecific nature of these symptoms may cause a woman to delay a trip to the hospital, interfere with her diagnosis, and thus delay treatment. In fact, a 2000 study of 5,888 men and women age 65 and older found that 22 percent of the people had experienced a heart attack but were not aware of it. In that same year, a study of 43,000 heart attack patients found that a third of them did not have chest pain at the time of their heart attack.

Complications of a Heart Attack

Serious complications can accompany or follow a heart attack. The ischemia (inadequate blood supply) associated with a heart attack results in the death of heart muscle cells in the area supplied by the occluded vessel. Loss of heart muscle can limit the heart's ability to exert the pressure needed to pump blood. Poor pumping may lead to congestive heart failure (see page 224) or an insufficient supply of blood to other tissues, such as the brain. Damage to the electrical system of the heart can lead to rhythm disturbances (see page 102).

A severe form of heart failure termed cardiogenic shock can be an early complication of a heart attack when more than 40 percent of the heart muscle is jeopardized. In addition, the damaged tissue in the injured portion of the heart may become so weak that the heart ruptures, a condition that requires immediate open heart surgery to save the patient's life. More commonly, the development of a bulge (aneurysm) in the heart wall at the site of the damaged muscle decreases the pumping efficiency of the heart.

Cardiac efficiency may also suffer from damage to the papillary muscles regulating the action of the mitral valve, which is located between two of the heart's chambers. Blood clots may form on areas of the heart where muscle tissue has been damaged or has died. If pieces of these clots break off and travel through the circulatory system (at which point they are called emboli), they can block distant blood vessels in the brain or elsewhere. Finally, pericarditis, an inflammation of the membrane on the surface of the heart, may complicate a heart attack and cause further pain.

Diagnosis

When patients experience symptoms of a heart attack, the diagnosis can usually be confirmed by an electrocardiogram and by measuring blood levels of proteins—creatine kinase MB (CK-MB) and troponin—released from damaged heart muscle. Measuring the blood levels of these substances may help diagnose a heart attack, as well as provide

H

prognostic information on the amount of myocardial damage. These tests are becoming more common and are now available in many hospitals.

Treatment

Treatment of a heart attack is often begun in an ambulance during transport to the hospital. Members of an emergency rescue squad can administer oxygen, provide nitrates and aspirin, begin cardiopulmonary resuscitation (CPR) in the event of cardiac arrest, and treat rhythm disturbances. At the hospital, heart attack patients are taken to a coronary care unit. Morphine is commonly given to relieve pain, sedate the patient, and reduce the heart's need for oxygen. The patient is attached to an ECG to verify the diagnosis and provide constant monitoring to detect rhythm disturbances that may require immediate treatment.

Thrombolytic Therapy

When a diagnosis is made early in the course of a heart attack, usually within 12 hours of the onset of symptoms, injection of streptokinase or tissue-type plasminogen activator (t-PA) will often reopen an occluded coronary artery by dissolving the blood clot that is blocking the flow of blood. Controlled studies have shown that such thrombolytic (clot-dissolving) therapy can restore blood flow through the blocked artery, reduce the amount of damage to the heart muscle, and improve survival after a heart attack. Drawbacks of thrombolytic therapy include a failure to reopen the artery in about 20 percent of cases and serious bleeding, especially into the brain, in less than 5 percent of patients.

Aspirin and intravenous heparin are usually administered after thrombolytic therapy to reduce the likelihood of further clot formation. Heparin is generally continued for 24 to 48 hours, and a daily dose of aspirin is given indefinitely thereafter.

Emergency Angioplasty/Bypass Surgery

If thrombolytic therapy fails, emergency surgery may be carried out—either angioplasty (in which a balloon attached to a atheter is inflated at the site where a coronary artery has been narrowed) or bypass surgery (which grafts a leg vein or artery from the chest to channel blood around the blocked segment of the artery).

Immediate angioplasty is probably preferable to thrombolytic therapy, especially for those at highest risk of death—patients older than 75 and those with an anterior infarction or sustained low blood pressure. Emergency bypass surgery is considered when thrombolytic treatment has not succeeded and coronary angiography—the "gold standard" for detecting blockages within coronary arteries—shows that a patient is unsuitable for angioplasty.

Risk Stratification

Early in their hospital stay, all patients should be "risk stratified," which means that they undergo tests to assess the risk of future coronary events. The results of these tests help doctors determine whether angioplasty or bypass surgery is necessary. Coronary angiography (see page 240) is commonly used for risk stratification. In some cases of mild heart attacks with no apparent complications during recovery, or when angiography is strongly contraindicated, a low-level exercise stress test is carried out five to seven days after the heart attack. Assessment of left ventricular function by echocardiography is also important in risk stratification.

Treatment of Complications of Heart Attack

Complications are most likely to occur when a heart attack is severe or an individual waits

Aspirin Therapy for the Heart

The effects of aspirin include its ability to make blood platelets less likely to stick together and form blood clots that may lead to heart attack. Aspirin is the only nonsteroidal anti-inflammatory drug, or NSAID—a group of drugs that also includes ibuprofen and naproxen—that has this benefit.

Because of this antiplatelet effect, aspirin therapy has long been recommended to patients after a first heart attack to help reduce the risk of additional heart attacks. For anyone who has had a heart attack, low-dose aspirin should always be taken unless there is a specific reason not to. Indeed, the Food and Drug Administration (FDA) has approved low-dose aspirin therapy for patients with a previous history of heart attack or unstable angina.

Aspirin can also help with acute heart attack: If an aspirin is chewed shortly after the onset of a heart attack, the risk of imminent death declines by 25 percent.

Guidelines from the U. S. Preventive Task Force also strongly recommend that healthy people take aspirin, but only if they have a significant risk of a heart attack within the next 10 years. This limitation was placed on aspirin because it can trigger potentially serious side effects, especially gastrointestinal bleeding in some individuals and in rare cases hemorrhagic stroke. Thus, it is crucial that candidates for low-dose aspirin therapy discuss the benefits and risks with a physician.

Potential candidates for taking aspirin to prevent a heart attack include men 40 years and older, postmenopausal women, smokers, and people with high blood pressure, diabetes, abnormal cholesterol levels, or a family history of premature heart attacks. Certain people should not take aspirin at all—for example, those with a history of gout, gastric ulcers or gastric bleeding, liver disease, uncontrolled high blood pressure, hemorrhagic stroke, or bleeding disorders.

In reviewing the research data, the Task Force found that lower doses of aspirin—ranging from 75 to 160 mg taken daily or 325 mg (a standard tablet) taken every other day—were effective for primary prevention of heart disease. The analysis also revealed that the more heart attack risk factors an individual has, the more effective aspirin is in preventing a heart attack or sudden death. The Task Force concluded that the heart-protective benefits of low-dose aspirin outweigh the side effects of gastrointestinal bleeding and hemorrhagic stroke for people who have at least a 6% chance of a heart attack in the next 10 years.

too long before getting to a hospital. The most common complications of heart attack are congestive heart failure (see page 224) and abnormal heart rhythms (arrhythmias, see page 102).

Other possibilities include severe dysfunction of the mitral valve due to rupture of the papillary muscles that hold the valve leaflets in place; rupture of the septum (wall) that separates the left from the right ventricle; rupture of the left ventricular free wall (almost always immediately fatal); ballooning of the wall of the left ventricle (ventricular aneurysm) due to scar tissue formation; and emboli to the brain, legs, or kidneys.

Recovery and Rehabilitation

If recovery is uneventful and angioplasty or bypass surgery is not necessary, patients are usually discharged from the hospital after about a week. Activities are slowly increased over the following eight weeks, and resumption of a full schedule is generally possible about two months after leaving the hospital.

Unless there are contraindications to their use, patients should be placed on

H

long-term treatment with aspirin and a beta-blocker after a heart attack. Therapy with cholesterol-lowering statin drugs is also recommended. (Indeed, statin therapy is so safe and effective that any heart attack survivor who isn't on it should ask their doctor why.) Patients with significant damage to the front wall of the left ventricle are often treated with warfarin for up to three months in an effort to prevent the formation of blood clots that may lead to a stroke caused by an embolus (a detached blood clot that moves through the circulatory system) to the brain.

In the past few decades, a new understanding has emerged concerning the importance of rehabilitation after a heart attack. For years, popular belief held that having a heart attack signaled the end of an active, healthy life. Today, however, better knowledge of how the heart works has made cardiac rehabilitation the cornerstone of recovery after a heart attack (as well as after bypass surgery or angioplasty). Indeed, many patients who follow a prescribed rehabilitation plan—usually with supervised exercise as the cornerstone—find that their lives are healthier and more active than before.

Hemorrhoids are swollen but normally present blood vessels in and around the anus and lower rectum that stretch under pressure, similar to varicose veins in the legs.

The increased pressure and swelling may result from straining to move the bowel. Other contributing factors include pregnancy, heredity, aging, and chronic constipation or diarrhea.

Hemorrhoids are either inside the anus (internal) or under the skin around the anus (external).

How Are Hemorrhoids Prevented?

The best way to prevent hemorrhoids is to keep stools soft so they pass easily, thus decreasing pressure and straining, and to empty bowels as soon as possible after the urge occurs. Exercise, including walking, and increased fiber in the diet help reduce constipation and straining by producing stools that are softer and easier to pass.

What Are the Symptoms of Hemorrhoids?

Many anorectal problems, including fissures, fistulae, abscesses, or irritation and itching (pruritus ani), have similar symptoms and are incorrectly referred to as hemorrhoids.

Hemorrhoids usually are not dangerous or life threatening. In most cases, hemorrhoidal symptoms will go away within a few days.

Although many people have hemorrhoids, not all of them experience symptoms. The most common symptom of internal hemorrhoids is bright red blood covering the stool, on toilet paper, or in the toilet bowl. However, an internal hemorrhoid may protrude through the anus outside the body, becoming irritated and painful. This is known as a protruding hemorrhoid.

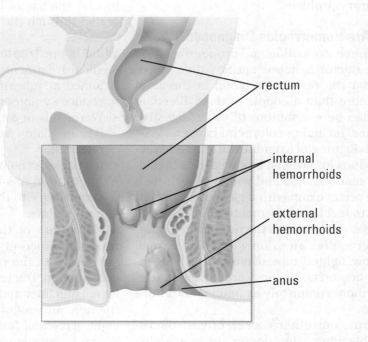

rectum

internal hemorrhoids

external hemorrhoids

anus

Hemorrhoids result when veins in the rectum or anus become inflamed. Internal hemorrhoids occur in veins of the rectum; external hemorrhoids, in veins of the anus.

Symptoms of external hemorrhoids may include painful swelling or a hard lump around the anus that results when a blood clot forms. This condition is known as a thrombosed external hemorrhoid.

In addition, excessive straining, rubbing, or cleaning around the anus may cause irritation with bleeding and/or itching, which may produce a vicious cycle of symptoms. Draining mucus may also cause itching.

How Common Are Hemorrhoids?

Hemorrhoids are very common in both men and women. About half of the population have hemorrhoids by age 50. Hemorrhoids are also common among pregnant women. The pressure of the fetus in the abdomen, as well as hormonal changes, cause the hemorrhoidal vessels to enlarge. These vessels are also placed under severe pressure during childbirth. For most women, however, hemorrhoids caused by pregnancy are a temporary problem.

How Are Hemorrhoids Diagnosed?

A thorough evaluation and proper diagnosis by the doctor is important any time bleeding from the rectum or blood in the stool lasts more than a couple of days. Bleeding may also be a symptom of other digestive diseases, including colorectal cancer.

The doctor will examine the anus and rectum to look for swollen blood vessels that indicate hemorrhoids and will also perform a digital rectal exam with a gloved, lubricated finger to feel for abnormalities.

Closer evaluation of the rectum for hemorrhoids requires an exam with an anoscope, a hollow, lighted tube useful for viewing internal hemorrhoids, or a proctoscope, useful for more completely examining the entire rectum.

To rule out other causes of gastrointestinal bleeding, the doctor may examine

---

Self-Care Measures

Self-care can lessen discomfort and facilitate healing of a hemorrhoid. Good hygiene is important. Gently wipe the anal area with damp toilet paper, or a premoistened wipe, and pat dry. If hemorrhoids aren't bleeding, petroleum jelly or zinc oxide ointment can soothe itching and help bowel movements pass easily. Topical creams such as lidocaine and oral analgesics like acetaminophen (Tylenol) can ease pain. Hemorrhoid preparations are fine, but they cost more and contain the same types of ingredients as listed above. If symptoms last beyond a week, see your doctor.

The Editors

---

the rectum and lower colon (sigmoid) with sigmoidoscopy or the entire colon with colonoscopy. Sigmoidoscopy and colonoscopy are diagnostic procedures that also involve the use of lighted, flexible tubes inserted through the rectum.

What Is the Treatment?

Medical treatment of hemorrhoids initially is aimed at relieving symptoms. Measures to reduce symptoms include:

- Warm tub or sitz baths several times a day in plain, warm water for about 10 minutes;
- Ice packs to help reduce swelling;
- Application of a hemorroidal cream or suppository to the affected area for a limited time.

Prevention of the recurrence of hemorrhoids is aimed at changing conditions associated with the pressure and straining of constipation. Doctors will often recommend increasing fiber and fluids in the diet. Eating the right amount of fiber and drinking six to eight glasses of fluid (not alcohol) result in softer, bulkier stools. A softer stool makes emptying the bowels easier and lessens the pressure on hemorrhoids caused by straining. Eliminating straining also helps prevent the hemorrhoids from protruding.

Good sources of fiber are fruits, vegetables, and whole grains. In addition, doctors may suggest a bulk stool softener or a fiber supplement such as psyllium (Metamucil) or methylcellulose (Citrucel).

In some cases, hemorrhoids must be treated surgically. These methods are used to shrink and destroy the hemorrhoidal tissue and are performed under anesthesia. The doctor will preform the surgery during an office or hospital visit.

A number of surgical methods may be used to remove or reduce the size of internal hemorrhoids. These techniques include:

- **Rubber band ligation.** A rubber band is placed around the base of the hemorrhoid inside the rectum. The band cuts off circulation, and the hemorrhoid withers away within a few days.
- **Sclerotherapy.** A chemical solution is injected around the blood vessel to shrink the hemorrhoid.

Techniques used to treat both internal and external hemorrhoids include:

- **Electrical or laser heat (laser coagulation) or infrared light (infrared photo coagulation).** Both techniques use special devices to burn hemorrhoidal tissue.
- **Hemorrhoidectomy.** Occasionally, extensive or severe internal or external hemorrhoids may require removal by surgery known as hemorrhoidectomy. This procedure is the best method for permanent removal of hemorrhoids.

National Institute of Diabetes and Digestive and Kidney Diseases

High blood pressure, also called hypertension, is sometimes referred to as the silent killer because it initially produces few, if any, symptoms but causes or contributes to the deaths of 210,000 Americans a year. The condition is a primary cause of stroke, heart disease, heart failure, kidney disease, and blindness. Currently, hypertension affects at least 65 million Americans, but those numbers are likely to increase dramatically as baby boomers begin moving into the hypertension age bracket. Fortunately, the condition is easily detected and usually controllable with diet, exercise, and medication.

Understanding Blood Pressure

Blood does not flow through the circulatory system in a steady stream; instead, it is pushed through the blood vessels with every heartbeat. Each time the heart contracts—a period known as systole—blood pressure rises as more blood is forced through the arteries. Each systole is followed by a moment of relaxation, or diastole, when pressure drops as the heart refills with blood and rests before its next contraction. Thus, pressure in the arteries rises and falls with each heartbeat. For this reason, blood pressure readings include two values: Systolic pressure, the higher number, corresponds with the peak pressure in the arteries during the heart's contraction; diastolic pressure, the lower number, reflects the lowest pressure in the arteries as the heart relaxes.

Blood pressure also fluctuates throughout the day under the direct influence of the heart, the arteries, and the kidneys. Variations in the strength of each heartbeat can lower or raise blood pressure—more powerful contractions produce greater pressure. During exercise, for example, increased blood flow is needed to provide extra oxygen and nutrients to the muscles,

so the heart beats faster and more forcefully to raise blood pressure and keep up with the demand. On the other hand, blood pressure drops as the heart slows during sleep.

The smooth muscle cells that encircle the small arteries permit them to expand (dilate) to decrease blood pressure or narrow (constrict) to increase it. Stress or anger can raise blood pressure by triggering the release of hormones that constrict blood vessels. Three hormones produced by the adrenal gland, epinephrine, norepinephrine, and aldosterol, all raise blood pressure. Finally, the volume of blood depends largely on its content of water; the kidneys can reduce blood pressure by eliminating excess salt and water.

An elaborate network of nerves and hormones control these processes. Special nerve endings called baroreceptors, residing in

the walls of arteries, monitor blood pressure. An increase in pressure stretches the artery wall and the baroreceptors signal the central nervous system to lower the pressure. Blood pressure is similarly monitored at sites in

the kidneys where blood is filtered (the glomeruli).

Normally, this complex regulatory system allows blood pressure to rise or fall as needed while staying within a desirable range. In many people, however, abnormalities in this system lead to chronically elevated blood pressure, or hypertension.

Causes

No specific cause can be identified in 90 percent to 95 percent of patients with hypertension—a condition called essential, or primary, hypertension. While hypertension is common in virtually all economically developed countries, it is uncommon in several isolated societies. When individuals from those societies migrate to developed countries, they often develop hypertension. These findings suggest that environmental factors, such as eating habits and level of physical activity, play an important role in hypertension.

A number of risk factors are associated with essential hypertension. These include high levels of sodium consumption; a diet low in fruits, vegetables, and dairy products and high in fat; obesity; excessive alcohol intake; a lack of exercise; and metabolic syndrome. Studies have also shown that essential hypertension has a genetic component—though it isn't clear how large a role genetics play in causing essential hypertension.

Secondary Hypertension

A number of disorders, as well as drugs, can cause secondary hypertension, which affects less than 5 percent of people with hypertension. It is particularly important to identify secondary causes of hypertension because the high blood pressure might be cured or better controlled by eliminating the underlying problem.

Disorders. Health problems that can produce hypertension include kidney disease that leads to chronic kidney (renal) failure; narrowing of the arteries supplying blood to one or both kidneys; and several types of adrenal tumors.

Narrowing of a portion of the aorta in the chest, called coarctation of the aorta, is associated with hypertension in the upper part of the body and low blood pressure in the abdomen and legs. This disorder, which can be corrected by surgery, is the most common secondary cause of hypertension in young individuals.

Drugs. Some prescription drugs that can raise blood pressure include corticosteroids, cyclosporine, tacrolimus, and nonsteroidal anti-inflammatory drugs (NSAIDs) such as indomethacin. Over-the-counter NSAIDs and nsasal decongestants can also raise blood pressure, as can weight loss products containing ephedra. (The Food and Drug Administration banned the sale of ephedra products in 2004, but the ban was challenged and products continued to be sold on Internet sites.) Illegal drugs such as cocaine and amphetamines can increase blood pressure as well.

Symptoms and Signs

Hypertension may produce no early symptoms and can go undetected for many years. Although some patients complain of headaches, most often hypertension is discovered during a routine physical examination or, less commonly, when a patient experiences one of its complications: transient ischemic attack (TIA), stroke, visual abnormalities, angina, heart attack, congestive heart failure, claudication (intermittent pain in the leg muscles associated with physical exertion), or symptoms of kidney disease.

Another situation that may cause symptoms from hypertension is a *hypertensive crisis*, which may occur when blood pressure reaches very high levels (diastolic pressure above 120 mm Hg). This condition occurs in about 1 percent of people with hypertension—usually around age 40—and may be precipitated by abrupt cessation of antihypertensive medication.

The most common type of hypertensive crisis is termed *hypertensive urgency*, which typically produces headaches and nosebleeds. It requires medical treatment within a few hours to prevent organ damage.

A more serious condition is a *hypertensive emergency*, signaled by chest pain, shortness of breath, seizures, back pain, headache with blurred vision, nausea, and vomiting—symptoms indicating damage to body organs. Anyone suspected of experiencing a

H

hypertensive emergency should be taken to a hospital immediately.

Classifying Blood Pressure

Blood pressure levels used to be classified as optimal, normal, high-normal, and hypertension (stage 1, stage 2, and stage 3). But with the publication of the Seventh Report of the Joint National Committee on Prevention, Detection, Evaluation, and Treatment of High Blood Pressure—more commonly known as JNC 7—a new system of classifying blood pressure was adopted in 2003. This classification system has the following categories: normal, prehypertension, and hypertension (stage 1 and stage 2).

The JNC report provides guidelines on diagnosing and managing hypertension (see chart page 387).

Systolic vs. Diastolic Pressure

Historically, doctors focused on diastolic blood pressure for the diagnosis and treatment of hypertension. But today the focus is on both systolic and diastolic blood pressure, since systolic pressure is an important determinant of hypertension complications, particularly in people older than age 50.

In contrast to diastolic blood pressure, which tends to rise until about age 55 and then begins to fall, systolic blood pressure continues to rise with age. Previously, such elevations were thought to be a normal part of aging—caused by a gradual loss of elasticity in the arterial walls. Now, however, a substantial body of evidence shows that high systolic blood pressure with a diastolic blood pressure under 90 mm Hg carries a high risk of heart attack and stroke. In light of such findings, the JNC 7 guidelines recommend using systolic blood pressure as the standard measure for the evaluation and treatment of hypertension, especially for people age 50 and older.

In addition, blood pressure should be kept below 140/90 mm Hg, regardless of age. In people with diabetes or kidney disease, blood pressure should be maintained below 130/80 mm Hg.

Isolated Systolic Hypertension

A high systolic blood pressure is very common in older adults. In fact, 65 percent of people over age 60 with hypertension have a condition called isolated systolic hypertension, defined as a systolic blood pressure of 140 mm Hg or higher and a diastolic blood pressure under 90 mm Hg, which is associated with an increased risk of stroke, coronary heart disease (CHD), and kidney disease.

White Coat Hypertension

Many people exhibit "white coat hypertension," that is, consistently high readings that are present only when they are examined by a physician or are in a medical environment. Blood pressure measurements are normal when taken at home by the patients themselves, family members, or friends. As many as 20 to 35 percent of people have white coat hypertension.

Whether or not to treat white coat hypertension with antihypertensive drugs is a controversial issue. In general, people with white coat hypertension and no other risk factors for cardiovascular disease (disease of the arteries supplying the heart or other organs) may not require aggressive treatment but should be especially careful to avoid other risk factors and, like all adults, to adopt healthy lifestyle habits. However, any person with white coat hypertension and organ damage from hypertension (for example, kidney or heart damage) requires treatment.

Some patients experience the opposite problem: Their average daytime blood pressure is high, but it is normal when measured

Evaluating and Managing Blood Pressure Levels

The JNC 7 blood pressure guidelines from the Joint National Committee on Prevention, Detection, Evaluation, and Treatment of High Blood Pressure are summarized in the table below. To determine your blood pressure category, average your blood pressure readings from at least two doctor visits. If your systolic and diastolic blood pressures fall into different categories, use the more elevated reading. For example, an average reading of 165 mm Hg systolic and 95 mm Hg diastolic means that you have stage 2—rather than stage 1—hypertension.

Blood Pressure Category	Systolic Blood Pressure (mm Hg)	Diastolic Blood Pressure (mm Hg)	What To Do
Normal	<120	<80	Lifestyle measures encouraged.
Prehypertension	120–139	80–89	Lifestyle measures only. If you have diabetes or kidney disease, you may need to take medication to lower your blood pressure to less than 130/80 mm Hg.
Stage 1 hypertension	140–159	90–99	Lifestyle measures. Blood pressure medication is also required—usually a thiazide diuretic. Other types of blood pressure medication may be considered if you have heart disease, diabetes, or kidney problems or if you've had a stroke.
Stage 2 hypertension	≥160	≥100	Lifestyle measures. Also, two blood pressure medications are typically required—usually a thiazide diuretic with an ACE inhibitor, angiotensin II receptor blocker, beta-blocker, or calcium channel blocker. Other combinations may be used if you have heart disease, diabetes, or kidney problems or if you've had a stroke.

in a medical setting. Such patients are unlikely to be treated for high blood pressure and therefore may miss out on the benefits of treatment. People with borderline in-office measurements are at greater risk for inaccurate diagnoses.

Complications from Hypertension
The excessive force of blood moving through arteries can damage both large and small arteries, leading to disease in the tissues or organs supplied by these blood vessels.

Hypertension is strongly associated with an increased risk of developing—and dying from—heart disease and stroke. It is also an important risk factor for atrial fibrillation (a type of irregular heartbeat that originates in the atria, the upper chambers of the heart) and left ventricular hypertrophy (thickening of the muscular wall of the left ventricle, which supplies blood to all parts of the body except the lungs). People with left ventricular hypertrophy are more likely to have angina, heart attacks, and congestive heart failure.

Hypertension also increases the risk of an aneurysm, a sac-like bulging in an artery of the brain or in the abdominal aorta that can rupture and cause catastrophic bleeding into the area of the brain surrounding the aneurysm (called a hemorrhagic stroke) or into the abdomen.

Another complication of hypertension is damage to the kidneys, which can occur in two ways: atherosclerotic narrowing of the arteries supplying the kidneys (the renal arteries) and damage to the small arteries within the kidneys. Either of these effects can lead to progressive loss of kidney function and, eventually, kidney failure with retention of waste products in the body (uremia).

Persistent elevation of blood pressure can also cause vision loss through damage to the tiny arteries that supply blood to the retina. This condition, known as hypertensive retinopathy, typically evolves gradually, and many years may pass before patients notice any visual symptoms. Treating high blood pressure usually prevents further damage to the retina.

Prevention

Prevention of any rise in blood pressure is important because organ damage can begin when pressures exceed 110 mm Hg systolic and 70 mm Hg diastolic—long before hypertension is present. Prevention of hypertension also eliminates the possible side effects and substantial costs of antihypertensive medications. Moreover, even when medications significantly lower blood pressure, studies have shown that treated hypertensive patients maintain a much higher risk of hypertensive complications than their normotensive counterparts with similar blood pressures. Therefore, prevention is the best way to reduce the risk of complications.

The keys to preventing hypertension are weight loss, regular exercise, improved diet with plenty of fruits and vegetables, lower sodium intake, and moderation in alcohol consumption. Such relatively simple steps can have a considerable impact. Even a moderate weight loss, for example, decreased the development of hypertension by 50 percent in one study of individuals with a systolic blood pressure between 130 and 139 mm Hg or a diastolic blood pressure between 85 and 89 mm Hg. The benefits of prevention appear to be more substantial when all of the recommended lifestyle modifications are adopted.

Diagnosis

Hypertension is most often discovered during a routine visit to the doctor. The instrument used to evaluate blood pressure in a doctor's office, known as a sphygmomanometer, originally consisted of an air pump, an inflatable cuff, and a mercury column gauge. Blood pressure was measured by wrapping the cuff around the upper arm and determining how high a pressure reading on the mercury column was needed to compress the brachial artery—the major artery in the arm. Thus, blood pressures are expressed in terms of millimeters of mercury, or mm Hg. Mercury-column manometers have now been largely replaced by digital devices—which when used properly can be as accurate as mercury instruments.

The following steps will help ensure accurate results. Do not smoke or consume caffeine in the 30 minutes prior to having blood pressure measured. Be seated and at rest for at least five minutes before the measurement. In addition, the results of two or more readings, taken at least one minute apart, should be averaged. Hypertension is diagnosed when the average blood pressure

Lowering Blood Pressure Through Diet

Results from the DASH (Dietary Approaches to Stop Hypertension) trial—a major study published in 1998—indicate that a dietary approach to reducing blood pressure may be as effective as a single antihypertensive medication. The diet provides a well-balanced menu of essential nutrients, particularly potassium, magnesium, and calcium. A large part of the success of the diet may be due to its high potassium content of about 4,400 mg daily. Recent research indicates that potassium lowers blood pressure by relaxing the arteries.

The diet calls for eating 8 to 10 servings (about five cups) of fruits and vegetables and three cups of low-fat dairy foods daily, twice the amount consumed by most Americans. It's also important to restrict sodium intake by avoiding processed foods and limiting restaurant food, both of which are typically high in sodium. A more recent study, the DASH-Sodium Trial, showed that the DASH diet and reduced sodium consumption—1,500 mg per day (compared to 3,300 in a typical American diet)—each lowered blood pressure independently in subjects with either normal or high blood pressure. But combining the two strategies produced the greatest decreases.

reading is 140/90 mm Hg or higher on at least two separate doctor visits.

Home and Ambulatory Monitoring

Home monitoring of blood pressure can be useful in determining the presence of white coat hypertension and can help people with established hypertension keep track of the effects of lifestyle changes and medication on their blood pressure. Two types of devices are available for home measurements: aneroid monitors (mechanical) and electronic monitors, which provide a digital readout.

A more detailed record of blood pressure can be obtained with ambulatory blood pressure monitors that automatically measure and record blood pressures at 15- to 60-minute intervals throughout a 24-hour period. Such measurements may help to identify white coat hypertension in people who cannot manage a home monitor or individuals whose blood pressure does not drop during sleep, a phenomenon that may increase cardiovascular risk. Many experts, however, feel strongly that office blood pressures, not ambulatory readings, should guide treatment.

Because home monitors can come with many features, consult your doctor for guidance when choosing a model. Then, before using the device you select, have someone in your doctor's office check to be sure it produces accurate readings and show you how to use it. Cuff size and placement, how you read the gauge, and many other variables can affect accuracy.

Medical Evaluation of Blood Pressure

Proper diagnosis of hypertension requires a thorough medical history, a physical examination, and laboratory tests. Blood pressure levels determined by a doctor to be lower than 120 mm Hg systolic and 80 mm Hg diastolic should be rechecked within two years. Pressures between 120 and 139 mm Hg systolic or 80 and 89 mm Hg diastolic should be rechecked within one year.

When blood pressures are consistently 140/90 mm Hg or above, the next step is to determine whether the hypertension is primary or secondary. Although secondary hypertension is uncommon, the possibility of secondary causes of high blood pressure should always be considered, since these forms of hypertension are potentially correctable and their identification may spare the patient a lifetime of antihypertensive medication. Precise diagnosis of a secondary cause usually requires special laboratory tests and procedures.

The other aims of a complete evaluation are to determine whether hypertension has caused tissue or organ damage, to detect lifestyle habits that may be contributing to hypertension, and to identify any additional risk factors for cardiovascular disease.

Treatment

Treatment of primary hypertension involves both lifestyle modifications and antihypertensive medications. The goal of treatment is to lower blood pressure and reduce the risk of complications from hypertension—specifically strokes, heart attacks, heart failure, and kidney disease. Most people with hypertension should aim to lower their blood pressure to less than 140/90 mm Hg. Those with diabetes or kidney disease have an even lower goal—less than 130/80 mm Hg.

The same blood pressure goals apply to people with secondary hypertension. In these individuals, however, doctors often try to treat the underlying disorder, especially if blood pressure is difficult to control with lifestyle modifications and medications.

People experiencing a hypertensive emergency (see page 385) must seek immediate medical attention and have their blood pressure lowered with intravenous antihypertensive medication in the hospital. Blood pressure is lowered gradually to avoid precipitous drops in pressure that could lead to a stroke.

Treating hypertension in older adults requires lowering blood pressure neither too far nor too rapidly. An abrupt drop in blood pressure on standing (orthostatic hypotension) is more common in elderly people when elevated systolic pressure is reduced too much or too fast. Orthostatic hypertension can cause dizziness and may lead to falls, which increase the risk of broken bones. Organ damage may also occur when blood pressure is reduced too quickly in older people. To prevent these complications, blood pressure should be reduced cautiously in elderly patients. For example, medications may be started at half the usual dosage, and increases in dosage made more slowly.

Lifestyle Modifications

Lifestyle modifications are essential for both the prevention and treatment of hypertension. Modifications proven to lower blood pressure include weight loss for those who are overweight, reduced salt intake, regular physical activity, and moderation in alcohol intake. An ample intake of potassium also can lower blood pressure. In studies, people with and without hypertension substantially lowered their blood pressure by reducing sodium intake and following the DASH (Dietary Approaches to Stop Hypertension) diet, which is low in both saturated and total fat and rich in fruits, vegetables, and low-fat dairy foods (see text box on page 389).

Adopting these lifestyle changes may not only help lower blood pressure, but also improve the effectiveness of antihypertensive medication and lower the risk of cardiovascular disease.

Medications

When lifestyle modifications are insufficient to lower blood pressure to target levels, doctors add medications. Each of the various classes of antihypertensive drugs lowers blood pressure in a different way (see text box above). The availability of a wide variety

How Blood Pressure Drugs Work

The following classes of drugs—which include more than 100 individual medications—work in different ways to lower high blood pressure. The drugs have a wide range of side effects, and people can respond very differently to the same drug. Thus, most patients must go through a trial period to find out which drugs are most effective for them while causing the fewest side effects.

- Diuretics increase sodium and water excretion. By reducing the overall fluid volume in the body, diuretics ease pressure exerted against blood vessel walls.

- Beta-blockers inhibit the action of the hormones adrenaline (epinephrine) and noradrenaline (norepinephrine). This effect lowers blood pressure by slowing the rate and force of the heart's contractions.

- Angiotensin converting enzyme (ACE) inhibitors block an enzyme that produces angiotensin II, a substance that causes blood vessels to constrict. These drugs relax blood vessels, lower blood pressure, and decrease the heart's work.

- Angiotensin II receptor blockers work like ACE inhibitors by blocking the actions of angiotensin II.

- Calcium channel blockers interfere with the movement of calcium into heart muscle cells and smooth muscle cells in arterial walls. These actions relax blood vessels, lower blood pressure, and decrease the heart's workload.

- Alpha-blockers and central alpha agonists block nerve impulses that constrict small arteries, thereby lowering resistance to blood flow through these arteries.

- Peripheral-acting adrenergic antagonists reduce resistance to blood flow in small arteries by inhibiting the release of adrenaline and noradrenaline from nerves.

- Direct vasodilators widen blood vessels by acting directly on the smooth muscle of small arteries.

- An aldosterone blocker, eplerenone (Inspra), works by blocking the activity of the hormone aldosterone.

H

of antihypertensive medications provides several valuable therapeutic advantages. Although the drugs in each class are about equally effective in lowering blood pressure at comparable dosages, some individuals or groups of individuals respond better to one class of drugs than to another. If a drug is ineffective, switching drugs rather than adding a second one may also reduce the possibility of side effects. Moreover, people unable to tolerate the side effects of one antihypertensive drug may do better with a different medication. Finally, combinations of drugs from two different classes usually improve blood pressure control when a single drug proves inadequate (see text box on page 392).

Depending on the stage of hypertension, satisfactory control of blood pressure can be achieved with the first medication tried in about 50 percent of people with hypertension. Some 76 percent of patients will respond to either a first or a second single drug, and about 80 percent of patients respond to a combination of two drugs.

In patients with lipid abnormalities, the effects of antihypertensive medications on levels of HDL cholesterol and triglycerides should be considered. Thiazides and beta-blockers can have a modestly adverse effect; alpha-blockers have a beneficial effect; and calcium channel blockers and ACE inhibitors have no effect.

Combination Therapy

Most people with hypertension require two or more antihypertensive medications to get their blood pressure under control. Combining medications from different classes often results in greater reductions in blood pressure than using a single drug, because the actions of the drugs may complement each other. For example, diuretics reduce blood pressure by increasing the excretion of sodium and water by the kidneys. But in some people this effect stimulates the release of certain blood pressure-raising hormones to compensate for the drop in blood volume. Adding an ACE inhibitor blocks the actions of these hormones and improves blood pressure control.

Combination therapy can be achieved by taking a separate dose of each drug or using fixed-dose combination drugs (two different drugs combined in a single pill). Most fixed-dose combinations contain a thiazide diuretic (most often hydrochlorothiazide) and an ACE inhibitor, beta-blocker, angiotensin II receptor blocker, or central alpha agonist. A fixed combination of an ACE inhibitor and a calcium channel blocker is also available.

Fixed-dose combination drugs are more convenient (fewer pills to take each day) and are less expensive than taking each drug individually. Because the fixed-dose combination tends to contain smaller doses of each drug than if the drugs were taken separately, the risk of side effects may be lower as well. In some cases, one drug in the combination prevents the side effects of the other. For example, ACE inhibitors can reduce the leg swelling that often occurs with calcium channel blockers.

However, fixed-dose combinations reduce dosing flexibility—that is, the dosage of each medication in the combination cannot be varied separately. In addition, no large, long-term studies have proven that fixed-dose combinations offer any benefits over taking the two drugs separately. Therefore, fixed-dose combination drugs are most appropriate for people who have found that the the two drugs effectively control their blood pressure when taken separately at the same doses as in the combination pill.

H

Selection of Antihypertensive Medications

The best blood pressure-lowering medication(s) for a particular person depends on how severe the hypertension is and whether other health problems are present. For people with stage 1 hypertension (140 to 159 mm Hg systolic or 90 to 99 mm Hg diastolic) who have no other health problems, a thiazide diuretic is most often prescribed along with lifestyle modifications. In the case of healthy people with stage 2 hypertension (160 mm Hg or higher systolic or 100 mm Hg or higher diastolic), a combination of two drugs is typically prescribed in addition to lifestyle modifications. The drug combination usually consists of a thiazide diuretic and an ACE inhibitor, angiotensin II receptor blocker, beta-blocker, or calcium channel blocker.

Many people with hypertension have other health conditions, and these individuals may require different or additional antihypertensive medications to control their blood pressure and manage their other health problems. For example, people with angina are usually prescribed a beta-blocker or calcium channel blocker to help relieve symptoms. People who have suffered a heart attack typically take an ACE inhibitor, beta-blocker, and aldosterone blocker to prevent another heart attack. In people with diabetes, at least two medications are usually required to reach the goal of 130/80 mm Hg.

Medical Follow-up During Treatment

People with stage 1 hypertension who are otherwise healthy are typically seen by their doctor once a month until they reach their blood pressure goal. Those with other health problems or stage 2 hypertension need to visit their doctor more frequently—every two to four weeks. At these visits, the doctor may adjust drug doses, add another drug, switch a medication if side effects are troublesome, and inquire about lifestyle modifications.

Once blood pressure is at goal or stabilizes, doctor visits are usually reduced to every three to six months, though people with other health conditions (such as diabetes or heart disease) may need to visit their doctor more often. Levels of blood sodium, potassium, and creatinine should be measured at least once or twice a year to detect any adverse effects from antihypertensive drugs and any deterioration in kidney function.

Only about a third of people with hypertension have reached the blood pressure goal of 140/90 mm Hg. One reason is that some doctors are not treating hypertension aggressively enough; another is that some people are not taking their antihypertensive medications as prescribed or are not adopting the recommended lifestyle modifications.

A significant number of drugs—over-the-counter as well as prescription—may decrease the effectiveness of antihypertensive medications. Before beginning antihypertensive therapy, you should always inform your doctor of any medications you take regularly. Also be sure to mention any new medications you start taking while on therapy for hypertension.

Poor compliance with antihypertensive therapy is understandable, considering that many people with hypertension have no or minimal symptoms yet are expected to make lifestyle modifications and take medication that may be costly or cause unpleasant side effects. Nonetheless, compliance is crucial to prevent the complications that may result from high blood pressure. On average, antihypertensive therapy is associated with a 35% to 40% lower risk of a stroke, a 20% to 25% reduced risk of a heart attack, and a 50% decrease in the risk of heart failure.

H

Hodgkin's disease is one of a group of cancers called lymphomas. Lymphoma is a general term for cancers that develop in the lymphatic system. Hodgkin's disease, an uncommon lymphoma, accounts for less than 1 percent of all cases of cancer in this country. Other cancers of the lymphatic system are called non-Hodgkin's lymphomas.

The lymphatic system is part of the body's immune system. It helps the body fight disease and infection. The lymphatic system includes a network of thin lymphatic vessels that branch, like blood vessels, into tissues throughout the body. Lymphatic vessels carry lymph, a colorless, watery fluid that contains infection-fighting cells called lymphocytes. Along this network of vessels are small organs called lymph nodes. Clusters of lymph nodes are found in the underarms, groin, neck, chest, and abdomen. Other parts of the lymphatic system are the spleen, thymus, tonsils, and bone marrow. Lymphatic tissue is also found in other parts of the body.

In Hodgkin's disease, cells in the lymphatic system become abnormal. They divide too rapidly and grow without any order or control. Because lymphatic tissue is present in many parts of the body, Hodgkin's disease can start almost anywhere. Hodgkin's disease may occur in a single lymph node, a group of lymph nodes, or, sometimes, in other parts of the lymphatic system such as the bone marrow and spleen. This type of cancer tends to spread in a fairly orderly way from one group of lymph nodes to the next group. For example, Hodgkin's disease that arises in the lymph nodes in the neck spreads first to the nodes above the collarbones, and then to the lymph nodes under the arms and within the chest. Eventually, it can spread to almost any other part of the body.

Cancer research has led to real progress against Hodgkin's disease—increased survival rates and improved quality of life. Most people diagnosed with Hodgkin's disease can now be cured, or their disease can be controlled for many years. Continuing research offers hope that, in the future, even more people with this disease will be treated successfully. Each achievement in laboratories and clinics brings researchers closer to the eventual control of Hodgkin's disease.

Risk Factors

Scientists at hospitals and medical centers all across the country are studying Hodgkin's disease. They are trying to learn more about what causes the disease and more effective methods of treatment.

At this time, the cause or causes of Hodgkin's disease are not known, and doctors can seldom explain why one person gets this disease and another does not. It is clear, however, that Hodgkin's disease is not caused by an injury, and it is not contagious; no one can "catch" this disease from another person.

By studying patterns of cancer in the population, researchers have found certain risk factors that are more common in people who get Hodgkin's disease than in those who do not. However, most people with these risk factors do not get Hodgkin's disease, and many who do get this disease have none of the known risk factors.

The following are some of the risk factors associated with this disease:

- **Age/Sex.** Hodgkin's disease occurs most often in people between 15 and 34 and in people over the age of 55. It is more common in men than in women.
- **Family History.** Brothers and sisters of those with Hodgkin's disease have a higher-than-average chance of developing this disease.

- **Viruses.** Epstein-Barr virus is an infectious agent that may be associated with an increased chance of getting Hodgkin's disease.

People who are concerned about the chance of developing Hodgkin's disease should talk with their doctor about the disease, the symptoms to watch for, and an appropriate schedule for checkups. The doctor's advice will be based on the person's age, medical history, and other factors.

Symptoms

Symptoms of Hodgkin's disease may include the following:

- A painless swelling in the lymph nodes in the neck, underarm, or groin
- Unexplained recurrent fevers
- Night sweats
- Unexplained weight loss
- Itchy skin

When symptoms like these occur, they are not sure signs of Hodgkin's disease. In most cases, they are actually caused by other, less serious conditions, such as the flu. When symptoms like these persist, however, it is important to see a doctor so that any illness can be diagnosed and treated. Only a doctor can make a diagnosis of Hodgkin's disease. Do not wait to feel pain; early Hodgkin's disease may not cause pain.

Diagnosis and Staging

If Hodgkin's disease is suspected, the doctor asks about the person's medical history and performs a physical exam to check general signs of health. The exam includes feeling to see if the lymph nodes in the neck, underarm, or groin are enlarged. The doctor may order blood tests.

The doctor may also order tests that produce pictures of the inside of the body. These may include:

- **X-rays:** High-energy radiation used to take pictures of areas inside the body, such as the chest, bones, liver, and spleen.
- **CT (or CAT) scan:** A series of detailed pictures of areas inside the body. The pictures are created by a computer linked to an x-ray machine.
- **MRI (magnetic resonance imaging):** Detailed pictures of areas inside the body produced with a powerful magnet linked to a computer.

The diagnosis depends on a biopsy. A surgeon removes a sample of lymphatic tissue (part or all of a lymph node) so that a pathologist can examine it under a microscope to check for cancer cells. Other tissues may be sampled as well. The pathologist studies the tissue and checks for Reed-Sternberg cells, large abnormal cells that are usually found with Hodgkin's disease.

If the biopsy reveals Hodgkin's disease, the doctor needs to learn the stage, or extent, of the disease. Staging is a careful attempt to find out whether the cancer has spread and, if so, what parts of the body are affected. Treatment decisions for Hodgkin's disease depend on these findings.

The doctor considers the following to determine the stage of Hodgkin's disease:

- The number and location of affected lymph nodes;
- Whether the affected lymph nodes are on one or both sides of the diaphragm (the thin muscle under the lungs and heart that separates the chest from the abdomen);
- Whether the disease has spread to the bone marrow, spleen, or places outside the lymphatic system, such as the liver.

In staging, the doctor may use some of the same tests used for the diagnosis of Hodgkin's disease. Other staging procedures may include additional biopsies of lymph nodes, the liver, bone marrow, or other tissue. A bone marrow biopsy involves removing a

Staging for Hodgkin's Disease

Once Hodgkin's disease is found, more tests will be done to find out if the cancer has spread from where it started to other parts of the body. This testing is called staging. A doctor needs to know the stage of the disease to plan treatment.

- **Stage I.** Cancer is found in only one lymph node area or in only one area or organ outside of the lymph nodes.
- **Stage II.** Either of the following means the disease is stage II: Cancer is found in two or more lymph node areas on the same side of the diaphragm (the thin muscle under the lungs that helps us breathe). Cancer is found in only one area or organ outside of the lymph nodes and in the lymph nodes around it. Other lymph node areas on the same side of the diaphragm may also have cancer.

- **Stage III.** Cancer is found in lymph node areas on both sides of the diaphragm. The cancer may also have spread to an area or organ near the lymph node areas and/or to the spleen.
- **Stage IV.** Either of the following means the disease is stage IV: Cancer has spread in more than one spot to an organ or organs outside the lymph system. Cancer cells may or may not be found in the lymph nodes near these organs. Cancer has spread to only one organ outside the lymph system, but lymph nodes far away from that organ are involved.
- **Recurrent.** Recurrent disease means that the cancer has come back after it has been treated. It may come back in the area where it first started or in another part of the body.

sample of bone marrow through a needle inserted into the hip or another large bone. Rarely, an operation called a laparotomy may be performed. During this operation, a surgeon makes an incision through the wall of the abdomen and removes samples of tissue. A pathologist examines tissue samples under a microscope to check for cancer cells.

Treatment

The doctor develops a treatment plan to fit each patient's needs. Treatment for Hodgkin's disease depends on the stage of the disease, the size of the enlarged lymph nodes, which symptoms are present, the age and general health of the patient, and other factors.

Patients with Hodgkin's disease may be vaccinated against the flu, pneumonia, and meningitis. They should discuss a vaccination plan with their health-care provider.

Hodgkin's disease is often treated by a team of specialists that may include a medical oncologist, oncology nurse, and/or radiation oncologist. Hodgkin's disease is usually treated with radiation therapy or chemotherapy. The doctors may decide to use one treatment method or a combination of methods. Taking part in a clinical trial (research study) to evaluate promising new ways to treat Hodgkin's disease is an important option for many people with this disease (page 181).

Radiation therapy and chemotherapy are the most common treatments for Hodgkin's disease, although bone marrow transplantation, peripheral stem cell transplantation, and biological therapies are being studied in clinical trials.

Radiation therapy (also called radiotherapy) is the use of high-energy rays to kill cancer cells. Depending on the stage of the disease, treatment with radiation may be given alone or with chemotherapy. Radiation therapy is local therapy; it affects cancer cells only in the treated area. Radiation treatment for Hodgkin's disease usually involves external radiation, which comes from a machine that aims the rays at a specific area of the body. External radiation does not cause the body to become radioactive. Most often, treatment is given on an outpatient basis in a hospital or clinic.

Chemotherapy is the use of drugs to kill cancer cells. Chemotherapy for Hodgkin's disease usually consists of a combination of several drugs. It may be given alone or followed by radiation therapy.

Chemotherapy is usually given in cycles: a treatment period followed by a recovery period, then another treatment period, and so on. Most anticancer drugs are given by injection into a blood vessel (IV); some are given by mouth. Chemotherapy is a systemic therapy, meaning that the drugs enter the bloodstream and travel throughout the body.

Usually, a patient has chemotherapy as an outpatient (at the hospital, at the doctor's office, or at home). However, depending on which drugs are given and the patient's general health, a short hospital stay may be needed.

Side Effects of Treatment
Treatments for Hodgkin's disease are very powerful. It is hard to limit the effects of therapy so that only cancer cells are destroyed. Because treatment also damages healthy cells and tissues, it often causes side effects.

The side effects of cancer treatment depend mainly on the type and extent of the therapy. Side effects may not be the same for everyone, and they may even change from one treatment to the next. Doctors and nurses can explain the possible side effects of treatment. They can also lessen or control many of the side effects that may occur during and after treatment.

Radiation Therapy
The side effects of radiation depend on the treatment dose and the part of the body that is treated. During radiation therapy, people are likely to become extremely tired, especially in the later weeks of treatment. Rest is important, but doctors usually advise patients to try to stay as active as they can.

It is common to lose hair in the treated area and for the skin to become red, dry, tender, and itchy. There may also be permanent darkening or "bronzing" of the skin in the treated area.

When the chest and neck are treated, patients may have a dry, sore throat and some trouble swallowing. Sometimes, they have shortness of breath or a dry cough. Radiation therapy to the abdomen may cause nausea, vomiting, diarrhea, or urinary discomfort. Often, changes in diet or medicine can ease these problems.

Radiation therapy also may cause a decrease in the number of white blood cells, cells that help protect the body against infection, or platelets, cells that help the blood to clot. If that happens, patients need to be careful to avoid possible sources of infection or injury. The doctor monitors a patient's blood count very carefully during radiation treatment. If necessary, treatment may have to be postponed to let the blood counts return to normal.

Although the side effects of radiation therapy can be difficult, they can usually be treated or controlled. It may also help to know that, in most cases, side effects are not permanent. However, patients may want to discuss with their doctor the possible long-term effects of radiation treatment on fertility (the ability to produce children) and the increased chance of second cancers after treatment is over. (The "Follow-up Care" section includes more information about the chance for second cancers.) Loss of fertility may be temporary or permanent, depending on whether the testes or ovaries received radiation and the patient's age. For men, sperm

H

banking before treatment may be a choice. Women's menstrual periods may stop, and they may have hot flashes and vaginal dryness. Menstrual periods are more likely to return for younger women.

Chemotherapy

The side effects of chemotherapy depend mainly on the specific drugs and the doses the patient receives. As with other types of treatment, side effects may vary from person to person.

Anticancer drugs generally affect cells that divide rapidly. In addition to cancer cells, these include blood cells, which fight infection, help the blood to clot, and carry oxygen to all parts of the body. When blood cells are affected, the patient is more likely to get infections, may bruise or bleed easily, and may feel unusually weak and tired.

Cells in hair roots also divide rapidly; therefore, chemotherapy may lead to hair loss. Hair loss is a major concern for many patients. Some anticancer drugs only cause the hair to thin out, while others may result in the loss of all body hair. People may cope with hair loss better if they decide how to handle hair loss before starting treatment.

Cells that line the digestive tract also divide rapidly, and are often damaged by chemotherapy. As a result, side effects may include poor appetite, nausea and vomiting, and/or mouth and lip sores.

Most side effects go away gradually during the recovery periods between treatments or after treatment is over. Sometimes, however, chemotherapy results in a permanent loss of fertility.

Follow-up Care

People who have had Hodgkin's disease should have regular follow-up examinations after their treatment is over and for the rest of their lives. Follow-up care is an important part of the overall treatment process, and people who have had cancer should not hesitate to discuss it with their health-care provider. Patients treated for Hodgkin's disease have an increased chance of developing leukemia; non-Hodgkin's lymphoma; and cancers of the colon, lung, bone, thyroid, and breast. Regular follow-up care ensures that patients are carefully monitored, any changes in health are discussed, and new or recurrent cancer can be detected and treated as soon as possible. Between follow-up appointments, people who have had Hodgkin's disease should report any health problems as soon as they appear.

National Cancer Institute

At least 45,000 Americans die of flu-related complications (most often pneumonia) every year—and 90 percent of them are age 65 or older. The flu can lead to other complications, such as dehydration, and worsen underlying chronic medical conditions (such as congestive heart failure or asthma). Nearly a third of all people over 50 have a chronic medical problem—such as diabetes; heart, lung, or kidney ailments; or a suppressed immune system (usually from cancer treatment)—that places them at high risk for flu-related hospitalization and death. For these reasons, the Centers for Disease Control and Prevention (CDC) recommends an annual flu vaccination for every person over 50.

Causes

Known more properly as influenza, the flu is a respiratory infection caused by the influenza virus. The two main types are influenza A and influenza B. Both typically spread when an infected person coughs or sneezes and expels the virus into the air, where it can linger for as long as three hours. People become infected by either inhaling the virus or touching a contaminated object, such as a phone, that the flu sufferer has used.

Symptoms

After infection, symptoms usually appear within two to four days. These include fever of up to 104°F, chills, headache, dry cough, runny or stuffy nose, sore throat, muscle aches (particularly in the back and legs), and extreme fatigue.

Treatment

If you do contract the flu, over-the-counter medications can treat the symptoms but not the underlying illness. The prescription antibiotics used to treat bacterial infections are not effective against viral infections. But two prescription antiviral drugs—zanamivir (Relenza) and oseltamivir (Tamiflu)—can speed recovery. They work by blocking an enzyme that flu viruses need to reproduce, which may reduce the severity and duration of symptoms and inhibit the spread of infection to members of the same household. Zanamivir is inhaled; oseltamivir is taken as a pill.

Two other prescription pills—amantadine (the anti-Parkinson's drug Symmetrel and others) and rimantadine (Flumadine)—can also reduce the duration of symptoms but only for influenza A. In addition, they are 70 percent to 90 percent effective when used for prevention. These medications may be particularly helpful for people who cannot be vaccinated or who require extra protection, perhaps because of other medical problems.

All four medications shorten the duration of symptoms by about 24 hours—to a little less than 6 days from 7—when otherwise healthy adults take them within 48 hours of infection. For unknown reasons, zanamivir and oseltamivir seem to be less effective in older people. Zanamivir appears to be more helpful in patients with a high temperature or severe symptoms. The cost of treatment is significant—about $50 for one day of relief.

Side Effects of Treatment

Rimantadine and especially amantadine can cause lightheadedness, nervousness, difficulty concentrating, and inability to sleep. Older people are particularly vulnerable. One study in the *Archives of Internal Medicine* evaluated 156 nursing home patients, average age 84, with influenza A, who were administered both drugs sequentially. While only 3 experienced adverse side effects while using rimantadine, 29 did with amantadine. Confusion was the most common complication, followed by agitation and hallucinations.

Zanamivir and oseltamivir were developed to eliminate the side effects of amantadine and rimantadine, but they can present their own problems. Zanamivir may cause a decline in respiration rate and volume, as well as bronchospasm (spasmodic contractions of the airways), which makes the drug inappropriate for people with breathing disorders such as asthma or chronic obstructive pulmonary disease. Oseltamivir may cause nausea and vomiting, which can be avoided by taking it with food.

Prevention

The CDC stresses that no medication is a substitute for preventive measures. When taken for treating the flu, none of the four antiviral medications has been proven effective in preventing or minimizing serious influenza-related complications such as pneumonia or the worsening of chronic diseases. Furthermore, each can cause troublesome side effects. Thus, prevention remains the best strategy.

The best way to prevent flu is annual vaccination, along with healthy lifestyle measures that include getting enough sleep, eating right, stress reduction, moderate exercise, and frequent hand washing. Yearly vaccination is vital because immunity is believed to last only about 12 months. Even if protection does persist, flu viruses constantly mutate. Therefore, the vaccine, which is given by injection, must be reformulated annually.

Vaccination is 70 percent to 90 percent effective in healthy young adults. While it will not prevent illness in everyone, it can reduce the severity of symptoms and the risk of complications. Moreover, vaccination is covered by Medicare, as well as by most health maintenance organizations and other types of insurance plans.

Vaccination may protect against other serious health risks, too. A study of 233 people with coronary heart disease found that flu vaccination reduced the risk of heart attack by 67 percent.

Since it typically takes one to two weeks for the immune system to respond to the vaccine, it's wise to get your shot as soon as the year's formulation becomes available—usually in October. People allergic to eggs should abstain because the vaccine contains a protein (albumin) derived from eggs. Those with certain other allergies or medical problems, such as bronchitis or pneumonia, should consult their doctor first.

Irritable bowel syndrome (IBS) is a common disorder of the intestines that leads to crampy pain, gassiness, bloating, and changes in bowel habits. Some people with IBS have constipation (difficult or infrequent bowel movements); others have diarrhea (frequent loose stools, often with an urgent need to move the bowels); and some people experience both. Sometimes the person with IBS has a crampy urge to move the bowels but cannot do so.

Through the years, IBS has been called by many names—colitis, mucous colitis, spastic colon, spastic bowel, and functional bowel disease. Most of these terms are inaccurate. Colitis, for instance, means inflammation of the large intestine (colon). IBS, however, does not cause inflammation and should not be confused with another disorder, ulcerative colitis.

The cause of IBS is not known, and as yet there is no cure. Doctors call it a functional disorder because there is no sign of disease when the colon is examined. IBS causes a great deal of discomfort and distress, but it does not cause permanent harm to the intestines and does not lead to intestinal bleeding of the bowel or to a serious disease such as cancer. Often IBS is just a mild annoyance, but for some people it can be disabling. They may be unable to go to social events, to go out to a job, or to travel even short distances. Most people with IBS, however, are able to control their symptoms through medications prescribed by their physicians, diet, and stress management.

What Causes IBS?

The colon, which is about six feet long, connects the small intestine with the rectum and anus. The major function of the colon is to absorb water and salts from digestive products that enter from the small intestine. Two quarts of liquid matter enter the colon from the small intestine each day. This material may remain there for several days until most of the fluid and salts are absorbed into the body. The stool then passes through the colon by a pattern of movements to the left side of the colon, where it is stored until a bowel movement occurs.

Colon motility (contraction of intestinal muscles and movement of its contents) is controlled by nerves and hormones and by electrical activity in the colon muscle. The electrical activity serves as a "pacemaker" similar to the mechanism that controls heart function.

Movements of the colon propel the contents slowly back and forth but mainly toward the rectum. A few times each day strong muscle contractions move down the colon pushing fecal material ahead of them. Some of these strong contractions result in a bowel movement.

Because doctors have been unable to find an organic cause, IBS often has been thought to be caused by emotional conflict or stress. While stress may worsen IBS symptoms, research suggests that other factors also are important. Researchers have found that the colon muscle of a person with IBS begins to spasm after only mild stimulation. The person with IBS seems to have a colon that is more sensitive and reactive than usual, so it responds strongly to stimuli that would not bother most people.

Ordinary events such as eating and distention from gas or other material in the colon can cause the colon to overreact in the person with IBS. Certain medicines and foods may trigger spasms in some people. Sometimes the spasm delays the passage of stool, leading to constipation. Chocolate, milk products, or large amounts of alcohol are frequent offenders. Caffeine causes loose stools in many people, but it is more likely to affect those with IBS. Researchers also have found that women with IBS may have more symptoms during their menstrual periods, suggesting that reproductive hormones can increase IBS symptoms.

What Are the Symptoms of IBS?

If you are concerned about IBS, it is important to realize that normal bowel function varies from person to person. Normal bowel movements range from as many as three stools a day to as few as three a week. A normal movement is one that is formed but not hard, contains no blood, and is passed without cramps or pain.

People with IBS, on the other hand, usually have crampy abdominal pain with painful constipation or diarrhea. In some people, constipation and diarrhea alternate. Sometimes people with IBS pass mucus with their bowel movements. Bleeding, fever, weight loss, and persistent severe pain are not symptoms of IBS but may indicate other problems.

How Is IBS Diagnosed?

IBS usually is diagnosed after doctors exclude the presence of disease. To get to that point, the doctor will take a complete medical history that includes a careful description of symptoms. A physical examination and laboratory tests will be done. A stool sample will be tested for evidence of bleeding. The doctor also may do diagnostic procedures such as x-rays or endoscopy (viewing the colon through a flexible tube inserted through the anus) to find out if there is disease.

How Do Diet and Stress Affect IBS?

The potential for abnormal function of the colon is always present in people with IBS, but a trigger also must be present to cause symptoms. The most likely culprits seem to be diet and emotional stress. Many people report that their symptoms occur following a meal or when they are under stress. No one is sure why this happens, but scientists have some clues.

Eating causes contractions of the colon. Normally, this response may cause an urge to have a bowel movement within 30 to 60 minutes after a meal. In people with IBS, the urge may come sooner with cramps and diarrhea.

The strength of the response is often related to the number of calories in a meal and especially the amount of fat in a meal. Fat in any form (animal or vegetable) is a strong stimulus of colonic contractions after a meal. Many foods contain fat, especially meats of all kinds, poultry skin, whole milk, cream, cheese, butter, vegetable oil, margarine, shortening, avocados, and whipped toppings.

Stress also stimulates colonic spasm in people with IBS. This process is not completely understood, but scientists point out that the colon is controlled partly by the nervous system. Stress reduction (relaxation) training or counseling and support help relieve IBS symptoms in some people. However, doctors are quick to note that this does not mean IBS is the result of a personality disorder. IBS is at least partly a disorder of colon motility.

How Does a Good Diet Help IBS?

For many people, eating a proper diet lessens IBS symptoms. Before changing your diet, it is a good idea to keep a journal noting which foods seem to cause distress. Discuss your findings with your doctor. You also may want to consult a registered dietitian, who can help you make changes in your diet. For instance, if dairy products cause your symptoms to flare up, you can try eating less of those foods. Yogurt might be tolerated better because it contains organisms that supply lactase, the enzyme needed to digest lactose, the sugar found in milk products.

Because dairy products are an important source of calcium and other nutrients that your body needs, be sure to get adequate nutrients in the foods that you substitute.

Dietary fiber may lessen IBS symptoms in many cases. Whole grain breads and cereals, beans, fruits, and vegetables are good sources of fiber. Consult your doctor before using an over-the-counter fiber supplement. High-fiber diets keep the colon mildly distended, which may help to prevent spasms from developing. Some forms of fiber also keep water in the stools, thereby preventing hard stools that are difficult to pass. Doctors usually recommend that you eat just enough fiber so that you have soft, easily passed, and painless bowel movements. High-fiber diets may cause gas and bloating, but within a few weeks, these symptoms often go away as your body adjusts to the diet.

Large meals can cause cramping and diarrhea in people with IBS. Symptoms may be eased if you eat smaller meals more frequently or just eat smaller portions at mealtime. This should help, especially if your meals are low in fat and high in carbohydrates such as pasta, rice, whole-grain breads and cereals, fruits, and vegetables.

Can Medicines Relieve IBS Symptoms?

Your doctor may prescribe fiber supplements or occasional laxatives if you are constipated. Some doctors prescribe drugs that control colon muscle spasms, drugs that slow the movement of food through the digestive system, tranquilizers, or anti-depressant drugs, all of which may relieve symptoms.

It is important to follow the physician's instructions when taking IBS medications—particularly laxatives, which can be habit forming if not used carefully.

Is IBS Linked to Other Diseases?

IBS has not been shown to lead to any serious, organic diseases. No link has been established between IBS and inflammatory bowel diseases such as Crohn's disease or ulcerative colitis. IBS does not lead to cancer. Some patients have a more severe form of IBS, and the pain and diarrhea may cause them to withdraw from normal activities. These patients need to work with their physicians to find the best combination of medicine, diet, counseling, and support to control their symptoms.

National Institute of Diabetes and Digestive and Kidney Diseases

The kidneys are two reddish-brown, bean-shaped organs located just above the waist, one on each side of the spine. They are part of the urinary system. Their main function is to filter blood and produce urine to rid the body of waste. As blood flows through the kidneys, they remove waste products and unneeded water. The resulting liquid, urine, collects in the middle of each kidney in an area called the renal pelvis. Urine drains from each kidney through a long tube, the ureter, into the bladder, where it is stored. Urine leaves the body through another tube, called the urethra.

The kidneys also produce substances that help control blood pressure and regulate the formation of red blood cells.

Several types of cancer can develop in the kidney. *This entry discusses renal cell cancer, the most common form of kidney cancer in adults.* Transitional cell cancer (carcinoma), which affects the renal pelvis, is a less common form of kidney cancer. It is similar to cancer that occurs in the bladder and is often treated like bladder cancer. Wilms' tumor, the most common type of childhood kidney cancer, is different from kidney cancer in adults.

As kidney cancer grows, it may invade organs near the kidney, such as the liver, colon, or pancreas. Kidney cancer cells may also break away from the original tumor and spread (metastasize) to other parts of the body. When kidney cancer spreads, cancer

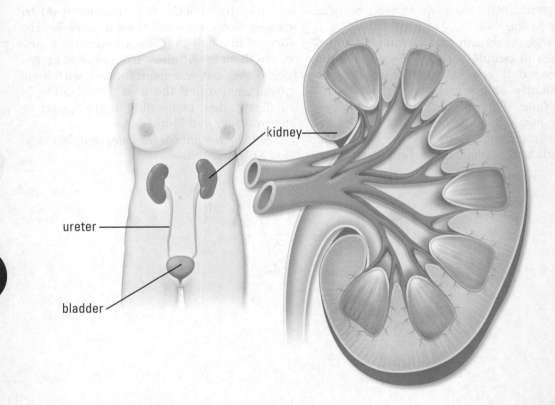

kidney

ureter

bladder

The kidneys are bean-shaped organs that produce urine to eliminate wastes, chemicals, and excess water from the body. Tumors of the kidney tend to form on the organ's top outer edge.

cells may appear in the lymph nodes. For this reason, lymph nodes near the kidney may be removed during surgery. If the pathologist finds cancer cells in the lymph nodes, it may mean that the disease has spread to other parts of the body. Kidney cancer may spread and form new tumors, most often in the bones or lungs. The new tumors have the same kind of abnormal cells and the same name as the original (primary) tumor in the kidney. For example, if kidney cancer spreads to the lungs, the cancer cells in the lungs are kidney cancer cells. The disease is metastatic kidney cancer; it is not lung cancer.

Possible Causes and Prevention

Scientists at hospitals and medical centers all across the country are studying kidney cancer. They are trying to learn what causes this disease and how to prevent it. At this time, scientists do not know exactly what causes kidney cancer, and they can seldom explain why one person gets this disease and another does not. However, it is clear that this disease is not contagious; no one can "catch" kidney cancer from another person.

Researchers study patterns of cancer in the population to look for factors that are more common in people who get kidney cancer than in people who don't. These studies help researchers find possible risk factors for kidney cancer. It is important to know that most people with these risk factors do not get cancer, and people who do get kidney cancer may have none of these factors.

As with most other types of cancer, studies show that the risk of kidney cancer increases with age. It occurs most often between the ages of 50 and 70. It affects almost twice as many men as women. In addition, kidney cancer is somewhat more common among African-American men than white men. Other risk factors for kidney cancer include:

- **Tobacco use.** Research shows that smokers are twice as likely to develop kidney cancer as nonsmokers. In addition, the longer a person smokes, the higher the risk. However, the risk of kidney cancer decreases for those who quit smoking.
- **Obesity.** Obesity may increase the risk of developing kidney cancer. In several studies, obesity has been associated with increased risk in women. One report suggests that being overweight may be a risk factor for men, too. The reasons for this possible link are not clear.
- **Occupational exposure.** A number of studies have examined occupational exposures to see whether they increase workers' chances of developing kidney cancer. Studies suggest, for example, that coke oven workers in steel plants have above-average rates of kidney cancer. In addition, there is some evidence that asbestos in the workplace, which has been linked to cancers of the lung and mesothelium (a membrane that surrounds internal organs of the body), also increases the risk of some kidney cancers.
- **Radiation.** Women who have been treated with radiation therapy for disorders of the uterus may have a slightly increased risk of developing kidney cancer. Also, people who were exposed to thorotrast (thorium dioxide), a radioactive substance used in the 1920s with certain diagnostic x-rays, have an increased rate of kidney cancer. However, this substance is no longer in use, and scientists think that radiation accounts for an extremely small percentage of the total number of kidney cancers.
- **Phenacetin.** Some people have developed kidney cancer after heavy, long-term use of this drug. This painkilling drug is no longer sold in the United States.
- **Dialysis.** Patients on long-term use of dialysis to treat chronic kidney failure have

K

an increased risk of developing renal cysts and renal cancer. Further study is needed to learn more about the long-term effects of dialysis on patients with kidney failure.

- **Von Hippel-Lindau (VHL) disease.** Researchers have found that people who have this inherited disorder are at greater risk of developing renal cell carcinoma, as well as tumors in other organs.Researchers have found the gene responsible for VHL, and they believe that the isolation of this gene may lead to improved methods of diagnosis, treatment, and even prevention of some kidney cancers.

People who think they may be at risk for developing kidney cancer should discuss this concern with their doctor. The doctor may suggest ways to reduce the risk and help plan an appropriate schedule for checkups.

Symptoms

In its early stages, kidney cancer usually causes no obvious signs or troublesome symptoms. However, as a kidney tumor grows, symptoms may occur. These may include:

- Blood in the urine. Blood may be present one day and not the next. In some cases, a person can actually see the blood, or traces of it may be found in urinalysis, a lab test often performed as part of a regular medical checkup.
- A lump or mass in the kidney area.

Other less common symptoms may include:

- Fatigue
- Loss of appetite
- Weight loss
- Recurrent fevers
- A pain in the side that doesn't go away
- A general feeling of poor health

High blood pressure (hypertension) or a lower than normal number of red cells in the blood (anemia) may also signal a kidney tumor; however, these symptoms occur less often.

These symptoms may be caused by cancer or by other, less serious problems such as an infection or a cyst. Only a doctor can make a diagnosis. People with any of these symptoms may see their family doctor or a urologist, a doctor who specializes in diseases of the urinary system. Usually, early cancer does not cause pain; it is important not to wait to feel pain before seeing a doctor.

In most cases, the earlier cancer is diagnosed and treated, the better a person's chance for a full recovery.

Diagnosis

To find the cause of symptoms, the doctor asks about the patient's medical history and does a physical exam. In addition to checking for general signs of health, the doctor may perform blood and urine tests. The doctor may also carefully feel the abdomen for lumps or irregular masses.

The doctor usually orders tests that produce pictures of the kidneys and nearby organs. These pictures can often show changes in the kidney and surrounding tissue. For example, an IVP (intravenous pyelogram) is a series of x-rays of the kidneys, ureters, and bladder after the injection of a dye. The dye may be placed in the body through a needle or a narrow tube called a catheter. The pictures produced can show changes in the shape of these organs and nearby lymph nodes.

Another test, arteriography, is a series of x-rays of the blood vessels. Dye is injected into a large blood vessel through a catheter. X-rays show the dye as it moves through the network of smaller blood vessels in and around the kidney.

Other imaging tests may include CT scan, MRI, and ultrasonography, which can show

K

the difference between diseased and healthy tissues.

If test results suggest that kidney cancer may be present, a biopsy may be performed; it is the only sure way to diagnose cancer. During a biopsy for kidney cancer, a thin needle is inserted into the tumor and a sample of tissue is withdrawn. A pathologist then examines the tissue under a microscope to check for cancer cells.

Once kidney cancer is diagnosed, the doctor will want to learn the stage, or extent, of the disease. Staging is a careful attempt to find out whether the cancer has spread and, if so, what parts of the body are affected. This information is needed to plan treatment.

To stage kidney cancer, the doctor may use additional MRI and x-ray studies of the tissues and blood vessels in and around the kidney. The doctor can check for swollen lymph nodes in the chest and abdomen through CT scans. Chest x-rays can often show whether cancer has spread to the lungs. Bone scans reveal changes that may be a sign that the cancer has spread to the bones.

Treatment

Treatment for kidney cancer depends on the stage of the disease, the patient's general health and age, and other factors. The doctor develops a treatment plan to fit each patient's needs.

People with kidney cancer are often treated by a team of specialists, which may include a urologist, an oncologist, and a radiation oncologist. Kidney cancer is usually treated with surgery, radiation therapy, biological therapy, chemotherapy, or hormone therapy. Sometimes a special treatment called arterial embolization is used. The doctors may decide to use one treatment method or a combination of methods.

Some people take part in a clinical trial (research study) using new treatment methods. Such studies are designed to improve cancer treatment.

Surgery is the most common treatment for kidney cancer. An operation to remove the kidney is called a nephrectomy. Most often, the surgeon removes the whole kidney along with the adrenal gland and the tissue around the kidney. Some lymph nodes in the area may also be removed. This procedure is called a radical nephrectomy. In some cases, the surgeon removes only the kidney (simple nephrectomy). The remaining kidney generally is able to perform the work of both kidneys. In another procedure, partial nephrectomy, the surgeon removes just the part of the kidney that contains the tumor.

Arterial embolization is sometimes used before an operation to make surgery easier. It also may be used to provide relief from pain or bleeding when removal of the tumor is not possible. Small pieces of a special gelatin sponge or other material are injected through a catheter to clog the main renal blood vessel. This procedure shrinks the tumor by depriving it of the oxygen-carrying blood and other substances it needs to grow.

Radiation therapy (also called radiotherapy) uses high-energy rays to kill cancer cells. Doctors sometimes use radiation therapy to relieve pain (palliative therapy) when kidney cancer has spread to the bone.

Radiation therapy for kidney cancer involves external radiation, which comes from radioactive material outside the body. A machine aims the rays at a specific area of the body. Most often, treatment is given on an outpatient basis in a hospital or clinic five days a week for several weeks. This schedule helps protect normal tissue by spreading out the total dose of radiation. The patient does not need to stay in the hospital for radiation therapy, and patients are not radioactive during or after treatment.

K

Surgery and arterial embolization are local therapy; they affect cancer cells only in the treated area. Biological therapy, chemotherapy, and hormone therapy, explained below, are systemic treatments because they travel through the bloodstream and can reach cells throughout the body.

Biological therapy (also called immunotherapy) is a form of treatment that uses the body's natural ability (immune system) to fight cancer. Interleukin-2 and interferon are types of biological therapy used to treat advanced kidney cancer. Clinical trials continue to examine better ways to use biological therapy while reducing the side effects patients may experience. Many people having biological therapy stay in the hospital during treatment so that these side effects can be monitored.

Chemotherapy is the use of drugs to kill cancer cells. Although useful in the treatment of many other cancers, chemotherapy has shown only limited effectiveness against kidney cancer. However, researchers continue to study new drugs and new drug combinations that may prove to be more useful.

Hormone therapy is used in a small number of patients with advanced kidney cancer. Some kidney cancers may be treated with hormones to try to control the growth of cancer cells. More often, it is used as palliative therapy.

Side Effects of Treatment

It is hard to limit the effects of therapy so that only cancer cells are removed or destroyed. Because treatment also damages healthy cells and tissues, it often causes unwanted side effects. The side effects of cancer therapy depend mainly on the type and extent of the treatment. Also, side effects may not be the same for each person, and they may even change from one treatment to the next. Doctors and nurses can explain the possible side effects of therapy, and they can help relieve problems that may occur during and after treatment. Patients should notify a doctor of the side effects they are having, as some may require immediate medical attention.

Surgery

The side effects of kidney surgery depend on the type of operation, the patient's general health, and other factors. Nephrectomy is major surgery, and after the operation most people have pain and discomfort. Patients may find it difficult to breathe deeply due to discomfort from surgery; they may have to do special coughing and breathing exercises to help keep their lungs clear. It is also common for patients who have had surgery to feel tired or weak for a while.

In addition, patients may need intravenous (IV) feeding and fluids for several days before and after the operation. When a kidney is removed, the one remaining kidney takes over the work of both. Nurses will monitor the amount of fluid a person takes in and the amount of urine produced. The length of time it takes to recover from an operation varies for each person.

Arterial Embolization

Arterial embolization can cause pain, fever, nausea, or vomiting. Often, people need IV fluids as the body recovers from this procedure.

Radiation Therapy

With radiation therapy, the side effects depend on the treatment dose and the part of the body that is treated. Patients are likely to become very tired, especially in the later weeks of treatment. Resting is important, but doctors usually advise patients to try to stay as active as they can.

It is common for the skin in the treated area to become red, dry, tender, and itchy. There may be permanent darkening or "bronzing" of the skin in the treated area. Radiation to the kidney and nearby areas may cause nausea, vomiting, diarrhea, or urinary discomfort. It may also cause a decrease in the number of white blood cells, cells that help protect the body against infection.

Biological Therapy

The side effects caused by biological therapy vary with the type of treatment. These treatments may cause flu-like symptoms such as chills, fever, muscle aches, weakness, loss of appetite, nausea, vomiting, and diarrhea. Patients often feel very tired after treatment, and they may bleed or bruise easily. Some people also get a skin rash. In addition, interleukin therapy can cause swelling and can interfere with normal liver or kidney function. These problems can be severe, but they go away after the treatment stops.

Chemotherapy

The side effects of chemotherapy depend on the drugs that are given. In general, anticancer drugs affect rapidly growing cells, such as blood cells that fight infection, cells that line the digestive tract, and cells in the hair follicles. As a result, patients may have side effects such as lower resistance to infection, loss of appetite, nausea, vomiting, or mouth sores. They may also have less energy and may lose their hair.

Hormone Therapy

The side effects of hormone therapy are usually mild. Progesterone is the hormone most often used to treat kidney cancer. Drugs containing progesterone may cause changes in appetite and weight. They may also cause swelling or fluid retention. These side effects generally go away after treatment.

Follow-up Care

Regular follow-up by the doctor is important after treatment for kidney cancer. The doctor will suggest appropriate follow-up that may include a physical exam, chest x-rays, and laboratory tests. The doctor sometimes orders scans and other tests. Patients should continue to have follow-up visits. They should also report any problem as soon as it appears.

National Cancer Institute

K

Your two kidneys are vital organs, performing many functions to keep your blood clean and chemically balanced. Understanding how your kidneys work can help you to keep them healthy.

What Do the Kidneys Do?

The kidneys remove wastes and extra water from the blood to form urine. Urine flows from the kidneys to the bladder through the ureters.

Your kidneys are bean-shaped organs, each about the size of your fist. They are located near the middle of your back, just below the rib cage. The kidneys are sophisticated reprocessing machines. Every day, your kidneys process about 200 quarts of blood to sift out about 2 quarts of waste products and extra water. The waste and extra water become urine, which flows to your bladder through tubes called ureters. Your bladder stores urine until you go to the bathroom.

The wastes in your blood come from the normal breakdown of active tissues and from the food you eat. Your body uses the food for energy and self-repair. After your body has taken what it needs from the food, waste is sent to the blood. If your kidneys did not remove these wastes, the wastes would build up in the blood and damage your body.

The actual filtering occurs in tiny units inside your kidneys called nephrons. Every kidney has about a million nephrons. In the nephron, a glomerulus—which is a tiny blood vessel, or capillary—intertwines with a tiny urine-collecting tube called a tubule. A complicated chemical exchange takes place, as waste materials and water leave your blood and enter your urinary system.

At first, the tubules receive a combination of waste materials and chemicals that your body can still use. Your kidneys measure out chemicals like sodium, phosphorus, and potassium and release them back to the blood to return to the body. In this way, your kidneys regulate the body's level of these substances. The right balance is necessary for life, but excess levels can be harmful.

What Is "Renal Function"?

Your health-care team may talk about the work your kidneys do as renal function. If you have two healthy kidneys, you have 100 percent of your renal function. This is more renal function than you really need. Some people are born with only one kidney, and these people are able to lead normal, healthy lives. Many people donate a kidney for transplantation to a family member or friend. Small declines in renal function do not cause a problem. In fact, you can be healthy with 50 percent of your renal function if it remains stable.

But many people with 50 percent of their renal function have a kidney disease that will get worse. You will have some serious health problems if you have less than 20 percent of your renal function. If your renal function drops below 10 percent to 15 percent, you cannot live long without renal replacement therapy (dialysis or transplantation).

Why Do Kidneys Fail?

Most kidney diseases attack the nephrons, causing them to lose their filtering capacity. Damage to the nephrons may happen quickly, often as the result of injury or poisoning. But most kidney diseases destroy the nephrons slowly and silently. It may take years or even decades for the damage to become apparent. The two most common causes of kidney disease are diabetes and high blood pressure. If your family has a history of any kidney problems, you may be at risk for kidney disease.

K

Diabetic Nephropathy
Diabetes is a disease that keeps the body from using glucose (sugar) as it should. If glucose stays in your blood instead of breaking down, it can act like a poison. Damage to the nephrons from unused glucose in the blood is called diabetic nephropathy. If you keep your blood glucose levels down, you can delay or prevent diabetic nephropathy.

High Blood Pressure
High blood pressure can damage the small blood vessels in your kidneys. The damaged vessels cannot filter poisons from your blood as they are supposed to.

Your doctor may prescribe blood pressure medication. A group of blood pressure medicines called angiotensin converting enzyme (ACE) inhibitors have been found to protect the kidneys even more than other medicines that lower blood pressure to similar levels. A related group of drugs called angiotensin II receptor blockers (ARBs) may also be effective. The National Heart, Lung, and Blood Institute recommends that people with reduced kidney function--anyone who has 1 gram or more of protein in a 24-hour urine collection--should keep their blood pressure at or below 125/75 mm Hg.

Glomerulonephritis
Several different types of kidney disease are grouped together under this category. Protein, blood, or both in the urine are often the first signs of these diseases. They can slowly destroy kidney function. Blood pressure control is important, and different treatments for the different types of glomerulonephritis may be used.

Inherited and Congenital Kidney Diseases
Some kidney diseases result from hereditary factors. Polycystic kidney disease (PKD),

for example, is a genetic disorder in which many cysts grow in the kidneys. PKD cysts can slowly replace much of the mass of the kidneys, reducing kidney function and leading to kidney failure.

Some kidney problems may show up when a child is still developing in the womb. Examples include autosomal recessive PKD, a rare form of PKD, and other developmental problems that interfere with the normal formation of the nephrons. The signs of kidney disease in children vary. A child may grow unusually slowly, may vomit often, or may have back or side pain. Some kidney diseases may be "silent" for months or even years.

Some hereditary kidney diseases may not be detected until adulthood. The most common form of PKD was once called "adult PKD" because the symptoms of high blood pressure and renal failure usually do not occur until patients are in their twenties or thirties. But with advances in imaging technology, doctors have found cysts in children and adolescents before any symptoms appear.

Other Causes of Kidney Disease
Poisons and trauma, for example a direct and forceful blow to your kidneys, can lead to kidney disease.

Some over-the-counter medicines can be poisonous to your kidneys if taken regularly over a long period of time. Products that combine aspirin, acetaminophen, and other medicines such as ibuprofen have been found to be the most dangerous to the kidneys. If you take painkillers regularly, check with your doctor to make sure you are not putting your kidneys at risk.

How Do Kidneys Fail?
Many factors that influence the speed of kidney failure are not completely understood.

Researchers are still studying how protein in the diet and cholesterol levels in the blood affect kidney function.

Acute Renal Failure

Some kidney problems happen quickly, like an accident that injures the kidneys. Losing a lot of blood can cause sudden kidney failure. Some drugs or poisons can make your kidneys stop working. These sudden drops in kidney function are called acute renal failure (ARF).

ARF may lead to permanent loss of kidney function. But if your kidneys are not seriously damaged, acute renal failure may be reversed.

Chronic Kidney Disease

Most kidney problems, however, happen slowly. You may have "silent" kidney disease for years. Gradual loss of kidney function is called chronic renal failure or chronic renal disease.

End-Stage Renal Disease

The condition of total or nearly total and permanent kidney failure is called end-stage renal disease (ESRD). People with ESRD must undergo dialysis or transplantation to stay alive.

What Are the Signs of Kidney Disease?

People in the early stages of kidney disease may not feel sick at all. The first signs that you are sick may be general: frequent headaches or feeling tired or itchy all over your body.

If your kidney disease gets worse, you may need to urinate more often or less often. You may lose your appetite or experience nausea and vomiting. Your hands or feet may swell or feel numb. You may get drowsy or have trouble concentrating. Your skin may darken. You may have muscle cramps.

How Will My Doctor Detect Kidney Disease?

First, your doctor will probably send blood and urine samples to a lab to test for substances that should not be there. If the blood contains too much creatinine or urea nitrogen and the urine contains protein, your kidneys may not be functioning properly.

Creatinine

Creatinine is a waste product in the blood created by the normal breakdown of muscle during activity. Healthy kidneys take creatinine out of the blood and put it in the urine to leave the body. When kidneys are not working well, creatinine builds up in the blood.

In the lab, your blood will be tested to see how many milligrams of creatinine are in one deciliter of blood (mg/dL). Creatinine levels in the blood can vary, and each laboratory has its own normal range. In many labs, the normal creatinine range is 0.6 to 1.2 mg/dL. If your creatinine level is only slightly above this normal range, you probably will not feel sick, but the elevation is a sign that your kidneys are not working at full strength. One formula for estimating kidney function equates a creatinine level of 1.7 mg/dL for most men and 1.4 mg/dL for most women to 50 percent of normal kidney function. But, because creatinine values are so variable and can be affected by diet, you may need to have your creatinine measured regularly to see whether your kidney function is decreasing. (The doctor may refer to the measure of creatinine in your blood as your serum creatinine. Do not confuse your serum creatinine number with your creatinine clearance number.)

Creatinine Clearance

Creatinine clearance is a measure of how fast your kidneys remove creatinine from the blood. Clearance is measured in milliliters per minute (mL/min). Doctors used to require a 24-

hour collection of urine to measure creatinine clearance directly, but they have discovered a formula that uses your serum creatinine measurement, your age, weight, BUN (see below), and race to calculate your creatinine clearance accurately.

For men, a normal creatinine clearance rate is 97 to 137 mL/min. For women, the normal rate is 88 to 128 mL/min. If your number is below this normal range, your kidneys are not working at full strength.

Blood Urea Nitrogen (BUN)

Blood carries protein for use by cells throughout the body. After the cells use the protein, the remaining waste product is returned to the blood as urea, a compound containing nitrogen. Healthy kidneys take urea out of the blood and send it to the bladder in the urine. If your kidneys are not working well, the urea will stay in the blood.

A deciliter of normal blood contains 7 to 20 milligrams of urea. If your BUN is more than 20 mg/dL, your kidneys may not be working at full strength. Other possible causes of an elevated BUN include dehydration and heart failure.

Proteinuria

Healthy kidneys take wastes out of the blood but leave protein. Impaired kidneys may fail to separate the protein from the wastes. Proteinuria means protein in the urine, and it is a sign of poor kidney function. If your urine makes foam in the toilet, it may contain high levels of protein. Your doctor may test for protein using a dipstick in a small sample of your urine taken in the doctor's office. The color of the dipstick indicates the presence or absence of proteinuria.

Additional Tests

Renal imaging. If blood and urine tests indicate reduced kidney function, your doctor may recommend additional tests to help identify the cause of the problem. Renal imaging (taking pictures of the kidneys) methods include ultrasound, computed tomography (CT scan), and magnetic resonance imaging (MRI). These tools are most helpful in finding unusual growths or blockages to the flow of urine.

Renal biopsy. Your doctor may want to see a tiny piece of your kidney tissue under a microscope. To obtain this tissue sample, the doctor will perform a renal biopsy—a hospital procedure in which the doctor inserts a needle through your skin into the back of the kidney. The needle retrieves a strand of tissue about 1/2 to 3/4 of an inch long. You will lie prone (on your stomach) on a table and will receive local anesthetic to numb the skin. The sample tissue will help the doctor identify problems at the cellular level.

What Can Be Done About Kidney Disease?

Unfortunately, chronic kidney disease often cannot be cured. But if you are in the early stages of a kidney disease, you may be able to make your kidneys last longer by taking certain steps.

- If you have diabetes, watch your blood glucose closely to keep it under control. Consult your doctor for the latest in treatment.
- Avoid pain pills that may make your kidney disease worse. Check with your doctor before taking any medicine.

Blood Pressure

People with reduced kidney function (a high creatinine level in the blood or a low creatinine clearance) should have their blood pressure controlled, and an ACE inhibitor should be one of their medications. If they also have proteinuria, the blood pressure should be maintained below 125/75 mm Hg.

K

Diet

People with reduced kidney function need to be aware that some parts of a normal diet may speed their kidney failure.

Protein

Protein is important to your body. It helps your body repair muscles and fight disease. Protein comes mostly from meat. As discussed in an earlier section, healthy kidneys take wastes out of the blood but leave protein. Impaired kidneys may fail to separate the protein from the wastes.

Some doctors tell their kidney patients to limit the amount of protein they eat so that the kidneys have less work to do. But you cannot avoid protein entirely. You may need to work with a dietitian to find the right food plan.

Cholesterol

Another problem that may be associated with kidney failure is too much cholesterol in your blood. High levels of cholesterol may result from a high-fat diet. Cholesterol can build up on the inside walls of your blood vessels. The buildup makes pumping blood through the vessels harder for your heart and can cause heart attacks and strokes.

Sodium

Sodium is a chemical found in salt and other foods. Sodium in your diet may raise your blood pressure, so you should limit foods that contain high levels of sodium. High-sodium foods include canned or processed foods like frozen dinners and hot dogs.

Potassium

Potassium is a mineral found naturally in many fruits and vegetables, like potatoes, bananas, dried fruits, dried beans and peas, and nuts. Healthy kidneys measure potassium in your blood and remove excess amounts. Diseased kidneys may fail to remove excess potassium, and with very poor kidney function, high potassium levels can affect the heart rhythm.

Treating Anemia

Anemia is a condition in which the blood does not contain enough red blood cells. These cells are important because they carry oxygen throughout the body. If you are anemic, you will feel tired and look pale. Healthy kidneys make the hormone EPO, which stimulates the bones to make red blood cells. Diseased kidneys may not make enough EPO. You may need to take injections of a manmade form of EPO.

Preparing for End-Stage Renal Disease

As your kidney disease progresses, you will need to make several decisions. You will need to learn about your options for treating ESRD so that you can make an informed choice between hemodialysis, peritoneal dialysis, and transplantation.

What Happens if Kidneys Fail Completely?

Complete and irreversible kidney failure is sometimes called end-stage renal disease, or ESRD. If your kidneys stop working completely, your body fills with extra water and waste products. This condition is called uremia. Your hands or feet may swell. You will feel tired and weak because your body needs clean blood to function properly.

Untreated uremia may lead to seizures or coma and will ultimately result in death. If your kidneys stop working completely, you will need to undergo dialysis or a kidney transplant.

Dialysis

The two major forms of dialysis are hemodialysis and peritoneal dialysis. In hemodialysis, your blood is sent through a machine that filters away waste products. The clean blood

Living Kidney Donors

Nearly half of all kidney transplants are made possible by the contributions of living donors. But the decision to make a living donation should be carefully considered. Each institution determines its own procedures and criteria, so these need to be ascertained. Making a living donation involves undergoing a major surgical procedure, which may be associated with pain and the risk—however small—of complications and death. The estimated risk of death is 3 per 10,000 for living kidney donors. There is also a slight chance that someone who donates a kidney to a close relative will experience the same medical problem that led to the family member needing a transplant. Be sure to discuss these possibilities with the donor team (a group comprising doctors and other health-care professionals). *The Editors*

is returned to your body. Hemodialysis is usually performed at a dialysis center three times per week for three or four hours.

In peritoneal dialysis, a fluid is put into your abdomen. This fluid, called dialysate, captures the waste products from your blood. After a few hours, the dialysate containing your body's wastes is drained away. Then, a fresh bag of dialysate is dripped into the abdomen. Patients can learn to do this themselves without going to a doctor's office each time. Patients using continuous ambulatory peritoneal dialysis (CAPD), the most common form of peritoneal dialysis, change dialysate four times a day. Another form of peritoneal dialysis, however, can be performed at night with a machine that drains and refills the abdomen automatically.

Kidney Transplantation

A donated kidney may come from an anonymous donor who has recently died or from a living person, usually a relative. The kidney that you receive must be a good match for your body. The more the new kidney is like you, the less likely your immune system is to reject it. Your immune system protects you from disease by attacking anything that is not recognized as a normal part of your body. So your immune system will attack a kidney that appears too "foreign." Special drugs can help trick your immune system so it does not reject a transplanted kidney.

National Institute of Diabetes and Digestive and Kidney Diseases

K

The pain begins as an ache in the back and side (the flank). Then it becomes constant and severe as the urinary system tries to rid itself of the stone. Sometimes there is burning during urination, blood in the urine, or a frequent urge to urinate. Nausea and vomiting may occur, and the lower abdomen or flank may be painful if touched.

All these symptoms are hallmarks of kidney stones, a condition that may affect up to 10 percent of Americans in their lifetimes. More than half a million people will develop kidney stones this year, and over one third of these patients will be hospitalized.

The Urinary System and How it Works

The urinary system includes two kidneys, two tube-like ureters that connect the kidneys to the bladder, and another tube, the urethra, that connects the bladder to the outside of the body.

Each kidney is bean-shaped and about the size of an adult's fist. The kidneys are located below the ribs and toward the back. They contain nearly 40 miles of tubes, most of them tiny, that process some 100 gallons of blood each day. The kidneys filter and clean the blood, and they produce urine from excess water and dissolved solids.

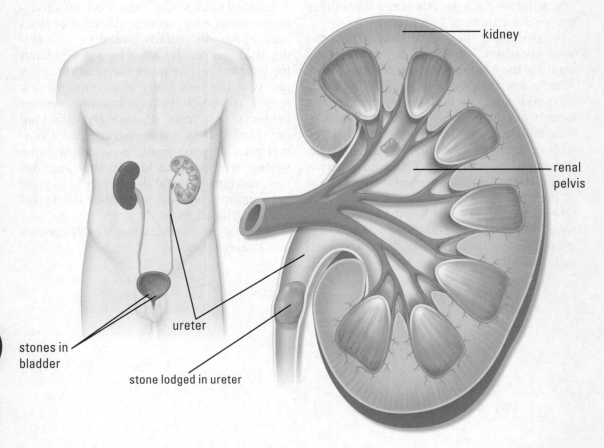

kidney

renal pelvis

ureter

stones in bladder

stone lodged in ureter

Renal calculi—kidney stones—can form in the kidney and pass spontaneously through the urinary tract. Stones cause severe pain when they become lodged in the ureter.

The ureters carry waste, as urine, from the kidneys to the bladder. The bladder, located in the lower abdomen, is a balloon-like organ that stores urine. A bladder can hold over a pint of urine. During urination, the urethra carries urine from the bottom of the bladder out of the body.

What Causes Kidney Stones?

Kidney stones are hardened crystal clumps that can develop in the urinary system. They usually form because there is a breakdown in the balance of liquids and dissolved solids in the urine. The kidneys must keep the right amount of water in the body while they remove materials that the body cannot use. If this balance is disturbed, the urine can become overloaded with substances (usually small crystals) that won't dissolve in water. Crystals begin to stick together and slowly add layer upon layer to form a stone. A kidney stone may grow for months or even years before it causes a problem.

What Does a Kidney Stone Look Like?

Kidney stones don't all look the same. The color depends on what chemicals are in it. Most are yellow or brown, but they can be tan, gold, or black. Stones can be round, jagged, or even have branches. They vary in size from specks to pebbles to stones as big as golf balls.

Can Kidney Stones Damage the Kidney?

Kidney stones can cause kidney damage. Whether there is damage and, if so, how much there is depends on the location of the stone in the urinary system. To avoid or minimize damage, it is important to eliminate stones that form and to prevent new ones from developing. Therefore, your family doctor may refer you to a urologist, a doctor who specializes in urinary diseases.

Who Gets Kidney Stones?

Anyone can get kidney stones, but some people are more likely to develop stones than others. Typically, a person with a kidney stone is a man 20 to 60 years old. Although four out of five kidney stone sufferers are men, women also get kidney stones. Often, there is a family history of kidney stones. Chronic dehydration (lack of body water) can lead to kidney stones. Very hot weather, heavy sweating, or too little fluid intake contribute to the formation of kidney stones. People who work outdoors in hot weather and who do not drink enough fluids may increase their risk of getting stones.

Some physicians believe that our rich diet in the U.S. may promote the development of kidney stones. Experts note that the incidence of kidney stones has tripled in Japan since World War II—at the same time the Japanese diet has become more like our own.

A variety of other conditions are linked with kidney stone development. These include urinary tract blockage, urinary infections that recur, bowel disease, and certain inherited disorders. People who are paralyzed or who have to rest in bed for long periods of time are also at increased risk for kidney stones, as are men and women who fly long space missions.

Types of Stones and Their Causes

Calcium oxalate and phosphate stones. Calcium oxalate and phosphate stones are made up of a hard crystal compound. These stones have become more common in recent years with about 70 percent to 80 percent of all kidney stones currently made up of calcium oxalate and phosphate. Calcium oxalate is often mixed with phosphate, but either pure calcium oxalate or calcium phosphate stones may occur.

K

Calcium and Kidney Stones

In the past, people who had developed calcium stones were encouraged to restrict their intake of calcium-rich foods. However, one study strongly suggested that a high calcium intake might actually protect against the formation of calcium oxalate stones. In an effort to determine the effect of dietary calcium intake on stone formation, Italian researchers conducted a five-year prospective study comparing two diets in 120 men with recurrent calcium oxalate stones. Half the group followed a diet that contained a normal amount of calcium but reduced amounts of animal protein and salt, while the other half consumed a low-calcium diet. After five years, almost twice as many men on the low-calcium diet had developed new kidney stones compared with those on the normal-calcium, low-meat, low-salt diet. Both diets reduced the amount of calcium in the urine. Men following the normal calcium, low-meat, low-salt diet, however, had decreased levels of oxalate in the urine, which probably contributed to the lower risk of stones in this group. (By contrast, urinary levels of oxalate actually rose in the men following the low-calcium diet.) *The Editors*

Hypercalciuria (too much calcium in the urine) often causes calcium oxalate stones to develop. Almost 40 percent of patients with calcium oxalate stones have an inherited metabolic disorder that causes a build-up of calcium in the urine. Certain drugs, such as furosemide (a diuretic), antacids, and steroids, also may cause an overload of calcium in the urine. Other factors associated with hypercalciuria include overactive parathyroid glands, too much vitamin A or D, and a diet high in purine from meat, fish, and poultry.

Another cause of calcium oxalate stones is too much oxalate in the urine. This can result from too much oxalate production by the body or not enough calcium in your diet. Large doses of vitamin C or not enough vitamin B can also lead to excess oxalate in the urine.

Struvite (or infection) stones. About 10 percent to 28 percent of all stones are associated with bacterial urinary infections. Such stones are called struvite stones, and like urinary infections, are more common in women. In patients with struvite stones, it is important not only to remove the stone but also to prevent recurrence of the urinary infection.

Uric acid stones. About 5 percent to 13 percent of kidney stones contain uric acid, which arises when the body breaks down certain foods, especially meats. These stones are more common among men and develop when there is too much uric acid in the urine. Patients with gout (see page 354), a metabolic disorder associated with high uric acid levels, are especially prone to uric acid stones.

Cystine stones. Another inherited condition can cause too much cystine (produced by the breakdown of protein from your diet) to collect in the urine. The cystine tends to form crystals that develop into cystine stones. These stones are relatively rare, accounting for only about 1 percent to 3 percent of all kidney stones.

Rare stones. Other rare stones (xanthine, silicate) may occur.

How Kidney Stones Are Found

People with kidney stones usually see their doctors because of back pain or blood in their urine. If your doctor thinks that you have a stone, its location, size, and type need to be determined for proper treatment to occur. Your doctor will start by asking you questions about your medical and family history and by doing a physical examination. Analyses of your blood and urine will help determine whether there is an infection or whether high levels of stone-forming substances are present.

Kidney stones can become stuck in any part of the urinary system. To begin to locate a stone, doctors may perform an x-ray or ultrasound study. This gives a good idea of the stone's size and where it is located. Many patients also receive an intravenous pyelogram (IVP). For an IVP, a special dye is injected into the patient's vein. The dye eventually collects in the urinary system. There, it produces a white contrast when an x-ray is taken. The dye allows the doctor to precisely locate the stone and to determine the condition of the kidneys, ureters, and bladder.

It is very important that the stone, if passed, be saved, so that it can be sent to a laboratory for evaluation. Long-term treatment and prevention plans depend on the type of stone. Between 70 percent and 80 percent of stones pass on their own in the urine, usually within 48 hours of the start of the symptoms. To catch a stone, patients are asked to urinate into a strainer, a cup with mesh in the bottom. All pieces of stone, no matter how small, should be collected and given to the doctor. If one stone is analyzed, more may not be needed, since most people develop just one type of stone.

Treatment

Although kidney stones, especially calcium stones, are very hard, most of the 20 percent to 30 percent that do not pass out of the body on their own can be eliminated without surgery. A process called lithotripsy (from the Greek word for "stone crushing") breaks into tiny fragments most stones that are less than three-quarters of an inch across. (Lithotripsy also is called extra-corporeal shock wave lithotripsy.)

Lithotripsy has been used in the U.S. since 1984. It is performed using a machine called a lithotripter. There are different types of lithotripters, but all focus shock waves from outside the body on the kidney stone. Repeated shock waves cause the kidney stone to disintegrate into tiny particles. These particles pass easily out of the body in the urine.

Before receiving lithotripsy, the patient's history is reviewed and the physical examination is completed. Laboratory tests also are performed, and the patient may be given some medication. Just before lithotripsy, most patients receive a sedative to help them relax. Occasionally, a patient is given anesthesia—either general anesthesia, which induces a sleep-like state, or a regional anesthesia, which numbs the lower body. The choice depends on physician and patient preference. Shock waves are then focused on the kidney stone for a total time of one-half hour to two hours. As the shock waves travel through body tissue, they may cause some mild bruising, which heals in a few days.

Lithotripsy alone doesn't work for all patients or for all kidney stones. In addition to lithotripsy, some patients may need to have a tube (catheter) inserted via a needle through the back muscles into the kidney to help drain the kidney. This tube may later be used to remove stones through a small telescopic device. Also, stones located in the lower portions of the urinary system may be removed with a small telescope inserted through the urethra. In fewer than 5 percent of cases, surgery through an incision may be required to remove kidney stones.

Can Kidney Stones Recur?

People who have had one kidney stone are prone to develop others. Without preventive

K

treatment or changes in lifestyle, patients can develop a new stone within a year or two of the first one. About half of patients do develop a stone again within 5 to 10 years, and 80 percent do so sometime in their lives.

What You Can Do to Prevent Future Kidney Stones

There definitely are things you can do to reduce your chances of developing another stone. One of the most important is simply getting into the life-long habit of drinking a lot of liquid—mainly water. Everyone who has had a kidney stone should drink at least 8 ounces of fluid at each meal, between each meal, before bed, and during the night if awakened to urinate. In other words, you should drink a minimum of 7, and preferably 10 to 12, large glasses of fluid in the course of each day. At least half of these should be glasses of water.

Your fluid intake should be spread out as evenly as possible throughout the day. This keeps the urine from becoming concentrated and reduces the chances that crystals—the building blocks of kidney stones—will form. Since the goal is to produce at least 2 quarts of urine a day, you should drink more fluid in very hot weather to make up for that lost by sweating.

A good way to judge whether you're drinking enough is to watch the color of your urine. If your urine is dark and yellow, drink more. It should be pale, almost watery. Urine has more color in the morning when it is most concentrated, but the rest of the time, the less color, the better.

Drinking plenty of fluids also reduces the risk of developing urinary tract infections—a major cause of struvite stones. Any infections that do occur should be treated promptly and completely.

Depending on the kind of stone involved and the results of laboratory tests, your doctor may advise you to eat less of certain kinds of foods. For example, patients with calcium oxalate or uric acid stones may need to reduce the amount of meat products and table salt in their diets and increase the amount of fiber. You and your physician may work with a dietitian to develop a diet suited to your particular needs.

There are prescription medications that help some patients. Diuretics, such as hydrochlorothiazide, decrease calcium excretion. Potassium citrate binds calcium and helps to remove it safely. Allopurinol, which causes the body to produce less uric acid, is sometimes prescribed for patients with gout. It also reduces their risk of forming uric acid or calcium oxalate stones. Patients taking medications still need to drink at least ten 8-ounce glasses of fluid per day. When cystine stone formation can't be controlled by increased fluid levels alone, penicillamine or tiopronin may be prescribed to make it easier for the body to dissolve cystine. Other specific medications may be prescribed by your doctor.

American Foundation for Urologic Disease

Leukemia is cancer of the blood cells. To better understand leukemia, it is helpful to know about normal blood cells and what happens to them when leukemia develops.

The blood is made up of fluid called plasma and three types of cells. Each type has special functions.

- **White blood cells** (also called WBCs or leukocytes) help the body fight infections and other diseases.
- **Red blood cells** (also called RBCs or erythrocytes) carry oxygen from the lungs to the body's tissues and take carbon dioxide from the tissues back to the lungs. The red blood cells give blood its color.
- **Platelets** (also called thrombocytes) help form blood clots that control bleeding.

Blood cells are formed in the bone marrow, the soft, spongy center of bones. New (immature) blood cells are called blasts. Some blasts stay in the marrow to mature. Some travel to other parts of the body to mature.

Normally, blood cells are produced in an orderly, controlled way, as the body needs them. This process helps keep us healthy.

When leukemia develops, the body produces large numbers of abnormal blood cells. In most types of leukemia, the abnormal cells are white blood cells. The leukemia cells usually look different from normal blood cells, and they do not function properly.

Types of Leukemia

There are several types of leukemia. They are grouped in two ways. One way is by how quickly the disease develops and gets worse. The other way is by the type of blood cell that is affected.

Leukemia is either acute or chronic. In acute leukemia, the abnormal blood cells are blasts that remain very immature and cannot carry out their normal functions. The number of blasts increases rapidly, and the disease gets worse quickly. In chronic leukemia, some blast cells are present, but in general, these cells are more mature and can carry out some of their normal functions. Also, the number of blasts increases less rapidly than in acute leukemia. As a result, chronic leukemia gets worse gradually.

Leukemia can arise in either of the two main types of white blood cells—lymphoid cells or myeloid cells. When leukemia affects lymphoid cells, it is called lymphocytic leukemia. When myeloid cells are affected, the disease is called myeloid or myelogenous leukemia.

These are the most common types of leukemia:

- **Acute lymphocytic leukemia (ALL)** is the most common type of leukemia in young children. This disease also affects adults, especially those age 65 and older.
- **Acute myeloid leukemia (AML)** occurs in both adults and children. This type of leukemia is sometimes called acute non-lymphocytic leukemia (ANLL).
- **Chronic lymphocytic leukemia (CLL)** most often affects adults over the age of 55. It sometimes occurs in younger adults, but it almost never affects children.
- **Chronic myeloid leukemia (CML)** occurs mainly in adults. A very small number of children also develop this disease.

Hairy cell leukemia is an uncommon type of chronic leukemia. This and other uncommon types of leukemia are not discussed in this entry. The Cancer Information Service can supply information about them.

Possible Causes

At this time, we do not know what causes leukemia. Researchers are trying to solve this problem. Scientists know that leukemia occurs in males more often than in females

L

and in whites more often than in African Americans. However, they cannot explain why one person gets leukemia and another does not.

By studying large numbers of people all over the world, researchers have found certain risk factors that increase a person's risk of getting leukemia. For example, exposure to large amounts of high-energy radiation increases the risk of getting leukemia. Such radiation was produced by the atomic bomb explosions in Japan during World War II. In nuclear power plants, strict safety rules protect workers and the public from exposure to harmful amounts of radiation.

Some research suggests that exposure to electromagnetic fields is a possible risk factor for leukemia. (Electromagnetic fields are a type of low-energy radiation that comes from power lines and electric appliances.) However, more studies are needed to prove this link.

Certain genetic conditions can increase the risk for leukemia. One such condition is Down's syndrome; children born with this syndrome are more likely to get leukemia than other children.

Workers exposed to certain chemicals over a long period of time are at higher risk for leukemia. Benzene is one of these chemicals. Also, some of the drugs used to treat other types of cancer may increase a person's risk of getting leukemia. However, this risk is very small when compared with the benefits of chemotherapy.

Scientists have identified a virus that seems to increase the risk for one very uncommon type of leukemia. However,

this virus has no known association with common forms of leukemia. Scientists throughout the world continue to study viruses and other possible risk factors for leukemia. By learning what causes this disease,

researchers hope to better understand how to prevent and treat it.

Symptoms

Leukemia cells are abnormal cells that cannot do what normal blood cells do. They cannot help the body fight infections. For this reason, people with leukemia often get infections and have fevers.

Also, people with leukemia often have less than the normal amount of healthy red blood cells and platelets. As a result, there are not enough red blood cells to carry oxygen through the body. With this condition, called anemia, patients may look pale and feel weak and tired. When there are not enough platelets, patients bleed and bruise easily.

Like all blood cells, leukemia cells travel through the body. Depending on the number of abnormal cells and where these cells collect, patients with leukemia may have a number of symptoms.

In acute leukemia, symptoms appear and get worse quickly. People with this disease go to their doctor because they feel sick. In chronic leukemia, symptoms may not appear for a long time; when symptoms do appear, they generally are mild at first and get worse gradually. Doctors often find chronic leukemia during a routine checkup—before there are any symptoms.

These are some of the common symptoms of leukemia:

- Fever, chills, and other flu-like symptoms
- Weakness and fatigue
- Frequent infections
- Loss of appetite and/or weight
- Swollen or tender lymph nodes, liver, or spleen
- Easy bleeding or bruising
- Tiny red spots (called petechiae) under the skin
- Swollen or bleeding gums

- Sweating, especially at night
- Bone or joint pain

In acute leukemia, the abnormal cells may collect in the brain or spinal cord (also called the central nervous system or CNS). The result may be headaches, vomiting, confusion, loss of muscle control, and seizures. Leukemia cells also can collect in the testicles and cause swelling. Also, some patients develop sores in the eyes or on the skin. Leukemia also can affect the digestive tract, kidneys, lungs, or other parts of the body.

In chronic leukemia, the abnormal blood cells may gradually collect in various parts of the body. Chronic leukemia may affect the skin, central nervous system, digestive tract, kidneys, and testicles.

Diagnosis

To find the cause of a person's symptoms, the doctor asks about the patient's medical history and does a physical exam. In addition to checking general signs of health, the doctor feels for swelling in the liver; the spleen; and the lymph nodes under the arms, in the groin, and in the neck.

Blood tests also help in the diagnosis. A sample of blood is examined under a microscope to see what the cells look like and to determine the number of mature cells and blasts. Although blood tests may reveal that a patient has leukemia, they may not show what type of leukemia it is.

To check further for leukemia cells or to tell what type of leukemia a patient has, a hematologist, oncologist, or pathologist examines a sample of bone marrow under a microscope. The doctor withdraws the sample by inserting a needle into a large bone (usually the hip) and removing a small amount of liquid bone marrow. This procedure is called bone marrow aspiration. A bone marrow biopsy is performed with a larger needle and removes a small piece of bone and bone marrow.

If leukemia cells are found in the bone marrow sample, the patient's doctor orders other tests to find out the extent of the disease. A spinal tap (lumbar puncture) checks for leukemia cells in the fluid that fills the spaces in and around the brain and spinal cord (cerebrospinal fluid). Chest x-rays can reveal signs of disease in the chest.

Treatment

Treatment for leukemia is complex. It varies with the type of leukemia and is not the same for all patients. The doctor plans the treatment to fit each patient's needs. The treatment depends not only on the type of leukemia, but also on certain features of the leukemia cells, the extent of the disease, and whether the leukemia has been treated before. It also depends on the patient's age, symptoms, and general health.

Whenever possible, patients should be treated at a medical center that has doctors who have experience in treating leukemia. If this is not possible, the patient's doctor should discuss the treatment plan with a specialist at such a center. Also, patients and their doctors can call the Cancer Information Service to request up-to-date treatment information from the National Cancer Institute's PDQ database.

Acute leukemia needs to be treated right away. The goal of treatment is to bring about a remission. Then, when there is no evidence of the disease, more therapy may be given to prevent a relapse. Many people with acute leukemia can be cured.

Chronic leukemia patients who do not have symptoms may not require immediate treatment. However, they should have frequent checkups so the doctor can see whether the disease is progressing. When treatment is needed, it can often control the

L

disease and its symptoms. However, chronic leukemia can seldom be cured.

Methods of Treatment

Most patients with leukemia are treated with chemotherapy. Some also may have radiation therapy and/or bone marrow transplantation (BMT) or biological therapy. In some cases, surgery to remove the spleen (an operation called a splenectomy) may be part of the treatment plan. When discussing treatment, the patient may want to talk with the doctor about research studies of new treatment methods. Such studies, called clinical trials, are designed to improve cancer treatment (see page 181).

Chemotherapy is the use of drugs to kill cancer cells. Depending on the type of leukemia, patients may receive a single drug or a combination of two or more drugs.

Some anticancer drugs can be taken by mouth. Most are given by IV injection (injected into a vein). Often, patients who need to have many IV treatments receive the drugs through a catheter.

One end of this thin, flexible tube is placed in a large vein, often in the upper chest. Drugs are injected into the catheter, rather than directly into a vein, to avoid the discomfort of repeated injections and injury to the skin.

Anticancer drugs given by IV injection or taken by mouth enter the bloodstream and affect leukemia cells in most parts of the body. However, the drugs often do not reach cells in the central nervous system because they are stopped by the blood-brain barrier. This protective barrier is formed by a network of blood vessels that filter blood going to the brain and spinal cord. To reach leukemia cells in the central nervous system, doctors use intrathecal chemotherapy. In this type of treatment, anticancer drugs are injected directly into the cerebrospinal fluid.

Intrathecal chemotherapy can be given in two ways. Some patients receive the drugs by injection into the lower part of the spinal column. Others, especially children, receive intrathecal chemotherapy through a special type of catheter called an Ommaya reservoir. This device is placed under the scalp, where it provides a pathway to the cerebrospinal fluid. Injecting anticancer drugs into the reservoir instead of into the spinal column can make intrathecal chemotherapy easier and more comfortable for the patient.

Chemotherapy is given in cycles: a treatment period followed by a recovery period, then another treatment period, and so on. In some cases, the patient has chemotherapy as an outpatient at the hospital, at the doctor's office, or at home. However, depending on which drugs are given and the patient's general health, a hospital stay may be necessary.

Radiation therapy is used along with chemotherapy for some kinds of leukemia. Radiation therapy (also called radiotherapy) uses high-energy rays to damage cancer cells and stop them from growing. The radiation comes from a large machine.

Radiation therapy for leukemia may be given in two ways. For some patients, the doctor may direct the radiation to one specific area of the body where there is a collection of leukemia cells, such as the spleen or testicles. Other patients may receive radiation that is directed to the whole body. This type of radiation therapy, which is called total-body irradiation, usually is given before a bone marrow transplant.

Bone marrow transplantation (BMT) also may be used for some patients. The patient's leukemia-producing bone marrow is destroyed by high doses of drugs and radiation and is then replaced by healthy bone marrow.

The healthy bone marrow may come from a donor, or it may be marrow that has been removed from the patient and stored before the high-dose treatment. If the patient's own bone marrow is used, it may first be treated outside the body to remove leukemia cells. Patients who have a bone marrow transplant usually stay in the hospital for several weeks. Until the transplanted bone marrow begins to produce enough white blood cells, patients have to be carefully protected from infection.

Biological therapy involves treatment with substances that affect the immune system's response to cancer. Interferon is a form of biological therapy that is used against some types of leukemia.

Supportive Care

Leukemia and its treatment can cause a number of complications and side effects. Patients receive supportive care to prevent or control these problems and to improve their comfort and quality of life during treatment.

Because leukemia patients get infections very easily, they may receive antibiotics and other drugs to help protect them from infections. They are often advised to stay out of crowds and away from people with colds and other infectious diseases. If an infection develops, it can be serious and should be treated promptly. Patients may need to stay in the hospital to treat the infection.

Anemia and bleeding are other problems that often require supportive care. Transfusions of red blood cells may be given to help reduce the shortness of breath and fatigue that anemia can cause. Platelet transfusions can help reduce the risk of serious bleeding.

Dental care also is very important. Leukemia and chemotherapy can make the mouth sensitive, easily infected, and likely to bleed. Doctors often advise patients to

---

Questions for Your Doctor

Here are some questions patients and their families may want to ask the doctor about bone marrow transplantation:

- What are the benefits of this treatment?
- What are the risks and side effects? What can be done about them?
- How long will I be in the hospital? What care will be needed after I leave the hospital?
- What changes in normal activities will be necessary?
- How will we be able to know if the treatment is working?

---

have a complete dental exam before treatment begins. Dentists can show patients how to keep their mouth clean and healthy during treatment.

Side Effects of Treatment

It is hard to limit the effects of therapy so that only leukemia cells are destroyed. Because treatment also damages healthy cells and tissues, it causes side effects.

The side effects of cancer treatment vary. They depend mainly on the type and extent of the treatment. Also, each person reacts differently. Side effects may even be different from one treatment to the next. Doctors try to plan the patient's therapy to keep side effects to a minimum.

Doctors and nurses can explain the side effects of treatment and can suggest medicine, diet changes, or other ways to deal with them.

Chemotherapy

The side effects of chemotherapy depend mainly on the drugs the patient receives. In addition, as with other types of treatment, side effects may vary from person to

L

person. Generally, anticancer drugs affect dividing cells. Cancer cells divide more often than healthy cells and are more likely to be affected by chemotherapy. Still, some healthy cells also may be damaged. Healthy cells that divide often, including blood cells, cells in hair roots, and cells in the digestive tract, are likely to be damaged. When chemotherapy affects healthy cells, it may lower patients' resistance to infection, and patients may have less energy and may bruise or bleed easily. They may lose their hair. The also may have nausea, vomiting, and mouth sores. Most side effects go away gradually during the recovery periods between treatments or after treatment stops.

Some anticancer drugs can affect a patient's fertility. Women's menstrual periods may become irregular or stop, and women may have symptoms of menopause, such as hot flashes and vaginal dryness. Men may stop producing sperm. Because these changes may be permanent, some men choose to have their sperm frozen and stored. Most children treated for leukemia appear to have normal fertility when they grow up. However, depending on the drugs and doses used and on the age of the patient, some boys and girls may not be able to have children when they mature.

Radiation Therapy

Patients receiving radiation therapy may become very tired. Resting is important, but doctors usually suggest that patients remain as active as they can.

When radiation is directed to the head, patients often lose their hair. Radiation can cause the scalp or the skin in the treated area to become red, dry, tender, and itchy. Patients will be shown how to keep the skin clean. They should not use any lotion or cream on the treated area without the doctor's advice. Radiation therapy also may cause nausea, vomiting, and loss of appetite. These side effects are temporary, and doctors and nurses can often suggest ways to control them until the treatment is over.

Some side effects may be lasting. Children, especially young ones, who receive radiation to the brain may develop problems with learning and coordination. For this reason, doctors use the lowest possible doses of radiation, and they give this treatment only to children who cannot be treated successfully with chemotherapy alone.

Also, radiation to the testicles is likely to affect both fertility and hormone production. Most boys who have this form of treatment are not able to have children later on. Some may need to take hormones.

Bone Marrow Transplantation

Patients who have a bone marrow transplant face an increased risk of infection, bleeding, and other side effects of the large doses of chemotherapy and radiation they receive. In addition, graft-versus-host disease (GVHD) may occur in patients who receive bone marrow from a donor. In GVHD, the donated marrow reacts against the patient's tissues (most often the liver, the skin, and the digestive tract). GVHD can be mild or very severe. It can occur any time after the transplant (even years later). Drugs may be given to reduce the risk of GVHD and to treat the problem if it occurs.

Potential long-term risks of bone marrow transplant include infertility (the inability to produce children); cataracts (clouding of the lens of the eye, which causes loss of vision); secondary (new) cancers; and complications in the liver, kidneys, lungs, and/or heart.

Follow-up Care

Regular follow-up exams are very important after treatment for leukemia. The doctor will continue to check the patient closely to be sure that the cancer has not returned. Checkups usually include exams of the blood, bone marrow, and cerebrospinal fluid. From time to time, the doctor does a complete physical exam.

Cancer treatment may cause side effects many years later. For this reason, patients should continue to have regular checkups and should also report health changes or problems to their doctor as soon as they appear.

National Cancer Institute

L

The lungs, a pair of sponge-like, cone-shaped organs, are part of the respiratory system. The right lung has three sections, called lobes; it is a little larger than the left lung, which has two lobes. When we breathe in, the lungs take in oxygen, which our cells need to live and carry out their normal functions. When we breathe out, the lungs get rid of carbon dioxide, which is a waste product of the body's cells.

Cancers that begin in the lungs are divided into two major types, non-small cell lung cancer and small cell lung cancer, depending on how the cells look under a microscope. Each type of lung cancer grows and spreads in different ways and is treated differently. Non-small cell lung cancer is more common than small cell lung cancer, and it generally grows and spreads more slowly. There are three main types of non-small cell lung cancer, each named for the type of cells in which the cancer develops: squamous cell carcinoma (also called epidermoid carcinoma), adenocarcinoma, and large cell carcinoma.

Small cell lung cancer, sometimes called oat cell cancer, is less common than non-small cell lung cancer. This type of lung cancer grows more quickly and is more likely to spread to other organs in the body.

Who's at Risk?

Researchers have discovered several causes of lung cancer; most are related to the use of tobacco.

Cigarettes. Smoking cigarettes causes lung cancer. Harmful substances, called carcinogens, in tobacco damage the cells in the lungs. Over time, the damaged cells may become

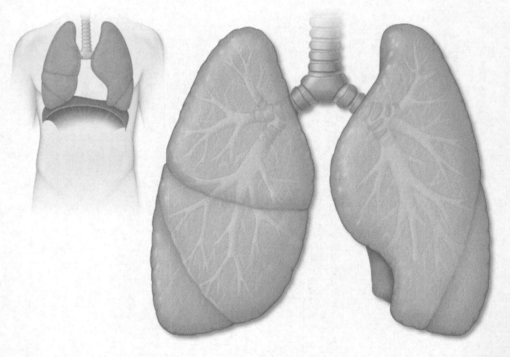

The trachea (windpipe) divides into two bronchi, one in each lung. The most common type of lung cancer begins in the bronchi.

L

Smoking Cessation

More than 80 percent of lung cancers result from smoking; quitting smoking—even after age 60—can greatly reduce your risk. Indeed, most individuals who stop smoking relapse within a few days, and only 2 percent to 3 percent of smokers quit successfully each year. Don't give up if the first attempt is unsuccessful; research has shown that the chance of quitting increases with each try.

Smoking cessation experts agree that the following measures improve the success rate:

- Select a specific target date (no more than a week or two ahead).
- Choose a time when stress levels are low, perhaps when on vacation and away from your usual environment.
- Get the support of friends and family in advance.
- Throw away all ashtrays, matches, and cigarettes on the night before the "quit date" so that the next day is started as a nonsmoker.
- Avoid caffeine-containing coffee and colas, which increase the craving to smoke.
- Keep alcoholic drinks to a minimum.
- Change habits associated with smoking, such as drinking alcohol and going to places where one tended to smoke a lot.

Formal stop-smoking group programs, which are widely available throughout the country, can be found by calling the local office of the American Lung Association or American Cancer Society. *The Editors*

cancerous. The likelihood that a smoker will develop lung cancer is affected by the age at which smoking began, how long the person has smoked, the number of cigarettes smoked per day, and how deeply the smoker inhales. Stopping smoking greatly reduces a person's risk for developing lung cancer.

Cigars and pipes. Cigar and pipe smokers have a higher risk of lung cancer than nonsmokers. The number of years a person smokes, the number of pipes or cigars smoked per day, and how deeply the person inhales all affect the risk of developing lung cancer. Even cigar and pipe smokers who do not inhale are at increased risk for lung, mouth, and other types of cancer.

Environmental tobacco smoke. Lung cancer risk is increased by exposure to environmental tobacco smoke (ETS)—the smoke in the air when someone else smokes. Exposure to ETS, or secondhand smoke, is called involuntary or passive smoking.

Radon. Radon is an invisible, odorless, and tasteless radioactive gas that occurs naturally in soil and rocks. It can cause damage to the lungs that may lead to lung cancer. People who work in mines may be exposed to radon and, in some parts of the country, radon is found in houses. Smoking increases the risk of lung cancer even more for those already at risk because of exposure to radon. A kit available at most hardware stores allows homeowners to measure radon levels in their homes. The home radon test is relatively easy to use and inexpensive. Once a radon problem is corrected, the hazard is gone for good.

Asbestos. Asbestos is the name of a group of minerals that occur naturally as fibers and are used in certain industries. Asbestos fibers tend to break easily into particles that can float in the air and stick to clothes. When the particles are inhaled, they can lodge in the lungs, damaging cells and increasing the risk for lung cancer. Studies have shown that workers who have been exposed to large amounts of asbestos have a risk of developing lung cancer that is three

L

to four times greater than that for workers who have not been exposed to asbestos. This exposure has been observed in such industries as shipbuilding, asbestos mining and manufacturing, insulation work, and brake repair. The risk of lung cancer is even higher among asbestos workers who smoke. Asbestos workers should use protective equipment provided by their employers and follow recommended work practices and safety procedures.

Pollution. Researchers have found a link between lung cancer and exposure to certain air pollutants, such as by-products of the combustion of diesel and other fossil fuels. However, this relationship has not been clearly defined, and more research is being done.

Lung diseases. Certain lung diseases, such as tuberculosis (TB), increase a person's chance of developing lung cancer. Lung cancer tends to develop in areas of the lung that are scarred from TB.

Personal history. A person who has had lung cancer once is more likely to develop a second lung cancer compared with a person who has never had lung cancer. Quitting smoking after lung cancer is diagnosed may prevent the development of a second lung cancer.

Researchers continue to study the causes of lung cancer and to search for ways to prevent it. We already know that the best way to prevent lung cancer is to quit (or never start) smoking. The sooner a person quits smoking the better. Even if you have been smoking for many years, it's never too late to benefit from quitting.

The best way to prevent lung cancer is to quit, or never start, smoking.

Symptoms

Common signs and symptoms of lung cancer include:

- A cough that doesn't go away and gets worse over time
- Constant chest pain
- Coughing up blood
- Shortness of breath, wheezing, or hoarseness
- Repeated problems with pneumonia or bronchitis
- Swelling of the neck and face
- Loss of appetite or weight loss
- Fatigue

These symptoms may be caused by lung cancer or by other conditions. It is important to check with a doctor.

Diagnosis

To help find the cause of symptoms, the doctor evaluates a person's medical history, smoking history, exposure to environmental and occupational substances, and family history of cancer. The doctor also performs a physical exam and may order a chest x-ray and other tests. If lung cancer is suspected, sputum cytology (the microscopic examination of cells obtained from a deep-cough sample of mucus in the lungs) is a simple test that may be useful in detecting lung cancer. To confirm the presence of lung cancer, the doctor must examine tissue from the lung. A biopsy—the removal of a small sample of tissue for examination under a microscope by a pathologist—can show whether a person has cancer. A number of procedures may be used to obtain this tissue:

- **Bronchoscopy.** The doctor puts a bronchoscope (a thin, lighted tube) into the mouth or nose and down through the windpipe to look into the breathing passages. Through this tube, the doctor can collect cells or small samples of tissue.
- **Needle aspiration.** A needle is inserted through the chest into the tumor to remove a sample of tissue.

- **Thoracentesis.** Using a needle, the doctor removes a sample of the fluid that surrounds the lungs to check for cancer cells.
- **Thoracotomy.** Surgery to open the chest is sometimes needed to diagnose lung cancer. This procedure is a major operation performed in a hospital.

Staging

If the diagnosis is cancer, the doctor will want to learn the stage (or extent) of the disease. Staging is done to find out whether the cancer has spread and, if so, to what parts of the body. Lung cancer often spreads to the brain or bones. Knowing the stage of the disease helps the doctor plan treatment. Some tests used to determine whether the cancer has spread include:

- **CAT (or CT) scan (computed tomography).** A computer linked to an x-ray machine creates a series of detailed pictures of areas inside the body.
- **MRI (magnetic resonance imaging).** A powerful magnet linked to a computer makes detailed pictures of areas inside the body.
- **Radionuclide scanning.** Scanning can show whether cancer has spread to other organs, such as the liver. The patient swallows or receives an injection of a mildly radioactive substance. A machine (scanner) measures and records the level of radioactivity in certain organs to reveal abnormal areas.
- **Bone scan.** A bone scan, one type of radionuclide scanning, can show whether cancer has spread to the bones. A small amount of radioactive substance is injected into a vein. It travels through the bloodstream and collects in areas of abnormal bone growth. An instrument called a scanner measures the radioactivity levels in these areas and records them on x-ray film.
- **Mediastinoscopy/Mediastinotomy.** A mediastinoscopy can help show whether the cancer has spread to the lymph nodes in the chest. Using a lighted viewing instrument called a scope, the doctor examines the center of the chest (mediastinum) and nearby lymph nodes. In mediastinoscopy, the scope is inserted through a small incision in the neck; in mediastinotomy, the incision is made in the chest. In either procedure, the scope is also used to remove a tissue sample. The patient receives a general anesthetic.

Treatment

Treatment depends on a number of factors, including the type of lung cancer (non-small or small cell lung cancer), the size, location, and extent of the tumor, and the general health of the patient. Many different treatments and combinations of treatments may be used to control lung cancer, and/or to improve quality of life by reducing symptoms. Clinical trials (research studies) to evaluate new ways to treat cancer are an option for many lung cancer patients (see page 181).

Surgery is an operation to remove the cancer. The type of surgery a doctor performs depends on the location of the tumor in the lung. An operation to remove only a small part of the lung is called a segmental or wedge resection. When the surgeon removes an entire lobe of the lung, the procedure is called a lobectomy. Pneumonectomy is the removal of an entire lung. Some tumors are inoperable (cannot be removed by surgery) because of their size or location, and some patients cannot have surgery for other medical reasons.

Chemotherapy is the use of anticancer drugs to kill cancer cells throughout the body. Even after cancer has been removed from the lung, cancer cells may still be

L

present in nearby tissue or elsewhere in the body. Chemotherapy may be used to control cancer growth or to relieve symptoms. Most anticancer drugs are given by injection directly into a vein (IV) or by means of a catheter, a thin tube that is placed into a large vein and remains there as long as it is needed. Some anticancer drugs are given in the form of a pill.

Radiation therapy, also called radiotherapy, involves the use of high-energy rays to kill cancer cells. Radiation therapy is directed to a limited area and affects the cancer cells only in that area. Radiation therapy may be used before surgery to shrink a tumor, or after surgery to destroy any cancer cells that remain in the treated area. Doctors also use radiation therapy, often combined with chemotherapy, as primary treatment instead of surgery. Radiation therapy may also be used to relieve symptoms such as shortness of breath. Radiation for the treatment of lung cancer most often comes from a machine (external radiation). The radiation can also come from an implant (a small container of radioactive material) placed directly into or near the tumor (internal radiation).

Photodynamic therapy (PDT), a type of laser therapy, involves the use of a special chemical that is injected into the bloodstream and absorbed by cells all over the body. The chemical rapidly leaves normal cells but remains in cancer cells for a longer time. A laser light aimed at the cancer activates the chemical, which then kills the cancer cells that have absorbed it. Photodynamic therapy may be used to reduce symptoms of lung cancer—for example, to control bleeding or to relieve breathing problems due to blocked airways when the cancer cannot be removed through surgery. Photodynamic therapy may also be used to treat very small tumors in patients for whom the usual treatments for lung cancer are not appropriate.

Treating Non-Small Cell Lung Cancer

Patients with non-small cell lung cancer may be treated in several ways. The choice of treatment depends mainly on the size, location, and extent of the tumor. Surgery is the most common way to treat this type of lung cancer. Cryosurgery, a treatment that freezes and destroys cancer tissue, may be used to control symptoms in the later stages of non-small cell lung cancer. Radiation therapy and chemotherapy may also be used to slow the progress of the disease and to manage the symptoms.

Treating Small Cell Lung Cancer

Small cell lung cancer spreads quickly. In many cases, cancer cells have already spread to other parts of the body when the disease is diagnosed. In order to reach cancer cells throughout the body, doctors almost always use chemotherapy. Treatment may also include radiation therapy aimed at the tumor in the lung or tumors in other parts of the body (such as in the brain). Some patients have radiation therapy to the brain even though no cancer is found there. This treatment, called prophylactic cranial irradiation (PCI), is given to prevent tumors from forming in the brain. Surgery is part of the treatment plan for a small number of patients with small cell lung cancer.

Side Effects of Treatment

The side effects of cancer treatment depend on the type of treatment and may be different for each person. Side effects are often only temporary. Doctors and nurses can explain the possible side effects of treatment, and can suggest ways to help relieve symptoms that may occur during and after treatment.

Surgery for lung cancer is a major operation. After lung surgery, air and fluid tend to collect in the chest. Patients often need help turning over, coughing, and breathing deeply. These activities are important for recovery because they help expand the remaining lung tissue and get rid of excess air and fluid. Pain or weakness in the chest and the arm and shortness of breath are common side effects of lung cancer surgery. Patients may need several weeks or months to regain their energy and strength.

Chemotherapy affects normal as well as cancerous cells. Side effects depend largely on the specific drugs and the dose (amount of drug given). Common side effects of chemotherapy include nausea and vomiting, hair loss, mouth sores, and fatigue.

Radiation therapy, like chemotherapy, affects normal as well as cancerous cells. Side effects of radiation therapy depend mainly on the part of the body that is treated and the treatment dose. Common side effects of radiation therapy are a dry, sore throat; difficulty swallowing; fatigue; skin changes at the site of treatment; and loss of appetite. Patients receiving radiation to the brain may have headaches, skin changes, fatigue, nausea and vomiting, hair loss, or problems with memory and thought processes.

Photodynamic therapy makes the skin and eyes sensitive to light for six weeks or more after treatment. Patients are advised to avoid direct sunlight and bright indoor light for at least six weeks. If patients must go outdoors, they need to wear protective clothing, including sunglasses. Other temporary side effects of PDT may include coughing, trouble swallowing, and painful breathing or shortness of breath. Patients should talk with their doctor about what to do if the skin becomes blistered, red, or swollen.

The Importance of Follow-up Care

Follow-up care after treatment for lung cancer is very important. Regular checkups ensure that changes in health are noticed, and if the cancer returns or a new cancer develops, it can be treated as soon as possible. Checkups may include physical exams, chest x-rays, or lab tests. Between scheduled appointments, people who have had lung cancer should report any health problems to their doctor as soon as they appear.

National Cancer Institute

Systemic lupus erythematosus (SLE), also known as lupus, is a chronic autoimmune disorder. It typically causes fatigue and joint pain, can injure nearly any internal organ, and increases the risk of cardiovascular disease. Although SLE usually strikes young women in their childbearing years, a large number of older adults have the condition—about 15 percent of cases are first diagnosed after age 55.

Causes

Normally, the immune system makes antibodies that protect the body by attacking foreign invaders such as viruses and bacteria. In SLE, however, the body produces so-called autoantibodies that attack and destroy normal cells, causing inflammation, injury, and pain in various tissues and organs.

Although the exact cause of SLE is unknown, genetic and environmental factors are thought to play a role. In addition to SLE, there are two other forms of lupus: drug-induced and cutaneous lupus. Drug-induced lupus may appear after the use of medications such as hydralazine (an antihypertensive) or procainamide (used to treat abnormal heart rhythms). Although the symptoms of this form of lupus are similar to those of SLE, they usually resolve within a few days to weeks after the offending drug is stopped. Cutaneous lupus erythematosus, a milder form sometimes manifested by coin-shaped lesions on the face, neck, and scalp, evolves into systemic disease in about 10 percent of patients.

Symptoms

SLE manifests itself in many ways and can affect virtually any part of the body. Onset may be sudden or gradual over years. Hallmarks of the disease include:

- **Joint pain.** Frequently accompanied by redness and swelling, especially in the fingers, hands, wrists, and knees, joint pain occurs in 90 percent of patients—sometimes years before other symptoms.
- **Skin disorders.** They may be manifested as a butterfly-shaped rash across the cheeks and bridge of the nose (50 percent of patients); coin-shaped lesions, often on the face (25 percent of patients); recurrent ulcers in the mouth and nose; and transient hair loss. About 30 percent develop Raynaud phenomenon, a disorder marked by poor circulation in the small blood vessels of the extremities.
- **Fatigue or fever.** Both occur in 90 percent of patients. Caused by inflammation rather than infection, fever is often low grade but may rise during flare-ups.
- **Kidney involvement.** About half of patients develop lupus nephritis, a persistent inflammation of the kidneys. Such individuals may eventually experience renal failure and require dialysis or kidney transplantation.
- **Blood disorders.** Almost 85 percent of patients experience low red cell, white cell, and platelet counts or other blood disorders. Low platelets may cause easy bleeding and bruising. An antibody paradoxically called the lupus anticoagulant can predispose the blood to clot, raising the risk of venous and arterial thrombosis, heart attack, and stroke.
- **Lung involvement.** Many patients develop pleurisy (an inflammation of the membrane lining the lung) and pleural effusion (an accumulation of fluid between the lung and its lining). Symptoms include chest pain, difficulty breathing, and coughing.
- **Nervous system involvement.** Neurologic disorders affect about a quarter of patients.

Symptoms typically include anxiety, irritability, depression, and mild impairment of memory and concentration, but seizures and psychosis can also occur. For some patients,

Lupus and Cardiovascular Disease

According to several recent studies, certain nontraditional risk factors—including low bone density and high homocystine levels—may be tied to heart disease and stroke in people with lupus.

A study in *Arthritis and Rheumatism* reported that women with SLE who had decreased bone mineral density had increased amounts of plaque in their carotid arteries and signs of calcification in their coronary arteries, factors that raise the risk of stroke and heart disease. And a recent Swedish study, reported in *Circulation*, also found that high homocystine levels and osteoporosis (very low bone density) appeared to increase the risk of heart disease and stroke in people with SLE. The study identified two other nontraditional risk factors for cardiovascular disease: the lupus anticoagulant and antibodies to oxidized low-density lipoprotein (LDL).

Long-term corticosteroid therapy, though often needed to control disease symptoms, may also contribute greatly to the higher cardiovascular risk among SLE patients. High doses of corticosteroids for long periods can raise blood pressure, increase lipid levels, cause weight gain, and raise the risk of diabetes down the road—all factors that put lupus patients at greater risk for heart disease and stroke. In addition, prolonged corticosteroid therapy can lead to low bone density, cataracts, and mood swings.

the limitations imposed by their disease may also lead to depression.

Flare-ups interspersed with periods of improvement or remission are typical for SLE. Symptoms remain mild in about 20 percent to 30 percent of patients. They may have only a skin rash and achy joints but no evidence of major organ involvement. In about 50 percent to 75 percent of patients, however, vital organs such as the kidney, heart, or lungs are affected. Symptoms can be exacerbated by infections, ultraviolet light, certain drugs, and hormones, especially estrogen—as a result, symptoms often increase before menstruation and during pregnancy. In addition, both physical and emotional stress may trigger episodes.

Treatment

Early diagnosis and treatment can greatly improve outcome in those who suffer from lupus. With treatment, the 20-year survival rate is about 80 percent, and many individuals can look forward to a normal life span. Regular monitoring of organ function and heart disease risk factors is necessary.

Patients with traditional and nontraditional risk factors should receive aggressive treatment to ward off cardiovascular disease (see text box above). Patients should generally be followed by a rheumatologist—even when they feel well. Although there is no cure, combination therapy can control symptoms.

Medications

For some patients with mild disease, the only medication needed may be aspirin or a nonsteroidal anti-inflammatory drug (NSAID) to relieve muscle and joint pain. Those with more severe symptoms may require stronger medications, at least on a short-term basis.

Corticosteroids reduce inflammation and suppress the immune system. They are used to control severe or life-threatening complications such as kidney disease, central nervous system involvement, and hemolytic anemia. Some people need corticosteroids for brief periods; others may require long-term therapy. Combining corticosteroids with other drugs can sometimes reduce the

L

risk of serious side effects by reducing the required corticosteroid dose.

Cytotoxic drugs also suppress immune function; they are most commonly used to manage widespread lupus flareups and to treat serious kidney, neurologic, and arthritic symptoms. Cytotoxic drugs can, however, produce anemia, a low white blood count, and an increased risk of infection; they may also increase the risk of cancer later in life, although the risk appears to be very small.

Antimalarial drugs are frequently given to treat the skin and joint symptoms associated with lupus. Side effects, though rare, include diarrhea and rashes. Because about 1 of every 5,000 people taking hydroxychloroquine may develop retinal changes, periodic eye examinations are recommended.

Lifestyle Measures
Conservative measures that discourage episodes include avoiding excessive sun exposure and using a sunscreen with a Sun Protection Factor (SPF) of at least 15. All patients with lupus should obtain sufficient rest (8 to 10 hours of sleep nightly and a nap, if needed, during the day), exercise regularly to help fend off muscle weakness and fatigue, and follow a healthy diet. Because lupus patients have limited energy, they should pace themselves by spreading out work and other activities over a longer period of time and slowing down before they become too tired. Immunizations to protect against influenza and pneumonia are generally recommended, and prompt treatment of infections is essential.

Stress management is also important. Some effective strategies for coping with stress include sharing your feelings with family, friends, and/or members of a support group, and exercising regularly and/or practicing relaxation techniques such as yoga or meditation.

In people over age 50, age-related macular degeneration (AMD)—also referred to as senile macular degeneration—is the leading cause of severe, irreversible loss of central vision. As the name suggests, the prevalence of severe visual loss from AMD increases with age, and most people with visual impairment owing to AMD are 60 or older.

Anatomy of the Retina

The retina is the light-sensitive layer of nerve tissue that lines the inner eye. It is made up of millions of tiny nerve receptor cells called cones and rods. Light rays reflected from an object are focused onto the retina; the cones and rods send impulses through the optic nerve to the brain in response to light.

The most sensitive portion of the retina is a small area at its center, called the macula. In the middle of the macula is a small indentation, the fovea. It contains the highest concentration of cones (the most sensitive receptors of light) and is the area of most acute vision. Central and detailed vision depend on an intact macula. If function of the macula is lost, the eye must rely on less sensitive peripheral vision, and activities such as reading normal-sized print are impossible without low-vision aids. At best, peripheral

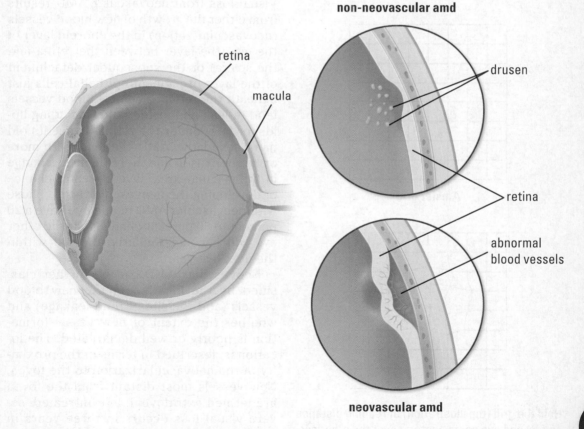

Non-neovascular age-related macular degeneration (AMD) is characterized by the formation of drusen (debris) under the retina. Neovascular AMD is characterized by the development of abnormal blood vessels that leak blood and fluid beneath the retina.

M

vision allows 20/200 visual acuity or the ability to read the big "E" on an eye chart, a common definition for severe visual loss.

Types of AMD

The two forms of AMD are non-neovascular (also known as nonexudative, atrophic, or dry) and neovascular (exudative or wet). The causes of both types are unknown. In addition to age, risk factors for dry AMD include farsightedness, cigarette smoking, light-colored iris, and a family history of the disorder. High blood pressure appears to be a risk factor for neovascular AMD.

Non-Neovascular AMDabnormal blood vesselsAbout 90 percent of people with

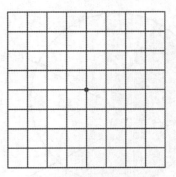

Amsler grid

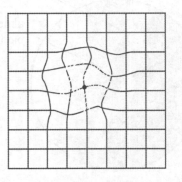

Hold the grid (top illustration) at reading distance and fix one eye on its center; cover the other eye. Distorted or wavy lines (bottom) indicate AMD.

AMD have the non-neovascular form, characterized by a breakdown or thinning of macular tissues. Most often, atrophy of retinal tissues and the formation of drusen (small accumulations of debris underneath the retina) are the distinguishing features of AMD. Although this form of the disease cannot be prevented or reversed, the changes occur slowly and may stabilize for periods of time; often vision is not impaired.

Neovascular AMD

Neovascular AMD, the more serious form of the disorder, is the primary cause of AMD-related visual loss. It may develop at any time in people with non-neovascular AMD. Visual loss from neovascular AMD results from either the growth of new blood vessels (neovascularization) in the choroid layer of the eye (the layer between the retina and the sclera) or the subsequent detachment of the layer of pigment epithelial cells just beneath the retina. The new blood vessels tend to leak and exude fluid (including lipids, or fats) under the retina, hence its old name "exudative AMD." Patients with more or larger drusen and more pigment change in the macular area have a greater chance of developing the neovascular form. Those with neovascular AMD in one eye have a 20 percent to 60 percent chance that the other eye will become similarly affected within the next five years.

Neovascular AMD can be further classified by the location of the new blood vessels (and the site of fluid leakage) and whether the extent of new vessel formation is poorly or well demarcated. The location is described in terms of the proximity of the neovascularization to the fovea. New vessels most distant from the fovea are termed extrafoveal; left untreated, severe visual loss occurs in three years in about 60 percent of eyes with this form of neovascularization. New vessels at

Low-Vision Aids

Despite timely detection and treatment (if indicated), AMD leads to low vision in some patients. The loss of vision is often accompanied by depression, poor self-image, grief, and even suicide.

A number of low-vision optical aids can optimize remaining vision. The perceived benefits of these aids—such as a pair of high-power reading glasses (available at a local drugstore)—depend on the expectations of patients. Patients with unrealistic expectations are likely to be disappointed, while many with more realistic hopes will recognize significant benefits. Also essential is proper training in the use of these devices. Many devices to aid vision are available through low-vision clinics and rehabilitation services.

In addition to these aids, the Low Vision Enhancement System (LVES) has been developed by collaborators at Johns Hopkins, the National Aeronautics and Space Administration (NASA), and the Veterans Administration. The LVES is a battery-powered, head-mounted (to free the user's hands) video device with a camera and a handset that allows the user to control the magnification, contrast, and brightness of an image seen on a monitor.

Recently, the manufacturers of LVES developed a smaller and lighter device, called the Aurora imaging system. Another system, the V-max (from Enhanced Vision Systems), uses a color camera instead of the monochrome display of LVES. The control box for V-max is also smaller and simpler to use than that of the LVES. While helpful, these devices are expensive and can be unwieldy. Other systems now in development will be smaller and lighter and display higher quality images.

---

the fovea itself are called subfoveal. Vessels in between are named juxtafoveal; 70 percent of eyes with subfoveal neovascularization experience severe visual loss within two years. An overgrowth of connective tissue, which accompanies the neovascularization, produces the scarring that is responsible for loss of vision.

Symptoms

Most AMD patients are asymptomatic. When symptoms occur, they usually present as an otherwise unexplained distortion of objects and mild loss of visual acuity that develops gradually (non-neovascular); less often symptoms can be severe and occur in a matter of days or weeks (neovascular). A grayness, haziness, or blank spot may appear in the area of central vision; words may be blurred on a page; straight lines may appear to have a kink in them; and objects may seem smaller than they are. Alternatively, color vision may become dimmer, since the receptors involved in color discrimination (cones) are most dense in the fovea.

Visual distortion can be detected by self-monitoring with an Amsler grid (see page 438). The Amsler grid alone, however, is not a reliable indicator of AMD. Because many patients may not notice gradual changes in vision, they are advised to monitor their vision in several ways, such as during reading, while watching television, and by noting the appearance of various objects.

Prevention

Certain factors within an individual's control might play a role in the prevention or development of AMD. These include dietary supplements, diet, and exposure to sunlight. In addition, a study published in 2000 suggested that people with high blood pressure may be at increased risk for the neovascular form of AMD.

M

Results of a major research trial published in 2001 found that a dietary supplement containing high levels of antioxidants and zinc significantly reduced the risk of developing advanced AMD. Other studies have suggested that eating fruits and vegetables high in carotenoids (carrots, spinach, and cantaloupe, for example), might help prevent AMD.

Avoiding excessive exposure to sunlight was shown to be protective in one large study. Men and women who spent more than three quarters of their time outdoors in the summer were more than twice as likely to develop neovascular AMD than those who spent less than one quarter of their time outside. Moreover, men in the study who regularly wore sunglasses and a hat with a brim reduced their risk of developing advanced AMD by 40 percent.

Based on these findings, it is worthwhile to take steps to protect the eyes from UV rays and to eat plenty of fruits and vegetables rich in carotenoids. Taking vitamin and mineral supplements to prevent or treat AMD may also be helpful for people at high risk of developing advanced AMD .

The more large drusen one has, the greater the risk of developing a leaky vessel. Laser treatment can cause many of the drusen to regress, but it is not yet known whether this reduces the risk of developing neovascular AMD.

Diagnosis

Non-neovascular AMD is diagnosed when the ophthalmologist observes drusen or other pigment changes in the macula. Angiography generally is not required for this form of AMD. Neovascular AMD is suspected when a person notes the onset of new symptoms and an eye examination shows an exudate (fluid deposit) or hemorrhage in the macular area. The diagnosis is confirmed by fluorescein angiography, an examination of blood vessels after a special dye, called fluorescein, is injected into a vein in the arm; photographs of the retina are taken as the dye circulates through the blood vessels of the eye. This test must be performed and interpreted promptly because the disorder can progress within days.

In some cases, it may be necessary first to remove cataracts that obstruct the view of the back of the eye to aid in the diagnosis and treatment of AMD. Removal of cataracts alone can improve vision in some patients, even when retinal treatment is not possible.

Treatment

Neovascular AMD can only be treated about 20 percent of the time, though many low-vision aids can help patients go about their daily activities despite visual loss in both eyes. Non-neovascular AMD is usually not treated; instead, patients are followed for the possible development of neovascular AMD. In addition, people with advanced AMD or vision loss due to AMD in one eye should consider taking supplemental antioxidants and zinc.

Photocoagulation

The standard treatment of neovascular AMD when the new blood vessels are outside the center of the retina is laser coagulation of the new blood vessels, a procedure referred to as photocoagulation. Because of its difficulty, the procedure must be carried out by an ophthalmologist with special training and experience. While photocoagulation decreases the risk of visual loss when well-demarcated new vessels can be identified in extrafoveal, juxtafoveal, or subfoveal sites, such treatment has not proven useful in patients with poorly demarcated new vessels. A variant of this technique, macular scatter ("grid") photocoagulation, was not beneficial

Treatments Under Study

A variety of treatments are being evaluated for patients whose pattern of new blood vessels is not amenable to laser photocoagulation or photodynamic therapy. These include medical therapy with different anti-angiogenic drugs (drugs that may shrink the abnormal vessels) and low-dose radiation. Other potential new therapies also may offer hope to people with neovascular AMD. For example, the abnormal vessels can be removed surgically from beneath the retina, and researchers are investigating this method—called subfoveal surgery—with the hope that the scar that forms after surgery may be smaller than the scar from natural healing. A smaller scar could preserve more vision.

---

and even appeared to be harmful, according to study results.

The high recurrence rate of AMD necessitates careful follow-up and periodic fluorescein angiography. Immediate reexamination is required if a person notes new symptoms of visual loss or distortion by self-monitoring with an Amsler grid. A close watch must be maintained on the other eye as well.

Photodynamic Therapy

The U.S. Food and Drug Administration (FDA) approved photodynamic therapy as a new treatment for neovascular AMD in 2000. Photodynamic therapy is a two-step procedure that can be performed in a doctor's office. In the first step, the patient receives an injection of a drug called verteporfin (Visudyne), which selectively binds to proteins in the tissue affected by abnormal blood vessel growth. Next, a low-powered laser is beamed into the eye, which activates verteporfin to destroy abnormal tissue (but leaves normal tissue intact). Photodynamic therapy appears to stop the leakage of abnormal blood vessels with minimal damage to the retina (one of the dangers of photocoagulation). This approach halts further visual loss and may improve visual acuity in some patients. Because it does not repair retinal tissue that is already damaged, however, photodynamic therapy usually cannot restore lost vision.

Researchers are working on a number of new treatments that may one day help prevent vision loss—or even improve vision—in people with AMD. The most promising medications under investigation are vascular endothelial growth factor (VEGF) inhibitors (including rhuFab V2 and pegatanib [Macugen]) and angiostatic corticosteroids (such as anecortave, triamcinolone, and flucinolone). These treatments may help prevent new blood vessel growth as well as leakage from blood vessels in the eye. Other treatments under investigation are radiation therapy, thermotherapy, and surgery.

M

Menopause, or the "change of life," affects each woman in a different way. Hot flashes and sleep problems troubled your sister. You felt a new sense of freedom and energy. Your best friend was hardly aware of a change at all.

What Is Menopause?

Menopause is a normal part of life. It is one step in a long, slow process of reproductive aging. For most women this process begins silently somewhere around age 40 when periods may start to be less regular. Declining levels of the hormones estrogen and progesterone cause changes in your periods.

These hormones are important for keeping the vagina and uterus healthy as well as for normal menstrual cycles and for successful pregnancy. Estrogen also helps to keep bones healthy. It helps women keep good cholesterol levels in their blood.

Some types of surgery can bring on menopause. For instance, removal of your uterus (hysterectomy) will make your periods stop. When both ovaries are removed (oophorectomy), menopause symptoms may start right away, no matter what your age.

Hormones and Change

A woman's body changes throughout her lifetime. Many of those changes are due to varying hormone levels that happen at different stages in life.

Puberty often starts when a girl is about 12 years old. Her body changes—breasts and pubic hair develop, monthly periods begin.

Menopausal transition, commonly called perimenopause, is the time when a woman's body is closer to menopause. At this time, a woman's periods may become less regular and she may start to feel menopause symptoms, such as hot flashes and night sweats. Perimenopause usually begins about 2 to 4 years before the last menstrual period. It lasts for about 1 year after your last period.

Menopause is marked by a woman's last menstrual period. You cannot know for sure what is your last period until you have been period free for 1 full year.

Postmenopause follows menopause and lasts the rest of your life. Pregnancy is no longer possible. There may be some symptoms, such as vaginal dryness, which may continue long after you have passed through menopause.

What Are the Signs of Menopause?

Changing hormone levels can cause a variety of symptoms that may last from a few months to a few years or longer. Some women have slight discomfort or worse. Others have little or no trouble. If any of these changes bother you, check with your doctor. The most common symptoms are:

Changes in periods. One of the first signs may be a change in a woman's periods. Many women become less regular; some have a lighter flow than normal; others have a heavier flow and may bleed a lot for many days. Periods may come less than 3 weeks apart or last more than a week. There may be spotting between periods. Women who have had problems with heavy menstrual periods and cramps will find relief from these symptoms when menopause starts.

Hot flashes. A hot flash is a sudden feeling of heat in the upper part or all of your body. Your face and neck become flushed. Red blotches may appear on your chest, back, and arms. Heavy sweating and cold shivering can follow. Flashes can be as mild as a light blush or severe enough to

M

wake you from a sound sleep (called night sweats). Most flashes last between 30 seconds and 5 minutes.

Problems with the vagina and bladder. The genital area can get drier and thinner as estrogen levels change. This dryness may make sexual intercourse painful. Vaginal infections can become more common. Some women have more urinary tract infections. Other problems can make it hard to hold urine long enough to get to the bathroom. Some women find that urine leaks during exercise, sneezing, coughing, laughing, or running.

Sex. Some women find that their feelings about sex change with menopause. Some have changes to the vagina, such as dryness, that make sexual intercourse painful. Others feel freer and sexier after menopause— relieved that pregnancy is no longer a worry.

Until you have had one full year without a period, you should still use birth control if you do not want to become pregnant. After menopause a woman can still get sexually transmitted diseases (STDs), such as HIV/AIDS or gonorrhea. If you are worried about STDs, make sure your partner uses a condom each time you have sex.

Sleep problems. Some women find they have a hard time getting a good night's sleep—they may not fall asleep easily or may wake too early. They may need to go to the bathroom in the middle of the night and then find they aren't able to fall back to sleep. Hot flashes also may cause some women to wake up.

Mood changes. There may be a relationship between changes in estrogen levels and a woman's mood. Shifts in mood may also be caused by stress, family changes such as children leaving home, or feeling tired. Depression is not a symptom of menopause.

Changes in your body. Some women find that their bodies change around the time of menopause. With age, waists thicken, muscle mass is lost, fat tissue may increase, skin may get thinner. Other women have memory problems, or joint and muscle stiffness and pain. With regular exercise and attention to diet, many of these changes may be eased or prevented.

There is no way to know when hot flashes will start, when they will end, or how frequent or severe they will be. Each woman's response to fluctuating estrogen levels is highly individual. On average, monthly periods stop sometime around age 51. Hot flashes generally start several years earlier, peak 3 to 24 months after they begin, and persist for 3 to 5 years thereafter. However, some women report experiencing hot flashes in their 70s. Hot flashes also can be caused by medical problems, notably thyroid disorders and infection. They may also be a side effect of some medications, including raloxifene (Evista), which is prescribed to prevent osteoporosis in women who have decided not to take HRT. These causes should be ruled out before hot flashes are attributed to menopause.

What About Heart and Bones?
You may not even notice two important changes that happen with menopause:
- Loss of bone tissue can weaken your bones and cause osteoporosis.
- Heart disease risk may grow, due to age-related increases in weight, blood pressure, and cholesterol levels.

Osteoporosis
To maintain strong bones, the body is always breaking down old bone and replacing it with new healthy bone. For women,

the loss of estrogen around the time of menopause causes more bone to be lost than is replaced. If too much bone is lost, bones become thin and weak and can break easily.

Many people do not know they have weak bones until they break a wrist, hip, or spine bone (vertebrae). Doctors can test bone density (bone densitometry) to find out if you are at risk of osteoporosis.

You can lower your risk of bone loss and osteoporosis by making changes to your lifestyle—regular weight-bearing exercise and getting plenty of calcium and vitamin D can help. There are also drugs available that prevent bone loss. Talk to your doctor to find out what is best for you.

Heart Disease

Younger women have a lower risk of heart disease than do men of the same age. But after menopause, a woman's risk of heart disease is almost the same as a man's. In fact, heart disease is the major cause of death in women, killing more women than lung or breast cancer. It's important to know your blood pressure, and levels of cholesterol, HDL, triglycerides, and fasting blood glucose.

You can lower your chance of heart disease by eating a healthy diet, not smoking, losing weight, and exercising regularly. There are also drugs that can help. Talk to your doctor to be sure you are doing everything possible to protect your heart.

How Can I Stay Healthy Throughout Menopause?

To stay healthy you can make some changes in the way you live. For example:
- Don't smoke.
- Eat a healthy diet that is low in fat and cholesterol and moderate in total fat.

Your diet should aim to be high in fiber and include fruits, vegetables, and whole-grain foods. It should also be well balanced in vitamins and minerals, including calcium.

- Lose weight if you are overweight.
- Take part in weight-bearing exercise, such as walking, jogging, running, or dancing, at least 3 days each week.
- Take medicine to lower your blood pressure if your doctor prescribes it for you.
- For vaginal discomfort, use a water-based vaginal lubricant (not petroleum jelly) or an estrogen cream.
- If you frequently feel an urgent need to urinate, ask your doctor about techniques such as pelvic muscle exercises, biofeedback, and bladder training that can help you improve muscle control.
- Be sure to get regular pelvic and breast exams, Pap tests, and mammograms. Contact your doctor right away if you notice a lump in your breast.
- If you are having hot flashes, keep a diary to track when they happen. You may be able to use this information to help find out what triggers them.

Try these tips to help manage hot flashes:
- When a hot flash starts, go somewhere cool.
- If hot flashes wake you at night, try sleeping in a cool room.
- Dress in layers that you can take off if you get too warm.
- Use sheets and clothing that let your skin "breathe."
- Have a cold drink (water or juice) at the beginning of a flash.

What About Hormone Replacement?

In perimenopause, your doctor might suggest birth control pills, especially if you are having problems with very heavy, frequent or unpredictable menstrual periods. This medication will make your periods more regular. It may also help with symptoms like hot flashes.

However, birth control pills can hide the arrival of menopause. If you think you might have reached menopause, you can stop taking the pill for a while and see if you start having regular periods again. But if you were using birth control pills to prevent pregnancy, you should remember to use another type of contraceptive until you have gone 12 months without a period.

In menopause, your doctor might suggest taking estrogen and progesterone, known as hormone replacement therapy or HRT. HRT involves taking estrogen plus progestin. Estrogen alone, or ERT, is for women who have had the uterus removed. Estrogen plus progestin is for women with a uterus. Progestin, when used with estrogen, helps reduce the risk of uterine cancer. These hormones can be taken in a variety of forms such as pills, skin patches, creams, or vaginal inserts, depending on a woman's needs.

HRT or ERT may relieve menopause-related symptoms, such as hot flashes, and reduce loss of bone. However, HRT has risks. It should not be used for long-term prevention of heart disease. Taking HRT increases, rather than reduces, the risk for heart disease and stroke. It also increases the risk of breast cancer and blood clots. But it appears to decrease the risk of colon cancer. Scientists are still studying the effects of HRT—the final answers are not yet available. Talk to your doctor about taking estrogen/progestin or about other treatments (for example, biofeedback) that may ease menopausal symptoms.

Although no other prescription medications are approved for relieving hot flashes, a few drugs that are approved for other purposes may be helpful, particularly the selective serotonin reuptake inhibitors (SSRIs). A recent double-blind trial conducted at Hopkins and 17 other centers found that a slow-release form of paroxetine (Paxil) reduced hot flashes in a group of menopausal women by 3.3 episodes per day, or 65%, with few bothersome side effects. When an SSRI is going to be effective for hot flashes, the benefit is apparent within a few days. In contrast, when SSRIs are taken for depression—their approved use—it often takes about 6 weeks for symptoms to improve. Other possibilities include the antihypertensive medications clonidine (Catapres), which is also prescribed to relieve premenstrual stress, and methyldopa (Aldomet), and the antiseizure drug gabapentin (Neurontin). But research is limited and the drugs' side effects or patients' existing medical problems may preclude their use.

What About Phytoestrogens?

Phytoestrogens are estrogen-like substances found in cereals, vegetables, legumes (beans), and some herbs. They may work in the body like a weak form of estrogen. Some may lower cholesterol levels. Soy, wild yams, and herbs such as black cohosh and dong quai, contain phytoestrogens and may relieve some symptoms of menopause. The government does not regulate phytoestrogens. Scientists are studying some of these plant estrogens to find out if they really work and are safe.

Be sure to tell your doctor if you decide to eat more foods with phytoestrogens. Any food or over-the-counter product that you use for its drug-like effects could inter-

M

act with other prescribed drugs or cause an overdose.

How Do I Decide What to Do?

Talk to your doctor to decide how to best manage your menopause. Think about your symptoms and how much they bother you. You also need to consider your medical history—your risk of heart disease, osteoporosis, and breast cancer. Remember that your decisions are never final. You can, and should, review them with your doctor every year during your checkup.

You can see a gynecologist, geriatrician, general practitioner, or internist.

For your grandmother and great-grandmother, life expectancy was shorter. Reaching menopause often meant that their life was nearing an end. But this is no longer true. Today women are living longer—on average, until age 78. By making wise decisions about menopause and a healthy lifestyle, you can make the most of the 20, 30, or more years you have ahead.

National Institute on Aging

M

Multiple myeloma is a type of cancer that affects certain white blood cells called plasma cells. Each year, nearly 13,000 people in the United States learn that they have multiple myeloma.

To understand multiple myeloma, it is helpful to know about normal cells, especially plasma cells, and what happens when they become cancerous.

Plasma cells and other white blood cells are part of the immune system, which helps protect the body from infection and disease. All white blood cells begin their development in the bone marrow, the soft, spongy tissue that fills the center of most bones. Certain white blood cells leave the bone marrow and mature in other parts of the body. Some of these develop into plasma cells when the immune system needs them to fight substances that cause infection and disease.

Plasma cells produce antibodies, proteins that move through the bloodstream to help the body get rid of harmful substances. Each type of plasma cell responds to only one specific substance by making a large amount of one kind of antibody. These antibodies find and act against that one substance. Because the body has many types of plasma cells, it can respond to many substances.

When cancer involves plasma cells, the body keeps producing more and more of these cells. The unneeded plasma cells—all abnormal and all exactly alike—are called myeloma cells.

Myeloma cells tend to collect in the bone marrow and in the hard, outer part of bones. Sometimes they collect in only one bone and form a single mass, or tumor, called a plasmacytoma. In most cases, however, the myeloma cells collect in many bones, often forming many tumors and causing other problems. This is called multiple myeloma.

(It is important to keep in mind that cancer is classified by the type of cell or the part of the body in which the disease begins. Although plasmacytoma and multiple myeloma affect the bones, they begin in cells of the immune system. These cancers are different from bone cancer, which actually begins in cells that form the hard, outer part of the bone. This fact is important because the diagnosis and treatment of plasmacytoma and multiple myeloma are different from the diagnosis and treatment of bone cancer.)

Because people with multiple myeloma have an abnormally large number of identical plasma cells, they also have too much of one type of antibody. These myeloma cells and antibodies can cause a number of serious medical problems:

- As myeloma cells increase in number, they damage and weaken bones, causing pain and sometimes fractures. Bone pain can make it difficult for patients to move.
- When bones are damaged, calcium is released into the blood. This may lead to hypercalcemia—too much calcium in the blood. Hypercalcemia can cause loss of appetite, nausea, thirst, fatigue, muscle weakness, restlessness, and confusion.
- Myeloma cells prevent the bone marrow from forming normal plasma cells and other white blood cells that are important to the immune system. Patients may not be able to fight infection and disease.
- The cancer cells also may prevent the growth of new red blood cells, causing anemia. Patients with anemia may feel unusually tired or weak.
- Multiple myeloma patients may have serious problems with their kidneys. Excess antibody proteins and calcium can prevent the kidneys from filtering and cleaning the blood properly.

M

Possible Causes

Scientists at hospitals, medical schools, and research laboratories across the country are studying multiple myeloma. At this time, we do not know what causes this disease or how to prevent it. However, we do know that no one can "catch" multiple myeloma from another person; cancer is not contagious.

Although scientists cannot explain why one person gets multiple myeloma and another doesn't, we do know that most multiple myeloma patients are between 50 and 70 years old. This disease affects African Americans more often than whites and men more often than women.

Some research suggests that certain risk factors increase a person's chance of getting multiple myeloma. For example, a person's family background appears to affect the risk of developing multiple myeloma; children and brothers and sisters of patients who have this disease have a slightly increased risk. Farmers and petroleum workers exposed to certain chemicals also seem to have a higher-than-average chance of getting multiple myeloma. In addition, people exposed to large amounts of radiation (such as survivors of the atomic bomb explosions in Japan) have an increased risk for this disease. Scientists have some concern that smaller amounts of radiation (such as those to which radiologists and workers in nuclear plants are exposed) also may increase the risk. At this time, however, scientists do not have clear evidence that large numbers of medical x-rays increase the risk for multiple myeloma. In fact, most people receive a fairly small number of x-rays, and scientists believe that the benefits of medical x-rays far outweigh the possible risk for multiple myeloma.

In most cases, people who develop multiple myeloma have no clear risk factors. The disease may be the result of several factors (known and/or unknown) acting together.

Symptoms

Symptoms of multiple myeloma depend on how advanced the disease is. In the earliest stage of the disease, there may be no symptoms. When symptoms do occur, patients commonly have bone pain, often in the back or ribs. Patients also may have broken bones, weakness, fatigue, weight loss, or repeated infections. When the disease is advanced, symptoms may include nausea, vomiting, constipation, problems with urination, and weakness or numbness in the legs. These are not sure signs of multiple myeloma; they can be symptoms of other types of medical problems. A person should see a doctor if these symptoms occur. Only a doctor can determine what is causing a patient's symptoms.

Diagnosis

Multiple myeloma may be found as part of a routine physical exam before patients have symptoms of the disease. When patients do have symptoms, the doctor asks about their personal and family medical history and does a complete physical exam. In addition to checking general signs of health, the doctor may order a number of tests to determine the cause of the symptoms. If a patient has bone pain, x-rays can show whether any bones are damaged or broken. Samples of the patient's blood and urine are checked to see whether they contain high levels of antibody proteins called M proteins. The doctor also may do a bone marrow aspiration and/or a bone marrow biopsy to check for myeloma cells. In an aspiration, the doctor inserts a needle into the hip bone or breast bone to withdraw a sample of fluid and cells from the bone marrow. To do a biopsy, the doctor uses a larger needle to remove a sample of solid tissue from the marrow. A pathologist examines the samples under a microscope to see whether myeloma cells are present.

Staging

To plan a patient's treatment, the doctor needs to know the stage, or extent, of the disease. Staging is a careful attempt to find out what parts of the body are affected by the cancer. Treatment decisions depend on these findings. Results of the patient's exam, blood tests, and bone marrow tests can help doctors determine the stage of the disease. In addition, staging usually involves a series of x-rays to determine the number and size of tumors in the bones. In some cases, a patient will have MRI if closeup views of the bones are needed.

Treatment

Treatment depends on the extent of the cancer and the patient's symptoms. Plasmacytoma and multiple myeloma are very hard to cure. Although patients who have a plasmacytoma may be free of symptoms for a long time after treatment, many eventually develop multiple myeloma. For those who have multiple myeloma, treatment can improve the quality of a patient's life by controlling the symptoms and complications of the disease.

People who have multiple myeloma but do not have symptoms of the disease usually do not receive treatment. For these patients, the risks and side effects of treatment are likely to outweigh the possible benefits. However, these patients are watched closely, and they begin treatment when symptoms appear. Patients who need treatment for multiple myeloma usually receive chemotherapy and sometimes radiation therapy. Also, the patient may want to talk with the doctor about taking part in a research study of new treatment methods. Such studies, called clinical trials, are designed to improve the treatment of this type of cancers (see page 181).

Chemotherapy is the use of drugs to treat cancer. It is the main treatment for multiple myeloma. Doctors may prescribe two or more drugs that work together to kill myeloma cells. Many of these drugs are taken by mouth; others are injected into a blood vessel. Either way, the drugs travel through the bloodstream, reaching myeloma cells all over the body. For this reason, chemotherapy is called systemic therapy.

Anticancer drugs often are given in cycles—a treatment period followed by a rest period, then another treatment and rest period, and so on. Most patients take their chemotherapy at home, as outpatients at the hospital, or at the doctor's office. However, depending on their health and the drugs being given, patients may need to stay in the hospital during treatment.

Radiation therapy (also called radiotherapy) uses high-energy rays to damage cancer cells and stop them from growing. In this form of treatment, a large machine aims the rays at a tumor and the area close to it. Treatment with radiation is local therapy; it affects only the cells in the treated area.

Radiation therapy is the main treatment for people who have a single plasmacytoma. They usually receive radiation therapy every weekday for four to five weeks in the outpatient department of a hospital or clinic.

People who have multiple myeloma sometimes receive radiation therapy in addition to chemotherapy. The purpose of the radiation therapy is to help control the growth of tumors in the bones and relieve the pain that these tumors cause. Treatment usually lasts for one to two weeks.

Side Effects of Treatment

The methods used to treat multiple myeloma are very powerful. Treatment can help patients feel better by relieving symptoms such as bone pain. However, it is hard to limit the effects of therapy so that only cancer cells are destroyed. Because healthy cells also may be damaged, treatment can cause unpleasant side effects.

The side effects that patients have during cancer treatment vary for each person. They may even be different from one treatment to the next. Doctors try to plan treatment to keep side effects to a minimum. They also monitor patients very carefully so they can help with any problems that occur.

The side effects of chemotherapy depend on the drugs that are given. In general, anticancer drugs affect rapidly growing cells, such as blood cells that fight infection, cells that line the digestive tract, and cells in hair follicles. As a result, patients may have lower resistance to infection, loss of appetite, nausea, vomiting, or mouth sores. Patients also may have less energy and may lose their hair. One drug used to treat multiple myeloma, called prednisone, may cause swelling of the face and feet, burning indigestion, mood swings, restlessness, and acne. The side effects of chemotherapy usually go away over time after treatment stops.

During radiation therapy, the patient may be more tired than usual. Resting is important, but doctors usually advise patients to stay as active as they can. Also, the skin in the treated area may become red or dry. The skin should be exposed to the air but protected from the sun, and patients should avoid wearing clothes that rub the treated area. They should not use any lotion or cream on the skin without the doctor's advice. Patients may have other side effects, depending upon the areas treated. For example, radiation to the lower back may cause nausea, vomiting, or diarrhea because the lower digestive tract is exposed to radiation. The doctor often can prescribe medicine or suggest changes in diet to ease these problems. Side effects usually disappear gradually after radiation therapy is over.

Loss of appetite can be a problem for patients with multiple myeloma. People may not feel hungry when they are uncomfortable or tired. Some of the common side effects of cancer treatment, such as nausea and vomiting, can also make it hard to eat. Yet patients who eat well often feel better and have more energy, so good nutrition is important. Eating well means getting enough calories and protein to prevent weight loss, regain strength, and rebuild normal tissues. Many patients find that having several small meals and snacks during the day works better than having three regular meals. Doctors, nurses, and dietitians can explain the side effects of cancer treatment and can suggest ways to deal with them.

Supportive Care

The complications of multiple myeloma can affect many parts of the body. Chemotherapy and radiation therapy often can help control complications such as pain, bone damage, and kidney problems. However, from time to time, most patients need additional treatment to manage these and other problems caused by the disease. This type of treatment, called supportive care, is given to improve patients' comfort and quality of life.

Patients with multiple myeloma frequently have pain caused by bone damage or by tumors pressing on nerves. Doctors often suggest that patients take pain medicine and/or wear a back or neck brace to help relieve their pain. Some patients find that techniques such as relaxation and imagery can reduce their pain.

Preventing or treating bone fractures is another important part of supportive care. Because exercise can reduce the loss of calcium from the bones, doctors and nurses encourage patients to be active, if possible. They may suggest appropriate forms of exercise. If a patient has a fracture or a breakdown of certain bones, especially those in the spine, a surgeon may need to operate to remove as much of the cancer as possible and to strengthen the bone.

Patients who have hypercalcemia may be given medicine to reduce the level of calcium in the blood. They also are encouraged to drink large amounts of fluids every day; some may need intravenous (IV) fluids. Getting plenty of fluids helps the kidneys get rid of excess calcium in the blood. It also helps prevent problems that occur when calcium collects in the kidneys.

If the kidneys aren't working well, dialysis or plasmapheresis may be necessary. In dialysis, the patient's blood passes through a machine that removes wastes, and the blood is then returned to the patient. Plasmapheresis is used to remove excess antibodies produced by the myeloma cells. This process thins the blood, making it easier for the kidneys and the heart to function.

Multiple myeloma weakens the immune system. Patients must be very careful to protect themselves from infection. It is important that they stay out of crowds and away from people with colds or other infectious diseases. Any sign of infection (fever, sore throat, cough) should be reported to the doctor right away. Patients who develop infections are treated with antibiotics or other drugs.

Patients who have anemia may have transfusions of red blood cells. Transfusions can help reduce the shortness of breath and fatigue that can be caused by anemia.

Follow-up Care

Regular follow-up is very important for anyone who has multiple myeloma. Checkups generally include a physical exam, x-rays, and blood and urine tests. Regular follow-up exams help doctors detect and treat problems promptly if they should arise. It is also important for the patient to tell the doctor about any new symptoms or problems that develop between checkups.

National Cancer Institute

M

N

The lymphatic system is part of the body's immune system. It helps the body fight disease and infection. The lymphatic system includes a network of thin tubes that branch, like blood vessels, into tissues throughout the body. Lymphatic vessels carry lymph, a colorless, watery fluid that contains infection-fighting cells called lymphocytes. Along this network of vessels are small organs called lymph nodes. Clusters of lymph nodes are found in the underarms, groin, neck, chest, and abdomen. Other parts of the lymphatic system are the spleen, thymus, tonsils, and bone marrow. Lymphatic tissue is also found in other parts of the body, including the stomach, intestines, and skin.

In non-Hodgkin's lymphoma, cells in the lymphatic system become abnormal. They divide and grow without any order or control, or old cells do not die as cells normally do. Because lymphatic tissue is present in many parts of the body, non-Hodgkin's lymphoma can start almost anywhere in the body. Non-Hodgkin's lymphoma may occur in a single lymph node, a group of lymph nodes, or in another organ. This type of cancer can spread to almost any part of the body, including the liver, bone marrow, and spleen.

Non-Hodgkin's lymphoma is a type of cancer. Lymphoma is a general term for cancers that develop in the lymphatic system. Hodgkin's disease is one type of lymphoma. All other lymphomas are grouped together and are called non-Hodgkin's lymphoma. Lymphomas account for about 5 percent of all cases of cancer in this country.

Risk Factors

The incidence of non-Hodgkin's lymphoma has increased dramatically over the last couple of decades. This disease has gone from being relatively rare to being the fifth most common cancer in the United States. At this time, little is known about the reasons for this increase or about exactly what causes non-Hodgkin's lymphoma.

Doctors can seldom explain why one person gets non-Hodgkin's lymphoma and another does not. It is clear, however, that cancer is not caused by an injury, and is not contagious; no one can "catch" non-Hodgkin's lymphoma from another person.

By studying patterns of cancer in the population, researchers have found certain risk factors that are more common in people who get non-Hodgkin's lymphoma than in those who do not. However, most people with these risk factors do not get non-Hodgkin's lymphoma, and many who do get this disease have none of the known risk factors.

The following are some of the risk factors associated with this disease:

- **Age/Sex.** The likelihood of getting non-Hodgkin's lymphoma increases with age and is more common in men than in women.
- **Weakened immune system.** Non-Hodgkin's lymphoma is more common among people with inherited immune deficiencies, autoimmune diseases, or HIV/AIDS, and among people taking immunosuppressant drugs following organ transplants.
- **Viruses.** Human T-lymphotropic virus type I (HTLV-1) and Epstein-Barr virus are two infectious agents that increase the chance of developing non-Hodgkin's lymphoma.
- **Environment.** People who work extensively with or are otherwise exposed to certain chemicals, such as pesticides, solvents, or fertilizers, have a greater chance of developing non-Hodgkin's lymphoma.

People who are concerned about non-Hodgkin's lymphoma should talk with their doctor about the disease, the symptoms to watch for, and an appropriate schedule for checkups. The doctor's advice will be based on the person's age, medical history, and other factors.

Symptoms

The most common symptom of non-Hodgkin's lymphoma is a painless swelling of the lymph nodes in the neck, underarm, or groin.

Other symptoms may include:

- Unexplained fever
- Night sweats
- Constant fatigue
- Unexplained weight loss
- Itchy skin
- Reddened patches on the skin

When symptoms like these occur, they are not sure signs of non-Hodgkin's lymphoma. They may also be caused by other, less serious conditions, such as the flu or other infections. Only a doctor can make a diagnosis. When symptoms are present, it is important to see a doctor so that any illness can be diagnosed and treated as early as possible. Do not wait to feel pain; early non-Hodgkin's lymphoma may not cause pain.

Diagnosis

If non-Hodgkin's lymphoma is suspected, the doctor asks about the person's medical history and performs a physical exam. The exam includes feeling to see if the lymph nodes in the neck, underarm, or groin are enlarged. In addition to checking general signs of health, the doctor may perform blood tests.

The doctor may also order tests that produce pictures of the inside of the body. These may include:

- **X-rays:** Pictures of areas inside the body created by high-energy radiation.
- **CT (or CAT) scan:** A series of detailed pictures of areas inside the body. The pictures are created by a computer linked to an x-ray machine.

- **MRI (magnetic resonance imaging):** Detailed pictures of areas inside the body produced with a powerful magnet linked to a computer.
- **Lymphangiogram:** Pictures of the lymphatic system taken with x-rays after a special dye is injected to outline the lymph nodes and vessels.

A biopsy is needed to make a diagnosis. A surgeon removes a sample of tissue so that a pathologist can examine it under a microscope to check for cancer cells. A biopsy for non-Hodgkin's lymphoma is usually taken from a lymph node, but other tissues may be sampled as well. Sometimes, an operation called a laparotomy may be performed. During this operation, a surgeon cuts into the abdomen and removes samples of tissue to be checked under a microscope.

Types of Non-Hodgkin's Lymphoma

Over the years, doctors have used a variety of terms to classify the many different types of non-Hodgkin's lymphoma. Most often, they are grouped by how the cancer cells look under a microscope and how quickly they are likely to grow and spread. Aggressive lymphomas, also known as intermediate and high-grade lymphomas, tend to grow and spread quickly and cause severe symptoms. Indolent lymphomas, also referred to as low-grade lymphomas, tend to grow quite slowly and cause fewer symptoms.

Staging

If non-Hodgkin's lymphoma is diagnosed, the doctor needs to learn the stage, or extent, of the disease. Staging is a careful attempt to find out whether the cancer has spread and, if so, what parts of the body are affected. Decisions about treatment depend on these findings.

The doctor considers the following to determine the stage of non-Hodgkin's lymphoma:

N

- The number and location of affected lymph nodes;
- Whether the affected lymph nodes are above, below, or on both sides of the diaphragm (the thin muscle under the lungs and heart that separates the chest from the abdomen); and
- Whether the disease has spread to the bone marrow, spleen, or to organs outside the lymphatic system, such as the liver.

In staging, the doctor may use some of the same tests used for the diagnosis of non-Hodgkin's lymphoma. Other staging procedures may include additional biopsies of lymph nodes, the liver, bone marrow, or other tissue. A bone marrow biopsy involves removing a sample of bone marrow through a needle inserted into the hip or another large bone. A pathologist examines the sample under a microscope to check for cancer cells.

Treatment

The doctor develops a treatment plan to fit each patient's needs. Treatment for non-Hodgkin's lymphoma depends on the stage of the disease, the type of cells involved, whether they are indolent or aggressive, and the age and general health of the patient.

Non-Hodgkin's lymphoma is often treated by a team of specialists that may include a hematologist, medical oncologist, and/or radiation oncologist. Non-Hodgkin's lymphoma is usually treated with chemotherapy, radiation therapy, or a combination of these treatments. In some cases, bone marrow transplantation, biological therapies, or surgery may be options.

For indolent lymphomas, the doctor may decide to wait until the disease causes symptoms before starting treatment. Often, this approach is called "watchful waiting."

Chemotherapy and radiation therapy are the most common treatments for non-Hodgkin's lymphoma, although bone marrow transplantation, biological therapies, or surgery are sometimes used. Taking part in a clinical trial (research study) to evaluate promising new ways to treat non-Hodgkin's lymphoma is an important option for many people with this disease (see page 181).

Chemotherapy is the use of drugs to kill cancer cells. Chemotherapy for non-Hodgkin's lymphoma usually consists of a combination of several drugs. Patients may receive chemotherapy alone or in combination with radiation therapy.

Chemotherapy is usually given in cycles: a treatment period followed by a recovery period, then another treatment period, and so on. Most anticancer drugs are given by injection into a blood vessel (IV); some are given by mouth. Chemotherapy is a systemic treatment because the drugs enter the bloodstream and travel throughout the body.

Usually a patient has chemotherapy as an outpatient (at the hospital, at the doctor's office, or at home). However, depending on which drugs are given and the patient's general health, a short hospital stay may be needed.

Radiation therapy (also called radiotherapy) is the use of high-energy rays to kill cancer cells. Treatment with radiation may be given alone or with chemotherapy. Radiation therapy is local treatment; it affects cancer cells only in the treated area. Radiation therapy for non-Hodgkin's lymphoma comes from a machine that aims the high-energy rays at a specific area of the body. There is no radioactivity in the body when the treatment is over.

Sometimes patients are given chemotherapy and/or radiation therapy to kill undetected cancer cells that may be present in the central nervous system (CNS). In this treatment, called central nervous system prophylaxis, the doctor injects anticancer drugs directly into the cerebrospinal fluid.

Bone marrow transplantation (BMT) may also be a treatment option, especially for patients whose non-Hodgkin's lymphoma has recurred. BMT provides the patient with healthy stem cells (very immature cells that produce blood cells) to replace cells damaged or destroyed by treatment with very high doses of chemotherapy and/or radiation therapy. The healthy bone marrow may come from a donor, or it may be marrow that was removed from the patient, treated to destroy cancer cells, stored, and then given back to the person following the high-dose treatment. Until the transplanted bone marrow begins to produce enough white blood cells, patients have to be carefully protected from infection. They usually stay in the hospital for several weeks.

Biological therapy (also called immunotherapy) is a form of treatment that uses the body's immune system, either directly or indirectly, to fight cancer or to lessen the side effects that can be caused by some cancer treatments. It uses materials made by the body or made in a laboratory to boost, direct, or restore the body's natural defenses against disease. Biological therapy is sometimes also called biological response modifier therapy.

Surgery may be performed to remove a tumor. Tissue around the tumor and nearby lymph nodes may also be removed during the operation.

Side Effects of Treatment

Treatments for non-Hodgkin's lymphoma are very powerful. It is hard to limit the effects of therapy so that only cancer cells are removed or destroyed. Because treatment also damages healthy cells and tissues, it often causes side effects.

The side effects of cancer treatment depend mainly on the type and extent of the therapy. Side effects may not be the same for everyone, and they may even change from one treatment to the next. Doctors and nurses can explain the possible side effects of treatment. They can also lessen or control many of the side effects that may occur during and after treatment.

Chemotherapy

The side effects of chemotherapy depend mainly on the drugs and the doses the patient receives. As with other types of treatment, side effects may vary from person to person.

Anticancer drugs generally affect cells that divide rapidly. In addition to cancer cells, these include blood cells, which fight infection, help the blood to clot, or carry oxygen to all parts of the body. When blood cells are affected, the patient is more likely to get infections, may bruise or bleed easily, and may feel unusually weak and tired. The patient's blood count is monitored during chemotherapy and, if necessary, the doctor may decide to postpone treatment to allow blood counts to recover.

Cells in hair roots also divide rapidly; therefore, chemotherapy may lead to hair loss. Patients may have other side effects such as poor appetite, nausea and vomiting, or mouth and lip sores. They may also experience dizziness and darkening of the skin and fingernails.

Most side effects go away gradually during the recovery periods between treatments or after treatment is over. However, certain anticancer drugs can increase the risk of developing a second cancer later in life.

In some men and women, chemotherapy causes a loss of fertility (the ability to

N

produce children). Loss of fertility may be temporary or permanent, depending on the drugs used and the patient's age. For men, sperm banking before treatment may be an option. Women's menstrual periods may stop, and they may have hot flashes and vaginal dryness. Menstrual periods are more likely to return in young women.

Radiation Therapy
The side effects of radiation depend on the treatment dose and the part of the body that is treated. During radiation therapy, people are likely to become extremely tired, especially in the later weeks of treatment. Rest is important, but doctors usually advise patients to try to stay as active as they can.

It is common to lose hair in the treated area and for the skin to become red, dry, tender, or itchy. There may also be permanent darkening or "bronzing" of the skin in the treated area.

When the chest and neck are treated, patients may have a dry, sore throat and trouble swallowing. Some patients may have tingling or numbness in their arms, legs, and lower back. Radiation therapy to the abdomen may cause nausea, vomiting, diarrhea, or urinary discomfort. Often, changes in diet or medicine can ease these problems.

Radiation therapy also may cause a decrease in the number of white blood cells, cells that help protect the body against infection. If that happens, patients need to be careful to avoid possible sources of infection. The doctor monitors a patient's blood count during radiation therapy. In some cases, treatment may have to be postponed to allow blood counts to recover.

Although the side effects of radiation therapy can be difficult, they can usually be treated or controlled. It may also help to know that, in most cases, side effects are not permanent. However, patients may want to discuss with their doctor the possible long-term effects of radiation treatment on fertility and the increased chance of second cancers after treatment is over.

Bone Marrow Transplantation
Patients who have a bone marrow transplant face an increased risk of infection, bleeding, and other side effects from the large doses of chemotherapy and radiation they receive. In addition, graft-versus-host disease (GVHD) may occur in patients who receive bone marrow from a donor. In GVHD, the donated marrow attacks the patient's tissues (most often the liver, the skin, and the digestive tract). GVHD can range from mild to very severe. It can occur any time after the transplant (even years later). Drugs may be given to reduce the risk of GVHD and to treat the problem if it occurs.

Biological Therapy
The side effects caused by biological therapy vary with the specific type of treatment. These treatments may cause flu-like symptoms such as chills, fever, muscle aches, weakness, loss of appetite, nausea, vomiting, and diarrhea. Patients also may bleed or bruise easily, get a skin rash, or retain fluid. These problems can be severe, but they usually go away after treatment stops.

Surgery
The side effects of surgery depend on the location of the tumor, the type of operation, the patient's general health, and other factors. Although patients are often uncomfortable during the first few days after surgery, the pain can usually be controlled with medicine. People can talk with their doctor or nurse about pain relief. It is also common for patients to feel tired or weak for a while. The length of time it takes to recover from an operation varies for each patient.

Follow-up Care

People who have had non-Hodgkin's lymphoma should have regular follow-up examinations after their treatment is over. Follow-up care is an important part of the overall treatment plan, and people should not hesitate to discuss it with their healthcare provider. Regular follow-up care ensures that patients are carefully monitored, any changes in health are discussed, and new or recurrent cancer can be detected and treated as soon as possible. Between follow-up appointments, people who have had non-Hodgkin's lymphoma should report any health problems as soon as they appear.

National Cancer Institute

More than 60 percent of Americans aged 20 years and older are overweight. One-quarter of American adults are also obese, putting them at increased health risk for chronic diseases such as heart disease, type 2 diabetes, high blood pressure, stroke, and some forms of cancer.

To most people, the term "obesity" means to be very overweight. Health professionals define "overweight" as an excessive amount of body weight that includes muscle, bone, fat, and water. "Obesity" specifically refers to an excessive amount of body fat. Some people, such as bodybuilders or other athletes with a lot of muscle, can be overweight without being obese.

How Is Obesity Measured?

Everyone needs a certain amount of body fat for stored energy, heat insulation, shock absorption, and other functions. As a rule, women have more body fat than men. Most health-care providers agree that men with more than 25 percent body fat and women with more than 30 percent body fat are obese.

Measuring the exact amount of a person's body fat is not easy. The most accurate measures are to weigh a person underwater or to use an x-ray test called Dual Energy X-ray Absorptiometry (DEXA). These methods are not practical for the average person, and are done only in research centers with special equipment.

There are simpler methods to estimate body fat. One is to measure the thickness of the layer of fat just under the skin in several parts of the body. Another involves sending a harmless amount of electricity through a person's body. Both methods are used at health clubs and commercial weight-loss programs. Results from these methods, however, can be inaccurate if done by an inexperienced person or on someone with severe obesity.

Because measuring a person's body fat is difficult, health-care providers often rely on other means to diagnose obesity. Weight-for-height tables, which have been used for decades, usually have a range of acceptable weights for a person of a given height. One problem with these tables is that there are many versions, all with different weight ranges. Another problem is that they do not distinguish between excess fat and muscle. A very muscular person may appear obese, according to the tables, when he or she is not.

In recent years, body mass index (BMI) has become the medical standard used to measure overweight and obesity.

Body Mass Index

BMI uses a mathematical formula based on a person's height and weight. BMI equals weight in kilograms divided by height in meters squared (BMI = kg/m2).

Another way to determine your BMI is to multiply your weight in pounds by 704 and divide the result by your height in inches squared.

A BMI of 25 to 29.9 indicates a person is overweight. A person with a BMI of 30 or higher is considered obese.

Like the weight-to-height tables, BMI does not show the difference between excess fat and muscle. BMI, however, is closely associated with measures of body fat. It also predicts the development of health problems related to excess weight. For these reasons, BMI is widely used by health-care providers.

Body Fat Distribution: "Pears" vs. "Apples"

Health-care providers are concerned not only with how much fat a person has, but

Medications for Weight Loss

Whether the treatment of obesity requires medication is a decision that must be made on a case-by-case basis. Generally, though, drugs should be used only by people who are obese—in other words, those whose BMI is greater than 30—or have a BMI greater than 27 accompanied by serious medical conditions that could be improved by weight loss.

For significant weight loss, you must combine medication with diet, exercise, and behavioral modification. Several classes of prescription medications are used to treat obesity.

Serotonin/norepinephrine reuptake inhibitors. By enhancing both serotonin and norepinephrine levels in the brain, sibutramine (Meridia) promotes feelings of satiation and thus reduces appetite. Sibutramine can increase blood pressure, so patients taking this drug should have their blood pressure monitored regularly.

Lipase inhibitors. The lipase inhibitor orlistat (Xenical) blocks the intestinal absorption of about 30 percent of dietary fat. Side effects—such as cramping, oily anal leakage, and explosive diarrhea—tend to be worse when patients eat greater quantities of fatty foods. This discourages the consumption of such foods and contributes to the effectiveness of the drug.

Noradrenergics. These drugs—which include benzphetamine (Didrex), diethylproprion (Tenuate), mazindol (Mazanor, Sanorex), and phentermine (Fastin, Ionamin)—increase levels of norepinephrine in the brain. Norepinephrine reduces appetite by stimulating the central nervous system. Tolerance to these drugs may develop after a few weeks, slowing the rate of weight loss. Serious side effects include rapid heartbeat and high blood pressure.

Antidepressants. Although not approved by the Food and Drug Administration (FDA) for weight control, selective serotonin reuptake inhibitors (SSRIs), such as fluoxetine (Prozac) or sertraline (Zoloft), often contribute to weight loss in patients taking them for depression. Typically, these drugs are prescribed for weight loss if a patient is also depressed. Patients taking SSRIs report feeling less hungry, less concerned with food, and better able to control their appetites; however, the effect may not last long. Side effects include insomnia and fatigue.

Bear in mind that without adopting and maintaining an appropriate lifestyle, people taking medications for weight loss tend to regain any lost weight as soon as they stop the medication.

The Editors

---

also where the fat is located on the body. Women typically collect fat in their hips and buttocks, giving them a "pear" shape. Men usually build up fat around their bellies, giving them more of an "apple" shape. Of course, some men are pear-shaped and some women become apple-shaped, especially after menopause. If you carry fat mainly around your waist, you are more likely to develop obesity-related health problems. Women with a waist measurement of more than 35 inches or men with a waist measurement of more than 40 inches have a higher health risk because of their body fat distribution.

Causes of Obesity

In scientific terms, obesity occurs when a person consumes more calories than he or she burns. What causes this imbalance between calories in and calories out may differ from one person to another. Genetic, environmental, psychological, and other factors may all play a part.

Genetic Factors

Obesity tends to run in families, suggesting a genetic cause. Yet families also share diet and lifestyle habits that may contribute to obesity. Separating these from genetic factors is often difficult. Even so, science shows that obesity is linked to heredity.

In one study, adults who were adopted as children were found to have weights closer to their biological parents than to their adoptive parents. In this case, the person's genetic makeup had more influence on the development of obesity than the environment in the adoptive family home.

Environmental Factors

Genes do not destine people to a lifetime of obesity, however. Environment also strongly influences obesity. This includes lifestyle behaviors such as what a person eats and his or her level of physical activity. Americans tend to eat high-fat foods, and they put taste and convenience ahead of nutrition. Also, most Americans do not get enough physical activity.

Although you cannot change your genetic makeup, you can change your eating habits and levels of activity. Try these techniques that have helped some people lose weight and keep it off:

- Learn how to choose more nutritious meals that are lower in fat.
- Learn to recognize and control environmental cues (like inviting smells) that make you want to eat when you're not hungry.
- Become more physically active.
- Keep records of your food intake and physical activity.

Psychological Factors

Psychological factors may also influence eating habits. Many people eat in response to negative emotions such as boredom, sadness, or anger.

Most overweight people have no more psychological problems than people of average weight. Still, up to 10 percent of people who are mildly obese and try to lose weight on their own or through commercial weight-loss programs have binge eating disorder. This disorder is even more common in people who are severely obese.

During a binge eating episode, people eat large amounts of food and feel that they cannot control how much they are eating. Those with the most severe binge eating problems are also likely to have symptoms of depression and low self-esteem. These people may have more difficulty losing weight and keeping it off than people without binge eating problems.

If you are upset by binge eating behavior and think you might have binge eating disorder, seek help from a health professional such as a psychiatrist, psychologist, or clinical social worker.

Other Causes of Obesity

Some illnesses can lead to obesity or a tendency to gain weight. These include hypothyroidism, Cushing's syndrome, depression, and certain neurological problems that can lead to overeating. Also, drugs such as steroids and some antidepressants may cause weight gain. A doctor can tell whether there are underlying medical conditions that are causing weight gain or making weight loss difficult.

Consequences of Obesity

Obesity is more than a cosmetic problem; it is a health hazard. Approximately 280,000 adult deaths in the United States each year are related to obesity. Several serious medical conditions have been linked to obesity, including type 2 diabetes, heart disease,

Gastric Surgery

Gastric surgery is considered in morbidly obese patients—BMI of 40 or more (or less than 40 with significant complications of obesity)—who have failed to lose weight through other methods. Two types of procedures are commonly available: vertical banded gastroplasty and gastric bypass. A third, less common type of operation is called gastric banding. All three operations encourage caloric restriction by reducing the size of the stomach, thus limiting the amount of food that can be consumed at one time; but gastric bypass also interferes with the digestive process (food bypasses part of the small intestine) and reduces calorie and nutrient absorption.

The risks associated with gastric bypass are similar to those of vertical banded gastroplasty. However, approximately 30% of bypass patients also develop nutritional deficiencies because many nutrients are normally absorbed in the upper part of the jejunum.

Gastric surgery is most effective when patients receive the dietary, exercise, and behavioral instructions that are the hallmarks of successful weight loss and weight maintenance. Gastric restriction surgery leads to substantial reductions in weight—averaging 80 to 150 lbs, depending on the initial weight—in the first year. Some weight may be regained during the next two to five years. (Typically, vertical banded gastroplasty results in less weight loss than gastric bypass.) Most of the complications of obesity improve: Blood glucose, triglyceride, and cholesterol levels fall; blood pressure is lowered; sleep apnea is eliminated; and arthritic pain is lessened. Moreover, gastric surgery increases the chance that morbidly obese patients will lose enough weight to increase life expectancy by avoiding serious complications of obesity.

Because gastric surgery is highly specialized, it should be performed only by skilled, experienced surgeons in hospitals with proven records of safety and efficacy. Under these conditions, the risk of dying from gastric surgery is less than 1 percent. Complications (such as nutritional deficiencies and vomiting) occur in about 10 percent of patients. *The Editors*

---

high blood pressure, and stroke. Obesity is also linked to higher rates of certain types of cancer. Obese men are more likely than non-obese men to die from cancer of the colon, rectum, or prostate. Obese women are more likely than non-obese women to die from cancer of the gallbladder, breast, uterus, cervix, or ovaries. Other diseases and health problems linked to obesity include:

- Gallbladder disease and gallstones;
- Liver disease;
- Osteoarthritis, a disease in which the joints deteriorate; this is possibly the result of excess weight on the joints;
- Gout, another disease affecting the joints;

- Pulmonary (breathing) problems, including sleep apnea, in which a person can stop breathing for a short time during sleep;
- Reproductive problems in women, including menstrual irregularities and infertility; health-care providers generally agree that the more obese a person is, the more likely he or she is to develop health problems.

Psychological and Social Effects
Emotional suffering may be one of the most painful parts of obesity. American society emphasizes physical appearance and often equates attractiveness with slimness, especially for women. Such messages make overweight people feel unattractive.

0

Many people think that obese individuals are gluttonous, lazy, or both, even though this is not true. As a result, obese people often face prejudice or discrimination in the job market, at school, and in social situations. Feelings of rejection, shame, or depression are common.

Who Should Lose Weight?

Health-care providers generally agree that people who have a BMI of 30 or more can improve their health through weight loss. This is especially true for people who are severely obese.

Preventing additional weight gain is recommended if you have a BMI between 25 and 29.9, unless you also have other additional risk factors. Obesity experts recommend you try to lose weight if you have two or more of the following:

- **Family history of certain chronic diseases.** If you have close relatives who have had heart disease or diabetes, you are more likely to develop these problems if you are obese.
- **Pre-existing medical conditions.** High blood pressure, high cholesterol levels, or high blood sugar levels are all warning signs of some obesity-associated diseases.
- **"Apple" shape.** If your weight is concentrated around your waist, you may have a higher risk of heart disease, diabetes, or cancer than people of the same weight who have a "pear" shape.

Fortunately, a weight loss of 5 percent to 10 percent can do much to improve health by lowering blood pressure and cholesterol levels. In addition, recent research has shown that a 5- to 7-percent weight loss can prevent type 2 diabetes in people at high risk for the disease.

How Is Obesity Treated?

The method of treatment depends on the patient's level of obesity, overall health condition, and motivation to lose weight. Treatment may include a combination of diet, exercise, behavior modification, and sometimes weight-loss drugs. In some cases of severe obesity, gastrointestinal surgery may be recommended. Remember, weight control is a life-long effort.

Weight-Control Information Network

For information on implementing dietary changes and other lifestyle measures to control weight, along with advice on how to maintain weight loss, see pages 37-43. Appetite-suppressing medication and surgery are options, but only for some patients, as discussed in the text boxes on pages 459 and 461.

Cancer may originate in the oral cavity (mouth) and the oropharynx (the part of the throat at the back of the mouth). The oral cavity includes many parts: the lips; the lining inside the lips and cheeks, called the buccal mucosa; the teeth; the bottom (floor) of the mouth under the tongue; the front two-thirds of the tongue; the bony top of the mouth (hard palate); the gums; and the small area behind the wisdom teeth. The oropharynx includes the back one-third of the tongue, the soft palate, the tonsils, and the part of the throat behind the mouth. Salivary glands throughout the oral cavity make saliva, which keeps the mouth moist and helps digest food.

When oral cancer spreads, it usually travels through the lymphatic system. Cancer cells that enter the lymphatic system are carried along by lymph, an almost colorless, watery fluid containing cells that help the body fight infection and disease. Along the lymphatic channels are groups of small, bean-shaped organs called lymph nodes (sometimes called lymph glands). Oral cancer that spreads usually travels to the lymph nodes in the neck. It can also spread to other parts of the body. Cancer that spreads is the same disease and has the same name as the original (primary) cancer.

Causes and Prevention

Scientists at hospitals and medical centers all across the country are studying this disease to learn more about what causes it and how to prevent it. Doctors do know that no one can "catch" cancer from another person: it is not contagious. Two known causes of oral cancer are tobacco and alcohol use.

Tobacco use—smoking cigarettes, cigars, or pipes; chewing tobacco; or dipping snuff—accounts for 80 to 90 percent of oral cancers. A number of studies have shown that cigar and pipe smokers have the same risk as cigarette smokers. Studies indicate that smokeless tobacco users are at particular risk of developing oral cancer. For long-time users, the risk is much greater, making the use of snuff or chewing tobacco among young people a special concern.

People who stop using tobacco—even after many years of use—can greatly reduce their risk of oral cancer. Special counseling or self-help groups may be useful for those who are trying to give up tobacco. Some hospitals have groups for people who want to quit. Also, the Cancer Information Service and the American Cancer Society may have information about groups in local areas to help people quit using tobacco.

Chronic and/or heavy use of alcohol also increases the risk of oral cancer, even for people who do not use tobacco. However, people who use both alcohol and tobacco have an especially high risk of oral cancer. Scientists believe that these substances increase each other's harmful effects.

Cancer of the lip can be caused by exposure to the sun. The risk can be avoided with the use of a lotion or lip balm containing a sunscreen. Wearing a hat with a brim can also block the sun's harmful rays. Pipe smokers are especially prone to cancer of the lip.

Some studies have shown that many people who develop oral cancer have a history of leukoplakia, a whitish patch inside the mouth. The causes of leukoplakia are not well understood, but it is commonly associated with heavy use of tobacco and alcohol. The condition often occurs in irritated areas, such as the gums and mouth lining of people who use smokeless tobacco and the lower lip of pipe smokers.

Another condition, erythroplakia, appears as a red patch in the mouth. Erythroplakia

O

Screening for Oral Cancer

Early detection and treatment of oral cancer significantly improve prognosis. In one study, 64 percent of people whose oral cancers were diagnosed before they spread to nearby lymph nodes were alive after five years, compared with just 15 percent of those diagnosed after spread. Regular oral self-examination, coupled with an annual professional examination, are the best ways to increase the potential for cure.

To perform the exam yourself, use a mirror to inspect the lips, gums, insides of the cheeks, tongue, back of the throat, and floor and roof of the mouth. See a doctor or dentist if you notice sores, especially those that bleed easily; color changes, particularly red or white patches; unexplained lumps, thickening, or erosion; loose teeth; or a change in how teeth fit together. *The Editors*

occurs most often in people 60 to 70 years of age. Early diagnosis and treatment of leukoplakia and erythroplakia are important because cancer may develop in these patches.

People who think they might be at risk for developing oral cancer should discuss this concern with their doctor or dentist, who may be able to suggest ways to reduce the risk and plan an appropriate schedule for checkups.

Lifestyle changes are just as important after diagnosis as before—perhaps more so. For example, after treatment, only 6 percent of smokers with oral cancer who break the habit are stricken with another head and neck cancer, compared with nearly 40 percent of those who continue to smoke.

Early Detection

Regular checkups that include an examination of the entire mouth can detect precancerous conditions or the early stages of oral cancer. Your doctor and dentist should check the tissues in your mouth as part of your routine exams.

Symptoms

Oral cancer usually occurs in people over the age of 45 but can develop at any age. These are some symptoms to watch for:

- A sore on the lip or in the mouth that does not heal
- A lump on the lip or in the mouth or throat
- A white or red patch on the gums, tongue, or lining of the mouth
- Unusual bleeding, pain, or numbness in the mouth
- A sore throat that does not go away, or a feeling that something is caught in the throat
- Difficulty or pain with chewing or swallowing
- Swelling of the jaw that causes dentures to fit poorly or become uncomfortable
- A change in the voice
- Pain in the ear

These symptoms may be caused by cancer or by other, less serious problems. It is important to see a dentist or doctor about any symptoms like these, so that the problem can be diagnosed and treated as early as possible.

Diagnosis

If an abnormal area has been found in the oral cavity, a biopsy is the only way to know whether it is cancer. Usually, the patient is referred to an oral surgeon or an ear, nose, and throat surgeon, who removes part or all of the lump or abnormal-looking area. A pathologist examines the tissue under a microscope to check for cancer cells.

Almost all oral cancers are squamous cell carcinomas. Squamous cells line the oral cavity. If the pathologist finds oral cancer, the patient's doctor needs to know the stage, or extent, of the disease in order to plan the best treatment. Staging tests and exams help the doctor find out whether the cancer has spread and what parts of the body are affected.

Staging

Staging generally includes dental x-rays and x-rays of the head and chest. The doctor may also want the patient to have a CT (or CAT) scan. A CT scan is a series of x-rays put together by a computer to form detailed pictures of areas inside the body. Ultrasonography is another way to produce pictures of areas in the body. High-frequency sound waves (ultrasound), which cannot be heard by humans, are bounced off organs and tissue. The pattern of echoes produced by these waves creates a picture called a sonogram. Sometimes the doctor asks for MRI (magnetic resonance imaging), a procedure in which pictures are created using a magnet linked to a computer. The doctor also feels the lymph nodes in the neck to check for swelling or other changes. In most cases, the patient will have a complete physical examination before treatment begins.

Treatment

After diagnosis and staging, the doctor develops a treatment plan to fit each patient's needs. Treatment for oral cancer depends on a number of factors. Among these are the location, size, type, and extent of the tumor and the stage of the disease. The doctor also considers the patient's age and general health. Treatment involves surgery, radiation therapy, or, in many cases, a combination of the two. Some patients receive chemotherapy, treatment with anticancer drugs. Also, the patient may want to talk with the doctor about taking part in a research study of new treatment methods. Such studies, called clinical trials, are designed to improve cancer treatment (see page 181).

For most patients, it is important to have a complete dental exam before cancer treatment begins. Because cancer treatment may make the mouth sensitive and more easily infected, doctors often advise patients to have any needed dental work done before treatment begins.

Patients with oral cancer may be treated by a team of specialists. The medical team may include an oral surgeon; an ear, nose, and throat surgeon; a medical oncologist; a radiation oncologist; a prosthodontist; a general dentist; a plastic surgeon; a dietitian; a social worker; a nurse; and a speech therapist.

Surgery to remove the tumor in the mouth is the usual treatment for patients with oral cancer. If there is evidence that the cancer has spread, the surgeon may also remove lymph nodes in the neck. If the disease has spread to muscles and other tissues in the neck, the operation may be more extensive.

Radiation therapy (also called radiotherapy) is the use of high-energy rays to damage cancer cells and stop them from growing. Like surgery, radiation therapy is local therapy; it affects only the cells in the treated area. The energy may come from a large machine (external radiation). It can also come from radioactive materials placed directly into or near the tumor (internal radiation).

0

Questions for Your Doctor

Before surgery, the patient may want to ask the doctor these questions:

- What kind of operation will it be?
- How will I feel after the operation? If I have pain, how will you help me?
- Will I have trouble eating?
- Where will the scars be? What will they look like?
- Do you expect that there will be long-term effects from the surgery?

- Will there be permanent changes in my appearance?
- Will I lose my teeth? Can they be replaced? How soon?
- If I need to have plastic surgery, when can that be done?
- Will I need to see a specialist for help with my speech?
- When can I get back to my normal activities?

Radiation therapy is sometimes used instead of surgery for small tumors in the mouth. Patients with large tumors may need both surgery and radiation therapy.

Radiation therapy may be given before or after surgery. Before surgery, radiation can shrink the tumor so that it can be removed. Radiation after surgery is used to destroy cancer cells that may remain.

For external radiation therapy, the patient goes to the hospital or clinic each day for treatments. Usually, treatment is given 5 days a week for five to six weeks. This schedule helps protect healthy tissues by dividing the total amount of radiation into small doses.

Implant radiation therapy puts tiny "seeds" containing radioactive material directly into the tumor or in tissue near it. Generally, an implant is left in place for several days, and the patient will stay in the hospital in a private room. The length of time nurses and other caregivers, as well as visitors, can spend with the patient will be limited. The implant is removed before the patient goes home.

Chemotherapy is the use of drugs to kill cancer cells. Researchers are looking for effective drugs or drug combinations to treat oral cancer. They are also exploring ways to combine chemotherapy with other forms of cancer treatment to help destroy the tumor and prevent the disease from spreading.

Side Effects of Treatment

It is hard to limit the effects of cancer treatment so that only cancer cells are removed or destroyed. Because healthy cells and tissues may also be damaged, treatment often causes side effects.

The side effects of cancer treatment vary. They depend mainly on the type and extent of the treatment and the specific area being treated. Also, each person reacts differently. Some side effects are temporary; others are permanent. Doctors try to plan the patient's therapy to keep side effects to a minimum. They also watch patients very carefully so they can help with any problems that occur.

Surgery

Surgery to remove a small tumor in the mouth usually does not cause any lasting problems. For a larger tumor, however, the surgeon may need to remove part of the palate, tongue, or jaw. Such surgery is likely to change the patient's ability to chew, swallow, or talk. The patient's appearance may also be different.

After surgery, the patient's face may be swollen. This swelling usually goes away within a few weeks. However, removing lymph nodes can slow the flow of lymph, which may collect in the tissues; this swelling may last for a long time.

Radiation

Before starting radiation therapy, a patient should see a dentist who is familiar with the changes this therapy can cause in the mouth. Radiation therapy can make the mouth sore. It can also cause changes in the saliva and may reduce the amount of saliva, making it hard to chew and swallow. Because saliva normally protects the teeth, mouth dryness can promote tooth decay. Good mouth care can help keep the teeth and gums healthy and can make the patient feel more comfortable. The health care team may suggest the use of a special kind of toothbrush or mouthwash. The dentist usually suggests a special fluoride program to keep the teeth healthy. To help relieve mouth dryness, the health-care team may suggest the use of artificial saliva and other methods to keep the mouth moist. Mouth dryness from radiation therapy goes away in some patients, but in others it can be permanent.

Weight loss can be a serious problem for patients being treated for oral cancer because a sore mouth may make eating difficult. Your doctor may suggest ways to maintain a healthy diet. In many cases, it helps to have food and beverages in very small amounts. Many patients find that eating several small meals and snacks during the day works better than trying to have three large meals. Often, it is easier to eat soft, bland foods that have been moistened with sauces or gravies; thick soups, puddings, and high protein milkshakes are nourishing and easy to swallow. It may be helpful to prepare other foods in a blender. The doctor may also suggest special liquid dietary supplements for patients who have trouble chewing. Drinking lots of fluids helps keep the mouth moist and makes it easier to eat.

Some patients are able to wear their dentures during radiation therapy. Many, however, will not be able to wear dentures for up to a year after treatment. Because the tissues in the mouth that support the denture may change during or after treatment, dentures may no longer fit properly. After treatment is over, a patient may need to have dentures refitted or replaced.

Radiation therapy can also cause sores in the mouth and cracked and peeling lips. These usually heal in the weeks after treatment is completed. Often, good mouth care can help prevent these sores. Dentures should not be worn until the sores have healed.

During radiation therapy, patients may become very tired, especially in the later weeks of treatment. Resting is important, but doctors usually advise their patients to try to stay reasonably active. Patients should match their activities to their energy level. It's common for radiation to cause the skin in the treated area to become red and dry, tender, and itchy. Toward the end of treatment, the skin may become moist and "weepy." There may be permanent darkening or "bronzing" of the skin in the treated area. This area should be exposed to the air as much as possible but should also be protected from the sun. Good skin care is important at this time, but patients should not use any lotions or creams without the doctor's advice. Men may lose all or part of their beard, but facial hair generally grows back after treatment is done. Usually, men

O

shave with an electric razor during treatment to prevent cuts that may lead to infection. Most effects of radiation therapy on the skin are temporary. The area will heal when the treatment is over.

Chemotherapy

The side effects of chemotherapy depend on the drugs that are given. In general, anticancer drugs affect rapidly growing cells, such as blood cells that fight infection, cells that line the mouth and the digestive tract, and cells in hair follicles. As a result, patients may have side effects such as lower resistance to infection, loss of appetite, nausea, vomiting, or mouth sores. They also may have less energy and may lose their hair.

The side effects of cancer treatment are different for each person, and they may even be different from one treatment to the next. Doctors, nurses, and dietitians can explain the side effects of cancer treatment and can suggest ways to deal with them.

Rehabilitation

Rehabilitation is a very important part of treatment for patients with oral cancer. The goals of rehabilitation depend on the extent of the disease and the treatment a patient has received. The health care team makes every effort to help the patient return to normal activities as soon as possible. Rehabilitation may include dietary counseling, surgery, a dental prosthesis, speech therapy, and other services.

Sometimes, a patient needs reconstructive and plastic surgery to rebuild the bones or tissues of the mouth. If this is not possible, a prosthodontist may be able to make an artificial dental and/or facial part (prosthesis). Patients may need special training to use the device.

Speech therapy generally begins as soon as possible for a patient who has trouble speaking after treatment. Often, a speech therapist visits the patient in the hospital to plan therapy and teach speech exercises. Speech therapy usually continues after the patient returns home.

Follow-up Care

Regular follow-up exams are very important for anyone who has been treated for oral cancer. The physician and the dentist watch the patient closely to check the healing process and to look for signs that the cancer may have returned. Patients with mouth dryness from radiation therapy should have dental exams three times a year.

The patient may need to see a dietitian if weight loss or eating problems continue. Most doctors urge their oral cancer patients to stop using tobacco and alcohol to reduce the risk of developing a new cancer.

National Cancer Institute

A rthritis, literally joint inflammation, refers to more than 100 different diseases characterized by pain, swelling, and limited movement in the joints. Osteoarthritis (OA), also known as degenerative joint disease, is the most common form of arthritis and the most frequent cause of disability in the United States. This condition results from the gradual deterioration of cartilage, the smooth elastic layer of connective tissue that encases the ends of bones, helping to absorb the shock of joint motion and permit fluid, easy movement. Over time, as the cartilage continues to break down, the smooth surface of the cartilage roughens, pieces of cartilage can break off and float in the joint space, and bony growths, or spurs, can develop at the edges of the bone—changes that contribute to the stiffness and soreness typical of OA.

By age 40, about 90 percent of all people have x-ray evidence of OA in the weight-bearing joints, such as the hips and knees. But most people don't experience symptoms until later in life. More than 20 million Americans currently have symptoms of OA.

The progression of OA varies from person to person. For many people, the deterioration results in only moderate discomfort. In some people, however, a complete wearing down of the cartilage allows the two adjacent bones to rub against each other, which produces a great deal of pain,

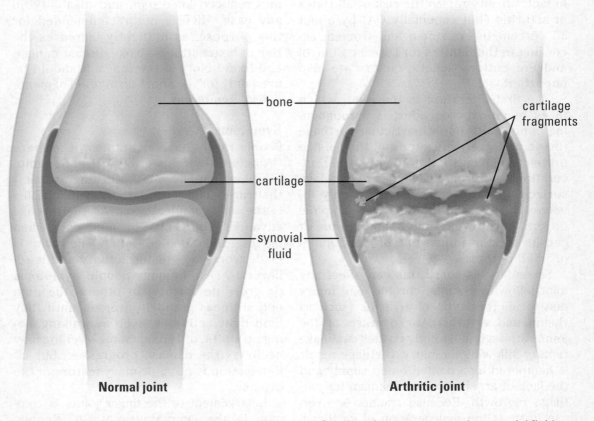

Normal joint   bone   cartilage   synovial fluid   **Arthritic joint**   cartilage fragments

In an osteoarthritic joint, the cartilage gradually erodes. Cartilage fragments enter the synovial fluid and cause irritation. If the cartilage wears down completely, adjacent bones rub against each other.

O

even at rest. While OA has no impact on life expectancy, severe involvement of the hips, knees, and spinal column may greatly limit activity and diminish overall quality of life.

Currently, there is no cure for OA; treatment is aimed at relieving pain and improving joint mobility. In severe cases, the damaged joint may be removed and replaced with an artificial joint to restore mobility.

Causes
Primary osteoarthritis, the gradual breakdown of cartilage that occurs with age, is the most common type of OA. It is caused by cartilage damage due mostly to stress on the joint—for example, from obesity. In fact, obesity raises the risk of all types of arthritis (but especially OA) by about 30 percent in both men and women, according to the Centers for Disease Control and Prevention. Genetic factors are also important.

The first alteration in the joint, which takes place over decades, is a roughening of normally smooth articular cartilage (made up largely of water and the gel-like protein collagen), followed by pitting, ulceration, and progressive loss of cartilage surface. Primary OA most commonly involves the joints of the hips, knees, spine, fingers, base of the thumb, and big toe. It can be present in just one of these joints or in all of them.

Secondary osteoarthritis can affect any joint following trauma, chronic joint injury due to another type of arthritis (such as rheumatoid arthritis), or overuse of the joint. Although most body tissues can make repairs following an injury, cartilage repair is hampered by a limited blood supply and the lack of an effective mechanism for cartilage regrowth. Because trauma or overuse hastens the degeneration of cartilage,

secondary OA can cause symptoms at a much younger age than primary OA.

Prevention
The only preventive measures for OA are avoidance of repetitive joint injury that may produce secondary OA and weight control. and, possibly, the use of estrogen replacement therapy (ERT). Several studies have shown evidence of reduced signs of OA on hip and knee x-rays in women taking estrogen replacement therapy (ERT) or hormone replacement therapy (HRT, which includes a progesterone-like hormone to lower the risk of uterine cancer from estrogen). Any protective effect disappears within 10 years of stopping the hormones, however, and does not appear to translate into reduced knee pain and disability. In any case, HRT is not recommended for this purpose, as it slightly increases the risk of heart attack, stroke, breast cancer, and blood clots in the lungs. It should be used only for the short-term relief of menopausal symptoms.

Symptoms
People rarely have symptoms of primary OA before their 40s or 50s. At first, symptoms are usually mild: Morning stiffness that rarely lasts for more than 15 minutes is the only manifestation. As the disease advances, there may be mild pain when moving the affected joint. The pain is made worse by greater activity and is relieved by rest. In many people, symptoms progress no further; in others, the pain and stiffness gradually worsen until they limit daily activities, such as walking, going up stairs, or typing. Some swelling may occur as the disease progresses, but inflammation is not a primary feature of the disease.

Enlargement of the finger joints is common in the later stages of OA. Knobby overgrowths of the joints nearest the fingertips (Heberden nodes) occur most often in women and tend to run in families. Enlargements of the middle joints of the fingers are referred to as Bouchard nodes. A crackling (crepitus) may be heard or felt when an affected joint is moved.

Diagnosis

When a patient complains of joint pain and stiffness, the doctor will obtain a complete medical history and conduct a thorough physical examination. These diagnostic procedures are important for two reasons: first, to identify the type of arthritis and second, to eliminate the possibility that the symptoms are caused by a more generalized disorder. The doctor will ask questions such as:

- Which joints are involved?
- What triggers pain?
- When is pain at its worst?
- Does anything provide relief? For example, OA pain gets better with rest, whereas stiffness due to rheumatoid arthritis (RA) improves with activity.
- Have the joints been red and swollen? (This could be a sign of gout or RA.)
- Do you have morning stiffness, and how long does it last? (Patients with OA usually have stiffness that lasts only a few minutes in the morning; in RA, by contrast, the morning stiffness can last for hours.)
- What are some of your current and past work and recreational activities? (Work involving a great deal of lifting, for example, might lead to knee OA.)

The physical exam includes inspection of all the joints of the hands, arms, legs, feet, and spine to see how many are affected and whether the arthritis involves joints symmetrically (on both sides of the body). The physician may also ask questions about the person's skin, heart, lungs, eyes, and digestion, because these can be involved with different rheumatic conditions.

In most cases, the diagnosis of OA is apparent from the history and physical examination. A group of tests called an arthritis panel can be used but may give a false-positive result (indicating arthritis when none is actually present), so it is not recommended by the American College of Rheumatology as a screening test in all patients with musculoskeletal discomfort. Since no lab test can confirm the presence of OA, part of the diagnostic process involves eliminating other possibilities (called differential diagnosis).

For example, unlike RA, at first OA generally involves joints only on one side of the body and produces enlargements in joints of the fingers, no signs of joint inflammation (warmth or redness), and no generalized symptoms (fever, fatigue, weight loss, or poor appetite). A tender hip or knee may indicate bursitis rather than OA. X-ray findings of a narrowed joint space and thickened bone with spurs and cysts help to distinguish OA from other forms of arthritis (although x-rays are usually not necessary for diagnosis). Also, marked deformity in a joint is much less common with OA than with RA or gout.

When the diagnosis is in doubt, it may be useful to obtain synovial fluid—a lubricating fluid secreted by the synovial membrane—from the affected joint. Examination of synovial fluid can often identify the type of arthritis and is essential to detect infectious arthritis, a condition caused by a bacterial infection within the joint space (joints with any preexisting type of arthritis are at greater risk for infection, as are joints in patients with diabetes). After sterilization of the skin and injection of a local anesthetic, a needle (similar to the type used to draw blood) is inserted into the

0

joint space, and a small amount of fluid is withdrawn into a syringe. The fluid is examined for the type and number of white blood cells, bacteria or other infectious agents, and uric acid crystals (suggestive of gout) to determine the cause of the joint pain.

Treatment

The rate of development and ultimate severity of OA are unpredictable. No treatment can stop or reverse its progression. But discomfort and incapacitation are not inevitable. In fact, research shows that the prognosis is generally good, especially among patients whose initial symptoms were mild or moderate, which is the case for most people with OA.

The goals of OA treatment are to relieve pain and maintain as much normal joint function as possible. To accomplish these goals, physicians apply a combination of treatment approaches. The most common are the careful use of medication for pain management; physical and occupational therapy to maintain flexibility and strengthen the muscles around the joint; and weight loss to lessen stress on the weight-bearing joints. In some cases, surgery may be beneficial. If possible, treatment should start with nondrug/nonsurgical options, although OA may worsen over time, eventually making surgery or long-term use of medication necessary. (By delaying the use of medications when possible, patients can reduce their lifetime exposure to drugs and their side effects.)

Weight Loss

Because excess weight puts additional stress on the joints, losing weight may benefit people with osteoarthritis by reducing stress on the joints and limiting further injury. A balanced, reduced-calorie diet and regular exercise help with weight loss.

Assistive devices can ease daily activities. For example, a cane, crutches, or a walker can help protect joints and minimize pain by taking weight off your hips and knees. Your doctor or a physical therapist may prescribe and teach you how to use them. A splint or brace can provide support, prevent overextension of the joint, and help you rest and protect joints when they are inflamed (though prolonged use of splints may promote weakness and stiffness).

Heat and Ice

While drugs are effective for pain, a warm bath or shower, a heat lamp, or warm compresses also may relieve pain and ease stiffness by relaxing muscles. Paraffin (warm wax) baths can lessen pain and stiffness in the fingers and feet. In some cases, however, application of cold packs provides better relief of pain. Ice should be wrapped in a towel and applied for no longer than 20 minutes to avoid the risk of frostbite.

Using heat and cold is also a component of physical therapy. Heat can be applied to an affected joint before exercise to aid stretching and relieve minor aches. Cold packs can be applied after exercise to reduce swelling and help to relieve minor pain.

Exercise

The treatment of arthritis requires both rest and exercise. The right balance between the two must be tailored to the individual and stage of the disease. While rest is important when joints ache, when symptoms subside appropriate exercise is equally essential to maintain joint motion, muscle strength, and fitness. Exercise can also help to improve balance, which may be impaired in people with knee OA, and assist with weight loss and maintenance.

An exercise program should be started with the approval of a physician and, preferably, under the guidance of a physical therapist who can design and teach exercises to do at home, as well as provide periodic monitoring of progress.

Aquatic exercise can particularly benefit people with arthritis. Like other forms of exercise, it can increase joint flexibility, strengthen muscles, provide a good aerobic workout, and boost self-confidence.

In general, improvements in symptoms may only become evident after two months of exercise, but improvements can continue for up to six months. Ideally, patients should exercise four to five times a week. The three forms of exercise are range-of-motion, muscle-strengthening, and endurance (or "fitness").

Range-of-motion exercises. These exercises involve moving a joint as far as possible in every direction without causing pain. Their purpose is to maintain flexibility, reduce pain and stiffness, and improve joint function. In range-of-motion exercises, muscles and joints are moved to a point that is just mildly uncomfortable. They are recommended as a warm-up before workouts.

Muscle-strengthening exercises. Strengthening muscles increases structural support for the joints, stabilizing the joints and lessening the load on them. Your physical therapist can recommend a strength training program using small free weights, exercise machines, isometrics, elastic bands, or resistive water exercises. Correct form is crucial to avoid injury.

Endurance exercises. Aerobic activities—such as swimming, walking, running, and bicycling—improve overall body fitness. Despite concern that such exercises could accelerate the breakdown of cartilage in weight-bearing joints, studies have not shown this is the case. Patients should be sure to warm up properly before exercising by walking briskly for a few minutes (to increase the heart rate) and then doing some gentle stretches (which should be easier once the muscles are warmed up). Wearing comfortable, supportive exercise shoes will help to absorb the shock of weight-bearing exercise.

Rest

Rest is more than simply avoiding an activity that causes pain. Equally significant are methods that reduce strain on a joint, such as using a cane, splinting the joint, using special shoe inserts, or wearing running shoes. Although items such as canes and running shoes are available over-the-counter, consulting a physical or occupational therapist may prevent aggravation of arthritis symptoms caused by selecting the wrong item or using it improperly.

Although rest is an important part of the treatment for osteoarthritis, the pain can lead people to rest their joints too much and to avoid certain movements. Excessive rest contributes to further stiffness and weakening of the muscles around the joint, and a worsening of symptoms. To combat these effects, experts recommend that people with arthritis exercise regularly. Though arthritis sufferers may fear that their symptoms will worsen with physical activity, exercise—when performed correctly and in moderation—usually does not aggravate pain and often improves symptoms.

0

Medications

Pain relief can usually be achieved with acetaminophen (Tylenol). Nonsteroidal anti-inflammatory drugs (NSAIDs)—including aspirin, ibuprofen (Advil, Motrin), naproxen (Aleve), and ketoprofen (Actron, Orudis KT), which are available over-the-counter—can be used if acetaminophen does not provide sufficient relief.

Until recently, a newer class of NSAIDs called cyclooxygenase-2 (COX-2) inhibitors was widely prescribed for arthritis and inflammation. But because of studies showing that COX-2 inhibitors may increase the risk of heart attack and stroke, their use has been greatly restricted (see page 477). Rarely, corticosteroids are injected into an affected joint. Another option for severe pain is opiates.

Trying a number of medications may be necessary before OA patients achieve optimal pain relief.

Acetaminophen. Since inflammation plays only a minor role in OA, the anti-inflammatory effect of NSAIDs is usually not required. In most cases, OA pain can be treated with acetaminophen, which is not an NSAID but can provide adequate pain relief with fewer side effects. The maximum daily dosage is 4,000 mg.

As is true with any drug, however, acetaminophen can cause dangerous side effects if taken regularly at dosages exceeding the recommended amount or if taken by patients with liver disease or those who drink excessive amounts of alcohol. Several years ago, a study linked a higher risk of end-stage kidney disease to heavy daily use of acetaminophen—no doubt leading to frustration among OA sufferers who had been told to take this drug to avoid the side effects of other agents. Despite this finding, it is important to realize that acetaminophen remains the drug with the lowest overall risk of side effects. Since

end-stage kidney disease is rare (only 1 of 5,000 people develop the condition each year), even regular acetaminophen users are unlikely to develop this disorder. Patients who use acetaminophen on a regular basis should avoid heavy alcohol consumption, because this combination may adversely affect the liver, and they should see their doctor periodically to be monitored for side effects.

Traditional nonsteroidal anti-inflammatory drugs (NSAIDs). If non-drug measures and/or acetaminophen fail to control OA pain, NSAIDs are the next option. How well symptoms respond to a specific NSAID varies greatly from person to person. As a result, finding the right drug depends largely on trial and error, and since each drug's effects are cumulative, at least two weeks of therapy are necessary to evaluate its effectiveness. Moderate doses of NSAIDs are usually enough to control the pain of OA.

Although NSAIDs can provide effective treatment, long-term use of these drugs, even in moderate doses, may carry an increased risk of cardiovascular events—and labels on all NSAIDs (except aspirin) carry a warning highlighting the potential risk. NSAIDs can also cause side effects. The most common of these are stomach irritation, bleeding, and ulceration caused by the drug's interference with the formation of protective mucus that normally coats the stomach. Some degree of gastrointestinal bleeding occurs in more than half of patients taking NSAIDs.

Certain groups of patients—for example, those over age 65, those taking corticosteroids, and those with a history of stomach ulcers or adverse reactions to NSAIDs—are at higher risk for side effects from NSAIDs and should either be carefully monitored while taking these drugs or avoid them completely. Since NSAIDs are metabolized in the liver, patients with hepatitis, cirrhosis of the liver, alcohol addiction, or other diseases that put them at greater risk for liver failure must use these drugs with care. Also, NSAIDs can lead to excessively low blood glucose (sugar) levels in people with diabetes who are taking oral hypoglycemic drugs. Because patients with diabetes are also more prone to kidney disease, they should have their kidney function monitored closely while taking NSAIDs. People with asthma should be aware that NSAIDs, especially aspirin, sometimes can exacerbate the disease. And patients with coronary heart disease taking the anticoagulant drug warfarin (Coumadin) should not use NSAIDs because the combination may lead to excessive bleeding.

Other, less common side effects of NSAIDs are being uncovered. Large amounts of NSAIDs, except for aspirin, may increase the risk of high blood pressure or cause kidney damage, especially in older individuals, those with heart failure or a history of kidney disease, or those taking diuretics. This finding does not mean that everyone using an NSAID will get hypertension. Rather, the risk for the disorder is increased, and frequent NSAID users should have their blood pressure monitored regularly, especially if they have one of the risk factors noted above.

Some evidence indicates that NSAIDs may either speed the degeneration of cartilage or slow the regeneration of damaged cartilage. And one adverse effect of NSAIDs may be indirectly due to their pain-relieving benefits: A study found that the NSAID piroxicam (available only by prescription) may encourage patients with OA of the knees to put too much pressure on their affected joints, possibly because the reduced pain makes them feel that they can do more than they should. (Studies have shown that patients who put less load on their knees prior to knee surgery generally have more favorable outcomes.) Arthritis patients should remember that pain serves an important function—it reminds them not to overwork and risk further damage to an injured joint.

Avoiding NSAID side effects. All patients on long-term NSAID treatment should have tests to monitor their blood count and potassium levels, and to check kidney function on a regular basis. Liver function should also be tested during the first six months but usually does not need to be tested again. Patients should tell their doctor of any NSAID side effects, such as gastrointestinal discomfort, red blood in the stool, or black, tarry stools. NSAIDs can also cause the kidneys to retain water.

The risk of NSAID side effects can be minimized in several ways. Adequate pain relief can often be obtained with NSAIDs that have fewer side effects, such as aspirin, salsalate (Disalcid), or low-dose naproxen (Naprosyn). Tolmetin (Tolectin) and indomethacin (Indocin) should be avoided if possible because of a relatively high number of side effects. Another option is enteric-coated NSAIDs—pills specially coated to dissolve in the intestine rather than in the stomach—taken with meals.

Several medications may reduce the risk of developing an ulcer when taking NSAIDs. These agents—called cytoprotective drugs—can reduce the acid content of the stomach; they include omeprazole (Prilosec), sucralfate (Carafate), and the histamine H2 receptor antagonists ranitidine (Zantac), cimetidine (Tagamet), nizatidine (Axid), and famotidine (Pepcid). All four histamine H2 receptor antagonists are now available over-the-counter. Only one drug, misoprostol (Cytotec), has been specifically approved by the U.S. Food and Drug Administration (FDA) for use with NSAIDs

0

Does Weather Affect Arthritis Pain?

Many people with arthritis feel that their pain is influenced by the weather—specifically, that they experience more pain on cold, rainy days and less pain on warm, dry days. Research studies (including two recent reports) on whether climate really does affect arthritis pain have produced conflicting results.

The first study looked for a relationship between weather and pain in 151 people with osteoarthritis (OA), rheumatoid arthritis (RA), or fibromyalgia, as well as 32 people without arthritis. All participants lived in Cordoba City, Argentina, which has a warm climate. Participants kept a journal for one year recording symptoms, and these daily reports were matched with weather conditions. Patients in all three disease groups experienced more pain on days when the temperature was low, while people in the control group were unaffected by any of the weather conditions. In addition, RA patients were affected by high humidity and high pressure; OA patients by high humidity; and fibromyalgia patients by high pressure. However, the associations were not strong enough to allow pain to predict weather, or vice versa.

The other study looked at 154 people (average age 72) who lived in Florida and had OA of the neck, hand, shoulder, knee, or foot. Participants reported their pain scores for up to two years, then researchers matched the scores with the daily temperature, barometric pressure, and precipitation status. No significant associations were found between any of the weather conditions and OA pain at any site, except for a slight association between rising barometric pressure and hand pain in women.

Although some evidence exists that people living in warmer, drier climates experience fewer episodes of arthritis pain, climate does not affect the course of the disease. At most, it may affect symptoms. One theory holds that a drop in air pressure (which often accompanies cold, rainy weather) allows tissues in the body to expand to fill the space, meaning that already inflamed tissue can swell even more and cause increased pain. Other possibilities: Pain thresholds drop in colder weather; cold, rainy days affect mood; and during colder weather people are less likely to be outside and get the exercise that normally helps keep arthritis pain in check.

Does this possible link mean that people with arthritis should move to a dry, warm climate such as Arizona? Not necessarily, especially if it means leaving family, friends, and support system behind. If you are thinking of moving, first spend a considerable amount of time in any new location to see if the weather affects your symptoms.

But bear in mind that no environment is arthritis-proof: Even though the people in these research studies live in warm climates, they still struggle with arthritis. Similarly, it's possible to get relief from arthritis symptoms in any climate. For example, even if cold weather means you can't spend time outdoors, you can still get valuable exercise in a gym or heated pool with similar effectiveness.

---

to prevent stomach ulcers. A combination of the NSAID diclofenac and misoprostol, called Arthrotec, was recently approved by the FDA.

Misoprostol can reduce the occurrence of ulcers in the upper part of the small intestine by two thirds and stomach ulcers by three fourths in regular NSAID users. Doses of misoprostol typically range from 100 to 200 micrograms (mcg or µg), taken up to four times a day. But these drugs can be expensive, data on their effectiveness against NSAID-caused ulcers are limited, and they carry side effects of their own.

COX-2 inhibitors. COX-2 inhibitors are a type of NSAID that can alleviate arthritis symptoms while carrying a lower risk of bleeding or stomach ulcers—the major drawbacks of other NSAIDs. But in 2004, one of the drugs, rofecoxib (Vioxx), was pulled from the market after being linked to an increased risk of heart attack and stroke in people taking the drug for a year and a half or longer. Another COX-2 inhibitor, valdecoxib (Bextra), was subsequently removed from the market after trials showed that it, too, was linked to an increased risk of cardiovascular complications. Valdecoxib has also been associated with a rare but serious skin reaction.

In addition, the Food and Drug Administration (FDA) required a third COX-2 inhibitor, celecoxib (Celebrex), to include a boxed warning highlighting an increased risk of cardiovascular events and other side effects.

Some patients who cannot take other NSAIDs (such as those who have ulcers) may still be candidates for celecoxib. Otherwise, a traditional NSAID is the better choice—though any decision about drug use should be based on the individual patient. Guidelines concerning the use of COX-2 inhibitors may change in response to ongoing findings about the drugs.

Hyaluronan. Viscosupplementation is a relatively new treatment option for people with osteoarthritis of the knee. The procedure involves the injection of hyaluronan, a natural component of synovial fluid, directly into the knee joint. It may provide improvements in pain relief and knee function for up to one year, but its long-term effects are unknown.

To date, the FDA has approved three hyaluronan derivatives—sodium hyaluronate (Hyalgan, Supartz) and hylan G-F 20 (Synvisc)—for the treatment of knee OA. Hyalgan and Supartz are injected into the knee once a week for five weeks, while Synvisc is administered once a week for three weeks. The cost for a series of injections averages about $500. If the results following the initial course of therapy are unsatisfactory, a second course of injections (after about eight months) may prove more beneficial.

One major advantage of viscosupplementation is that it appears to have few, if any, serious side effects. The most common side effects are local reactions at the injection site, such as pain, swelling, rash, and itching; these reactions are temporary and may result from the injections rather than the agent itself.

For now, viscosupplementation has a limited role in the treatment of OA. It should be considered only by people who cannot tolerate basic pain relievers like acetaminophen or anti-inflammatory medications, who are unable to have joint replacement surgery, or who wish to delay surgery, if possible.

Injections and irrigation. Patients who cannot take NSAIDs or acetaminophen, or who have taken them and not benefited, may wish to have a corticosteroid injection into the joint, or joint irrigation. Injection of corticosteroids directly into the joint may also help in uncommon situations, such as an acute worsening of OA symptoms or treatment of patients who are poor candidates for joint replacement surgery. This technique can also provide temporary relief from discomfort and increased mobility for rare and special situations, such as a parent wanting to dance at a child's wedding. Corticosteroids relieve pain by reducing inflammation, and one injection can provide pain relief lasting from a few weeks to several months—enough time to initiate physical therapy. Pain returning within a few weeks may indicate some problem other than inflammation.

A six-week self-help program sponsored by the Arthritis Foundation (www.arthritis.org) is available to help individuals with arthritis learn how to reduce and overcome joint pain. Graduates come away with a better understanding of the basics of joint anatomy, the causes and types of arthritis, how to take medications, and how to make educated decisions about alternative therapies. Studies have shown that course participants may experience a 15 percent to 25 percent decline in pain, as well as a significant reduction in their health-care expenses over time.

Eventually, other similar options may become available. One small study found that injections of 1 mg of morphine into the knee joint of patients with OA provided pain relief for at least one week. Additional studies might find that longer-acting pain medication results in more prolonged relief. However, these therapies only provide pain relief and do not reverse the underlying degenerative process in the joint. Because more frequent use increases the risk of damage to the cartilage, corticosteroid injections should be performed no more than two or three times a year.

Tidal irrigation also may provide relief for patients with OA of the knee. In this procedure, a saline solution is repeatedly injected and then withdrawn from the joint space. Irrigation may break up areas where the synovial membrane has attached to itself, and may also help to remove debris from the joint. The American College of Rheumatology currently does not recommend tidal irrigation, citing the need for further study.

Surgery

A number of available surgical procedures may be helpful when arthritis becomes severely disabling.

Arthroscopy. This procedure is performed by an orthopedic surgeon in a hospital operating room or an outpatient surgical suite. It entails the insertion of an arthroscope—a thin, lighted tube with a camera attached that allows the surgeon to see into a joint. Arthroscopy is now performed in the shoulder, wrist, and elbow, as well as in the knee and hip. It may be used to diagnose the type of arthritis and to determine the amount of damage. It can also be used—by means of tiny, specially-designed instruments inserted into the joint—to repair torn cartilage, smooth roughened cartilage, and remove loose bone fragments. Overall, the rate of complications—such as blood clots or infection—is less than 1 percent.

Osteotomy. Damaged bone tissue in the knee or spine is cut away and the remaining bones are realigned. An osteotomy is usually performed in cases of OA to remove areas of bone that cause misalignment of the joint. In appropriately selected patients, removal of this bone permits a more even distribution of weight across the joint. This procedure can be a good option for more active patients who wish to continue high-impact activities, such as skiing, which may exceed the limits of a prosthetic joint. An osteotomy requires a hospital stay and several weeks of recovery but provides good relief of pain. Recovery is 80 percent complete in about six weeks, and 100 percent complete within six months. About 1 percent of patients who undergo osteotomy of the knee experience a complication called foot drop when the muscles on top of the foot become weakened or paralyzed as a result of nerve damage.

Resection. All or part of a bone is removed from a joint in the hand, wrist, elbow, toe, or ankle. The procedure is most commonly performed to relieve pain in rheumatoid arthritis patients. Recovery times vary, but may be as long as several weeks.

Topical Products for Arthritis

Topical preparations for arthritis won't "banish" pain, as some advertisers claim, but they can provide temporary relief. They work in two ways. When applied to the skin over an affected joint, they mask pain by stimulating a warm or cool sensation that sometimes distracts users from the underlying discomfort (and frequently causes a harmless, temporary reddening of the skin). Alternatively, they offer limited, direct pain relief by reducing the amount of specific neurotransmitters (chemicals that transmit pain impulses to the central nervous system and may encourage inflammation) found inside aching joints.

Preparations that mask pain, called counterirritants, are available over-the-counter. Their active ingredient is camphor, menthol, or turpentine oil. These preparations should be rubbed gently but thoroughly into the skin over the aching joint. A counterirritant can be applied three or four times a day, but patients who find they are using one regularly more than two or three times a week should consult their physician to develop a more comprehensive treatment program.

One topical preparation contains capsaicin, the compound that gives hot peppers their "bite." This compound reduces the amount of a neurotransmitter called substance P, which is thought to release inflammation-causing enzymes and possibly carry pain impulses to the central nervous system.

Capsaicin-containing ointment (Zostrix) is now available over-the-counter. This ointment must be applied to affected joints three or four times a day. It usually takes about two weeks for pain to diminish, although some cases might require up to six weeks of treatment. Unlike counterirritants, capsaicin does not usually cause redness, but it may induce a burning sensation that disappears after the first few applications. Patients must keep using the product to realize its benefit. Pain quickly returns after capsaicin is discontinued.

Topical treatments are not dangerous and have few side effects, but some precautions apply. The medications should not come in contact with patients' eyes, nose, or mouth, or any open cuts. Patients should never tightly bandage or apply heat to a treated area. If irritation develops, the product should be discontinued immediately. Patients using pain relief creams that contain trolamine salicylate or methyl salicylate should know that these substances are sometimes absorbed into the body from the skin. Persons sensitive to salicylates (which include aspirin) or who are taking medication that might interact with them—for example, warafin—should use these creams with caution. Symptoms of salicylate toxicity, including ringing in the ears, blurred vision, and shortness of breath, should be reported to a doctor.

Arthrodesis. In this procedure, a surgeon fuses together two bones in a finger, wrist, ankle, or foot joint. While this operation results in loss of flexibility, it relieves the pain caused by two bones rubbing against each other in the damaged joint. The "new" fused bone is more stable and can bear weight much better than before. This procedure provides an alternative to joint replacement (see below) for arthritis patients whose bones are not strong enough to support a prosthesis or who have frequent joint infections that preclude the use of a prosthesis. Arthrodesis may also be used in small joints, such as the thumb, where replacements are performed less often.

Resurfacing. Resurfacing, also referred to as bone relining, is actually a type of joint replacement. In this procedure, the damaged cartilage and bone ends in the hip joint are removed and capped with metal; the joint capsule is sometimes lined with plastic.

Joint Replacement (Arthroplasty)

In arthroplasty, also called joint replacement, the entire diseased or damaged joint is removed and replaced with a mechanical one in order to relieve pain and restore function. Between 80 percent and 90 percent of joint replacements are of the hip and knee, although joints in the shoulder, elbow, hand, ankle, and foot can also be replaced. New technology and improved operative techniques and materials have made joint replacement the best treatment alternative for many patients. Each year approximately 750,000 joint replacements are done in the United States, primarily (but not exclusively) for patients suffering from arthritis. For hip replacement—the most common type—the success rate is almost 95 percent during the first 5 to 10 years, according to the Arthritis Foundation.

Before considering surgery, patients should consult their physician about more conservative treatments—rest, ice or heat, muscle-strengthening exercises, and pain medication.

Reasons for joint replacement include the following:

- Failure of arthritis to respond adequately to the various antiarthritic drugs or drug combinations and lifestyle changes within six months;
- Joint pain severe enough to cause awakening at night;
- Joint pain that limits walking to about one block;
- Evidence of substantial joint degeneration on x-ray, but only if accompanied by severe pain. (Even when x-rays show significant joint deterioration, some arthritis patients have little or no pain.)

If arthroplasty is deemed necessary, patients should get as much information as they can about the procedure, recovery, and rehabilitation. In one study, patients who participated in a two-hour educational program prior to knee replacement showed markedly greater and faster improvement after surgery than another group of patients who had the same operation but did not participate in the program. The patients in the educational program spent an average of two fewer days in the hospital and required fewer sessions of physical therapy to attain full recovery.

To ensure the most satisfaction from the results of arthroplasty, patients should discuss with their surgeon before the operation the kinds of activities (including sports) they intend to continue afterwards. This information will aid the surgeon in selecting the type of prosthesis, implantation technique, and rehabilitation, as well as make the patient more aware of the risks and limitations of his or her chosen activities. Recommended activities after surgery include golfing, swimming, cycling, bowling, and sailing. Not recommended are such activities as running, racquetball, and basketball.

Arthroplasty requires hospitalization and, usually, general anesthesia. (In some cases, spinal anesthesia to numb the lower body may be used for knee replacement.)

Joint replacement options. Two types of hip and knee joint replacements are available: cemented and uncemented. Cemented joints are glued to the natural bone; uncemented joints are covered with a porous, "bumpy" material into which the natural bone eventually grows and attaches itself. Cemented joints offer the advantage of faster healing, but they tend to loosen over time. At some point this loosening may necessitate a second joint replacement, called a revision, to remove the implant and replace it with a new one. With many advances in cement technology, only about 10 percent of all cemented hip and knee joints have to be revised within 10 to 15 years. One way to minimize the need for revision is to postpone the initial replacement procedure for as long as possible.

In contrast, an uncemented joint is initially not physically connected to the natural bone but instead wedged tightly in the proper place. Recovery takes longer, but this type of replacement is believed to last longer than cemented joints and to get stronger over time (although this has not been proven). As many as 30 percent of patients with uncemented total hip prostheses develop thigh pain, but this usually goes away in two or three years. (Pain generally occurs less often in cemented prostheses.)

In general, uncemented joints are probably better for patients under age 65, who are more likely to need revision of a cemented joint due to the longer time the implant may be in place. After 65, when natural bone gets thinner, a cemented joint may be safer. Deciding on the type of joint replacement depends not only on an individual's age, but also on his or her lifestyle and general health. For example, an uncemented prosthesis may be best for an active 65-year-old, while a sedentary 55-year-old with low bone density (osteoporosis) may opt for a cemented joint.

Revisions tend to be riskier and technically more difficult operations than the initial replacement surgery. The revision procedure is basically a more complicated version of the first one: More bone is cut away, the surgery takes longer, and blood loss is greater. In addition, since revisions take place up to 20 years after the original surgery, patients are older and perhaps less healthy.

Significant complications occur in about 5 percent of cases. The most frequent is blood clots in leg veins, although surgeons take extra precautions to help prevent this problem, such as using aspirin, heparin or similar blood thinners, or leg compression devices. A potentially more serious but less common complication is infection, which usually requires removal of the prosthesis and several weeks in the hospital for antibiotic therapy.

Rehabilitation. Pain may be considerable immediately after the surgery—from muscles disturbed during the operation, rather than from the joint itself. Rehabilitation begins in the hospital, usually the day after surgery, with passive-motion exercises to strengthen the muscles supporting the joint. Recovery from a hip replacement is 80 percent complete within four weeks and 100 percent complete within six months. Recovery from a knee replacement is 80 percent complete within four weeks and 100 percent complete after one year. During this time, a strict timetable of exercise, rest, and medication is crucial to the success of the surgery.

Continuous passive motion (CPM) may be used when the knee joint is replaced. This therapy utilizes a device that slowly but continuously bends and straightens the patient's leg for several hours a day, gradually increasing the range of movement. In one study, combining CPM with standard therapy improved early recovery of joint function, decreased postoperative swelling, and ultimately cost substantially less than standard therapy alone, eliminating most of the need for expensive treatment by a physical therapist.

The success of arthroplasty depends greatly on the motivation and participation of the patient after the operation. In fact, the decision to have joint replacement surgery should be accompanied by a commitment to this period of recuperation. Successful joint replacement, especially knee replacement, requires quite an investment of time and energy in postsurgical rehabilitation, but the rewards are great and not exclusively physical. Joint replacement patients improve their psychological well-being and life satisfaction, as well as reduce their pain.

Treatments Under Development

To date, treatments for OA have provided only symptomatic relief and do not prevent or reverse the underlying damage to the joint itself. Researchers are investigating new methods that may halt or actually repair the damage done by OA.

Glucosamine and chondroitin. These two naturally occurring substances play important roles in the formation and maintenance of cartilage within joints—and may initiate repair.

A review article in *American Family Physician* in 2003 suggested that glucosamine and chondroitin reduce the symptoms of OA, but there was no evidence that the supplements slow disease progression or regenerate damaged cartilage. (A study published in 2004 did find that glucosamine slowed disease progression, but one study is by no means conclusive.) The review also concluded that glucosamine and chondroitin cause fewer gastrointestinal side effects than NSAIDs, and that the combination of glucosamine and chondroitin appeared to be no better than taking either supplement separately.

Products containing glucosamine and chondroitin sulfate are available without a prescription in health food stores, but the FDA does not regulate the purity of these dietary supplements. Although they appear to cause few or no side effects, further studies are needed to determine their long-term benefits and safety.

People with diabetes should be cautious about using glucosamine. In one study, even in very low doses, it had adverse effects on blood sugar levels. Chondroitin might also interact with the anticoagulant drug warfarin (Coumadin) and cause excessive bleeding.

Disease-modifying osteoarthritis drugs. Human studies are under way on a new class of medications called disease-modifying osteoarthritis drugs (DMOADs). DMOADs may eventually offer relief by inhibiting the release of enzymes that break down cartilage.

Gene therapy. Another option being examined to treat OA entails removing cells from the body, genetically changing them, and then injecting them back into the affected joint, where the re-engineered cells protect the joint from damaging enzymes.

Osteoporosis, literally "porous bone" in Latin, is characterized by a decrease in bone density and deterioration of bone tissue—changes that result in fragile bones that fracture easily, most commonly in the hip and spine. The disorder affects nearly 10 million people in the United States, and another 18 million Americans are at risk for osteoporosis due to low bone mass. Postmenopausal women are at highest risk, but older men can also get osteoporosis. One panel of experts convened by the National Osteoporosis Foundation estimated that at least 90 percent of all spine and hip fractures in older women are caused by osteoporosis.

Due to the increasing age of our population (more than 25 percent of Americans will be age 50 or older by 2011), the emergence of osteoporosis as a societal problem is only beginning. Osteoporosis-related fractures are estimated to account for $13.8 billion in hospital and nursing home costs each year, and these costs are increasing.

To complicate matters, people at risk for osteoporosis often go unidentified: As many as half of American women who have thinning bones do not realize it, according to the findings of a major osteoporosis trial published in 2001 in the *Journal of the American Medical Association*. Unfortunately, many older women learn they have the disease only after fracturing a wrist, hip, or spine. Knowing if you are at risk for osteoporosis is crucial to starting preventive measures early—and prevention is the best line of defense against this disorder.

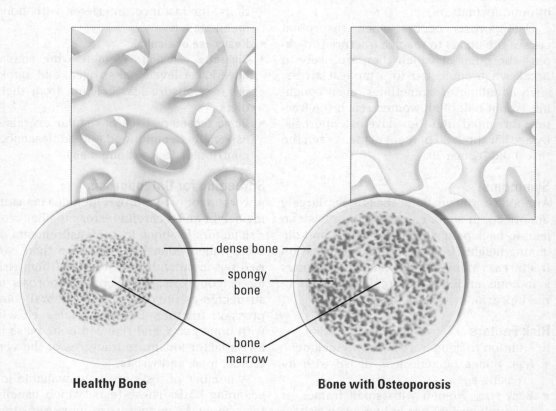

dense bone

spongy bone

bone marrow

Healthy Bone

Bone with Osteoporosis

If the amount of calcium stored in healthy bone decreases, the bone's dense outer layer becomes smaller, while the spongy inner layer increases, eventually making the bone more porous and fragile.

0

How Osteoporosis Develops

Many people think of bones as stable structure structures that don't change with time. But bone is a living tissue that undergoes constant renewal. In this process, known as bone remodeling, old bone is broken down (resorbed) and new bone is formed. Bones are strongest in a person's early 30s, when most people reach maximum bone density. After that, bone starts to erode, beginning a slow but inexorable decline in bone mass. In women, the process accelerates around menopause because of the decline in estrogen (a hormone that helps prevent bone loss). In men, bone density declines more slowly because the production of testosterone remains relatively constant. (Like estrogen, testosterone is a hormone that plays a role in bone formation.)

Osteoporosis occurs when resorption causes the bones to reach a fracture threshold—the point at which they are likely to break when subjected to a modest stress, such as falling or, sometimes, even coughing. About half of all women reach the fracture threshold, and thus have osteoporosis, by age 65; about 20 percent of men reach the threshold by age 70.

Symptoms

Although reduced bone mass goes largely unnoticed, in some cases osteoporosis can lead to back pain, stooped posture, and declining height (from vertebral compression fractures). Many people have no obvious symptoms until a bone breaks, typically in the hip, arm, or wrist.

Risk Factors

In addition to gender, risk factors include:

- **Age.** Bones become less dense with increasing age.
- **Body size.** Women with small frames or low body weight are at increased risk.

- **Ethnicity.** White and Asian women are at highest risk.
- **Family history.** Susceptibility to fractures may be hereditary.
- **Low levels of sex hormones.** Menopause, characterized by low estrogen levels, amenorrhea (abnormal absence of menstrual periods), and low testosterone level in men all increase the risk of osteoporosis. Early menopause is also associated with increased risk.
- **Hyperthyroidism.** An overactive thyroid is associated with increased bone loss.
- **A diet low in calcium and vitamin D.** Calcium is the main component of bone and vitamin D is necessary for the absorption of calcium.
- **Certain medications.** The use of corticosteroid drugs or anticonvulsant medications, for instance, interferes with bone maintenance.
- **Heavy use of alcohol.**
- **Cigarette smoking.** Women who smoke have lower levels of estrogen, and smokers may absorb less calcium from their diets.
- **Being sedentary.** Lack of regular exercise, especially in childhood and adolescence, contributes to low bone mass.

Screening for Osteoporosis

A workup for osteoporosis includes measuring height and a careful history to check for risk factors for bone loss. Measurements of bone mineral density (BMD) are then carried out in individuals who are at high risk for osteoporosis, or when osteoporosis is suspected as the cause of a vertebral compression fracture. BMD correlates closely with bone mass, and reduced bone mass is a risk factor for future fractures of the vertebrae, hips, and wrists.

A number of tests are now available for scanning BMD. These tests, which usually take about 15 minutes, are more sensitive

Drugs That Can Cause Bone Loss

Osteoporosis can result from the long-term use of certain medications—a condition known as secondary osteoporosis. The most common medications associated with secondary osteoporosis are the corticosteroids, a class of drugs that act like cortisol, a hormone produced by the adrenal glands. Cortisone, prednisone, and dexamethasone are examples of corticosteroid drugs.

Thyroid hormones, antacids that contain aluminum, methotrexate (an arthritis drug), and heparin (an anticlotting medication) are some of the other drugs that can cause secondary osteoporosis. In addition, the side effects of many medications such as muscle relaxants and blood pressure drugs include dizziness or lightheadedness, which increase risk for falls. People with osteoporosis are at greater risk for fractures when they fall.

What To Do

Before starting any treatment that has bone loss as a side effect, your doctor should evaluate your risk of osteoporosis. If you begin treatment, your doctor should monitor your bone mineral density while on the treatment.

For those at risk, one way your doctor can prevent or limit secondary osteoporosis is to prescribe the lowest possible dose that still controls the symptoms of the disease. If it improves, patients may benefit from discontinuing the medication. (Medications should be discontinued only under the supervision of a doctor.)

Because some medications within a class of drugs do not cause bone loss, your doctor may be able to switch you to another medication if you are at risk for osteoporosis. If patients need to continue taking corticosteroids over the long term, non-oral modes of administration should be used whenever possible.

Your doctor can also determine if medications for treating osteoporosis are appropriate for you. Exercise, a healthy diet, and not smoking are other measures you can take to reduce your risk.

---

than x-rays for assessing bone mineral content; they also involve little or no exposure to radiation.

Dual energy x-ray absorptiometry (DEXA) has become the gold standard for measuring bone density. It works by aiming two x-ray beams at the spine or femoral neck (part of the hip joint) and using a computer to calculate the amount of energy that passes through the bone. The test provides values that make it possible to estimate fracture risk. Not all insurers will cover the cost of DEXA, however, and some medical facilities do not have the equipment. If DEXA is unavailable, several other tests can be used and cost significantly less. A newer test, quantitative ultrasound (QUS), relies on passing high-frequency sound waves through bone to assess BMD and involves no exposure to radiation. Regardless of the type of test, a result indicating low bone density mandates working with one's doctor to preserve bone health and prevent fractures.

Guidelines from the National Osteoporosis Foundation recommend bone mineral density screening for all women age 65 and older and for postmenopausal women younger than age 65 who are considering osteoporosis treatment, have additional risk factors (such as smoking or a family history of osteoporosis), or have sustained a fracture.

0

Prevention

Preventing osteoporosis can help people avoid bone fractures and back problems later in life. While women are more likely than men to develop osteoporosis, men, too, should get regular exercise and an adequate calcium intake (see the text box on page 488 for information on osteoporosis in men).

Exercise

Exercise is extremely important for preventing osteoporosis. An exercise routine should include weight-bearing exercise, such as walking, which helps strengthen bones. Strength training using dumbbells or exercise tubes or bands to provide resistance is also recommended since building muscle stimulates bone growth (to support the extra weight). Some reports suggest that people who perform weight-bearing exercises have a 10 percent greater bone mass than those who do not exercise. Check with your doctor before beginning an exercise program.

Calcium and Vitamin D

About 99 percent of calcium in the body is in the bones and teeth; the rest is present in the blood, other body fluids, and cells, and is needed for vital functions including contractions of the heart and other muscles. When calcium intake is low (or when calcium is improperly absorbed), the body, through complex mechanisms regulated by parathyroid hormone, removes calcium from the bones to maintain these vital functions. A lifetime of inadequate calcium intake can result in low bone density because more calcium is taken from the bones than is deposited.

For men and women age 19 to 50, the recommended amount for calcium is 1,000 mg per day. After age 50, the amount increases to 1,200 mg per day.

Food sources. The best sources of calcium are low-fat milk and other dairy products. Smaller amounts of calcium are found in foods such as canned salmon with bones, some leafy green vegetables (collard or turnip greens for example), and almonds. In addition, certain fruit juices and grain products are fortified with calcium.

Supplements. Surveys show that most people get less than the recommended amount for calcium from their diet, often as little 400 mg of calcium per day. While careful dietary planning can help people meet the recommendations for calcium intake, many people need to take supplements that provide 500 to 1,000 mg of calcium to achieve recommended calcium levels. In addition, most postmenopausal women should take a daily supplement of 400 to 800 IU of vitamin D to enhance calcium absorption.

A variety of calcium supplements are available. The two most common types are calcium carbonate and calcium citrate. Calcium citrate is more readily absorbed from the intestine; calcium carbonate pills should be taken with meals because calcium absorption from such tablets is improved by the presence of gastric acid.

Generally, calcium citrate is more expensive than calcium carbonate, and more tablets are required because calcium citrate contains less pure, or "elemental," calcium. For these reasons, calcium carbonate is often recommended.

Calcium, whether from the diet or from a supplement, is best absorbed in amounts under 500 mg. Therefore, steer away from supplements that provide more than 500 mg per dose.

The female hormone estrogen has the benefit of reducing the rapid loss of bone and increased risk of fracture that accompanies menopause. For many years, doctors prescribed estrogen to prevent and treat osteoporosis. However, when taken for several years, hormone replacement therapy (HRT)—either estrogen alone or in combination with the hormone progesterone (which counteracts the increased risk of uterine cancer in women taking estrogen alone)—has been linked to an increased risk of breast cancer and cardiovascular events (such as heart attacks, strokes, and blood clots). For this reason, women who are concerned about bone loss should consider alternate forms of treatment after discussing their personal risk and benefit profile with their doctor. (Women who use HRT to treat menopausal symptoms such as hot flashes and vaginal dryness should take it for as short a time as possible.)

Medications

Nearly all of the currently available medications are antiresorptive drugs, so named because they reduce the excessive bone resorption that leads to fragile bones. Alendronate (Fosamax), risedronate (Actonel), and raloxifene (Evista) have been approved by the FDA for both the prevention and treatment of osteoporosis, but they only should be used for prevention in people who are at high risk for osteoporosis. Women who take medication to prevent osteoporosis should still be sure to get plenty of exercise, calcium, and vitamin D.

Bisphosphonates. Alendronate and risedronate are both members of the drug class known as bisphosphonates. By slowing down bone resorption, they help to preserve bone mass.

Clinical trials of alendronate and risedronate have focused on their effect on bone mineral density (BMD) and fracture risk in women with and without osteoporosis. So far, the drugs have proved effective as a preventive and treatment option for osteoporosis by increasing BMD in postmenopausal women. Although researchers assume that fracture risk decreases with a higher BMD (which indicates stronger bones), in some studies the drugs only decreased the risk of fracture in women already at high risk (who have sustained at least one fracture or have severe osteoporosis).

Alendronate and risedronate are not easily absorbed, which may lead to gastrointestinal side effects such as stomach pain, diarrhea, indigestion, heartburn, ulcers, and nausea, as well as muscle cramps. Also, slow movement of the drug through the esophagus can cause irritation. To improve the absorption of alendronate and risedronate, and lessen the chances of side effects, the manufacturers of the drugs have issued specific instructions on the proper dosing procedure. In addition, a once-weekly alendronate tablet (70 mg for treatment and 35 mg for prevention) makes it even easier to take the drug.

Selective estrogen receptor modulators. A member of a class of drugs called selective estrogen receptor modulators (SERMs), raloxifene mimics some, but not all, of the actions of estrogen. In fact, it seems to provide benefits similar to the hormone without some of its drawbacks (for example, growth of endometrial cells in the uterus). The drug is administered once a day in 60 mg doses and can be taken with or without food.

A serious adverse effect of raloxifene is a significantly greater risk of venous thromboembolic events (such as blood clots in a

Osteoporosis in Men

Men have a lower risk of osteoporosis than women because men generally start with a higher bone mineral density (BMD), their bone loss occurs later and progresses more slowly, and they have no period of rapid hormonal change (such as menopause for women) to accelerate bone loss. But more than 1.5 million American men age 65 and older are affected by osteoporosis. In addition, worldwide, one third of all osteoporosis-related hip fractures occur in men.

In general, men should be evaluated for osteoporosis if they have one or more of the major risk factors (see page 484), have bone fractures after a relatively minor trauma, or experience sudden back pain or a humpbacked posture.

Osteoporosis can be managed with a treatment program that includes exercise, calcium supplementation, and/or medication. Men with low levels of testosterone, which may cause osteoporosis, can receive supplements of the hormone. In the past, testosterone could only be delivered by injections, usually every two weeks; however, the FDA has approved skin patches for testosterone administration.

The nonestrogen drugs prescribed for women (see page 487) also work for men. Most research has focused on women, but studies of calcitonin (Calcimar, Miacalcin) suggest it works for both sexes. And preliminary findings indicate that alendronate (Fosamax), which has been FDA-approved for treatment of osteoporosis in men, works with comparable effectiveness to reduce fractures in men and women within one year of treatment.

---

leg vein that can break off and travel to the lungs), particularly in the first four months of therapy.

Alternative Therapy

Ipriflavone, a synthetic isoflavone that is structurally similar to soy isoflavones, has garnered much interest recently for the prevention and treatment of osteoporosis. Soy contains a number of compounds called isoflavones, which have weak estrogen-like activity and are thought to relieve menopausal symptoms and decrease the risk of osteoporosis. Because ipriflavone does not appear to have the same negative effects on reproductive organs as estrogen, such as stimulating breast or uterine tissue growth, it may be an alternative to conventional HRT. All research on ipriflavone is still preliminary, however, and more studies are needed to determine both its safety and effectiveness.

Treatment

Treatment of osteoporosis starts with exercise, calcium and vitamin D supplements, and estrogen replacement—the same measures used for prevention.

Calcium and Vitamin D. In 1993, a thorough review of all published studies concluded that bone loss after menopause was slowed or stopped by calcium supplements in 16 of the 19 studies that carefully controlled the amount of calcium intake. Calcium supplements even proved beneficial when started as long as five years after menopause.

Perhaps even more important was the finding that bone fractures decreased when patients' diets were supplemented with vitamin D alone or with a combination of vitamin D and calcium. (Older people tend to have low blood levels of vitamin D and its active products, which promote the absorption of calcium from the intestine.) The author of this review concluded that it would be prudent for most menopausal women to increase calcium intake to 1,000 or 1,500 mg per day and to add 400 to 800 IU of vitamin D daily.

These recommendations are similar to those from a National Institutes of Health Consensus Conference, which recommended 1,500 mg of calcium daily for postmenopausal women not taking estrogen and for men over age 65. Check with your doctor before starting supplements, especially if you have a history of kidney stones or elevated levels of blood calcium.

Medications. Alendronate, risedronate, raloxifene, calcitonin, and hormone replacement therapy are approved medications for treating osteporosis. Recently, two new drugs —ibandronate (Boniva) and teriparatide (Forteo)—were approved as treatments for the disease. Although not approved for this purpose, four other bisphosphonate drugs (etidronate, pamidronate, tiludronate, and zoledronic acid) have also been used.

Alendronate and risedronate reduce the incidence of vertebral fractures, slow bone loss, and often improve bone mass in the spine and hip. Ibandronate is also a bisphosphonate that appears to be as effective as alendronate and risedronate. Like the two older drugs, it carries side effects that include gastrointestinal (GI) symptoms such as acid reflux and constipation. But ibandronate comes in a once-a-month dose, and this less frequent dosing (compared to once-weekly doses) helps reduce GI distress. Therefore, patients who cannot tolerate alendronate or risedronate can consider ibandronate as an alternative.

Teriparatide, a type of recombinant human parathyroid hormone, is different from previous medications in that it stimulates bone formation rather then preventing bone resorption. A daily injection of teriparatide dramatically improves BMD and moderately reduces fracture risk.

One troubling potential side effect of teriparatide is an increased risk of bone cancer observed in rats injected with high doses of the medication. Although this type of cancer has not been observed in people treated with the medication, people at increased risk for bone cancer should not use teriparatide. Furthermore, since teriparatide may raise blood calcium levels, those with high levels of calcium in the blood should not use teriparatide.

High doses of calcitonin slow bone loss in the spine and may even add some bone mass. Calcitonin appears to provide some modest fracture reduction in the spine, but does not appear to protect against hip fractures. The usual dose is an injection every day or every other day or one puff of nasal spray (Miacalcin) daily. Although Miacalcin is well tolerated, some patients may develop rhinitis (nasal inflammation).

The ovaries are a pair of organs in the female reproductive system. They are located in the pelvis, one on each side of the uterus (the hollow, pear-shaped organ where a baby grows). Each ovary is about the size and shape of an almond. The ovaries have two functions: they produce eggs and female hormones (chemicals that control the way certain cells or organs function).

Every month, during the menstrual cycle, an egg is released from one ovary in a process called ovulation. The egg travels from the ovary through the fallopian tube to the uterus.

The ovaries are also the main source of the female hormones estrogen and progesterone. These hormones influence the development of a woman's breasts, body shape, and body hair. They also regulate the menstrual cycle and pregnancy.

A malignant tumor that begins in the ovaries is called ovarian cancer. There are several types of ovarian cancer. Ovarian cancer that begins on the surface of the ovary (epithelial carcinoma) is the most common type. This is the type of cancer discussed in this entry. Ovarian cancer that begins in the egg-producing cells (germ cell tumors) and cancer that begins in the supportive tissue surrounding the ovaries (stromal tumors) are rare and are not discussed in this entry.

Ovarian cysts are a different type of growth. They are fluid-filled sacs that form on the surface of an ovary. They are not cancer. Cysts often go away without treatment. If a cyst does not go away, the doctor may suggest removing it, especially if it seems to be growing.

Ovarian cancer cells can break away from the ovary and spread to other tissues and organs in a process called shedding. When

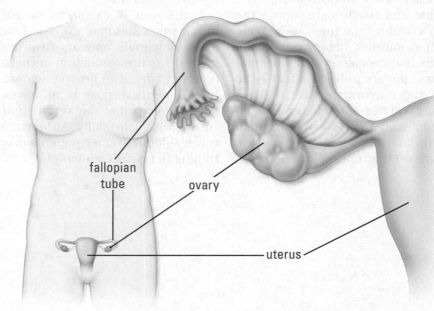

fallopian tube
ovary
uterus

The ovaries are a pair of female organs located at the end of the fallopian tubes on each side of the uterus. Ovarian cancer is rarely detected early since it can grow for some time before it produces symptoms.

When to Consider Genetic Testing

Although ovarian cancer usually occurs for unknown reasons, experts estimate that hereditary factors account for 5 percent to 10 percent of cases. Three distinct hereditary patterns have emerged: ovarian cancer that occurs alone; ovarian cancer with breast cancer; and ovarian cancer with a family history of breast, colorectal, bladder, or uterine cancer. Among the many genes thought to play a role in these cases, only BRCA1 (which is also associated with breast cancer) has been firmly established. Many major medical centers offer BRCA 1 testing, which is appropriate only for patients with a personal or family history of these cancers. Because findings are difficult to interpret, genetic counseling is essential. Patients who have the BRCA' gene should be carefully monitored with pelvic examination, a blood test for CA-125, and transvaginal ultrasound. *The Editors*

ovarian cancer sheds, it tends to seed (form new tumors) on the peritoneum (the large membrane that lines the abdomen) and on the diaphragm (the thin muscle that separates the chest from the abdomen). Fluid may collect in the abdomen. This condition is known as ascites. It may make a woman feel bloated, or her abdomen may look swollen.

Ovarian cancer cells can also enter the bloodstream or lymphatic system (the tissues and organs that produce and store cells that fight infection and disease). Once in the bloodstream or lymphatic system, the cancer cells can travel and form new tumors in other parts of the body.

Who's at Risk?

The exact causes of ovarian cancer are not known. However, studies show that the following factors may increase the chance of developing this disease:

- **Family history.** First-degree relatives (mother, daughter, sister) of a woman who has had ovarian cancer are at increased risk of developing this type of cancer themselves. The likelihood is especially high if two or more first-degree relatives have had the disease. The risk is somewhat less, but still above average, if other relatives (grandmother, aunt, cousin) have had ovarian cancer. A family history of breast cancer or colon cancer is also associated with an increased risk of developing ovarian cancer.

- **Age.** The likelihood of developing ovarian cancer increases as a woman gets older. Most ovarian cancers occur in women over the age of 50, with the highest risk in women over 60.

- **Childbearing.** Women who have never had children are more likely to develop ovarian cancer than women who have had children. In fact, the more children a woman has had, the less likely she is to develop ovarian cancer.

- **Personal history.** Women who have had breast or colon cancer may have a greater chance of developing ovarian cancer than women who have not had breast or colon cancer.

- **Fertility drugs.** Drugs that cause a woman to ovulate may slightly increase a woman's chance of developing ovarian cancer. Researchers are studying this possible association.

- **Talc.** Some studies suggest that women who have used talc in the genital area for many years may be at increased risk of developing ovarian cancer.

O

- **Hormone replacement therapy (HRT).** Some evidence suggests that women who use HRT after menopause may have a slightly increased risk of developing ovarian cancer.

About 1 in every 57 women in the United States will develop ovarian cancer. Most cases occur in women over the age of 50, but this disease can also affect younger women.

As we learn more about what causes ovarian cancer, we may also learn how to reduce the chance of getting this disease. Some studies have shown that breast feeding and taking birth control pills (oral contraceptives) may decrease a woman's likelihood of developing ovarian cancer. These factors decrease the number of times a woman ovulates, and studies suggest that reducing the number of ovulations during a woman's lifetime may lower the risk of ovarian cancer.

Women who have had an operation that prevents pregnancy (tubal ligation) or have had their uterus and cervix removed (hysterectomy) also have a lower risk of developing ovarian cancer. In addition, some evidence suggests that reducing the amount of fat in the diet may lower the risk of developing ovarian cancer.

Women who are at high risk for ovarian cancer due to a family history of the disease may consider having their ovaries removed before cancer develops (prophylactic oophorectomy). This procedure usually, but not always, protects women from developing ovarian cancer. The risks associated with this surgery and its side effects should be carefully considered. A woman should discuss the possible benefits and risks with her doctor based on her unique situation.

Having one or more of the risk factors mentioned here does not mean that a woman is sure to develop ovarian cancer, but the chance may be higher than average.

Women who are concerned about ovarian cancer may want to talk with a doctor who specializes in treating women with cancer: a gynecologist, a gynecologic oncologist, or a medical oncologist. The doctor may be able to suggest ways to reduce the likelihood of developing ovarian cancer and can plan an appropriate schedule for checkups.

Symptoms

Ovarian cancer often shows no obvious signs or symptoms until late in its development. Signs and symptoms of ovarian cancer may include:

- General abdominal discomfort and/or pain (gas, indigestion, pressure, swelling, bloating, cramps)
- Nausea, diarrhea, constipation, or frequent urination
- Loss of appetite
- Feeling of fullness even after a light meal
- Weight gain or loss with no known reason
- Abnormal bleeding from the vagina

These symptoms may be caused by ovarian cancer or by other, less serious conditions. It is important to check with a doctor about any of these symptoms.

Diagnosis

To help find the cause of symptoms, a doctor evaluates a woman's medical history. The doctor also performs a physical exam and orders diagnostic tests. Some exams and tests that may be useful are described below:

- **Pelvic exam** includes feeling the uterus, vagina, ovaries, fallopian tubes, bladder, and rectum to find any abnormality in their shape or size. (A Pap test, a good test for cancer of the cervix, is often done along with the pelvic exam, but it is not a reliable way to find or diagnose ovarian cancer.)
- **Ultrasound** refers to the use of high-frequency sound waves. These waves, which

Detecting Ovarian Cancer

The sooner ovarian cancer is found and treated, the better a woman's chance for recovery. But ovarian cancer is hard to detect early. Many times, women with ovarian cancer have no symptoms or just mild symptoms until the disease is in an advanced stage. That's why many experts believe that all women with persistent, unexplained abdominal or gastrointestinal discomfort—or a personal history of ovarian, breast, colorectal, uterine, or bladder cancer—should be evaluated with two tests: CA-125, a blood test that detects a protein sometimes produced by ovarian tumors; and transvaginal ultrasound (TVS), a non-invasive imaging technique that takes about 15 minutes to complete. These tests are not appropriate for general screening because, when used indiscriminately, they produce false-positive results that frequently lead to unnecessary surgery. However, using them together in high-risk situations increases the likelihood that a positive finding will be accurate. Any woman with risk factors for ovarian cancer should discuss with her doctor the possibility of regular screening. *The Editors*

cannot be heard by humans, are aimed at the ovaries. The pattern of the echoes they produce creates a picture called a sonogram. Healthy tissues, fluid-filled cysts, and tumors look different on this picture.

- **CA-125** assay is a blood test used to measure the level of CA-125, a tumor marker that is often found in higher-than-normal amounts in the blood of women with ovarian cancer.
- **Lower GI series, or barium enema,** is a series of x-rays of the colon and rectum. The pictures are taken after the patient is given an enema with a white, chalky solution containing barium. The barium outlines the colon and rectum on the x-ray, making tumors or other abnormal areas easier to see.
- **CT (or CAT)** scan is a series of detailed pictures of areas inside the body created by a computer linked to an x-ray machine.
- **Biopsy** is the removal of tissue for examination under a microscope. A pathologist studies the tissue to make a diagnosis. To obtain the tissue, the surgeon performs a laparotomy (an operation to open the abdomen). If cancer is suspected, the surgeon performs an oophorectomy (removal of the entire ovary). This is important because, if cancer is present, removing just a sample of tissue by cutting through the outer layer of the ovary could allow cancer cells to escape and cause the disease to spread.

If the diagnosis is ovarian cancer, the doctor will want to learn the stage (or extent) of disease. Staging is a careful attempt to find out whether the cancer has spread and, if so, to what parts of the body. Staging may involve surgery, x-rays and other imaging procedures, and lab tests. Knowing the stage of the disease helps the doctor plan treatment.

Treatment

Treatment depends on a number of factors, including the stage of the disease and the general health of the patient. Patients are often treated by a team of specialists. The team may include a gynecologist, a gynecologic oncologist, a medical oncologist, and/or a radiation oncologist. Many different treatments and combinations of treatments are used to treat ovarian cancer. Clinical trials (research studies) to evaluate new ways

0

to treat cancer are also an important treatment option for many women with ovarian cancer (see page 181).

Surgery is the usual initial treatment for women diagnosed with ovarian cancer. The ovaries, the fallopian tubes, the uterus, and the cervix are usually removed. This operation is called a hysterectomy with bilateral salpingo-oophorectomy. Often, the surgeon also removes the omentum (the thin tissue covering the stomach and large intestine) and lymph nodes (small organs located along the channels of the lymphatic system) in the abdomen.

Staging during surgery (to find out whether the cancer has spread) generally involves removing lymph nodes, samples of tissue from the diaphragm and other organs in the abdomen, and fluid from the abdomen. If the cancer has spread, the surgeon usually removes as much of the cancer as possible in a procedure called tumor debulking. Tumor debulking reduces the amount of cancer that will have to be treated later with chemotherapy or radiation therapy.

Chemotherapy is the use of drugs to kill cancer cells. Chemotherapy may be given to destroy any cancerous cells that may remain in the body after surgery, to control tumor growth, or to relieve symptoms.

Most drugs used to treat ovarian cancer are given by injection into a vein (intravenously, or IV). The drugs can be injected directly into a vein or given through a catheter, a thin tube. The catheter is placed into a large vein and remains there as long as it is needed. Some anticancer drugs are taken by mouth. Whether they are given intravenously or by mouth, the drugs enter the bloodstream and circulate throughout the body.

Another way to give chemotherapy is to put the drug directly into the abdomen through a catheter. With this method, called intraperitoneal chemotherapy, most of the drug remains in the abdomen.

After chemotherapy has been completed, second-look surgery may be performed to examine the abdomen directly. The surgeon may remove fluid and tissue samples to determine whether the anticancer drugs have been successful.

Radiation therapy, also called radiotherapy, involves the use of high-energy rays to kill cancer cells. Radiation therapy affects the cancer cells only in the treated area. The radiation may come from a machine (external radiation). Some women receive a treatment called intraperitoneal radiation therapy in which radioactive liquid is put directly into the abdomen through a catheter.

Side Effects of Treatment

The side effects of cancer treatment depend on the type of treatment and may be different for each woman. Doctors and nurses will explain the possible side effects of treatment, and they can suggest ways to help relieve problems that may occur during and after treatment.

Surgery causes short-term pain and tenderness in the area of the operation. Discomfort or pain after surgery can be controlled with medicine. Patients should feel free to discuss pain relief with their doctor. For several days after surgery, the patient may have difficulty emptying her bladder and having bowel movements.

When both ovaries are removed, a woman loses her ability to become pregnant. Some women may experience feelings of loss that may make intimacy difficult. Counseling or support for both the patient and her partner may be helpful.

Also, removing the ovaries means that the body's natural source of estrogen and progesterone is lost, and menopause occurs.

Symptoms of menopause, such as hot flashes and vaginal dryness, are likely to appear soon after the surgery. Some form of hormone replacement therapy may be used to ease such symptoms. Deciding whether to use it is a personal choice; women with ovarian cancer should discuss with their doctors the possible risks and benefits of using hormone replacement therapy.

Chemotherapy affects normal as well as cancerous cells. Side effects depend largely on the specific drugs and the dose. Common side effects of chemotherapy include nausea and vomiting, loss of appetite, diarrhea, fatigue, numbness and tingling in hands or feet, headaches, hair loss, and darkening of the skin and fingernails. Certain drugs used in the treatment of ovarian cancer can cause some hearing loss or kidney damage. To help protect the kidneys while taking these drugs, patients may receive extra fluid intravenously.

Radiation therapy, like chemotherapy, affects normal as well as cancerous cells. Side effects of radiation therapy depend mainly on the treatment dose and the part of the body that is treated. Common side effects of radiation therapy to the abdomen are fatigue, loss of appetite, nausea, vomiting, urinary discomfort, diarrhea, and skin changes on the abdomen. Intraperitoneal radiation therapy may cause abdominal pain and bowel obstruction (a blockage of the intestine).

Follow-up Care

Follow-up care after treatment for ovarian cancer is important. Regular checkups generally include a physical exam, as well as a pelvic exam and Pap test. The doctor also may perform additional tests such as a chest x-ray, CT scan, urinalysis, complete blood count, and CA-125 assay.

In addition to having follow-up exams to check for the return of ovarian cancer, patients may also want to ask their doctor about checking them for other types of cancer. Women who have had ovarian cancer may be at increased risk of developing breast or colon cancer. In addition, treatment with certain anticancer drugs may increase the risk of second cancers, such as leukemia.

National Cancer Institute

The pancreas is located in the abdomen. It is surrounded by the stomach, intestines, and other organs. The pancreas is about six inches long and is shaped like a long, flattened pear—wide at one end and narrow at the other. The wide part of the pancreas is called the head, the narrow end is the tail, and the middle section is called the body of the pancreas.

The pancreas is a gland that has two main functions. It makes pancreatic juices, and it produces several hormones, including insulin.

Pancreatic juices contain proteins called enzymes that help digest food. The pancreas releases these juices, as they are needed, into a system of ducts. The main pancreatic duct joins the common bile duct from the liver and gallbladder. (The common bile duct carries bile, a fluid that helps digest fat.) Together these ducts form a short tube that empties into the duodenum, the first section of the small intestine.

Pancreatic hormones help the body use or store the energy that comes from food. For example, insulin helps control the amount of sugar (a source of energy) in the blood. The pancreas releases insulin and other hormones when they are needed. The hormones enter the bloodstream and travel throughout the body.

More than 100 different types of cancer are known—and several types of cancer can develop in the pancreas. Cancer of the pancreas is also called pancreatic cancer or carcinoma of the pancreas. Most pancreatic cancers begin in the ducts that carry pancreatic juices. A rare type of pancreatic cancer begins in the cells that produce insulin and other hormones. These cells are called islet cells, or the islets of Langerhans. Cancers that begin in these cells are called islet cell cancers.

As pancreatic cancer grows, the tumor may invade organs that surround the pancreas, such as the stomach or small intestine.

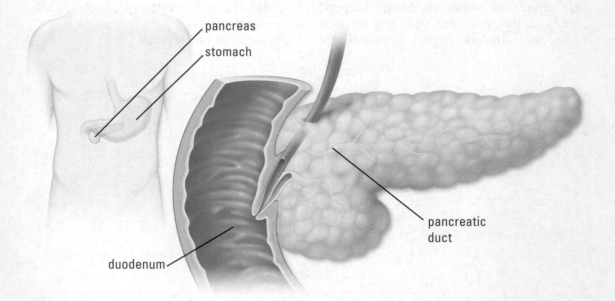

pancreas
stomach
pancreatic duct
duodenum

The pancreas secretes digestive juices into the duodenum and makes insulin and glucagon, hormones essential to maintain blood sugar levels. Tumors usually arise in the ducts that carry pancreatic juices.

Pancreatic cancer cells also may break away from the tumor and spread to other parts of the body. When pancreatic cancer cells spread, they often form new tumors in lymph nodes and the liver, and sometimes in the lungs or bones. The new tumors have the same kind of abnormal cells and the same name as the primary (original) tumor in the pancreas. For example, if pancreatic cancer spreads to the liver, the cancer cells in the liver are pancreatic cancer cells. The disease is metastatic pancreatic cancer; it is not liver cancer.

Causes and Prevention

Scientists across the country are studying pancreatic cancer and trying to learn what causes this disease. The more they can find out about the cause of this disease, the better the chance of finding ways to prevent it.

Scientists have learned that some things increase a person's chance of getting this disease. As with most other types of cancer, studies show that the risk of pancreatic cancer increases with age. This disease rarely occurs before age 40; the average age at diagnosis is about 70.

Research also shows that smoking is a risk factor for several types of cancer, including cancer of the pancreas. Cigarette smokers develop this disease two to three times more often than nonsmokers. Quitting smoking reduces the risk of pancreatic, lung, and certain other cancers, as well as a number of other diseases.

Having diabetes is another risk factor for pancreatic cancer. People who have diabetes develop pancreatic cancer about twice as often as people who do not have diabetes.

Research suggests that a person's diet may affect the chances of getting some types of cancer. In several studies, the risk of pancreatic cancer was higher among people whose diet was high in fat and low in fruits and vegetables. Although the possible link between diet and cancer of the pancreas is still under study, some scientists believe that choosing a low-fat diet and eating well-balanced meals with plenty of fruits and vegetables may lower a person's risk.

Some studies suggest that occupational exposure to petroleum and certain chemicals may increase the risk of pancreatic cancer. These possible links have not been proven, but workers should follow safety rules provided by their employers.

People who think they may be at risk for pancreatic cancer should discuss this concern with their doctor. The doctor may be able to suggest ways to reduce the risk and can suggest an appropriate schedule of checkups.

Symptoms

Pancreatic cancer has been called a "silent" disease because it usually does not cause symptoms early on. The cancer may grow for some time before it causes pressure in the abdomen, pain, or other problems. When symptoms do appear, they may be so vague that they are ignored at first. For these reasons, pancreatic cancer is hard to find early. In many cases, the cancer has spread outside the pancreas by the time it is found.

When symptoms appear, they depend on the location and size of the tumor. If the tumor blocks the common bile duct so that bile cannot pass into the intestines, the skin and whites of the eyes may become yellow, and the urine may become dark. This condition is called jaundice.

As the cancer grows and spreads, pain often develops in the upper abdomen and sometimes spreads to the back. The pain may become worse after the person eats or lies down. Cancer of the pancreas can also cause nausea, loss of appetite, weight loss, and weakness.

P

Islet cell cancer can cause the pancreas to make too much insulin or other hormones. When this happens, the person may feel weak or dizzy and may have chills, muscle spasms, or diarrhea.

These symptoms may be caused by cancer or by other, less serious problems. Only a doctor can tell for sure.

Diagnosis and Staging

To find the cause of a person's symptoms, the doctor performs a physical exam and asks about the person's medical history. In addition to checking general signs of health, the doctor may perform blood, urine, and stool tests.

The doctor usually orders procedures that produce pictures of the pancreas and the area around it. Pictures can help the doctor diagnose cancer of the pancreas. They also can help the doctor determine the stage, or extent, of the disease by showing whether the cancer affects nearby organs. Pictures that show the location and extent of the cancer help the doctor decide how to treat it. Procedures to produce pictures of the pancreas and nearby organs may include:

- **An upper GI series,** sometimes called a barium swallow. A series of x-rays of the upper digestive system is taken after the patient drinks a barium solution. The barium shows an outline of the digestive organs on the x-rays.
- **CT scanning,** the use of an x-ray machine linked with a computer. The x-ray machine is shaped like a doughnut with a large hole. The patient lies on a bed that passes through the hole, and the machine moves along the patient's body, taking many x-rays. The computer puts the x-rays together to produce detailed pictures.
- **MRI,** the use of a powerful magnet linked to a computer. The MRI machine is very

large, with space for the patient to lie in a tunnel inside the magnet. The machine measures the body's response to the magnetic field, and the computer uses this information to make detailed pictures of areas inside the body.

- **Ultrasonography,** the use of high-frequency sound waves that cannot be heard by humans. An instrument sends sound waves into the patient's abdomen. The echoes that the sound waves produce as they bounce off internal organs create a picture called a sonogram. Healthy tissues and tumors produce different echoes.
- **ERCP,** a method for taking x-rays of the common bile duct and pancreatic ducts. The doctor passes a long, flexible tube (endoscope) down the throat, through the stomach, and into the small intestine. The doctor then injects dye into the ducts and takes x-rays.
- **PTC,** in which a thin needle is put into the liver through the skin on the right side of the abdomen. Dye is injected into the bile ducts in the liver so that blockages in the ducts can be seen on x-rays.
- **Angiography,** x-rays of blood vessels taken after the injection of dye that makes the blood vessels show up on the x-rays.

The doctor can explain what is involved in each of these exams and what will be done to keep the patient comfortable.

Pictures of the pancreas and nearby organs provide important clues as to whether a person has cancer. However, doing a biopsy is the only sure way for the doctor to learn whether pancreatic cancer is present. In a biopsy, the doctor removes a tissue sample. A pathologist looks at the tissue under a microscope to check for cancer cells.

There are several ways to do a biopsy to diagnose pancreatic cancer, and some people may need to have more than one type of biopsy. One way to remove tissue is called a needle biopsy. The doctor inserts a long needle through the skin of the abdomen into the pancreas. Ultrasonography or x-rays guide the placement of the needle. Another type of biopsy is a brush biopsy. This is done at the same time as ERCP. The doctor inserts a very small brush through the endoscope into the opening from the bile duct and main pancreatic duct to rub off cells to examine under a microscope.

Sometimes, the biopsy to diagnose pancreatic cancer is done during surgery. In one type of surgery, called laparoscopy, the doctor inserts a lighted instrument shaped like a thin tube into the abdomen through a small incision. In addition to removing tissue samples to be examined under the microscope, the doctor can see inside the abdomen to determine the location and extent of the disease. During the laparoscopy, the doctor can decide whether a larger operation called a laparotomy is needed to remove the tumor or to relieve symptoms caused by the cancer.

In some cases, a laparotomy is necessary to make a diagnosis. In this operation, the doctor makes a larger incision and directly examines the organs in the abdomen. If cancer is found, the doctor can go ahead with further surgery.

Treatment

Cancer of the pancreas is very hard to control. This disease can be cured only when it is found at an early stage, before it has spread. However, treatment can improve the quality of a person's life by controlling the symptoms and complications of this disease.

People with pancreatic cancer are often treated by a team of specialists, which may include surgeons, medical oncologists, radiation oncologists, and endocrinologists. The choice of treatment depends on the type of cancer, the location and size of the tumor, the extent (stage) of the disease, the person's age and general health, and other factors. Cancer that begins in the pancreatic ducts may be treated with surgery, radiation therapy, or chemotherapy. Doctors sometimes use combinations of these treatments. Researchers are also studying biological therapy to see whether it can help when pancreatic cancer has spread to other parts of the body or has recurred. Islet cell cancer is usually treated with surgery or chemotherapy. Doctors may decide to use one method or a combination of treatment methods.

Some people take part in a clinical trial (research study) using new treatment methods. Such studies are designed to improve cancer treatment (see page 181).

Surgery may be done to remove all or part of the pancreas and other nearby tissue. The type of surgery depends on the type of pancreatic cancer, the location of the tumor in the pancreas, the person's symptoms, whether the cancer involves other organs, and whether the cancer can be completely removed. In the Whipple procedure, the surgeon removes the head of the pancreas, the duodenum, part of the stomach, and other nearby tissue. A total pancreatectomy is surgery to remove the entire pancreas as well as the duodenum, common bile duct, gallbladder, spleen, and nearby lymph nodes.

Sometimes, the cancer cannot be completely removed. However, surgery can help to relieve symptoms that occur if the duodenum or bile duct is blocked. To relieve such symptoms, the surgeon creates a bypass around the blockage.

Radiation therapy (also called radiotherapy) is the use of high-energy rays to damage cancer cells and stop them from growing and dividing. Like surgery, radiation therapy is local therapy; the radiation can affect cancer cells only in the treated area. The radiation to treat pancreatic cancer comes from a

P

Surgical Options

Surgery may be used to remove the tumor. A doctor may take out the cancer using one of the following operations:

- A Whipple procedure removes the head of the pancreas, part of the small intestine, and some of the tissues around it. Enough of the pancreas is left to continue making digestive juices and insulin.
- Total pancreatectomy takes out the whole pancreas, part of the small intestine, part of the stomach, the bile duct, the gallbladder, spleen, and most of the lymph nodes in the area.
- Distal pancreatectomy takes out the body and tail of the pancreas.

If the cancer has spread and it cannot be removed, the doctor may do surgery to relieve symptoms. If the cancer is blocking the small intestine and bile builds up in the gallbladder, the doctor may do surgery to go around (bypass) all or part of the small intestine. During this operation, the doctor will cut the gallbladder or bile duct and sew it to the small intestine. This is called biliary bypass. Surgery or x-ray procedures may also be done to put in a tube (catheter) to drain bile that has built up in the area. During these procedures, the doctor may make the catheter drain through a tube to the outside of the body or the catheter may go around the blocked area and drain the bile to the small intestine. In addition, if the cancer is blocking the flow of food from the stomach, the stomach may be sewn directly to the small intestine so the patient can continue to eat normally.

machine that aims the rays from radioactive material at a specific area of the body.

Doctors may use radiation therapy before surgery to shrink a tumor so that it is easier to remove or after surgery to destroy cancer cells that may remain in the area. Radiation also may be given alone or with chemotherapy to relieve pain or digestive problems if the tumor cannot be removed. In most cases, patients receive treatment as an outpatient in a hospital or clinic five days a week for several weeks.

Chemotherapy is the use of drugs to kill cancer cells. It may be given alone or along with radiation therapy to relieve symptoms of the disease if the cancer cannot be removed. When the cancer can be removed, doctors sometimes give chemotherapy after surgery to help control the growth of cancer cells that may remain in the body. The doctor may use one drug or a combination of drugs.

Chemotherapy is usually given in cycles: a treatment period followed by a recovery period, then another treatment period, and so on. Most anticancer drugs are given by injection into a vein (IV); some are given by mouth. Chemotherapy is a systemic therapy, meaning that the drugs flow through the body in the bloodstream.

Usually a person has chemotherapy as an outpatient (at the hospital, at the doctor's office, or at home). However, depending on which drugs are given and the person's general health, a short hospital stay may be needed.

Biological therapy (also called immunotherapy) is a form of treatment that uses the body's natural ability (immune system) to fight disease or to protect the body from treatment side effects. Researchers are testing several types of biological therapy, alone or in combination with chemotherapy. These treatments may be used when pancreatic cancer has spread to other organs or when it has recurred. People receiving biological therapy may need to stay in the hospital so that the side effects of their treatment can be watched.

Side Effects of Treatment

It is hard to limit the effects of therapy so that only cancer cells are removed or destroyed. Because treatment also damages healthy cells and tissues, it often causes unpleasant side effects.

The side effects of cancer treatment depend mainly on the type and extent of the treatment. Also, they may not be the same for each person, and they may even change from one treatment to the next. Doctors monitor patients closely so they can help with any problems that occur. Doctors and nurses can explain the possible side effects of treatment and suggest ways to help relieve symptoms that may occur during and after treatment.

Surgery

Surgery for cancer of the pancreas is a major operation. The side effects of surgery depend on the extent of the operation, the person's general health, and other factors. Although patients often have pain during the first few days after surgery, their pain can be controlled with medicine. People should feel free to discuss pain relief with the doctor or nurse. (For more information about pain control see page 502).

It is also common for patients to feel tired or weak for a while. The length of time it takes to recover from an operation varies for each person.

During recovery from surgery, a patient's diet and weight are checked carefully. At first, patients may be fed only liquids and may be given extra nourishment by IV. Foods are added gradually.

When the entire pancreas is removed, and even sometimes when only part of the pancreas is removed, people with pancreatic cancer may not have enough pancreatic juices or hormones. When a patient does not have enough pancreatic juices, problems with digestion may occur. The doctor can suggest an appropriate diet and prescribe medicine to help relieve diarrhea or other problems such as pain, feelings of fullness, or cramping. (For more information about nutrition for people with pancreatic cancer, see page 503.) Patients who do not have enough pancreatic hormones may develop other problems. For example, those who do not have enough insulin may develop diabetes. The doctor can treat this problem by giving patients hormones to replace those no longer produced by the pancreas.

Radiation Therapy

With radiation therapy, the side effects depend on the treatment dose and the part of the body that is treated. During radiation therapy people are likely to become very tired, especially in the later weeks of treatment. Getting plenty of rest is important.

It is common to lose hair in the treated area and for the skin to become red, tender, and itchy. There may be permanent darkening or "bronzing" of the skin in the treated areas. This area should be exposed to the air as much as possible but protected from the sun, and it is important to avoid wearing clothes that rub. Patients will be shown how to take care of the treated area. Lotion or cream should not be used on the treated skin without the doctor's advice.

Radiation therapy to the pancreas and nearby tissues and organs may cause nausea, vomiting, diarrhea, or problems with digestion. Usually, the doctor can suggest certain diet changes or medicine to treat or control these problems. In most cases, side effects go away when treatment is over.

Chemotherapy

The side effects of chemotherapy depend mainly on the specific drugs and the doses received. As with other types of treatment, side effects also vary from person to person. Generally, anticancer drugs affect cells that divide rapidly. These include blood cells, which fight infection, help the blood to clot, or carry oxygen to all parts of the body. When blood cells are affected, people are more likely to get infections, may bruise or bleed easily, and may have less energy. Cells in hair roots and cells that line the digestive tract also divide rapidly. As a result, people may lose their hair and may have other side effects such as poor appetite, nausea and vomiting, diarrhea, or mouth sores. Usually these side effects go away gradually during the recovery periods between treatments or after treatment is over.

Biological Therapy

The side effects caused by biological therapy vary with the type of treatment. These treatments may cause flu-like symptoms such as chills, fever, muscle aches, weakness, loss of appetite, nausea, vomiting, and diarrhea. Patients also may bleed or bruise easily, get a rash, or have swelling. These problems can be severe, but they usually go away after the treatment stops.

Pain Control

Pain is a common problem for people with pancreatic cancer, especially when the cancer grows outside the pancreas and presses against nerves and other organs. However, the doctor can usually relieve or reduce pain. It is important for patients to report their pain so the doctor can take steps to help relieve it.

There are several ways to control pain caused by pancreatic cancer. In most cases, the doctor prescribes medicine to control the pain. Sometimes a combination of pain medicines is needed. Medicines that relieve pain may make people drowsy and constipated, but resting and taking laxatives can

help. In some cases, pain medicine is not enough. The doctor may use other treatments that affect nerves in the abdomen. For example, the doctor may inject alcohol into the area around certain nerves to block the feeling of pain. The injection can be done during surgery or by using a long needle inserted through the skin into the abdomen. This procedure rarely causes problems and usually provides pain relief. Sometimes, the doctor cuts nerves in the abdomen during surgery to block the feeling of pain. In addition, radiation therapy can help relieve pain by shrinking the tumor.

Nutrition for Pancreatic Cancer Patients

Eating well during cancer treatment means getting enough calories and protein to help prevent weight loss and maintain strength. Eating well often helps people feel better and have more energy.

Some people with cancer find it hard to eat well. They may lose their appetite. In addition, common side effects of treatment, such as nausea, vomiting, or mouth sores, can make eating difficult. Often, foods taste different. Also, people being treated for cancer may not feel like eating when they are uncomfortable or tired.

Cancer of the pancreas and its treatment may interfere with production of pancreatic enzymes and insulin. As a result, patients may have problems digesting food and maintaining the proper blood sugar level. They may need to take medicines to replace the enzymes and hormones normally produced by the pancreas. These medicines must be given in just the right amount for each patient. The doctor will watch the patient closely and adjust the doses or suggest diet changes when needed. Careful planning and checkups are important to help avoid nutrition problems leading to weight loss, weakness, and lack of energy.

Doctors, nurses, and dietitians can offer advice on how to eat properly during cancer treatment.

Follow-up Care

Regular follow-up exams are very important after treatment for pancreatic cancer. The doctor will continue to check the person closely so that, if the cancer returns or progresses, it can be treated. Checkups may include a physical exam; blood, urine, and stool tests; chest x-rays; and CT scans.

People taking medicine to replace pancreatic hormones or digestive juices need to see their doctor regularly so that the dose can be adjusted if necessary. Also, it is important for the patient to let the doctor know about pain or any changes or problems that occur.

National Cancer Institute

Your pancreas is a large gland behind your stomach and close to your duodenum. The pancreas secretes powerful digestive enzymes that enter the small intestine through a duct. These enzymes help you digest fats, proteins, and carbohydrates. The pancreas also releases the hormones insulin and glucagon into the bloodstream. These hormones play an important part in metabolizing sugar.

Pancreatitis is a disease in which the pancreas becomes inflamed. Damage to the gland occurs when digestive enzymes are activated and begin attacking the pancreas. In severe cases, there may be bleeding into the gland, serious tissue damage, infection, and cysts. Enzymes and toxins may enter the bloodstream and seriously injure organs, such as the heart, lungs, and kidney.

There are two forms of pancreatitis. The acute form occurs suddenly and may be a severe, life-threatening illness with many complications. Usually, the patient recovers completely. If injury to the pancreas continues, such as when a patient persists in drinking alcohol, a chronic form of the disease may develop, bringing severe pain and reduced functioning of the pancreas that affects digestion and causes weight loss.

What Is Acute Pancreatitis?

An estimated 50,000 to 80,000 cases of acute pancreatitis occur in the United States each year. This disease occurs when the pancreas suddenly becomes inflamed and then gets better. Some patients have more than one attack but recover fully after each one. Most cases of acute pancreatitis are caused either by alcohol abuse or by gallstones. Other causes may be use of prescribed drugs, trauma or surgery to the abdomen, or abnormalities of the pancreas or intestine. In rare cases, the disease may result from infections, such as mumps. In about 15 percent of cases, the cause is unknown.

What Are the Symptoms of Acute Pancreatitis?

Acute pancreatitis usually begins with pain in the upper abdomen that may last for a few days. The pain is often severe. It may be constant pain, just in the abdomen, or it may reach to the back and other areas. The pain may be sudden and intense, or it may begin as a mild pain that is aggravated by eating and slowly grows worse. The abdomen may be swollen and very tender. Other symptoms may include nausea, vomiting, fever, and an increased pulse rate. The person often feels and looks very sick.

About 20 percent of cases are severe. The patient may become dehydrated and have low blood pressure. Sometimes the patient's heart, lungs, or kidneys fail. In the most severe cases, bleeding can occur in the pancreas, leading to shock and sometimes death.

How Is Acute Pancreatitis Diagnosed?

During acute attacks, high levels of amylase (a digestive enzyme formed in the pancreas) are found in the blood. Changes may also occur in blood levels of calcium, magnesium, sodium, potassium, and bicarbonate. Patients may have high amounts of sugar and lipids (fats) in their blood too. These changes help the doctor diagnose pancreatitis. After the pancreas recovers, blood levels of these substances usually return to normal.

What Is the Treatment for Acute Pancreatitis?

The treatment a patient receives depends on how bad the attack is. Unless complications occur, acute pancreatitis usually gets better on its own, so treatment is supportive in most cases. Usually the patient goes into the hospital. The doctor prescribes fluids by vein to restore blood volume. The kidneys and lungs may be treated to prevent failure of those organs. Other problems, such as cysts in the pancreas, may need treatment too.

Sometimes a patient cannot control vomiting and needs to have a tube through the nose to the stomach to remove fluid and air. In mild cases, the patient may not have food for three or four days but is given fluids and pain relievers by vein. An acute attack usually lasts only a few days, unless the ducts are blocked by gallstones. In severe cases, the patient may be fed through the veins for three to six weeks while the pancreas slowly heals.

Antibiotics may be given if signs of infection arise. Surgery may be needed if complications such as infection, cysts, or bleeding occur. Attacks caused by gallstones may require removal of the gallbladder or surgery of the bile duct. Surgery is sometimes needed for the doctor to be able to exclude other abdominal problems that can simulate pancreatitis or to treat acute pancreatitis. When there is severe injury with death of tissue, an operation may be done to remove the dead tissue.

After all signs of acute pancreatitis are gone, the doctor will determine the cause and try to prevent future attacks. In some patients the cause of the attack is clear, but in others further tests need to be done.

What if the Patient Has Gallstones?
Ultrasound is used to detect gallstones and sometimes can provide the doctor with an idea of how severe the pancreatitis is. When gallstones are found, surgery is usually needed to remove them. When they are removed depends on how severe the pancreatitis is. If it is mild, the gallstones often can be removed within a week or so. In more severe cases, the patient may wait a month or more, until he improves, before the stones are removed. The CAT (computer axial tomography) scan may also be used to find out what is happening in and around the pancreas and how severe the problem is. This is important information that the doctor needs to determine when to remove the gallstones.

After the gallstones are removed and inflammation subsides, the pancreas usually returns to normal. Before patients leave the hospital, they are advised not to drink alcohol and not to eat large meals.

What Is Chronic Pancreatitis?
Chronic pancreatitis has many causes but 70 percent to 80 percent of cases are due to chronic alcohol abuse. The disorder may develop after only one acute attack, especially if the ducts of the pancreas become damaged. Damage to the pancreas from drinking alcohol may cause no symptoms for many years, and then the patient suddenly has an attack of pancreatitis. It is more common in men than women and often develops between 30 and 40 years of age. In other cases, pancreatitis may be inherited. Inherited forms appear to be due to abnormalities of the pancreas enzymes that cause the enzymes to autodigest the pancreas.

In the early stages of pancreatitis, the doctor cannot always tell whether the patient has acute or chronic disease. The symptoms may be the same. Patients with chronic pancreatitis tend to have three kinds of problems: pain, malabsorption of food leading to weight loss, or diabetes.

Some patients do not have any pain but most do. Pain may be constant in the back and abdomen, and for some patients, the pain attacks are disabling. In some cases, the abdominal pain goes away as the condition advances. Doctors think this happens because pancreatic enzymes are no longer being made by the pancreas.

P

Patients with this disease often lose weight, even when their appetite and eating habits are normal. This occurs because the body does not secrete enough pancreatic enzymes to break down food, so nutrients are not absorbed normally. Poor digestion leads to loss of fat, protein, and sugar into the stool. Diabetes may also develop at this stage if the insulin-producing cells of the pancreas (islet cells) have been damaged.

How Is Chronic Pancreatitis Diagnosed?
Diagnosis may be difficult but is aided by a number of new techniques. Pancreatic function tests help the physician decide if the pancreas still can make enough digestive enzymes. The doctor can see abnormalities in the pancreas using several techniques: ultrasonic imaging, endoscopic retrograde cholangiopancreatography (ERCP), and the CAT scan. In more advanced stages of the disease, when diabetes and malabsorption (a problem due to lack of enzymes) occur, the doctor can use a number of blood, urine, and stool tests to help in the diagnosis of chronic pancreatitis and to monitor its progression.

How Is Chronic Pancreatitis Treated?
The doctor treats chronic pancreatitis by relieving pain and managing the nutritional and metabolic problems. The patient can reduce the amount of fat and protein lost in stools by cutting back on dietary fat and taking pills containing pancreatic enzymes. This will result in better nutrition and weight gain. Sometimes insulin or other drugs must be given to control the patient's blood sugar.

In some cases, surgery is needed to relieve pain by draining an enlarged pancreatic duct. Sometimes, part or most of the pancreas is removed in an attempt to relieve chronic pain.

Patients must stop drinking, adhere to their prescribed diets, and take the proper medications in order to have fewer and milder attacks.

National Institute of Diabetes and Digestive and Kidney Diseases

P
arkinson's disease may be one of the most baffling and complex of the neurological disorders. Its cause remains a mystery but research in this area is active, with new and intriguing findings constantly being reported.

Parkinson's disease was first described in 1817 by James Parkinson, a British physician who published a paper on what he called "the shaking palsy." In this paper, he set forth the major symptoms of the disease that would later bear his name. For the next century and a half, scientists pursued the causes and treatment of the disease. They defined its range of symptoms, distribution among the population, and prospects for cure.

In the early 1960s, researchers identified a fundamental brain defect that is a hallmark of the disease: the loss of brain cells that produce a chemical—dopamine— that helps direct muscle activity. This discovery pointed to the first successful treatment for Parkinson's disease and suggested ways of devising new and even more effective therapies.

Society pays an enormous price for Parkinson's disease. According to the National Parkinson Foundation, each patient spends an average of $2,500 a year for medications. After factoring in office visits, Social Security payments, nursing home expenditures, and lost income, the total cost to the nation is estimated to exceed $5.6 billion annually.

What Is Parkinson's Disease?

Parkinson's disease belongs to a group of conditions called motor system disorders. The four primary symptoms are:

- Tremor or trembling in hands, arms, legs, jaw, and face
- Rigidity or stiffness of the limbs and trunk
- Bradykinesia or slowness of movement
- Postural instability or impaired balance and coordination

As these symptoms become more pronounced, patients may have difficulty walking, talking, or completing other simple tasks.

The disease is both chronic, meaning it persists over a long period of time, and progressive, meaning its symptoms grow worse over time. It is not contagious nor is it usually inherited—that is, it does not pass directly from one family member or generation to the next.

Parkinson's disease is the most common form of parkinsonism, the name for a group of disorders with similar features (see "What Are The Other Forms of Parkinsonism?" on page 512). These disorders share the four primary symptoms described above, and

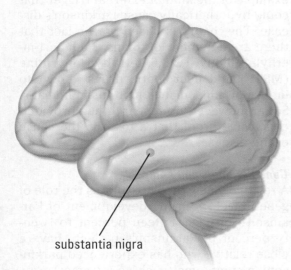

substantia nigra

The loss of nerve cells from the brain's substantia nigra region is thought to be responsible for the symptoms of Parkinson's Disease.

P

all are the result of the loss of dopamine-producing brain cells. Parkinson's disease is also called primary parkinsonism or idiopathic Parkinson's disease; idiopathic is a term describing a disorder for which no cause has yet been found. In the other forms of parkinsonism either the cause is known or suspected or the disorder occurs as a secondary effect of another, primary neurological disorder.

What Causes the Disease?

Parkinson's disease occurs when certain nerve cells, or neurons, in an area of the brain known as the substantia nigra die or become impaired. Normally, these neurons produce an important brain chemical known as dopamine. Dopamine is a chemical messenger responsible for transmitting signals between the substantia nigra and the next "relay station" of the brain, the corpus striatum, to produce smooth, purposeful muscle activity. Loss of dopamine causes the nerve cells of the striatum to fire out of control, leaving patients unable to direct or control their movements in a normal manner. Studies have shown that Parkinson's patients have a loss of 80 percent or more of dopamine-producing cells in the substantia nigra. The cause of this cell death or impairment is not known but significant findings by research scientists continue to yield fascinating new clues to the disease.

Free Radicals

One theory holds that free radicals—unstable and potentially damaging molecules generated by normal chemical reactions in the body—may contribute to nerve cell death thereby leading to Parkinson's disease. Free radicals are unstable because they lack one electron; in an attempt to replace this missing electron, free radicals react with neighboring molecules (especially

metals such as iron), in a process called oxidation. Oxidation is thought to cause damage to tissues, including neurons. Normally, free radical damage is kept under control by antioxidants, chemicals that protect cells from this damage. Evidence that oxidative mechanisms may cause or contribute to Parkinson's disease includes the finding that patients with the disease have increased brain levels of iron, especially in the substantia nigra, and decreased levels of ferritin, which serves as a protective mechanism by chelating or forming a ring around the iron and isolating it.

Environmental Toxins

Some scientists have suggested that Parkinson's disease may occur when either an external or an internal toxin selectively destroys dopaminergic neurons. An environmental risk factor, such as exposure to pesticides or a toxin in the food supply, is an example of the kind of external trigger that could hypothetically cause Parkinson's disease. The theory is based on the fact that there are a number of toxins, such as 1-methyl-4-phenyl-1,2,3,6,-tetrahydropyridine (MPTP) and neuroleptic drugs known to induce parkinsonian symptoms in humans. So far, however, no research has provided conclusive proof that a toxin is the cause of the disease.

Genetic Factors and Aging

A relatively new theory explores the role of genetic factors in the development of Parkinson's disease. Fifteen percent to twenty percent of Parkinson's patients have a close relative who has experienced parkinsonian symptoms (such as a tremor). Several causative genes have been identified, usually causing young onset parkinsonism. Mutations in the gene for the protein alpha-synuclein, located on chromosome 4, result in autosomal dominant parkinsonism.

The function of this protein is not known. The most commonly occurring genetic defect affects the gene for the protein called parkin on chromosome 6. Mutations in this gene result in autosomal recessive parkinsonism that is slowly progressive with onset before the age of 40. After studies in animals showed that MPTP interferes with the function of mitochondria within nerve cells, investigators became interested in the possibility that impairment in mitochondrial DNA may be the cause of Parkinson's disease, and families with maternal inheritance of parkinsonism, suggesting mitochondrial DNA defects, are being actively investigated. Mitochondria are essential organelles found in all animal cells that convert the energy in food into fuel for the cells.

Yet another theory proposes that Parkinson's disease occurs when, for unknown reasons, the normal, age-related wearing away of dopamine-producing neurons accelerates in certain individuals. This theory is supported by the knowledge that loss of antioxidative protective mechanisms is associated with both Parkinson's disease and increasing age.

Many researchers believe that a combination of these four mechanisms—oxidative damage, environmental toxins, genetic predisposition, and accelerated aging—may ultimately be shown to cause the disease.

Who Gets Parkinson's Disease?

About 50,000 Americans are diagnosed with Parkinson's disease each year, with more than half a million Americans affected at any one time. Getting an accurate count of the number of cases may be impossible, however, because many people in the early stages of the disease assume their symptoms are the result of normal aging and do not seek help from a physician. Also, diagnosis is sometimes difficult and uncertain because other conditions may produce some of the symptoms of Parkinson's disease. People with Parkinson's disease may be told by their doctors that they have other disorders or, conversely, people who have similar diseases may be initially diagnosed as having Parkinson's disease.

Parkinson's disease strikes men and women in almost equal numbers and it knows no social, economic, or geographic boundaries. Some studies show that African Americans and Asians are less likely than whites to develop Parkinson's disease. Scientists have not been able to explain this apparent lower incidence in certain populations. It is reasonable to assume, however, that all people have a similar probability of developing Parkinson's disease.

Age, however, clearly correlates with the onset of symptoms. Parkinson's disease is a disease of late middle age, usually affecting people over the age of 50. The average age of onset is 60 years. However, some physicians have reportedly noticed more cases of "early-onset" Parkinson's disease in the past several years, and some have estimated that 5 percent to 10 percent of patients are under the age of 40.

What Are the Early Symptoms?

Early symptoms of Parkinson's disease are subtle and occur gradually. Patients may be tired or notice a general malaise. Some may feel a little shaky or have difficulty getting out of a chair. They may notice that they speak too softly or that their handwriting looks cramped and spidery. They may lose track of a word or thought, or they may feel irritable or depressed for no apparent reason. This very early period may last a long

P

time before the more classic and obvious symptoms appear.

Friends or family members may be the first to notice changes. They may see that the person's face lacks expression and animation (known as "masked face") or that the person remains in a certain position for a long time or does not move an arm or leg normally. Perhaps they see that the person seems stiff, unsteady, and unusually slow.

As the disease progresses, the shaking, or tremor, that affects the majority of Parkinson's patients may begin to interfere with daily activities. Patients may not be able to hold utensils steady or may find that the shaking makes reading a newspaper difficult. Parkinson's tremor may become worse when the patient is relaxed. A few seconds after the hands are rested on a table, for instance, the shaking is most pronounced. For most patients, tremor is usually the symptom that causes them to seek medical help.

What Are the Major Symptoms?

Parkinson's disease does not affect everyone the same way. In some people the disease progresses quickly, in others it does not. Although some people become severely disabled, others experience only minor motor disruptions. Tremor is the major symptom for some patients, while for others tremor is only a minor complaint and different symptoms are more troublesome.

Tremor. The tremor associated with Parkinson's disease has a characteristic appearance. Typically, the tremor takes the form of a rhythmic back-and-forth motion of the thumb and forefinger at three beats per second. This is sometimes called "pill rolling." Tremor usually begins in a hand, although sometimes a foot or the jaw is affected first. It is most obvious when the hand is at rest or when a person is under stress. In three out of four patients, the tremor may affect only one part or side of the body, especially during the early stages of the disease. Later it may become more general. Tremor is rarely disabling and it usually disappears during sleep or improves with intentional movement.

Rigidity. Rigidity, or a resistance to movement, affects most parkinsonian patients. A major principle of body movement is that all muscles have an opposing muscle. Movement is possible not just because one muscle becomes more active, but because the opposing muscle relaxes. In Parkinson's disease, rigidity comes about when, in response to signals from the brain, the delicate balance of opposing muscles is disturbed. The muscles remain constantly tensed and contracted so that the person aches or feels stiff or weak. The rigidity becomes obvious when another person tries to move the patient's arm, which will move only in ratchet-like or short, jerky movements known as "cogwheel" rigidity.

Bradykinesia. Bradykinesia, or the slowing down and loss of spontaneous and automatic movement, is particularly frustrating because it is unpredictable. One moment the patient can move easily. The next moment he or she may need help. This may well be the most disabling and distressing symptom of the disease because the patient cannot rapidly perform routine movements. Activities once performed quickly and easily— such as washing or dressing—may take several hours.

Postural instability. Postural instability, or impaired balance and coordination, causes patients to develop a forward or backward lean and to fall easily. When bumped from the front or when starting to walk, patients with a backward lean have a tendency to step backwards, which is known as retropulsion. Postural instability can cause patients to have a stooped posture in which the head is bowed and the shoulders are drooped. As the disease progresses, walking may be affected. Patients may halt in mid-stride and "freeze" in place, possibly even toppling over. Or patients may walk with a series of quick, small steps as if hurrying forward to keep balance. This is known as festination.

Are There Other Symptoms?

Various other symptoms accompany Parkinson's disease; some are minor, others are more bothersome. Many can be treated with appropriate medication or physical therapy. No one can predict which symptoms will affect an individual patient, and the intensity of the symptoms also varies from person to person. None of these symptoms is fatal, although swallowing problems can cause choking.

Depression. This is a common problem and may appear early in the course of the disease, even before other symptoms are noticed. Depression may not be severe, but it may be intensified by the drugs used to treat other symptoms of Parkinson's disease. Fortunately, depression can be successfully treated with antidepressant medications.

Emotional changes. Some people with Parkinson's disease become fearful and insecure. Perhaps they fear they cannot cope with new situations. They may not want to travel, go to parties, or socialize with friends. Some lose their motivation and become dependent on family members. Others may become irritable or uncharacteristically pessimistic. Memory loss and slow thinking may occur, although the ability to reason remains intact. Whether people actually suffer intellectual loss (also known as dementia) from Parkinson's disease is a controversial area still being studied.

One of the most demoralizing aspects of the disease is how completely the patient's world changes. The most basic daily routines may be affected—from socializing with friends and enjoying normal and congenial relationships with family members to earning a living and taking care of a home. Faced with a very different life, people need encouragement to remain as active and involved as possible. That's when support groups can be of particular value to parkinsonian patients, their families, and their caregivers.

Difficulty in swallowing and chewing. Muscles used in swallowing may work less efficiently in later stages of the disease. In these cases, food and saliva may collect in the mouth and back of the throat, which can result in choking or drooling. Medications can often alleviate these problems.

Speech changes. About half of all parkinsonian patients have problems with speech. They may speak too softly or in a monotone, hesitate before speaking, slur or repeat their words, or speak too fast. A speech therapist may be able to help patients reduce some of these problems.

Urinary problems or constipation. In some patients bladder and bowel problems can occur due to the improper functioning of the autonomic nervous system, which is responsible for regulating smooth muscle activity. Some people may become incontinent while others have trouble urinating. In others, constipation may occur because the intestinal tract operates more slowly. Constipation can also be caused by inactivity, eating a poor diet, or drinking too little fluid. It can be a persistent problem and, in rare cases, can be serious enough to require hospitalization.

P

P

Patients should not let constipation last for more than several days before taking steps to alleviate it.

Skin problems. In Parkinson's disease, it is common for the skin on the face to become very oily, particularly on the forehead and at the sides of the nose. The scalp may become oily too, resulting in dandruff. In other cases, the skin can become very dry. These problems are also the result of an improperly functioning autonomic nervous system. Standard treatments for skin problems help. Excessive sweating, another common symptom, is usually controllable with medications used for Parkinson's disease.

Sleep problems. These include difficulty staying asleep, restless sleep, nightmares and emotional dreams, and drowsiness during the day. It is unclear if these symptoms are related to the disease or to the medications used to treat Parkinson's disease. Patients should never take over-the-counter sleep aids without consulting their physicians.

What Are the Other Forms of Parkinsonism?

Postencephalitic parkinsonism. Just after the first World War, a viral disease, encephalitis lethargica, attacked almost 5 million people throughout the world, and then suddenly disappeared in the 1920s. Known as sleeping sickness in the United States, this disease killed one third of its victims and in many others led to postencephalitic parkinsonism, a particularly severe form of movement disorder in which some patients developed, often years after the acute phase of the illness, disabling neurological disorders, including various forms of catatonia. (In 1973, neurologist Oliver Sacks published Awakenings, an account of his work in the late 1960's with surviving post-encephalitic patients in a New York City hospital. Using the then-experimental drug levodopa, Dr. Sacks was able to temporarily "awaken" these patients from their statue-like state. A film by the same name was released in 1990.) In rare cases, other viral infections, including western equine encephalomyelitis, eastern equine encephalomyelitis, and Japanese B encephalitis, can leave patients with parkinsonian symptoms.

Drug-induced parkinsonism. A reversible form of parkinsonism sometimes results from use of certain drugs—chlorpromazine and haloperidol, for example—prescribed for patients with psychiatric disorders. Some drugs used for stomach disorders (metoclopramide) and high blood pressure (reserpine) may also produce parkinsonian symptoms. Stopping the medication or lowering the dosage causes the symptoms to abate.

Striatonigral degeneration. In this form of parkinsonism, the substantia nigra is only mildly affected, while other brain areas show more severe damage than occurs in patients with primary Parkinson's disease. People with this type of parkinsonism tend to show more rigidity and the disease progresses more rapidly.

Arteriosclerotic parkinsonism. Sometimes known as pseudoparkinsonism, arteriosclerotic parkinsonism involves damage to brain vessels due to multiple small strokes. Tremor is rare in this type of parkinsonism, while dementia—the loss of mental skills and abilities—is common. Antiparkinsonian drugs are of little help to patients with this form of parkinsonism.

Toxin-induced parkinsonism. Some toxins —such as manganese dust, carbon disulfide, and carbon monoxide—can also cause parkinsonism. A chemical that is known as MPTP (1-methyl-4-phenyl-1,2,5,6- tetrahydropyridine) causes a permanent form of parkinsonism that closely resembles Parkinson's disease. Investigators discovered this reaction in the 1980s when heroin addicts in California who had taken an illicit street drug contaminated with MPTP began to develop severe parkinsonism. This discovery, which demonstrated that a toxic substance could damage the brain and produce parkinsonian symptoms, caused a dramatic breakthrough in Parkinson's research: for the first time scientists were able to simulate Parkinson's disease in animals and conduct studies to increase understanding of the disease.

Parkinsonism accompanying other conditions. Parkinsonian symptoms may also appear in patients with other, clearly distinct neurological disorders such as Shy-Drager syndrome (sometimes called multiple system atrophy), progressive supranuclear palsy, Wilson's disease, Huntington's disease, Hallervorden-Spatz syndrome, Alzheimer's disease, Creutzfeldt-Jakob disease, olivopontocerebellar atrophy, and post-traumatic encephalopathy.

How Do Doctors Diagnose Parkinson's Disease?

Even for an experienced neurologist, making an accurate diagnosis in the early stages of Parkinson's disease can be difficult. There are, as yet, no sophisticated blood or laboratory tests available to diagnose the disease. The physician may need to observe the patient for some time until it is apparent that the tremor is consistently present and is joined by one or more of the other classic symptoms. Since other forms of parkinsonism have similar features but require different treatments, making a precise diagnosis as soon as possible is essential for starting a patient on proper medication.

How Is the Disease Treated?

At present, there is no cure for Parkinson's disease. But a variety of medications provide dramatic relief from the symptoms.

When recommending a course of treatment, the physician determines how much the symptoms disrupt the patient's life and then tailors therapy to the person's particular condition. Since no two patients will react the same way to a given drug, it may take time and patience to get the dose just right. Even then, symptoms may not be completely alleviated. In the early stages of Parkinson's disease, physicians often begin treatment with one or a combination of the less powerful drugs—such as the anticholinergics or amantadine (see section entitled "Are There Other Medications Available?" on page 515), saving the most powerful treatment, specifically levodopa, for the time when the patient needs it most.

Levodopa

Without doubt, the gold standard of present therapy is the drug levodopa (also called L-dopa). L-Dopa (from the full name L-3,4-dihydroxyphenylalanine) is a simple chemical found naturally in plants and animals. Levodopa is the generic name used for this chemical when it is formulated for drug use in patients. Nerve cells can use levodopa to make dopamine and replenish the brain's dwindling supply. Dopamine itself cannot be given because it doesn't cross the blood-brain barrier, the elaborate meshwork of fine blood vessels and cells that filters blood reaching the brain. Usually, patients are given levodopa combined with carbidopa. When added to levodopa, carbidopa delays the conversion of levodopa into dopamine until it reaches the brain, preventing or diminishing some of the side effects that often accompany levodopa therapy. Carbidopa also reduces the amount of levodopa needed.

Levodopa's success in treating the major symptoms of Parkinson's disease is a triumph of modern medicine. First introduced in the 1960s, it delays the onset of debilitating symptoms and allows the majority of parkinsonian patients—who would otherwise be very disabled—to extend the period of time in which they can lead relatively normal, productive lives.

Although levodopa helps at least three-quarters of parkinsonian cases, not all symptoms respond equally to the drug. Bradykinesia and rigidity respond best, while tremor may be only marginally reduced. Problems with balance and other symptoms may not be alleviated at all.

People who have taken other medications before starting levodopa therapy may have to cut back or eliminate these drugs in order to feel the full benefit of levodopa. Once levodopa therapy starts people often respond dramatically, but they may need to increase the dose gradually for maximum benefit.

Because a high-protein diet can interfere with the absorption of levodopa, some physicians recommend that patients taking the drug restrict protein consumption to the evening meal.

Levodopa is so effective that some people may forget they have Parkinson's disease. But levodopa is not a cure. Although it can diminish the symptoms, it does not replace lost nerve cells and it does not stop the progression of the disease.

Side Effects of Levodopa

Although beneficial for thousands of patients, levodopa is not without its limitations and side effects. The most common side effects are nausea, vomiting, low blood pressure, involuntary movements, and restlessness. In rare cases patients may become confused. The nausea and vomiting caused by levodopa are greatly reduced by the combination of levodopa and carbidopa, which enhances the effectiveness of a lower dose. A slow-release formulation of the drug, which provides a longer lasting effect, is also available.

Prolonging Levodopa Action

Recent studies revealed that when the drug tolcapone is added to the standard drug treatment for Parkinson's disease, levodopa-carbidopa, symptom relief is prolonged greatly. This promising new drug that blocks the breakdown of dopamine and levodopa would allow patients to take fewer doses and smaller amounts of levodopa-carbidopa and to decrease the problems of the wearing-off effect.

Dyskinesias, or involuntary movements such as twitching, nodding, and jerking, most commonly develop in people who are taking large doses of levodopa over an extended period. These movements may be either mild or severe and either very rapid or very slow. The only effective way to control these drug-induced movements is to lower the dose of levodopa or to use drugs that block dopamine, but these remedies usually cause the disease symptoms to reappear. Doctors and patients must work together closely to find a tolerable balance between the drug's benefits and side effects.

Other more troubling and distressing problems may occur with long-term levodopa use. Patients may begin to notice more pronounced symptoms before their first dose of medication in the morning, and they can feel when each dose begins to wear off (muscle spasms are a common effect). Symptoms gradually begin to return. The period of effectiveness from each dose may begin to shorten, called the wearing-off effect. Another potential problem is referred to as the on-off effect—sudden, unpredictable changes in movement, from normal to parkinsonian movement and back again, possibly occurring several times during the day. These effects probably indicate that the patient's response to the drug is changing or that the disease is progressing.

Parkinson's Disease and Nicotine

Several population studies have shown that smokers have a lower incidence of Parkinson's disease than non-smokers. But this doesn't mean that people who suffer from Parkinson's disease should start smoking; cigarette smoking causes lung cancer and heart disease.

However, scientists are investigating nicotine as a possible therapeutic agent for Parkinson's disease. In a small study, patients suffering from mild to moderate Parkinson's disease experienced improved motor function and cognition after receiving a nicotine injection and wearing a nicotine patch for two weeks. Another small study found that a nicotine patch improved movement and memory deficits. However, another study, using a nicotine patch in addition to conventional treatment, found no effect.

How nicotine might protect the brain is not entirely clear. One theory is that nicotine binds to certain brain receptors and enhances levels of dopamine—a brain chemical that affects motor control and is responsible for the jerky movements and slowness that characterize Parkinson's disease.

Those studies that found nicotine was therapeutically beneficial in treating Parkinson's disease were too short—and used too few patients—to determine whether nicotine would be useful as a long-term treatment. Further careful studies are needed before a recommendation for nicotine can be made. *The Editors*

One approach to alleviating these side effects is to take levodopa more often and in smaller amounts. Sometimes, physicians instruct patients to stop levodopa for several days in an effort to improve the response to the drug and to manage the complications of long-term levodopa therapy. This controversial technique is known as a "drug holiday." Because of the possibility of serious complications, drug holidays should be attempted only under a physician's direct supervision, preferably in a hospital. Parkinson's disease patients should never stop taking levodopa without their physician's knowledge or consent because of the potentially serious side effects of rapidly withdrawing the drug.

Are There Other Medications Available?

Levodopa is not a perfect drug. Fortunately, physicians have other treatment choices for particular symptoms or stages of the disease. Other therapies include the following:

Bromocriptine, pergolide, pramipexole and ropinirole. These four drugs mimic the role of dopamine in the brain, causing the neurons to react as they would to dopamine. They can be given alone or with levodopa and may be used in the early stages of the disease or started later to lengthen the duration of response to levodopa in patients experiencing wearing-off or on-off effects. They are generally less effective than levodopa in controlling rigidity and bradykinesia. Side effects may include paranoia, hallucinations, confusion, dyskinesias, nightmares, nausea, and vomiting.

Selegiline. Studies supported by the the National Institute of Neurological Disorders and Stroke (NINDS) shown that this drug (also known as deprenyl) delays the need for levodopa therapy by an average of nine months. When selegiline is given with levodopa, it appears to enhance and prolong the response to levodopa and thus may reduce wearing-off fluctuations. Selegiline inhibits the activity of the enzyme monoamine oxidase B (MAO-B), the enzyme that metabolizes dopamine in the brain, delaying the breakdown of naturally occurring dopamine and of dopamine formed from levodopa, and also provides mild symptomatic relief from parkinsonism in and of itself. Selegiline is an easy drug to take, although side effects may include nausea, orthostatic hypotension, or insomnia (when taken late in the day). Also, toxic reactions have occurred in some patients who took selegiline with fluoxetine (an antidepressant) and meperidine (used as a sedative and an analgesic).

Anticholinergics. These drugs were the main treatment for Parkinson's disease until the introduction of levodopa. Their benefit is limited, but they may help control tremor and rigidity. They are particularly helpful in reducing drug-induced parkinsonism. Anticholinergics appear to act by blocking the action of another brain chemical, acetylcholine, whose effects become more pronounced when dopamine levels drop. Only about half the patients who receive anticholinergics respond, usually for a brief period and with only a 30 percent improvement. Although not as effective as levodopa or bromocriptine, anticholinergics may have a therapeutic effect at any stage of the disease when taken with either of these drugs. Common side effects include dry mouth, constipation, urinary retention, hallucinations, memory loss, blurred vision, changes in mental activity, and confusion.

Amantadine. An antiviral drug, amantadine, helps reduce symptoms of Parkinson's disease. It is often used alone in the early stages of the disease or with an anticholinergic drug or levodopa. After several months amantadine's effectiveness wears off in a third to a half of the patients taking it, although effectiveness may return after a brief withdrawal from the drug. Amantadine has several side effects, including mottled skin, edema, confusion, blurred vision, and depression.

Is Surgery Ever Used to Treat Parkinson's Disease?

Treating Parkinson's disease with surgery was once a common practice. But after the discovery of levodopa, surgery was restricted to only a few cases. Currently, surgery is reserved for patients who have failed to respond satisfactorily to drugs. One of the procedures used, called cryothalamotomy, requires the surgical insertion of a supercooled metal tip of a probe into the thalamus (a "relay station" deep in the brain) to destroy the brain area that produces tremors. This and related procedures, such as thalamic stimulation, are coming back into favor for patients who have severe tremor or have the disease only on one side of the body. Investigators have also revived interest in a surgical procedure called pallidotomy in which a portion of the brain called the globus pallidus is lesioned. Some studies indicate that pallidotomy may improve symptoms of tremor, rigidity, and bradykinesia, possibly by interrupting the neural pathway between the globus pallidus and the striatum or thalamus. Further research on the value of surgically destroying these brain areas is currently being conducted. Restorative surgery, using nerve cell transplants to supplement the patient's own dopamine-producing nerve cells, is also under investigation.

Can Diet or Exercise Programs Help Relieve Symptoms?
Diet
Eating a well-balanced, nutritious diet can be beneficial for anybody. But for preventing or curing Parkinson's disease, there does not seem to be any specific vitamin, mineral, or other nutrient that has any therapeutic value. A high protein diet, however, may limit levodopa's effectiveness.

Despite some early optimism, recent studies have shown that tocopherol (a form of vitamin E) does not delay Parkinson's disease. This conclusion came from a carefully conducted study supported by the NINDS called DATATOP (Deprenyl and Tocopherol Antioxidative Therapy for Parkinson's Disease) that examined, over five years, the effects of both deprenyl and vitamin E on early Parkinson's disease. While deprenyl was found to slow the early symptomatic progression of the disease and delay the need for levodopa, there was no evidence of therapeutic benefit from vitamin E.

Exercise

Because movements are affected in Parkinson's disease, exercising may help people improve their mobility. Some doctors prescribe physical therapy or muscle-strengthening exercises to tone muscles and to put underused and rigid muscles through a full range of motion. Exercises will not stop disease progression, but they may improve body strength so that the person is less disabled. Exercises also improve balance, helping people overcome gait problems, and can strengthen certain muscles so that people can speak and swallow better. Exercises can also improve the emotional well-being of parkinsonian patients by giving them a feeling of accomplishment. Although structured exercise programs help many patients, more general physical activity, such as walking, gardening, swimming, calisthenics, and using exercise machines, is also beneficial.

Can Scientists Predict or Prevent Parkinson's Disease?

As yet, there is no way to predict or prevent the disease. However, researchers are now looking for a biomarker—a biochemical abnormality that all patients with Parkinson's disease might share—that could be picked up by screening techniques or by a simple chemical test given to people who do not have any parkinsonian symptoms.

Positron emission tomography (PET) scanning may lead to important advances in our knowledge about Parkinson's disease. PET scans of the brain produce pictures of chemical changes as they occur in the living brain. Using PET, research scientists can study the brain's dopamine receptors (the sites on nerve cells that bind with dopamine) to determine if the loss of dopamine activity follows or precedes degeneration of the neurons that make this chemical. This information could help scientists better understand the disease process and may potentially lead to improved treatments.

National Institute of Neurological Disorders and Stroke

P

A peptic ulcer is a sore on the lining of the stomach or duodenum, which is the beginning of the small intestine. Peptic ulcers are common: One in 10 Americans develops an ulcer at some time in his or her life. One cause of peptic ulcer is bacterial infection, but some ulcers are caused by long-term use of nonsteroidal anti-inflammatory agents (NSAIDs), such as aspirin and ibuprofen. In a few cases, cancerous tumors in the stomach or pancreas can cause ulcers. Peptic ulcers are not caused by spicy food or stress.

What Is *H. Pylori*?

Helicobacter pylori (*H. pylori*) is a type of bacteria. Researchers believe that *H. pylori* is responsible for the majority of peptic ulcers.

H. pylori infection is common in the United States: About 20 percent of people under 40 years old and half of those over 60 have it. Most infected people, however, do not develop ulcers. Why *H. pylori* does not cause ulcers in every infected person is not known. Most likely, infection depends on characteristics of the infected person, the type of *H. pylori*, and other factors yet to be discovered.

Researchers are not certain how people contract *H. pylori*, but they think it may be through food or water.

Researchers have found *H. pylori* in some infected people's saliva, so the bacteria may also spread through mouth-to-mouth contact such as kissing.

How Does *H. Pylori* Cause a Peptic Ulcer?

H. pylori weakens the protective mucous coating of the stomach and duodenum, which allows acid to get through to the sensitive lining beneath. Both the acid and the bacteria irritate the lining and cause a sore, or ulcer.

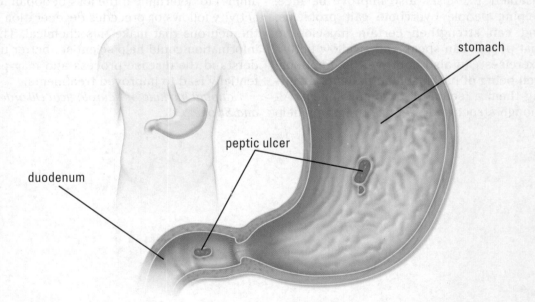

stomach

peptic ulcer

duodenum

Peptic ulcers are raw spots or sores that can occur anywhere on the lining of the stomach (where they are called gastric ulcers) or the duodenum (where they are called duodenal ulcers).

H. pylori is able to survive in stomach acid because it secretes enzymes that neutralize the acid. This allows *H. pylori* to make its way to the "safe" area--the protective mucous lining. Once there, the bacterium's spiral shape helps it burrow through the lining.

What Are the Symptoms of an Ulcer?

Abdominal discomfort is the most common symptom. This discomfort usually:

- is a dull, gnawing ache;
- comes and goes for several days or weeks;
- occurs two to three hours after a meal;
- occurs in the middle of the night (when the stomach is empty);
- is relieved by food;
- is relieved by antacid medications.

Other symptoms include:

- weight loss
- poor appetite
- bloating
- burping
- nausea
- vomiting

Some people experience only very mild symptoms, or none at all.

The symptoms above refer primarily to duodenal ulcers. People with gastric ulcers experience pain 15 to 30 minutes after eating, are frequently afraid to eat, and often lose weight. Pain at night and pain during fasting are rare.

How Is an *H. Pylori*-related Ulcer Diagnosed?

Diagnosing an Ulcer

To see whether symptoms are caused by an ulcer, the doctor may do an upper gastrointestinal (GI) series or an endoscopy. An upper GI series is an x-ray of the esophagus,

Emergency Symptoms

Call your doctor right away if you have any of these symptoms:

- Sharp, sudden, persistent stomach pain
- Bloody or black stools
- Bloody vomit or vomit that looks like coffee grounds

They could be signs of a serious problem, such as:

- Perforation—when the ulcer burrows through the stomach or duodenal wall
- Bleeding—when acid or the ulcer breaks a blood vessel
- Obstruction—when the ulcer blocks the path of food trying to leave the stomach

stomach, and duodenum. The patient drinks a chalky liquid called barium to make these organs and any ulcers show up more clearly on the x-ray.

An endoscopy is an exam that uses an endoscope, a thin, lighted tube with a tiny camera on the end. The patient is lightly sedated, and the doctor carefully eases the endoscope into the mouth and down the throat to the stomach and duodenum. This allows the doctor to see the lining of the esophagus, stomach, and duodenum. The doctor can use the endoscope to take photos of ulcers or remove a tiny piece of tissue to view under a microscope.

Diagnosing H. Pylori

If an ulcer is found, the doctor will test the patient for *H. pylori*. This test is important because treatment for an ulcer caused by *H. pylori* is different from that for an ulcer caused by NSAIDs.

H. pylori is diagnosed through blood, breath, stool, and tissue tests. Blood tests

P

NSAIDs and Ulcers

Long-term use of nonsteroidal anti-inflammatory drugs (NSAIDs) is associated with an increased risk of stomach irritation, bleeding, and ulceration caused by the drug's interference with the formation of protective mucus that normally coats the stomach. Some degree of gastrointestinal (GI) bleeding occurs in more than half of patients taking NSAIDs—which include familiar pain relievers such as aspirin, ibuprofen, and naproxen, as well as less familiar prescription medications such as fenoprofen calcium, etodolac, and indomethacin.

People at highest risk for GI side effects include those over age 65, those taking corticosteroids, and those with a history of stomach ulcers or adverse reactions to NSAIDs.

The risk of such side effects can be minimized by selecting an enteric-coated NSAID (pills specially coated to dissolve in the intestine rather than the stomach). In addition, there are several medications that, taken along with an NSAID, may reduce the risk of developing an ulcer. These agents—called cytoprotective drugs—can reduce the acid content of the stomach; they include omeprazole, sucralfate, and the histamine H2 receptor antagonists ranitidine, cimetidine, nizatidine, and famotidine.

Another medication, misoprostol, can reduce the occurrence of ulcers in the upper part of the small intestine by two thirds and stomach ulcers by three fourths in regular NSAID users. A combination of the NSAID diclofenac and misoprostol, called Arthrotec, is also available.

---

are most common. They detect antibodies to *H. pylori* bacteria. Blood is taken at the doctor's office through a finger stick.

Urea breath tests are mainly used after treatment to see whether it worked, but they can be used in diagnosis too. In the doctor's office, the patient drinks a urea solution that contains a special carbon atom. If *H. pylori* is present, it breaks down the urea, releasing the carbon. The blood carries the carbon to the lungs, where the patient exhales it. The test is 96 percent to 98 percent accurate.

Stool tests may be used to detect *H. pylori* infection in the patient's fecal matter. Studies have shown that the test, called the Helicobacter pylori stool antigen (HpSA) test, is accurate for diagnosing *H. pylori*.

Tissue tests are usually done using the biopsy sample that is removed with the endoscope. There are three types:
• The rapid urease test detects the enzyme urease, which is produced by *H. pylori*.

• A histology test allows the doctor to find and examine the actual bacteria.
• A culture test involves allowing *H. pylori* to grow in the tissue sample.

Blood, breath, and stool tests are often done before tissue tests because they are less invasive. However, blood tests are not used to detect *H. pylori* following treatment because a patient's blood can show positive results even after *H. pylori* has been eliminated.

How Are *H. Pylori* Peptic Ulcers Treated?

H. pylori peptic ulcers are treated with drugs that kill the bacteria, reduce stomach acid, and protect the stomach lining. Antibiotics are used to kill the bacteria. Two types of acid-suppressing drugs might be used: H2 blockers and proton pump inhibitors.

H2 blockers work by blocking histamine, which stimulates acid secretion. They help reduce ulcer pain after a few weeks. Proton pump inhibitors suppress acid production by halting the mechanism that pumps the acid into the stomach. H2 blockers and proton pump inhibitors have been prescribed alone for years as treatments for ulcers. But used alone, these drugs do not eradicate *H. pylori* and therefore do not cure *H. pylori*-related ulcers. Bismuth subsalicylate, a component of Pepto-Bismol, is used to protect the stomach lining from acid. It also kills *H. pylori*.

Treatment usually involves a combination of drugs that include antibiotics, acid suppressors, and stomach protectors. Antibiotic regimens recommended for patients may differ across regions of the world because bacteria in different areas have begun to show resistance to particular antibiotics.

The use of only one medication to treat *H. pylori* is not recommended. At this time, the most proven effective treatment is a two-week course of treatment called triple therapy. It involves taking two antibiotics to kill the bacteria and either an acid suppressor or stomach-lining shield. Two-week triple therapy reduces ulcer symptoms, kills the bacteria, and prevents ulcer recurrence in more than 90 percent of patients.

Unfortunately, patients may find triple therapy complicated because it involves taking as many as 20 pills a day. Also, the antibiotics used in triple therapy may cause mild side effects such as nausea, vomiting, diarrhea, dark stools, metallic taste in the mouth, dizziness, headache, and yeast infections in women. (Most side effects can be treated with medication withdrawal.) Nevertheless, recent studies show that two weeks of triple therapy is ideal.

Early results of studies in other countries suggest that one week of triple therapy may be as effective as the two-week therapy, with fewer side effects.

Another option is two weeks of dual therapy. Dual therapy involves two drugs: an antibiotic and an acid suppressor. It is not as effective as triple therapy.

Two weeks of quadruple therapy, which uses two antibiotics, an acid suppressor, and a stomach-lining shield, looks promising in research studies. It is also called bismuth triple therapy.

Can *H. Pylori* Infection Be Prevented?

No one knows for sure how *H. pylori* spreads, so prevention is difficult. Researchers are trying to develop a vaccine to prevent infection.

National Institute of Diabetes and Digestive and Kidney Diseases

P

If you have been told you have periodontal (gum) disease, you're not alone. An estimated 80 percent of American adults currently have some form of the disease.

Periodontal diseases range from simple gum inflammation to serious disease that results in major damage to the soft tissue and bone that support the teeth. In the worst cases, teeth are lost.

Gum disease is a threat to your oral health. Research is also pointing to possible health effects of periodontal diseases that go well beyond your mouth (more about this later). Whether it is stopped, slowed, or gets worse depends a great deal on how well you care for your teeth and gums every day, from this point forward.

Causes

Our mouths are full of bacteria. These bacteria, along with mucus and other particles, constantly form a sticky, colorless "plaque" on teeth. Brushing and flossing help get rid of plaque. Plaque that is not removed can harden and form bacteria-harboring "tartar" that brushing doesn't clean. Only a professional cleaning by a dentist or dental hygienist can remove tartar.

Gingivitis

The longer plaque and tartar are on teeth, the more harmful they become. The bacteria cause inflammation of the gums that is called "gingivitis." In gingivitis, the gums become red, swollen and can bleed easily. Gingivitis is a mild form of gum disease that can usually be reversed with daily brushing and flossing, and professional cleaning. This form of gum disease does not include any loss of bone and tissue that hold teeth in place.

Periodontitis

When gingivitis is not treated, it can advance to periodontitis (which means "inflammation around the tooth.") In periodontitis,

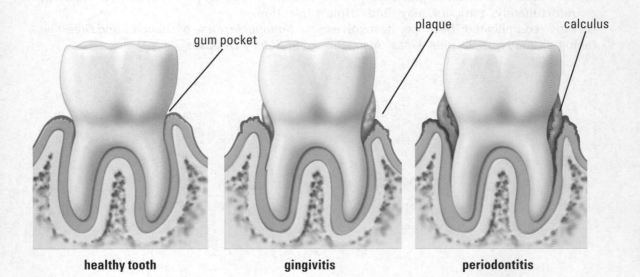

healthy tooth　　　　　**gingivitis**　　　　　**periodontitis**

With gingivitis, plaque builds up and irritates the gums. As gum disease advances, gums gradually pull away from affected teeth, and underlying tissue and bone are destroyed (periodontitis).

gums pull away from the teeth and form "pockets" that are infected. The body's immune system fights the bacteria as the plaque spreads and grows below the gum line. Bacterial toxins and the body's enzymes fighting the infection actually start to break down the bone and connective tissue that hold teeth in place. If not treated, the bones, gums, and connective tissue that support the teeth are destroyed. The teeth may eventually become loose and have to be removed.

Who Gets It?
People usually don't show signs of gum disease until they are in their 30s or 40s. Men are more likely to have periodontal disease than women. Although teenagers rarely develop periodontitis, they can develop gingivitis, the milder form of gum disease. Most commonly, gum disease develops when plaque is allowed to build up along and under the gum line.

Prevention
Here are some things you can do to prevent periodontal diseases:
- Brush your teeth twice a day (with a fluoride toothpaste).
- Floss once a day.
- Visit the dentist routinely for a check-up and professional cleaning.
- Eat a well balanced diet.
- Don't use tobacco products.

Don't brush with plain baking soda or rush out to buy a toothpaste containing baking soda, unless you're more likely to brush regularly because you like the taste or feel of such products. A mild abrasive, baking soda is a weak tooth cleaner, and it does not help prevent periodontal disease.

Risk Factors
- **Smoking.** Need another reason to quit smoking? Smoking is one of the most significant risk factors associated with the development of periodontitis. Additionally, smoking can lower the chances of success of some treatments.
- **Hormonal changes in girls/women.** These changes can make gums more sensitive and make it easier for gingivitis to develop.
- **Diabetes.** People with diabetes are at higher risk for developing infections, including periodontal disease.
- **Stress.** Research shows that stress can make it more difficult for our bodies to fight infection, including periodontal disease.
- **Medications.** Some drugs, such as oral contraceptives, antidepressants, and some heart medicines can affect oral health because they lessen the flow of saliva. (Saliva has a protective effect on teeth and gums.)
- **Poor nutrition.** A poor diet, especially one low in calcium, can lower your resistance to gum disease.
- **Illnesses.** Diseases like cancer or AIDS and their treatments can also affect the health of gums.
- **Genetic susceptibility.** Some people are more prone to severe periodontal disease than others.

Sjögren's syndrome (see page 570)—characterized by dry mouth and dry eyes, either alone (termed sicca syndrome), or accompanied by dryness in other parts of the body, including the skin, nose, throat, and vagina—is another condition that increases the risk of periodontal disease.

How Do I Know if I Have Periodontal Disease?
Symptoms are often not noticeable until the disease is advanced. They include:
- Bad breath that won't go away

P

- Red or swollen gums
- Tender or bleeding gums
- Painful chewing
- Loose teeth
- Sensitive teeth

Any of these symptoms may signal a serious problem, which should be checked by a dentist. At your dental visit:

- The dentist will ask about your medical history to identify underlying conditions or risk factors (such as smoking) that may contribute to periodontal disease.
- The dentist or hygienist will examine your gums and note any signs of inflammation.
- The dentist or hygienist will use a probe to check for periodontal pockets and to measure any pockets. In a healthy mouth, the depth of these pockets is usually between 1 and 3 millimeters.
- The dentist or hygienist may take an x-ray to see whether there is any bone loss.
- The dentist may refer you to a periodontist, a specialist who treats gum diseases.

Treatment

The main goal of treatment is to control the infection. Treatment will vary, depending on the extent of the gum disease. Any type of treatment requires that the patient keep up good daily care at home. Additionally, modifying certain behaviors, such as quitting tobacco use, might be suggested as a way to improve treatment outcome.

Deep Cleaning

The dentist, periodontist, or dental hygienist removes the plaque through a deep-cleaning method called scaling and root planing. Scaling means scraping off the tartar from above and below the gum line. Root planing gets rid of rough spots on the tooth root where the germs gather, and helps remove bacteria that contribute to the disease.

Although "tartar-control" toothpastes appear to reduce tartar buildup by about a third, they don't remove all tartar (the hardened plaque that may lead to periodontal disease). See your dentist regularly for a professional cleaning, which is the only way to remove most or all tartar buildup.

Medications

A number of medications are now available to control the infection and reduce inflammation. Medications are generally used with treatment that includes scaling and root planing. Long-term studies will be needed to determine whether using medications reduces the need for surgery and whether they are effective over a long period of time. Here are some that are currently used.

Surgery

Flap Surgery. Surgery might be necessary if inflammation and deep pockets remain following treatment with deep cleaning and medications. A periodontist may perform flap surgery to remove tartar deposits in deep pockets or to reduce the periodontal pocket and make it easier for the patient, dentist, and hygienist to keep the area clean. This common surgery involves lifting back the gums and removing the tartar. The gums are then sutured back in place so that the tissue fits snugly around the tooth again.

Bone and Tissue Grafts. In addition to flap surgery, your periodontist may suggest placing bone or tissue grafts. Grafting is a way to replace or encourage new growth of bone or gum tissue destroyed by periodontitis. A technique that can be used with bone grafting is called guided tissue regeneration, in which a small piece of mesh-like fabric is inserted between the

Periodontal Disease Medications

A number of medications are now available to control the infection and reduce inflammation. Medications are generally used with treatment that includes scaling and root planing. Long-term studies will be needed to determine whether using medications reduces the need for surgery and whether they are effective over a long period of time. This chart describes some of the medications that are currently used.

Medications	What is it?	Why is it used?	How is it used?
Antimicrobial mouthrinse	A prescription mouthrinse containing an antimicrobial called chlorhexidine	To control bacteria when treating gingivitis and after gum surgery	It's used like a regular mouthwash.
Antiseptic "chip"	A tiny piece of gelatin filled with the medicine chlorhexidine	To control bacteria and reduce the size of periodontal pockets	After root planing, it's placed in the pockets where the medicine is slowly released over time.
Antibiotic gel	A gel that contains the antibiotic doxycycline	To control bacteria and reduce the size of periodontal pockets	The periodontist puts it in the pockets after scaling and root planing. The antibiotic is released slowly over a period of about seven days.
Antibiotic fiber	Thread-like fiber that contains the antibiotic tetracycline	To control bacteria and reduce the size of periodontal pockets	These fibers are placed in the pockets. The medicine is released slowly over 10 days. The fibers are then removed.
Antibiotic microspheres	Tiny, round particles that contain the antibiotic minocycline	To control bacteria and reduce the size of periodontal pockets	The periodontist puts the microspheres into the pockets after scaling and root planing. The particles release minocycline slowly over time.
Enzyme suppressant	A low dose of the medication doxycycline that keeps destructive enzymes in check	To hold back the body's enzyme response—if not controlled, certain enzymes can break down gum tissue	This medication is in pill form. It is used in combination with scaling and root planing.

bone and gum tissue. This keeps the gum tissue from growing into the area where the bone should be, allowing the bone and connective tissue to regrow.

Since each case is different, it is not possible to predict with certainty which grafts will be successful over the long term. Treatment results depend on many things, including severity of the disease, ability to maintain oral hygiene at home, and certain risk factors, such as smoking, which may lower the chances of success. Ask your periodontist what the level of success might be in your particular case.

P

Second Opinion

When considering any extensive dental or medical treatment options, you should think about getting a second opinion. To find a dentist or periodontist for a second opinion, call your local dental society. They can provide you with names of practitioners in your area. Dental schools are also a good source for getting a second opinion.

Can Periodontal Disease Cause Health Problems Beyond The Mouth?

Maybe. But so far the research is inconclusive. Studies are ongoing to try to determine whether there is a cause-and-effect relationship between periodontal disease and:

- an increased risk of heart attack or stroke;
- an increased risk of delivering preterm, low birth weight babies;
- difficulty controlling blood sugar levels in people with diabetes.

In the meantime, it's a fact that controlling periodontal disease can save your teeth—a very good reason to take care of your teeth and gums.

National Institute of Dental and Craniofacial Research

The mechanism underlying peripheral arterial disease (PAD)—also referred to as peripheral vascular disease—is similar to that of angina, a classic symptom of coronary heart disease (CHD), which is characterized by insufficient blood flow to the heart muscle (see page 233). PAD is characterized by insufficient blood flow to the legs; its hallmark is intermittent claudication, an angina-like pain in the legs. About 8 million Americans have PAD, which affects about 8 percent of people in their 60s and 20 percent of those over age 70.

Although PAD is not immediately life-threatening, people who have it are also at increased risk for CHD and cerebrovascular disease (CVD), an insufficient blood flow to the brain. CHD is the most common cause of heart attacks, while CVD is the most common cause of strokes (see page 592). People with PAD may be vulnerable to one or both of these life-threatening medical emergencies. Symptoms of PAD itself can be highly disabling. Many sufferers experience such severe leg pain that they are unable to walk more than a few steps, and some develop open sores (ulcers) on the legs or feet. Gangrene may develop in a small number of severe cases.

Causes

Like CAD and CVD, PAD is usually caused by atherosclerosis, the accumulation of plaques (deposits of fat and other material) within arterial walls. Plaque build-up narrows arteries and reduces the flow of oxygen-enriched blood to the muscles—especially during exercise, when oxygen demand is high. Oxygen deprivation, also known as ischemia, leads to muscle pain, and over time, the affected muscles may weaken and waste away (atrophy). Male gender, diabetes, and smoking are the three most significant risk factors for PAD. Other risk factors include high blood pressure, high cholesterol, and obesity—which all contribute to arterial narrowing.

Symptoms

Like angina, the pain of intermittent claudication is predictable: It nearly always develops after the same amount of exertion (such as walking a specific distance); generally occurs in the same area of the feet, legs, or buttocks; and usually improves rapidly with rest. In some patients, pain begins after only a few steps; in others, it may not start for more than a mile. Sometimes, sufferers experience pain only when walking uphill or climbing stairs. Other symptoms include coldness or numbness in the lower extremities and, sometimes, impotence in men.

About 3.4 million people with PAD experience these symptoms. But arteries can become significantly blocked without causing discomfort, a phenomenon called silent ischemia. Even though silent ischemia is not associated with symptoms, it poses the same threats as overt ischemia. PAD causes silent ischemia in about 4.2 million people. It is strongly suspected when systolic blood pressure is lower at the ankle than in the arm. If PAD appears likely, diagnostic studies to measure blood flow, such as Doppler ultrasound, may be recommended.

Long-Term Consequences of PAD

After five years, 73 percent of patients diagnosed with PAD remain stable—and many improve. But about 20 percent have a heart attack or stroke. In the aftermath of these events, five-year mortality is between 20 percent and 30 percent, and ten-year mortality climbs to 62 percent in men and 33 percent in women. About 4 percent eventually require amputation due to ulcers or

P

P

Walking Away the Pain

If you have muscle pain brought on by walking, see your doctor before starting an exercise program (other conditions may mimic peripheral vascular disease but require different treatments). The following tips should help to increase the distance you can walk without pain:

- Spend several minutes stretching before you walk, and walk on level ground.

- When walking, note how far you can go before pain starts (the initial claudication distance). Continue from this point until pain becomes so severe that you have to stop.

- Rest for a few minutes until pain subsides, then resume walking.

- Repeat this pattern for 40 to 60 minutes.

- Try to walk at least four times a week. In inclement weather, walk in a mall or other indoor space.

- Keep track of initial claudication distances and the stopping distances. Both should increase within a few weeks.

- If you have heart disease, check with your physician about how much you should walk. Even if you don't have a history of heart disease but experience chest pain, shortness of breath, or rapid heartbeat while walking, stop and call your doctor.

gangrene. A poor prognosis is more likely in those who have leg pain at rest or do not pursue treatment.

Treatment

The most effective treatments for PAD are lifestyle measures. Not smoking is the single most important step sufferers can take. Exercise—especially walking—is also essential. The idea is to set a brisk but comfortable pace until claudication begins; then rest and resume walking when the pain subsides. After a few months, many patients can complete the entire workout without pain or rest breaks.

It is also important for people with PAD to be evaluated for CHD and CVD. If either condition is found, treatment should proceed accordingly. In addition, many physicians recommend low-dose aspirin for PAD patients.

Finally, when applicable, diabetes, high blood pressure, and high cholesterol should be controlled, and patients who are obese should try to lose weight. (Controlling diabetes and high blood pressure, both risk factors for PAD, won't necessarily improve symptoms, but may reduce disease progression and the risk of heart attack and stroke.) Elevating the head of the bed a few inches to increase blood flow to the legs may also help relieve symptoms.

Despite proper care, about 7 percent of PAD patients require angioplasty or bypass surgery to restore blood flow to the legs. If lifestyle changes are unsatisfactory, the benefits of these procedures may outweigh the small possibility of complications.

Pneumonia is a serious infection or inflammation of your lungs. The air sacs in the lungs fill with pus and other liquid. Oxygen has trouble reaching your blood. If there is too little oxygen in your blood, your body cells can't work properly. Because of this and spreading infection through the body, pneumonia can cause death.

Until 1936, pneumonia was the number-one cause of death in the U.S. Since then, the use of antibiotics has brought it under control. In 1997, pneumonia and influenza combined ranked as the sixth leading cause of death.

Pneumonia affects your lungs in two ways. Lobar pneumonia affects a section (lobe) of a lung. Bronchial pneumonia (or bronchopneumonia) affects patches throughout both lungs.

Causes of Pneumonia

Pneumonia is not a single disease. It can have more than 30 different causes. There are five main causes of pneumonia:

- Bacteria
- Viruses
- Mycoplasmas
- Other infectious agents, such as fungi— including pneumocystis
- Various chemicals

Bacterial Pneumonia

Bacterial pneumonia can attack anyone from infants through the very old. Alcoholics, the debilitated, post-operative patients, people with respiratory diseases or viral infections and people who have weakened immune systems are at greater risk.

Pneumonia bacteria are present in some healthy throats. When body defenses are weakened in some way, by illness, old age, malnutrition, general debility or impaired immunity, the bacteria can multiply and cause serious damage. Usually, when a person's resistance is lowered, bacteria work

their way into the lungs and inflame the air sacs.

The tissue of part of a lobe of the lung, an entire lobe, or even most of the lungs' five lobes becomes completely filled with liquid (this is called "consolidation"). The infection quickly spreads through the bloodstream and the whole body is invaded.

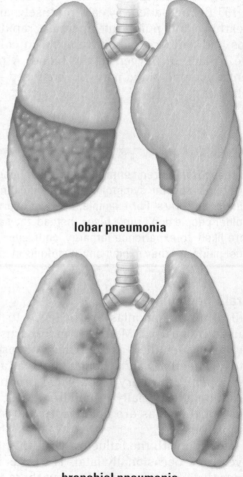

lobar pneumonia

bronchial pneumonia

Lobar pneumonia affects a section (or lobe) of a single lung; bronchial pneumonia can affect patches throughout both lungs.

P

The streptococcus pneumoniae is the most common cause of bacterial pneumonia. It is one form of pneumonia for which a vaccine is available.

Symptoms: The onset of bacterial pneumonia can vary from gradual to sudden. In the most severe cases, the patient may experience shaking chills, chattering teeth, severe chest pain, and a cough that produces rust-colored or greenish mucus.

A person's temperature may rise as high as 105°F. The patient sweats profusely, and breathing and pulse rate increase rapidly. Lips and nailbeds may have a bluish color due to lack of oxygen in the blood. A patient's mental state may be confused or delirious.

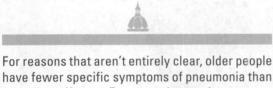

For reasons that aren't entirely clear, older people have fewer specific symptoms of pneumonia than younger sufferers. For example, nearly a quarter of older people don't run a fever. Instead, they are more likely to experience lethargy, confusion, or chest pains—if they exhibit any symptoms at all.

Viral Pneumonia

Half of all pneumonias are believed to be caused by viruses. More and more viruses are being identified as the cause of respiratory infection, and though most attack the upper respiratory tract, some produce pneumonia, especially in children. Most of these pneumonias are not serious and last a short time.

Infection with the influenza virus may be severe and occasionally fatal. The virus invades the lungs and multiplies, but there are almost no physical signs of lung tissue becoming filled with fluid. It finds many of its victims among those who have pre-existing heart or lung disease or are pregnant.

Symptoms: The initial symptoms of viral pneumonia are the same as influenza symptoms: fever, a dry cough, headache, muscle pain, and weakness. Within 12 to 36 hours, there is increasing breathlessness; the cough becomes worse and produces a small amount of mucus. There is a high fever and there may be blueness of the lips.

In extreme cases, the patient has a desperate need for air and extreme breathlessness. Viral pneumonias may be complicated by an invasion of bacteria, with all the typical symptoms of bacterial pneumonia.

Mycoplasma Pneumonia

Because of its somewhat different symptoms and physical signs, and because the course of the illness differed from classical pneumococcal pneumonia, mycoplasma pneumonia was once believed to be caused by one or more undiscovered viruses and was called "primary atypical pneumonia."

Identified during World War II, mycoplasmas are the smallest free-living agents of disease in humankind, unclassified as to whether bacteria or viruses, but having characteristics of both. They generally cause a mild and widespread pneumonia. They affect all age groups, occurring most frequently in older children and young adults. The death rate is low, even in untreated cases.

Symptoms: The most prominent symptom of mycoplasma pneumonia is a cough that tends to come in violent attacks, but produces only sparse whitish mucus. Chills and fever are early symptoms, and some patients experience nausea or vomiting. Patients may experience profound weakness that lasts for a long time.

Other Kinds of Pneumonia

Pneumocystis carinii pneumonia (PCP) is caused by an organism believed to be a fungus. PCP is the first sign of illness in many persons with AIDS.

PCP can be successfully treated in many cases. It may recur a few months later, but treatment can help to prevent or delay its recurrence.

Other less common pneumonias may be quite serious and are occurring more often. Various special pneumonias are caused by the inhalation of food, liquid, gases or dust, and by fungi. Foreign bodies or a bronchial obstruction such as a tumor may promote the occurrence of pneumonia, although they are not causes of pneumonia.

Rickettsia (also considered an organism somewhere between viruses and bacteria) cause Rocky Mountain spotted fever, Q fever, typhus and psittacosis, diseases that may have mild or severe effects on the lungs.

Tuberculosis pneumonia is a very serious lung infection and extremely dangerous unless treated early.

Treating Pneumonia

If you develop pneumonia, your chances of a fast recovery are greatest under certain conditions: if you're young, if your pneumonia is caught early, if your defenses against disease are working well, if the infection hasn't spread, and if you're not suffering from other illnesses.

In the young and healthy, early treatment with antibiotics can cure bacterial pneumonia and speed recovery from mycoplasma pneumonia and a certain percentage of rickettsia cases. There is not yet a general treatment for viral pneumonia, although antiviral drugs are used for certain kinds. Most people can be treated at home.

The drugs used to fight pneumonia are determined by the germ causing the pneumonia and the judgment of the doctor. After a patient's temperature returns to normal, medication must be continued according to the doctor's instructions,

otherwise the pneumonia may recur. Relapses can be far more serious than the first attack.

Besides antibiotics, patients are given supportive treatment: proper diet and oxygen to increase oxygen in the blood when needed. In some patients, medication to ease chest pain and to provide relief from violent cough may be necessary.

The vigorous young person may lead a normal life within a week of recovery from pneumonia. For the middle-aged, however, weeks may elapse before they regain their accustomed strength, vigor, and feeling of well being. A person recovering from mycoplasma pneumonia may be weak for an extended period of time.

In general, a person should not be discouraged from returning to work or carrying out usual activities but must be warned to expect some difficulties. Adequate rest is important to maintain progress toward full recovery and to avoid relapse.

Preventing Pneumonia Is Possible

Because pneumonia is a common complication of influenza (flu), getting a flu shot every fall is good pneumonia prevention.

Vaccine is also available to help fight pneumococcal pneumonia, one type of bacterial pneumonia. Your doctor can help you decide if you or a member of your family needs the vaccine. It is usually given only to people at high risk of getting the disease and suffering its life-threatening complications.

The greatest risk of pneumococcal pneumonia is usually among people who:
• Have chronic illnesses such as lung disease, heart disease, kidney disorders, sickle cell anemia, or diabetes
• Are recovering from severe illness
• Are in nursing homes or other chronic care facilities

P

P

- Are age 65 or older

If you are at risk, ask your doctor for the vaccine. The vaccine is generally given only once. Ask your doctor about any revaccination recommendations. The vaccine is not recommended for pregnant women or children under age two.

Experts estimate that at least half of pneumonia-related deaths could be avoided if everyone age 65 and older received a vaccination against pneumonia. In the past, the vaccine was given only once. A booster every five years may be appropriate, however, particularly for people who were first vaccinated before age 65.

Since pneumonia often follows ordinary respiratory infections, the most important preventive measure is to be alert to any symptoms of respiratory trouble that linger more than a few days. Good health habits, proper diet and hygiene, rest, and regular exercise increase resistance to all respiratory illnesses. They also help promote fast recovery when illness does occur.

If You Have Symptoms of Pneumonia

Call your doctor immediately. Even with the many effective antibiotics, early diagnosis and treatment are important.

Follow your doctor's advice. In serious cases, your doctor may advise a hospital stay. Or recovery at home may be possible.

Continue to take the medicine your doctor prescribes until told you may stop. This will help prevent recurrence of pneumonia and relapse.

Remember, even though pneumonia can be treated, it is an extremely serious illness. Don't wait, get treatment early.

American Lung Association

B y midlife, many people begin to notice that they cannot focus clearly on near objects and need the assistance of reading glasses or bifocals. This problem, known as presbyopia, is due to an age-related disorder of the lens of the eye. To see objects up close, contraction of the ciliary muscles surrounding the lens cause it to change its shape to focus on the near object—a process called accommodation. As we age, the lens gradually becomes thicker and more rigid and is less able to change its shape to bring close objects into focus.

Vision may also become impaired by structural abnormalities of the eye that prevent the light rays from focusing on the retina. Normally, the lens changes shape to focus light rays so they converge exactly on the retina. For example, to see a distant object, the ciliary muscles tighten to flatten the lens and focus light coming from afar. Whereas, to read, these muscles relax, and the lens reverts to its naturally rounder shape, which focuses light from close objects onto the retina. Refractive errors result from irregularities in the shape or refractive strength of certain eye structures.

Types of Refractive Errors

There are three types of refractive errors; presbyopia, while a common cause of blurred vision, is not technically a refractive disorder.

- **Nearsightedness (myopia).** In nearsighted people, the eyeball is too long or the cornea has too much curvature. As a result, light focuses on a point in front of the retina; near objects can be seen clearly but distant ones do not come into proper focus. Nearly 30 percent of Americans are nearsighted.
- **Farsightedness (hyperopia).** If the eyeball is too short or the cornea is too flat, the focal point for light is behind the retina.

In this condition, distant objects can be seen clearly but close ones do not come into proper focus.
- **Astigmatism.** Astigmatism occurs when the cornea or lens is slightly irregular in shape. This unequal curvature causes

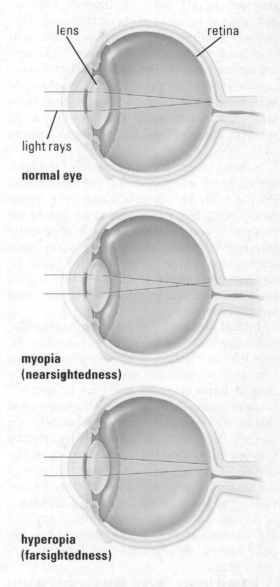

lens   retina

light rays

normal eye

**myopia
(nearsightedness)**

**hyperopia
(farsightedness)**

In a normal eye, light focuses precisely on the retina. In nearsightedness, light focuses short of the retina; in farsightedness, beyond the retina.

P

P

light to focus at different points in the eye. The result is blurred or distorted vision.

Non-Surgical Treatment

To correct for presbyopia, most people need nothing more than reading glasses. For individuals with presbyopia who do not need a distance prescription, over-the-counter reading glasses are available, and may be a good choice. They come in varying strengths and are labeled with the same power system as prescription glasses. Be sure to get the correct prescription from your ophthalmologist and update it as needed, since presbyopia tends to worsen over time.

Refractive errors can be corrected with prescription eyeglasses or contact lenses. People with presbyopia along with coexisting refractive errors, such as nearsightedness or astigmatism, have traditionally required bifocals. Because bifocals have limitations, newer types of multifocal lenses have been developed. These new lenses include trifocals, progressive lenses, and specialty lenses.

Bifocal lenses have two segments. The lower part of the lens corrects vision for reading and other close work, while the top part corrects for distance. Usually the largest percentage of the lens is devoted to near vision. (For people who have good distance vision but want to wear bifocals so they don't have to remove their reading glasses every time they need to see in the distance, the top half contains plain glass.) An aesthetic problem is the visible line between the two sections. Another drawback is having only two focus points, near and far; objects at intermediate distances appear blurry. Bifocals are the least expensive option.

Trifocal lenses have a third segment that focuses on objects 18 to 24 inches away, such as a computer screen or the dashboard of a car. While wearing these lenses,

---

Adjusting to Multifocal Lenses

Multifocal lenses can be disconcerting at first, so here are a few tips to ease the adjustment period:

- Wear the multifocals continuously until you're accustomed to them, even though you may not need them all the time.
- Look straight ahead, not at your feet, when walking.
- Hold reading material close to your body and lower your eyes so you're looking through the bottom part of the lens. Move the book, rather than your head, while reading.

---

you look down for close objects, straight ahead for ones at intermediate distances, and slightly up for distant objects. Trifocals have two visible lines. They usually cost more than bifocals but less than progressive lenses.

Progressive lenses, also called invisible or "no-line" bifocals, aren't really bifocals at all. Instead of focusing at only two distances, they allow you to focus on an infinite number of points. Progressive lenses offer the closest thing to natural vision before the onset of presbyopia; they're also the most visually appealing, since no line is visible between segments. However, progressive lenses are the most expensive. Some people find it difficult to adjust to the undefined focus segments, although most new progressive-lens wearers are able to adapt quickly. Some manufacturers allow you to exchange progressive lenses for bifocals if you're unable to adjust within a few weeks.

Specialty lenses give you the option of changing the near-focus segment of the lens, which is traditionally located in the lower section. Depending on your occupation and hobbies, a different location might be preferred. For example, a golfer might benefit from glasses with a near-focus segment that is lower and in the inside corner of one lens, allowing him to see the scorecard without compromising his ability to hit the ball. Specialty lenses are not meant for everyday wear; you will also need regular multifocal lenses.

Like eyeglasses, prescription contact lenses can correct presbyopia with coexisting refractive errors. The two options for contact lenses are monovision lenses and bifocal lenses. Monovision contact lenses correct one eye for near vision and the other for distance (or not at all, if the person is not nearsighted). Bifocal lenses, which correct both near and far vision in each lens, have dramatically improved in recent years.

Both types of contact lenses eliminate the need to wear glasses; each type, however, has its disadvantages. A recent study found that 41 percent of people were unable to adjust to monovision contact lenses. Bifocal contacts usually don't provide perfect vision, and satisfaction with them depends largely on the skill of the optometrist fitting the lenses. Another drawback is that some people have difficulty handling, removing, and cleaning contact lenses. The frequent handling of contact lenses may also increase the long-term risk of eye infections.

Surgical Treatment

An increasingly popular alternative to glasses and contacts is laser vision correction, especially for nearsightedness. Three types of laser surgery have been developed to sharpen vision. PRK (photorefractive keratectomy) and LASIK (laser-assisted in-situ keratomileusis) can be performed to correct nearsightedness, astigmatism, and presbyopia. PRK can also be used to correct farsightedness. During surgery, a special machine known as an excimer laser is used to produce pulses of light energy that can alter the shape of the cornea so that light rays from distant objects will focus on the retina with greater precision. The same type of laser is used for LASIK and PRK. The main difference between the two surgeries is the way that the middle layer of the cornea is exposed before it is vaporized with the laser. In PRK, the top layer of the cornea is scraped away to expose the middle layer, whereas in LASIK, a hinged flap is cut in the outer layer of the cornea. This flap is then folded back to expose the corneal tissue.

When LASIK or PRK are used for nearsightedness, both eyes can be corrected for distance. But when these procedures are used for presbyopia, correcting both eyes for close work compromises distance vision. So instead, the nondominant eye is corrected for near vision and, if necessary, the dominant eye is corrected for distance, producing an arrangement known as monovision.

LASIK is often preferred because of its shorter recovery period (about one to three days compared with five to seven for PRK). But PRK is sometimes the better choice because it offers more protection from subsequent eye injury. PRK may also be more appropriate for people with dry eyes or corneal abnormalities.

The third type of surgery, laser thermal keratoplasty (LTK), is approved for farsightedness, and can also be used for presbyopia. LTK involves the use of a holmium laser to strategically place thermal spots of energy on the periphery of the cornea. This also changes the curvature of the cornea to improve vision. When LTK is used, there is no need for monovision because both eyes can be corrected for close work. Although the procedure is associated with excellent results and few complications, improvements may wear off in one to two years.

The average cost per eye is $1,500, which is not reimbursed by most insurance plans.

Side Effects of Surgery

Information about the long-term complications of laser eye surgery is scarce, since no procedure has been available for more than ten years.

Side effects include seeing halos around lights or ghost images, especially at night. Contrast sensitivity (the ability to see objects clearly against a similar background or in dim lighting conditions) may narrow in some individuals. Sometimes, the level of correction achieved is temporary, and in some cases, vision is under-corrected, in which case additional treatments or prescription lenses may be necessary. There's a small risk of eye infection with the surgery, though this is may not be serious. In addition, eyes may be very dry after surgery, and this condition may be permanent. The most troublesome complications—sensitivity to glare and difficulty seeing at night—usually improve over time.

Furthermore, while laser surgery can help you cope with presbyopia, it can't reverse the condition, and can't prevent it from advancing. (Laser surgery can, however, correct refractive errors). Therefore, you may need surgery again as presbyopia progresses, or you may require prescription lenses. Another drawback is adjusting to monovision, which can be difficult since it involves some loss of depth perception. A trial with monovision contact lenses is often helpful. In addition, neither eye will have the best possible near or distant vision.

To reduce the risk of complications, select an experienced surgeon who tracks personal success and complication rates and willingly shares them. Your evaluation should rule

out potential contraindications, including cataracts, glaucoma, macular degeneration, severe nearsightedness or farsightedness, unusually large pupils, diabetes, and implantable cardiac devices (pacemakers and defibrillators). Also, the benefit of surgery for presbyopia is maximized if your reading prescription has been stable for at least six months.

Because the equipment used for laser eye surgery is expensive, some practitioners emphasize volume over quality. Be alert to the warning signs of questionable practices. Avoid clinics that aggressively advertise and emphasize low prices; don't tell you in advance who your surgeon will be; assign you to a different doctor at each appointment; or solicit an "upgrade" to better equipment, better aftercare, or a better surgeon.

The prostate is a gland in a man's reproductive system. It makes and stores seminal fluid, a milky fluid that nourishes sperm. This fluid is released to form part of semen.

The prostate is about the size of a walnut. It is located below the bladder and in front of the rectum. It surrounds the upper part of the urethra, the tube that empties urine from the bladder. If the prostate grows too large, the flow of urine can be slowed or stopped. To work properly, the prostate needs male hormones, which are responsible for male sex characteristics. The main male hormone is testosterone, which is made mainly by the testicles. Some male hormones are produced in small amounts by the adrenal glands.

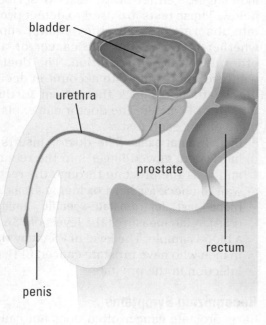

bladder

urethra

prostate

rectum

penis

The prostate is a chestnut-shaped gland that sits at the base of the bladder, in front of the rectum and surrounding the urethra.

The prostate, like all other organs of the body, is made up of many types of cells. Normally, cells divide to produce more cells only when they are needed. This orderly process helps keep the body healthy. When cells divide without control, they form too much tissue. This tissue can be benign (noncancerous) or malignant (cancerous). When cancer spreads outside the prostate, it often shows up in nearby lymph nodes. If the cancer has reached these nodes, it means that cancer cells may have spread to other parts of the body—other lymph nodes and other organs, such as the bones, bladder, or rectum. When cancer spreads from its original location to another part of the body, the new tumor has the same kind of abnormal cells and the same name as the primary tumor. For example, if prostate cancer spreads to the bones, the cancer cells in the new tumor are prostate cancer cells. The disease is metastatic prostate cancer; it is not bone cancer.

Who's at Risk?

The causes of prostate cancer are not well understood. Doctors cannot explain why one man gets prostate cancer and another does not.

Researchers are studying factors that may increase the risk of this disease. Studies have found that the following risk factors are associated with prostate cancer:

- **Age.** In the United States, prostate cancer is found mainly in men over age 55. At the time of diagnosis the average age of patients is 70.
- **Family history of prostate cancer.** A man's risk for developing prostate cancer is higher if his father or brother has had the disease.
- **Race.** This disease is much more common in African-American men than in white men. It is less common in Asian and Native American men.

P

Evaluating Prostate Cancer

A decision on prostate cancer treatment can be guided by several measures that help show how advanced and aggressive the tumor is, including:

Palpability. Whether the tumor can be felt during a digital rectal exam, in which the doctor inserts a gloved finger into the rectum to feel the prostate.

PSA. A measure of a protein released by the prostate into the bloodstream. PSAs of less than 4 ng/ml are considered normal; 4 to 10 ng/ml are viewed as mild elevations that indicate early cancer in one-third of men. PSAs of more than 10 ng/ml are high and indicate cancer in two-thirds of men; more than half will have tumors that have already spread beyond the prostate.

Biopsy results. A biopsy is performed as an outpatient procedure under local anesthesia. Samples, or "cores," of prostate tissue are usually obtained from six different areas of the gland.

Gleason score. A measure of cancer aggressiveness determined by looking at biopsied prostate cancer cells under a microscope. Cancers with a Gleason score of less than 6 or 7 are considered less aggressive, and are less likely to have spread beyond the prostate.

In sum, early cancers, ones less likely to have spread, usually have a PSA of less than 10 ng/ml; a Gleason score of less than 7; and two or fewer cancer-containing cores on biopsy. *The Editors*

- **Diet and dietary factors.** Some evidence suggests that a diet high in animal fat may increase the risk of prostate cancer and a diet high in fruits and vegetables may decrease the risk. Studies are in progress to learn whether men can reduce their risk of prostate cancer by taking certain dietary supplements.

Although a few studies suggested that having a vasectomy might increase a man's risk for prostate cancer, most studies do not support this finding. Scientists have studied whether benign prostatic hyperplasia (BPH), obesity, lack of exercise, smoking, radiation exposure, or a sexually transmitted virus might increase the risk for prostate cancer. At this time, there is little evidence that these factors contribute to an increased risk.

Detecting Prostate Cancer

A man who has any of the risk factors described in "Who's at Risk?" may want to ask a doctor whether to begin screening for prostate cancer (even though he does not have any symptoms), what tests to have,

and how often to have them. The doctor may suggest either of the tests described below. These tests are used to detect prostate abnormalities, but they cannot show whether abnormalities are cancer or another, less serious condition. The doctor will take the results into account in deciding whether to check the patient further for signs of cancer. The doctor can explain more about each test.

- **Digital rectal exam.** The doctor inserts a lubricated, gloved finger into the rectum and feels the prostate through the rectal wall to check for hard or lumpy areas.
- **Blood test for prostate-specific antigen (PSA).** A lab measures the levels of PSA in a blood sample. The level of PSA may rise in men who have prostate cancer, BPH, or infection in the prostate.

Recognizing Symptoms

Early prostate cancer often does not cause symptoms. But prostate cancer can cause any of these problems:

- A need to urinate frequently, especially at night

- Difficulty starting urination or holding back urine
- Inability to urinate
- Weak or interrupted flow of urine
- Painful or burning urination
- Difficulty in having an erection
- Painful ejaculation
- Blood in urine or semen
- Frequent pain or stiffness in the lower back, hips, or upper thighs

Any of these symptoms may be caused by cancer or by other, less serious health problems, such as BPH or an infection. A man who has symptoms like these should see his doctor or a urologist (a doctor who specializes in diagnosing and treating diseases of the genitourinary system).

Diagnosing Prostate Cancer

If a man has symptoms or test results that suggest prostate cancer, his doctor asks about his personal and family medical history, performs a physical exam, and may order laboratory tests. The exams and tests may include a digital rectal exam, a urine test to check for blood or infection, and a blood test to measure PSA. In some cases, the doctor also may check the level of prostatic acid phosphatase (PAP) in the blood, especially if the results of the PSA indicate there might be a problem.

The doctor may order exams to learn more about the cause of the symptoms. These may include:

- **Transrectal ultrasonography.** Sound waves that cannot be heard by humans (ultrasound) are sent out by a probe inserted into the rectum. The waves bounce off the prostate, and a computer uses the echoes to create a picture called a sonogram.
- **Intravenous pyelogram.** A series of x-rays of the organs of the urinary tract.
- **Cystoscopy.** A procedure in which a doctor looks into the urethra and bladder through a thin, lighted tube.

Biopsy

If test results suggest that cancer may be present, the man will need to have a biopsy. During a biopsy, the doctor removes tissue samples from the prostate, usually with a needle. A pathologist looks at the tissue under a microscope to check for cancer cells. If cancer is present, the pathologist usually reports the grade of the tumor. The grade tells how much the tumor tissue differs from normal prostate tissue and suggests how fast the tumor is likely to grow. One way of grading prostate cancer, called the Gleason system, uses scores of 2 to 10. Another system uses G1 through G4. Tumors with higher scores or grades are more likely to grow and spread than tumors with lower scores.

If the physical exam and test results do not suggest cancer, the doctor may recommend medicine to reduce the symptoms caused by an enlarged prostate. Surgery is another way to relieve these symptoms. The surgery most often used in such cases is called transurethral resection of the prostate (TURP or TUR). In TURP, an instrument is inserted through the urethra to remove prostate tissue that is pressing against the upper part of the urethra and restricting the flow of urine. (Patients may want to ask whether other procedures might be appropriate.)

Staging

If cancer is found in the prostate, the doctor needs to know the stage, or extent, of the disease. Staging is a careful attempt to find out whether the cancer has spread and, if so, what parts of the body are affected. The doctor may use various blood and imaging tests to learn the stage of the disease. Treatment decisions depend on these findings.

Prostate cancer staging is a complex process. The doctor may describe the stage using Roman numerals (I-IV) or a capital letter

P

P

(A-D). These are the main features of each stage:

- **Stage I or Stage A.** The cancer cannot be felt during a rectal exam. It may be found by accident when surgery is done for another reason, usually for BPH. There is no evidence that the cancer has spread outside the prostate.
- **Stage II or Stage B.** The tumor involves more tissue within the prostate, it can be felt during a rectal exam, or it is found with a biopsy that is done because of a high PSA level. There is no evidence that the cancer has spread outside the prostate.
- **Stage III or Stage C.** The cancer has spread outside the prostate to nearby tissues.
- **Stage IV or Stage D.** The cancer has spread to lymph nodes or to other parts of the body.

Treatment

The doctor develops a treatment plan to fit each man's needs. Treatment for prostate cancer depends on the stage of the disease and the grade of the tumor (which indicates how abnormal the cells look, and how likely they are to grow or spread). Other important factors in planning treatment are the man's age and general health and his feelings about the treatments and their possible side effects.

Prostate cancer can be managed in a number of ways (with watchful waiting, surgery, radiation therapy, and hormonal therapy). If the doctor recommends watchful waiting, the man's health will be monitored closely, and he will be treated only if symptoms occur or worsen. Patients considering surgery, radiation therapy, or hormonal therapy may want to consult doctors who specialize in these types of treatment.

The patient and his doctor may want to consider both the benefits and possible side effects of each option, especially the effects on sexual activity and urination, and other concerns about quality of life. Also, the patient may want to talk with his doctor about taking part in a research study to help determine the best approach or to study new kinds of treatment (see pages 181 and 546).

Watchful waiting may be suggested for some men who have prostate cancer that is found at an early stage and appears to be slow growing. Also, watchful waiting may be advised for older men or men with other serious medical problems. For these men, the risks and possible side effects of surgery, radiation therapy, or hormonal therapy may outweigh the possible benefits.

Surgery is a common treatment for early stage prostate cancer. The doctor may remove all of the prostate (a type of surgery called radical prostatectomy) or only part of it. In some cases, the doctor can use a new technique known as nerve-sparing surgery. This type of surgery may save the nerves that control erection. However, men with large tumors or tumors that are very close to the nerves may not be able to have this surgery.

If the pathologist finds cancer cells in the lymph nodes, it is likely that the disease has spread to other parts of the body. Sometimes the doctor removes the lymph nodes before doing a prostatectomy. If the prostate cancer has not spread to the lymph nodes, the doctor then removes the prostate. But if cancer has spread to the nodes, the doctor usually does not remove the prostate, but may suggest other treatment.

Radiation therapy (also called radiotherapy) uses high-energy x-rays to kill cancer cells. Like surgery, radiation therapy is local therapy; it can affect cancer cells only in the treated area. In early stage prostate cancer, radiation can be used instead of surgery, or it may be used after surgery to destroy any cancer cells that may remain in the area. In advanced stages, it may be given to relieve pain or other problems.

Who Is an Ideal Candidate for Brachytherapy?

Research suggests brachytherapy—also known as seed therapy because it involves the surgical implantation of dozens of tiny radioactive isotopes, or "seeds," directly into the prostate—can offer favorable outcomes for prostate cancer when the following criteria are met:

Prostate size. The prostate should not exceed 60 cubic centimeters (or less than 2 oz). Unfortunately, some in the medical community have ignored this criterion, which is one of the reasons men experience side effects from seed therapy. The larger the prostate, the more seeds required and the greater the dose of radiation. In particular, the middle lobe of the prostate should not be overly enlarged. When this lobe, which surrounds the urethra, is enlarged, the higher number of seeds required increases the risk that radiation will cause urethral contraction and scarring that leads to urinary difficulty.

Early detection. The cancer must be detected at an early, localized stage. Gleason score must be 6 or less and PSA level should be less than 10. This combination of favorable stage, grade, and PSA value is important because it increases the likelihood that the cancer is confined to the prostate. By definition, brachytherapy is aimed at destroying cancer cells within the prostate, not cancer that extends outside the prostate.

The Editors

Radiation may be directed at the body by a machine (external radiation), or it may come from tiny radioactive seeds placed inside or near the tumor (internal or implant radiation, or brachytherapy). Men who receive radioactive seeds alone usually have small tumors. Some men with prostate cancer receive both kinds of radiation therapy.

For external radiation, patients go to the hospital or clinic, usually five days a week for several weeks. Patients may stay in the hospital for a short time for implant radiation.

Hormonal therapy keeps cancer cells from getting the male hormones they need to grow. It is called systemic therapy because it can affect cancer cells throughout the body. Systemic therapy is used to treat cancer that has spread. Sometimes this type of therapy is used to try to prevent the cancer from coming back after surgery or radiation treatment.

There are several forms of hormonal therapy in use:

- Orchiectomy is surgery to remove the testicles, which are the main source of male hormones.
- Drugs known as a luteinizing hormone-releasing hormone (LH-RH) agonists can prevent the testicles from producing testosterone. Examples are leuprolide, goserelin, and buserelin.
- Drugs known as antiandrogens can block the action of androgens. Two examples are flutamide and bicalutamide.
- Drugs that can prevent the adrenal glands from making androgens include ketoconazole and aminoglutethimide.

After orchiectomy or treatment with an LH-RH agonist, the body no longer gets testosterone from the testicles. However, the adrenal glands still produce small amounts of male hormones. Sometimes, the patient is also given an antiandrogen, which blocks the effect of any remaining male hormones. This combination of treatments is known as total androgen blockade. Doctors do not know for sure whether total androgen blockade is more effective than orchiectomy or LH-RH agonist alone.

Prostate cancer that has spread to other parts of the body usually can be controlled with hormonal therapy for a period of time, often several years. Eventually, however, most prostate cancers are able to grow with very little or no male hormones. When this happens, hormonal therapy is no longer effective, and the doctor may suggest other forms of treatment that are under study.

Side Effects of Treatment

It is hard to limit the effects of treatment so that only cancer cells are removed or destroyed. Because healthy cells and tissues may be damaged, treatment often causes unwanted side effects. Doctors and nurses will explain the possible side effects of treatment to the patient.

The side effects of cancer treatment depend mainly on the type and extent of the treatment. Also, each patient reacts differently to treatment.

Watchful Waiting

Although men who choose watchful waiting avoid the side effects of surgery and radiation, there can be some negative aspects to this choice. Watchful waiting may reduce the chance of controlling the disease before it spreads. Also, older men should keep in mind that it may be harder to manage surgery and radiation therapy as they age.

Some men may decide against watchful waiting because they feel they would be uncomfortable living with an untreated cancer, even one that appears to be growing slowly or not at all. A man who chooses watchful waiting but later becomes concerned or anxious should discuss his feelings with his doctor. A different treatment approach is nearly always available.

Surgery

Patients are often uncomfortable for the first few days after surgery. Their pain usually can be controlled with medicine, and patients should discuss pain relief with the doctor or nurse. The patient will wear a catheter (a tube inserted into the urethra) to drain urine for 10 days to 3 weeks. The nurse or doctor will show the man how to care for the catheter.

It is also common for patients to feel extremely tired or weak for a while. The length of time it takes to recover from an operation varies.

Surgery to remove the prostate may cause long-term problems, including rectal injury or urinary incontinence. Some men may have permanent impotence. Nerve-sparing surgery is an attempt to avoid the problem of impotence. When the doctor can use nerve-sparing surgery and the operation is fully successful, impotence may be only temporary. Still, some men who have this procedure may be permanently impotent.

Men who have a prostatectomy no longer produce semen, so they have dry orgasms. Men who wish to father children may consider sperm banking or a procedure for sperm retrieval.

Spontaneous erections often return within a year or two after prostate surgery. Until they do, a variety of treatment options are available for overcoming erectile dysfunction (impotence). For more information on the treatment of erectile dysfunction, see page 317.

Radiation Therapy

Radiation therapy may cause patients to become extremely tired, especially in the later

Questions for Your Doctor

These are some questions a patient may want to ask the doctor before treatment begins:

- What is the stage of the disease?
- What is the grade of the disease?
- What are my treatment choices? Is watchful waiting a good choice for me?
- Are new treatments under study? Would a clinical trial be appropriate for me?
- What are the expected benefits of each kind of treatment?
- What are the risks and possible side effects of each treatment? How can the side effects be managed?
- Is treatment likely to affect my sex life?
- Am I likely to have urinary problems?
- Am I likely to have bowel problems, such as diarrhea or rectal bleeding?
- Will I need to change my normal activities? If so, for how long?

The doctor can describe the types of surgery and can discuss and compare their benefits and risks.

- In radical retropubic prostatectomy, the doctor removes the entire prostate and nearby lymph nodes through an incision in the abdomen.
- In radical perineal prostatectomy, the doctor removes the entire prostate through an incision between the scrotum and the anus. Nearby lymph nodes are sometimes removed through a separate incision in the abdomen.
- In transurethral resection of the prostate (TURP), the doctor removes part of the prostate with an instrument that is inserted through the urethra. The cancer is cut from the prostate by electricity passing through a small wire loop on the end of the instrument. This method is used mainly to remove tissue that blocks urine flow.

weeks of treatment. Resting is important, but doctors usually encourage men to try to stay as active as they can. Some men may have diarrhea or frequent and uncomfortable urination.

When men with prostate cancer receive external radiation therapy, it is common for the skin in the treated area to become red, dry, and tender. External radiation therapy can also cause hair loss in the treated area. The loss may be temporary or permanent, depending on the dose of radiation.

Both types of radiation therapy may cause impotence in some men, but internal radiation therapy is not as likely as external radiation therapy to damage the nerves that control erection. However, internal radiation therapy may cause temporary incontinence. Long-term side effects from internal radiation therapy are uncommon.

Hormonal Therapy

The side effects of hormonal therapy depend largely on the type of treatment. Orchiectomy and LH-RH agonists often cause side effects such as impotence, hot flashes, and loss of sexual desire. When first taken, an LH-RH agonist may make a patient's symptoms worse for a short time. This temporary problem is called "flare." Gradually, however, the treatment causes a man's testosterone level to fall. Without testosterone, tumor growth slows down and the patient's condition improves. (To prevent flare, the doctor may give the man an antiandrogen for a while along with the LH-RH agonist.)

Antiandrogens can cause nausea, vomiting, diarrhea, or breast growth or tenderness. If used a long time, ketoconazole may cause liver problems, and aminoglutethimide

Urinary Incontinence

One of the most common complications of treatment for prostate cancer is urinary incontinence, since radiation and surgery may damage the urethra or the nerves and muscles necessary for urinary control. Rarely, the degree of incontinence is severe. Most commonly, men suffer from stress incontinence—where some event that increases intra-abdominal pressure, such as coughing, causes light to moderate leakage. Fortunately, a variety of methods are available for managing urinary incontinence. Certain devices may not be recommended immediately following treatment since they may interfere with independent muscle control that is needed to regain urinary continence. Discuss the risks and benefits of each method with your doctor.

Lifestyle measures. Both constipation and obesity cause increased pressure on the bladder. Adding high-fiber foods, like leafy greens, fruits, whole grains, and beans to your diet can reduce constipation and help with weight loss. Limit caffeine and alcohol, which increase urination frequency. Before bedtime reduce liquid consumption to 1 cup.

Kegel exercises. Strengthening the muscles that support the bladder and surround the urethra may improve bladder control. Kegel exercises are performed by squeezing and relaxing the pelvic floor muscles.

Absorbent products. Wearing absorbent pads or undergarments is the most common solution for men with light to severe incontinence.

Penile clamp. This device compresses the penis to prevent urine from leaking and may be an option for men with severe incontinence.

External collection device. This condom-like device can be pulled over the penis and held in place with adhesive, Velcro straps, or elastic bands. A tube drains fluid from the device to a bag secured on the leg.

Catheters. A small tube inserted through the urethra allows urine to flow continuously from the bladder into a bag.

Collagen injections. Collagen can be injected around the bladder neck to increase bulk and provide increased resistance to urine flow at times of stress.

Artificial sphincter implantation. In this procedure, a rubber cuff is implanted around the urethra to keep urine in the bladder. The fluid-filled cuff is connected by a thin tube to a bulb implanted in the scrotum; the bulb, in turn, is connected to a reservoir within the abdomen. The fluid remains in the cuff and creates pressure around the urethra to hold urine inside the bladder. When the urge to urinate is felt, squeezing the scrotal bulb transfers fluid from the cuff to the reservoir, and deflates the cuff for 3 minutes so urine can drain through the urethra. Afterward, the cuff automatically refills and urine flow is again stopped.

Medications. Certain medications may improve mild to moderate incontinence either by increasing constriction at the outlet of the bladder into the urethra or by preventing excessive contractions in the bladder itself. *The Editors*

can cause skin rashes. Men who receive total androgen blockade may experience more side effects than men who receive a single method of hormonal therapy. Any method of hormonal therapy that lowers androgen levels can contribute to weakening of the bones in older men.

Follow-up Care

During and after treatment, the doctor will continue to follow the patient. The doctor will examine the man regularly to be sure that the disease has not returned or progressed, and will decide what other medical care may be needed. Follow-up exams may include x-rays, scans, and lab tests, such as the PSA blood test.

The Promise of Prostate Cancer Research
Causes

Although researchers know several risk factors for prostate cancer, they still are not sure why one man develops the disease and another doesn't. (Known risk factors, which include aging, are listed in the "Who's at Risk?" section on page 537)

Some aspects of a man's lifestyle may affect his chances of developing prostate cancer. For example, some evidence suggests a link between diet and this disease. These studies show that prostate cancer is more common in populations that consume a high-fat diet (particularly animal fat), and in populations that have diets lacking certain nutrients. Although it is not known whether a diet low in fat will prevent prostate cancer, a low-fat diet may have many other health benefits.

Some research suggests that high levels of testosterone may increase the risk of prostate cancer. The difference between racial groups in prostate cancer risk could be related to high testosterone levels, but it also could result from diet or other lifestyle factors.

Researchers also are looking for changes in genes that may increase the risk for developing prostate cancer. They are studying the genes of men who were diagnosed with prostate cancer at a relatively young age (less than 55 years old) and the genes of families who have several members with the disease. Much more work is needed, however, before scientists can say exactly how changes in these genes are related to prostate cancer. Men with a family history of prostate cancer who are concerned about an inherited risk for this disease should talk with their doctor. The doctor may suggest seeing a health professional trained in genetics.

Prevention

Several studies are under way to explore how prostate cancer might be prevented. These include the use of dietary supplements, such as vitamin E and selenium. In addition, recent studies suggest that a diet that regularly includes tomato-based foods may help protect men from prostate cancer.

The drug finasteride is being studied in the Prostate Cancer Prevention Trial, which involves thousands of men across the country who are participating until 2004 (for a total of seven years).

Scientists are also looking at ways to prevent recurrence among men who have been treated for prostate cancer. These approaches involve the use of drugs such as finasteride, flutamide, and LH-RH agonists. Studies have shown that hormonal therapy after radiation therapy or after radical prostatectomy can benefit certain men whose cancer has spread to nearby tissues.

Researchers also are investigating whether diets that are low in fat and high in soy, fruits, vegetables, and other food products might prevent a recurrence.

Screening/Early Detection

Researchers are studying ways to screen men for prostate cancer (check for the disease in men who have no symptoms). At this time, it is not known whether screening for prostate cancer actually saves lives, even if the disease is found at an earlier stage. The NCI-supported Prostate, Lung, Colorectal, and Ovarian Cancer Screening Trial is designed to show whether certain detection tests can reduce the number of deaths from these cancers. This trial is looking at the usefulness of prostate cancer screening by performing a digital rectal exam and checking the PSA level in the blood in men ages 55 to 74. The results of this trial may change the way men are screened for prostate cancer. The Cancer

Information Service can provide information about this trial.

New Treatments

Through research, doctors try to find new, more effective ways to treat prostate cancer. Many studies of new approaches for men with prostate cancer are under way. When laboratory research shows that a new treatment method has promise, cancer patients receive the new approach in treatment clinical trials. These studies are designed to answer important questions and to find out whether the new approach is safe and effective. Often, clinical trials compare a new treatment with a standard approach.

Cryosurgery is under study as an alternative to surgery and radiation therapy. The doctor tries to avoid damaging healthy tissue by placing an instrument known as a cryoprobe in direct contact with the tumor to freeze it. The extreme cold destroys the cancer cells.

Doctors are studying new ways of using radiation therapy and hormonal therapy. They also are testing the effectiveness of chemotherapy and biological therapy for men whose cancer does not respond or stops responding to hormonal therapy. In addition, scientists are exploring new treatment schedules and new ways of combining various types of treatment. For example, they are studying the usefulness of hormonal therapy before primary therapy (surgery or radiation) to shrink the tumor.

For men with early stage prostate cancer, researchers also are comparing treatment with watchful waiting. The results of this work will help doctors know whether to treat early stage prostate cancer immediately or only later on, if symptoms occur or worsen.

National Cancer Institute

The term prostatitis is used to describe a group of diverse disorders that involve inflammation of the prostate, the walnut-sized gland located below the bladder in men. The symptoms, which vary from person to person, range from urinary problems to pain in the perineum (the area between the rectum and testicles) to painful ejaculation. Some forms of prostatitis produce no symptoms at all.

Prostatitis is a common condition, affecting nearly half of all men at some point in their lives. And it can cause major discomfort; according to one study, prostatitis may erode quality of life as dramatically as other better-known chronic conditions, such as diabetes and congestive heart failure.

Part of the problem in treating prostatitis is that the disease comes in several forms. Some patients experience acute flare-ups, with sudden and continuous pain that lasts for several days at a time. More common, however, is chronic prostatitis, which may go on for several weeks, only to disappear and then start up again. It usually affects men in their early 40s, and it is one of the leading reasons why men visit a urologist.

Prostatitis is further differentiated by bacterial and nonbacterial causes. Nearly 95 percent of patients are thought to develop prostatitis from nonbacterial origins, which have yet to be identified. In addition, some men may have signs of inflammation, such as white blood cells in their semen, but none of the painful symptoms of prostatitis. A related condition, called prostatodynia, causes the same symptoms as prostatitis, but with no laboratory signs of infection or inflammation.

Causes
Both acute and chronic bacterial prostatitis are usually caused by various strains of Escherichia coli, a species of bacteria that ordinarily resides in the intestines. However, the cause of the more prevalent, nonbacterial form is not yet known. Some men find that stress, emotional problems, or even drinking coffee seems to trigger flare-ups. Other possible culprits include zinc deficiency, tight sphincter muscles, insufficient ejaculation, and dehydration. Scientists have attempted to confirm these potential causes, but the evidence is inconclusive.

Some experts suggest that nonbacterial prostatitis is not really a prostate problem at all. Rather, flare-ups could be the result of a pelvic muscle spasm or some other cause that mimics symptoms originating in the prostate. Another theory under investigation is that prostatitis is caused by an autoimmune disorder. In this scenario, the immune system mistakenly attacks healthy prostate tissue and promotes inflammation, not unlike the way rheumatoid arthritis targets the joints. Indeed, researchers recently found that men with chronic prostatitis had increased levels of the same pro-inflammatory molecules that are elevated in the joint tissue of rheumatoid arthritis patients.

Symptoms
Acute bacterial prostatitis comes on suddenly and is usually accompanied by fever. Other symptoms include chills, bloody urine, and pain in the lower back and perineum. Some men also experience extreme pain, burning, and urgency or difficulty urinating, which can lead to urinary retention.

Chronic bacterial prostatitis usually presents as repeated urinary tract infections (UTIs), along with episodes of urinary problems (difficult, frequent, urgent, burning, or painful urination), and pain in the lower back, perineum, penis, scrotum, or

P

pubic region. Symptoms must be present for at least three months to qualify for the diagnosis.

Noninfectious prostatitis is associated with an excess of inflammatory cells, but no history of UTIs or evidence of bacteria. The symptoms are virtually identical to those of the chronic bacterial form. Episodes may wax and wane, occurring frequently, or at intervals of months or years. For unknown reasons, the condition sometimes permanently resolves on its own.

Diagnosis

As part of the initial evaluation, the patient's urine is examined to determine if the disease stems from a bacterial cause. Cultures are taken from normal urine flow (both urethral and bladder specimens), and from urine voided after a prostate massage, which involves methodical stroking of the prostate by the doctor until fluid is pushed out into the urethra during a digital rectal examination, or DRE. In a DRE a gloved, lubricated finger is inserted into the rectum. Comparing cultures of urine and prostatic fluid can show if bacteria are present and whether they reside in the urethra, bladder, or prostate. A prostate massage is not performed if fever and chills accompany a bout of acute prostatitis. Acute flare-ups may also cause a steep rise in prostate specific antigen (PSA) levels, so PSA testing for prostate cancer should not be performed during these episodes.

A symptom questionnaire recently developed by the National Institutes of Health (NIH) may also help in assessing the disease through answers to questions on three different aspects of prostatitis: pain, urinary symptoms, and quality of life. After scoring the answers, a physician can determine the impact of a patient's symptoms and how well treatments are working.

When persistent symptoms do not respond to treatment, magnetic resonance imaging can detect abscesses in acute cases, and ultrasound can rule out infected cysts in chronic cases.

Treatment

Treatment is fairly straightforward for bacterial prostatitis. A patient is given antibiotics for a period of 8 to 12 weeks—considerably longer than the standard 7- to 10-day course prescribed for most other infections. Prolonged antibiotic therapy is necessary because antibiotics do not diffuse well into the prostate. Thus, if they are stopped too soon, the infection will recur. Appropriate antibiotics include carbenicillin (Geocillin, Geopen), trimethoprim/sulfamethoxazole (Bactrim, Cotrim), and doxycycline (Apo-Doxy, Doryx). Bacterial prostatitis is the most curable form of the disease, although some patients may not respond to treatment, or relapse once the antibiotics are stopped.

Acute bacterial prostatitis also requires bed rest, increased fluid intake, and stool softeners if constipation is a problem, because straining can worsen prostate pain. If urinary retention develops, catheterization may be necessary to empty the bladder. Severe cases may require hospitalization.

While antibiotics are typically reserved for bacterial diseases, many patients with persistent symptoms receive antibiotics and a prostate massage for nonbacterial prostatitis and prostatodynia, followed by high doses of alpha-blocker drugs (the medications used for benign prostatic hyperplasia, or BPH). Prostatodynia may improve when treated with muscle relaxants and alpha-blockers. Men who experience pain are usually helped by anti-inflammatory medications, such as aspirin, ibuprofen (Motrin and others), or naproxen (Aleve and others). A hot bath may also work for some, while ice packs are better for others.

If ejaculation is not painful, sex or masturbation may improve symptoms. One recent study found that prostatitis patients who ejaculated at least twice a week over a six-month period were likely to experience greater relief of symptoms than those who ejaculated less frequently.

It's also helpful to avoid caffeinated and alcoholic beverages until symptoms subside. These drinks have a diuretic effect, which promotes an increase in urinary frequency.

Expressing as much prostate fluid as possible by massaging the prostate may ease pain for several weeks in some men. Although it is possible for some men to accomplish the task on their own or with the aid of a partner, the process is best performed by a doctor as part of a DRE. However, not all doctors provide this treatment or believe it to be helpful.

Many men remain frustrated because there is no breakthrough therapy that provides consistent relief from nonbacterial prostatitis. Fortunately, major research efforts are currently under way, and experts are optimistic that these studies will provide important new insights on improving the management of chronic prostatitis.

Psoriasis is a persistent skin disease that got its name from the Greek word for "itch." The skin becomes inflamed, producing red, thickened areas with silvery scales, most often on the scalp, elbows, knees, and lower back.

In some cases, psoriasis is so mild that people don't know they have it. At the opposite extreme, severe psoriasis may cover large areas of the body. Doctors can help even the most severe cases.

Psoriasis cannot be passed from one person to another, though it is more likely to occur in people whose family members have it. In the United States two out of every hundred people have psoriasis (four to five million people). Approximately 150,000 new cases occur each year.

What Causes Psoriasis?

The cause is unknown. However, recent discoveries point to an abnormality in the functioning of key white cells in the blood stream triggering inflammation in the skin. Because of the inflammation, the skin sheds too rapidly, every three to four days.

People often notice new spots 10 to 14 days after the skin is cut, scratched, rubbed, or severely sunburned. Psoriasis can also be activated by infections, such as strep throat, and by certain medicines. Flare-ups sometimes occur in the winter, as a result of dry skin and lack of sunlight.

Types of Psoriasis

Psoriasis comes in many forms. Each differs in severity, duration, location, and in the shape and pattern of the scales. The most common form begins with little red bumps. Gradually these grow larger and scales form. While the top scales flake off easily and often, scales below the surface stick together. When they are removed, the tender, exposed skin bleeds. These small red areas then grow, sometimes becoming quite large.

Elbows, knees, groin and genitals, arms, legs, palms and soles, scalp and face, body folds and nails are the areas most commonly affected by psoriasis. It will often appear in the same place on both sides of the body.

Nails with psoriasis have tiny pits on them. Nails may loosen, thicken or crumble and are difficult to treat.

Inverse psoriasis occurs in the armpit, under the breast and in skin folds around the groin, buttocks, and genitals.

Guttate psoriasis usually affects children and young adults. It often shows up after a sore throat, with many small, red, drop-like, scaly spots appearing on the skin. It often clears up by itself in weeks or a few months.

Up to 30 percent of people with psoriasis may have symptoms of arthritis and 5 percent to 10 percent may have some functional disability from arthritis of various joints. In some people, the arthritis is worse when the skin is very involved. Sometimes the arthritis improves when the condition of the patient's skin improves.

How Is Psoriasis Diagnosed?

Dermatologists diagnose psoriasis by examining the skin, nails, and scalp. If the diagnosis is in doubt, a skin biopsy may be helpful.

How Is Psoriasis Treated?

The goal is to reduce inflammation and to control shedding of the skin. Moisturizing creams and lotions loosen scales and help control itching. Special diets have not been successful in treating psoriasis, except in isolated cases.

Treatment is based on the patient's health, age, lifestyle, and the severity of the psoriasis. Different types of treatments and several visits to the dermatologist may be needed.

The doctor may prescribe medications to apply on the skin containing cortisone-like compounds, synthetic vitamin D, tar, or anthralin. These may be used in combination with natural sunlight or ultraviolet light. The most severe forms of psoriasis may require oral medications, with or without the use of light treatment.

Sunlight exposure helps the majority of people with psoriasis but it must be used cautiously. Ultraviolet light therapy may be given in a dermatologist's office, a psoriasis center or a hospital.

Types of Treatment

Steroids (Cortisone). Cortisone creams, ointments, and lotions may clear the skin temporarily and control the condition in many patients. Weaker preparations should be used on more sensitive areas of the body such as the genitals, groin, and face. Stronger preparations will usually be needed to control lesions on the scalp, elbow, knees, palms and soles, and parts of the torso and may need to be covered with dressings. These must be used cautiously and with the dermatologist's instruction. Side effects of the stronger cortisone preparations include thinning of the skin, dilated blood vessels, bruising, and skin color changes. Stopping these medications suddenly may result in a flare-up of the disease. After many months of treatment, the psoriasis may become resistant to the steroid preparations.

The dermatologist may inject cortisone in difficult-to-treat spots. These injections must be used in very small amounts to avoid side effects.

Scalp treatment. The treatment for psoriasis of the scalp depends on the seriousness of the disease, hair length, and the patient's lifestyle. A variety of non-prescription and prescription shampoos, oils, solutions, and sprays are available. Most contain coal tar or cortisone. The patient must take care to avoid harsh shampooing and scratching the scalp.

Anthralin. A medication that works well on tough-to-treat thick patches of psoriasis. It can cause irritation and temporary staining of the skin and clothes. Newer preparations and methods of treatment have lessened these side effects.

Vitamin D. A synthetic Vitamin D, calcipotriene, is now available in prescription form. It is useful for individuals with localized psoriasis and can be used with other treatments. Limited amounts should be used to avoid side effects. Ordinary Vitamin D, such as one would buy in a drug store or health food store, is of no value in treating psoriasis.

Retinoids (oral). Prescription vitamin A-related gels may be used alone or in combination with topical steroids for treatment of localized psoriasis. Women who are or may become pregnant should not use topical retinoids.

Coal tar. For more than 100 years, coal tar has been used to treat psoriasis. Today's products are greatly improved and less messy. Stronger prescriptions can be made to treat difficult areas.

Goeckerman treatment. Named after the Mayo Clinic dermatologist who first reported it in 1925. Combining coal tar dressings and ultraviolet light, it is used for patients with severe psoriasis. The treatment is performed daily in specialized centers. Ultraviolet exposure times vary with the kind of psoriasis and the sensitivity of the patient's skin.

Light therapy. Sunlight and ultraviolet light slow the rapid growth of skin cells. Although ultraviolet light or sunlight can cause skin wrinkling, eye damage, and skin cancer, light treatment is safe and effective under a doctor's care. People with psoriasis all over their bodies may require treatment in a medically approved center equipped with light boxes for full body exposure. Psoriasis patients who live in warm climates may be directed to carefully sunbathe. Seek the advice of a dermatologist before self-treating with natural or artificial sunlight.

PUVA. When psoriasis has not responded to other treatments or is widespread, PUVA is effective in 85 percent to 90 percent of cases. The treatment name comes from "Psoralen + UVA," the two factors involved. Patients are given a drug called Psoralen, then are exposed to a carefully measured amount of a special form of ultraviolet (UVA) light. It takes approximately 25 treatments, over a two- or three-month period, before clearing occurs. About 30-40 treatments a year are usually required to keep the psoriasis under control. Because Psoralen remains in the lens of the eye, patients must wear UVA-blocking eyeglasses when exposed to sunlight from the time of exposure to Psoralen until sunset that day. PUVA treatments over a long period increase the risk of skin aging, freckling, and skin cancer. Dermatologists and their staff must monitor PUVA treatment very carefully.

Methotrexate. an oral anti-cancer drug that can produce dramatic clearing of psoriasis when other treatments have failed. Because it can produce side effects, particularly liver disease, regular blood tests are performed. Chest x-rays and occasional liver biopsies may be required. Other side effects include upset stomach, nausea and dizziness.

Retinoids (oral). Prescription oral vitamin A-related drugs may be prescribed alone or in combination with ultraviolet light for severe cases of psoriasis. Side effects include dryness of the skin, lips and eyes, elevation of fat levels in the blood, and formation of tiny bone spurs. Oral retinoids should not be used by pregnant women or women of childbearing age who intended to become pregnant during or within three years of discontinuation of therapy, as birth defects may result. Close monitoring is required together with regular blood tests.

Cyclosporine. An immunosuppressant drug used to prevent rejection of transplanted organs (liver, kidneys). It is used for treatment of widespread psoriasis when other methods have failed. Because of potential effects on the kidneys and blood pressure, close medical monitoring is required together with regular blood tests.

New Therapies Under Investigation
The above treatments alone or in combination can clear or greatly improve psoriasis in most cases, but no treatment permanently "cures" it. Dermatologists and other researchers are continually testing new drugs and treatments.

American Academy of Dermatology

About two million Americans have rheumatoid arthritis (RA), a chronic disease that causes pain, stiffness, swelling, and loss of function in the joints, as well as fatigue and low-grade fever. Unlike osteoarthritis, which affects mainly cartilage and bone (see page 469), RA affects numerous structures in the joint and also has systemic effects, meaning that it affects other tissues and organs throughout the body. There is no cure for RA, but treatment can reduce pain and inflammation and prevent deformities.

RA is an autoimmune disorder. Such disorders result when the body initiates an immunologic response to protect against some natural body constituent mistakenly recognized as "foreign." The joint damage caused by RA begins with inflammation of the synovial membrane that lines the joint. The inflammation leads to a thickening of the synovial membrane (a pannus),

due to overgrowth of synovial cells and accumulation of white blood cells. Release of enzymes and growth factors by these cells, along with continuing growth of the pannus, can erode cartilage as well as bones, tendons, and ligaments within the joint capsule. As RA progresses, the production of excess fibrous tissue can further limit joint motion. Inflammation of tissues surrounding the joint also contributes to joint damage.

Although RA often develops before age 50, the risk of the condition increases with age. RA affects two to three times more women than men; however, late-onset disease strikes men and women equally. It also tends to progress more quickly than early-onset disease and is more likely to attack larger joints. The good news is that late-onset RA frequently has a better prognosis than early-onset disease. Symptoms are likely to improve within 18 months, and

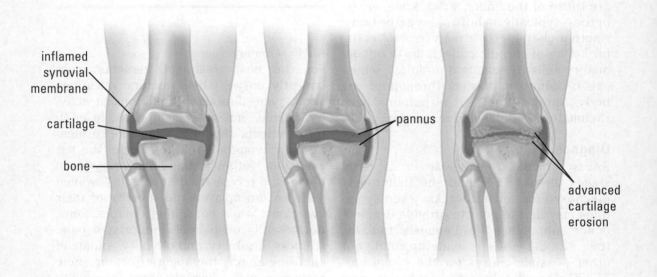

In early rheumatoid arthritis (A), the synovial membrane becomes inflamed. Next, a pannus—a group of abnormal inflammatory cells—forms (B). Finally, the cartilage erodes and the two bones rub together (C).

sufferers typically experience less permanent joint damage, deformity, and functional decline.

Causes

The exact cause of RA is unknown, but a tendency to develop it can be inherited. Some researchers believe that a virus or some other infection may trigger the onset of RA. Because the ratio of women to men with RA is three to one, some experts believe that hormonal factors play a role.

Symptoms

Most often the onset of RA is marked by fatigue, weakness, low-grade fever, or loss of appetite and weight. Such symptoms may or may not be accompanied by mild joint stiffness or pain. Stiffness is most prominent in the morning and improves during the day; the period of stiffness lengthens when the disease is more active and tends to increase after strenuous activity.

The joints that most often become inflamed (red, warm, swollen, and painful) are those of the finger, wrist, knee, ankle, or toe—typically on both sides of the body. Another characteristic feature of RA is the formation of chronic collections of inflammatory cells (rheumatoid nodules), which can be found in tissues throughout the body. About 20 percent of patients have rheumatoid nodules under the skin.

Diagnosis

RA is difficult to diagnose in its early stages. In fact, it cannot be definitively diagnosed for several weeks, when symptoms may first appear to provide firm evidence supporting the diagnosis. Initially, then, the diagnosis is made by ruling out other possible causes for the symptoms. The doctor will take a medical history and conduct a physical examination similar to the one used to diagnose osteoarthritis. The presence of RA can be confirmed later with x-rays and laboratory tests.

The finding of multiple red, swollen joints that are warm to the touch is strongly suggestive of RA, particularly if joints are involved symmetrically on both sides of the body. However, these signs are only present during active stages of the disease (which can go into remission periodically) and may not be detectable in joints that are deeply buried in the body, such as the hip.

People with rheumatoid arthritis who consult a rheumatologist—a medical doctor who specializes in rheumatic diseases—are more likely to receive state-of-the-art care than those who see a general practitioner. This is because the regimens recommended for RA are relatively new, may be complicated, and frequently require careful adjustment.

Medical History

For the best treatment, patients must honestly answer their doctors' questions about pain, disability, limitations in activity, fatigue, and other symptoms. In addition, patients should not hesitate to mention any symptoms that the doctor did not ask about. Although this advice may seem obvious, a recent study found that women with RA downplayed the severity of their symptoms when consulting doctors. Since doctors rely on patients' reports of pain, stiffness, disability, and other symptoms in choosing among therapeutic options, stoic responses may adversely affect the quality of treatment.

People with arthritis who suspect they are depressed should consult their doctor. While the pain and disability associated with arthritis can trigger depression, evidence also indicates that arthritis pain is worse when accompanied by symptoms of depression. Therefore, treating depression can have far-reaching benefits for people with arthritis. The two main treatments for depression—medication and psychotherapy—are often effective alone, but are generally most effective when used in combination for mild to moderate depression. Group therapy, particularly arthritis support groups, may provide another helpful option.

Laboratory Tests

The diagnosis of RA can be made more certain by documenting synovitis—inflammation of the synovial membrane. Synovitis can be detected by withdrawing a small amount of fluid from the joint and counting the number of white blood cells, which fight infection but can also cause inflammation. Other causes of synovitis must still be considered. Although x-rays of affected joints are not useful during the early stages of RA, those taken more than six months after the onset of active disease can show characteristic narrowing of the joint space and bony erosions that point to a diagnosis of RA.

A lab test to check for the presence of rheumatoid factor is also useful. Rheumatoid factor is an abnormal protein present in the blood of about 85 percent of patients with RA; larger amounts of this protein are found when the disease is most severe. Many patients with RA who initially test negative for rheumatoid factor will test positive as the disease progresses. However, this test is not definitive because elevated levels of rheumatoid factor can be found at times in a number of unrelated disorders, as well as in other autoimmune diseases. Other common laboratory abnormalities are mild anemia, elevated sedimentation rate (a nonspecific sign of inflammation), and a low white blood cell count.

Prognosis

About 10 percent of patients diagnosed with RA experience a complete remission within one year. Another 40 percent to 65 percent go into remission within two years. In these two groups of patients, rheumatoid factor levels are often low or absent, and symptoms are relatively mild, even when the disease is active. The prognosis is much worse if the disease remains active for more than two years. Such patients have a far greater chance of significant joint deformity.

If the disease progresses for months or years, affected joints eventually become deformed and their range of motion is increasingly limited. There may also be atrophy of the skin and muscles around affected joints, carpal tunnel syndrome (see page 189), and dryness of the eyes, mouth, and other mucous membranes. Less frequently, patients may experience more serious systemic problems (that is, problems affecting other sites in the body). These include an enlarged spleen and inflammation of the heart, the membrane covering the heart (pericarditis), the membranes surrounding the lung (pleurisy), and the outer layers of the eye (which can lead to blindness).

RA and Heart Disease

People with RA have a shorter lifespan than the general population, largely due to an increased risk of heart disease. This increase might be explained by the fact that people with RA tend to get less exercise. It is also possible that the inflammatory component of RA contributes to the high rate of heart disease. In recent years, researchers have found that inflammation accelerates the buildup of atherosclerotic plaque in arteries.

For this reason, RA patients need to take extra steps to prevent heart disease, such as eating a diet low in fat and cholesterol and exercising several times a week (physical activity can help with arthritis symptoms as well). In addition, RA patients may need to take medications to lower their cholesterol or blood pressure.

Treatment

The goals in the treatment of RA are to relieve pain, reduce inflammation, maintain function, and prevent deformities. Medications are required to control pain and diminish inflammation. Other therapeutic components include an appropriate mixture of rest periods and gentle exercise, as well as physical therapy and protection of the joints (for example, by using splints). A thorough understanding of the disease and a positive attitude are also tremendous assets. One current change in the standard approach to treating RA is a movement among physicians to prescribe stronger anti-rheumatic drugs (see page 558) earlier in the course of the disease, in an effort to control symptoms more quickly and minimize joint damage.

Patients with RA can benefit from many of the treatments for OA: application of ice to affected joints to reduce pain and inflammation, exercise to build strength and flexibility, and surgery to replace damaged joints. (However, topical products do not work for RA.) Additional medications may be needed to control inflammation. And patients with RA must pay special attention to combating fatigue, which can be the most incapacitating feature of the disease. Developing strategies to cope with the emotional and psychological factors associated with RA is also a key part of treatment that should not be overlooked.

Rest

Proper rest and the use of splints and other assistive devices when joints are inflamed can help relieve fatigue. Complete bed rest may be necessary during periods of severe inflammation involving multiple joints. Listed below are five general ways to relieve fatigue:

- Get ample rest—at least 10 hours of sleep a day, either all at night or about 8 hours at night and 2 hours during daytime naps.
- Relieve pain promptly—with joint rest, application of heat or cold, and medications—since continued pain causes fatigue.
- Prioritize all daily activities and carry out only the most essential ones; postpone nonessential activities until flare-ups subside.
- Spread out your work by thinking of your energy in terms of a budget that you must balance against daily activities. Just as you would not spend all of your money at the beginning of the month, do not carry out all vigorous work at one time of the day; rather, spread it out with rest periods between jobs.
- Try not to waste energy. For example, instead of making numerous trips up and down stairs during the day, consolidate activities and complete all of the tasks on one floor before moving on to the next.

Resting Joints

When inflammation is present, but not severe enough to require complete bed rest, joints should be rested properly to avoid flexion contracture. Flexion contracture is a loss of joint motion due to shortening of the surrounding tissues, especially in the hips and knees. Listed below are three tips for proper resting technique:

- Do not sit in a flexed position for a long time.
- If weight-bearing joints are involved, protect them by using crutches or braces when starting to walk after periods of severe inflammation.
- Apply removable splints to inflamed joints to alleviate muscle spasm and diminish the likelihood of deformities.

Splints and Assistive Devices
Braces, splints, and other supports are all examples of orthotic devices, or orthotics. They are designed to relieve pain and stabilize and protect joints during periods of inflammation, when joints (especially those in the hands and wrists) are more prone to injury. They help the user to perform everyday activities (such as walking, climbing stairs, turning doorknobs, and pouring beverages) that are affected by arthritis. Other special aids, called assistive devices (such as faucet turners or openers for jars), also help with the performance of daily activities.

Orthotics are most commonly composed of elastic, plastic, leather, moldable foam, and metal. Some orthotic devices can be purchased over-the-counter at medical supply stores or pharmacies, while others are custom designed and typically made and fitted by a specialist called an orthotist.

Many people find that over-the-counter orthotic devices are sufficient to improve their condition. These come in a variety of sizes for all the major joints and are typically inexpensive (less than $100). Because they are not custom made, however, they may

not fit properly and could cause problems ranging from skin irritation to restricted use of healthy joints adjacent to the problem joint. In such cases, a custom-fitted orthotic should be chosen. To obtain a custom-fitted orthotic device, ask your primary care doctor, rheumatologist, or orthopedic surgeon to write you a prescription and refer you to an orthotist. Occupational therapists are also experts in fabricating splints, recommending assistive devices, and instructing patients on their proper use.

Exercise
When joints are inflamed, only passive range-of-motion exercises are appropriate. Hydrotherapy (exercise in water) is also a good exercise option for people with RA, since the buoyancy of the water helps alleviate excessive stress on the joints. Also, water temperature is typically warm—between 83°F and 88°F—which relaxes the muscles and can reduce pain and stiffness.

More strenuous resistance exercises can be introduced gradually as joint inflammation subsides. However, an exercise should be avoided if it worsens pain an hour later. When joints are not inflamed, moderate aerobic exercises should be performed to help increase endurance, keep joints flexible, and reduce the risk of heart disease.

Drug Treatment: NSAIDs
Unless there is some reason not to use it, such as an allergy, aspirin is usually the first drug tried in RA. Aspirin is effective in reducing inflammation and is less expensive than the other nonsteroidal anti-inflammatory drugs (NSAIDs). Dosage depends on a balance between the large amounts of aspirin that may be needed to control symptoms and the development of side effects.

R

Other NSAIDs are employed when aspirin is ineffective or causes serious side effects. These drugs are more expensive than aspirin, but compliance may be better because they are taken less often each day. None of the NSAIDs has proved most effective for the treatment of RA, although some patients respond better to one drug than to others. The goal is to use the NSAID that provides the greatest benefit while producing the fewest side effects; some trial and error may be needed.

Drug Treatment: Anti-Rheumatics
The current trend is to move patients rapidly to other, more potent anti-rheumatic drugs when the basic anti-inflammatories fail to control symptoms adequately. The more potent drugs are usually referred to as disease-modifying anti-rheumatic drugs (DMARDs) but are also called SAARDs (slow-acting anti-rheumatic drugs).

Antimalarials. The most commonly used antimalarial is hydroxychloroquine sulfate (Plaquenil). Between 30 percent and 40 percent of patients with RA respond to this drug, but improvement does not start for three to six months. A typical dosage is 200 mg per day. The advantage of this drug is its low incidence of side effects. The most serious risk—vision loss due to retinal damage—is rare at low dosages, but regular eye exams are required during long-term treatment. Other side effects are gastrointestinal problems and, in rare instances, inflammation of the nervous system and skeletal and cardiac muscles.

Azathioprine. Azathioprine (Imuran) is an antimetabolite (a substance that blocks a normal metabolic process) most commonly employed as an immunosuppressant to prevent rejection of transplanted kidneys and hearts. The dosage depends upon body weight. Azathioprine's mechanism

of action in RA is unknown; because it can cause dangerous suppression of the immune system that may lead to serious infection, it is used only when severe symptoms fail to respond to safer drugs. Digestive side effects, such as loss of appetite, nausea, or, rarely, vomiting, may develop. In addition, the agent can take several months to work.

Corticosteroids. The corticosteroid drug prednisone usually produces rapid and dramatic symptomatic improvement by reducing inflammation and suppressing the immune system, but disease manifestations frequently recur once the steroid is discontinued. As a result, physicians and patients alike have been tempted to continue steroid use for long periods, despite many serious side effects.

Corticosteroid use is best reserved for the acute treatment of incapacitating flare-ups of joint disease, for severe manifestations of RA affecting other organs, or when alternative drugs are unsuccessful or cause intolerable side effects.

When corticosteroids are discontinued after being used at high doses or for a long time, the dose must be reduced very slowly. This will help to prevent a flare-up of arthritis and to avoid the symptoms of adrenal insufficiency, since corticosteroid administration stops the normal formation of steroids by the adrenal glands.

Cyclophosphamide. The anti-cancer drug cyclophosphamide (Cytoxan) has proven beneficial in experimental studies with RA patients who have not responded adequately to any other therapeutic measures. People taking this drug must drink plenty of fluids to maintain good urine flow, since serious inflammation of the bladder (hemorrhagic cystitis) is one of its side effects. Cyclophosphamide can cause fetal damage if administered to a pregnant woman, an important concern because many RA patients are women of childbearing age. The dosage may vary considerably, depending on the patient.

Cyclosporine. Cyclosporine is an immunosuppressant that is most commonly used to prevent rejection of newly transplanted organs. It relieves symptoms of RA by inhibiting the growth and action of immune system cells, including those that cause joint pain and swelling. Because it is highly toxic and can cause high blood pressure and damage to the kidneys, however, patients on cyclosporine must be monitored closely while it is administered in low doses over a period of time. A combination of cyclosporine and methotrexate has been shown to improve symptoms in patients who have not responded to methotrexate therapy alone. The correct dosage is based on a number of individual factors.

Gold salts. Therapy with gold salts (chrysotherapy), used in patients who do not respond to NSAIDs and are unable to take methotrexate (see right), is beneficial about 60 percent of the time. Gold salts appear to act by suppressing synovial inflammation during active RA. The benefits of treatment are not apparent for about three to six months. Gold is administered either by weekly intramuscular injections or by twice-daily oral dosages—though injected gold is more effective overall than oral treatment. Initial oral dosages are about 6 mg a day. The injections start at 10 mg, then range from 25 to 50 mg a week. If no benefit is seen after giving a total of 1 g, consideration is given to discontinuance of gold treatment.

Side effects, which occur in about a third of patients receiving gold injections, include inflammation of the skin and mucous membranes of the mouth, protein in the urine, and a drop in white blood cell levels. Diarrhea (which can be reduced by bulk diets and by starting with low doses that are increased slowly) occurs more often with oral treatment; the other side effects, especially protein in the urine, occur more often with injections. About 4 percent to 5 percent of patients must stop gold therapy because of digestive side effects. Even those who have tolerated gold injections for several years need to watch for adverse symptoms. These include dizziness, nausea, and pain occurring within an hour of the injection. Regular blood tests are necessary to monitor side effects.

Methotrexate. Methotrexate (Rheumatrex), which acts as a mild immunosuppressant, was first used to treat various forms of cancer. It is now recognized as the drug of choice for people with severe RA that does not respond to NSAIDs. It often leads to improvement within a month—much more quickly than antimalarials, gold, or penicillamine. About 7.5 to 15 mg is taken orally once a week and is usually well tolerated. Combinations of methotrexate and cyclosporine are used for cases of hard-to-treat RA.

The most common side effects of methotrexate are irritation of the stomach and inflammation of the mucous membranes of the mouth. Rarely, the drug produces an extremely dangerous toxic reaction that may include lung inflammation, bone marrow suppression, and severe liver damage.

Based on recent studies, low-dose folic acid supplements are recommended as an inexpensive way to reduce methotrexate side effects. Because high doses of folic acid can mask the warning symptoms of vitamin B12 deficiency, patients should not start on supplements without first checking with their doctor.

Because methotrexate may harm the liver, experts recommend periodic blood

R

R

tests to monitor liver function. A biopsy is performed only if blood tests indicate liver damage. Doctors may also take a baseline chest x-ray for comparison purposes should lung complications develop from the drug, especially if the patient has underlying lung disease.

Despite some concern that methotrexate might increase the risk of such blood cancers as leukemia or lymphoma, this association appears unlikely, according to a recent study. If any link does exist, the authors of the study state that it would be small and unrelated to the dosage or length of methotrexate therapy.

Research on the use of methotrexate to treat RA may in fact foreshadow a major change in the approach rheumatologists take in starting drug therapy. An analysis of results from 11 clinical trials indicates that, contrary to current practice, RA should be treated aggressively in the initial stages of the disease. If these findings are borne out by further research, potent drugs may be prescribed early to gain control of symptoms. Additional studies have shown that methotrexate is more effective when combined with other drugs, such as cyclosporine, leflunomide, etanercept, infliximab, or adalimumab.

Penicillamine. Penicillamine has proven effective—particularly in studies carried out in the United Kingdom—in patients who are unresponsive to all other measures. Its use is limited, however, by reactions that occur in about half the people taking this drug. Side effects include fever, rash, mouth ulcers, loss of taste, protein in the urine, and low blood levels of white blood cells and platelets. The usual dosage is 250 to 1,500 mg per day.

Sulfasalazine. Sulfasalazine (Azulfidine EN-tabs) appears to suppress the immune system response that is activated in RA and also acts as an anti-inflammatory agent. The usual dosage of sulfasalazine is 2 g per day; the drug generally does not take effect for four weeks. The dosage may be raised after 12 weeks if the patient still does not feel better. Because of adverse effects—which include skin rash, headache, nausea, vomiting, stomach problems, loss of appetite, and decreased sperm count—patients should be monitored closely for the first three months of therapy. Less frequent side effects include itching, fever, anemia, and skin eruptions and discoloration. Based on x-ray results, clinical trials have shown sulfasalazine to be as effective as gold salts.

New Drug Treatments

Etanercept (Enbrel), leflunomide (Arava), anakinra (Kineret), and adalimumab (Humira) are drugs that not only treat the symptoms of RA but also have been shown to slow the associated structural damage in the joint that occurs over time.

Etanercept, anakinra, and adalimumab must be injected (leflunomide comes in pill form). At first, a health care professional should administer the injections. Only with a physician's approval and after instruction by a health care professional should people self-inject the medication. The drug is injected into the layer of fat directly under the skin, and the site of the injection should be rotated regularly. (Common injection sites include the upper arm, thigh, and abdomen.) The drugs must be refrigerated but should not be frozen.

Infliximab (Remicade), a third new medication for RA, was originally approved for the treatment of Crohn's disease. It has since been approved for the treatment of RA as well. While this medication can treat the symptoms of RA, it is not known to slow the progression of the disease. The drug must be administered intravenously by a doctor or nurse.

Prosorba Column

The Prosorba column, which was approved by the FDA in 1999, is an alternative for RA patients who do not respond to medication. Similar in procedure to kidney dialysis, this unusual type of therapy removes from the blood immune proteins believed to cause inflammation. The whole procedure takes approximately two hours and must be performed once a week for 12 weeks to be effective. No clinical studies have yet proven the long-term effectiveness or safety of the Prosorba column.

Surgery

Patients with RA can benefit from the same surgical procedures used in those with OA (see page 478). Also, a synovectomy may be effective when RA involves the elbow, shoulder, hip, or knee.

Synovectomy. This procedure—performed mostly in patients whose RA has not responded to medication—involves the removal of the inflamed synovial membrane. Synovectomy prevents the joint stiffness and destruction of cartilage, ligaments, tendons, and bone caused by substances released from the diseased synovial cells. Synovectomy is not as involved a procedure as joint replacement; it is not considered a permanent cure because the synovial membrane can grow back within several years. The procedure can be performed through either arthroscopy or open surgery, depending on the size of the joint. Unless the disease is brought under control with medication, synovitis is likely to recur.

Resection. In this procedure, all or part of a bone is removed from a joint in the hand, wrist, elbow, toe, or ankle. Resection is most commonly performed to relieve pain in people with RA. Recovery times vary but may be as long as several weeks.

R

When the itchy red spots of childhood chickenpox disappear and life returns to normal, the battle with the virus that causes chickenpox seems to be won. But for all too many of us this triumph of the body's immune system over the virus that causes chickenpox is only temporary. The virus has not been destroyed, but lays low, ready to strike again later in life. This second eruption of the chickenpox virus is the disease called shingles.

You cannot develop shingles unless you have had an earlier bout of chickenpox, and everyone who has had chickenpox is at risk for shingles. While young people do develop shingles, the disease most often strikes in later years.

Scientists call the chickenpox/shingles-causing agent varicella zoster. Varicella is a Latin word meaning "little pox" to distinguish the virus from smallpox, the highly contagious and often fatal scourge that disfigured or killed millions of people, especially during the Middle Ages. Zoster is the Greek word for "girdle;" shingles often produces a girdle of blisters or lesions around the waist. This striking pattern also gives the disease its common name: the word shingles comes from cingulum, the Latin word for belt or girdle.

What Is Shingles?

Scientists believe that in the original battle with the chickenpox virus some of the virus particles leave the skin blisters and move into the nervous system. There the viruses settle down in an inactive (latent) form inside specific nerve cells (neurons) that relay information to the brain about what your body is sensing—whether your skin feels hot or cold, whether you've been touched or feel pain. These lie in clusters (ganglia) adjacent to the spinal cord and brain and are one type of sensory neurons.

When the chickenpox virus reactivates, the virus moves down the long nerve fibers that extend from the sensory cell bodies to the skin. The viruses multiply, the telltale rash erupts, and the person now has herpes zoster, or shingles. With shingles, the nervous system is more deeply involved than it was during the bout with chickenpox, and the symptoms are often more complex and severe.

The virus responsible for shingles and chickenpox belongs to a group of viruses called herpesviruses. This group includes the herpes simplex virus that causes cold sores, fever blisters, mononucleosis, genital herpes—a sexually transmitted disease—and the Epstein-Barr virus involved in infectious mononucleosis. Like the shingles-causing virus, many other herpesviruses can take refuge in the nervous system after an individual has suffered an initial infection.

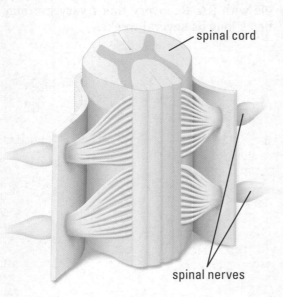

spinal cord

spinal nerves

The shingles virus can hide, dormant, inside spinal nerves. If the virus is reactivated, it travels along the nerve to the skin, causing a painful rash.

These viruses may remain latent for years, then travel down nerve cell fibers to cause a renewed infection.

The varicella zoster virus looks as though it was designed by a mathematician. It is a microscopic sphere encasing a 20-sided geometric figure called an icosahedron. Inside the icosahedron is the genetic material of the virus, deoxyribonucleic acid (DNA). When activated, the virus reproduces inside the nucleus of an infected cell. It acquires its spherical wrapping as it buds through the nuclear membrane.

Who's at Risk?

About 10 percent of normal adults can be expected to get shingles during their lifetimes, usually after age 50. The incidence increases with age so that shingles is 10 times more likely to occur in adults over 60 than in children under 10. Most people who get shingles develop immunity to the virus and will not get the disease again, however, shingles may recur in some individuals. These cases usually involve people with declining or compromised immune systems, such as those infected with HIV or receiving chemotherapy.

A person who is suffering from a disease that damages the immune system, or who is taking anticancer drugs that suppress the immune system, is a prime candidate for an attack of shingles. Even among healthy individuals, temporary depression of the immune system because of stress, a cold, and even sunburn may be associated with an attack of shingles.

Youngsters whose mothers had chickenpox late in pregnancy—5 to 21 days before giving birth—are also vulnerable to shingles. Sometimes these children are born with chickenpox or develop a typical case within a few days (see section "Do Women Have Special Risks from Shingles?" on page 566).

What Are the Symptoms of Shingles?

The first sign of shingles is often burning or tingling pain, or sometimes numbness, in or under the skin. The individual may also feel ill with fever, chills, headache, or stomach upset. After several days, a rash of small fluid-filled blisters, reminiscent of chickenpox, appears on reddened skin. The pain associated with shingles can be intense and is often described as "unrelenting." People with lesions on the torso may feel spasms of pain at the gentlest touch or breeze. The blisters are usually limited to a band, called dermatomes, spanning one side of the trunk, around the waistline, or clustered on one side of the face.

The distribution of the shingles spots is a telltale clue to where the chickenpox virus has been hiding since the initial infection. Scientists now know that the shingles lesions correspond to the dermatome supplied by a specific sensory nerve that exits from the brain or spinal cord.

For the majority of healthy individuals, this second bout with the chickenpox virus is almost always a second triumph of the body's immune system. The shingles attack may last longer than chickenpox, and the patient may need medication for pain, but in most cases the body has the inner resources to fight back. The lesions heal, the pain subsides within three to five weeks, and for most patients the blisters leave no scars.

How Is it Treated?

The severity and duration of an attack of shingles can be significantly reduced by immediate treatment with antiviral drugs, which include acyclovir, valacyclovir, or famcyclovir. Antiviral drugs may also help stave off the painful aftereffects of shingles known as postherpetic neuralgia. Doctors now recommend starting antiviral drugs within 72 hours of the first sign of the shingles rash.

S

Early treatment is believed to reduce the risk of postherpetic neuralgia and may speed up the healing process. Other treatments for post-herpetic neuralgia include steroids, antidepressants, anticonvulsants, and topical agents. Scientists continue to work toward developing newer antiviral agents and more effective pain killers.

Is Shingles Contagious?

As early as 1909 a German scientist suspected that the viruses causing chickenpox and shingles were one and the same. In the 1920s and 1930s the case was strengthened. In an experiment, children were inoculated with fluid from the lesions of patients with shingles. Within two weeks about half the children came down with chickenpox. Finally in 1958 detailed analyses of the viruses taken from patients with either chickenpox or shingles confirmed that the viruses were identical.

This study also proved that a person with shingles can pass the virus to individuals who have never had chickenpox, but these individuals will develop chickenpox, not shingles. A person with chickenpox cannot communicate shingles to someone else. In order for people to develop shingles they must already harbor the virus in their nervous system, and for those who do harbor the virus, having contact with someone with chickenpox will not trigger shingles. Additionally, a person with shingles cannot communicate shingles to another individual.

What Are the Complications?

People with "optical" shingles (where the virus has invaded an ophthalmic nerve) may suffer painful eye inflammations that leave them temporarily blind or impair their vision. Individuals with this type of shingles should see an ophthalmologist immediately. If shingles appears on the face and affects the auditory nerves, it can also lead to complications in hearing. Infections of facial nerves can lead to temporary paralysis.

Postherpetic Neuralgia

Sometimes, particularly in older people, symptoms of shingles persist long after the rash is healed. In these cases, facial paralysis, headache, and persistent pain can be the aftermath. Possibly because the nerve cells conveying pain sensations are hardest hit, or

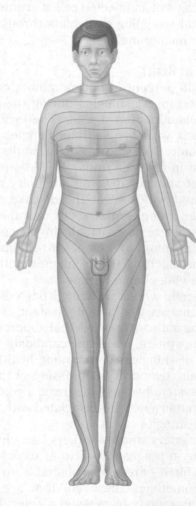

The lines mark the areas of skin served by individual brain or spinal nerves. The rash from shingles typically follows one of these narrow bands.

are exquisitely sensitized by the virus attack, pain is the principal persistent complication of shingles. This pain, called postherpetic neuralgia, is among the most devastating known to mankind—the kind of pain that leads to insomnia, weight loss, depression, and that total preoccupation with unrelenting torment that characterizes the chronic pain sufferer.

Although it can be extraordinarily painful, postherpetic neuralgia is not life-threatening. Doctors treating the pain currently employ a variety of medications. Powerful narcotic pain relievers can offer relief but, because they can have serious side effects, doctors often prescribe newer nonaddictive but potent painkillers. Ointments containing capsaicin, the heat-producing ingredient found in hot chili peppers, are effective in relieving pain from postherpetic neuralgia, as well as pain from other disorders such as arthritis. Such ointments are currently available by prescription. Although these creams contain less than 1 percent capsaicin, new research suggests that patients may be able to tolerate creams containing 5 percent to 10 percent of this active ingredient if used in combination with other pain killers. More research is needed before these higher-dose ointments will be available to patients.

In 1999, the Food and Drug Administration approved a new method of treating the pain of postherpetic neuralgia. The product is an adhesive patch containing lidocaine, a commonly used local anesthetic. The patch allows lidocaine to be released into the top layers of the skin, reducing pain from the damaged nerves. Because it delivers the drug via the skin, it does not produce any significant levels of the drug in the blood and, therefore, does not cause serious systemic side effects if used appropriately.

Studies have also shown that some anticonvulsant drugs used to treat epilepsy, such as carbamazepine, are sometimes effective in relieving the pain of postherpetic neuralgia. Antidepressants can help also. In addition to their effects on mood, the antidepressants appear to relieve pain. Some doctors report that patients occasionally benefit from alternative treatments for pain, such as acupuncture and electrical stimulation of nerve endings.

It is important to realize that individuals with postherpetic neuralgia no longer have shingles: their infection is over. Instead, they are suffering from damage to the nervous system. Scientists believe that the virus attack has led to scarring or other lesions affecting the cells in sensory ganglia and associated nerves. Even in such severe cases, however, the paralysis, headaches, and pain generally subside, although it may take time.

Is Shingles Life-Threatening?

Shingles is a serious threat to life in immunosuppressed individuals—for example, those with HIV infection or patients with cancer who are receiving treatments that can weaken their immune systems. These treatments destroy cancerous tissue but unfortunately they also have the potential to damage cells of the immune system that normally fight invading organisms. Patients who receive organ transplants (for kidney disease, for example) are also vulnerable to shingles. To prevent the body from rejecting the foreign tissue of the transplant, these patients are given drugs that suppress the immune system. Should any of these patients contract shingles, there is a possibility that the zoster virus will spread throughout the body, reaching vital organs like the lungs. If unchecked, such disseminated zoster can lead to death from viral pneumonia or secondary bacterial infection.

Do Women Have Special Risks from Shingles?

Many mothers-to-be are concerned about any infection contracted during pregnancy, and rightly so. It is well known that certain viruses can be transmitted across the mother's bloodstream to the fetus, or can be acquired by the baby during the birth process.

Maternal chickenpox poses some risk to the unborn child, depending upon the stage of pregnancy during which the mother contracts the disease. During the first 30 weeks, maternal chickenpox may, in some cases, lead to congenital malformations. Such cases are rare and experts differ in their opinions on how great the risk is.

If the mother gets chickenpox from 21 to 5 days before giving birth, the newborn may have chickenpox at birth or develop it within a few days, as noted earlier. But the time lapse between the start of the mother's illness and the birth of the baby generally allows the mother's immune system to react and produce antibodies to fight the virus. These antibodies can be transmitted to the unborn child and thus help fight the infection. Still, a third of the babies exposed to chickenpox in the 21 to 5 days before birth develop shingles in the first 5 years of life because the virus must also be fought by immune cells.

What if the mother contracts chickenpox at precisely the time of birth? In that case, the mother's immune system has not had a chance to mobilize its forces. And although some of the mother's antibodies will be transmitted to the newborn via the placenta, the newborn will have little ability to fight off the attack because the immune system is immature. For these babies chickenpox can be fatal. They must be given "zoster immune globulin," a preparation made from the antibody-rich blood of adults who have recently recovered from chickenpox or shingles.

National Institute of Neurological Disorders and Stroke

The sinuses are air-filled cavities in the bones surrounding the nose and around the eyes. Although their exact role is unknown, sinuses probably help to keep the respiratory system free from infection by producing mucus, which normally drains through the nose into the throat. During a cold or allergic reaction, the sinuses often become inflamed and swollen. As a result, the opening between the sinuses and the nose narrows or becomes blocked, hindering drainage. Reduced drainage permits congestion, which provides a breeding ground for bacteria. These developments can lead to acute bacterial sinusitis.

Causes

Most cases of sinusitis follow a cold or a period when allergies have worsened. Other precipitating causes might be asthma; exposure to toxic fumes or air pollutants such as tobacco smoke; nasal obstruction caused by such factors as a deviated septum, polyp, tumor, or even scar tissue that may have formed after repeated bouts of sinusitis; and infection from an upper tooth that has extended into the sinuses.

Symptoms

If you have a cold that lasts more than 10 days, you may be suffering from acute bacterial sinusitis. Although the symptoms of acute bacterial sinusitis sometimes mimic those of a cold or allergy, certain characteristics distinguish it from other respiratory problems. The American Academy of Otolaryngology-Head and Neck Surgery, a professional association of ear, nose, and throat doctors,

S

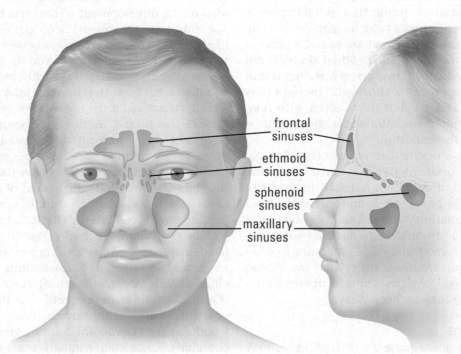

frontal
sinuses

ethmoid
sinuses

sphenoid
sinuses

maxillary
sinuses

There are four sets of sinus cavities. The maxillary sinuses—the largest—account for most sinus problems in adults. Pain occurs when the thin drainage channels between the sinuses and the nose becomes blocked.

recommends seeing a doctor if you have three or more of the following symptoms:

- Facial pressure/pain
- Headache
- Congestion/stuffy nose
- Postnasal drip
- Thick nasal discharge
- Cold symptoms for more than 10 days
- Low-grade fever
- Bad breath
- Pain in the upper teeth

Diagnosis

Because the symptoms of acute sinusitis frequently mimic those of a cold or allergy, many people do not realize they have the condition. And some who think they have sinusitis decide to ride out the illness on their own, believing that treatment is unnecessary or unavailable. One survey conducted by the Academy found that of 1,002 people who said they had a cold, allergy, or sinus infection during the previous year, 39 percent of those who thought they had sinusitis did not see a doctor. The survey also found that nearly 80 percent of those who thought they had sinusitis treated themselves with nonprescription medications that should not be used for the condition.

Seeing a doctor can ensure that you get the appropriate medication and increase the likelihood of symptom relief. A diagnosis of sinusitis is based on symptoms and physical examination. When sinusitis is severe or chronic, additional tests such as computer assisted tomography (CT scanning) or an endoscopic examination (visual inspection of the nasal cavities using a fiberoptic instrument) may be necessary.

Treatment

Although some patients with sinusitis may get better on their own, many continue to feel ill or become vulnerable to repeat episodes, severe symptoms, and chronic sinusitis (a diagnosis made after the condition has persisted for at least three months). If not treated, chronic inflammation or rare complications, such as bacterial spread to the orbital tissues around the eyes or to the brain, may require surgery. For these reasons, the Academy of Otolaryngology recommends proper antibiotic treatment for all cases of acute bacterial sinusitis.

The initial goal of therapy is to eliminate infection and improve drainage. The first and most important step toward recovery is antibiotic therapy, which should be taken for at least 10 to 14 days. Patients generally feel better in about four days but should continue taking antibiotics as prescribed. The Academy of Otolaryngology estimates that at least 40 percent of patients stop taking their medication prematurely, which may lead to the development of bacteria that resist antibiotic treatment. Such patients are likely to have repeat episodes, severe symptoms, or chronic sinusitis. If you do not feel better after five days, tell your doctor. He or she may wish to switch medications.

Unfortunately, it is not always easy to choose the proper antibiotic. Doctors who have not kept abreast of developments sometimes continue to prescribe antibiotics that have little or no effect on the drug-resistant bacteria that cause most of today's sinus infections. Familiar standbys such as erythromycin, cephalexin (Keflex), and ampicillin (Polycillin) generally should not be used. Instead, one of several newer antibiotics should be selected. These include amoxicillin clavulanate (Augmentin), cefuroxime (Ceftin), cefpodoxime proxetil (Vantin), cefprozil (Cefzil), azithromycin (Zithromax), levofloxacin (Levaquin), and loracarbef (Lorabid). Amoxicillin (Amoxil) is also sometimes effective. The proper choice of drug depends on which bacteria are prevalent in your particular geographic area. Your doctor can obtain this information from a nearby or regional hospital.

Guaifenesin, a medication that thins mucus secretions and is more commonly used as a cough expectorant, may also be recommended. Although guaifenesin is available over-the-counter (OTC), the prescription-strength version is required for sinus problems. Congestion can be relieved with prescription or OTC decongestants in pill, spray, or drop form. However, using them for more than three or four days may slow recovery. A saline nasal spray or inhaling steam may also help relieve discomfort. Antihistamines are ineffective for sinusitis and should generally be avoided.

It's also important to control or eliminate any precipitating conditions that you may have. If sinusitis persists, a longer course of antibiotic therapy may be prescribed along with corticosteroid sprays or pills. If the sinuses remain blocked despite these efforts, surgery may be needed to drain the sinuses, remove inflamed tissue, or create new outlets for mucus. Such procedures can be performed endoscopically, thus reducing the need for hospitalization.

Between one and four million people in the United States suffer from Sjögren's (SHOW-grins) syndrome, an autoimmune disorder that mostly affects women over the age of 40. Two types of Sjögren's syndrome have been identified: primary and secondary. Primary Sjögren's is characterized by symptoms of dry mouth and dry eyes. In secondary Sjögren's—the more common type—these symptoms occur along with another autoimmune disease such as rheumatoid arthritis or lupus. About 10 percent to 15 percent of people with rheumatoid arthritis develop Sjögren's syndrome.

Causes

Sjögren's syndrome occurs when the immune system mistakenly attacks and damages glands that produce moisture such as tears and saliva. Researchers are not sure why this happens. One possibility is that a viral or bacterial infection triggers the immune system to act. But instead of fighting the infection, the immune system turns against the body's own cells. Genetic and hormonal factors may play a role in this faulty response.

Symptoms

The damage to the moisture-producing glands leads to a decreased production of tears and saliva that results in dry eyes and dry mouth, the hallmark symptoms of Sjögren's. In some cases, the dryness can be so severe that it feels like sand is in the eyes and the mouth is full of cotton. Other parts of the body that can experience dryness include the skin, nose, throat, and vagina.

Such dryness can lead to additional complications. For instance, people with dry eyes are at increased risk for eye infections; signs of an infection are pus, excessive redness, and pain. People with dry mouth are susceptible to tooth decay and difficulty swallowing. Dry mouth also increases your risk of mouth infections. A common one is candidiasis, which appears as white patches or red, burning areas in the mouth. It can be treated with an antifungal drug.

Sjögren's syndrome can also cause inflammation and pain in the joints and muscles, and, less commonly, inflammation of the lungs, kidneys, and blood vessels. Some people experience extreme fatigue. In rare cases, people with Sjögren's develop lymphoma, a cancer of the lymph nodes.

Diagnosis

Diagnosis of Sjögren's syndrome is complicated since the symptoms of dry eyes and dry mouth can be due to other factors, such as medications or other diseases. Your doctor will first take a detailed medical history and then perform a complete physical exam that includes an examination of the mouth and eyes. If Sjögren's is suspected, one or more of the following tests may be done to help confirm the diagnosis and determine the severity of the disease:

Schirmer test. A small strip of filter paper is placed between the lower eyelid and the eyeball in order to measure the amount of tears produced.

Slit lamp exam. After a special dye is put into the eye, a device is used for a magnified view of the eye to see how dry it is and whether there is any inflammation

Salivary gland biopsy. Salivary glands are removed from the lower lip and examined under a microscope to look for inflammation.

Blood tests. Blood samples are taken to detect certain antibodies (substances produced by the immune system) that are often present in people with Sjögren's syndrome.

Treatment

There is no cure for Sjögren's syndrome, but the symptoms can be relieved using over-the-counter and prescription medications, and by making simple changes in your behavior and environment. The approach to treatment depends on which parts of the body are affected.

Dry eyes. The most common treatment for dry eyes is artificial tears; preservative-free tears are the most comfortable. At night, an eye ointment can be used to help keep the eyes lubricated. You should also use a humidifier, avoid cigarette smoke, protect your eyes from the wind, and blink several times a minute while reading or using the computer.

If these measures do not provide sufficient relief, a punctal occlusion—a surgical procedure that closes the ducts that drain tears from the eyes—might be helpful. The surgeon can close the ducts temporarily using collagen plugs that dissolve over time or more permanently with silicone plugs that can be removed if necessary. For permanent closure of the ducts, laser or heat is used.

Dry mouth. Dry mouth can be controlled in a number of ways. Taking small sips of water throughout the day can help keep your mouth moist. Saliva production can be stimulated by chewing gum or sucking on hard candy. However, gum and candy should be sugar-free to avoid increasing the risk of dental cavities. Drugs can also be used to stimulate saliva production. Two are available: pilocarpine (Salagen) and cevimeline (Evoxac). Studies show that cevimeline may last longer and have fewer adverse side effects than pilocarpine. If you produce little or no saliva, a saliva substitute can be tried. A gel-based substitute is best.

Other types of dryness. Heavy moisturizing creams or ointments can be used for dry skin. Saline (salt water) nasal sprays work well for a dry nose. For vaginal dryness, estrogen creams or vaginal moisturizers are recommended. If needed, a water-based vaginal lubricant can be used during sexual intercourse. Dry, cracked lips can be relieved with oil- or petroleum-based lip balms.

Other symptoms. Nonsteroidal anti-inflammatory drugs are prescribed for joint or muscle pain. Corticosteroids are used to suppress the immune system if other parts of the body, such as the lungs, kidneys, or blood vessels, are affected.

When to See a Doctor

Make an appointment to see your doctor if you develop persistent dryness in the mucous membranes of the eyes, mouth, nasal passages, or vagina. Also, contact your doctor if you notice any signs of an eye or mouth infection.

People with dry mouth are susceptible to tooth decay. Be sure to visit your dentist three times per year, brush your teeth with a fluoride-containing toothpaste after each meal and before going to bed, floss your teeth daily, and limit your consumption of sugary foods. If you do eat sugary foods, brush your teeth immediately afterward.

S

The skin is the body's outer covering. It protects us against heat, light, injury, and infection. It regulates body temperature and stores water, fat, and vitamin D. Weighing about six pounds, the skin is actually the body's largest organ. It is made up of two main layers: the epidermis and the inner dermis.

The epidermis (outer layer of the skin) is mostly made up of flat, scale-like cells called squamous cells. Under the squamous cells are round cells called basal cells. The deepest part of the epidermis also contains melanocytes. These cells produce melanin, which gives the skin its color.

The dermis (inner layer of skin) contains blood and lymph vessels, hair follicles, and glands. These glands produce sweat, which helps regulate body temperature, and sebum, an oily substance that helps keep the skin from drying out. Sweat and sebum reach the skin's surface through tiny openings called pores.

Types of Skin Cancer

The two most common kinds of skin cancer are basal cell carcinoma and squamous cell carcinoma. (Carcinoma is cancer that begins in the cells that cover or line an organ.) Basal cell carcinoma accounts for more than 90 percent of all skin cancers in the United States. It is a slow-growing cancer that seldom spreads to other parts of the body. Squamous cell carcinoma also rarely spreads, but it does so more often than basal cell carcinoma. However, it is important that skin cancers be found and treated early because they can invade and destroy nearby tissue.

Basal cell carcinoma and squamous cell carcinoma are sometimes called non-melanoma skin cancer. Another type of cancer that occurs in the skin is melanoma, which begins in the melanocytes.

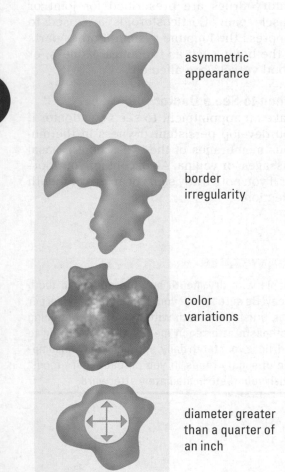

asymmetric appearance

border irregularity

color variations

diameter greater than a quarter of an inch

Warning signs of melanoma include recent changes in shape, border contours, color, or size.

Non-melanoma skin cancers arise in different regions of the epidermis. Basal cell carcinoma begins in the lower epidermis. It usually develops on the head and neck and grows slowly. Squamous cell carcinoma starts in the mid-epidermis. While it, too, commonly appears on sun-exposed areas, squamous cell carcinoma can also develop within scars, skin ulcers, and elsewhere on the body.

Melanoma

Melanoma is the most deadly of the three main types of skin cancer, and its incidence is rising faster than that of any other cancer in the United States. Although melanoma accounts for only about 4 percent of all skin cancer diagnoses, it is responsible for about 80 percent of all skin cancer deaths. Of the estimated 9,600 skin cancer deaths predicted annually, nearly 8,000 will be attributable to melanoma. If detected and treated early, melanoma is highly curable. But left untreated, it can spread rapidly and prove fatal.

All melanomas arise from melanocytes, cells that produce the pigment melanin, which darkens the skin and helps protect it from the harmful effects of the sun. Melanocytes are scattered throughout the thin, top layer of skin known as the epidermis. They may also collect and form moles, or nevi. Melanoma can develop from scattered melanocytes or from those collected in nevi.

Ninety-five percent of all melanomas develop on sun-exposed parts of the body. In men, this is usually the torso. In women, it is usually the arms and legs. But melanoma can occur anywhere on the body, including areas that are never exposed to the sun.

The large majority of melanomas do not spread right away. Many begin as a "melanoma in situ," in which growth does not extend beneath the epidermis. In the second stage, or vertical growth phase, melanoma can penetrate the dermis (the thicker, deeper layer of skin located under the epidermis). Finally, the cancer can metastasize (spread) throughout the body. Once this process begins, the malignancy can progress quickly. Some patients develop large masses of melanoma in the lymph nodes, lungs, brain, gastrointestinal tract, or liver, even though the original skin tumor is still small.

Treatment of melanoma usually begins with surgical removal of the tumor. To minimize the chances that the cancer will spread, surrounding tissue is also excised. However, if the cancer has spread to other parts of the body, surgery is not effective. In these cases, chemotherapy to destroy cancer cells and radiation to provide symptom relief are the traditional treatment methods. But chemotherapy rarely cures advanced disease, and until recently, the prognosis was often poor for people with advanced melanoma. However, a new treatment called immunotherapy, biological therapy, or biochemotherapy offers hope for people with melanoma. This new technique uses drugs to encourage the immune system to destroy cancer cells more effectively than chemotherapy and, in some cases, produces long-term remissions. *The Editors*

Causes and Prevention

Skin cancer is the most common type of cancer in the United States. According to current estimates, 40 percent to 50 percent of Americans who live to age 65 will have skin cancer at least once. Although anyone can get skin cancer, the risk is greatest for people who have fair skin that freckles easily—often those with red or blond hair and blue or light-colored eyes.

Ultraviolet (UV) radiation from the sun is the main cause of skin cancer. Artificial sources of UV radiation, like sunlamps and tanning booths, can also cause skin cancer.

The risk of developing skin cancer is affected by where a person lives. People who live in areas that get high levels of UV radiation from the sun are more likely to get skin cancer. In the United States, for example, skin cancer is more common in Texas than it is in Minnesota, where the sun is not as strong. Worldwide, the highest rates of skin cancer are found in South Africa and Australia, areas that receive high amounts of UV radiation.

How to Do a Skin Self-Exam

You can improve your chances of finding skin cancer promptly by performing a simple skin self-exam regularly.

The best time to do this self-exam is after a shower or bath. You should check your skin in a well-lighted room using a full-length mirror and a hand-held mirror. It's best to begin by learning where your birthmarks, moles, and blemishes are and what they usually look like. Check for anything new—a change in the size, texture, or color of a mole, or a sore that does not heal.

Check all areas, including the back, the scalp, between the buttocks, and the genital area.

- Look at the front and back of your body in the mirror, then raise your arms and look at the left and right sides.
- Bend your elbows and look carefully at your palms; forearms, including the undersides; and the upper arms.
- Examine the back and front of your legs. Also look between your buttocks and around your genital area.
- Sit and closely examine your feet, including the soles and the spaces between the toes.
- Look at your face, neck, and scalp. You may want to use a comb or a blow dryer to move hair so that you can see better.

By checking your skin regularly, you will become familiar with what is normal. If you find anything unusual, see your doctor right away. Remember, the earlier skin cancer is found, the better the chance for cure.

In addition, skin cancer is related to lifetime exposure to UV radiation. Most skin cancers appear after age 50, but the sun's damaging effects begin at an early age. Therefore, protection should start in childhood to prevent skin cancer later in life.

Whenever possible, people should avoid exposure to the midday sun (from 10 a.m. to 2 p.m. standard time, or from 11 a.m. to 3 p.m. daylight saving time). Keep in mind that protective clothing, such as sun hats and long sleeves, can block out the sun's harmful rays. Also, lotions that contain sunscreens can protect the skin. Sunscreens are rated in strength according to a sun protection factor (SPF), which ranges from 2 to 30 or higher. Those rated 15 to 30 block most of the sun's harmful rays.

Symptoms

The most common warning sign of skin cancer is a change on the skin, especially a new growth or a sore that doesn't heal. Skin cancers don't all look the same. For example, the cancer may start as a small, smooth, shiny, pale, or waxy lump. Or it can appear as a firm red lump. Sometimes, the lump bleeds or develops a crust. Skin cancer can also start as a flat, red spot that is rough, dry, or scaly.

Both basal and squamous cell cancers are found mainly on areas of the skin that are exposed to the sun—the head, face, neck, hands, and arms. However, skin cancer can occur anywhere.

Actinic keratosis, which appears as rough, red or brown scaly patches on the skin, is known as a precancerous condition because it sometimes develops into squamous cell cancer. Like skin cancer, it usually appears on sun-exposed areas but can be found elsewhere.

Changes in the skin are not sure signs of cancer; however, it is important to see a doctor if any symptom lasts longer than two weeks. Don't wait for the area to hurt—skin cancers seldom cause pain.

Detection

The cure rate for skin cancer could be 100 percent if all skin cancers were brought to a doctor's attention before they had a chance to spread. Therefore, people should check themselves regularly for new growths or other changes in the skin. (See "How To Do a Skin Self-Exam" on page 574.) Any new, colored growths or any changes in growths that are already present should be reported to the doctor without delay.

Doctors should also look at the skin during routine physical exams. People who have already had skin cancer should be sure to have regular exams so that the doctor can check the skin—both the treated areas and other places where cancer may develop.

Diagnosis

Basal cell carcinoma and squamous cell carcinoma are generally diagnosed and treated in the same way. When an area of skin does not look normal, the doctor may remove all or part of the growth. This is called a biopsy. To check for cancer cells, the tissue is examined under a microscope by a pathologist or a dermatologist. A biopsy is the only sure way to tell if the problem is cancer.

Doctors generally divide skin cancer into two stages: local (affecting only the skin) or metastatic (spreading beyond the skin). Because skin cancer rarely spreads, a biopsy often is the only test needed to determine the stage. In cases where the growth is very large or has been present for a long time, the doctor will carefully check the lymph nodes in the area. In addition, the patient may need to have additional tests, such as special x-rays, to find out whether the cancer has spread to other parts of the body. Knowing the stage of a skin cancer helps the doctor plan the best treatment.

Treatment

In treating skin cancer, the doctor's main goal is to remove or destroy the cancer completely with as small a scar as possible. To plan the best treatment for each patient, the doctor considers the location and size of the cancer, the risk of scarring, and the person's age, general health, and medical history.

Treatment for skin cancer usually involves some type of surgery. In some cases, doctors suggest radiation therapy or chemotherapy. Sometimes a combination of these methods is used. In clinical trials (research studies with cancer patients), doctors are studying new treatments for skin cancer (see page 577). This is an important option for people with skin cancer.

Surgery

Many skin cancers can be cut from the skin quickly and easily. In fact, the cancer is sometimes completely removed at the time of the biopsy, and no further treatment is needed.

Curettage and Electrodesiccation. Doctors commonly use a type of surgery called curettage. After a local anesthetic numbs the area, the cancer is scooped out with a curette, an instrument with a sharp, spoon-shaped end. The area is also treated by electrodesiccation. An electric current from a special machine is used to control bleeding and kill any cancer cells remaining around the edge of the wound. Most patients develop a flat, white scar.

Mohs' Surgery. Mohs' technique is a special type of surgery used for skin cancer. Its purpose is to remove all of the cancerous tissue and as little of the healthy tissue as possible. It is especially helpful when the doctor is not sure of the shape and depth of the tumor. In addition, this method is used to remove large tumors, those in hard-to-treat places, and cancers that have recurred. The patient is given a local anesthetic, and the cancer is

Questions for Your Doctor

Skin cancer has a better prognosis, or outcome, than most other types of cancer. Although skin cancer is the most common type of cancer in this country, it accounts for much less than 1 percent of all cancer deaths. It is cured in 85 percent to 95 percent of all cases. Still, any diagnosis of cancer can be frightening, and it's natural to have concerns about medical tests, treatments, and doctors' bills.

Be sure to ask your doctor the following:

- What types of treatment are available?
- Are there any risks or side effects of treatment?
- Will there be a scar?
- Will I have to change my normal activities?
- How can I protect myself from getting skin cancer again?
- How often will I need a checkup?

Some patients become concerned that treatment may change their appearance, especially if the skin cancer is on their face. Patients should discuss this important concern with their doctor. And they may want to have a second opinion before treatment.

---

shaved off one thin layer at a time. Each layer is checked under a microscope until the entire tumor is removed. The degree of scarring depends on the location and size of the treated area. This method should be used only by doctors who are specially trained in this type of surgery.

Cryosurgery. Extreme cold may be used to treat precancerous skin conditions, such as actinic keratosis, as well as certain small skin cancers. In cryosurgery, liquid nitrogen is applied to the growth to freeze and kill the abnormal cells. After the area thaws, the dead tissue falls off. More than one freezing may be needed to remove the growth completely. Cryosurgery usually does not hurt, but patients may have pain and swelling after the area thaws. A white scar may form in the treated area.

Laser Therapy. Laser therapy uses a narrow beam of light to remove or destroy cancer cells. This approach is sometimes used for cancers that involve only the outer layer of skin.

Grafting. Sometimes, especially when a large cancer is removed, a skin graft is needed to close the wound and reduce the amount of scarring. For this procedure, the doctor takes a piece of healthy skin from another part of the body to replace the skin that was removed.

Radiation

Skin cancer responds well to radiation therapy (also called radiotherapy), which uses high-energy rays to damage cancer cells and stop them from growing. Doctors often use this treatment for cancers that occur in areas that are hard to treat with surgery. For example, radiation therapy might be used for cancers of the eyelid, the tip of the nose, or the ear. Several treatments may be needed to destroy all of the cancer cells. Radiation therapy may cause a rash or make the skin in the area dry or red. Changes in skin color and/or texture may develop after the treatment is over and may become more noticeable many years later.

Topical Chemotherapy

Topical chemotherapy is the use of anticancer drugs in a cream or lotion applied to the skin. Actinic keratosis can be treated effectively with the anticancer drug fluorouracil (also called 5-FU). This treatment is also useful for cancers limited to the top layer of skin.

The 5-FU is applied daily for several weeks. Intense inflammation is common during treatment, but scars usually do not occur.

In clinical trials (research studies with cancer patients), doctors are studying new treatments for skin cancer. For example, they are exploring photodynamic therapy, a treatment that destroys cancer cells with a combination of laser light and drugs that make the cells sensitive to light. Biological therapy (also called immunotherapy) is a form of treatment to improve the body's natural ability to fight cancer. Interferon and tumor necrosis factor are types of biological therapy under study for skin cancer.

Follow-up Care

Even though most skin cancers are cured, the disease can recur in the same place. Also, people who have been treated for skin cancer have a higher-than-average risk of developing a new cancer elsewhere on the skin. That's why it is so important for them to continue to examine themselves regularly, to visit their doctor for regular checkups, and to follow the doctor's instructions on how to reduce the risk of developing skin cancer again.

National Cancer Institute

Early in life, you probably fell asleep quickly and slept soundly. As you've grown older, you may find settling down to sleep more difficult; you may awaken more often and then take longer to go back to sleep. The honk of a car horn or the bark of a neighbor's dog may be enough to disturb your sleep. Maybe you find yourself dozing off more easily while watching TV or reading the newspaper.

Repeated sleep troubles—whether it is difficulty failing asleep at night or falling asleep often during the day—are not normal at any age.

Normal age-related changes sometimes hide sleep disorders that become more common as people grow older. Medical or psychiatric illnesses—especially those involving pain or depression—go hand-in-hand with sleep disorders. It is often difficult for healthcare professionals to tell which problem came first.

As you have aged, you've probably heard others say that people need less sleep as they grow older. Actually, older people still need about the same amount of sleep, but they are likely to sleep less in one stretch than they did when they were younger. As you age, your body becomes less skilled at maintaining sound sleep.

On the other hand, you may be finding it easier to nap during the day, since your schedule may be less busy. Recent research suggests that our bodies are designed for at least one afternoon nap a day. Only later in life, freed from the pressures of work and other heavy responsibilities, can we let ourselves do what comes naturally, nap.

Although older people spend about the same amount of time in dreaming sleep (also known as REM, or rapid eye movement sleep) as younger people do, they get less of the deeper stages of sleep they need and awaken more often. Studies show that some people over age 60 awaken briefly an amazing 150 times a night!

Young adults, on the other hand, wake up briefly about five times a night. Even though these awakenings usually aren't remembered the next morning, they may create the impression of restless sleep.

In addition, most people over 65 wake up at least once a night for a trip to the bathroom.

Common Causes

According to a panel of experts from the National Institutes of Health, more than half of all people age 65 or over experience disturbed sleep. Insomnia is the most common of these complaints.

Medication. The overuse of prescription drugs and over-the-counter medications by elderly people to aid sleep is of serious concern. While people over age 65 make up only about 13 percent of the American population, they take more than 30 percent of all prescription drugs and 40 percent of all sleeping pills. Studies show that a number of commonly used drugs may not work well in older people, and may even make sleep-related problems worse.

Not only is the sleep process less complete as we get older, but we are also more likely to develop chronic medical illnesses that can interfere with sleep. Asthma and other respiratory diseases, heart disease, and arthritis are notorious offenders. Pain, fever, itching, and coughing often contribute to insomnia. Many drugs used to treat these problems can disrupt sleep. If you take medication for any of the above problems, you should discuss its effects with your healthcare professional. Even a slight change in the timing or amount of your medication may bring about an improvement in your sleep. Paying close attention to your sleep habits and using relaxation techniques before going to bed may also help. Some people benefit by having sleeping pills on hand for occasional use.

Alcohol. Waking too early may represent a "rebound" from the use of alcohol at bedtime or from certain types of sleeping medications. Waking too early may also be the result of aging.

Depression. Difficulty falling asleep, sleep disruption, and waking up too early in the morning can be caused by depression, which is common as we grow older. For some people, depression begins gradually and progresses until "feeling blue" becomes a chronic way of life. Others focus on their poor sleep and become convinced that their lives would be better if they could just get a decent night's sleep. As poor sleep progresses, some people may stop eating regularly and may lose their usual interest and pleasure in the activities of daily life.

Loss of loved one. Loss of a loved one often triggers insomnia and depression. Surveys show that three quarters of newly widowed people report trouble sleeping a month after the death of their spouse. One year later, half report that their sleep problems continue.

Other causes and what you can do. While some older people may focus on trouble with sleep, others may have trouble with mood or performance during the day. Not all sleep disorders have symptoms that are obvious to individuals or to their families.

Trouble sleeping sometimes stems from simple, easily correctable causes, such as use of caffeine, eating heavy meals, or exercising too late in the day. Sleep problems can be the result of hospitalization, recovery after an operation, or travel. They may flare up during times of worry, or may smolder under constant stress.

In the quiet of the bedroom, some people find that their minds race and their worries overwhelm them. It can be helpful to set aside a time during the day for "worry time," to allow for the consideration of problems and the formulation of solutions. With worry out of the way, bedtime can be devoted to focusing on sleep.

Our schedules program our bodies to sleep and wake at the same time each day. if you still work but have irregular work hours, you may notice that it takes longer to adapt to schedule changes. It may also take you longer to adjust to the changes brought about by jet lag, especially when several time zones are crossed.

If you lead a quiet or restricted life, you may doze more during the day than you suspect. People with insomnia are often less active during the day than those who are better sleepers. A Gallup survey found that active retirees had fewer sleep problems than those who were less active. A general rule to follow is to try to confine your sleep to nighttime or nap time. Some people who feel extremely tired during the day don't suspect that anything is wrong with their sleep. They may find sleep unsatisfactory without being able to pinpoint the nature of their problem.

Specific Sleep Disorders

Sleep apnea: In this disorder, breathing stops for brief periods of time over and over again during sleep. Sleep apnea may cause problems while sleeping or awake. Sleep apnea disrupts sleep to varying degrees for an estimated one in four people over age 60.

In some cases, disturbed breathing is obvious to bedpartners because the sleeper snores loudly. Snoring reflects a partial blockage of the airway during sleep and generally increases with age. Although snoring may seem harmless, it can be a sign of a medical problem.

Driving with a sleep disorder may be as dangerous as driving while intoxicated. When researchers compared the reaction times between 80 people with blood alcohol levels at or above the legal driving limit and 113 patients with sleep apnea, the reaction times of the sleep apnea participants were the same or worse than the intoxicated ones.

Obstructive sleep apnea (OSA): A particular type of snoring—that caused by OSA—demands a visit to a health-care professional. Such snoring consists of loud snorts and gasping, followed by pauses in breathing due to a narrowing or closure (obstruction) of the throat. The breathing disturbance causes brief awakenings that disrupt sleep, but are not usually remembered in the morning.

Some people with OSA awaken hundreds of times a night, and feel excessively sleepy during the day. Sleep apnea may contribute to difficulty thinking and concentrating during waking hours, and may cause heart or lung disease if left untreated.

Weight loss and sleeping on one's side can be helpful in some cases. Severe OSA requires treatment. A device that uses air pressure to keep the throat open (CPAP) is the most effective treatment. Surgery and oral appliances can help some patients.

Central sleep apnea (CSA): People with CSA may or may not snore. When the central nervous system breathing processes fail to work properly, sleepers may sigh frequently or appear to breathe shallowly. In the morning, they may remember the frequent awakenings and complain of light and fragmented sleep. Acetazolamide, theophylline, CPAP, and hypnotics are some treatments for CSA. Some of these have side effects and should not be used without consulting with a healthcare professional.

Advanced sleep phase syndrome (ASPS): The tendency to be "early to bed and early to rise" increases as we grow older. Many people adapt successfully, but some people find that their bodies are ready for bed earlier than they desire, often well before 9 p.m.

ASPS can disrupt a person's social life, since it is frustrating to be awake early in the morning while others are still sleeping, and difficult to stay awake later in the evening when others are engaged in social activities.

People with ASPS often try various strategies to stay up later. Even if they are successful in pushing back bedtime, however, they may not be able to sleep any later since their body clocks still awaken them early. One solution sometimes used by healthcare professionals to treat patients with this condition involves exposure to outdoor light late in the afternoon and, when possible, in the early evening. Bright light affects the timing of the sleep/wake cycle and causes a delay in the feeling of sleepiness in the early evening. It also postpones early morning awakenings.

Periodic limb movement disorder and restless leg syndrome (PLMD): Perhaps half of all people age 65 and over experience twitching in the legs, and sometimes in the arms, during the night. These muscle jerks may occur infrequently or as often as once or twice each minute for an hour or two at a time. PLMD usually doesn't completely awaken the sleeper, but it does interfere with sound sleep.

S

When PLMD is mild, the person may be unaware of any impact on sleep or daytime functioning. When it is moderate, sleepers often complain of insomnia, reporting restless nights and waking to find the bedsheets in a tangle. When it is more severe, people often feel very sleepy during the day.

People who have PLMD during sleep may also experience restless legs when awake. This syndrome causes a peculiar crawling sensation in the calves or thighs, and occurs when the person is sitting or lying down. A variety of medications can ease this problem. A healthcare professional should determine the best medication or treatment.

REM sleep behavior disorder: Ordinarily the body is virtually paralyzed during dreaming sleep. This normal paralysis does not occur in people with REM sleep behavior disorder.

People with this disorder literally act out their dreams. They may crash into furniture, break windows, or fall down stairs, injuring themselves and sometimes others. Such forceful behavior challenges the traditional view of sleep as a time of rest.

Most sufferers are men over age 50, which suggests that age plays a role in this disorder. The drug clonazepam can improve sleep in people with this problem, and may eliminate the dream disturbances.

Wandering and other disturbances: Seventy percent of caregivers who decide to institutionalize an older person refer to sleep disturbances, wandering and confusion (sometimes called sundowning) as a factor in their decision. Most caregivers report that their loved one's problems disrupt their own sleep as well.

Two thirds of people living in long-term care facilities suffer sleep disturbances. In a nursing home or hospital, nighttime problems usually continue or increase, prompting widespread use of tranquilizing drugs. Unfortunately, these drugs can contribute to further confusion and an increased likelihood of falls.

When Should I Seek Professional Help?

Poor sleep for a month or longer and sleepiness during the day that interferes with normal activities may warrant a visit to a health-care professional. You may then be referred to a sleep specialist, who will conduct a medical history, a physical exam, and laboratory tests, such as those of hormone function, to help identify certain sleep disorders. The specialist may ask your bedpartner or other members of your household about your sleeping and waking behavior.

After an appointment is made at a sleep center, a sleep log of your sleeping and waking patterns may be needed before you are seen at the center.

You may also be asked to spend a night undergoing sleep monitoring. Monitoring is sometimes the only way to uncover a disorder that occurs during sleep. Before bedtime, a technician will place dime-sized sensors at various locations on your body to record brain waves, muscle activity, leg and arm movements, heart rhythms, breathing, and other body functions during sleep. These monitoring devices cause little or no discomfort, and do not hamper your movements during the night. Sleep specialists may also want to study your sleep during the day by asking you to nap at two-hour intervals. The rate at which people fall asleep on this test, known as the multiple sleep latency test, records the level of daytime sleepiness.

How to Sleep Well

These guidelines from the American Academy of Sleep Medicine can be used for a variety of sleep disorders. They will help most people sleep better. For more specific guidelines for your particular sleep disorder, consult your health-care professional.

- Maintain a regular wake time, even on days off work and on weekends.
- Try to go to bed only when you are drowsy.
- If you are not drowsy and are unable to fall asleep for about 20 minutes, leave your bedroom and engage in a quiet activity elsewhere. Do not permit yourself to fall asleep outside the bedroom. Return to bed when, and only when, you are sleepy. Repeat this process as often as necessary throughout the night.
- Use your bedroom only for sleep, sex and times of illness.
- Avoid napping during the daytime. If you nap, try to do so at the same time every day and for no more than one hour. Mid-afternoon (no later than 3:00 P.M.) is best for most people.
- Exercise regularly. Confine vigorous exercise to early hours, at least six hours before bedtime,

and do mild exercise at least four hours prior to bedtime.

- Keep a regular schedule. Regular times for meals, medications, chores, and other activities help keep the inner clock running smoothly.
- Establish relaxing pre-sleep rituals such as a warm bath, light bedtime snack, or ten minutes of reading.
- While a light snack before bedtime can help promote sound sleep, avoid large meals.
- Avoid ingestion of caffeine within six hours of bedtime.
- Don't drink alcohol when sleepy. Even a small dose of alcohol can have a potent effect when combined with tiredness.
- Avoid the use of nicotine close to bedtime or during the night.
- Sleeping pills should be used only conservatvely. Most doctors avoid prescribing sleeping pills for periods longer than three weeks.
- Do not drink alcohol while taking sleeping pills or other medications.

Should I Use Medications to Help Me Sleep?

Sleeping pills. As we grow older, our bodies break down drugs less efficiently than when we were younger. Because drugs stay in the body longer as we age, their effects may last longer, too.

For example, drowsiness—which is desirable at bedtime—is not welcome when driving a car the next day. Ideally, a sleeping pill should help you fall asleep faster and wake up less often, with no "hangover" the next day. The sleeping pills prescribed most often today—members of the benzodiazepine chemical family—come in both short- and long-acting forms. Short-acting drugs help

bring about sleep, but their effects usually wear off quickly. Long-acting drugs help maintain sleep through the night, but sometimes cause sleepiness the next day. Your healthcare professional will prescribe the type of drug and the particular dosage that is right for you. Short-acting drugs commonly used to aid sleep include triazolam and temazepam. A frequently prescribed long-acting drug is flurazepam.

A new class of medications has shown some usefulness in the geriatrics population. These medications include zolpidem and zaleplon. They are effective in inducing sleep in the elderly population, but may not necessarily promote longer or less interrupted sleep during the middle and late parts of the night.

Sleeping pills bought without a prescription—known as over-the-counter (OTC) drugs—get their drowsiness-inducing effect from antihistamines. Like prescription sleep aids, OTC drugs may cause sleepiness the next day, and require similar caution.

Warning: A complaint of insomnia sometimes signals disturbed breathing during sleep. It may be a mistake to use sleeping pills, since they tend to make interruptions in breathing occur more often and last longer. A person who complains of more than an occasional bad night should discuss this with a health-care professional.

Melatonin. Melatonin is a naturally occurring hormone that helps tell the brain when it is time to sleep. Some older people with insomnia may have lower than normal amounts of melatonin. Melatonin may be useful for treating some sleep problems but it has not been well tested. Melatonin has many other functions and its use can worsen some common medical conditions. Since melatonin does not help all people with insomnia and it can potentially cause harm, you should consult your health-care professional before using melatonin.

Medication problems. The use of inappropriate or multiple medications can cause problems. One 81-year-old woman, for example, who entered the hospital for a gallbladder operation, informed her physician that she had been taking barbiturates every night for years, and felt that "going to sleep" meant "taking a pill." The physician switched her to a safer benzodiazepine.

After the patient returned home, she became agitated and irritable, and another doctor prescribed a tranquilizer. Meanwhile, she continued a longtime habit of drinking an evening vodka martini. The result was confusion, forgetfulness, and depression. When her doctors recognized that her medications could be the cause of her problems, they stopped them. She quickly returned to her former alert self.

American Academy of Sleep Medicine

Smell and taste problems can have a big impact on our lives. Because these senses contribute substantially to our enjoyment of life, our desire to eat, and to be social, smell and taste disorders can be serious. When smell and taste are impaired, life loses some zest. We eat poorly, socialize less, and as a result, feel worse. Many older people experience this problem.

Smell and taste also warn us about dangers, such as fire, poisonous fumes, and spoiled food. Certain jobs require that these senses be accurate—chefs and firemen rely on taste and smell. One study estimates that more than 200,000 people visit a doctor with smell and taste disorders every year, but many more cases go unreported.

Loss of the sense of smell may be a sign of sinus disease, growths in the nasal passages, or, in rare circumstances, brain tumors.

How Do Smell and Taste Work?

Smell and taste belong to our chemical sensing system (chemosensation). The complicated processes of smelling and tasting begin when molecules released by the substances around us stimulate special nerve cells in the nose, mouth, or throat. These cells transmit messages to the brain, where specific smells or tastes are identified.

Olfactory (small nerve) cells are stimulated by the odors around us—the fragrance from a rose, the smell of bread baking. These nerve cells are found in a tiny patch of tissue high up in the nose, and they connect directly to the brain.
Gustatory (taste nerve) cells react to food or drink mixed with saliva and are clustered in the taste buds of the mouth and throat. Many of the small bumps that can be seen on the tongue contain taste buds. These surface cells send taste information to nearby nerve fibers, which send messages to the brain.

The common chemical sense, another chemosensory mechanism, contributes to our senses of smell and taste. In this system, thousands of free nerve endings—especially on the moist surfaces of the eyes, nose, mouth, and throat—identify sensations like the sting of ammonia, the coolness of menthol, and the "heat" of chili peppers.

Flavor
We can commonly identify four basic taste sensations:
- Sweet
- Sour
- Bitter
- Salty

Certain combinations of these tastes—along with texture, temperature, odor, and the sensations from the common chemical sense—produce a flavor. It is flavor that lets us know whether we are eating peanuts or caviar.

Many flavors are recognized mainly through the sense of smell. If you hold your nose while eating chocolate, for example, you will have trouble identifying the chocolate flavor, even though you can distinguish the food's sweetness or bitterness. This is because the familiar flavor of chocolate is sensed largely by odor. So is the well-known flavor of coffee. This is why a person who wishes to fully savor a delicious flavor (e.g., an expert chef testing his own creation) will exhale through his nose after each swallow.

Taste and smell cells are the only cells in the nervous system that are replaced when they become old or damaged. Scientists are examining this phenomenon while studying ways to replace other damaged nerve cells.

What Causes Smell and Taste Disorders?
Scientists have found that the sense of smell is most accurate between the ages of 30 and

Coping with a Severe Olfactory Deficit

Severe, irreversible olfactory impairment can lead to serious problems, including malnutrition and depression. Other potential problems include food poisoning because sufferers are insensitive to odors that may indicate spoilage; poor personal hygiene because body odors that prompt washing are not perceived; and a decline in personal safety because sufferers are oblivious to smoke, gas leaks, and other potential hazards. Incorporating the following lifestyle measures can help decrease these risks:

• Challenge taste buds with different spices and flavorings.
• Eat regular, planned meals.
• Dine with other people as often as possible.

• Label stored foods with a throw-away date; visually inspect foods for signs of spoilage.
• Install smoke and carbon monoxide detectors.
• Ask someone to inspect your home periodically for unusual odors.
• Wash often and on a regular schedule (at least twice a week).

People with olfactory impairment can continue to enjoy food by varying food textures and taste sensations (e.g., alternating crunchy and soft or sweet and sour); avoiding cigarettes, caffeine, and food that is very hot or very cold; eating slowly; displaying food attractively; and brushing teeth after meals rather than before, since toothpaste can mask food flavors. *The Editors*

60 years. It begins to decline after age 60, and a large proportion of elderly people lose their smelling ability. Women of all ages are generally more accurate than men in identifying odors.

Some people are born with a poor sense of smell or taste. Upper respiratory infections are blamed for some losses, and injury to the head can also cause smell or taste problems.

Loss of smell and taste may result from polyps in the nasal or sinus cavities, hormonal disturbances, or dental problems. They can also be caused by prolonged exposure to certain chemicals such as insecticides and by some medicines.

Tobacco smoking is the most concentrated form of pollution that most people will ever be exposed to. It impairs the ability to identify odors and diminishes the sense of taste. Quitting smoking improves the smell function.

Radiation therapy patients with cancers of the head and neck later complain of lost smell and taste. These senses can also be lost in the course of some diseases that affect the nervous system.

Patients who have lost their larynx (voice box) commonly complain of poor ability to smell and taste. Laryngectomy patients can use a special "bypass" tube to breathe through the nose again. The enhanced air flow through the nose helps smell and taste sensation to be reestablished.

How Are Smell and Taste Disorders Diagnosed?
The extent of loss of smell or taste can be tested using the lowest concentration of a chemical that a person can detect and recognize. A patient may also be asked to compare the smells or tastes of different chemicals, or how the intensities of smells or tastes grow when a chemical concentration is increased.

• **Smell.** Scientists have developed an easily administered "scratch-and-sniff" test to evaluate the sense of smell.

- **Taste.** Patients react to different chemical concentrations in taste testing; this may involve a simple "sip, spit, and rinse" test, or chemicals may be applied directly to specific areas of the tongue.

Can Smell and Taste Disorders Be Treated?

Sometimes a certain medication is the cause of smell or taste disorders, and improvement occurs when that medicine is stopped or changed. Although certain medications can cause chemosensory problems, others—particularly anti-allergy drugs—seem to improve the senses of taste and smell. Some patients, notably those with serious respiratory infections or seasonal allergies, regain their smell or taste simply by waiting for their illness to run its course. In many cases, nasal obstructions, such as polyps, can be removed to restore airflow to the receptor area and can correct the loss of smell and taste. Occasionally, chemosenses return to normal just as spontaneously as they disappeared.

What Can I Do to Help Myself?

If you experience a smell or taste problem, try to identify and record the circumstances surrounding it. When did you first become aware of it? Did you have a "cold" or "flu" then? A head injury? Were you exposed to air pollutants, pollens, danders, or dust to which you might be allergic? Is this a recurring problem? Does it come in any special season, like hayfever time?

Bring all this information with you when you visit a physician who deals with diseases of the nose and throat (an otolaryngologist-head and neck surgeon). Proper diagnosis by a trained professional can provide reassurance that your illness is not imaginary. You may even be surprised by the results. For example, what you may think is a taste problem could actually be a smell problem, because much of what you think you taste you really smell.

Diagnosis may also lead to treatment of an underlying cause for the disturbance. Many types of smell and taste disorders are reversible. But, if yours is not, it is important to remember that you are not alone. Thousands of other patients have faced the same situation.

American Academy of Otolaryngology—Head and Neck Surgery

The stomach is part of the digestive system. It is located in the upper abdomen, under the ribs. The upper part of the stomach connects to the esophagus, and the lower part leads into the small intestine.

Stomach cancer (or gastric cancer) can develop in any part of the stomach and may spread throughout the stomach and to other organs. It may grow along the stomach wall into the esophagus or small intestine.

It also may extend through the stomach wall and spread to nearby lymph nodes and to organs such as the liver, pancreas, and colon. Stomach cancer also may spread to distant organs, such as the lungs, the lymph nodes above the collar bone, and the ovaries.

When cancer spreads to another part of the body, the new tumor has the same kind of abnormal cells and the same name as the primary tumor. For example, if stomach cancer spreads to the liver, the cancer cells in the liver are stomach cancer cells. The disease is metastatic stomach cancer (it is not liver cancer). However, when stomach cancer spreads to an ovary, the tumor in the ovary is called a Krukenberg tumor. (This tumor, named for a doctor, is not a different disease; it is metastatic stomach cancer. The cancer cells in a Krukenberg tumor are stomach cancer cells, the same as the cancer cells in the primary tumor.)

Causes

The stomach cancer rate in the United States and the number of deaths from this disease have gone down dramatically over the past 60 years. Still, stomach cancer is a serious disease, and scientists all over the world are trying to learn more about what causes this disease and how to prevent it. At this time, doctors cannot explain why one person gets stomach cancer and another does not. They do know, however, that stomach cancer is not contagious; no one can "catch" cancer from another person.

Researchers have learned that some people are more likely than others to develop stomach cancer. The disease is found most often in people over age 55. It affects men twice as often as women, and is more common in African Americans than in whites. Also, stomach cancer is more common in some parts of the world—such as Japan, Korea, parts of Eastern Europe, and Latin America—than in the United States. People in these areas eat many foods that are preserved by drying, smoking, salting, or pickling. Scientists believe that eating foods preserved in these ways may play a role in the development of stomach cancer. On the other hand, fresh foods (especially fresh fruits and vegetables and properly frozen or refrigerated fresh foods) may protect against this disease.

Stomach ulcers do not appear to increase a person's risk of getting stomach cancer. However, some studies suggest that a type of bacteria, Helicobacter pylori, which may cause stomach inflammation and ulcers, may be an important risk factor for this disease. Also, research shows that people who have had stomach surgery or have pernicious anemia, achlorhydria, or gastric atrophy (which generally result in lower than normal amounts of digestive juices) have an increased risk of stomach cancer.

Exposure to certain dusts and fumes in the workplace has been linked to a higher than average risk of stomach cancer. Also, some scientists believe smoking may increase stomach cancer risk.

People who think they might be at risk for stomach cancer should discuss this concern with their doctor. The doctor can suggest an appropriate schedule of checkups so that, if

S

cancer appears, it can be detected as early as possible.

Symptoms

Stomach cancer can be hard to find early. Often there are no symptoms in the early stages and, in many cases, the cancer has spread before it is found. When symptoms do occur, they are often so vague that the person ignores them. Stomach cancer can cause the following:

- Indigestion or a burning sensation
- Discomfort or pain in the abdomen
- Nausea and vomiting
- Diarrhea or constipation
- Bloating of the stomach after meals
- Loss of appetite
- Weakness and fatigue
- Bleeding (vomiting blood or having blood in the stool)

Any of these symptoms may be caused by cancer or by other, less serious health problems, such as a stomach virus or an ulcer. Only a doctor can tell the cause. People who have any of these symptoms should see their doctor. They may be referred to a gastroenterologist, a doctor who specializes in diagnosing and treating digestive problems. These doctors are sometimes called gastrointestinal (or GI) specialists.

Diagnosis

To find the cause of symptoms, the doctor asks about the patient's medical history, does a physical exam, and may order laboratory studies. The patient may also have one or all of the following exams:

Fecal occult blood test—a check for hidden (occult) blood in the stool. This test is done by placing a small amount of stool on a plastic slide or on special paper. It may be tested in the doctor's office or sent to a laboratory. This test is done because stomach cancer sometimes causes bleeding that cannot be seen. However, noncancerous conditions also may cause bleeding, so having blood in the stool does not necessarily mean that a person has cancer.

Upper GI series—x-rays of the esophagus and stomach (the upper gastrointestinal, or GI, tract). The x-rays are taken after the patient drinks a barium solution, a thick, chalky liquid. (This test is sometimes called a barium swallow.) The barium outlines the stomach on the x-rays, helping the doctor find tumors or other abnormal areas. During the test, the doctor may pump air into the stomach to make small tumors easier to see.

Endoscopy—an exam of the esophagus and stomach using a thin, lighted tube called a gastroscope, which is passed through the mouth and esophagus to the stomach. The patient's throat is sprayed with a local anesthetic to reduce discomfort and gagging. Patients also may receive medicine to relax them. Through the gastroscope, the doctor can look directly at the inside of the stomach. If an abnormal area is found, the doctor can remove some tissue through the gastroscope. Another doctor, a pathologist, examines the tissue under a microscope to check for cancer cells. This procedure—removing tissue and examining it under a microscope—is called a biopsy. A biopsy is the only sure way to know whether cancer cells are present.

Staging

If the pathologist finds cancer cells in the tissue sample, the patient's doctor needs to know the stage, or extent, of the disease. Staging exams and tests help the doctor find out whether the cancer has spread and, if so, what parts of the body are affected. Because stomach cancer can spread to the liver, the pancreas, and other organs near the stomach as well as to the lungs, the doctor may order a CT (or CAT) scan, an ultrasound exam, or other tests to check these areas.

Staging may not be complete until after surgery. The surgeon removes nearby lymph nodes and may take samples of tissue from other areas in the abdomen. All of these samples are examined by a pathologist to check for cancer cells. Decisions about treatment after surgery depend on these findings.

Treatment

The doctor develops a treatment plan to fit each patient's needs. Treatment for stomach cancer depends on the size, location, and extent of the tumor; the stage of the disease; the patient's general health; and other factors.

Cancer of the stomach is difficult to cure unless it is found in an early stage (before it has begun to spread). Unfortunately, because early stomach cancer causes few symptoms, the disease is usually advanced when the diagnosis is made. However, advanced stomach cancer can be treated and the symptoms can be relieved. Treatment for stomach cancer may include surgery, chemotherapy, and/or radiation therapy. A patient may have one form of treatment or a combination of treatments. New treatment approaches such as biological therapy and improved ways of using current methods are being studied in clinical trials. When talking about treatment choices, the patient may want to ask about taking part in a research study. Such studies are designed to improve cancer treatment. (More information about clinical trials is in the text box on page 181).

Surgery is the most common treatment for stomach cancer. The operation is called gastrectomy. The surgeon removes part (subtotal or partial gastrectomy) or all (total gastrectomy) of the stomach, as well as some of the tissue around the stomach. After a subtotal gastrectomy, the doctor connects the remaining part of the stomach to the esophagus or the small intestine. After a total gastrectomy, the doctor connects the esophagus directly to the small intestine. Because cancer can spread through the lymphatic system, lymph nodes near the tumor are often removed during surgery so that the pathologist can check them for cancer cells. If cancer cells are in the lymph nodes, the disease may have spread to other parts of the body.

Chemotherapy is the use of drugs to kill cancer cells. This type of treatment is called systemic therapy because the drugs enter the bloodstream and travel through the body.

Clinical trials are in progress to find the best ways to use chemotherapy to treat stomach cancer. Scientists are exploring the benefits of giving chemotherapy before surgery to shrink the tumor, or as adjuvant therapy after surgery to destroy remaining cancer cells. Combination treatment with chemotherapy and radiation therapy is also under study. Doctors are testing a treatment in which anticancer drugs are put directly into the abdomen (intraperitoneal chemotherapy). Chemotherapy also is being studied as a treatment for cancer that has spread, and as a way to relieve symptoms of the disease.

Most anticancer drugs are given by injection; some are taken by mouth. The doctor may use one drug or a combination of drugs. Chemotherapy is given in cycles: a treatment period followed by a recovery period, then another treatment, and so on. Usually a person receives chemotherapy as an outpatient (at the hospital, at the doctor's office, or at home). However, depending on which drugs are given and the patient's general health, a short hospital stay may be needed.

Radiation therapy (also called radiotherapy) is the use of high-energy rays to damage cancer cells and stop them from growing. Like surgery, it is local therapy; the radiation can affect cancer cells only in the treated area. Radiation therapy is sometimes given after surgery to destroy cancer cells that may remain in the area. Researchers are conducting clinical trials to find out whether it is helpful to give radiation therapy during surgery (intraoperative radiation therapy). Radiation therapy may also be used to relieve pain or blockage.

The patient goes to the hospital or clinic each day for radiation therapy. Usually treatments are given five days a week for five to six weeks.

Biological therapy (also called immunotherapy) is a form of treatment that helps the body's immune system attack and destroy cancer cells; it may also help the body recover from some of the side effects of treatment. In clinical trials, doctors are studying biological therapy in combination with other treatments to try to prevent a recurrence of stomach cancer. In another use of biological therapy, patients who have low blood cell counts during or after chemotherapy may receive colony-stimulating factors to help restore the blood cell levels. Patients may need to stay in the hospital while receiving some types of biological therapy.

Side Effects of Treatment

It is hard to limit the effects of therapy so that only cancer cells are removed or destroyed. Because healthy cells and tissues also may be damaged, treatment can cause unpleasant side effects.

The side effects of cancer treatment are different for each person, and they may even be different from one treatment to the next. Doctors try to plan treatment in ways that keep side effects to a minimum; they can help with any problems that occur. For this reason, it is very important to let the doctor know about any problems during or after treatment.

Surgery

Gastrectomy is major surgery. For a period of time after the surgery, the person's activities are limited to allow healing to take place. For the first few days after surgery, the patient is fed intravenously (through a vein). Within several days, most patients are ready for liquids, followed by soft, then solid, foods. Those who have had their entire stomach removed cannot absorb vitamin B12, which is necessary for healthy blood and nerves, so they need regular injections of this vitamin. Patients may have temporary or permanent difficulty digesting certain foods, and they may need to change their diet. Some gastrectomy patients will need to follow a special diet for a few weeks or months, while others will need to do so permanently. The doctor or a dietitian (a nutrition specialist) will explain any necessary dietary changes.

Some gastrectomy patients have cramps, nausea, diarrhea, and dizziness shortly after eating because food and liquid enter the small intestine too quickly. This group of symptoms is called the dumping syndrome. Foods containing high amounts of sugar often make the symptoms worse. The dumping syndrome can be treated by changing the patient's diet. Doctors often advise patients to eat several small meals throughout the day, to avoid foods that contain sugar, and to eat foods high in protein. To reduce the amount of fluid that enters the small intestine, patients are usually encouraged not to drink at mealtimes. Medicine also can help control the dumping syndrome. Symptoms usually disappear in 3 to 12 months, but they may be permanent.

Following gastrectomy, bile in the small intestine may back up into the remaining part of the stomach or into the esophagus, causing the symptoms of an upset stomach. The patient's doctor may prescribe medicine or suggest over-the-counter products to control such symptoms.

Chemotherapy

The side effects of chemotherapy depend mainly on the drugs the patient receives. As with any other type of treatment, side effects also vary from person to person. In general, anticancer drugs affect cells that divide rapidly. These include blood cells, which fight infection, help the blood to clot, or carry oxygen to all parts of the body. When blood cells are affected by anticancer drugs, patients are more likely to get infections, may bruise or bleed easily, and may have less energy. Cells in hair roots and cells that line the digestive tract also divide rapidly. As a result of chemotherapy, patients may have side effects such as loss of appetite, nausea, vomiting, hair loss, or mouth sores. For some patients, the doctor may prescribe medicine to help with side effects, especially with nausea and vomiting. These effects usually go away gradually during the recovery period between treatments or after the treatments stop.

Radiation Therapy

Patients who receive radiation to the abdomen may have nausea, vomiting, and diarrhea. The doctor can prescribe medicine or suggest dietary changes to relieve these problems. The skin in the treated area may become red, dry, tender, and itchy. Patients should avoid wearing clothes that rub; loose-fitting cotton clothes are usually best. It is important for patients to take good care of their skin during treatment, but they should not use lotions or creams without the doctor's advice.

Patients are likely to become very tired during radiation therapy, especially in the later weeks of treatment. Resting is important, but doctors usually advise patients to try to stay as active as they can.

Biological Therapy

The side effects of biological therapy vary with the type of treatment. Some cause flu-like symptoms, such as chills, fever, weakness, nausea, vomiting, and diarrhea. Patients sometimes get a rash, and they may bruise or bleed easily. These problems may be severe, and patients may need to stay in the hospital during treatment.

Nutrition

It is sometimes difficult for patients who have been treated for stomach cancer to eat well. Cancer often causes loss of appetite, and people may not feel like eating when they are uncomfortable or tired. It is hard for patients to eat when they have nausea, vomiting, mouth sores, or the dumping syndrome. Patients who have had stomach surgery are likely to feel full after eating only a small amount of food. For some patients, the taste of food changes. Still, good nutrition is important. Eating well means getting enough calories and protein to help prevent weight loss, regain strength, and rebuild normal tissues.

Doctors, nurses, and dietitians can offer advice for healthy eating during and after cancer treatment.

National Cancer Institute

E ach year about 700,000 people in the United States suffer a new or recurrent stroke—a "brain attack" that damages part of the brain when blood vessels in the brain either burst or become blocked, depriving brain cells of vital oxygen and nutrients. In addition to being the third-leading cause of death of American adults (behind cardiovascular disease and cancer), stroke is a major cause of disability. About 537,000 Americans survive a stroke each year, and stroke survivors total some 4.7 million; most have some degree of lasting impairment, such as speech difficulties, visual problems, and paralysis.

Over the past two decades, the number of strokes per 100,000 people has fallen—a decline that is probably the result of earlier diagnosis of risk factors (such as hypertension) and more aggressive treatment of them. The news from stroke researchers is likewise encouraging. In addition to alteplase (Activase)—the first drug capable of halting a stroke in progress if administered soon enough after onset—other medications may soon be available for emergency treatment of a stroke. Other forms of treatment are also under investigation, as are new approaches to rehabilitation.

Still, the best weapon against stroke remains prevention. More than half of all strokes could be averted if people took the appropriate steps to control risk factors.

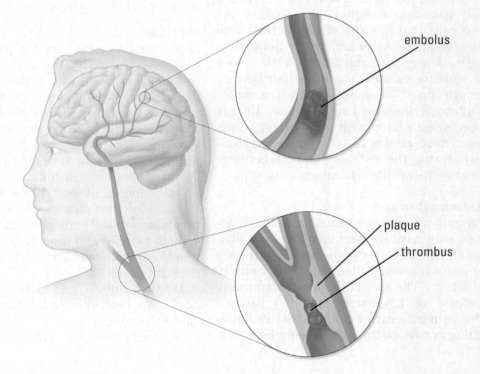

An ischemic stroke occurs when a blockage interrupts blood supply to the brain. The blockage may be caused either by an embolus (a blood clot that travels to the brain from an outside artery) or a thrombus (a clot that forms in an artery, often narrowed by atherosclerotic plaque, leading to or within the brain).

Types of Stroke

Strokes occur when an artery supplying blood to a portion of the brain becomes blocked or ruptures, so that neurons (nerve cells) in affected area are starved of the oxygen and nutrients normally provided by blood. Although the brain performs no physical functions and accounts for only 2 percent of the body's total weight, it consumes about 25 percent of the oxygen and 70 percent of the glucose (sugar) in the bloodstream.

Since neurons do not regenerate once they are destroyed, nerve damage due to a stroke is usually permanent. Despite the death of neurons, however, some improvement usually occurs over time as other neurons are recruited to take over the functions of those that were lost.

There are two basic types of stroke, ischemic and hemorrhagic. Within each of these two major categories of stroke are several subcategories. Proper diagnosis of the specific type of stroke is essential for determining the right course of treatment.

Ischemic Strokes

Approximately 88 percent of all strokes are ischemic. An ischemic stroke occurs when blood flow is interrupted by blockage of an artery supplying blood to the brain. This situation can arise in one of two ways. A blood clot, or thrombus, can form in an artery leading to or within the brain, a condition called cerebral thrombosis. These blood clots tend to develop in arteries already narrowed by atherosclerotic plaques—the same fatty deposits that cause coronary heart disease (CHD).

Less frequently, a blood clot from the heart or a fragment of atherosclerotic plaque in an artery outside of the brain— typically in the aorta or carotid artery in the neck—breaks loose and travels through the bloodstream (embolus) until it lodges in a smaller artery in the brain. Such an event is called a cerebral embolism.

When an ischemic stroke occurs, neurons are damaged not only by the lack of oxygen, but also by a powerful chain of chemical reactions known as the ischemic (or glutamate) cascade, which leads to a buildup of toxins that further compounds cell destruction. The large accumulation of glutamate from injured neurons excites other neurons to release excessive amounts of nitric oxide. The combination of high levels of both substances results in further nerve cell damage. The degree and duration of the ischemic event determine whether the brain suffers only temporary impairment, irreversible injury to a few highly vulnerable neurons, or extensive neurological damage.

Transient ischemic attacks (TIAs). TIAs are short-lived (lasting less than 24 hours) neurological deficits due to ischemia. Most episodes subside within 5 to 20 minutes, and they rarely continue for more than a few hours. By definition, TIAs do not result in permanent neurological deficits and are almost never painful. Hence, they tend to be ignored. TIAs are, however, an important warning sign of an impending stroke and thus warrant prompt medical attention. Patients may have repetitive spells of TIAs days or weeks before a stroke, and one third of those who experience a TIA have a stroke within five years.

Recognition of the cause of TIAs may help to prevent a stroke and its complications. For example, if carotid stenosis (a narrowing of one of the arteries supplying the brain) is detected, an endarterectomy can be performed to remove the blockage (see the text box on page 596).

Hemorrhagic Strokes

Accounting for approximately 12 percent of all strokes, hemorrhagic strokes occur when

S

an artery in the brain suddenly bursts and blood leaks out into the surrounding tissue. The bleeding can take place either into the brain itself (intracerebral hemorrhage) or into the space between the brain and the skull (subarachnoid hemorrhage).

Damage occurs in two ways. First, the blood supply is cut off to the parts of the brain beyond the site of the arterial rupture (comparable to ischemic strokes). Second—and posing the greatest danger—the escaped blood forms a mass that, within the rigid skull, exerts excessive pressure on the brain. Blood continues to leak until it coagulates, or until the pressure inside the skull is equal to the blood pressure in the ruptured artery. Massive hemorrhages are usually fatal; the death rate from an intracerebral hemorrhage is as high as 50 percent in some studies.

Aneurysms—blood-filled pouches ballooning out from weak spots in a blood vessel wall—cause many hemorrhagic strokes. Brain hemorrhage may also result from a congenital blood vessel defect known as an arteriovenous malformation, which is a complex, tangled web of arteries and veins. The walls of these abnormal blood vessels tend to be so thin that surges in blood pressure, or simply the wear and tear of normal blood circulation, may eventually cause a a blood vessel to rupture and bleed into the brain. Some people with an arteriovenous malformation experience seizures, usually during their 20s and 30s.

Symptoms of Stroke

Like a heart attack, a stroke is an emergency that requires immediate medical attention. Yet, while most people can recognize the characteristic symptoms of a heart attack, many are unaware of the symptoms of a stroke. Furthermore, symptoms of a TIA (see page 593) may appear suddenly

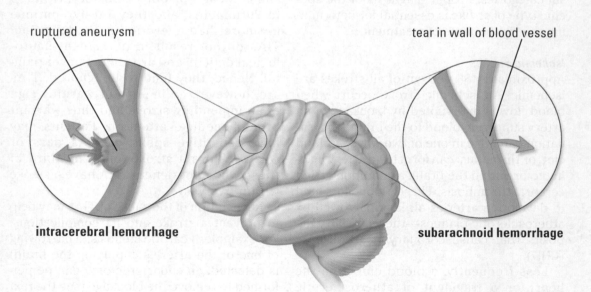

ruptured aneurysm

tear in wall of blood vessel

intracerebral hemorrhage

subarachnoid hemorrhage

A hemorrhagic stroke occurs when an artery in the brain breaks open and leaks blood into the brain itself (intracerebral hemorrhage) or into the space between the brain and the skull (subarachnoid hemorrhage).

Warning Signs and Actions

The following symptoms could indicate that a stroke is under way:

- Sudden numbness, weakness, or paralysis in the face or limbs (often on one side of the body
- Sudden loss, blurring, or dimness of vision
- Mental confusion, loss of memory, loss of consciousness, or unexplained drowsiness
- Slurred speech, loss of speech, or problem understanding others
- Sudden, severe headache
- Unexplained dizziness, lack of coordination, or fall
- Nausea and vomiting, especially when accompanied by any of the previous symptoms

Actions to take: It's common for people to deny the possibility that a stroke is occurring. Don't hesitate to take prompt action. Call or have someone call 911 for an ambulance.

The person suffering the stroke should be made comfortable while waiting for the ambulance and should not drink anything other than water. If an ambulance is not available, a friend or family member should drive the patient to the hospital. The patient should never drive himself or herself. At the hospital, be sure to inform hospital personnel if the patient has any known medical conditions or is taking any medications.

and subside so quickly that sufferers get the false impression that there is no serious problem.

Anyone who experiences the sudden onset and persistence of any of the symptoms of stroke (see the text box above) must call 911 for an ambulance or go straight to the hospital. Rapid diagnosis and treatment may minimize damage to brain tissue and save lives.

Long-Term Effects of a Stroke

In addition to the initial emergency symptoms, strokes generally produce lasting neurological deficits that may impair a patient's senses, motor skills, behavior, language ability, memory, or thought processes, depending on which portions of the brain are damaged (as well as on the type and severity of the stroke). A stroke may produce other long-term complications, including seizures, impaired concentration, poor judgment, erratic sleep cycles, loss of libido, emotional instability, and depression.

Prevention

A number of factors contribute to the overall chance of having a stroke. Some risk factors cannot be modified. These include age (the incidence of stroke more than doubles with each successive decade after age 55); gender (overall, the incidence of stroke is 25 percent higher in men than in women); and race (African Americans have about twice as high a risk of death and disability from a stroke as whites, and Hispanics are also at higher risk). Other risk factors are family history and a prior history of stroke: Stroke survivors are at substantially higher risk for a subsequent stroke.

Fortunately, though, a number of risk factors can be changed, and controlling or treating them through lifestyle measures or medical therapy is the best way to reduce the risk of stroke. The more of these factors you control, the lower your risk.

Medical Therapy for Stroke Prevention

Both medications and surgical procedures are used to prevent strokes in patients with certain risk factors.

Medications. Abnormal blood clotting can lead to ischemic stroke. Fortunately, two types of anti-clotting drugs may help prevent abnormal clot formation in people with atrial fibrillation or a history of prior stroke. Antiplatelet drugs (such as aspirin) reduce clot formation by inhibiting the aggregation of blood platelets. Anticoagulants (such as warfarin and heparin), which inhibit clot formation at a different stage in the clotting process, are the most effective agents for preventing embolic strokes.

Surgery. In people who have severe blockages in one or both carotid arteries (the major arteries in the neck), a surgical procedure called carotid endarterectomy can clear the arteries. This operation significantly reduces the risk of stroke and TIA in some patients. Because the procedure is associated with significant risks, it should be performed only by an experienced surgeon at a medical center known to have a complication rate of no more than 3 percent to 4 percent. Getting a second opinion before undergoing surgery is also strongly recommended.

Another method for opening a partially blocked carotid artery is angioplasty (see page 91), a procedure first used to open coronary arteries in people with coronary heart disease. Angioplasty may also involve implanting a stent—a flexible metal tube placed inside a clogged artery to keep it propped open. Thus far, stent implantation has had mixed results and some experts have raised concerns about it, especially because of a risk of blood clots. Angioplasty may be a good option for high-risk patients who are unable to undergo carotid endarterectomy, which is a more extensive surgical procedure.

Blood pressure. High blood pressure, the single greatest risk factor for stroke, is estimated to play a role in about 70% of all ischemic and hemorrhagic strokes. Elevations in either systolic or diastolic blood pressure increase the risk of stroke in both men and women and in people of all ages. Indeed, stroke risk is about four times greater in those with a blood pressure of 160/95 mm Hg or above than in those with a blood pressure of 140/90 mm Hg or below. A recent meta-analysis concluded that the risk of stroke was increased 10 to 12 times in people with a diastolic blood pressure of 105 mm Hg or higher compared with those with a diastolic pressure of less than 76 mm Hg.

Smoking. Cigarette smokers have a 50 percent higher risk of stroke than nonsmokers. The more cigarettes smoked, the greater the risk. Fortunately, within five years of quitting, the risk declines to that of a nonsmoker.

Diabetes. People with diabetes have a threefold higher risk of ischemic stroke than the general population. Women with diabetes are at greater risk than men. Evidence is growing that controlling blood sugar may lower stroke risk. Diabetes does not appear to increase the risk of hemorrhagic strokes.

Circulatory disorders. Strokes can be caused by any number of problems that interfere with the supply of blood to the brain. These include, most significantly, blockage of the carotid arteries (carotid artery stenosis), but also coronary heart disease, valvular heart disease, heart failure, and atrial fibrillation. Treatment of such problems with medication or surgery may help prevent strokes.

Alcohol. One to two alcoholic drinks daily is associated with a modest decline in the risk for ischemic stroke—though even this moderate level of consumption may raise the risk of hemorrhagic stroke. Habitually drinking larger amounts doubles the risk of stroke by producing cardiac arrhythmias, raising blood pressure, and promoting clot formation.

Oral contraceptives and hormone replacement therapy. The low-dose oral contraceptives used today are associated with a risk of stroke, but the risk is small compared to older, high-dose estrogen oral contraceptives.

Hormone replacement therapy (HRT) also increases stroke risk. Therefore, women taking hormone replacement therapy—either estrogen plus progestin or estrogen alone—for relief of menopausal symptoms should do so for the shortest time possible and at the smallest effective dose.

Abnormal lipid levels. High total and low-density lipoprotein (LDL, or "bad") cholesterol, elevated triglycerides, and low HDL ("good") cholesterol contribute to atherosclerosis and they are important risk factors for stroke as well. Reduction of total cholesterol, LDL cholesterol, and triglyceride levels using statin drugs substantially reduces the risk of ischemic stroke.

Sedentary lifestyle. Studies consistently show that regular physical activity lowers the risk of both ischemic and hemorrhagic stroke, possibly by reducing other stroke risk factors, such as obesity and hypertension. In general, people who are physically inactive are almost three times as likely to suffer a stroke than people who exercise regularly.

Obesity. Being extremely overweight (see page 458) increases the risk of fatal and non-fatal stroke by 50 to 100 percent. Although obesity is associated with other risk factors for stroke, such as hypertension and diabetes, it may also be an independent risk factor for stroke.

Diagnosis

When a patient arrives at an emergency room with symptoms of a stroke, time is of the essence: Fast action can minimize neurological damage and even mean the difference between life and death. The attending doctor must rule out other potential causes of the symptoms (such as seizure, brain tumor, diabetic coma, low blood sugar, or migraine headache) and determine the type of stroke (ischemic or hemorrhagic). It is also important to identify what caused the stroke and which part or parts of the brain are affected.

The patient will undergo both a general and a neurological examination to determine how the brain has been affected. Blood tests and urinalysis can also help to identify conditions that can mimic or cause a stroke.

To diagnose the type of stroke, physicians rely on imaging of brain and blood vessels. The standard procedure is a computer-assisted tomography (CT or CAT) scan, which can help to pinpoint the location and extent of a blockage, narrowing, or bleeding. Other diagnostic techniques include magnetic resonance imaging (MRI), ultrasound scanning, and cerebral angiography. This last technique, which entails the injection of a dye into the blood stream, provides more detailed information than the other imaging techniques. Because it is an invasive technique with a risk of complications, however, it is used only when noninvasive methods prove inadequate. Newer noninvasive techniques that utilize dyes to obtain improved images of blood vessels are being developed and tested.

S

Ischemic strokes may show up on an MRI scan as early as 6 to 12 hours after symptom onset. New developments in MRI technology may allow even earlier detection and the possibility of predicting the size, severity, and reversibility of neurological deficits. For instance, diffusion-weighted MRI can detect injury from an ischemic stroke within one to two hours based on alterations in water movement in the brain; perfusion-weighted MRI can show the degree of blood flow to areas in the brain.on.Combining diffusion and perfusion imaging may hold the key to determining which patients might benefit from thrombolytic therapy after a stroke.

Treatment

Emergency care for a stroke requires hospitalization, where life support systems are available, if needed, to maintain respiration and cardiac function. Specific avenues of treatment ultimately depend on whether the stroke is ischemic or hemorrhagic. In ischemic stroke, the primary goal is to restore or at least improve blood flow to the brain; the goal in hemorrhagic stroke is to relieve pressure on the brain and arrest bleeding.

Treatment of Ischemic Stroke
Careful monitoring and control of blood pressure are essential after a stroke. Following ischemic stroke, elevated pressure is generally acceptable, since it promotes the flow of blood through the partially blocked arteries to reach jeopardized regions of the brain. The exception is when blood pressure is so high that it may damage the brain, heart, or kidneys. In such cases, blood pressure should be lowered slowly. Otherwise, efforts are aimed at preventing low blood pressure (hypotension), which can limit the amount of blood reaching the brain. Body temperature must also be carefully monitored and

controlled, since a fever can compound damage to the brain.

Medications. Until recently, doctors could do little to intervene while an ischemic stroke was in progress. However, with the FDA approval of the first emergency stroke drug, alteplase (Activase), doctors now have a specific course of action to follow for an ischemic stroke. Alteplase—a member of a drug class known as thrombolytic ("clot-busting") agents—is a genetically engineered copy of the naturally occurring tissue-type plasminogen activator (tPA) that has been widely used to treat heart attacks. Prompt administration of alteplase can dissolve a clot that is blocking blood flow to the heart muscle, thereby preventing extensive tissue damage. Some (but not all) studies have shown similar results for strokes, even though thrombolytic drugs are associated with an increased risk of cerebral hemorrhage (a side effect in about 6 percent of patients).

Early treatment is essential. According to American Heart Association guidelines, alteplase should only be used when treatment starts within three hours of the onset of an ischemic stroke. If too much time has elapsed, cerebral bleeding may be more likely and it may be too late to prevent brain damage. Beforehand, all patients must have a neurological examination and a CT scan that is evaluated by an expert to ensure they are appropriate candidates.

Only hospitals equipped for immediate treatment of excessive bleeding should administer alteplase. And it cannot be used in certain individuals, including those who have a hemorrhagic stroke, had another stroke within the previous three months, have blood pressure greater than 185/110 mm Hg, or are currently taking the anticoagulant drugs heparin or warfarin (however, aspirin users are eligible if they fit all other criteria).

Rehabilitation for Stroke

The process of rehabilitation after a stroke starts almost immediately after admission to the hospital and often continues for at least one to two months afterward. At first, the main goal is to reduce or prevent stroke complications, such as stiffening of the limbs or deep vein thrombosis. As the patient's condition stabilizes, the focus turns toward the longer-term goals of restoring mental and physical function, adapting to disability, returning to an active life, and preventing additional strokes.

Although the exact approach depends on the specific loss of function caused by the stroke, rehabilitation typically consists of developing new strategies to overcome deficits and performing exercises designed to improve range of motion in joints, strengthen weak muscles, and restore function to the greatest extent possible.

The Agency for Health Care Policy and Research has made several recommendations to help patients get the most out of rehabilitation. These include beginning rehabilitation as soon as possible, carefully selecting the most appropriate program, setting realistic goals (to avoid later frustration), frequently assessing progress, and following up during the transition back to the community (when the family plays a major role). Individuals may need to accept some degree of disability, but optimal recovery depends on a combination of factors: the patient's determination to succeed, the support of family and friends, and the well-integrated efforts of specialists.

Because continuing medical treatment after a stroke is complicated, one doctor should be selected to oversee care. This approach will ensure there are no gaps in treatment and allow frequent assessments of progress and an eventual phaseout of rehabilitation when patients have progressed as far as they can. Throughout the poststroke period, all medications must be carefully monitored.

Some of the specially trained professionals involved in the rehabilitation process include occupational therapists, who teach patients new ways to perform day-to-day activities (writing, bathing, cooking, or job-related tasks) made difficult because of disability; physical therapists, who provide instruction and exercises to help patients regain the ability to walk and move about independently, as well as to improve strength, flexibility, balance, and overall fitness; registered nurses; social workers, who can provide information on the wide range of community services available to help stroke survivors and their families; and speech-language pathologists, who help patients regain as much as possible their lost swallowing ability and language skills.

For strokes due to cerebral embolism, the anticoagulant drug heparin is often administered intravenously for several days to prevent new clots from forming and to keep existing clots from getting any larger. Heparin is also the usual immediate medical therapy for strokes due to severe atherosclerotic stenosis in the carotid, vertebral, or basilar arteries (which branch off from the vertebral arteries), although its effectiveness in these situations is not clearly established. Patients with an embolic stroke due to atrial fibrillation may be treated with heart rhythm stabilizers (antiarrhythmic agents such as amiodarone and procainamide).

Surgery. Surgery is rarely part of the immediate treatment of ischemic stroke, although carotid endarterectomy (see the text box on page 596) is sometimes performed to treat minor strokes and prevent additional ones in patients with severe carotid stenosis. However, in the aftermath of a large ischemic stroke, the brain should be allowed to recover before the procedure is attempted. In such cases, surgery may be postponed for as long as six weeks after the stroke. Angioplasty with or without the use of stents is being increasingly used, especially in patients for whom standard carotid endarterectomy presents too great a risk.

Treatment of Hemorrhagic Stroke

Because hemorrhagic strokes often occur in association with excessive hypertension, doctors first attempt to lower blood pressure to minimize the amount of bleeding from the ruptured artery. Pressure is reduced carefully and conservatively, since, as with ischemic stroke, additional brain damage can occur when blood pressure is too low.

Medications. Mannitol (a type of sugar) and diuretics, which counteract fluid retention by increasing sodium and water loss in the urine, can be used to reduce cerebral edema (swelling of tissues in the brain), a serious and relatively common consequence of hemorrhagic stroke. Vasospasm (spasm of cerebral blood vessels—likely to occur in the first to second week after subarachnoid hemorrhage) causes further reduction of blood flow. Occurring in about one third of patients, vasospasm is now recognized as one of the most prevalent, serious complications and a major cause of death after a subarachnoid hemorrhage. Nimodipine, a calcium channel blocker widely used to treat hypertension, may reduce brain damage due to vasospasm.

Surgery. Surgical intervention is warranted in some cases of hemorrhagic stroke, such as those associated with aneurysms, which have a high risk of rebleeding. Depending on its location in the brain, an aneurysm that has leaked or ruptured can be clipped across its neck—to prevent future bleeding by stopping blood flow into the aneurysm; adjacent blood vessels are then surgically repaired. A newer, less invasive procedure may be tried in patients who are unable to undergo clipping: A platinum coil is fed into the aneurysm to seal it off from blood circulation.

Hemorrhagic strokes often produce an intracerebral hematoma—a pool of blood within the brain that damages brain cells and can dangerously increase intracranial pressure. (Indeed, large hematomas are usually fatal.) Emergency drainage of a hematoma, known as evacuation, can relieve the excess pressure and thus minimize brain damage.

Tendons are fibrous cords at the end of most muscles; they join muscles to bones. Tendinitis, literally inflammation of a tendon, is characterized by microscopic tears in a tendon—most commonly in the shoulder, elbow (tennis or golfer's elbow), wrist (de Quervain's tenosynovitis), the fingers (trigger finger), and the ankle (Achilles tendinitis)—that cause limited movement, pain and swelling in the affected area.

When the muscles in the affected area are used regularly despite the initial pain, the injured tendon may be slow to heal. While many cases of tendinitis last no more than two weeks, and are usually alleviated by rest and proper conditioning, repeated use of the injured area may lead to chronic tendinitis, characterized by scarring of the involved tissues and limited flexibility. People over 40 are most prone to chronic tendinitis.

Causes

Tendinitis is typically caused by overuse due to prolonged, repetitive movements, which can include playing a musical instrument or a slot machine for hours, regular participation in tennis or long distance running, or carrying a heavy briefcase every day. Such repetitive movements increase the tension on the tendons, resulting in the microscopic tears and inflammation that are the hallmarks of tendinitis. Other causes include:

- Physical injury, like twisting an ankle
- Inadequate conditioning or insufficient warm-up prior to exercise
- Degenerative changes due to increasing age and years of continual use
- Calcium deposits in a tendon (calcific tendinitis)
  Treatment
  If tendinitis is a recurring condition, self-help measures can reduce pain and inflammation. At the first signs of tendinitis—pain and swelling—you should stop any activity that aggravates the condition.

- For the first 72 hours, rest and periodically ice the affected area to reduce inflammation. A compression bandage can help minimize swelling.
- After 72 hours, apply hot compresses to soothe discomfort, increase circulation, and speed healing.
- Non-steroidal anti-inflammatory drugs, such as aspirin or other NSAIDS, may be used to alleviate pain.
- If you suspect high-impact exercise is responsible for the injury, temporarily switch to a low-impact exercise, such as bicycling or swimming.
- Stretching exercises will help to restore flexibility; gradually add exercises with light weights to strengthen muscles.

If muscle or joint pain persists for more than two weeks and interferes with ordinary activities despite self-treatment, notify your doctor, who may provide you with slings or splints to immobilize the injured area for a few days. In serious cases, corticosteroids may be injected directly into the affected area to ease pain and inflammation. (However, such therapy is not recommended for Achilles tendinitis, where injections may weaken or rupture the tendon.) A more seriously torn or ruptured tendon may require surgical repair.

Sudden pain in the back of the lower leg, often accompanied by a snapping sound, may signal the rupture of an Achilles tendon.

Prevention

The best way to prevent tendinitis is to avoid highly repetitious movements whenever possible. Regular, moderate exercise—including a proper warm-up, cool-down, and gentle stretches—is also helpful since tight muscles put extra stress on the tendons. Additional steps to prevent tendinitis include:

- **Don't overdo it.** Suddenly increasing the number of miles you normally run, or working out more strenuously or longer than usual, can produce muscle fatigue and lead to an injury.
- **Exercise caution as you grow older.** Starting as early as the thirties, tendons gradually lose elasticity and become more brittle.
- **Develop the right technique.** An improperly executed backhand is often the cause of tennis elbow, just as the wrong golf swing can lead to a rotator cuff injury. A coach, trainer, or professional can give you pointers on proper technique.
- **Get the right equipment.** A bike that's too small can cause tendinitis in the knee; running shoes with worn-down heels can lead to Achilles tendinitis.
- **Listen to your body.** If you feel pain or discomfort signaling a tendon injury, reduce the intensity of your workout or try a different activity until the tendon heals.
- **Compensate for musculoskeletal problems.** For instance, if your feet roll inward (overpronate) as you run, or your legs are different lengths, you may develop a form of tendinitis called runner's knee. You may need to consult a physical therapist, podiatrist, orthopedist, or other specialist about diagnosis and treatment.
- **Counter muscle imbalances.** If you have strong calf muscles but don't strengthen the opposing muscles in the shins, you increase the chances of injuring your Achilles tendon. Strengthen the muscle groups that are important for your activity.

The thyroid is a butterfly-shaped gland located at the front of the windpipe at the base of the throat. It controls metabolism (the rate at which the body converts food and oxygen into energy) by producing hormones called thyroxine, or T4, and triiodothyronine (T3). The body also converts T4 into the more biologically powerful and rapidly acting T3. Levels of these hormones influence heart rate, body temperature, alertness, mood, and many other functions.

The thyroid is controlled by the pituitary gland, located deep within the brain. The pituitary regulates the thyroid, working much like a thermostat by releasing or withholding thyroid-stimulating hormone (TSH), depending on blood levels of T4 and T3. For example, when blood levels of thyroid hormones are low, the pituitary secretes TSH, which signals the thyroid to increase hormone production. On the other hand, when blood levels of T4 and T3 are high, the pituitary restricts the output of TSH, which signals the thyroid to slow down hormone production. When any part of this process malfunctions, the thyroid can produce too little hormone (hypothyroidism) or too much hormone (a condition called hyperthyroidism).

Thyroid disorders are not always obvious since many symptoms of an underactive thyroid, such as weight gain and fatigue, are nonspecific and may be attributed to aging, menopause, or depression. And symptoms of hyperthyroidism, like nervousness, insomnia, and heart palpitations, may be attributed to anxiety. Consequently, thyroid disease is grossly underdiagnosed.

Hypothyroidism

Women are 10 times more likely to suffer from hypothyroidism than men, and an estimated 8 percent to 10 percent of women over age 50 have an underactive thyroid.

Causes

The condition is most frequently caused by Hashimoto's thyroiditis, an autoimmune disorder that prompts the body's immune system to attack the thyroid gland. In addition, previous thyroid surgery or radioactive iodine treatment can lead to an underactive thyroid. Too little iodine in the diet was once a major cause, but the introduction of iodized salt in the 1920s has practically eradicated this problem in the United States. Finally, certain medications such as lithium (prescribed to treat manic depressive disorder) and the antiarrhythmic drug amiodarone (Cordarone), and radiation treatment for disorders such as Hodgkin's disease or throat cancer, can also cause hypothyroidism.

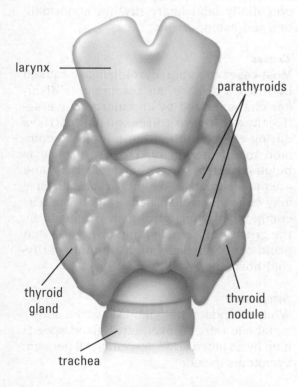

larynx

parathyroids

thyroid gland

thyroid nodule

trachea

Thyroid nodules are painless lumps that tend to grow slowly over many years. Only 5 percent of thyroid nodules are cancerous.

Symptoms

A mildly underactive thyroid (subclinical hypothyroidism) may be asymptomatic, but about 5 percent of patients with subclinical hypothyroidism progress to overt hypothyroidism—where symptoms surface—annually. Symptoms include:

- Weight gain
- Fatigue
- Constipation
- Cold Sensitivity
- Depression
- Impaired memory
- Dry brittle hair or hair loss
- Decreased sex drive
- Dry Skin
- Hoarseness
- Muscle Cramps

Diagnosis

A simple test that measures the amount of TSH in the blood can confirm or rule out an underactive thyroid. TSH levels are elevated in patients with overt hypothyroidism and in those whose thyroid gland is only mildly underactive. However, in rare cases, hypothyroidism is due to a disorder of the pituitary, and TSH levels are not high in these people.

Treatment

It is important to treat hypothyroidism even when it does not cause symptoms. An underactive thyroid gland—even a mild one—can be associated with high cholesterol, and thus is a risk factor for heart disease. Treating the condition can reverse elevated cholesterol levels and halt the progression to overt heart disease.

Most people with hypothyroidism require daily, lifetime therapy with synthetic T4 (or levothyroxine sodium, marketed under the brand names Levothroid, Synthroid, Levoxyl, and Eltroxin). Although T4 therapy is safe and effective, an abrupt increase in T4 levels may increase the demand for oxygen by the heart—which could lead to a heart attack, particularly in older people. Therefore, T4 treatment should be started at a low dose and gradually increased until T4 and TSH are in the normal range.

Hyperthyroidism

Roughly 2 percent of American adults suffer hyperthyroidism, most of them women—who are 10 times more likely to have an overactive thyroid compared to men. Although not nearly as common in those over 50, an overactive thyroid gland (hyperthyroidism or thyrotoxicosis) is another potentially dangerous thyroid condition. Left untreated, hyperthyroidism can cause potentially fatal heart rhythm abnormalities and osteoporosis.

Causes

Most cases of hyperthyroidism are caused by Grave's disease, an autoimmune disorder characterized by an enlarged, overactive thyroid. Grave's disease usually strikes during early adulthood or mid-life. A common manifestation of Grave's disease is bulging, watery eyes that feel gritty and are more sensitive to light. Grave's disease may cause a swollen neck (a goiter). Less commonly, hyperthyroidism is caused by the growth of a single lump or nodule that produces abnormally high amounts of thyroid hormone.

Symptoms

While an underactive gland slows the body's metabolic rate, an overactive gland speeds it up by as much as 60 percent to 80 percent. Symptoms include:

- Weight Loss
- Fatigue
- Nervousness

Multinodular Goiter Disease

Another common condition is multinodular goiter disease, which is characterized by soft nodules that slowly grow within the thyroid. As with other nodules, multinodular goiters are often asymptomatic. However, if they grow too large, they may compress the windpipe and cause difficulty breathing or swallowing.

The treatment of choice for symptomatic multinodular goiter disease is surgery. To prevent future recurrances, and a possible malignancy, both lobes of the thyroid may be removed.

While most multinodular goiters are non-cancerous, the presence of a dominant nodule is cause for suspicion. A fine-needle biopsy can indicate whether there is a malignancy. As with all thyroid malignancies, treatment involves surgical removal of one or both lobes of the thyroid.

- Insomnia
- Shaking
- Muscle weakness
- Diarrhea
- Heart palpitations
- Increased sensitivity to light
- Increased sweating
- Intolerance to heat
- Anxiety
- Unusually light or absent menstrual periods

Diagnosis

As with hypothyroidism, symptoms of hyperthyroidism can point to a number of disorders, and the disease can be easily missed—especially in older adults, who may not exhibit the symptoms that are characteristic of hyperthyroidism in younger people. Nevertheless, diagnosis can be made on the basis of low levels of TSH and T4 in a blood test.

The TSH test is a simple, inexpensive blood test that can identify even mild cases of thyroid disorder before symptoms appear. For more information on thyroid screening, see page 51.

Treatment

Hyperthyroidism is usually treated with radioactive iodine. As the thyroid absorbs the iodine, radiation destroys parts of the gland so that it produces less thyroid hormone. In about 50 percent of people, however, this renders the gland underactive, and patients then require life-long T4 therapy. An overactive thyroid can also be treated with medications, such as propylthiouracil and methimazole (Tapazol), but their effectiveness is often limited to about a year. If the gland is unusually large, surgery is an option, but one that is rarely used.

Thyroid Nodules and Thyroid Cancer

Thyroid nodules are solid, painless lumps arising in the thyroid gland; they affect nearly 4 percent of the adult population. Nodules tend to grow slowly over many years; the thyroid gland may contain only one or several nodules. Thyroid nodules are classified according to their production of thyroid hormone: "warm" nodules mimic normal thyroid cells in this regard; "hot" nodules overproduce thyroid hormone and are virtually always benign; "cold" nodules produce little thyroid hormone.

Thyroid nodules are usually asymptomatic. "Hot" nodules may produce symptoms of hyperthyroidism. The greatest concern of a thyroid nodule is the possibility of cancer, but only about 5 percent of thyroid nodules are cancerous.

Diagnosis

Thyroid nodules are often found during a routine physical examination. Imaging studies, such as ultrasound or MRI, can be used to confirm the diagnosis. In addition, a thyroid scan with radioactive iodine or technetium is sometimes used to identify whether the nodule is hot, warm, or cold. If the nodule is cold, fine-needle biopsy (use of a small-gauge needle and syringe to take a tissue sample for examination under a microscope) is used to rule out cancer.

Treatment

If a needle biopsy shows no evidence of cancer and thyroid function tests are normal,

regular follow-up with thyroid function tests is all that is required. "Hot" nodules may be treated with radioactive iodine or, rarely, surgery. Treatment for hypothyroidism may subsequently be needed if excess thyroid tissue is removed or destroyed by radioactive iodine therapy (see page 605).

If the biopsy is suspicious of or confirms a malignancy, one or both lobes of the thyroid are surgically removed (thyroidectomy). In the case of cancer, removal of surrounding lymph nodes and other tissues may also be warranted. Radioactive iodine therapy also may be used to destroy thyroid tissue left behind during a thyroidectomy or to treat thyroid cancer that has spread to the lungs or the bones.

All patients who have had their thyroid surgically removed require lifetime supplementation with synthetic thyroid hormone.

About 10 percent of older Americans live with a constant ringing, buzzing, or humming in their ears that is severe enough to interfere with everyday activities; another 30 percent complain of mild, intermittent noise. Called tinnitus, these so-called phantom noises can be a symptom of many disorders. But in most instances, no cause can be found and the noise persists indefinitely.

Chronic tinnitus can be highly disabling and usually develops after age 60. Because the problem can be difficult to treat, sufferers frequently become frustrated in their search for relief. Anxiety, depression, and disturbed sleep may result. But research is finally leading to a better understanding of the disorder and may even eventually produce a cure. Meanwhile, certain drugs, lifestyle measures, and behavioral therapies can help.

Causes

Tinnitus appears to be caused by abnormalities in two key areas: the brain and the inner ear. One study mapped the brain abnormalities using an imaging technique called positron emission tomography (PET) scanning in four patients with tinnitus and six without the problem. The resulting images showed that all of the subjects with tinnitus had heightened activity in two regions: the temporal lobe (the lower, back portion of the brain opposite the ear) that perceives the ringing and the hippocampus (the region responsible for emotions). Scans also showed that the brains of those with tinnitus were hypersensitive to external sound.

These findings suggest that the mechanisms that lead to phantom noise may be similar to those that produce phantom limb pain following amputation, which is associated with heightened brain activity and changes in circuitry. They speculate that tinnitus may be caused by an abnormal link between two brain networks: the

---

Self-Care Measures

The following lifestyle measures may help tinnitus sufferers manage their condition.

- Stop smoking and cut back on caffeine. Both can exacerbate tinnitus by constricting blood vessels.
- Avoid very loud noises, including loud music, and wear earplugs when exposed to them.
- Drink in moderation. Excessive alcohol consumption may damage tiny hair-like structures in the cochlea, which are important for hearing.
- Exercise. Among the benefits of exercise are improved blood flow, better sleep, less stress, and relief from depression.

---

central auditory system and the limbic system (which includes the hippocampus). Further, the characteristics and severity of the noises heard by sufferers may depend on how sensitive the brain is to external sound, as hypersensitivity can change brain circuitry. And tinnitus may be psychologically damaging because abnormalities occur in an area of the brain that regulates emotion.

Chronic tinnitus is frequently associated with some degree of hearing loss, usually due to aging or prolonged exposure to very loud noises. Men develop the disorder more often than women, probably because they're more likely to work in construction, manufacturing, and other noisy jobs. Tinnitus has also been associated with auditory problems such as Ménière's disease (an inner ear disturbance; see page 296), ear infection, and wax build-up in the ear canal. Tinnitus can also be caused by nonauditory disorders, such as high blood pressure; arthritis in the neck; head, neck, or ear injury (including whiplash); and migraine headaches. Physical and emotional stress, smoking, and high caffeine consumption may also play a role. Finally, tinnitus can be triggered by many medications including aspirin, naproxen (Anaprox), and alprazolam (Xanax), as well as excessive alcohol consumption.

Treatment

Anyone with persistent tinnitus should see a doctor for an evaluation and possible referral to an otolaryngologist (a physician specializing in ear, nose, and throat disorders). Being fitted with the proper hearing device, ridding the ear of wax, or changing medication is often all that's required. If no cause can be found, tinnitus rarely goes away; but sufferers often learn to ignore the noise.

As of yet, no effective medication has been found for treating tinnitus. But antidepressants and prescription sleep medications sometimes help by making sufferers more responsive to behavioral and lifestyle approaches.

Behavioral therapy capitalizes on the ability to learn new coping skills. The two most successful techniques are:

- **Masking.** Masking disguises tinnitus with an external noise of the same frequency, generated by a device much like a hearing aid.
- **Biofeedback.** This relaxation technique trains the patient to control specific muscles that may contribute to tinnitus.

Lifestyle measures may also help. Some sufferers have had success with alternative, albeit unproven, treatments such as acupuncture and ginkgo biloba (an herbal remedy said to improve blood flow to the brain), or supplementation with vitamin B12 (which the body uses to manufacture a fatty material that protects nerves in the inner ear).

Tuberculosis (often called TB) is an infectious disease that usually attacks the lungs, but can attack almost any part of the body. Tuberculosis is spread from person to person through the air.

When people with TB in their lungs or throat cough, laugh, sneeze, sing, or even talk, the germs that cause TB may be spread into the air. If other people breathe in these germs there is a chance that they will become infected with tuberculosis. Repeated contact is usually required for infection.

It is important to understand that there is a difference between being infected with TB and having TB disease. Someone who is infected with TB has the TB germs, or bacteria, in their body. The body's defenses are protecting them from the germs and they are not sick.

Someone with TB disease is sick and can spread the disease to other people. A person with TB disease needs to see a doctor as soon as possible.

It is not easy to become infected with tuberculosis. Usually a person has to be close to someone with TB disease for a long period of time. TB is usually spread between family members, close friends, and people who work or live together. TB is spread most easily in closed spaces over a long period of time. However, transmission in an airplane, although rare, has been documented.

Even if someone becomes infected with tuberculosis, that does not mean they will get TB disease. Most people who become infected do not develop TB disease because their body's defenses protect them.

Experts believe that about 10 million Americans are infected with TB germs. Only about 10 percent of these people will develop TB disease in their lifetimes. The other 90 percent will never get sick from the TB germs or be able to spread them to other people.

TB is an increasing and major worldwide problem, especially in Africa, where the spread is facilitated by AIDS. It is estimated that nearly 1 billion people will become infected, 200 million will become sick, and 70 million will die worldwide between now and 2020. In 1999, approximately 8.4 million cases and 2 million deaths were attributed to TB; 100,000 of those 2 million deaths occurred among children.

Who Gets TB?

Anyone can get it. People of all races and nationalities. The rich and poor. And at any age. But for many reasons, some groups of people are at higher risk to get active TB disease. The groups that are at high risk include:

- People with HIV infection (the AIDS virus)
- People in close contact with those known to be infectious with TB
- People with medical conditions that make the body less able to protect itself from disease (for example: diabetes, the dust disease silicosis, or people undergoing treatment with drugs that can suppress the immune system, such as long-term use of corticosteroids)
- People from countries with high TB rates
- Some racial or ethnic minorities
- People who work in or are residents of long-term care facilities (nursing homes, prisons, some hospitals)
- Health-care workers and others such as prison guards
- People who are malnourished
- Alcoholics and IV drug users

What Are the Symptoms of TB?

A person with TB infection will have no symptoms. A person with TB disease may have any, all or none of the following symptoms:

- A cough that will not go away
- Feeling tired all the time

- Weight loss
- Loss of appetite
- Fever
- Coughing up blood
- Night sweats

These symptoms can also occur with other types of lung disease so it is important to see a doctor and to let the doctor determine if you have TB. It is also important to remember that a person with TB disease may feel perfectly healthy or may only have a cough from time to time. If you think you have been exposed to TB, get a TB skin test.

How Does TB Disease Develop?

There are two possible ways a person can become sick with TB disease:

The first applies to a person who may have been infected with TB for years and has been perfectly healthy. The time may come when this person suffers a change in health. The cause of this change in health may be another disease like AIDS or diabetes. Or it may be drug or alcohol abuse or a lack of health care because of homelessness.

Whatever the cause, when the body's ability to protect itself is damaged, the TB infection can become TB disease. In this way, a person may become sick with TB disease months or even years after first breathing in the TB germs.

The other way TB disease develops happens much more quickly. Sometimes when a person first breathes in the TB germs the body is unable to protect itself against the disease. The germs then develop into active TB disease within weeks.

What Is the TB Skin Test?

The TB skin test is a way to find out if a person has TB infection. Although there is more than one TB skin test, the preferred method of testing is the Mantoux test.

For this test, a small amount of testing material is placed just below the top layers of skin, usually on the arm. Two to three days later a health-care worker checks the arm to see if a bump has developed and measures the size of the bump. If the bump is of a certain size (varying with group) the test is significant and the person is presumed to have TB infection.

Once the doctor knows that a person has TB infection he or she will want to determine if the person has TB disease. This is done by using several other tests including a chest x-ray and a test of the person's mucus (the material that is sometimes coughed up from the lungs).

The advice for most people is to get a tuberculin test if you have symptoms or if you are living in close contact or have otherwise been in close contact with someone who recently came down with TB disease. (Some people get skin tests because of their jobs, in a school or hospital, for example, to make sure they have not contracted TB and will not infect others if they have TB.)

However, if you fall into one or more of the high-risk categories for TB noted earlier, for example, if you are HIV-positive, or if you've never had a skin test before, or if there is no record of the last result, you should be tested.

If you're not sure, ask your doctor. TB can be prevented, even if you are at risk.

What Is the Treatment for TB?

Treatment for TB depends on whether a person has TB disease or only TB infection.

A person who has become infected with TB, but does not have TB disease, may be given preventive therapy. Preventive therapy aims to kill germs that are not doing any damage right now, but could break out later.

If a doctor decides a person should have preventive therapy, the usual prescription is a daily dose of isoniazid (also called "INH"), an inexpensive TB medicine. The person takes INH for six to nine months (up to a year for some patients), with periodic checkups to make sure the medicine is being taken as the doctor has prescribed.

Years ago a patient with TB disease would have been placed in a special hospital for months, maybe even years, and would often have surgery. Today, TB can be treated with very effective drugs.

Often the patient will only have to stay a short time in the hospital and can then continue taking medication at home. Sometimes the patient will not have to stay in the hospital at all. After a few weeks a person can probably even return to normal activities and not have to worry about infecting others.

The patient usually gets a combination of several drugs (most frequently INH plus two to three others), usually for nine months. The patient will probably begin to feel better only a few weeks after starting to take the drugs.

It is very important, however, that the patient continue to take the medicine correctly for the full length of treatment. If the medicine is taken incorrectly or stopped the patient may become sick again and will be able to infect others with TB. As a result, many public health authorities recommend Directly Observed Therapy (DOT), in which a health-care worker ensures that patients take their medicine.

If the medicine is taken incorrectly and the patient becomes sick with TB a second time, the TB may be harder to treat because it has become drug resistant. This means that the TB germs in the body are unaffected by some drugs used to treat TB.

Multi-drug resistant TB is very dangerous, so patients should be sure that they take all of their medicine correctly.

Regular checkups are needed to see how treatment is progressing. Sometimes the drugs used to treat TB can cause side effects. It is important both for people undergoing preventive therapy and people being treated for TB disease to immediately let a doctor know if they begin experiencing any unusual symptoms.

Can a TB Patient Infect Others?

Yes, if TB disease is present and it is not being treated. Normally, once treatment begins, a patient quickly becomes noninfectious; that is, they cannot spread the disease to others.

There is little danger from the TB patient who is being treated, is taking his or her medication continuously, and is responding well. The drugs usually make the patient noninfectious within weeks.

TB is spread by germs in the air, germs put there by coughing or sneezing. Handling a patient's bed sheets, books, furniture, or eating utensils does not spread the infection.

Brief exposure to a source of TB rarely infects a person. It's day-after-day close contact that usually does it.

What Is Multi-Drug Resistant TB?

Multi-drug resistant tuberculosis (called MDR TB for short) is a very dangerous form of tuberculosis. Some TB germs become resistant to the effects of some TB drugs. This happens when TB disease is not properly treated.

These resistant germs can then cause TB disease. The TB disease they cause is much harder to treat because the drugs do not kill the germs. MDR TB can be spread to others, just like regular TB.

It is important that patients with TB disease follow their doctor's instructions for taking their TB medicine so that they will not develop MDR TB.

T

TB: What You Should Do

Find out if you're infected. Certain people, such as those infected with HIV or health-care workers, should be tested regularly. You should also be tested if there's any chance you have been infected, recently or many years ago.

If the test is negative. A negative reaction usually means that you are not infected and no treatment is needed. However, if you have TB symptoms your doctor must continue to look for the cause. Sometimes, when a person has only recently been infected, or when his or her immune system isn't working properly, the test may be falsely negative.

If the test is positive. A significant reaction usually means that you have been infected with the TB germ. It does not necessarily mean that you have TB disease. Cooperate with the doctor when he or she recommends a chest x-ray and possibly other tests.

If the doctor recommends treatment to prevent sickness, follow the recommendations. If medicine is prescribed, be sure to take it as directed.

If you don't need treatment, do what the doctor tells you to do about follow-up. The doctor may simply say to return for another checkup if you get into a special risk situation for TB sickness or develop symptoms.

If you are sick with TB disease, follow the doctor's recommendations for treatment.

If you're a health worker. Your local American Lung Association can provide you with more comprehensive information developed for health professionals on the diagnosis, treatment, and control of TB.

American Lung Association

Urinary incontinence (UI)—the involuntary leakage of urine—affects some 17 million older Americans. One recent study showed that about one third of women and one fifth of men over age 65 are affected by overactive bladder. Yet sufferers often do not seek treatment, usually because they're embarrassed or mistakenly believe that medicine has nothing to offer. In fact, effective treatments include self-care measures, medication, and surgery. Most patients report a significant improvement—sometimes even a cure, defined as complete dryness.

Causes

Two muscles are mainly responsible for controlling urination: the detrusor muscle surrounding the bladder and the valve-like sphincter muscle that encircles the top of the urethra (the tube that empties the bladder). As the bladder fills, the detrusor muscle relaxes to accommodate more urine, and the sphincter contracts to prevent leakage. In addition, pelvic floor muscles support the base of the bladder and close off the bladder end of the urethra, further blocking urine flow. During urination, the brain signals the sphincter and pelvic muscles to relax, permitting urine to flow into the urethra, and the detrusor muscle tightens and squeezes the urine out of the bladder.

UI occurs when any step in this process goes wrong. Declining nerve function (often a complication of diabetes) or weakening of the pelvic floor muscles (perhaps due to aging, declining estrogen production, pregnancy, or obesity) may play a role. Also implicated are vaginal infections and the aftereffects of pelvic surgery (including removal of the prostate in men). The side effects of many medications and certain lifestyle habits (such as excessive beverage consumption near bedtime or excessive alcohol consumption at any time) also may interfere with control.

Types of Urinary Incontinence

There are three types of UI: stress incontinence, urge incontinence, and overflow incontinence. Many people with poor urinary control have problems of more than one type, a condition described as mixed incontinence.

- Stress incontinence, the most common form, occurs when urine leaks due to increased pressure on the bladder when coughing, sneezing, lifting heavy objects, rising from a seated or recumbent position, exercising, or performing other activities that increase pressure within the pelvis.
- Urge incontinence, or "overactive bladder," occurs when the need to urinate cannot be controlled and urine is lost before reaching the bathroom.
- Overflow incontinence describes the frequent loss of small amounts of urine because the bladder does not have enough room to contain it, perhaps owing to incomplete voiding. Men with urge incontinence sometimes experience a small amount of leakage after urination, a phenomenon called postmicturition dribble.

Treatment

Historically, about four out of five people with bladder control problems rely on absorbent products rather than seek treatment—even though approximately 80 percent of cases can be significantly improved or cured. Treatment options include lifestyle measures, medications, and surgery.

Lifestyle Measures

The first step toward gaining control is an evaluation by a urologist, gynecologist, or

U

Kegel Exercise

The Kegel exercise, named for the physician who first promoted it during the 1940s, improves control by increasing the strength of the pelvic floor muscles. The movement involves drawing in and lifting up these muscles, along with the anal sphincter, as if to control voiding with minimal contraction of abdominal, buttock, and inner thigh muscles. To be effective, the exercise must become part of your daily routine. About three quarters of those who practice "Kegels" every day report less leakage, and 12 percent are cured.

To get a sense of the muscles that must be used, try eliminating a very small amount of urine on a full bladder, starting and stopping the stream until the bladder is empty. You have just completed a series of Kegel exercises. Now that you have located the proper muscles, try activating them when you're not urinating. (Regularly performing the exercise during urination may actually weaken the muscles.) During the contraction phase of the movement, hold the muscles tight for about three seconds. Ideally, to improve control, the pelvic floor muscles must be contracted and released 15 times in a row, 6 times a day, though performing 20 repetitions twice daily is also acceptable.

urogynecologist. When mild to moderate stress incontinence (absorbent pads are sometimes needed to avoid accidents, but leakage generally does not interfere with daily activities) is diagnosed, lifestyle measures, such as avoiding liquids close to bedtime and curbing alcohol consumption often improve control.

Kegel exercises, muscle contractions that strengthen the pelvic floor muscles, also are useful for about half of women with stress incontinence, some women with urge incontinence, and some men with these problems. Because the correct muscles can be difficult to isolate, patients may be referred to a physical therapist for biofeedback training (using electrically amplified body signals to gain control of muscles that are ordinarily contracted unconsciously).

Overflow incontinence may improve by regular voiding every three to four hours during the day, since leakage is less likely when the bladder is not full. About half of those who try planned voiding report significant improvement, and 16 percent are cured.

Medications

It is always important to determine if UI is a side effect of any medications taken for other medical problems. Dosing adjustments made in consultation with a doctor are often successful. In addition, several medications are available to treat UI. Tolterodine tartrate (Detrol) and oxybutynin chloride (Ditropan) are effective for urge incontinence; amitriptyline (Elavil), a tricyclic antidepressant that relaxes the bladder and tightens the urethral sphincter, may also be considered. Estrogen replacement therapy has sometimes been prescribed for women, but no scientific studies have demonstrated its effectiveness.

Surgery

For incontinence caused by structural problems, two types of surgery may be effective for women who are bothered by persistent symptoms and excessive reliance on absorbent products:

- **Sling procedure.** This procedure, performed through the vagina and a small incision in the abdomen, places a supporting strip of material under the urethra and bladder neck and secures it to the abdominal wall and pelvic bone.

- **Retropubic suspension.** This procedure is performed through an incision in the lower abdomen. Sutures secure the bladder neck and urethra directly to the surrounding pelvic bone or other nearby structures.

Bear in mind that surgery cannot address issues such as infection, declining muscle tone, or neurological problems. In addition, because many patients have mixed incontinence, some degree of leakage may remain after surgery. This situation can be addressed with lifestyle measures, medication, and, when necessary, absorbent pads. An artificial sphincter can sometimes help men with persistent leakage after prostate surgery.

When incontinence persists as a complication of surgical repair, injection of a "bulking agent" (usually collagen) into the tissues around the urethra can sometimes improve the closing ability of the sphincter. Injections permit patients to avoid a second surgery, but they usually need to be repeated every 6 to 12 months.

Collagen is a fibrous protein. When injected into the urinary sphincter, it adds bulk and creates a more secure seal. The injections can be given in a doctor's office under local anesthesia, and at least three treatments are necessary. About 80 percent of women are dry or improved after three treatments. In men, the success rate is 88 percent after TURP, 25 percent after prostate removal, and 14 percent after radiation.

A new type of surgery known as sacral nerve stimulation may be highly effective for significant urge and overflow incontinence. A device called a neurostimulator is surgically placed under the skin of the abdomen. About the size of a stopwatch and similar to a cardiac pacemaker, the device generates small electrical pulses that are carried via a thin implanted wire to the sacral nerves (nerves in the lower back that control bladder function). The increased stimulation provided by the impulses improves bladder function and control. Studies have found that six months after implantation, up to half of patients are completely dry and up to three quarters experience a significant reduction in the number of leakage episodes.

U

One in three adults develops a urinary tract infection (UTI) sometime after age 50. Although younger women are affected far more often than younger men, this discrepancy gradually disappears after middle age for reasons that are not yet fully understood.

Causes

The kidneys remove waste products from the blood and excrete them in the urine, which is ordinarily sterile. The ureters carry urine from the kidneys to the bladder, where it is held until it is eliminated through the urethra. UTIs usually start at the entrance to the urethra, when microorganisms (bacteria, viruses, or fungi) cling to its opening and begin to multiply. The usual culprit is Escherichia coli, a bacterium that may be beneficial when confined to the colon (large intestine) but harmful in the urinary tract. From its toehold at the entrance to the urinary tract, E. coli can easily migrate up and cause infection in the urethra (urethritis) or the bladder (cystitis). From the bladder, the infection may then move through the ureters to the kidneys (pyelonephritis).

Ordinarily, the ureters and bladder prevent urine from backing up toward the kidneys, and the flow of urine from the bladder helps wash bacteria and other microorganisms out of the body. In men, the prostate gland produces secretions that slow bacterial growth. In both sexes, immune defenses also help thwart infection. But when infection occurs, these mechanisms cannot cope with the onslaught of pathogens.

Who's at Risk?

Women are thought to be more susceptible to UTIs because they have a relatively short urethra with an opening located close to the anus, where E. coli may be deposited during bowel movements. Researchers are investigating how estrogen and the absence

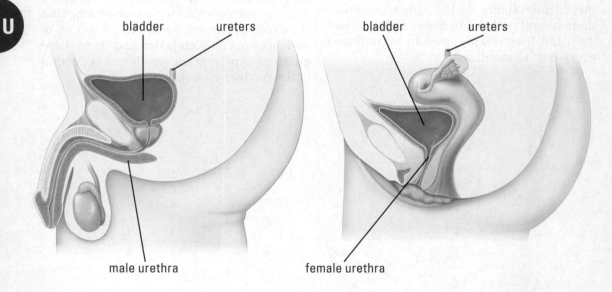

bladder   ureters   bladder   ureters

male urethra   female urethra

Urinary tract infections are more common in women than men since the location of a woman's urethra and its shorter length facilitate the entry of bacteria into the urinary tract.

of certain antibodies (infection-fighting proteins) may make cells lining the urethra more susceptible to colonization by these and other pathogens. In addition, postmenopausal changes in the acidity of the vagina may permit vaginal infections that then spread to the urinary tract.

In men, UTIs are often associated with acute prostatitis (sudden inflammation and infection of the prostate). Any problem that slows urine flow, such as prostate enlargement (benign prostatic hyperplasia), can also increase risk.

People with diabetes are vulnerable to UTIs because diabetes weakens the immune system and may damage nerves that control urinary structures. In addition, glucose commonly "spills" into the urine, where it may fuel bacterial growth. Urinary catheterization increases risk because, no matter how carefully the procedure is performed, bacteria may be introduced into the urinary tract. Sexual intercourse, which can introduce bacteria into the vagina, is also associated with an increased rate of UTI in women. Though rare, certain types of bladder cancer occasionally mimic chronic bladder infections.

Symptoms
- Frequent, urgent need to urinate
- Painful, burning sensation during urination in the area of the bladder or urethra
- Despite urge to urinate, only a small amount of urine passes
- In some cases, pain even when not urinating
- Urine may look milky, cloudy, or reddish (if blood is present)

These are symptoms of cystitis, the most common type of UTI, which involves infection of the bladder and lower urinary tract. Urethritis is an inflammation of the urethra and is often difficult to distinguish from cystitis. In women the two conditions usually occur together; in men, infection may be confined to the urethra.

UTIs can also spread to the kidney—a condition called pyelonephritis that may be accompanied by fever, back pain, nausea, and vomiting. In men, prostatitis can cause cystitis-like symptoms, though symptoms of prostatitis tend to wax and wane (see page 547).

Age-related erosion of bladder control due to urinary incontinence or prostate enlargement may prompt an urgent need to urinate, but burning and other symptoms are absent.

When to See a Doctor
All urinary symptoms require a visit to the doctor. An evaluation for pain, burning, and other symptoms suggestive of infection is imperative because UTIs may not clear up on their own and are easier to cure when treatment starts early. Without therapy, symptoms are likely to worsen and may recur. Over time, the kidneys may be affected—and pyelonephritis is far more difficult to eradicate than urethritis or cystitis. If ignored, UTIs can spread beyond the urinary tract via the circulation, leading to a systemic infection that may be life threatening.

Treatment
Although mild cystitis may clear up on its own, drug therapy is nearly always advisable. Occasional episodes can be treated by your regular doctor, but recurrent infections should be evaluated by a urologist. Numerous antibiotics are available. The one chosen, as well as its dosage and how long it should be taken, depends on your symptoms, how many episodes you've had and their frequency, and the specific microorganism involved (which can be determined with a urine culture).

U

In general, higher doses and a longer course of treatment are required for women with recurrent infections and for all men to prevent or cure prostatitis. Symptoms typically disappear within 48 hours of starting therapy. In the meantime, pain relievers and a heating pad can lessen discomfort. But even if you feel better after taking only a few doses, be sure to finish the prescription to ensure that the infection is eradicated.

When an infection is the cause, antibiotic therapy is highly effective—especially when started soon after symptoms appear. But patients typically feel better so quickly after starting treatment that they often stop the medication too soon. The result can be recurrences with potentially serious complications. Nearly 20 percent of women have a recurrence after their initial episode if they are not treated.

Prevention

Lifestyle measures may help prevent UTIs. Drink lots of fluids (about 64 oz. daily) to dilute urine, and urinate frequently to flush the bladder. Cranberry juice, which makes the urine acidic and kills bacteria, is a good choice—although it is not a cure and its high sugar content may make it a poor choice for people with diabetes. Keep the groin cool and dry to discourage bacterial growth, and wear breathable, cotton underwear and loose-fitting clothing.

Personal hygiene is also important, especially for women. When using toilet paper, wipe from front to back to keep from introducing bacteria from the anal opening into the urethral opening. Avoid perfumed soaps, bubble baths, douches, and laundry detergents, which can cause irritation and inflammation that may worsen symptoms. Urinating immediately after intercourse can help eliminate bacteria that may be introduced into the urethra at that time. It is not known whether hormone replacement therapy helps prevent UTI in women.

The uterus is part of a woman's reproductive system. It is the hollow, pear-shaped organ where a baby grows. The uterus is in the pelvis between the bladder and the rectum.

The narrow, lower portion of the uterus is the cervix. The broad, middle part of the uterus is the body, or corpus. The dome-shaped top of the uterus is the fundus. The fallopian tubes extend from either side of the top of the uterus to the ovaries.

The wall of the uterus has two layers of tissue. The inner layer, or lining, is the endometrium. The outer layer is muscle tissue called the myometrium.

In women of childbearing age, the lining of the uterus grows and thickens each month to prepare for pregnancy. If a woman does not become pregnant, the thick, bloody lining flows out of the body through the vagina. This flow is called menstruation.

Fibroids are common benign tumors that grow in the muscle of the uterus. They occur mainly in women who are in their forties. Women may have many fibroids at the same time. Fibroids do not develop into cancer. As a woman reaches menopause, fibroids are likely to become smaller, and sometimes they disappear.

Usually, fibroids cause no symptoms and need no treatment. But depending on their size and location, fibroids can cause bleeding, vaginal discharge, and frequent urination. Women with these symptoms should see a doctor. If fibroids cause heavy bleeding, or if they press against nearby organs and cause pain, the doctor may suggest surgery or other treatment.

Endometriosis is another benign condition that affects the uterus. It is most common in women in their thirties and forties, especially in women who have never been

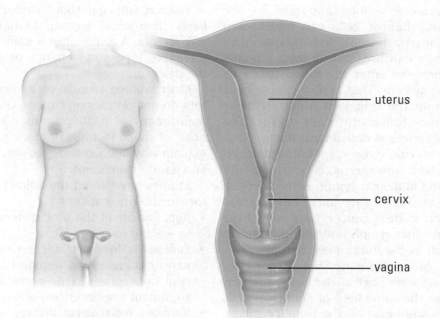

uterus

cervix

vagina

The uterus is a female reproductive organ. After menopause, the lining of the uterus thins and menstruation ceases. The risk of uterine cancer increases after menopause.

pregnant. It occurs when endometrial tissue begins to grow on the outside of the uterus and on nearby organs. This condition may cause painful menstrual periods, abnormal vaginal bleeding, and sometimes loss of fertility (ability to get pregnant), but it does not cause cancer. Women with endometriosis may be treated with hormones or surgery.

Endometrial hyperplasia is an increase in the number of cells in the lining of the uterus. It is not cancer. Sometimes it develops into cancer. Heavy menstrual periods, bleeding between periods, and bleeding after menopause are common symptoms of hyperplasia. It is most common after age 40.

To prevent endometrial hyperplasia from developing into cancer, the doctor may recommend surgery to remove the uterus (hysterectomy) or treatment with hormones (progesterone) and regular follow-up exams.

Malignant tumors are cancer. They are generally more serious and may be life threatening. Cancer cells can invade and damage nearby tissues and organs. Also, cancer cells can break away from a malignant tumor and enter the bloodstream or lymphatic system. That is how cancer cells spread from the original (primary) tumor to form new tumors in other organs. The spread of cancer is called metastasis.

When uterine cancer spreads (metastasizes) outside the uterus, cancer cells are often found in nearby lymph nodes, nerves, or blood vessels. If the cancer has reached the lymph nodes, cancer cells may have spread to other lymph nodes and other organs, such as the lungs, liver, and bones.

When cancer spreads from its original place to another part of the body, the new tumor has the same kind of abnormal cells and the same name as the primary tumor. For example, if cancer of the uterus spreads to the lungs, the cancer cells in the lungs are actually uterine cancer cells. The disease is metastatic uterine cancer, not lung cancer. It is treated as uterine cancer, not lung cancer. Doctors sometimes call the new tumor "distant" disease.

The most common type of cancer of the uterus begins in the lining (endometrium). It is called endometrial cancer, uterine cancer, or cancer of the uterus. In this entry, we will use the terms uterine cancer or cancer of the uterus to refer to cancer that begins in the endometrium.

A different type of cancer, uterine sarcoma, develops in the muscle (myometrium). Cancer that begins in the cervix is also a different type of cancer.

Who's at Risk?

No one knows the exact causes of uterine cancer. However, it is clear that this disease is not contagious. No one can "catch" cancer from another person.

Women who get this disease are more likely than other women to have certain risk factors. A risk factor is something that increases a person's chance of developing the disease.

Most women who have known risk factors do not get uterine cancer. On the other hand, many who do get this disease have none of these factors. Doctors can seldom explain why one woman gets uterine cancer and another does not.

Studies have found the following risk factors for uterine cancer.:

- **Age.** Cancer of the uterus occurs mostly in women over age 50.
- **Endometrial hyperplasia.** The risk of uterine cancer is higher if a woman has endometrial hyperplasia. This condition and its treatment are described above.
- **Hormone replacement therapy (HRT).** HRT is used to control the symptoms of

menopause, to prevent osteoporosis (thinning of the bones), and to reduce the risk of heart disease or stroke.

Women who use estrogen without progesterone have an increased risk of uterine cancer. Long-term use and large doses of estrogen seem to increase this risk. Women who use a combination of estrogen and progesterone have a lower risk of uterine cancer than women who use estrogen alone. The progesterone protects the uterus.

Women should discuss the benefits and risks of HRT with their doctor. Also, having regular checkups while taking HRT may improve the chance that the doctor will find uterine cancer at an early stage, if it does develop.

Obesity and related conditions. The body makes some of its estrogen in fatty tissue. That's why obese women are more likely than thin women to have higher levels of estrogen in their bodies. High levels of estrogen may be the reason that obese women have an increased risk of developing uterine cancer. The risk of this disease is also higher in women with diabetes or high blood pressure (conditions that occur in many obese women).

Tamoxifen. Women taking the drug tamoxifen to prevent or treat breast cancer have an increased risk of uterine cancer. This risk appears to be related to the estrogen-like effect of this drug on the uterus. Doctors monitor women taking tamoxifen for possible signs or symptoms of uterine cancer.

The benefits of tamoxifen to treat breast cancer outweigh the risk of developing other cancers. Still, each woman is different. Any woman considering taking tamoxifen should discuss with the doctor her personal and family medical history and her concerns.

Race. White women are more likely to get uterine cancer than African-American women

Colorectal cancer. Women who have had an inherited form of colorectal cancer have a higher risk of developing uterine cancer than other women.

Other risk factors are related to how long a woman's body is exposed to estrogen. Women who have no children, begin menstruation at a very young age, or enter menopause late in life are exposed to estrogen longer and have a higher risk.

Women with known risk factors or who are concerned about uterine cancer should ask their doctor about the symptoms to watch for and how often to have checkups. The doctor's advice will be based on the woman's age, medical history, and other factors.

Symptoms

Uterine cancer usually occurs after menopause. But it may also occur around the time that menopause begins. Abnormal vaginal bleeding is the most common symptom of uterine cancer. Bleeding may start as a watery, blood-streaked flow that gradually contains more blood. Women should not assume that abnormal vaginal bleeding is part of menopause.

A woman should see her doctor if she has any of the following symptoms:
- Unusual vaginal bleeding or discharge
- Difficult or painful urination
- Pain during intercourse
- Pain in the pelvic area

These symptoms can be caused by cancer or other less serious conditions. Most often they are not cancer, but only a doctor can tell for sure.

Diagnosis

If a woman has symptoms that suggest uterine cancer, her doctor may check general signs of health and may order blood and urine tests. The doctor also may perform one or more of the exams or tests described on the next pages.

- **Pelvic exam.** A woman has a pelvic exam to check the vagina, uterus, bladder, and rectum. The doctor feels these organs for any lumps or changes in their shape or size. To see the upper part of the vagina and the cervix, the doctor inserts an instrument called a speculum into the vagina.
- **Pap test.** The doctor collects cells from the cervix and upper vagina. A medical laboratory checks for abnormal cells. Although the Pap test can detect cancer of the cervix, cells from inside the uterus usually do not show up on a Pap test. This is why the doctor collects samples of cells from inside the uterus in a procedure called a biopsy.
- **Transvaginal ultrasound.** The doctor inserts an instrument into the vagina. The instrument aims high-frequency sound waves at the uterus. The pattern of the echoes they produce creates a picture. If the endometrium looks too thick, the doctor can do a biopsy.
- **Biopsy.** The doctor removes a sample of tissue from the uterine lining. This usually can be done in the doctor's office. In some cases, however, a woman may need to have a dilation and curettage (D&C). A D&C is usually done as same-day surgery with anesthesia in a hospital. A pathologist examines the tissue to check for cancer cells, hyperplasia, and other conditions. For a short time after the biopsy, some women have cramps and vaginal bleeding.

Staging

If uterine cancer is diagnosed, the doctor needs to know the stage, or extent, of the disease to plan the best treatment. Staging is a careful attempt to find out whether the cancer has spread, and if so, to what parts of the body.

The doctor may order blood and urine tests and chest x-rays. The woman also may have other x-rays, CT scans, an ultrasound test, magnetic resonance imaging (MRI), sigmoidoscopy, or colonoscopy.

In most cases, the most reliable way to stage this disease is to remove the uterus (hysterectomy). (The description of surgery in the "Methods of Treatment" section has more information.) After the uterus has been removed, the surgeon can look for obvious signs that the cancer has invaded the muscle of the uterus. The surgeon also can check the lymph nodes and other organs in the pelvic area for signs of cancer. A pathologist uses a microscope to examine the uterus and other tissues removed by the surgeon.

These are the main features of each stage of the disease:

- **Stage I.** The cancer is only in the body of the uterus. It is not in the cervix.
- **Stage II.** The cancer has spread from the body of the uterus to the cervix.
- **Stage III.** The cancer has spread outside the uterus, but not outside the pelvis (and not to the bladder or rectum). Lymph nodes in the pelvis may contain cancer cells.
- **Stage IV.** The cancer has spread into the bladder or rectum. Or it has spread beyond the pelvis to other body parts.

Treatment

The choice of treatment depends on the size of the tumor, the stage of the disease, whether female hormones affect tumor growth, and the tumor grade. (The grade tells how closely the cancer cells resemble normal cells and suggests how fast the cancer is likely to grow. Low-grade cancers are likely to grow and spread more slowly than high-grade cancers.) The doctor also considers other factors, including the woman's age and general health.

Women with uterine cancer have many treatment options. Most women with uterine cancer are treated with surgery. Some have radiation therapy. A smaller number of women may be treated with hormonal therapy. Some patients receive a combination of therapies.

The doctor is the best person to describe the treatment choices and discuss the expected results of treatment.

A woman may want to talk with her doctor about taking part in a clinical trial, a research study of new treatment methods. Clinical trials are an important option for women with all stages of uterine cancer (see page 624).

Most women with uterine cancer have surgery to remove the uterus (hysterectomy) through an incision in the abdomen. The doctor also removes both fallopian tubes and both ovaries. (This procedure is called a bilateral salpingo-oophorectomy.)

The doctor may also remove the lymph nodes near the tumor to see if they contain cancer. If cancer cells have reached the lymph nodes, it may mean that the disease has spread to other parts of the body. If cancer cells have not spread beyond the endometrium, the woman may not need to have any other treatment. The length of the hospital stay may vary from several days to a week.

In radiation therapy, high-energy rays are used to kill cancer cells. Like surgery, radiation therapy is a local therapy. It affects cancer cells only in the treated area.

Some women with Stage I, II, or III uterine cancer need both radiation therapy and surgery. They may have radiation before surgery to shrink the tumor or after surgery to destroy any cancer cells that remain in the area. Also, the doctor may suggest radiation treatments for the small number of women who cannot have surgery.

Doctors use two types of radiation therapy to treat uterine cancer:

External radiation: In external radiation therapy, a large machine outside the body is used to aim radiation at the tumor area. The woman is usually an outpatient in a hospital or clinic and receives external radiation five days a week for several weeks. This schedule helps protect healthy cells and tissue by spreading out the total dose of radiation. No radioactive materials are put into the body for external radiation therapy.

Internal radiation: In internal radiation therapy, tiny tubes containing a radioactive substance are inserted through the vagina and left in place for a few days. The woman stays in the hospital during this treatment. To protect others from radiation exposure, the patient may not be able to have visitors or may have visitors only for a short period of time while the implant is in place. Once the implant is removed, the woman has no radioactivity in her body.

Hormonal therapy involves substances that prevent cancer cells from getting or using the hormones they may need to grow. Hormones can attach to hormone receptors, causing changes in uterine tissue. Before therapy begins, the doctor may request a hormone receptor test. This special lab test of uterine tissue helps the doctor learn if estrogen and progesterone receptors are present. If the tissue has receptors, the woman is more likely to respond to hormonal therapy.

Hormonal therapy is called a systemic therapy because it can affect cancer cells throughout the body. Usually, hormonal therapy is a type of progesterone taken as a pill.

The doctor may use hormonal therapy for women with uterine cancer who are unable to have surgery or radiation therapy. Also, the doctor may give hormonal therapy to

The Promise of Cancer Research

In a large trial with hundreds of women, doctors are studying a less extensive method of surgery to remove the uterus. Normally, the doctor makes an incision in the abdomen to remove the uterus. In this study, doctors use a laparoscope (a lighted tube) to help remove the uterus through the vagina. Also, the doctor can use the laparoscope to help remove the ovaries and lymph nodes and to look into the abdomen for signs of cancer.

Other researchers are looking at the effectiveness of radiation therapy after surgery, as well as at the combination of surgery, radiation, and chemotherapy. Other trials are studying new drugs, new drug combinations, and biological therapies. Some of these studies are designed to find ways to reduce the side effects of treatment and to improve the quality of women's lives.

A woman who is interested in being part of a clinical trial should talk with her doctor. NCI's cancerTrials Web site at http://cancertrials.nci. nih.gov provides general information about clinical trials. (Also see page 181 for more on clinical trials.)

women with uterine cancer that has spread to the lungs or other distant sites. It is also given to women with uterine cancer that has come back.

Side Effects of Cancer Treatment

Because cancer treatment may damage healthy cells and tissues, unwanted side effects sometimes occur. These side effects depend on many factors, including the type and extent of the treatment. Side effects may not be the same for each person, and they may even change from one treatment session to the next. Before treatment starts, doctors and nurses will explain the possible side effects and how they will help you manage them.

Surgery

After a hysterectomy, women usually have some pain and feel extremely tired. Most women return to their normal activities within four to eight weeks after surgery. Some may need more time than that.

Some women may have problems with nausea and vomiting after surgery, and some may have bladder and bowel problems. The doctor may restrict the woman's diet to liquids at first, with a gradual return to solid food.

Women who have had a hysterectomy no longer have menstrual periods and can no longer get pregnant. When the ovaries are removed, menopause occurs at once. Hot flashes and other symptoms of menopause caused by surgery may be more severe than those caused by natural menopause. Hormone replacement therapy (HRT) is often given to women who have not had uterine cancer to relieve these problems. However, doctors usually do not give the hormone estrogen to women who have had uterine cancer. Because estrogen is a risk factor for this disease (see "Who's at Risk?" page 620), many doctors are concerned that estrogen may cause uterine cancer to return. Other doctors point out that there is no scientific evidence that estrogen increases the risk that cancer will come back. NCI is sponsoring a large research study to learn whether women who have had early stage uterine cancer can take estrogen safely.

For some women, a hysterectomy can affect sexual intimacy. A woman may have feelings of loss that may make intimacy difficult. Sharing these feelings with her partner may be helpful.

Radiation Therapy

The side effects of radiation therapy depend mainly on the treatment dose and the part of the body that is treated. Common side effects of radiation include dry, reddened skin and hair loss in the treated area, loss of appetite, and extreme tiredness. Some women may have dryness, itching, tightening, and burning in the vagina. Radiation also may cause diarrhea or frequent and uncomfortable urination. It may reduce the number of white blood cells, which help protect the body against infection.

Doctors may advise their patients not to have intercourse during radiation therapy. However, most can resume sexual activity within a few weeks after treatment ends. The doctor or nurse may suggest ways to relieve any vaginal discomfort related to treatment.

Hormonal Therapy

Hormonal therapy can cause a number of side effects. Women taking progesterone may retain fluid, have an increased appetite, and gain weight. Women who are still menstruating may have changes in their periods.

Follow-up Care

Follow-up care after treatment for uterine cancer is important. Women should not hesitate to discuss follow-up with their doctor. Regular checkups ensure that any changes in health are noticed. Any problem that develops can be found and treated as soon as possible. Checkups may include a physical exam, a pelvic exam, x-rays, and laboratory tests.

National Cancer Institute

U

Vaginitis is an inflammation of a woman's vagina. As many as one third of women will have symptoms of vaginitis sometime during their lives. Vaginitis affects women of all ages. There are many possible causes, and the type of treatment depends on the cause.

This entry tells you about the symptoms, causes and treatment of some of the most common types of vaginitis. It also explains how to prevent getting an infection.

The Vagina

The vagina has a normal discharge—fluid that passes out of the vagina—that is clear or cloudy and whitish. A healthy vagina keeps a balance of many organisms, such as bacteria and yeast.

Many factors can affect the normal balance of the vagina:

- Antibiotics
- Changes in hormone levels, such as those that occur with pregnancy or menopause
- Douches
- Spermicides
- Sexual intercourse
- Sexually transmitted diseases (STDs)

A change in the normal balance can allow either yeast or bacteria to increase and result in vaginitis. Vaginitis can result from irritation, from growth of organisms in the vagina, or from infection.

Common vaginal irritants include perfumed soaps, powders, feminine hygiene products, and spermicidal foams, gels, and creams. Friction from inadequately lubricated condoms also can irritate vaginal surfaces. Eliminating the source of irritation usually helps prevent vaginitis.

Diagnosis and Treatment

To diagnose vaginitis, your doctor will take a sample of the discharge from your vagina and look at it under a microscope. Your doctor may also suggest other tests. To ensure the results of the test are accurate, do not douche or use any vaginal medications or spermicide before you see your doctor.

Treatment may depend on the cause of the vaginitis, as well as on your special needs. For instance, some medications may not be used during pregnancy. Treatment may be either with a pill or by applying a cream or gel to the vagina.

Follow your doctor's instructions exactly, even if the discharge or other symptoms go away before you finish the medication. Even though the symptoms disappear, the infection could still be present. Stopping the treatment may cause symptoms to come back. If symptoms recur after the treatment is finished, see your doctor again—a different treatment may be needed.

Types of Vaginitis
Yeast Infection

Yeast infection is also known as candidiasis. It is one of the most common types of vaginal infection.

Cause. Yeast infection is caused by a fungus called *Candida*. It is found in small numbers in the normal vagina. However, when the balance of the vagina is changed, the yeast may overgrow and cause infection.

Many women who take antibiotics will get yeast infections. The antibiotics kill normal vaginal bacteria, and the yeast then has a chance to overgrow. A woman is more likely to get yeast infections if she is pregnant or has diabetes. Overgrowth of yeast can also occur if the body's immune system, which protects the body from disease, isn't working well. For example, in women infected with HIV (human immunodeficiency virus), yeast infections may be severe. They may not go away, even with treatment, or may recur often. In many cases, the cause of a yeast infection is not known.

Symptoms. The most common symptoms of a yeast infection are itching and burning of the vagina and vulva. The burning may be worse with urination or sex. The vulva may be red and swollen. The vaginal discharge is usually white and has no odor. It may look like cottage cheese. Some women with yeast infections notice an increase or change in discharge. Others do not notice a discharge at all. Some women may have no symptoms.

Treatment. Yeast infections are usually treated by placing medication into the vagina. Some doctors may prescribe a single dose you take by mouth. In most cases, treatment of male sex partners is not necessary.

You can buy over-the-counter yeast medication, but be sure to see your doctor if:

- this is the first time you've had a vaginal infection;
- your symptoms do not go away after treatment;
- your vaginal discharge is yellow or green or has a bad odor;
- there is a chance that you have an STD.

Sometimes a woman thinks she has a yeast infection when she actually has another problem. The medication may mask another cause for vaginitis. If there is another cause, it may be harder to find if a woman is taking medication for a yeast infection.

Bacterial Vaginosis

Causes. The bacteria that cause bacterial vaginosis occur naturally in the vagina. Bacterial vaginosis is caused by overgrowth of several of these bacteria. It is not clear whether it can be passed through sex.

Symptoms. The main symptom is increased discharge with a strong fishy odor. The odor

What You Can Do

There are a number of things you can do to lower the risk of getting infectious vaginitis:

- Do not use feminine hygiene sprays or scented, deodorant tampons. You should not try to cover up a bad odor. It could be a sign of infection that should prompt you to see your doctor. Do not douche. It is better to let the vagina cleanse itself.
- Thoroughly clean diaphragms, cervical caps and spermicide applicators after each use.
- Use condoms during sex.

Check with your doctor about preventing yeast infections if you are prescribed antibiotics for another type of infection.

is stronger during your menstrual period or after sex. The discharge is thin and dark or dull gray. Itching is not common, but may be present if there is a lot of discharge. Some women may have no symptoms.

Treatment. Two antibiotics are used to treat bacterial vaginosis. One is a drug called metronidazole. It can be taken by mouth or applied to the vagina as a gel. The other drug is called clindamycin. It can also be taken by mouth or applied to the vagina as a cream.

When metronidazole is taken by mouth, it can cause side effects in some patients. These include nausea, vomiting, and darkening of urine. Do not drink alcohol when taking metronidazole. The combination can cause severe nausea and vomiting.

Usually there is no need to treat a woman's sex partner. But if the woman has repeated infections, treatment of the partner may be helpful. Some doctors may suggest that the couple not have sex or that they use a condom during treatment.

Bacterial vaginosis often comes back. It may require long-term or repeated treatment.

In most cases, treatment eventually works in time. Sometimes when bacterial vaginosis keeps coming back it may mean that you have another STD. Your doctor may test you for other infections.

Trichomonas Vaginitis

Causes. Trichomonas is a parasite that is spread through sex. Women who have trichomonas vaginitis are at higher risk for infection with other STDs.

Symptoms. Signs of trichomoniasis may include a yellow-gray or green vaginal discharge. The discharge may have a fishy odor. There may be burning, irritation, redness and swelling of the vulva and vagina. Sometimes there is pain during urination.

Treatment. Trichomoniasis is usually treated with a single dose of metronidazole by mouth. Do not drink alcohol for 24 hours when taking this drug because it causes nausea and vomiting. Sexual partners must be treated at the same time for treatment to work.

Atrophic Vaginitis

This type of vaginitis is linked with not having enough estrogen. It can occur during breast-feeding and after menopause. Symptoms include vaginal dryness and burning. Atrophic vaginitis is treated with estrogen, either taken by mouth or applied as a vaginal cream. If for some reason a woman cannot take estrogen, she may find a water-soluble lubricant helpful.

At the first sign of any abnormal discharge or symptoms of vaginitis, contact your doctor so that the problem can be properly diagnosed and treated. Although vaginitis can be annoying and uncomfortable, it can almost always be successfully treated once the cause has been found.

American College of Obstetricians and Gynecologists

Varicose veins are distended, bulging veins that are typically located on the inside of the legs and the back of the calf. They result from a weakening in the wall of a vein. The term varicose, derived from the Latin word varix, refers to the twisted, rope-like shapes made by the veins. Spider veins, also known as telangiectasias, are smaller, dilated venous capillaries (tiny blood vessels) that lie closer to the skin surface. These threadlike vessels, red or bluish in color, generally appear on the legs and face—most often on the outside of the thighs, around the knees, and on the nose or cheeks. About 80 million Americans have spider veins, varicose veins, or a combination of both.

Symptoms

Some spider veins and varicose veins primarily pose a cosmetic problem, though even small spider veins can cause symptoms such as burning, swelling, throbbing, cramping, and leg fatigue. Patients with larger varicose veins may experience aching pain and heaviness in the legs, swelling in the lower legs, and persistent itching around the affected veins.

If left untreated, some varicose veins can lead to more serious problems, such as dermatitis (skin inflammation), bleeding, painful skin ulcers, and thrombophlebitis (formation of a blood clot inside an inflamed vein). Thrombophlebitis that affects the saphenous vein (a large vein in the middle of the leg that, like all veins, carries blood to the heart) or one of its branches—so-called superficial thrombophlebitis—usually heals within a few days. A clot that forms very high in a thigh vein, however, can sometimes progress into the deep venous system and lead to pulmonary embolism, a potentially life-threatening complication.

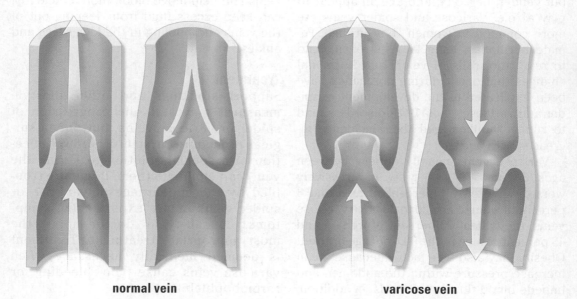

normal vein   **varicose vein**

In a normal vein, the valve opens to allow blood to flow toward the heart, then closes securely to prevent backflow in the opposite direction. A varicose vein occurs when these valves fail.

Causes

The superficial saphenous veins and the deep veins in the middle of the leg are the primary veins that carry blood from the legs to the heart. Perforating, or communicating, veins link the deep and superficial veins. Contractions of calf muscles help pump blood through the veins on the uphill journey to the heart. To counter the pull of gravity and prevent blood from flowing backward, leg veins are equipped with tiny valves that close at regular intervals. These valves may become defective and allow blood to flow back down the leg and pool in the veins. The increased pressure in the distended veins can cause fluid to leak out into the surrounding tissues and produce swelling. Varicose veins typically form in the greater and lesser saphenous veins and their branches.

Who's at Risk?

What causes the wall of a vein to weaken or a venous valve to malfunction is unknown, but gender, heredity, and age all appear to play a role. Varicose and spider veins are more common in women than in men. Female hormones, especially estrogen, tend to relax the walls of veins, and hormonal changes that occur during pregnancy have been implicated in the development of spider and varicose veins. Both disorders tend to run in families, and their incidence increases with age.

Varicose veins usually appear between ages 30 and 70 and grow progressively worse. While only 1 percent of men and 8 percent of women age 20 to 30 have varicose veins, they affect 72 percent of women and 43 percent of men in the 60 to 70 age bracket. Obesity may also be a factor because it can increase pressure within the abdomen and impede blood flow in the veins. In addition, prolonged standing or sitting, particularly with the legs bent or crossed, can worsen the problem.

Prevention

Although some predisposing factors for spider and varicose veins, such as age, heredity, and gender, obviously can't be changed, you can take several practical steps to reduce your risk:

- Exercise regularly by walking, jogging, bicycling, and swimming to improve blood circulation in your legs and help prevent pooling.
- Lose weight if you are overweight.
- Wear low-heeled shoes and avoid tight-fitting clothing.
- Elevate your legs above your heart several times a day by lying on your back and resting your feet on some pillows.
- Avoid prolonged periods of sitting or standing, and move your legs frequently. Periodically flexing the ankles helps pump blood out of the legs.

All the above measures can also help keep existing spider or varicose veins from getting worse. In addition, wearing elastic support stockings, which compress the veins and help move blood more efficiently, can keep excess fluid from seeping out of the veins and pooling in the lower legs and ankles.

Treatment

Support stockings and other lifestyle measures may stall the progression of spider or varicose veins, but only a surgical procedure or sclerotherapy (injection of a special solution to shrink the vein) can eliminate them. If you are troubled by the appearance of varicose or spider veins or are experiencing symptoms, consult your doctor about the most appropriate treatment. Treatment is deemed medically necessary when varicose veins cause pain, bleeding, or thrombophlebitis.

Dermatologists can eradicate spider and varicose veins with sclerotherapy and laser therapy; vascular surgeons carry out surgical ligation and stripping, ambulatory phlebectomy, and radiofrequency endovascular ablation. The choice of procedure depends on the size and extent of the abnormal veins as well as the patient's age, treatment history, presence of allergies, and ability to tolerate anesthesia and surgery.

In some cases, a Doppler or duplex ultrasound study (imaging techniques that measure blood flow) may be performed prior to the procedure to identify the incompetent valves and determine the degree of reflux (backward flow of blood). After the diseased vessel is eliminated, circulation in the legs typically improves as nearby healthy veins take over and restore normal blood flow.

Sclerotherapy. Sclerotherapy is an outpatient procedure used to treat spider veins and certain varicose veins. Sclerotherapy is generally reserved for smaller varicose veins, ranging from 2 to 3 mm in diameter. Several treatment sessions are often required. In this procedure, the physician injects a sclerosing, or hardening, agent into the affected veins through a fine needle. The agent may be a special chemical solution or a concentrated salt (saline) solution. The solution irritates the lining of the vein and causes it to collapse; the treated vein is absorbed by the body during the natural healing process.

After the procedure, the patient must wear compression bandages or graduated support stockings for two to three weeks. Walking and moderate exercise may hasten recovery. Side effects of sclerotherapy include slight swelling of the leg or foot, minor bruising, allergic reactions, and soreness. A yellow-brownish discoloration of the treated area may last for up to six months.

Laser therapy. Laser therapy and intense pulsed light therapy are useful for treating spider veins on the face and isolated spider veins on the legs. Laser or pulsed light therapy is a good option for people with spider veins who are afraid of needles or have had a poor response to sclerotherapy. The heat from the high-intensity laser beam or pulsed light device destroys the abnormal veins. Depending on the severity and density of the veins, from two to five laser treatments—each lasting about 15 minutes—are typically needed to remove the spider veins.

Any larger varicose veins present on the legs must be treated—for example, by surgery or sclerotherapy—before laser therapy is performed. If they are left untreated, reverse pressure from these enlarged veins can cause the spider veins to recur after laser therapy.

Surgical ligation and stripping. Larger and more extensive varicose veins—those measuring about 3 mm or more in diameter—can be treated with surgical ligation and stripping, a procedure usually performed in the hospital. It is important to identify and ligate any affected perforating veins because they could feed a whole cluster of varicose veins. In this procedure, the surgeon makes an incision, usually at the groin, and ties off, or ligates, the enlarged vein above the bulging section. The varicose section of the vein is then stripped, or removed, through another incision, generally at the level of the knee.

The procedure may be done either under local or general anesthesia, most often on an outpatient basis. The leg is bandaged after the surgery, and patients are usually able to resume their normal activities in about two weeks. The surgical approach leaves patients with some scars; but it eliminates the pain caused by varicose veins, and patients are generally pleased with the results.

Ambulatory phlebectomy. In this outpatient procedure, originally developed in Europe, a varicose vein is removed through a series of tiny incisions made along the path of the enlarged vein. Generally reserved for superficial varicose veins, ambulatory phlebectomy

V

A New Treatment Using Radiofrequency

Radiofrequency ablation is a relatively new, minimally invasive technique for treating varicose veins. Its primary role is to treat people with saphenous vein disease. It doesn't address isolated superficial varicose veins or incompetent perforating veins. This procedure involves insertion of a small tube, called a catheter, into the abnormal vein through a tiny puncture. When radiofrequency energy is delivered through the catheter to the vein wall, the resulting heat causes the vein to shrink and to seal shut. Generally, patients can walk right after the procedure and resume all their normal activities within 24 hours. Radiofrequency ablation produces good cosmetic results, but it is not yet widely available, and its long-term effectiveness is unknown.

is performed under tumescent anesthesia, a form of local anesthesia in which a dilute anesthetic solution is infiltrated along the course of the vein. No stitches are required to close the incisions. People who undergo this procedure experience much less pain than after traditional vein surgery, but there is mild bruising that usually disappears in a few weeks. Patients wear support stockings for two weeks, but they are usually able to resume their normal activities the day after the procedure.

Hepatitis is inflammation of the liver. Several different viruses cause viral hepatitis. They are named the hepatitis A, B, C, D, and E viruses.

All of these viruses cause acute, or short-term, viral hepatitis. The hepatitis B, C, and D viruses can also cause chronic hepatitis, in which the infection is prolonged, sometimes lifelong.

Other viruses may also cause hepatitis, but they have yet to be discovered and they are obviously rare causes of the disease.

Symptoms of Viral Hepatitis
Symptoms include:
- Jaundice (yellowing of the skin and whites of the eyes)
- Fatigue
- Abdominal pain
- Loss of appetite
- Nausea
- Diarrhea
- Vomiting

However, some people do not have symptoms until the disease is advanced.

Hepatitis A
Disease Spread
Primarily through food or water contaminated by feces from an infected person. Rarely, it spreads through contact with infected blood.

People at Risk
International travelers; people living in areas where hepatitis A outbreaks are common; people who live with or have sex with an infected person; and, during outbreaks, day care children and employees, sexually active gay men, and injection drug users.

Prevention
The hepatitis A vaccine; also, avoiding tap water when traveling internationally and practicing good hygiene and sanitation.

Treatment
Hepatitis A usually resolves on its own over several weeks.

Hepatitis B
Disease Spread
Through contact with infected blood, through sex with an infected person, and from mother to child during childbirth.

People at Risk
Injection drug users, people who have sex with an infected person, men who have sex with men, children of immigrants from disease-endemic areas, people who live with an infected person, infants born to infected mothers, health-care workers, and hemodialysis patients.

Prevention
The hepatitis B vaccine.

Treatment
Drug treatment with alpha interferon or lamivudine.

Hepatitis C
Disease Spread
Primarily through contact with infected blood; less commonly, through sexual contact and childbirth.

People at Risk
Injection drug users, hemodialysis patients, health-care workers, people who have sex with an infected person, people who have multiple sex partners, infants born to infected women, and people who received a transfusion of blood or blood products before July 1992 or clotting factors made before 1987.

Prevention
There is no vaccine for hepatitis C—the only way to prevent the disease is to reduce the

Liver Cancer

Hepatoma is a cancer that begins in the liver cells—and chronic infection with hepatitis B or hepatitis C is the chief risk factor. Also called hepatocellular carcinoma or liver cancer, hepatomas account for up to 90 percent of all primary liver cancers. (Cancer that originates in the liver is known as primary liver cancer. When cancer that originates in another site—such as the lung—spreads to the liver, it is known as metastatic cancer.) Hepatomas are more common in men, and typically occur in people 50 to 60 years old.

Risk Factors

The exact cause of liver cancer is unknown, but certain risk factors have been identified. In addition to hepatitis, cirrhosis of the liver—a disease that is characterized by scar tissue formation in the liver, most often owing to alcoholism or viral hepatitis—is another leading risk factor. Other risk factors include: hemachromatosis (a disease that results in the storage of excess iron in body tissues); chronic exposure to aflatoxin—a toxin produced by mold that contaminates peanuts, wheat, soybeans, ground nuts, corn, and rice; long-term use of anabolic steroids; and drinking water contaminated with arsenic. Research also suggests that long-term oral contraceptive use (more than eight years) is associated with an increased risk of liver cancer. Nevertheless, liver cancer is rare and occurs in less than one woman per million long-term users of birth control pills.

Symptoms

Signs of liver cancer include:

- Abdominal pain, especially in the right upper quadrant
- Bloated abdomen
- Weakness
- Jaundice (yellowing of the skin and eyes)
- Tendency to bruise easily
- Fever
- Loss of appetite

Treatment

The three main types of treatment for liver cancer are surgery, radiation, and chemotherapy. Sometimes, more than one type of treatment may be used. Which type of treatment is chosen depends on the stage of the cancer, the condition of the liver (if the patient has cirrhosis, the liver may not have enough healthy tissue to make certain treatments possible), and the patient's general health.

Surgical removal of the tumor offers the only hope of a cure. However, in most cases, it is not possible to completely remove the tumor since liver cancer is often not diagnosed until the tumor is too large to remove or has spread beyond the liver. Sometimes, surgical procedures are used to treat liver cancer without removing the tumor. Examples of such procedures include tumor ablation, which typically involves freezing the tumor (cryosurgery), and embolization, which reduces the blood supply to the tumor by blocking the artery that feeds the malignancy.

Chemotherapy may help shrink liver tumors, but there is little evidence that it improves the survival of hepatoma patients.

Radiation therapy can also shrink tumor cells and may provide pain relief for patients with liver cancer. However, radiation therapy can not cure cancer, nor has it been proven to help patients live longer. *The Editors*

risk of exposure to the virus. This means avoiding behaviors like sharing drug needles or sharing personal items like toothbrushes, razors, and nail clippers with a person who is infected.

Treatment

Drug treatment with alpha interferon or combination treatment with interferon and the drug ribavirin.

Hepatitis D

Disease Spread

Through contact with infected blood. This disease occurs only in people who are already infected with hepatitis B.

People at Risk

Anyone infected with hepatitis B. Injection drug users who have hepatitis B have the highest risk. People who have hepatitis B are also at risk if they have sex with a person infected with hepatitis D or if they live with an infected person.

Prevention

Immunization against hepatitis B for those not already infected; also, avoiding exposure to infected blood, contaminated needles, and an infected person's personal items (toothbrush, razor, nail clippers).

Treatment

Drug treatment with alpha interferon.

Hepatitis E

Disease Spread

Through food or water contaminated by feces from an infected person. This disease is uncommon in the United States.

People at Risk

International travelers; people living in areas where hepatitis E outbreaks are common; and people who live or have sex with an infected person.

Prevention

There is no vaccine for hepatitis E—the only way to prevent the disease is to reduce the risk of exposure to the hepatitis E virus. This means avoiding tap water when traveling internationally and practicing good hygiene and sanitation.

Treatment

Hepatitis E usually resolves on its own over several weeks to months.

Other Causes of Viral Hepatitis

Some cases of viral hepatitis cannot be attributed to the hepatitis A, B, C, D, or E viruses. This is called non A...E hepatitis or hepatitis X. Scientists have identified several candidate viruses, but none have been proven to cause hepatitis. The search for the virus responsible for hepatitis X continues.

National Institute of Diabetes and Digestive and Kidney Diseases

Over the years, everyone develops wrinkles. But age alone is not responsible: Most wrinkles are caused by overexposure to sunlight, an environmental factor that can be controlled. Although sun damage is cumulative, protective measures can help prevent future skin injury, and reduce the risk for skin cancer (see page 572). Precautions against the sun include avoiding direct sunlight, especially between 10 a.m. and 4 p.m.; liberally using a sunscreen with a sun protection factor (SPF) of 15 or higher that protects against UVA and UVB rays; and wearing sunglasses, hats and other protective clothing.

As for wrinkles that already exist, treatment—whether topical or surgical—is aimed at minimizing fine lines and tightening droopy skin. Bear in mind that no treatment can reverse aging or prevent new wrinkles from forming.

Causes

Only a few facial furrows—specifically the so-called "laugh lines" around the corners of the eyes and in between the nose and upper lip—are a natural consequence of aging. These tiny, hairline depressions probably occur because gradual loosening of elastic fibers that keep the skin taut allow it to sag. A few other depressions appear because of the patterns created by facial expressions. But the most bothersome wrinkles are caused by environmental factors, especially overexposure to the ultraviolet (UV) rays of sunlight. Two types of UV rays, which are not thoroughly filtered by the earth's protective (albeit threatened) ozone layer, play a role in skin damage:

• UVA is strongly associated with tanning, wrinkles, and melanoma (the most serious form of skin cancer);

• UVB is closely associated with sunburn and basal and squamous cell carcinoma (two other types of skin cancer).

Although it is not known how sun-associated skin damage occurs, some researchers think that UV rays attack the body's immune system and increase the production of enzymes that break down collagen, a protein in the connective tissue located underneath the dermis (the layer of skin below the outer layer, or epidermis).

Treatment

Several types of treatments are aimed at softening wrinkles. Topical ointments remove the top layer of skin cells, allowing the underlying cells—which have not been exposed to the sun—to emerge; topical procedures, such as laser resurfacing and dermabrasion, also remove the top layer of skin cells; injections, such as collagen or botox, temporarily plump up the wrinkles; surgical procedures can remove excess tissue and tighten the skin.

Topical Preparations

Special creams are useful for smoothing out fine lines and minimizing sun-associated roughness. They include products containing tretinoin (Renova) or high concentrations of alpha-hydroxy acid. Low-concentration alpha-hydroxy products are available over-the-counter, but they're relatively ineffective.

Tretinoin sloughs off dead skin, regenerates collagen, and allows cells in the top layer of skin, which are continuously replaced, to mature more normally than untreated sun-damaged cells. Side effects include temporary dryness, peeling, redness, blistering, and a permanent increase in sun sensitivity.

Alpha-hydroxy acids slough off dead skin and thicken the layer of underlying cells. Treatment causes redness and blistering that lasts a few weeks. Some preparations can be used at home, while others must be applied by a physician.

W

Topical Procedures

Laser resurfacing, dermabrasion, and chemical peels are generally performed in an outpatient clinic or physician's office. They all involve some discomfort, although medication can usually eliminate pain. Several weeks are required for healing and aftercare (such as changing dressings or applying ointment), and it may take several months for redness to disappear. Afterward, the skin is nearly always more sensitive to the sun, and vigilant lifelong sun protection is essential. In skilled hands, complications are rare. But all cosmetic procedures should be used judiciously, especially on people with dark complexions, who are more vulnerable to scarring and discoloration than those with light complexions.

No matter what technique you choose, be sure that the physician who will perform the procedure is highly experienced. Plastic and dermatologic surgeons are generally the best qualified. The technique that's best for you depends largely on your budget, goals, and the level of inconvenience you are willing to tolerate. The extent, depth, and location of the wrinkles should also be considered. Among the most effective procedures are:

Laser resurfacing. High-energy laser technology produces the most lasting and dramatic results of all the anti-wrinkle procedures; however, it's also the most expensive. The equipment produces short, high energy pulses that heat the water inside selected cells in the top layers of skin. This vaporizes the water and exposes the new, smoother, undamaged skin below. It also causes the remaining skin to tighten, possibly by shortening collagen fibers. Mild to moderate wrinkles disappear, while deeper ones are minimized.

The technique is precise and nearly painfree, although healing takes up to two weeks and redness may last for six months. While treated wrinkles do not recur, new wrinkles can emerge over time due to normal aging. The major risk is scarring, but in the hands of a skilled physician, the complication rate is less than 1 percent.

Dermabrasion. The physician freezes and then sands or scrapes away the outermost layer of skin with a motorized instrument. Dermabrasion causes redness, scaling, and peeling for about a week; swelling for about two weeks; and pinkness for two to three months. Treated wrinkles do not recur, but new age-associated wrinkles may appear.

Dermabrasion is generally used for wrinkles around the upper lip and chin; it cannot be used around the eyes. The principal complications, though rare, are infection, permanent discoloration, and scarring.

Chemical peels. This technique uses chemicals to strip away the outermost layer of skin. It causes redness, scaling, and swelling. Depending on the chemical used, full recovery takes three to six months. (Usual activities can gradually be resumed after two weeks.) Improvement may be temporary or permanent, again depending on the type of chemical.

Peels are most effective for fine wrinkles around the upper lip; they cannot be used around the eyes. The major risks, though rare, are whiteheads, infection, allergic reaction, cold sores, permanent discoloration, numbness, and scarring.

Injections

Fine wrinkles can be plumped up with injections of fat or collagen. Temporary stinging, throbbing, burning, faint redness, or swelling may occur for a short time immediately after treatment. Risks include allergic reactions, connective tissue or autoimmune disease, contour irregularities, and infection. Improvement lasts only about a year.

Injections of Botulinum toxin—a derivative of Clostridium botulinum, the bacterium that causes botulism—lessens facial wrinkles by weakening muscles. These injections are generally considered safe, although the Food and Drug Administration (FDA) has not approved them for cosmetic purposes. Botulinum toxin is most commonly used to minimize age-related wrinkles and sagging skin at the neck. It is not effective for wrinkles caused by sun exposure. Results typically last about three to six months. Potential side effects may be caused by muscle weakness, but they are rare, generally mild, and usually transitory.

Surgery

Facelift and eyelid surgery can be performed on an outpatient basis, usually with local anesthesia and, sometimes, sedation. Complications are rare with experienced physicians, but the true incidence of complications is unknown since there is no mandatory reporting or review of adverse events. Ethical and medical standards vary widely so make sure you select an experienced, reputable doctor.

Surgery can help tighten droopy skin, but it is important to note that neither procedure eliminates wrinkles around the eyes and other parts of the face. In addition, the face continues to age after treatment, and skin that has been surgically tightened may begin to sag. Scrupulous sun protection can help protect results and, if necessary, additional treatments can be considered.

Facelift (rhytidectomy). A facelift can minimize jowls, a double chin, and the crease that often develops where the cheek and lip meet. Facelifts take several hours to complete and may require general anesthesia. Patients can usually go back to work and gradually resume other activities within three weeks. Results last 5 to 10 years.

Temporary side effects may include swelling, numbness, tightness, tenderness, dry skin, and bruising. Risks include injury to the nerves that control facial muscles, infection, poor healing, excessive scarring, asymmetry, and changes in the hairline.

Eyelid surgery (blepharoplasty). Eyelid surgery is used to minimize droopy upper eyelids and puffy bags below the eyes. The procedure usually takes one to three hours. Patients can usually read again in two to three days, and can resume work in five to seven days. Results last years or even a lifetime.

Temporary side effects may include tightness of the lids, swelling, bruising, dryness, burning, and itching of the eyes. Excessive tearing and sensitivity to light, blurred or double vision, infection, swelling at the corners of the eyelids, and tiny whiteheads are also possible. Blindness is a rare complication. Slight asymmetry in healing or scarring may also occur. Some patients have difficulty closing their eyes completely, but this problem usually improves over time and may be correctable with a second procedure.

appendix

It's disconcerting to consider that, if you're like most Americans, you would have better luck finding reliable, quantitative information to help you pick out a new stereo or microwave oven than you would to choose a doctor, hospital, or health insurance plan. Fortunately, recent changes in legislation, along with increasing access to the Internet and other resources, have begun to rectify this situation. The general public now has access to more and more empiric performance data that were once difficult or impossible to procure—such as records of physician and hospital errors, malpractice verdicts, health plan "report cards," and the comparative success rates and mortality rates of various medical facilities.

However, interpreting data about the performance of health-care providers requires patience and some degree of sophistication. Although the information may be objective, it can reflect many different variables that must be considered for any of your conclusions to be valid. For example, some physicians and hospitals may treat sicker patients than others, which may preclude direct comparison of death or complication rates. Similarly, some procedures are inherently riskier than others, though they may be necessary. Perhaps worst of all, unscrupulous providers may be tempted to manipulate information so that poor performance is kept off the record. Despite these drawbacks, performance data can empower you to take greater control of your own health and medical care. But it's recommended that after gathering information, you discuss it with a trusted physician to clarify inconsistencies and ultimately make a decision about what the best health care is for you.

Information on Physicians

With the growth of managed care plans for health insurance, many Americans are asked to find a new doctor—and often are limited to choosing from a list of doctors who participate in a particular health-care plan. Hence, there is a need for people to obtain information about the doctors available to them. You can do this by getting referrals from people you trust, including health-care professionals who have treated you in the past. Many hospitals also have referral services that can recommend doctors who are on their staffs and provide information about their training. Also, the health information organizations listed on pages 645-653 will sometimes make referrals, so you should check with them.

Ruling out doctors who have been disciplined for serious infractions by state medical boards is one way to avoid incompetence. Such actions are taken against about 2,600 doctors a year (one half of 1 percent of all physicians). The actions are recorded in The National Practitioner's Data Bank (NPDB), created by Congress under the Health Care Quality Improvement Act (HCQIA) of 1986. The goal of the legislation is to prevent incompetent physicians and dentists from moving their practices across state lines without disclosing their records. At present, access to the NPDB is restricted, mostly to hospitals and health maintenance organizations (HMOs).

Patient advocacy groups are lobbying for public access, and Congress is considering the possibility. Meanwhile, some organizations are making physician disciplinary information available at a reasonable cost. The Federation of State Medical Boards (FSMB) operates a Web site it describes as "the most comprehensive nationally consolidated data bank of disciplinary histories on U.S. licensed physicians in existence." For a small fee, you can submit a search for records of the disciplinary actions taken against a particular doctor. Some information utilizing data from

Getting a Second Opinion

Second opinions are a standard part of good medical practice. When additional expertise is necessary, doctors routinely consult colleagues and encourage their patients to do so as well. As the complexity of medicine has increased, many patients have begun to seek second opinions on their own. In some cases, the practice is valuable; in others, it may be a waste of time and money.

If the medical history, physical examination, and diagnostic tests allow a near certain diagnosis, and the recommended treatment is appropriate and generally accepted, a second opinion is not necessary. Consider a second opinion when a clear diagnosis is elusive, the diagnosed disorder is rare or serious, the recommended treatment may have major adverse effects or entails an arduous recovery, or it's necessary to choose between several treatment options.

Consulting with more than one specialist can also make a patient aware of more treatment options, since specialists in different fields may recommend different treatments for the same problem. In deciding on treatment for prostate cancer, for example, a patient might get one opinion from a urologist (who can explain the pros and cons of prostate surgery) and a second opinion from a radiation oncologist (who can explain the variety of radiation techniques and their benefits and limitations).

Second opinions are also appropriate for patients who wish to explore the possibility of an experimental treatment or for those who do not appear to improve on a recommended course of treatment.

Your primary-care doctor and specialist (if you have seen one) are the best sources for a referral. Hospitals, local health departments, family, and friends are other possible sources. Also, before you start the referral process, ask your insurance carrier which services are covered.

If the recommendations from a second opinion differ from the first, ask each doctor to detail why they came to their respective conclusions. You can also suggest that they discuss the matter with each other. Sometimes such conversations produce an acceptable consensus. If not, ask your primary-care doctor to help you sort through the options.

---

the FSMB is available from Public Citizen (see page 644).

When You Need a Specialist
For doctors who are specialists, certification by the American Board of Medical Specialties (ABMS) can help ensure an acceptable level of professional training. Established in 1933, the ABMS evaluates physicians who voluntarily seek certification by any of 24 medical specialty boards. Doctors who are awarded certification have demonstrated competency and appropriate training in a particular field. Recertification is required every 7 to 10 years.

You can verify a particular specialist's board certification by contacting ABMS. Alternatively, you may look up a physician in the annually revised Official American Board of Medical Specialties Directory of Board Certified Medical Specialists, available in many libraries—or you can contact one of the medical specialty boards directly (phone numbers and Web sites are listed on the Web site for ABMS—see page 644). However, certification is not required for a licensed physician to practice a specialty. And certification by a medical specialty board is not a guarantee of excellence; in fact, many excellent physicians are not board certified. But a board-certified physician has passed a written exam, thereby demonstrating a certain amount of knowledge to other specialists in the same field. The boards might refer you to a "board eligible" physician—a specialist who has met a board's requirements but has not yet passed the written test.

Board-certification is one criterion to weigh against other information. You can also take the following steps:

- Call the medical licensing board in the state where the doctor now practices or used to practice (the number is available via directory assistance). The board can frequently supply information on the physician's education and specialty training, and whether the doctor has been disciplined or formally charged with misconduct.
- Look up the doctor in the American Medical Association's American Medical Directory or the Directory of Medical Specialists, which can be found in all medical libraries and many large public libraries. These directories list the physician's educational background and board-certification.
- Ask the doctor for the names of hospitals where he or she has admitting privileges. Your local university teaching hospital will probably be the most selective about the physicians it admits to its staff. Also, should you need to be hospitalized, you will want a doctor who can admit you to the best facility.
- Ask any surgeon you are considering about his or her track record. He or she should be willing to provide you with concrete figures; for example, morbidity and mortality (complication and death) rates for a particular procedure. He should explain what factors affect these rates and how they compare with colleagues.

Information on Hospitals

Most good hospitals participate in evaluation programs of the Joint Commission on Accreditation of Healthcare Organizations (JCAHO), which ensures that certain standards are met. These standards focus on the quality of staff and equipment, as well as the facility's success rates in treating and curing patients. If a hospital meets JCAHO standards, it receives accreditation. Reviews are done at least every three years. Performance reports and accreditation status of participating institutions are available from JCAHO.

In addition, many state governments and consumer organizations have developed hospital "report cards," designed to help people make informed choices about where they decide to be admitted for elective procedures. For example, California, New York, Ohio, and Pennsylvania—to name a few—have laws requiring hospitals to report data on their outcomes for specific procedures (such as coronary artery bypass graft surgery) and overall quality of care. Third-party groups, such as the Cleveland Health Quality Choice Program, which gather information on hospital performance and patient satisfaction, are another resource. You can find out what kind of information is available in your area from your state department of health or local hospital association. Also, ask your primary-care physician for his or her opinion of a hospital.

When preparing to undergo a specific procedure, look for a facility that performs a high volume of such procedures. As a general rule, high-volume facilities are associated with quicker recovery, lower complication and mortality rates, and, often, lower costs. In addition, when choosing a hospital, consider asking the following questions:

- Is the facility a general hospital that treats a wide range of common problems such as hernias or flu, or a specialized facility, which may be more appropriate for a particular therapy, such as cancer treatment or total joint replacement?
- Has the hospital been successful with your condition? How often is the type of care you need provided there? How does it compare with other hospitals you might consider?

- Has either the facility itself or your state health department published any "outcome studies," which report on how well certain types of patients fare after a specific procedure? Such studies can help you compare which hospitals and surgeons have had the most success with a procedure or condition.
- Does the hospital keep track of patient injuries and infections? A reputable institution not only should do this, but should make such information readily available.
- How does the facility's quality assurance department monitor the quality of care? Are results of patient satisfaction surveys available to get an idea of how other patients have rated the quality of their care?
- Does your health plan cover care at this facility? If not, is there an alternative way to pay for your care?

Information on Insurance Plans

An increasing number of organizations are dedicated to compiling and disseminating information about health insurance plans. Most of these organizations generate report cards designed to help guide large companies and government offices to purchase group insurance for their employees. Such reports are often available to the general public.

For example, the nonprofit National Committee for Quality Assurance (NCQA) is the

Evaluating Information Online

Thousands of sites on the Internet now provide health information, and finding the most appropriate ones can be challenging. Because the Internet has evolved so rapidly and is still relatively new, evaluating information can be frustrating. But the following guidelines can help Internet users obtain information that will improve, rather than hamper or undermine, their healthcare.

- **Consider the source.** You are most likely to get reliable information from government health agencies, such as the National Institutes of Health (NIH) or the Food and Drug Administration (FDA); major medical centers and university hospitals; professional associations; and major nonprofit organizations. Many of these sources are listed in the directory that follows.
- **Separate fact from opinion.** Both have value, as long as you know which is which. Factual information is based on published reports in leading medical journals. An absence of references indicates the information may be based on opinion or anecdote rather than research.
- **Look for different viewpoints.** No one organization has all the answers. Reputable Web sites reflect and explain differing views whenever appropriate.

- **Keep track of where you are.** It's easy to get lost by clicking on link after link. Several clicks later, you may find yourself at a site that has different standards than the one where you started.
- **Note when information was updated.** Treatments and diagnostic techniques can change rapidly. Health-related Web sites should be regularly updated to reflect these advances.
- **Get a second opinion.** Check out the information you obtain on the Internet with other sources of information, including different Web sites, traditional print publications, and your own doctor.
- **Avoid Web sites that attempt to practice medicine.** Providing an online diagnosis or prescribing therapies without benefit of a physical examination or established doctor-patient relationship is an obvious conflict of interest and serious breach of medical ethics—as well as potentially dangerous. The FDA is expected to establish regulations that prohibit such practices.

country's largest accreditor of managed care plans and the developer of the Health Plan Employer Data Information Set (HEDIS), a list of criteria used by more than 90 percent of the nation's health plans to measure their level of performance. Health plans earning a high rating from the NCQA, based on HEDIS standards, offer "best practice" services such as annual retinal exams to people with diabetes, a prescription for beta-blockers for post-heart attack patients, and so forth. Such measures indicate whether the plan is likely to be both cost-effective and high in patient satisfaction.

The NCQA has made its Health Plan Report Card available on a Web site (see listing at right). Designed expressly for consumers, the site offers helpful tips for using the information, along with definitions of terms. Health plans are rated for criteria such as customer service and satisfaction, physician qualifications, preventive and screening services offered, and quality of disease management programs.

Health Information Organizations

Organizations that provide health information and/or support vary greatly in what services they can provide. The smallest can provide literature on a specific illness. The major ones can do everything from keeping you up-to-date on the latest progress in treatment, to making referrals to physicians or hospitals, to helping you locate a support group. Because you want reliable health-related information, finding a good organization requires some careful checking. Start with your physician and ask if he or she can recommend a health information organization for you to contact.

The Federal Government provides a referral service called the National Health Information Center (listed below). Using their database, staff members can find a health information organization to help you, or they can answer questions about what a particular health information organization does.

For More Information

- Public Citizen's Health Research Group, Washington, DC. Phone: 202-588-1000; Web site: www.citizen.org/hrg/
- American Board of Medical Specialties, Evanston, IL. Phone: 847-491-9091; Web site: www.abms.org
- American Medical Association, Chicago, IL. Phone: 800-621-8335; Web site: www.ama-assn.org/
- Joint Commission on Accreditation of Healthcare Organizations, Oakbrook Terrace, IL. Phone: 630-792-5000; Web site: www.jcaho.org
- National Committee for Quality Assurance, Washington, DC. Phone: 888-275-7585; Web site: www.ncqa.org
- National Health Information Center, Washington, DC. Phone: 800-336-4797; Web site: www.health.gov/nhic

This listing comprises voluntary, nonprofit, and professional organizations listed by disorder; a section called General Organizations follows. These resources should be used to obtain background information, support, and/or referrals—but not as a substitute for a physician.

Autoimmune Disorders

Lupus Foundation of America
1300 Piccard Dr., Suite 200
Rockville, MD 20850-4303
800-558-0121
301-670-9292
www.lupus.org

The Alliance for Lupus Research
1270 Avenue of Americas, Suite 609
New York, NY 10020
800-867-1743
www.lupusresearch.org

Sjogren's Syndrome Foundation, Inc.
8120 Woodmont Ave., Suite 530
Bethesda, MD 20814
800-475-6473
301-718-0300
www.sjogrens.com

Cancer

AMC Cancer Research Center
1600 Pierce St.
Denver, CO 80214
800-525-3777
303-233-6501
www.amc.org

American Cancer Society, Inc.
2200 Lake Blvd.
Atlanta, GA 30319
800-ACS-2345
www.cancer.org

American College of Radiology
1891 Preston White Dr.
Reston, VA 20191-4397
703-648-8900
www.acr.org

Cancer Care, Inc.
275 7th Ave.
New York, NY 10001
800-813-HOPE (212-813-4673)
212-712-8080
www.cancercare.org

Cancer Research Institute, Inc.
681 Fifth Ave.
New York, NY 10022
212-688-7515
800-99CANCER
www.cancerresearch.org

National Alliance of Breast Cancer Organizations
9 East 37th St., 10th Fl.
New York, NY 10016
888-80-NABCO (888-806-2226)
212-889-0606
www.nabco.org

National Cancer Institute
Office of Cancer Communications, Bldg. 31, Rm. 10A24
Bethesda, MD 20892
800-4-CANCER (800-422-6237)
301-496-5583
www.cancer.gov

National Coalition for Cancer Survivorship
1010 Wayne Avenue, Suite 770
Silver Spring, MD 20910
301-650-9127
www.cansearch.org

Patient Advocates for Advanced Cancer Treatment
1143 Parmelee, NW
Grand Rapids, MI 49504
616-453-1477
www.paactusa.org

Rose Kushner Breast Cancer Advisory Center
PO Box 224
Kensington, MD 20895
www.rkbcac.org

The Leukemia & Lymphoma Society
1311 Mamaroneck Avenue
White Plains, NY 10605
914-949-5213
www.leukemia.org

The R. A. Bloch Cancer Foundation, Inc.
4400 Main St.
Kansas City, MO 64111
800-433-0464
816-932-8453
www.blochcancer.org

The Skin Cancer Foundation
245 Fifth Ave., Suite 1403
New York, NY 10016
212-725-5751
800-SKIN-490 (800-754-6490)
www.skincancer.org

United Ostomy Association, Inc.
19772 MacArthur Blvd., Suite 200
Irvine, CA 92612-2405
800-826-0826
www.uoa.org

Y-ME National Breast Cancer Organization
212 West Van Buren
Chicago, IL 60607
800-221-2141
312-986-8228
www.y-me.org

The Brain and Nervous System

Acoustic Neuroma Association
600 Peachtree Parkway, Suite 108
Cumming, GA 30041-6899
770-205-8211
www.ANAUSA.org

Alzheimer's Association, Inc.
919 N. Michigan Ave., Suite 1100
Chicago, IL 60611-1676
800-272-3900
312-335-8700
www.alz.org

Alzheimer's Disease Education and Referral (ADEAR) Center
PO Box 8250
Silver Spring, MD 20907-8250
800-438-4380
301-495-3311
www.alzheimers.org

American Association of Neurological Surgeons (AANS)
5550 Meadowbrook Drive
Rolling Meadows, IL 60088
888-566-AANS (888-566-2267)
847-378-0500
www.neurosurgery.org/aans

American Brain Tumor Association
2720 River Road
Des Plaines, IL 60018
800-886-2282
847-827-9910
www.abta.org

American Chronic Pain Association, Inc.
PO Box 850
Rocklin, CA 95677
916-632-0922
www.theacpa.org

American Council for Headache Education (ACHE)
19 Mantua Road
Mt. Royal, NJ 08061
800-255-ACHE (800-255-2243)
856-423-0258
www.achenet.org

American Parkinson's Disease Association, Inc. (APDA)
1250 Hylan Blvd., Suite 4B
Staten Island, NY 10305-1946
800-223-2732
718-981-8001
www.apdaparkinson.org

American Society of Anesthesiologists
520 N. Northwest Highway
Park Ridge, IL 60068-2573
847-825-5586
www.asahq.org

Christopher Reeve Paralysis Foundation
500 Morris Avenue
Springfield, NJ 07081
800-225-0292
www.paralysis.org

Epilepsy Foundation of America (EFA)
4351 Garden City Drive
Landover, MD 20785-7223
800-332-1000
www.efa.org

Huntington's Disease Society of America
158 West 29th Street, 7th Floor
New York, N.Y. 10001-5300
800-345-HDSA (800-345-4372)
www.hdsa.org

International Essential Tremor Foundation
7046 West 105th Street
Overland Park, KS 66212-1803
888-387-3667
913-341-3880
www.essentialtremor.org

National Ataxia Foundation
2600 Fernbrook Lane, Suite 119
Minneapolis, MN 55447
763-553-0020
www.ataxia.org

National Brain Tumor Foundation
414 Thirteenth Street, Suite 700
Oakland, CA 94612-2603
800-934-CURE (800-934-2873)
510-839-9777
www.braintumor.org

National Foundation for Brain Research
1250 24th Street, NW - Suite 300
Washington, DC 20037-1124
202-293-5453
www.brainnet.org

National Headache Foundation
428 West St. James Place, 2nd Floor
Chicago, IL 60614-2750
888-NHF-5552 (888-643-5552)
800-843-2256
www.headaches.org

National Institute of Neurological Disorders and Stroke
P.O. Box 5801
Bethesda, MD 20824
800-352-9424
www.nind.nih.gov

National Spinal Cord Injury Association (NSCIA)
6701 Democracy Boulevard
Suite 300-9
Bethesda, MD 20817
800-962-9629
301-588-6959
www.spinalcord.org

Parkinson's Disease Foundation, Inc.
710 W. 168th St.
New York, NY 10032-9982
800-457-6676
212-923-4700
www.pdf.org

The Alzheimer's Association
919 North Michigan Avenue
Suite 1100
Chicago, IL 60611-1676
800-272-3900
312-335-8700
www.alz.org

The Brain Tumor Society
124 Watertown Street, Suite 3-H
Watertown, MA 02472
800-770-TBTS (800-770-8287)
617-924-9997
www.tbts.org

The National Head Injury Foundation, Inc.
1776 Massachusetts Ave., NW, Suite 100
Washington, DC 20036
800-444-NHIF (800-444-6443)
202-296-6443
www.nhif.org

The National Parkinson Foundation, Inc.
1501 N.W. Ninth Avenue
Miami, FL 33136-1494
800-327-4545
305-547-6666
www.parkinson.org

The Vestibular Disorders Association (VEDA)
PO Box 4467
Portland, OR 97208-4467
503-229-7705
www.vestibular.org

Dental and Oral Disorders

American Association of Endodontists (AAE)
211 East Chicago Avenue
Suite 1100
Chicago, IL 60611-2691
800-872-3636
www.aae.org

American Association of Oral and Maxillofacial Surgeons (AAOMS)
9700 West Bryn Mawr Avenue
Rosemont, IL 60018-5701
847-678-6200
www.aaoms.org

American Board of Orthodontics
401 N. Lindbergh Blvd.
Suite 308
St. Louis MO 63141
314-432-6130
www.americanboardortho.com

American College of Prosthodontists
P.O. Box 271894
West Hartford CT 06127-1894
860-679-2649
www.prosthodontics.org

American Dental Association
211 E. Chicago Ave.
Chicago, IL 60611
312-440-2500
www.ada.org

American Society for Geriatric Dentistry
211 East Chicago Avenue, 5th Floor
Chicago, IL 60611
312-440-2660
www.SCDonline.org

Centers for Disease Control and Prevention
1600 Clifton Rd., MS F10
Atlanta, GA 30333
404-639-3534
800-311-3435
www.cdc.gov

National Institute of Dental and Craniofacial Research
NIDCR Information & Liaison Branch
45 Center Drive, MSC 6400
Bethesda, MD 20892-6400
301-496-4261
www.nidr.nih.gov

The American Academy of Periodontology
737 N. Michigan Ave., Suite 800
Chicago, IL 60611-2690
312-787-5518
www.perio.org

The Digestive System
About GERD
P.O. Box 170864
Milwaukee, WI 53217-8076
888-964-2001
www.aboutgerd.org

American College of Gastroenterology
4900 B South 31st. St.
Arlington, VA 22206
703-820-7400
www.acg.gi.org

American Liver Foundation
75 Maiden Lane, Suite 603
New York, NY 10038
800-GOLIVER (800-465-4837)
www.liverfoundation.org

Crohn's & Colitis Foundation of America, Inc. (CCFA)
386 Park Ave. South
New York, NY 10016
800-932-2423
800-343-3637
www.ccfa.org

Digestive Disease National Coalition
507 Capitol Court NE., Suite 200
Washington, DC 20002
202-544-7497
www.ddnc.org

Foundation for Digestive Health and Nutrition (FDHN)
7910 Woodmont Ave., Suite 910
Bethesda, MD 20814-3015
301-222-4002
www.fdhn.org

International Foundation for Functional Gastrointestinal Disorders
P.O. Box 170864
Milwaukee, WI 53217-8076
888-964-2001
www.iffgd.org

Intestinal Disease Foundation, Inc.
Landmarks Building, Suite 525
One Station Square
Pittsburgh, PA 15219-1138
877-587-9606
412-261-5888
www.intestinalfoundation.org

National Digestive Diseases Information Clearinghouse
2 Information Way
Bethesda, MD 20892-3570
800-891-5389
301-654-3810
www.niddk.nih.gov/health/digest/nddic.htm

National Institute of Diabetes and Digestive and Kidney Diseases
Office of Communications and Public Liason
NIDDK
NIH
Building 31, Rm. 9A04
31 Center Drive, MSC 2560
Bethesda, MD 20892
www.niddk.nih.gov

The American Gastroenterological Association
7910 Woodmont Ave. 7th Floor
Bethesda, MD 20814
301-654-2055
www.gastro.org

The American Society of Colon and Rectal Surgeons
85 West Algonquin Rd., Suite 550
Arlington Heights, IL 60005
847-290-9184
www.fascrs.org

The Ears, Nose, and Throat
Alexander Graham Bell Association for the Deaf and Hard of Hearing, Inc.
3417 Volta Place, NW
Washington, DC 20007-2778
202-337-5220
www.agbell.org

American Academy of Otolaryngology-Head and Neck Surgery
One Prince Street
Alexandria, VA 22314-3357
703-836-4444
www.entnet.org

American Hearing Research Foundation
55 E. Washington St., Suite 2022
Chicago, IL 60602
312-726-9670
www.american-hearing.org

American Speech-Language-Hearing Association
10801 Rockville Pike
Rockville, MD 20852
800-638-8255
www.asha.org

American Tinnitus Association (ATA)
P.O. Box 5
Portland, OR 97207-0005
800-634-8978
503-248-9985
www.ata.org

Better Hearing Institute
515 King Street, Suite 420
Alexandria, VA 22314
703-684-3391
www.betterhearing.org

Dial a Hearing Screening Test
P. O. Box 1880
Media, PA 19063
800-222-EARS (800-222-3277)
www.dialatest.com

Information on Deafness
Gallaudet University
800 Florida Avenue, NE
Washington, DC 20002
202-651-5051
clerccenter.gallaudet.edu/InfoToGo/

International Association of Laryngectomies
8900 Thornton Road
Box 99311
Stockton, CA 95209
866-IAL-FORU (866-425-3678)
www.larynxlink.com

International Hearing Society
16880 Middlebelt Rd.
Livonia, MI 48154
800-521-5247
734-522-7200
www.ihsinfo.org

National Association of the Deaf
814 Thayer Avenue
Silver Spring, MD 20910-4500
301-587-1788
www.nad.org

National Institute on Deafness and Other Communication Disorders
31 Center Drive MSC 2320
Bethesda, MD 20892-2320
800-241-1044
301-496-7243
301-402-0252 TDD
www.nidcd.nih.gov

Self-Help for Hard of Hearing People, Inc.
7910 Woodmont, Suite 1200
Bethesda, MD 20814
301-657-2248
301-657-2249
www.shhh.org

The Deafness Research Foundation
1050 17th Street NW, Suite 701
Washington, DC 20036
202-289-5850
drf.org

The Endocrine System

American Association of Diabetes Educators
100 West Monroe St., Suite 400
Chicago, IL 60603-1901
312-424-2426
www.aadenet.org

American Diabetes Association
1701 North Beauregard Street
Alexandria, VA 22311
800-DIABETES (800-342-2383)
www.diabetes.org

Joslin Diabetes Center, Inc.
One Joslin Place
Boston, MA 02215
617-732-2440
www.joslin.org

National Diabetes Information Clearinghouse
1 Information Way
Bethesda, MD 20892-3560
800-860-8747
301-654-3327
www.niddk.nih.gov/health/diabetes/ndic.htm

The Thyroid Foundation of America, Inc.
Ruth Sleeper Hall, Rsl. 350
40 Parkman Street
Boston, MA 02114-2698
800-832-8321
617-726-8500
www.allthyroid.org

The Eyes

American Academy of Ophthalmology
P.O. Box 7424
San Francisco, CA 94120
415-561-8500
www.aao.org

American Council of the Blind
1155 15th St., NW, Suite 1004
Washington, DC 20005
800-424-8666
202-467-5081
acb.org/acb

American Foundation for the Blind
11 Penn Plaza, Suite 300
New York, NY 10001
800-AFB-LINE (800-232-5463)
212-502-7600
www.afb.org

American Optometric Association (AOA)
243 North Lindbergh Blvd.
St. Louis, MO 63141
314-991-4100
www.aoanet.org

Associated Services for the Blind (ASB)
919 Walnut Street
Philadelphia, PA 19107
215-627-0600
www.asb.org

Association for Macular Diseases, Inc.
210 East 64th Street, 8th Floor
New York, NY 10021
212-605-3719
www.macula.org

Benign Essential Blepharospasm Research Foundation, Inc.
PO Box 12468
Beaumont, TX 77726-2468
409-832-0788
www.blepharospasm.org

Council of Citizens With Low Vision
1155 15th Street NW
Suite 1004
Washington, DC 20005
800-733-2258
www.cclvi.org

Eye Bank Association of America
1015 Eighteenth Street NW, Suite 1010
Washington, DC 20036
202-775-4999
www.restoresight.org

Eye Care America-National Eye Care Project
2318 Fillmore Street
San Francisco, CA 94142
800-222-EYES (800-222-3937)
www.aao.org

Glaucoma Research Foundation
200 Pine St., Suite 200
San Francisco, CA 94104
800-826-6693
415-986-3162
www.glaucoma.org
Guiding Eyes for the Blind, Inc.

611 Granite Springs Road
Yorktown Heights, NY 10598
800-942-0149
914-245-4024
www.guiding-eyes.org

Lighthouse International
111 E. 59th St.
New York, NY 10022
800-829-0500
212-821-9200
www.lighthouse.org

National Association for the Visually Handicapped
22 W. 21st Street
New York, NY 10010
212-255-2804
www.navh.org

National Eye Institute
2020 Vision Place
Bethesda, MD 20892-3655
301-496-5248
www.nei.nih.gov

National Federation of the Blind
1800 Johnson Street
Baltimore, MD 21230
410-659-9314
www.nfb.org

Prevent Blindness America
500 E. Remington Rd.
Schaumburg, IL 60173
800-331-2020
www.prevent-blindness.org

The Foundation Fighting Blindness
11435 Cronhill Drive
Owings Mills, MD 21117-2220
888-394-3937
410-568-0150
www.blindness.org

Vision Foundation
23A Elm St.
Watertown, MA 02472
617-926-4232
Vision World Wide, Inc.
5707 Brockton Dr., Suite 302
Indianapolis, IN 46220-5481
800-431-1739
317-254-1332
www.visionww.org

The Heart and Blood Vessels

American Heart Association
7272 Greenville Ave.
Dallas, TX 75231-4599
800-AHA-USA-1 (800-242-8721)
www.americanheart.org

American Stroke Association National Center
7272 Greenville Ave.
Dallas, TX 75231
888-4-STROKE (888-478-7653)
www.strokeassociation.org

CARF, The Rehabilitation Accreditation Commision
4891 E. Grant Road
Tuscon, AZ 85712
520-325-1044
www.carf.org

Mended Hearts
7272 Greenville Ave.
Dallas, TX 75231-4596
800-242-8721
214-706-1442
www.mendedhearts.org

National Aphasia Association
29 John Street, #1103
New York, NY 10038
800-922-4622
212-267-2812
www.aphasia.org

National Heart, Lung, and Blood Institute (NHLBI)
NHLBI Information Center
PO Box 30105
Bethesda, MD 20824-0105
301-496-4236
www.nhlbi.nih.gov

National Rehabilitation Information Center
1010 Wayne Ave., Suite 800
Silver Spring, MD 20910
800-346-2742
301-562-2400
www.naric.com

National Stroke Association
907 East Easter Lane
Englewood, CO 80112
800-STROKES (800-787-6537)
303-649-9299
www.stroke.org

The American College of Cardiology
Heart House
9111 Old Georgetown Rd.
Bethesda, MD 20814-1699
800-253-4636
301-897-5400
www.acc.org

The Kidneys and Urinary Tract

American Association of Kidney Patients (AAKP)
3505 East Frontage Road
Suite 315
Tampa, FL 33607
800-749-2257
www.aakp.org

American Foundation for Urologic Disease (AFUD)
1128 North Charles Street
Baltimore, MD 21201
410-468-1800
www.afud.org

American Kidney Fund
6110 Executive Blvd., Suite 1010
Rockville, MD 20852
800-638-8299
www.akfinc.org

American Urological Association
1120 North Charles Street
Baltimore, MD 21201
410-727-1100
www.auanet.org

National Association for Continence (NAFC)
P.O. Box 8310
Spartanburg, SC 29305-8310
800-BLADDER (800-252-3337)
864-579-7900
www.nafc.org

National Kidney Foundation
30 East 33rd Street, Suite 1100
New York, NY 10016
800-622-9010
212-889-2210
www.kidney.org

The National Kidney and Urologic Diseases Information Clearinghouse
3 Information Way
Bethesda, MD 20892-3580
800-891-5390
301-654-4415
www.niddk.nih.gov/health/kidney/nkudic.htm

The Lungs and Respiratory System

American Academy of Allergy Asthma and Immunology (AAAAI)
611 East Wells Street
Milwaukee, WI 53202
800-822-2762
414-272-6071
www.aaaai.org

Asthma and Allergy Foundation of America (AAFA)
1233 20th Street, NW, Suite 402
Washington, DC 20036
800-7ASTHMA (800-727-8462)
202-466-7643
www.aafa.org

National Institute of Allergy and Infectious Diseases
Bldg. 31, Rm. 7A-50
31 Center Dr., MSC 2520
Bethesda, MD 20892-2520
301-496-5717
www.niaid.nih.gov

National Jewish Center for Immunology and Respiratory Medicine
1400 Jackson Street
Denver, CO 80206
800-222-LUNG (800-222-5864)
www.njc.org

The American Lung Association
1740 Broadway
New York, NY 10019
800-LUNG-USA (800-586-4872)
212-315-8700
www.lungusa.org

The Muscles and Bones
American Academy of Orthopaedic Surgeons
6300 North River Road
Rosemont, IL 60018-4262
800-346-AAOS (800-346-2267)
847-823-7186
www.aaos.org

American Osteopathic Association
142 E. Ontario St.
Chicago, IL 60611
800-621-1773
www.aoa-net.org

American Podiatric Medical Association
9312 Old Georgetown Rd.
Bethesda, MD 20814-1621
301-581-9221
www.apma.org

Arthritis Foundation
P.O. Box 7669
Atlanta, GA 30357-0669
800-283-7800
www.arthritis.org

Back Pain Hotline
6300 W. Parker Rd.
Plano, TX 75093
800-247-2225
www.texasback.com

National Osteoporosis Foundation
1232 22nd Street N.W.
Washington, D.C. 20037-1292
202-223-2226
www.nof.org

Osteoporosis and Related Bone Diseases National Resource Center
1232 22nd St. NW
Washington, DC 20037-1292
800-624-BONE (800-624-2663)
202-223-0344
www.osteo.org

Spondylitis Association of America
14827 Ventura Blvd. # 222
Sherman Oaks, CA 91403
800-777-8189
818-981-1616
www.spondylitis.org

The Arthritis Society
393 University Ave., Suite 1700
Toronto, Ontario
M5G 1E6 Canada
416-979-7228
www.arthritis.ca

The Skin
American Academy of Dermatology
P.O. Box 4014
Schaumburg, IL 60168-4014
888-462-DERM (800-462-3376)
847-330-0230
www.aad.org

National Alopecia Areata Foundation
P. O. Box 150760
San Rafael, CA 94915-0760
415-472-3780
www.naaf.org

National Arthritis and Musculoskeletal and Skin Diseases Information Clearinghouse
National Institutes of Health
1 AMS Circle
Bethesda, MD 20892-3675
877-22-NIAMS (877-226-4267)
301-495-4484
www.niams.nih.gov

National Psoriasis Foundation
6600 SW 92nd Ave., Suite 300
Portland, OR 97223-7195
800-723-9166
503-244-7404
www.psoriasis.org

Health Problems of Men
Brady Urological Institute
1620 McElderry Street
Read Hall East, Suite 1131
Baltimore, MD 21205
410-614-3961
urology.jhu.edu/index.html

Impotence Institute of America
8201 Corporate Drive, Suite 320
Landover, MD 20785
800-669-1603
301-577-0660
www.impotence.org

Prostate Cancer Education Council
1800 Jackson St.
Golden, CO 80401
303-316-4685
www.pcaw.com

Health Problems of Women
American College of Obstetricians and Gynecologists
P.O. Box 96920
Washington, DC 20090-6920
202-638-5577
www.acog.org

HERS Foundation
422 Bryn Mawr Ave.
Bala Cynwyd, PA 19004
888-750-HERS (888-750-4375)
610-667-7757
www.hersfoundation.com

National Women's Health Network
514 10th St., NW, Suite 400
Washington, DC 20004
202-347-1140
www.womenshealthnetwork.org

Mental Health
Al-Anon Family Group Headquarters, Inc.
1600 Corporate Landing Parkway,
Virginia Beach, VA 23454-5617
757-563-1600
www.al-anon.alateen.org

Alcoholics Anonymous
P.O. Box 459
Grand Central Station
New York, NY 10163
212-870-3400
www.alcoholics-anonymous.org

American Academy of Sleep Medicine
6301 Bandel Road, NW, Suite 101
Rochester, MN 55901
507-287-6006
www.asda.org

American Mental Health Counselors Association (AMHCA)
801 N. Fairfax Street, Suite 304
Alexandria, VA 22314
800-326-2642
703-548-6002
www.amhca.org

American Psychiatric Association
1400 K Street, NW
Washington, DC 20005
888-357-7924
www.psych.org

American Psychological Association
Washington, DC 20002-4242
800-374-2721
202-336-5510
www.apa.org

American Sleep Apnea Association
1424 K Street NW, Suite 302
Washington, DC 20005
202-293-3650
www.sleepapnea.org

Depression and Related Affective Disorders Association (DRADA)
Meyer 3-181
600 North Wolfe Street
Baltimore, MD 21287-7381
410-955-4647
202-955-5800
www.drada.org

Emotions Anonymous
PO Box 4245
St. Paul, MN 55104-0245
651-647-9712
www.emotionsanonymous.org

National Alliance for the Mentally Ill
2107 Wilson Blvd, #300
Arlington, VA 22201
800-950-6264
703-524-7600
www.nami.org

National Council on Alcoholism and Drug Dependence, Inc. (NCADD)
20 Exchange Place, #2902
New York, NY 10005
800-NCA-CALL (800-622-2255)
212-269-7797
www.ncadd.org

National Depressive and Manic-Depressive Association
730 North Franklin Street, Suite 501
Chicago, IL 60610-7204
800-826-3632
www.ndmda.org

National Institute of Mental Health
6001 Executive Blvd., Rm. 8184, MSC 9663
Bethesda, MD 20892-9663
301-443-4513
www.nimh.nih.gov

National Mental Health Association
1021 Prince Street
Alexandria, VA 22314-2971
800-969-NMHA (800-969-6642)
703-684-7722
www.nmha.org

National Mental Health Consumer Self-Help Clearinghouse
1211 Chestnut Street, Suite 1207
Philadelphia, PA 19107
800-553-4539
215-751-1810
www.mhselfhelp.org

National Sleep Foundation
1522 K Street, NW, Suite 500
Washington DC 20005
202-347-3471
www.sleepfoundation.org

Older Women's League (OWL)
666 11th St., NW, Suite 700
Washington, DC 2000
800-825-3695
202-783-6686
www.owl-national.org

Substance Abuse and Mental Health Services Administration (SAMHSA)
5600 Fishers Lane, Parklawn Bldg., Rm. 12-105
Rockville, MD 20857
301-443-4795
www.samhsa.gov

Well Spouse Foundation
PO Box 30093
Elkins Park, PA 19027
800-838-0879
www.wellspouse.org

General Organizations

Administration on Aging
330 Independence Ave. SW
Washington, DC 20201
202-619-7501
www.aoa.dhhs.gov

Aerobics and Fitness Association of America (AFAA)
15250 Ventura Blvd., Suite 200
Sherman Oaks, CA 91403-3297
800-446-2322 ext. 215
1-877-YOURBODY (877-968-7263)
www.afaa.com

Alliance for Retired Americans
888 16th Street, NW
Washington DC 20006
888-373-6497
www.retiredamericans.org

American Association of Retired Persons (AARP)
601 E Street, NW
Washington, DC 20049
800-424-3410
202-434-2277
www.aarp.org

American College of Surgeons
633 North Saint Clair Street
Chicago, IL 60611-3211
312-202-5000
www.facs.org

American Dietetic Association
216 West Jackson Blvd.
Chicago, IL 60606-6995
800-745-0775
312-899-0040
www.eatright.org

American Health Foundation
300 East 42 Street
New York, NY 10017
212-953-1900
www.ahf.org

American Hospital Association (AHA)
One North Franklin, 27th Floor
Chicago, IL 60606-3421
800-242-2626
312-422-3000
www.aha.org

American Medical Association
515 North State Street
Chicago, IL 60610
800-262-3211
312-464-5000
www.ama-assn.org

American Music Therapy Association, Inc.
8455 Colesville Rd., Suite 1000
Silver Spring, MD 20910
301-589-3300
www.musictherapy.org

American Nurses Association
600 Maryland Ave., Suite 100 West
Washington, DC 20024
800-274-4ANA
www.nursingworld.org

American Physical Therapy Association (APTA)
1111 North Fairfax
Alexandria, VA 22314-1488
800-999-2782
703-684-2782
www.apta.org

American Red Cross
430 17th Street NW
Washington, DC 20006-5307
877-272-7337
www.redcross.org

American Society of Internal Medicine
190 N Independence Mall West
Philadelphia, PA 19106-1572
800-523-1546, x2600
215-351-2600
www.acponline.org

American Society of Ophthalmic Plastic and Reconstructive Surgery
1133 West Morse Blvd, #201
Winter Park, FL 32789
407-647-8839
www.asoprs.org

American Society on Aging (ASA)
833 Market Street, Suite 511
San Francisco, CA 94103-1824
415-974-9600
www.asaging.org

Association of American Medical Colleges
2450 N Street NW
Washington, DC 20037-1126
202-828-0400
www.aamc.org

Center for Medical Consumers
130 Macdougal St.
New York, NY 10012-5030
212-674-7105
www.medicalconsumers.org

Centers for Disease Control and Prevention
1600 Clifton Rd.
Atlanta, GA 30333
800-311-3435
404-639-3534
www.cdc.gov

Centers for Medicare & Medicaid Services
7500 Security Boulevard
Baltimore MD 21244-1850
410-786-3000
cms.hhs.gov

Community Health Accreditation Program, Inc. (CHAP)
61 Broadway
New York, NY 10006
800-656-9656
212-480-8828
www.chapinc.org

Consumer Information Center
P.O. Box 450
Camby, IN 46113
800-FED-INFO
800-688-9889
www.info.gov

Council of Better Business Bureaus
4200 Wilson Blvd., Suite 800
Arlington, VA 22203
703-276-0100
www.bbb.org

Department of Health and Human Services
200 Independence Ave., SW
Washington, DC 20201
877-696-6775
202-619-0257
www.hhs.gov

Food and Drug Administration
5600 Fishers Lane
Rockville, MD 20857-0001
888-463-6332
www.fda.gov

Foundation for Hospice and Home Care
2120 L Street, NW, Suite 200
Washington, DC 20037
202-223-0204
www.americanhospice.org

Gray Panthers
733 15th Street, NW
Suite 437
Washington, DC 20005
Washington, DC 20005
202-737-6637
www.graypanthers.org

Health Resources and Services Administration
Parklawn Building
5600 Fishers Lane
Rockville, MD 20857
888-275-4772
www.hrsa.gov

Hospice Education Institute
3 Unity Square
P.O. Box 98
Machiasport, ME 04655-0098
800-331-1620
207-255-8800
www.hospiceworld.org

Hospice Foundation of America
777 17 Street
Miami Beach, FL 33139
800-552-9963
305-538-9272
www.hospicefoundation.org

Joint Commission on Accreditation of Healthcare Organizations
One Renaissance Blvd.
Oakbrook Terrace, IL 60181
630-792-5000
www.jcaho.org

Let's Face It
P.O. Box 29972
Bellingham, WA 98228-1972
360-676-7325
www.faceit.org

National Adult Day Services Association
409 Third St., SW
Washington, DC 20024
202-479-1200
www.ncoa.orgnadsa

National Association for Home Care
228 7th Street, SE
Washington, DC 20003
202-547-7424
www.nahc.org

National Association of Area Agencies on Aging (N4A)
927 15th Street NW, 6th Floor
Washington, DC 20005
202-296-8130
www.n4A.org

National Association of State Units on Aging (NASUA)
1201 15th Street NW, #350
Washington, DC 20005
202-898-2578
www.nasua.org

National Consumers League
1701 K St., NW, Suite 1200
Washington, DC 20006
202-835-3323
www.natlconsumersleague.org

National Council Against Health Fraud Resource Center
119 Foster St.
Peabody, MA 01960
978-532-9383
www.ncahf.org

National Council on Disability
1331 F St., NW, Suite 850
Washington, DC 20004
202-272-2004
www.ncd.gov

National Council on the Aging, Inc.
409 Third Street SW, #200
Washington, DC 20024
202-479-1200
www.ncoa.org

National Dairy Council
10255 West Higgins Road, Suite 900
Rosemont, IL 60018-5616
www.nationaldairycouncil.org

National Hospice and Palliative Care Organization
1700 Diagonal Road, Suite 625
Alexandria, VA 22314
800-658-8898
703-243-5900
www.nhpco.org

National Institute of General Medical Sciences
45 Center Drive, MSC 6200
Bethesda, MD 20892-6200
301-496-7301
www.nigms.nih.gov

National Institute on Aging
Building 31, Room 5C27
31 Center Drive, MSC 2292
Bethesda, MD 20892
301-496-1752
www.nia.nih.gov

National Institutes of Health
Bethesda, MD 20892
301-496-4000
www.nih.gov

National Interfaith Coalition of Aging
409 Third Sreet, SW
Washington, DC 20024
202-479-1200
www.ncoa.orgnicanica.htm

National League for Nursing
61 Broadway, 33rd Floor
New York, NY 10006
800-669-1656
212-363-5555
www.nln.org

NIH Clinical Center
6100 Executive Blvd., Suite 3C01 MSC 7511
Bethesda, MD 20892-7511
301-496-2563
www.cc.nih.gov

Office of Disability Employment Policy
1331 F St., NW, Suite 300
Washington, DC 20004
202-376-6200
202-376-6205 TDD
www.dol.gov/dol/odep/

Office of Disease Prevention and Health Promotion
200 Independence Ave. SW, Room 738G
Washington, DC 20201
202-401-6295
odphp.osophs.dhhs.gov

Partnership for Caring
1620 Eye Street NW, Suite 202
Washington, DC 20006
800-989-9455
202-296-8071
www.partnershipforcaring.org

President's Council on Physical Fitness and Sports
Department W
200 Independence Ave., SW
Room 738-H
Washington, D.C. 20201-0004
202-690-9000
www.fitness.gov

Recovery, Inc.
802 N. Dearborn St.
Chicago, IL 60610
312-337-5661
www.recovery-inc.com

The American Geriatrics Society
The Empire State Building
350 Fifth Avenue, Suite 801
New York, NY 10118
212-308-1414
www.americangeriatrics.org

The American Occupational Therapy Association, Inc. (AOTA)
4720 Montgomery Lane., PO Box 31220
Bethesda, MD 20824-1220
800-377-8555
301-652-2682
www.aota.org

The American Trauma Society
8903 Presidential Parkway, Suite 512
Upper Marlboro, MD 20772
800-556-7890
301-420-4189
www.amtrauma.org

The Catholic Health Association of the United States
4455 Woodson Road
St. Louis, MO 63134-3797
314-427-2500
www.chausa.org

The Living Bank
PO Box 6725
Houston, TX 77265
800-528-2971
www.livingbank.org

The National Agricultural Library
10301 Baltimore Avenue
Beltsville, MD 20705
301-504-5755
www.nalusda.gov

The National Organization for Rare Disorders, Inc.
PO Box 8923
New Fairfield, CT 06812-8923
800-999-6673
203-746-6518
www.rarediseases.org

The Office of Special Education and Rehabilitative Services
400 Maryland Ave., SW
Washington, DC 20202
202-205-5465
www.ed.gov/offices/OSERS/

The Scleroderma Foundation, Inc.
12 Kent Way, Suite 101
Byfield, MA 01922
800-722-HOPE (877-722-4673)
978-463-5843
www.scleroderma.org

United Network for Organ Sharing
1100 Boulders Parkway, Suite 500
PO Box 13770
Richmond, VA 23225-8770
888-TXINFO1 (888-894-6361)
www.unos.org

United Way of America
701 North Fairfax Street
Alexandria, VA 22314-2045
703-836-7112
national.unitedway.org

Visiting Nurse Associations of America
11 Beacon Street, Suite 910
Boston, MA 092108
617-523-4042
www.vnaa.org

YWCA of the USA
350 Fifth Ave.
New York, NY 10128
212-273-7800
www.ywca.org

A

5-alpha-reductase inhibitors A class of drugs used to treat BPH. They block the conversion of testosterone into dihydrotestosterone, the major male sex hormone within the cells of the prostate.

abscess A localized accumulation of pus resulting from an infection.

acetylcholine A neurotransmitter that is crucial to memory and learning.

acute cholecystitis Inflammation of the gallbladder marked by severe pain, fever, nausea, and vomiting.

adrenergic agonist eye drops A treatment for glaucoma. The eye drops reduce intraocular pressure by decreasing the production of aqueous humor and increasing its drainage through the uveoscleral pathway.

adrenergic symptoms Symptoms, including sweating and palpitations, that occur when a low blood glucose level triggers the release of the hormone epinephrine (adrenaline) into the blood.

aerobic exercise Continuous rhythmic exercise using the large muscles of the body over an extended period of time. Aerobic exercise increases the body's demand for oxygen, thereby adding to the workload of the heart and lungs and elevating the heart rate.

age-associated memory impairment Normal forgetfulness that increases with age.

age-related macular degeneration A loss of central vision caused by changes in the macula. Commonly abbreviated as AMD and sometimes referred to as senile macular degeneration.

agnosia Loss of the ability to interpret incoming visual, auditory, or tactile stimuli, even though the senses of vision, hearing, and touch are mechanically intact and function normally.

agoraphobia Fear of being in public places.

aldosteronism A disorder caused by a tumor or overgrowth of cells in the adrenal gland that results in the overproduction of aldosterone (a hormone); can lead to hypertension.

alkaline phosphatase Enzyme released by bone-forming cells called osteoblasts. Blood levels are elevated in people with Paget's disease.

alpha-1-adrenergic blockers A class of drugs used to treat BPH that work by relaxing smooth muscle tissue within the prostate. Also called alpha-blockers.

alpha-blocker A drug that decreases blood pressure by blocking nerve impulses that constrict small arteries.

alpha-glucosidase inhibitors Oral diabetes drugs that lower the peak levels of blood glucose and insulin after a meal. Examples are acarbose (Precose) and miglitol (Glyset).

alteplase A drug used to treat heart attacks and strokes by dissolving blood clots.

amyloid plaques Dense deposits of beta-amyloid, pieces of damaged nerve cells, and other proteins. Found in the brains of virtually all people with Alzheimer's disease.

androgen A sex hormone, such as testosterone, found in higher levels in males than in females.

aneurysm A ballooning-out of the wall of a blood vessel caused by weakening of the wall.

angina Episodes of chest pain caused by an inadequate supply of oxygen and blood to the heart. It occurs most often during physical activity. Also called angina pectoris.

angioplasty A procedure in which a small balloon is inflated in a blocked artery to enlarge the path for blood flow.

angiotensin It has two forms: angiotensin I and angiotensin II. The latter is a hormone that raises blood pressure by causing arteries to constrict and triggering the release of aldosterone.

angiotensin II receptor blocker A type of drug that helps to lower blood pressure by interfering with the action of angiotensin II, a hormone that causes arteries to constrict and triggers the release of aldosterone.

angiotensin-converting enzyme (ACE) inhibitor A drug commonly prescribed to lower blood pressure by preventing the formation of angiotensin II, a hormone that causes arteries to constrict and triggers the release of aldosterone. Also used to slow the progression of kidney disease in patients with diabetes.

ankylosing spondylitis Chronic inflammation of the facet joints and sacroiliac joints (between the sacrum and the pelvis).

annulus fibrosus Tough, fibrous layers of tissue that cover an intervertebral disk.

antiandrogens Drugs that bind to androgen receptors in cells, preventing androgens from stimulating the cells.

anti-angiogenic drugs Drugs used to shrink blood vessels in the eyes of individuals with age-related macular degeneration.

anticoagulant drug An anticlotting drug that works by inhibiting the formation of fibrin, a protein required for clot development. Examples include heparin and warfarin.

antioxidants Substances that help the body neutralize free radicals, which can cause cell damage. Naturally occurring antioxidants include beta carotene, vitamin C, vitamin E, and selenium.

antiplatelet drug An anticlotting drug that works by inhibiting the clumping of blood cells called platelets. One example is aspirin.

antireflux barrier A mechanical impediment created by the lower esophageal sphincter and the diaphragm that prevents the contents of the stomach from entering the esophagus.

aphasia A partial or complete inability to use or understand spoken or written language.

apolipoprotein E (APOE) A gene on chromosome 19. The e4 version of this gene is associated with an increased risk of Alzheimer's disease.

aqueous humor A watery fluid that is located in front of the lens and provides nutrients to the lens and cornea.

arrhythmia An abnormal heart rhythm.

arteriovenous malformation A congenital disorder characterized by a complex, tangled web of arteries and veins.

arthroplasty Implantation of a mechanical joint to replace a diseased or damaged joint. Also called total joint replacement surgery.

arthroscopy A diagnostic and surgical technique that uses a thin tube with a light and tiny video camera at one end to view the inside of a joint.

A-scan ultrasonography A test that uses sound waves to measure the length of the eyeball.

aspiration pneumonia Pneumonia caused by the inhalation of food and other particles into the lungs.

atherosclerosis An accumulation of deposits of fat and fibrous tissue, called plaques, within the walls of arteries that can narrow vessels and reduce blood flow.

atrial fibrillation A common abnormal heart rhythm in which the heart contracts at a fast and chaotic rate.

autoimmune disorder A disorder, such as rheumatoid arthritis, that results when the body's tissues are attacked by its own immune system.

autonomic neuropathy Damage to nerves that control many involuntary actions in the body, such as the movement of food through the digestive tract, heart rate, and bladder control.

B

baroreceptors Special nerve endings in the walls of arteries that monitor blood pressure.

Barrett's esophagus A disorder in which the cells that line the esophageal mucosa are replaced by more acid-resistant cells; it is associated with an increased risk of esophageal cancer.

benzodiazepines A class of drugs used to relieve anxiety.

beta-blocker eye drops A treatment for glaucoma. The eye drops reduce intraocular pressure by decreasing the production of aqueous humor.

beta-blockers A class of drugs that impedes the actions of epinephrine and norepinephrine, slows heart rate, and lowers blood pressure by diminishing the cardiac output. Used to treat angina, high blood pressure, irregular heart rhythms, and migraine. Beta-blockers are also sometimes used to treat performance anxiety or used in combination with antidepressants.

biguanides Oral diabetes drugs that enhance the action of insulin to decrease glucose production by the liver and to increase glucose uptake by muscle and fat cells. Do not cause hypoglycemia when used alone. Metformin (Glucophage) is the only available biguanide.

bile Substances synthesized by the liver, stored and concentrated in the gallbladder, and then released into the duodenum to help in the digestion and absorption of dietary fat.

biliary colic Intermittent episodes of sharp pain in the right upper portion of the abdomen that occur when gallstones block the flow of bile from the gallbladder.

biofeedback Treatment in which the person practices different relaxation methods while using electronic sensors to measure bodily functions, such as muscle tension, breathing patterns, and heart rate.

bisphosphonate A class of drugs used to maintain or improve bone density.

bladder calculi Calcium stones that may occur in the bladder.

blood osmolarity The thickness of the blood. High blood glucose increases blood osmolarity, making a person thirsty.

b-mode imaging An imaging technique that uses high-frequency sound waves to produce a three-dimensional view of the carotid arteries.

bone scan Imaging test that involves the injection of radioactive technetium and then the measurement of how much radioactivity is taken up by specific areas of bone. This test can detect metastatic cancer, bony overgrowths in Paget's disease, bacterial infections of the spine, and small fractures that are not visible on x-rays.

Bouchard nodes Knobby overgrowths of the middle joint of the fingers in people with osteoarthritis.

bovine spongiform encephalopathy (BSE) An infectious disease of cows with manifestations similar to Creutzfeldt-Jakob disease in humans. More commonly known as mad cow disease.

brachytherapy A treatment for prostate cancer that involves the implantation of radioactive seeds into the prostate.

B-scan ultrasonography A test that uses sound waves to view structures in the back of the eye.

bursa A small, fluid-filled sac between a tendon and a bone that protects muscles and tendons from coming into direct contact with bones.

C

calcitriol A hormone formed from dietary vitamin D that increases the absorption of calcium from the intestine and plays a role in the regulation of blood pressure by constricting small arteries.

calcium channel blockers A class of drugs that lower blood pressure by dilating arteries and, in some cases, by decreasing cardiac output.

capillaries The intricate network of tiny blood vessels that permeate most of the body's tissues. Capillaries serve as the juncture between the arterial and venous systems and help cells to maintain a proper exchange of oxygen and carbon dioxide.

carbonic anhydrase inhibitors A class of medications used to treat glaucoma. Available in both oral and eye drop forms.

carotid endarterectomy A surgical procedure to remove plaque from the carotid arteries.

carotid stenosis A narrowing of the carotid arteries in the neck that supply blood to the brain.

cartilage The connective tissue that covers the ends of bones and acts as the body's shock absorber by cushioning the bones from weight-bearing stress. Contains water, chondrocytes, collagen, and proteoglycans.

cauda equina Bundle of nerve roots at the bottom of the spinal cord.

central alpha agonist A drug that lowers blood pressure by blocking brain nerve impulses that constrict small arteries.

cerebellum A fist-sized structure, located at the base of the brain beneath the cerebral cortex, that coordinates movement and balance.

cerebral angiography An invasive procedure involving the injection of an iodine-based contrast solution into the bloodstream to produce a high-quality x-ray image of the blood vessels within the brain.

cerebral cortex The convoluted outer layer of gray matter that constitutes the "thinking" portion of the brain.

cerebral edema Swelling of the brain due to bleeding, trauma, a stroke, or a tumor.

cerebral embolism A blockage of blood flow that occurs when part of a blood clot or a piece of atherosclerotic plaque breaks off and travels through the bloodstream until it lodges in an artery supplying blood to the brain.

cerebral thrombosis A blockage of blood flow that occurs when a blood clot forms at the site of an atherosclerotic plaque within the wall of a major artery supplying the brain. The most common cause of an ischemic stroke.

cerebrum The largest portion of the brain. It controls conscious thought, perception, voluntary movement, and integration of sensory input.

chiropractor Medical professional who uses such techniques as physical manipulation and adjustment of the spine, massage, application of heat or cold, and electrical stimulation to treat back problems.

cholangitis Infection inside the bile ducts.

cholecystectomy Surgical removal of the gallbladder.

cholinesterase inhibitors Medications that slow the breakdown of acetylcholine. Used in the treatment of Alzheimer's disease.

chondrocyte A cartilage cell.

chymopapain Enzyme obtained from the papaya plant. Injected into the disk to break down noncollagen components of the nucleus pulposus; controversial alternative to surgery for a herniated disk.

claudication Intermittent pain in the leg muscles caused by an inadequate supply of oxygen and blood to the legs. It most often occurs with walking.

coagulopathies A group of rare disorders of blood clotting that are inherited or result from other disorders such as cancer.

colchicine An anti-inflammatory drug commonly used to treat gout.

colectomy Surgical removal of part or all of the colon.

collagen The major protein of connective tissue, cartilage, and bone.

colonoscopy A diagnostic procedure in which an endoscope is inserted through the anus and rectum to view the colon and the final portion of the small intestine (terminal ileum).

common bile duct A tube that carries bile from the liver and gallbladder to the small intestine.

complete blood cell count Measures cellular elements of blood: red blood cells, white blood cells, and platelets. Helps rule out anemia, infections, and vitamin B12 deficiency as causes of dementia or factors that can exacerbate dementia.

computed tomography (CT) angiography An imaging method in which an iodine-based dye is injected into the patient and a rapid CT scan is performed through the region of interest. Computer-based software then shows images of the blood vessels that fill with dye.

computed tomography (CAT or CT) scan Imaging technique in which the person lies on a special table while x-rays are passed through the body and sensed by a detector that rotates 360° around the person. A computer combines the information into a cross-sectional picture that shows body structures and fluids, blood clots, tumors, and bones.

contact laser prostatectomy A method for treating BPH in which laser energy is used to vaporize prostate tissue.

cornea The transparent, dome-shaped disk covering the iris and pupil.

coronary heart disease A narrowing of the coronary arteries that results in inadequate blood flow to the heart.

corticosteroids Potent drugs that are used to reduce the pain and inflammation associated with rheumatoid arthritis and other autoimmune disorders. Also called steroids.

Creutzfeldt-Jakob disease (CJD) A rare, fatal brain disorder that causes a rapid, progressive dementia. Sometimes mistaken for Alzheimer's disease.

Crohn's disease A chronic inflammatory disorder that primarily affects the small intestine but can involve any segment of the gastrointestinal tract from the mouth to anus.

cryotherapy The application of extreme cold to treat a disease, such as prostate cancer.

CT myelogram CT scan carried out after contrast material is injected into the spinal canal. Offers good detail of bone and soft tissue.

Cushing syndrome A condition resulting from the secretion of excessive amounts of cortisone and related hormones by a tumor of the adrenal cortex (the outer portion of the adrenal gland). A potential cause of high blood pressure.

cyclodestructive surgery A treatment for glaucoma that destroys the ciliary body with a laser or other methods.

cyclooxygenase-2 (COX-2) inhibitors Anti-inflammatory drugs that work by blocking the COX-2 enzyme, which plays a role in inflammation, but not the COX-1 enzyme, which helps protect the digestive tract.

cystic duct A tube that carries bile from the gallbladder to the common bile duct.

cystoid macular edema A specific pattern of swelling of the central retina.

cystoscopy Passage of a cystoscope (a type of telescope) through the urethra into the bladder to directly view the urethra and bladder.

cytoprotective drugs A class of drugs designed to protect healthy tissue, for example, during an ischemic stroke.

D

deciliter (dl) A metric unit of volume, equal to 1/10 of a liter. (A liter is slightly smaller than a quart.) Deciliters are commonly used in laboratory test measurements. Cholesterol test results, for example, are often given as grams of cholesterol per deciliter of blood (g/dl).

deep vein thrombosis The formation of a blood clot in the legs. Also known as thrombophlebitis.

diabetic ketoacidosis An acute complication of diabetes, usually type 1, resulting from a nearly complete lack of insulin. The body is forced to use fatty acids instead of glucose as a major source of energy. The resulting excessive breakdown of fatty acids to ketone bodies raises the acidity of the blood to dangerous levels. Symptoms include nausea, vomiting, heavy breathing, and the symptoms of elevated blood glucose.

diabetic retinopathy Damage to small blood vessels in the retina resulting from chronic high blood glucose levels; more common in people with poorly controlled diabetes.

diaphragm The muscle that separates the chest from the abdomen; its movements play an important role in breathing.

diastolic blood pressure The lower number in a blood pressure reading. Represents pressure in the arteries when the heart relaxes between beats.

digital rectal exam (DRE) An examination used to screen for prostate and colorectal cancer in which a doctor inserts a lubricated, gloved finger into the rectum to feel for abnormalities of the prostate and rectum.

dihydrotestosterone (DHT) The most potent androgen inside prostate cells; formed from testosterone by the enzyme 5-reductase.

direct vasodilators Antihypertensive drugs that act directly on the smooth muscle of small arteries, causing them to widen.

disease-modifying anti-rheumatic drugs (DMARDs) Anti-inflammatory drugs that not only help relieve the pain and inflammation of rheumatoid arthritis but also slow the progression of the disease. Once considered a treatment of last resort, they are now prescribed earlier in the disease.

disease-modifying osteoarthritis drugs (DMOADs) A class of medications that prevent joint damage in patients with osteoarthritis by inhibiting the release of enzymes that break down cartilage.

diskectomy Surgical treatment for a herniated disk that takes pressure off a pinched nerve by making an incision in the annulus fibrosus and removing the extruded nucleus pulposus.

diuretics Drugs that increase urine production by enhancing loss of sodium through the kidneys. They are used to eliminate excess fluid from the body and to treat high blood pressure.

dopamine A neurotransmitter; low levels are linked to depression and Parkinson disease.

dopamine reuptake inhibitors Antidepressant drugs that decrease the reabsorption of dopamine by the cell that released the neurotransmitter.

Doppler ultrasound A technique using sound waves to measure how fast blood moves through arteries, such as the carotid arteries.

dowager's hump Kyphosis in the upper back. Common in older women, it can result from disk degeneration, the collapse of vertebrae due to osteoporosis, or both.

D-phenylalanine derivatives Oral diabetes drugs that stimulate rapid insulin secretion to reduce the rise in blood glucose levels that occurs soon after eating. The only available example is nateglinide (Starlix).

drusen Small accumulations of debris underneath the retina.

dual energy x-ray absorptiometry (DEXA) Test to measure bone density. Two x-ray beams are directed at the spine or hip joint, and a computer calculates the amount of energy that passes through the bone.

dual photon absorptiometry Test that measures bone absorption of radiation from a radioactive element. Used to measure bone density of the spine.

duodenum The first portion of the small intestine.

dyspepsia A condition marked by discomfort in the upper abdomen, nausea, and sometimes vomiting; also known as upset stomach or indigestion.

dysphagia Difficulty in swallowing food or liquid. Oropharyngeal dysphagia is marked by an inability to initiate swallowing, while esophageal dysphagia refers to problems that arise as food passes through the esophagus.

dysthymia A chronic mood disorder lasting two years or more, characterized by the presence of depressed mood for most of the day for more days than not. Symptoms are not severe enough to meet the criteria for major depression.

E

electrocardiogram (ECG, EKG) A test to record the electrical processes originating within the heart, such as heartbeat, and to assess heart problems. The test involves electrodes, or leads, attached to the chest, neck, arms, and legs.

electroconvulsive therapy (ECT) Involves a series of sessions in which a controlled seizure is produced by attaching electrodes to the head and then sending brief electrical impulses through the skull into the brain. Used to treat depression when other treatments have failed or when immediate relief of symptoms is needed.

embolus A blood clot or a piece of atherosclerotic plaque that travels through the bloodstream until it lodges in a narrowed vessel and blocks blood flow. The plural form is emboli.

endoscopic retrograde cholangiopancreatography (ERCP) A diagnostic test that combines endoscopy with x-rays to view the pancreatic ducts and bile ducts.

endoscopy A procedure that uses a thin, lighted viewing tube (telescope) to visually examine the interior of a hollow organ, such as the esophagus, stomach, small bowel, or colon.

endothelin A hormone that causes blood vessels to constrict.

epinephrine A hormone that increases blood pressure in response to stress. Also called adrenaline.

epithelial cells See glandular cells.

essential hypertension See primary hypertension.

external beam radiation therapy A therapy for prostate cancer that uses an x-ray machine to aim high-energy radiation at the prostate.

extracapsular surgery Cataract surgery that removes the capsule, cortex, and nucleus of the lens while sparing the posterior capsule.

exudate Fluid deposit.

F

facet joints Joints formed by the interlocking of bony projections at the rear of adjacent vertebrae.

fatty acids Chemical chains of carbon, hydrogen, and oxygen atoms that are part of a fat (lipid) and constitute the major component of triglycerides. Depending on the number and arrangement of these atoms, fatty acids are classified as either saturated, polyunsaturated, or monounsaturated. Also see trans fatty acids.

filling cystometry A test that involves filling the bladder with fluid, assessing the sensation of urinary urgency felt by the patient, and measuring the pressure within the bladder.

filtration surgery A treatment for glaucoma that uses conventional surgical instruments to open a passage through the clogged trabecular meshwork, so that excess aqueous humor

can drain into surrounding tissues.

fistula An abnormal channel or connection in the body caused by disease. May develop between different segments of the bowel, or between the bowel and other organs, usually the bladder, vagina, or skin.

fluorescein angiography A diagnostic procedure for age-related macular degeneration and other retinal diseases. A special dye, called fluorescein, is injected into a vein in the arm. Photographs of the retina are taken as the dye circulates through the blood vessels of the eye.

Foley catheter A small tube inserted through the urethra that allows urine to drain from the bladder into a bag. Has a balloon at its tip so that it remains in place when filled with water.

follicle-stimulating hormone (FSH) A pituitary hormone that stimulates sperm production by the testes.

fracture A break in a bone caused by injury or osteoporosis.

free beam laser prostatectomy A method for treating BPH in which a flexible fiber inserted through the urethra emits beams of laser energy into the prostate to destroy prostate tissue.

free radicals Chemical compounds that can damage cells and oxidize low density lipoproteins, making them more likely to deposit in the walls of arteries.

frontotemporal dementia A spectrum of disorders associated with impaired initiation of plans and goal setting, personality changes, language difficulties, and unawareness of any loss of mental function.

fructosamine test A test that measures protein-bound glucose and reflects average blood glucose levels over the prior two weeks.

G

gallbladder A pear-shaped sac located under the liver that stores bile, which plays an important role in the digestion and absorption of dietary fat.

gamma-aminobutyric acid (GABA) A neurotransmitter (chemical messenger) that suppresses the action of nerve cells. Decreased activity of GABA may contribute to anxiety disorders.

gastritis An inflammation of the inner lining of the stomach.

gastroesophageal junction The interface between the esophagus and the stomach.

gestational diabetes A type of diabetes that occurs first during pregnancy. It occurs in 2 percent to 5 percent of pregnant women, usually goes away when the pregnancy is over, and signals a high risk of developing type 2 diabetes later in life.

glandular cells Produce part of the fluid portion of semen. Also called epithelial cells.

Gleason score A classification system for prostate cancer, based on the microscopic appearance of cancer cells, that is used to predict the seriousness of the cancer; a lower score indicates a slower-growing tumor.

glomeruli Sites in the kidneys where blood contents other than cells and proteins are filtered from the blood into the excretory tubules of the kidneys.

glucagon A hormone that raises blood glucose levels by signaling the liver to convert amino acids and glycogen to glucose and to send the glucose into the bloodstream. Glucagon may be given by injection to raise blood glucose levels in the case of a severe insulin reaction.

glucose A simple sugar that circulates in the blood and provides energy to the body.

glucose transport proteins Proteins that carry glucose from the outside of a cell to the inside.

glutamate cascade See ischemic cascade.

glycogen A complex carbohydrate that is stored in the liver and muscles until it is needed for energy.

gonioscopy A technique used to distinguish between open- and closed-angle glaucoma. It involves an examination of the front part of the eye to check the angle where the iris meets the cornea.

H

H2-blockers Drugs that inhibit gastric acid secretion. Also known as histamine-receptor antagonists.

Heberden nodes Knobby overgrowths of the joint nearest the fingertips in patients with osteoarthritis.

hematoma A mass of clotted blood that forms as a result of a broken blood vessel.

hematuria Blood in the urine.

hemoglobin A1c (HbA1c) test A test that measures the amount of glucose attached to hemoglobin. The test is routinely used to assess blood glucose control over the previous two to three months. Also called a glycohemoglobin test.

hemorrhage Leakage of blood from blood vessels.

hemorrhagic stroke A stroke that occurs when an artery in the brain suddenly bursts and blood leaks into the surrounding tissue.

hepatobiliary scintigram A diagnostic test for acute cholecystitis in which a small amount of radioactive material is injected into a vein to visualize the bile duct system. Also called a hepato-iminodiacetic acid (HIDA) scan.

herniated disk Bulging of the nucleus pulposus through the annulus fibrosus of an intervertebral disk.

hiatal hernia A protrusion of the gastroesophageal junction and a portion of the stomach, which are normally located below the diaphragm, into the chest cavity.

high density lipoprotein (HDL) A particle in the blood that can protect against coronary heart disease by removing cholesterol from the body. Because of its protective benefit, HDL is sometimes referred to as "good" cholesterol.

HMG-CoA reductase inhibitors Drugs that reduce blood levels of cholesterol by blocking its formation. Also called statins.

hormones Chemical substances secreted by a variety of body organs that are carried by the bloodstream and usually influence cells some distance from the source of production. Hormones signal certain enzymes to perform their functions. In this way, hormones regulate such body functions as blood sugar levels, insulin levels, the menstrual cycle, and growth.

hormone replacement therapy Administration of low-dose estrogen with or without a progestin to reduce the symptoms and rapid loss of bone that accompany menopause in women.

Huntington's disease A disease of the central nervous system characterized by jerky movements, personality changes, and dementia.

hyperglycemia A condition characterized by an abnormally high blood glucose level; it occurs in people with untreated or inadequately controlled diabetes.

hyperinsulinemia Excess insulin in the blood.

hyperopia Farsightedness.

hyperosmolar nonketotic state A medical emergency characterized by extremely high blood glucose levels in people with type 2 diabetes. It is usually caused by the stress of an injury or a major illness accompanied by extreme dehydration.

hyperparathyroidism Excessive production of parathyroid hormone by the parathyroid gland. Weakens bones by promoting loss of calcium from bone.

hypertension The medical term for high blood pressure.

hypertensive encephalopathy A brain disorder that occurs in people experiencing a hypertensive emergency. Symptoms may include intense headaches, drowsiness, seizures, loss of consciousness, blurred vision, and even blindness.

hyperthyroidism Excessive production of thyroid hormone that can result in osteoporosis.

hyperuricemia Excess uric acid in the blood.

hypoglycemia Low blood glucose (sugar) levels.

hypomania Episodes of mild manic symptoms.

hypotension The medical term for low blood pressure.

I

ileostomy A surgical procedure that attaches the last part of the small intestine (ileum) to an opening in the skin of the abdomen so that fecal material can pass out of the body.

ileum The last portion of the small intestine.

imaging studies Tests that produce an image of the body; for example, ultrasound, computed tomography, magnetic resonance imaging, and x-rays.

immunosuppressant A medication that suppresses the body's immune response.

impaired fasting glucose A condition in which fasting blood glucose levels are above normal (110 to 125 mg/dL) but not quite in the diabetic range.

impaired glucose tolerance A condition in which the results of a glucose tolerance test are above normal (between 140 and 199 mg/dL two hours after ingesting 75 g of glucose) but not quite in the diabetic range.

incontinence An inability to control urination or defecation.

insulin A hormone normally produced by the pancreas that controls the manufacture of glucose by the liver and permits muscle cells to remove glucose from the blood. Also a medication taken by people with diabetes whose pancreas does not make enough insulin.

insulin resistance syndrome A group of findings, including elevated blood insulin levels, high triglycerides, low HDL cholesterol, increased risk of diabetes and atherosclerosis, and high blood pressure, that is caused by a genetic predisposition to insulin resistance and an accumulation of fat in the abdomen. Also called syndrome X or metabolic syndrome.

intermittent claudication Pain in the buttocks, thighs, or calves while walking. The pain, caused by impaired blood flow to the legs, stops promptly when the person rests. The pain of spinal stenosis may be confused with intermittent claudication.

intervertebral disk Flexible pad of tissue located between vertebrae. Acts as a cushion during movement and prevents vertebrae from grinding against each other.

intracerebral hemorrhage Leakage of blood into tissues deep within the brain.

intraocular pressure The pressure exerted by the fluids inside the eyeball.

ischemia A reduced supply of oxygen to any part of the body owing to obstruction of blood flow.

ischemic stroke A stroke resulting from blockage of an artery supplying blood to the brain.

isolated systolic hypertension A disorder in which the systolic blood pressure is 140 mm Hg or higher and the diastolic blood pressure is under 90 mm Hg.

Associated with an increased risk of stroke, coronary heart disease, and kidney disease.

J

joint capsule A sac-like envelope that encloses a joint. Consists of an inner synovial membrane and an outer fibrous membrane.

K

Kegel exercises A system of exercises that strengthen the pelvic floor muscles.

kyphosis An abnormal accentuation of the usual curvature of the upper back. Commonly referred to as a humpback or hunchback.

L

lacunar stroke A stroke that occurs when the tiny branches at the end of arteries in the brain become completely blocked by small emboli or atherosclerotic plaque.

laparoscopy A technique in which a tiny instrument containing a light and camera is inserted into the body through a small incision. Used for a variety of surgical and diagnostic procedures, including radical prostatectomy.

left ventricular hypertrophy A thickening of the muscular wall of the left ventricle that occurs when it must work harder to pump blood. Common in people with hypertension.

legal blindness Vision that is 20/200 or worse in both eyes. (20/200 vision is the ability to see at 20 feet what a normal eye can see at 200 feet.)

ligament A band of fibrous tissue that connects two bones.

limbic system A group of structures (including the hippocampus, amygdala, hypothalamus, and entorhinal cortex) in the brain responsible for primal urges and powerful emotions, such as hunger and terror, that help to ensure self-preservation.

lipids The technical term for fats, waxes, and fatty compounds.

lipoproteins Packages of proteins, cholesterol, and triglycerides assembled by the intestine and liver that circulate in the bloodstream. One of their chief functions is to carry cholesterol.

lordosis Spinal deformity in which the abdomen is thrust too far forward and the buttocks too far to the rear. Also known as swayback.

low density lipoprotein (LDL) A particle that transports cholesterol in the bloodstream. Its deposition in artery walls initiates plaque formation. A major contributor to coronary heart disease, it has been referred to as "bad" cholesterol.

lower esophageal sphincter (LES) A ring of muscle at the lower end of the esophagus that contracts to create a barrier that prevents the reflux of stomach contents into the esophagus.

luteinizing hormone (LH) A pituitary hormone that stimulates the release of testosterone from the testicles.

M

macula A small area at the center of the retina that is responsible for central and fine-detail vision.

magnetic resonance angiography (MRA) A technique for viewing the arteries in the neck, brain, or other organs by manipulating the scanner in a conventional MRI.

magnetic resonance imaging (MRI) An imaging technique that that employs magnetic fields and radio waves to generate a three-dimensional image of various areas of the body, including the brain.

malignant hypertension A condition characterized by extremely high blood pressure levels (diastolic pressure of 120 mm Hg or higher) that may lead to organ failure. Occurs in about 1 percent of people with hypertension. Also called a hypertensive emergency.

melatonin A hormone that appears to play a role in the body's daily rhythms.

metabolic syndrome See insulin resistance syndrome.

mild cognitive impairment (MCI) Forgetfulness that is more than normal for one's age but is not associated with certain cognitive problems common in dementia, such as disorientation or confusion. Severity falls between age-associated memory impairment and early dementia.

miotics Eye drops used to treat glaucoma. They increase the outflow of aqueous humor by improving its flow through the trabecular meshwork.

monoamine oxidase (MAO) inhibitors Antidepressant drugs that increase brain levels of the neurotransmitters norepinephrine, serotonin, and dopamine by blocking the action of the enzyme monoamine oxidase, which normally inactivates these neurotransmitters.

mononeuropathy Nerve damage resulting from disruption of the blood supply to one nerve. Leads to the sudden onset of pain or weakness in the area served by the affected nerve.

mucosal protectants Drugs that act to increase the resistance of the inner lining of the digestive tract to damaging acid from the stomach.

myopia Nearsightedness.

N

neovascularization The growth of new blood vessels.

nephropathy Kidney damage that can lead to kidney failure.

neuroleptics Antipsychotic drugs sometimes used to control the psychotic symptoms of bipolar disorder until other mood-stabilizing drugs begin to take effect.

neuron Nerve cell.

neuropathy Nerve damage due to diabetes. Most often affects the toes or feet, and can also cause erectile dysfunction.

neurotransmitter A specialized chemical that relays messages between nerve cells.

nitric oxide A substance secreted by cells lining the walls of blood vessels that causes arteries to dilate by relaxing smooth muscle cells.

nocturia Frequent nighttime urination; a symptom of BPH and other diseases.

nonsteroidal anti-inflammatory drugs (NSAIDs) A class of drugs (including ibuprofen and aspirin) that reduce pain and inflammation.

norepinephrine A neurotransmitter; low levels are linked to depression.

nuclear cataract A cataract affecting the nucleus of the lens.

nucleus pulposus Central part of an intervertebral disk. As we age, the nucleus pulposus slowly loses its water content and shrinks.

O

omega-3 fatty acids A unique group of polyunsaturated fatty acids found in fish oil and some seeds (such as in linseed oil). Omega-3s in fish oil significantly reduce blood clotting. They make platelets less likely to stick together and to blood vessels. Omega-3s may reduce the risk of heart attack or stroke.

opiates Narcotic pain relievers, such as morphine.

oral glucose tolerance test A test in which a person fasts overnight and then drinks a solution containing 75 g of glucose. A diabetes diagnosis is made if two hours later the blood glucose level is 200 mg/dL or more.

orthostatic hypertension An abrupt drop in blood pressure on standing.

osteophyte Bone spur.

P

pancreas An organ, located behind and beneath the lower part of the stomach, that produces and secretes insulin. The pancreas also makes digestive juices.

pancreatic islets Cellular masses in the pancreas that contain insulin-secreting cells.

pannus A thickening of the synovial membrane resulting from an overgrowth of synovial cells and an accumulation of white blood cells. Occurs as rheumatoid arthritis progresses.

parathyroid hormone A hormone that regulates calcium metabolism. It dilates small arteries that may play a role in the control of blood pressure.

parkinsonism The symptoms of Parkinson disease: tremors; rigid, stooped posture; slowness; and shuffling gait.

peripheral-acting adrenergic antagonist A type of drug that reduces resistance to blood flow in small arteries.

peripheral neuropathy A slow, progressive loss of function of the sensory nerves in the limbs that causes numbness, tingling, and pain in the legs and hands.

peripheral arterial disease A buildup of fatty deposits and fibrous tissue, called plaques, in the arteries leading to the legs and feet.

peristalsis A series of wavelike muscle contractions that occur automatically to move food and fluid through the digestive tract.

peritonitis Inflammation or infection inside the peritoneal cavity.

pH A measurement of acidity or alkalinity.

phytotherapy The use of plant-derived substances to treat a medical condition such as BPH.

pituitary gland A small gland at the base of the brain; releases hormones that regulate growth and metabolism.

plaque (arterial) An accumulation of fatty substances, such as cholesterol, in the inner lining of the artery walls. Plaque buildup can lead to atherosclerosis.

podagra Severe pain in the big toe caused by gout.

prednisone A steroid drug with powerful anti-inflammatory effects.

processes The seven bony projections that jut out from the rear of each vertebra.

progesterone A female sex hormone secreted by the ovaries. Progesterone and estrogen regulate changes that occur during the menstrual cycle.

prokinetic agents Drugs that increase removal of acid from the esophagus, raise lower esophageal sphincter pressure, and stimulate emptying of the stomach.

prostate A gland the size and shape of a chestnut that surrounds the upper portion of the male urethra. Its main function is to produce part of the fluid that makes up semen.

prostate-specific antigen (PSA) An enzyme produced by the glandular cells of the prostate and secreted into the seminal fluid that is released during ejaculation. High blood levels may indicate the presence of prostate cancer but can also be caused by BPH and infection.

prostatic intraepithelial neoplasia (PIN) A precancerous change within the prostate that is thought to have the potential to develop into cancer.

prostatitis An inflammation of the prostate that may cause pain in the lower back and in the area between the scrotum and rectum.

prostatodynia A condition that causes the same symptoms as prostatitis but is not associated with infection or inflammation.

proton-pump inhibitors Drugs that strongly suppress acid production in the stomach.

PSA density The PSA level divided by the volume of the prostate. Allows the doctor to better distinguish between BPH and cancer by taking prostate volume into account when assessing the PSA level.

PSA velocity A measurement of the changes in PSA values over time. PSA velocity is greater in men with prostate cancer than in those without the disease.

pulse pressure The difference between systolic and diastolic blood pressures. Reflects the stiffness of arteries.

pylorus A circular muscle that connects the opening at the end of the stomach with the duodenum (first portion of the small intestine).

R

radical prostatectomy A type of surgery for prostate cancer that removes the entire prostate and the seminal vesicles.

residual urine Urine retained in the bladder after voiding. It can become infected or lead to the formation of bladder stones.

retinal detachment A vision-threatening condition in which the retina becomes separated from the underlying layers of the eye.

retinopathy Damage to the retina caused by changes in the tiny blood vessels that supply the retina.

retrograde ejaculation Ejaculation of semen into the bladder rather than through the penis.

retropubic open prostatectomy An operation for BPH used when the prostate is too large for the surgeon to perform transurethral prostatectomy (TURP). It involves pushing aside the bladder so that the inner prostate tissue can be removed without entering the bladder.

reuptake The reabsorption of a neurotransmitter by the neuron that released it. Drugs that block reuptake leave the neurotransmitter in the synaptic cleft to continue stimulation of other neurons.

rubeosis iridis New blood vessel growth on the iris. It usually occurs in people with diabetes.

S

S-adenosylmethionine (SAM-e) A supplement marketed as a treatment for depression. Research has not supported its effectiveness in the treatment of depression.

sciatica Pain that radiates into the buttocks, down the thighs, and into the calves and often the feet. Caused by irritation of the sciatic nerve.

sciatic nerve Nerve arising from the lower spine that extends into the leg and foot.

sclera The white outer layer that covers and protects most of the eye.

scoliosis An abnormal sideways bend to the back caused by a twisting of the spine.

scotoma A blind spot in the visual field.

seasonal affective disorder (SAD) Episodes of depression only during certain times of the year, usually beginning in November when there is less sunlight.

secondary hypertension Hypertension caused by another heath condition or a medication. Responsible for less than 5 percent of cases of hypertension.

secondary osteoarthritis Osteoarthritis that results from trauma to the joint or from chronic joint injury due to another type of arthritis, such as rheumatoid arthritis.

selective serotonin reuptake inhibitors (SSRIs) Antidepressant drugs that inhibit the reuptake of serotonin and thereby raise its concentration in the synaptic cleft.

selegiline A medication used to treat Parkinson disease that is currently begin tested as a therapy for Alzheimer's disease. It has antioxidant effects similar to vitamin E but is associated with more side effects.

serotonin A neurotransmitter (chemical messenger); low levels are linked to depression.

sigmoidoscopy, flexible A procedure in which the last 25 inches of the colon is examined with a short, flexible endoscope inserted through the rectum.

simple prostatectomy A type of surgery for BPH that typically involves removing only the inner portion of the prostate. The procedure is performed either through the urethra (TURP) or by making an incision in the lower abdomen (retropubic or suprapubic prostatectomy).

single photon absorptiometry Test that indirectly measures bone density using low-energy radiation. Rarely used today.

slow-acting anti-rheumatic drugs (SAARDs) See disease-modifying anti-rheumatic drugs (DMARDs).

smooth muscle cells Muscle cells in the prostate that contract to push prostatic fluid into the urethra during ejaculation.

sphygmomanometer An instrument used to measure blood pressure. Consists of an air pump, inflatable cuff, and aneroid or mercury column gauge.

spinal canal Channel through which the spinal cord runs. Formed by the hole in each vertebra it protects the spinal cord.

spinal cord Long column of nerve tissue that extends from the base of the skull to the upper portion of the lower back. Protected by the surrounding vertebrae, the spinal cord carries sensory and motor signals to and from the brain.

spinal stenosis Narrowing of the spinal canal.

spine Column made up of 33 bones called vertebrae that support the body and protect the spinal cord. The spine comprises 7 cervical (neck) vertebrae, 12 thoracic (chest) vertebrae, 5 lumbar (lower back) vertebrae, 5 sacral (back of the pelvic wall) vertebrae, and 4 coccyx (tailbone) vertebrae.

spondylolisthesis Forward movement or dislocation of one vertebra in relation to an adjacent vertebra.

sprain Injury resulting from partial tearing of a ligament.

St. John's wort An herbal treatment used for mild to moderate depression. It is considered a dietary supplement, which means it is not approved by the U.S. Food and Drug Administration.

steatorrhea The presence of large amounts of undigested fat in the stool.

stent A wire mesh tube that is inserted into an artery to help keep it open.

strain Injury resulting from overstretching of a muscle.

stroke A sudden reduction in or loss of brain function that occurs when an artery supplying blood to a portion of the brain becomes blocked or ruptures. Neurons in the affected area are starved of oxygen and nutrients normally provided by the blood.

subarachnoid hemorrhage Leakage of blood into the space between the brain and the arachnoid membrane, the middle of the three membranes that envelop the brain. Most commonly results from trauma or a ruptured aneurysm.

subdural hematoma A collection of blood between the skull and the brain that can lead to memory problems and loss of consciousness.

subfoveal surgery A procedure that surgically removes the abnormal blood vessels beneath the retina in people with age-related macular degeneration.

sulfonylureas Oral diabetes drugs that stimulate the pancreas to secrete more insulin. Examples are chlorpropamide (Diabinese) and glyburide (DiaBeta, Glynase, Micronase).

suprapubic open prostatectomy An operation for BPH performed when the prostate is too large to allow for TURP. Involves opening the bladder and removing the inner portion of the prostate through the bladder.

synaptic cleft The small gap between neurons; sometimes referred to as a synapse.

syndrome X See insulin resistance syndrome.

synovectomy Removal of the synovial membrane of a joint.

synovial fluid Fluid secreted by the synovial membrane that lubricates the joints.

synovial membrane Connective tissue that lines the cavity of a joint and produces synovial fluid.

systemic lupus erythematosus (SLE) An inflammatory disease of connective tissue that is characterized especially by skin rash, arthritis, and inflammation of different organs. Occurs primarily in women.

systolic blood pressure The upper number in a blood pressure reading. Represents pressure in the arteries when the heart is pumping blood to the rest of the body.

T

tendons The strong, inelastic cords of connective tissue that anchor muscles to bones or, in some cases, to other tissues.

testosterone The principal male sex hormone that induces and maintains the changes that occur in males at puberty. In men, the testicles continue to produce testosterone throughout life, though there is some decline with age.

thiazolidinediones A class of oral diabetes drugs that increase the sensitivity of muscle cells to insulin. Examples are pioglitazone (Actos) and rosiglitazone (Avandia).

thrombolytic drug A medication that breaks up blood clots.

thrombus A blood clot. The plural form is thrombi.

tidal irrigation A treatment for osteoarthritis of the knee in which a saline solution is repeatedly injected and then withdrawn from the joint space

to remove debris from the joint and help break up the synovial membrane that has adhered to itself.

tolerance Decreased effectiveness of a given dose of a drug with its continued use.

tonometry A method of measuring intraocular pressure by determining the amount of force needed to make a slight indentation in a small area of the cornea.

tophi Deposits of uric acid crystals in the skin or around joints.

trabecular meshwork A spongy network of connective tissue through which aqueous humor drains from the eye. Blockage of the meshwork causes a buildup of intraocular pressure.

trachea The windpipe.

transcranial magnetic stimulation A procedure in which an electromagnetic coil is placed on the scalp and a high-intensity current is passed through the coil. It is currently being investigated for the treatment of depression.

transcutaneous electrical nerve stimulation (TENS) Application of low-energy electrical radiation to "numb" the nerves; not recommended as a treatment for back pain.

trans fatty acids Fats that are produced during the process of hydrogenation, which occurs when manufacturers add hydrogen to unsaturated fats to make them more solid or shelf stable. Studies have shown that trans fats act like saturated fatty acids, raising levels of total and LDL ("bad") cholesterol.

transient ischemic attack (TIA) Short-lived neurological deficits caused by insufficient

blood flow to the brain. Most episodes subside within 20 minutes.

transrectal ultrasonography A procedure that uses an ultrasound probe inserted into the rectum to develop images of the prostate. Used to guide needle biopsy of the prostate to diagnose prostate cancer.

tricyclics Antidepressant drugs that raise concentrations of the neurotransmitters norepinephrine and serotonin in the synaptic cleft by blocking their reuptake.

triglyceride A lipid (fat) in the bloodstream. Elevated levels are associated with an increased risk of coronary heart disease.

tumor necrosis factor A protein that plays an early and major role in the rheumatic disease process.

tumor, node, metastasis (TNM) system A system for describing the clinical stage of a cancerous tumor using T numbers that indicate whether the tumor is palpable or not and if palpable, the extent of the tumor (e.g., T1 and T2), as well as N+ for cancer that has spread to the lymph nodes and M+ for cancer that has spread to other parts of the body.

type 1 diabetes An autoimmune disease that destroys the ability of pancreatic beta cells to make insulin. Occurs most commonly in children and young adults. Daily insulin injections are necessary to stay alive.

type 2 diabetes The most common type of diabetes; accounts for about 95 percent of all cases in the United States. Develops when the pancreas cannot make enough insulin to overcome the body's resistance to insulin action. Occurs most often in overweight or obese people over the age of 40, but its occurrence in overweight children is on the rise.

U

ulcerative colitis A chronic inflammatory disease of the large intestine caused by an abnormal autoimmune reaction that causes the body to attack its own tissue.

ultrasound Use of high-frequency sound waves to detect osteoporosis and predict the risk of fractures.

upper GI series X-rays of the esophagus, stomach, and duodenum that are taken after the patient swallows a solution of barium, which makes the organs visible on the x-ray.

urethral stricture Narrowing of the urethra.

urethra The canal through which urine is transported from the bladder and out of the body. In men, the urethra also carries semen that is released during ejaculation.

uroflowmetry A noninvasive test for BPH that measures the speed of urine flow.

uveitis Inflammation of the uvea, the part of the eye that contains the iris, ciliary body, and choroid.

uveoscleral pathway An alternative drainage system for aqueous humor. It is located behind the trabecular meshwork.

V

vagus nerve stimulator A small, surgically implanted device that periodically stimulates the brain through the vagus nerve. It is used in the treatment of epilepsy and is being investigated for the treatment of depression.

vascular dementia A disorder, often resulting from a series of tiny strokes in the brain, that can lead to dementia.

vasodilator A drug that allows the penis to become engorged with blood by widening the blood vessels. Used as a treatment for erectile dysfunction. Examples are papaverine, phentolamine, and prostaglandin E-1 (alprostadil).

vasopressin A hormone produced by the hypothalamus and used as an alternative treatment to enhance memory.

vasospasm A sudden constriction of blood vessels in the brain that is likely to occur in the first two weeks after a subarachnoid hemorrhage.

vertebra, vertebrae (pl.) Any of the 33 interlocking bones that form the spinal column.

vertebral compression fracture Collapse of the front of a vertebra, often producing immediate and intense pain in the area of the fracture. Can be caused by even minor trauma in a vertebra weakened by cancer, osteoporosis, Paget's disease, or hyperparathyroidism.

vertebral osteomyelitis A serious bacterial infection of the spine. It can cause pain in the neck or back and is usually accompanied by fever.

viscosupplementation A treatment option for people with osteoarthritis of the knee that involves the injection of hyaluronan, a natural component of synovial fluid, directly into the knee joint.

visual laser ablation of the prostate (VLAP) See free beam laser prostatectomy.

vitrectomy A surgical treatment for diabetic retinopathy in which the the vitreous humor is removed and replaced with a saline solution.

vitreous humor A thick, gel-like substance that fills the back of the eyeball behind the lens.

W

white coat hypertension High blood pressure readings that are only present when the patient's blood pressure is recorded by a physician or in a medical environment. Blood pressure is normal when taken at home by the patient, family members, or friends.

Whitmore-Jewett system A system for describing the clinical stage of a cancerous tumor using the letters A, B, C, and D, with D denoting the most advanced stage.

Y

YAG laser A type of laser that contains yttrium, aluminum, and garnet. It is used to clear blurred vision that may occur after extracapsular surgery.

We wish to thank the following organizations, which so generously gave us permission to reprint material from their publications. Those publications are acknowledged below, preceded by the respective subject entry name as it appears in the Guide:

Organizations

BLADDER CANCER: *What You Need To Know About Bladder Cancer*, National Cancer Institute.

BRAIN TUMORS: *What You Need To Know About Brain Tumors*, National Cancer Institute.

BREAST CANCER: *What You Need To Know About Breast Cancer*, National Cancer Institute.

CANCER: *What You Need To Know About Cancer*, National Cancer Institute.

CERVICAL CANCER: *What You Need To Know About Cancer of the Cervix*, National Cancer Institute.

CIRRHOSIS OF THE LIVER: *Cirrhosis of the Liver*, National Institute of Diabetes and Digestive and Kidney Diseases.

COLORECTAL CANCER: *What You Need To Know About Cancer of the Colon and Rectum*, National Cancer Institute.

CONSTIPATION: *Constipation*, National Institute of Diabetes and Digestive and Kidney Diseases.

DIARRHEA: *Diarrhea*, National Institute of Diabetes and Digestive and Kidney Diseases.

DIVERTICULOSIS AND DIVERTICULITIS: *Diverticulosis and Diverticulitis*, National Institute of Diabetes and Digestive and Kidney Diseases.

DRY MOUTH: *Dry Mouth*, National Institute of Dental and Craniofacial Research.

EPILEPSY: *Seizures and Epilepsy: Hope Through Research*, National Institute of Neurological Disorders and Stroke.

ESOPHAGEAL CANCER: *What You Need To Know About Cancer of the Esophagus*, National Cancer Institute.

GASTROESOPHAGEAL REFLUX DISEASE: *Gastroesophageal Reflux Disease (Hiatal Hernia and Heartburn)*, National Institute of Diabetes and Digestive and Kidney Diseases.

HEADACHE: *Headache—Hope Through Research*, National Institute of Neurological Disorders and Stroke.

HEMORRHOIDS: *Hemorrhoids*, National Institute of Diabetes and Digestive and Kidney Diseases.

HODGKIN'S DISEASE: *What You Need To Know About Hodgkin's Disease*, National Cancer Institute.

IRRITABLE BOWEL SYNDROME: *Irritable Bowel Syndrome*, National Institute of Diabetes and Digestive and Kidney Diseases.

KIDNEY CANCER: *What You Need To Know About Kidney Cancer*, National Cancer Institute.

KIDNEY DISEASE: *Your Kidneys and How They Work*, National Institute of Diabetes and Digestive and Kidney Diseases.

KIDNEY STONES: *Kidney Stones*, American Foundation for Urologic Disease.

LEUKEMIA: *What You Need To Know About Leukemia*, National Cancer Institute.

LUNG CANCER: *What You Need To Know About Lung Cancer*, National Cancer Institute.

MENOPAUSE: *Menopause*, National Institute on Aging.

MULTIPLE MYELOMA: *What You Need To Know About Multiple Myeloma*, National Cancer Institute.

NON-HODGKIN'S LYMPHOMA: *What You Need To Know About Non-Hodgkin's Lymphoma*, National Cancer Institute.

OBESITY: *Understanding Adult Obesity*, Weight-Control Information Network.

ORAL CANCER: *What You Need To Know About Oral Cancer*, National Cancer Institute.

OVARIAN CANCER: *What You Need To Know About Ovarian Cancer*, National Cancer Institute.

PANCREATIC CANCER: *What You Need To Know About Cancer of the Pancreas*, National Cancer Institute.

PANCREATITIS: *Pancreatitis*, National Institute of Diabetes and Digestive and Kidney Diseases.

PARKINSON'S DISEASE: *Parkinson's Disease—Hope Through Research*, National Institute of Neurological Disorders and Stroke.

PEPTIC ULCER: *H. pylori and Peptic Ulcer*, National Institute of Diabetes and Digestive and Kidney Diseases.

PERIODONTAL DISEASE: *Periodontal (GUM) Diseases*, National Institute of Dental and Craniofacial Research.

PNEUMONIA: Reprinted with permission © 2002 American Lung Association. For more information on how you can support to fight lung disease, the third leading cause of death in the U.S., please contact The American Lung Association at 1-800-LUNG-USA (1-800-586-4872) or logon to the Web site at www.lungusa.org.

PROSTATE CANCER: *What You Need To Know About Prostate Cancer*, National Cancer Institute.

PSORIASIS: *Psoriasis*, © 1994, Reprinted with permission from the American Academy of Dermatology. All rights reserved.

SHINGLES: *Shingles: Hope Through Research*, National Institute of Neurological Disorders and Stroke.

SKIN CANCER: *What You Need To Know About Skin Cancer*, National Cancer Institute.

SLEEP DISORDERS: *Sleep as We Grow Older*, © 2000, American Academy of Sleep Medicine.

SMELL AND TASTE DISORDERS: *Smell and Taste Disorders*, © 2001, American Academy of Otolaryngology—Head and Neck Surgery, Inc.

STOMACH CANCER: *What You Need To Know About Stomach Cancer*, National Cancer Institute.

TUBERCULOSIS: Reprinted with permission © 2002 American Lung Association. For more information on how you can support to fight lung disease, the third leading cause of death in the U.S., please contact The American Lung Association at 1-800-LUNG-USA (1-800-586-4872) Web site at www.lungusa.org.

UTERINE CANCER: *What You Need To Know About Cancer of the Uterus*, National Cancer Institute.

VAGINITIS: *American College of Obstetricians and Gynecologists. Vaginitis: Causes and Treatments* (Patient Education Pamphlet No. AP028). Washington DC, © ACOG, April 1997.

VIRAL HEPATITIS: *Viral Hepatitis A to E and Beyond*, National Institute of Diabetes and Digestive and Kidney Diseases.